'I Succeeded Once':

The Aboriginal Protectorate on the Mornington Peninsula, 1839–1840

'I Succeeded Once':

The Aboriginal Protectorate on the Mornington Peninsula, 1839–1840

Marie Hansen Fels

ANU
THE AUSTRALIAN NATIONAL UNIVERSITY

E PRESS

Published by ANU E Press and Aboriginal History Incorporated
Aboriginal History Monograph 22

This title is also available online at: http://epress.anu.edu.au/succeeded_once_citation.html

National Library of Australia Cataloguing-in-Publication entry

Author: Fels, Marie Hansen, 1938-

Title: 'I succeeded once' : the Aboriginal Protectorate on the Mornington Peninsula, 1839-1840 / Marie Fels.

ISBN: 9781921862120 (pbk.) 978192186137 (ebook)

Series: Aboriginal history monograph ; 22

Notes: Includes bibliographical references.

Subjects: Thomas, William, 1791-1867.
         Aboriginal Australians--Victoria--Mornington Peninsula--History.
         Mornington Peninsula (Vic.)--History.

Dewey Number: 994.500499152

Aboriginal History Incorporated

Aboriginal History is administered by an Editorial Board which is responsible for all unsigned material. Views and opinions expressed by the author are not necessarily shared by Board members.

The Committee of Management and the Editorial Board

Contacting Aboriginal History

All correspondence should be addressed to Aboriginal History, Box 2837 GPO Canberra, 2601, Australia. Sales and orders for journals and monographs, and journal subscriptions: Thelma Sims, email: Thelma.Sims@anu.edu.au, tel or fax: +61 2 6125 3269, www.aboriginalhistory.org

Aboriginal History Inc. is a part of the Australian Centre for Indigenous Studies, Research School of Social Sciences, The Australian National University and gratefully acknowledges the support of the History Program, RSSS and the National Centre for Indigenous Studies, The Australian National University.

WARNING: Readers are notified that this publication may contain names or images of deceased persons.

Contacting ANU E Press

All correspondence should be addressed to: ANU E Press, The Australian National University, Canberra ACT 0200, Australia. Email: anuepress@anu.edu.au, Website: http://epress.anu.edu.au

Monograph 22 editors: Niel Gunson and Tikka Wilson

Copy editor: Geoff Hunt

Cover design: Richard Barwick.

Cover image: Map of Western Port District and William Thomas sketch

Contents

Foreword

Eleanor Bourke

Marie Fels has been working in ethno history since her study on the Native Police Corps. The thesis version of her previous publication *Good Men and True* is among the most widely consulted in the archives of The University of Melbourne. It contains over 100 pages of biographical details of individual Aboriginal men. The records she has used in this publication were written in the earliest years of contact with Europeans, before traditional life changed forever. These are rare and valuable records of interest to all Victorians. Though they were written for other purposes, mainly administrative, and by white males of the early 19th century, these early records are the closest we can get to the Indigenous people whose land was taken in the 1830s.

This book contains 20 sets of biographical details, mainly of Bonurong men: as Fels observes, the writers of the records didn't pay much attention to women. These biographical details add wonderfully to our knowledge. Eventually it may assist to bridge the gap of the 1850s between people identified according to custom, and the people at Coranderrk who had acquired European names.

It is all new work, based solely on primary sources, and asks the question 'why was there so little trouble, neither deaths nor hostilities on the Mornington Peninsula, when the rest of Victoria is characterised by trouble'? The reason Fels advances is the nature of the reciprocal relationships between the earliest European occupiers of the Mornington Peninsula and the original owners. In investigating this question, she has discovered much new information which will be of interest to all people with a connection to the land of the Mornington Peninsula. It is an unexpected bonus to find so much 'actual quoted Aboriginal speech' showing opinions and attitudes, which Thomas relates with the use of inverted commas: this is rare and precious.

Marie Fels has decided to present the original evidence to the reader. The observations are filtered through the eyes of the Assistant Protector William Thomas, and Fels has paraphrased his journal so that reading it is easy. Day by day, the little details of some people's lives draw us into understanding of contact experiences. They stood up for their rights; they protested in clear and logical language against the injustice of the white men taking their land; they continued to walk their country even when it displeased Thomas. They continued with their marriage customs, and they never forgave him for the one time he intervened; they continued to be in close contact with other Kulin nations and the messengers went back and forth in the time honoured way; they taught Thomas about navigating the bush and laughed at his stupidity; they applied their rules of food distribution to the new foods of tea and sugar, flour and damper and mutton; they looked after him as much as, if not more, than he looked after them. They engaged him and other local Mornington Peninsula white men in relationships of some reciprocity.

The book is place based: there are chapters on all three Protectorate sites, Tubberubbabel, Buckermitterwarrer and Kangerong, plus one on Kullurk which is the place the Bonurong themselves chose for their reserve, plus one on the site at McCrae where Johnny is buried, the young man whom many people know about from Georgiana McCrae's journal.

Ultimately, the Protectorate was a failure: Fels sees Thomas as a good man who tried his best to get justice for the people, Robinson as a bad administrator and the government as mean. Tragically, programs in Aboriginal affairs continue to receive a meagre portion of resources from governments and therefore like the Protectorate continue to fail.

Many people already interested in this area of Victoria will be keen to read this new publication and read the chapter on the abducted women for new information. This publication is accessible to anyone who is interested in learning more about the Mornington Peninsula and obtaining some understanding of this abduction because it has not been written about before, except in scholarly journals and reports. I hope Yankee Yankee's extraordinary story will move everyone's heart, so young to be kidnapped with his mother, so resourceful in all his travels, so reliable an informant. There will no doubt be interest in the evidence for infanticide. Fels accepts the records and suggests they look persuasive. In her view they appear to offer a different view on the population decline and resurgence.

The scientist Dr Holdgate was generous enough to allow his wonderful map of Lake Phillip to be published. It will be a source of great satisfaction to many that science has confirmed the oral tradition so carefully handed down (and recorded by Europeans) that in past times, Port Phillip was a hunting ground and people walked across it to Corio.

Today the Victorian Aboriginal Heritage Act of 2006 has altered the framework under which cultural heritage is managed in this State. The Act's objectives include that Aboriginal cultural heritage is to be recognised, protected and conserved in ways based on respect for Aboriginal knowledge and cultural and traditional practices; and that Traditional Owners are to be accorded appropriate status in protecting our heritage.

I am proud to be a member of the Victorian Aboriginal Heritage Council which is established by the Act and is the first decision making body of its kind in Australia. The Council encourages all Shires and Councils in Victoria to establish or revitalise engagement with Traditional Owners under the Act. Though it has a heritage framework for sites and places of European historical importance, the Mornington Peninsula Shire has yet to treat Aboriginal heritage in the same way. Perhaps this book will inspire efforts in this direction.

This book is important, and I have pleasure in recommending it as a good read.

Eleanor A Bourke

Chairperson, Victorian Aboriginal Heritage Council

About the Author

Marie Hansen Fels has a first class honours degree in History, including Archaeology and Anthropology, from the University of Melbourne: her thesis on the earliest Tasmanian colonial period, 1803–1811 was published by the Tasmanian Historical Research Association. Her PhD won the Harbison Higinbothom Scholarship for the best PhD submitted in the arts and social sciences for the period 1986–88, and was published by Melbourne University Press as *Good Men and True: the Aboriginal Police of the Port Phillip District 1837–1853*. She was awarded the Colonel George Johnston post doctoral scholarship to the University of Sydney in the Lenten Term 1987. In 1988 she researched the *Dandenong Police Paddocks* published in two volumes by Victoria Archaeological Survey (VAS) as *Early Use as Native Police Headquarters and Aboriginal Protectorate Station 1837–1853*, and *Land History and Use 1851– 1988*. In 1989 she was employed by VAS to research *Some Aspects of the History of Coranderrk Station* published in 1998. In 1990 she researched *A History of the Ebenezer Mission*, Occasional Report No 51 published by Aboriginal Affairs Victoria. A comparison of the early contact histories of Tasmania and Victoria was published in the *Bulletin of the Centre for Tasmanian Historical Studies* in 1991–92. In 1993 she produced a report for Telecom on the Acheron-Mohican Aboriginal Reserve. She was the expert witness, History, for the Victorian and New South Wales governments in the Yorta Yorta Native Title case. She is the author of numerous reviews.

Preface

Fig 1. 'Bungil's Cave, Flinders, 2006'

Reproduced with the permission of the Flinders District Historical Society.

This history started with maps. After a talk I gave to the Flinders District Historical Society (FDHS) in 2003, the president asked me to discover the real name of Stony Creek, Shoreham. My subsequent map research disclosed so many Aboriginal names that we formed a working group, and, confining ourselves only to the earliest records where the names came at first hand from the traditional owners of the land, we constructed the map entitled *The Boon-Wurrung Mornington Peninsula*: it was produced by Phil Hughes, Coordinator of the Mornington Peninsula Shire's Geographic Information Systems unit (GIS), and FDHS gave copies to all secondary schools on the Mornington Peninsula, as well as Aboriginal Affairs Victoria (AAV), Victorian Aboriginal Corporation for Languages, the Surveyor-General, the Public Record Office of Victoria, and the Mornington Peninsula Historical Societies: this earliest edition of the map has been reproduced in an Indigenous publication. We also constructed a bibliography of Bungil's Cave and gave it to AAV, who made a site inspection in conjunction with the Boon Wurrung Foundation Ltd, and the Bunurong Land Council Aboriginal Corporation, and FDHS: as a consequence, Bungil's Cave has been placed on the register.

The names, however, were of antiquarian interest only in the absence of detailed knowledge of the activities of the Bonurong on the Mornington Peninsula in the early contact period. The library purchased from the Mitchell Library the 28 reels of the microfilmed Papers of the Assistant Protector William Thomas, and five years later, this book is the product of the research. There is little interpretation in it, no conclusion: on the contrary, the aim was to tell the story of the people's use of their land in that one year, bringing into the public domain as much of the original records as possible. The people's use of their land then led to other stories, before and after that one year, which enlarge our understanding of them. I aimed to bring individuals out of obscurity, to make connections, so that we can know them as persons, however imperfectly. I wrote in 1986 that the small details of Aboriginal lives are as important to an understanding of Australia's past as are the small details of European lives. Ian Clark quoted that in 2005, and I still believe it to be true in 2010. This book is offered as a resource book, and a platform for further research.

Joe Cauchi, Director, Sustainable Communities, Mornington Peninsula Shire, made the decision to purchase the microfilm. Geoff Carson, Manager, Libraries, Arts and Culture, and his library staff obtained material, did not charge for Inter Library Loans, gave extended loans, home loans from the reserve collection, and purchased for the library items of interest such as the authentic version of Georgiana McCrae's manuscripts; I appreciated very much this practical support and I thank them. Phil Hughes, GIS Coordinator, took Thomas' written distance and mileage figures, applied them to Smythe's maps, then overlaid the cadastre, and thus identified the sites: this could not have been done without him, and I thank him. All readers would share my indebtedness to Guy Holdgate, School of Earth Sciences, University of Melbourne, for his generosity in permitting his research findings regarding the water levels of Port Phillip to be published here: though he has lectured on them, they have not yet been published in the scientific literature. I am deeply grateful for the privilege. Thanks are due to Lighthouses of Australia for permission to reproduce from its collection the unique stereoscopic photo of the 1854 and 1883 Eastern lighthouses standing together while the latter was being erected.

I am grateful to the staff of the State Library of Victoria, especially Kevin Molloy, the Manuscripts librarian, who gave permission to read some treasures in the original when checks were necessary, and to Judith Scurfield, the Map librarian who was, as ever, helpful in sharing her great knowledge of the collection and finding relevant maps, and to Jane Miller who pursued George Smith with me and for me. The recently retired Microforms Librarian in the Mitchell Library,

Martin Beckett, was generous in providing me with readable copies where the microfilm could not be read because of age or damage to the original, and the Manuscripts Librarian, Tracy Bradford, kindly allowed me to read originals when all other efforts failed: I am grateful to both. Sebastian Gurciullo of the Public Record Office helped me in the same manner with Thomas' letters, as did Tony Morabito, Crown Land Registry, with maps, and I thank them both. Aboriginal Affairs Victoria provided the subsidy to the publishers of the monograph series, *Aboriginal History*, without which publication would not have been possible. This book was honoured in that *Aboriginal History* asked Niel Gunson to edit it, and Richard Barwick to do the illustrations. Both distinguished scholars in their own right, they have a long history of commitment to early contact history, and I am most grateful for their work. Any errors of course, are mine.

Families of researchers get used to 'I'm working' and I am grateful to mine, particularly those who read drafts, and those who rescued me from computer disasters, taught me new skills when my primitive technology failed, took photographs for me, formatted the finished text and so on: I am pleased that they think it was worthwhile being short-changed for a few years - Bob, and Nick and Rebecca, Ben and Nysa, Emma and Leigh.

Marie Hansen Fels
16 February 2010

List of Illustrations

Glossary

Bemin	ring-tailed possum
Big one	elevated status, eg 'big one Governor' was the governor of New South Wales; 'big one talk' was Divine Service; 'big one Sunday' was the most important day of the week
Boo	shoot – not necessarily shoot to kill, includes shooting up in the air in high spirits, or shooting and missing
Bullito	greatness/much
Bungarlurly	wrong/stupid
Coolin	male person
Gammon	a truth/untruth dichotomy, eg plenty gammon – a big lie; no gammon – I am not deceiving you
Koem	kangaroo
Koogra	possum skin cloak
Lubra	female person
Marminata	good father
Meregeek	very good
Miam	dwelling, used also to describe European huts
Nerlingo	come back
No	commonly used in speaking instead of not
Pickaninny	small or little, as in child or miserable wages
Pilmularly	steal
Punjil	Creator of the universe
Quomby	to camp
Sleeps	measure of time as in contemporary usage
Sulky	angry
Tuin	flying squirrel
Wallert	possum
Willum	dwelling
Wonguim	wooden implement, used for striking or throwing, modern term boomerang, see fig. 23
Yangelly	be off with you
Yarraman	horse

1. The writings of William Thomas

This treasure trove of records created by Assistant Protector William Thomas can be divided into two categories – those which he wrote for other eyes to read, and his private journals.

The public record

In the course of his duties as Assistant Protector, Thomas wrote monthly summaries, quarterly reports, six monthly returns of births and deaths, and annual reports, plus single-subject letters, to the Chief Protector mainly, but also to others: in addition, he made formal submissions to several Parliamentary Select Committees of Enquiry, 1843 and 1849 (New South Wales) and 1859 (Victoria). His regular reports as Assistant Protector were submitted to the Chief Protector in Melbourne. Robinson forwarded them to La Trobe who read them before forwarding them to the Colonial Secretary in Sydney, for the information of the Governor of New South Wales: in some instances, the Governor forwarded them in their entirety to London, for the information of the Secretary of State for War and the Colonies. Some of these reports from Thomas were published in Parliamentary Papers in New South Wales and later Victoria, and in Great Britain.

After the Protectorate ended in 1849, Thomas was appointed Guardian of the Aborigines of Victoria. Then, after the establishment of the Central Board for the Protection of Aborigines in 1859, he was appointed the official Visitor: in the course of these duties his reports to the government were weekly. R Brough Smyth, the secretary to the Central Board, used much of Thomas' material in Smyth's two volume work, *The Aborigines of Victoria and other parts of Australia and Tasmania*, first published in 1876. Thomas also submitted a manuscript to La Trobe before he departed the Colony with the firm intention of writing a history of the early years of Port Phillip: La Trobe found himself unable to accomplish this history and sent all the manuscripts back to Victoria where they were eventually published in 1898 by the State Librarian, Thomas Francis Bride, as *Letters from Victorian Pioneers*, including Thomas' manuscripts.

Of these public records, by far the greatest proportion is at the Public Record Office of Victoria (PROV), in a collection which is now closed on the grounds of fragility, but accessible in full on 16 mm microfilm at present, with a portion of it now digitised. A surprising amount has finished up in the Port Phillip boxes in the Archives Authority of New South Wales, to some extent duplicating what is in the PROV, but not entirely. The La Trobe Library has a significant collection,[1] and the National Archives of Australia at Archives Victoria holds the Thomas papers from his time of reporting to the Central Board (1859).

The private record

These are Thomas' journals, 28 volumes and boxes dated from 1834–1868, intimate daily records of his work and travels with the Aboriginal people, his feelings, his relationships, his interior life. They are amongst the treasures of the Mitchell Library, exceedingly fragile now and available for reading only on 35mm microfilm copies. With the exception of the period January to December 1839, published in *Historical Records of Victoria (HRV)*,[2] Thomas' private journals have not been transcribed.[3] There is now an index available, and for this recent work, all researchers would be grateful.[4] The Mornington Peninsula Shire purchased a set of the microfilms in 2005, and the present work is based largely on information from these microfilmed journals with reference to the public record where necessary.

The aim of this research and writing is simple – to bring the Bonurong out of obscurity, in so far as it is possible, and to convey some sense of them living and moving and having their being in their own country in the earliest years of contact with Europeans. Necessarily, this meant recognising them as individuals and families, and the recovered biographical details of the lives of 26 people are inserted into the text.

We are accustomed on the Mornington Peninsula to the ritual of acknowledging the original inhabitants prior to formal meetings, and flying the Indigenous flag, but we have had very little specific knowledge of these original owners of the land. The Bonurong disappeared from the land quite quickly, but that they disappeared from memory is more puzzling. The obituary for James and Eliza Dunbar, universally accepted to be the last of the Bonurong, was published with an illustration captioned 'Jimmy Dunbar and his lubra – The last of the Mordialloc tribe':[5] not the last of the Bonurong, but the last of the Mordialloc tribe. This is a mistake on the magazine's part. There is no doubt that Europeans considered him as belonging to Mordialloc, but that was because Mordialloc

---

1 See 'The La Trobe Library collection of the papers of Assistant Protector William Thomas' (Fels 1989).
2 Edited by Michael Cannon (vol 2A, 1982, vol 2B, 1983). R Cotter's *A Cloud of Hapless Foreboding* (2005), is a re-publication of small selections from the complete published texts of Bride and Cannon.
3 Victorian Aboriginal Corporation for Languages (VACL) made a start but the funding was inadequate, Paul Paton, Manager, pers comm 11 October 2005.
4 See *The Thomas Papers in the Mitchell Library: A Comprehensive Index* (Byrt 2004).
5 *Illustrated Australian News*, 14 May 1877: 68.

was the designated reserve,[6] not because he was an original owner. Thomas
does not list him in the Family Connections Census of 1846 as belonging to
Mordialloc, and in fact a great deal more research is required into the Dunbars
and the presumed link Jimmy Dunbar/Big Jemmy/Yamerboke as both Thomas
and Native Police records list Yamerboke as a Yarra black, belonging to the Mt
Macedon section of the Waworong, not a Bonurong man at all. Thomas lists
him in the 1851 census as Yammerbook, male, Warwoorong, alias Jemmy, lubra
Koorrergrook alias Sally.[7] Redmond Barry defended *pro bono* Yamerboke and 11
other named men in January 1841, charged with assault and robbery at Peter
Snodgrass' station on the upper Yarra.[8] It is possible that there were two men
named Yamerboke so more research is needed.

We have the benefit of a 1981 archaeological survey,[9] and *Western Port
Chronology*,[10] and there is a thesis, virtually inaccessible,[11] and a two part
journal article.[12] There is also the substantial work of the anthropologist Diane
Barwick.[13] But apart from those, it is true to state that we have been forced to
rely on histories of local towns and areas and industries within the shire whose
authors were simply not in a position to go right back to primary sources. There
is as yet, no full length history of the Protectorate, though two pages of a recent
book on Merri Creek are devoted to the Protectorate at Arthurs Seat.[14] So not
only have we had little detailed information about the Bonurong as a group, still
less have we been able to recognise individuals and families speaking, acting,
living on identifiable tracts of land: worse, we have endlessly propagated errors,[15]
for example the Tal Tals as a tribal name – it is in fact, an original misreading
of Yal Yals which in turn is a corruption of Yearl Yearl, the name of the shellfish
which at the time of European contact covered the rock platform between Cape
Schanck and Point Nepean. Some histories of other municipalities contain good
general accounts of the Bonurong, but people in districts other than the local

---

6 640 acres first mentioned in Appendix 2 of the second Report of the Central Board for the Protection of
Aborigines (1862) as 'not gazetted' and carried forward each year remaining 'not gazetted'.

7 Thomas Journal, set 214, item 12: 143, ML.

8 Hart 1929: 141–142.

9 Sullivan 1981.

10 Cole 1984 has a small section on the Bonurong derived totally from original documents.

11 'William Thomas and the Port Phillip Protectorate, 1838–1849' (Crawford 1966).

12 Foxcroft 1940–1941.

13 For example, 'Mapping the past: An Atlas of Victorian clans, 1835–1904' (Barwick 1984); 'This most
resolute lady: a biographical puzzle' (Barwick 1985); 'Coranderrk and Cumeroogunga: pioneers and policy'
(Barwick 1972); 'Changes in the Aboriginal population of Victoria, 1863–1966' (Barwick 1971); 'Economic
absorption without assimilation: The case of some Melbourne part-Aboriginal families' (Barwick 1962); 'And
the lubras are ladies now' (Barwick 1974).

14 Clark and Heydon 2004.

15 *Mornington in the Wake of Flinders*, widely known, widely quoted, is a seriously misleading book
because of its inaccuracies.

shire or council can hardly be expected to be aware of them.[16] Mornington Peninsula Shire has commissioned an environmental thematic study to which the present work will make a substantial contribution.[17]

Most historians who have dipped into Thomas have generally regarded him as benign though ineffective. Mulvaney regards him positively:

> He concentrated on the practical tasks of keeping them alive ... was more successful than any other first generation settler in attempting to comprehend and sustain Aboriginal society. His charges knew him as Marminata (Good Father), and he always administered indirectly through influence on their leaders. He had striking success in settling intertribal disputes and preventing racial strife. His bravery and moral conviction were undoubted, but his advocacy of Aboriginal causes made him unpopular in colonial society.[18]

This is a view of Thomas that I share, but it needs to be noted that this view is criticised in an article which finds Thomas to be seriously flawed on the grounds of his 'whiteness' and 'maleness'.[19]

Thomas was as able to construct a good English sentence, and write a polished formal report, as any other educated man in Port Phillip. But his journals were neither – they are characterised by sentences without verbs, an abundance of

---

16 This list is not exhaustive: Niel Gunson, *The Good Country: Cranbourne Shire* (1968); Richard Broome, *Coburg: Between Two Creeks* (1987); Gillian Hibbins, *A History of the City of Springvale* (1984); Susan Priestley, *Altona: A Long View* (1988).

17 Graeme Butler and Associates, Draft Environmental History, 2008.

18 Derek J Mulvaney, 'Thomas, William (1793 – 1867)', *Australian Dictionary of Biography*, vol 2: 518.

19 Reed 2004: 87–99. In a section of this article headed 'White fantasy tropes in Thomas' writings', Reed uses the events of the night of 17 December 1839 to underpin her assertion that Thomas was afraid of Aboriginal sexuality. In fact, the night of 17 December 1839 is possibly the worst night of violence I have seen in the records. There were around 400 people encamped near the surveyor's paddock on the north side of the Yarra (the surveyors' paddock was located at what is now the corner of Flinders and Russell streets), including Barrabools from Geelong and Goulburn blacks: they had congregated in Melbourne since September, hoping for good things from La Trobe, the 'Big one Gubernor'. There had been night after night of drunkenness and violence, followed by corroborees. This night, Derrimut and Mr King arrived at the encampment drunk, and the Western Port chief Budgery Tom, irritated, threw a wonguim which happened to hit Derrimut. A fight ensued between Western Port men, unusual, very unusual. Budgery Tom was so badly wounded that Thomas thought he would die. The encampment settled down eventually, then about 11 pm two Western Port youths held down a thirteen year old Goulburn girl while ten or more ravished her. Thomas and Surveyor Smythe rescued her and Thomas proposed putting her in Mrs Thomas' tent. Her brother and sister refused, and insisted she be placed in their care. Then Thomas discovered that the alleged sister was negotiating with the males for a repeat. The encampment quietened down again, only to be disturbed half an hour later by a fight between the women, naked in front of banked up fires, the cause being the girl – some of the women were roundly abusing her for not keeping quiet while she was being assaulted. The sister was seriously cut open and a Western Port woman seriously injured as well. Thomas sent his own daughter out of the encampment, and it is for this action that Reed finds fault with him. My view is that it does not matter that Thomas was white and male: in this instance, with the chief believed to be mortally wounded, and normative behaviour gone by the wayside, it was simply prudent for Thomas to act as he did. To be fair to Reed who is a distinguished scholar, she was forced to work with general categories, there being no biographies available to her then. But Budgery Tom thought to be dying! No wonder there was chaos – had Reed had available to her biographical details of Budgery Tom, and his importance, she might have read the ensuing behaviours differently.

capital letters, abbreviations, eccentric spellings – they were basically notes of record for the book he intended to write. To publish the journals would require such editorial intervention by means of square brackets, sic, corrections, insertions and qualifiers and explanatory material, that the reading experience would be a trial; scholars would search it for facts relative to their own research, but few other readers would persevere.

Hence the decision to paraphrase, underpinned by what might seem an excessive use of footnotes, but in fact the notes function as an aid to further research: every observation can be found easily in the original and examined for what else Thomas might have written.

It would subvert the intention of the research to use the respectful and correct 'the Indigenous people' in this work. Blacks, natives, Aborigines, are Thomas' varied descriptors and they are used here with no disrespect. Likewise for Boon Wurrung, the most correct name accepted by the Victorian Aboriginal Corporation for Languages, to describe the people Thomas names variously as Bonurong, Bunerong, Boonorung, etc. As this history is mainly a record, albeit filtered through Thomas, and now through me, it would, in my view, amount to a distortion to use the modern spelling. Thomas called the people Bonurong on his 'more correct' census of 20 November 1839, and that spelling is used here in this work dealing with this earliest period; his first descriptor for the Yarra tribe was Waworong on that same census, so for the same reason, this spelling is used in this work.[20] In the same manner, I have followed Thomas' locational descriptors of other groups, for example Goulburns, Mt Macedons, instead of the correct language descriptors. These strategies are an aid in being faithful to the period of the record.

Likewise with personal names: there is no correct spelling of personal names, so Thomas' spelling, with all the variants, is followed. To standardise spelling would amount to subverting future identifications of individuals: one example will suffice. It has been published in a scholarly article that Mingaragon and Ningerranaro are one and the same person: in fact they are two separate Bonurong individuals, each a person of importance. Only the accumulation of all observations, with all spelling variants, and all collateral information could reveal this. Recording all variants is a methodological device which works in the direction of rigour in identification.

---

20 Thomas' Censuses. This 'more correct' census is to be found in its entirety in VPRS 10, unit 1/242, PROV, in Thomas' best writing, with covering letters from Thomas to Robinson and Robinson to La Trobe. The same census is to be found in Thomas' writing but not his best, at CY 3082, frames 47–52, ML. An incomplete and corrupt version (eg reading Winggolobin for Ninggolobin) of this same census is to be found in *Historical Records of Victoria* (*HRV*), vol 2B: 603–607. Thomas describes his census as 'more correct' in relation to Dredge's Census of 20 March 1839 (Robinson Papers, vol 54, A 7075/1, ML), and Thomas' own 'Names taken in encampment July 1839', (CY 2604, item 1, frame 31, ML).

In the interest of directing the reader's attention to thoughts and feelings, Aboriginal utterances are in **bold**. Square brackets [ ] are used for editorial insertions, and standard brackets ( ) are left for use by Thomas and other primary sources in direct quotations, as the sources used them.

Women's names do not appear often. A man of his times, Thomas most often referred to women as X's lubra, or by their European name, which clouds the identification because senior men had several wives. The most senior man of all the Bonurong, Mingaragon/Old Mr Man had three wives, sisters, of whom two shared the same name. Recovering female names will be a long-term project.

The major subject left out of Thomas' journal entries for the periods when he was on the Mornington Peninsula is his relationship with God. Thomas lived in the presence of God, his Heavenly Father: he began each day with scripture reading, and closed each day in prayer. He thanked God for every week, every month, every year of his life, and he began each year's journal with a recommitment of his life and work to the Divine Purpose: he wrote once that he really wanted to be a missionary. One of his earliest achievements, largely done at Tubberubbabel, was to translate into Bonurong Psalm cxxi, the Creed, the Lord's Prayer and the first chapter of Genesis, all reproduced in Chapter 12 as a mark of respect for the language, and for the time and scholarship that Thomas and his major informant, the clanhead Budgery Tom, put into the translations. These have been published before, in 1859 and 1876, but these publications are held now in reserved and rare book collections, virtually inaccessible. Quite early he preached to them in their own language, and it adds to our sense of immediacy, what the Bonurong experienced, to see these translations again in print.

Apart from Thomas' personal relationship with God which is left to his future biographer, the practical matter of religious services *is* important, for several reasons – Bonurong men would not allow the women to attend Divine Service initially, and later, when that prohibition was relaxed, attending or not attending Divine Service was a means of expressing approval or disapproval of Thomas by the Bonurong. Divine Service was also an activity to which they brought traditional behaviour, for example when the men eventually permitted the women to attend with them, the women sat with their backs to both Thomas and the men, and Thomas had to persuade the women to face him at the front.[21] So in this account, Divine Service is a constant, held twice every Sunday, morning and evening, noted when it was connected with significant action. There is later evidence of the Bonurong discussing the theological and philosophical concepts of God and Punjil, and requesting repeats of certain sermons, but it must wait till the later years of the history of the Protectorate are investigated so that the evidence can be read in its context.

21   30 May 1841 at Nerre Nerre Warren, CY 2605, frame 280, ML.

Another aspect of religious practice that *is* included is hymn singing, simply because the Bonurong gave every indication of enjoying it, as well as the flute played by Thomas' son. Thomas himself is quite matter of fact about his expectation that they would learn the hymns he taught them, but Samuel Rawson recorded that he was present at Jamieson's station on the river Kunnung (Yallock Creek) at Western Port in February 1840, when Thomas' Divine Service concluded with six white men and 'nearly all' of the 60 Bonurong singing the Halleluiah chorus:

> when the sound rose on the night air and went echoing thro' the forest, it filled one with greater awe and deeper religious feeling than I ever felt before on hearing the finest performed service in an English cathedral.[22]

I take that observation to mean that the Bonurong sang well and sang powerfully: a thin and miserable performance could not possibly have made such a profound impression on the 20 year old Rawson, an English youth just about to join his regiment at Parramatta.

Thomas' religious convictions intersected their lives in yet another important way, by sermons. In keeping with the judgemental theology of the early nineteenth century Thomas used threats of God's vengeance to condemn behaviours of which he disapproved – infanticide (Chapter 2), cannibalism (Chapter 8), the possibility of theft (see Toby's story in Chapter 4), and prevarication or deceit or dissembling (they did not apparently ever lie straight out): the use of emotional blackmail by Thomas is a part of the story, as is the reverse. In this story, as in the story of the Native Police, feelings matter.

Another aspect of behaviour which is mostly left out because it is a constant is good manners. Thomas and the blacks appear to have greeted each other every morning and closed the day with good wishes: when either party was 'sulky', that is angry, these formal courtesies were withheld, and this appears to have been experienced painfully by both Thomas and the people. Shaking hands appears frequently in the text.

Violence and drunkenness were two issues which set Thomas' pen flying, with anxiety about the consequences, condemnation of Europeans who provided alcohol, prayers of intercession for deliverance from it and imaginings of a homestation in the hinterland free of alcohol. But violence and drunkenness are scarcely mentioned in this account on the simple grounds that *he* scarcely mentions them in his record of the Bonurong on their own land. There are four instances of gratuitous violence, an immediate physical response by a male to wounded feelings.

---

22 Samuel Rawson, 'Journal from November 1839 kept while forming a new station at Western Port on the southern coast of New Holland', Ms 204/1, NLA.

As for drunkenness, there are perhaps three records of an Aboriginal man turning up drunk at Tubberubbabel: as it is not credible that a man could leave Melbourne drunk, walk the whole distance, or catch a lift in one of Edward Hobson's boats or drays, or even walk from the No Good Damper Inn near Dandenong, and still arrive drunk at Tubberubbabel, these sparse records of drunkenness probably attest more to social bonding than anything else. There must have been European friends within walking distance with whom to share a drink. On the contrary, 'happy', 'peaceful', 'settled' are the terms Thomas used about them when they were at Buckkermitterwarrer, Kangerong and Tubberubbabel.

Chapter 3 is the skeleton of the work: it only summarises the entries when he was in Melbourne concerned with all Aborigines from the various tribes, not just the Bonurong, but it does give a comprehensive account of all the activities in the periods when he was here on the Mornington Peninsula. This work concerns itself with the tiny details of place as well as people.

Because our knowledge of specific places of importance has been so scanty, for example the Martha Cove development has destroyed a major fishing site at the mouth of Brokil Creek,[23] three chapters have been devoted to amassing all the known records of the three Protectorate stations – Tubberubbabel, Kangerong and Buckkermitterwarrer. Under the provisions of the *Aboriginal Heritage Act 2006* (Vic), cultural heritage values are defined broadly; actions which leave no material trace, for example memories, stories, stated opinions, activities are all considered to contribute to the heritage values of a site.

Tubberubbabel is on private land off the Old Moorooduc Road, inaccessible of course, but Aboriginal Affairs Victoria (AAV) will investigate it in case there remain some traces of the Protectorate.[24]

Kangerong is securely identified at the flyover of Nepean Highway across the freeway, thoroughly disturbed in construction. Buckkermitterwarrer is adjacent to the Dromana drive-in, a site which has been placed as a result of this work on AAV's site register, though at the time of going to press, it has a planning permit for development.

A fourth place, Kullurk, also merits its own chapter. The observations on Kullurk were compiled because that place was the Bonurong's own choice in 1840 for a reserve of land for their imagined future. Coolart, owned by Parks Victoria is a part of that land which the Bonurong selected: it possesses the historical significance appropriate for a future interpretive centre.

---

23 The original archaeological consultant's report was simply unaware.
24 David Clark, Aboriginal Affairs Victoria, pers comm 1 September 2008.

Chapter 8, on the pre-contact massacres, is fundamental to understanding the prevailing fear of the Bonurong throughout the Protectorate year, a real fear which determined some of their actions. It has not been investigated in detail before, and it has led to consideration of contemporary evidence regarding the successive phases of inundation and drying out of Port Phillip over the last 10,000 years. For the first time, the evidence of the Bonurong that they walked across Port Phillip is confirmed by science.

The chapter on Johnny's death and burial is included because it is possible or even probable that we are walking over his grave at present, and that is unseemly. Johnny was closely engaged with George Smith (went to California with him), the person who in my view, helped to determine the nature of relationships on the Mornington Peninsula because of the bond he formed with Baddourup/Big Benbow from 1835.

Chapter 11 presents the astonishing story of Yankee Yankee, a son of the clanhead Benbow, a brother to Mary whose story is told in Chapter 6; Yankee Yankee married subsequently a daughter of the Warworong clanhead Billibellary. Yankee Yankee links the past with the present in profound ways, as some of the present people who claim the right to speak for the land are descended from the women abducted off the beach all those years ago.[25]

This chapter examines as well, the available evidence related to the issue of the women said to have been taken from Western Port, reported to be living at King George's Sound in 1839. Strange as it seems, there has been no previous investigation of the circumstances of the abduction, all previous researchers having as their primary aim the recovery of the names of the people, as part of the overarching enquiry to establish genealogical links between past and present. This would not be considered acceptable in historical research – raiding a source for names, without considering the provenance of the source, or the related detail. The circumstances of a report *do* matter, and in the present case, the truth matters enormously to both claimant groups and to residents of the Mornington Peninsula.

For example, one claim made is that three women were at Point Nepean, a 'special' place, the implication being for women's ceremonial business,[26] but the participant witness account of Matilda, which is reproduced in full, relates how the men who were present attempted to thwart the abduction, and the local people present at an interview with Robinson on 28 December 1836 told him that the tribe was down at Point Nepean hunting: knowledge of the primary sources which attest that men were present would not permit the abduction to be cast as a women only event. Another account states that Robert Cunningham joined

25   Barwick 1985.
26   Briggs 2000.

a whaling crew and eventually settled in Western Australia, which is definitely not so, as will be seen from his biographical details.[27] And if, as one source states,[28] the little girl claimed to be Louisa Briggs came back to Melbourne, aged 'about 18 years' at a time when 'there were only three houses', her return would have been in the short time frame of one year: that is between the arrival of the Europeans in 1835 when there were no buildings, and the Police Magistrate's report of 10 June 1836 which stated that there were 13 buildings.[29] As it is also believed that Louisa Briggs was born in 1836[30] there are problems with evidence that need to be reconciled.

Two separate applications to become a Registered Aboriginal Party, submitted by the Boon Wurrung Foundation Ltd, and the Bunurong Land Council Aboriginal Corporation, were declined on 27 August 2009 by the Victorian Aboriginal Heritage Council (VAHC). In its published reasons for the decision, the VAHC specifically stated that persons from both groups are descendants of the women abducted off the beach: there is no question about that. The VAHC did not however, come to a decision on the evidence before it, to register one applicant over the other. I infer from this that more primary research would be welcome, and the lengthy quotations in this chapter, mostly from primary sources, are intended as a contribution to knowledge, useful to the two groups, as well as broadly informative for the interested local reader.

As they stand, the biographical details of the 26 persons give some sense of the nature of relationships, of the complexities of individual lives, and the range of experiences. Some names appear in Thomas' record of early colonial experience, and appear again later in records from Coranderrk and in Indigenous genealogies. Only the patient accumulation of biographical details will make it apparent whether they are the same people.

The book concludes with the scholarly translations which Thomas made with the help of Indigenous people, only one of whom he names – the Western Port chief Budgery Tom. Although there is no summary statement of argument, my concluding remarks are given in an Afterword.

It remains only to permit Thomas to make his own assessment of the part played by Mrs Thomas in his work, and to have the second-last word – his claim of 'success'. It was written in 1843 as the Protectorate was re-locating for a second time from a designated Aboriginal station, this time from Nerre Nerre Warren to Merri Creek:

---

27   Rhodes and Compton 2005.
28   Briggs 2000.
29   *HRV*, vol 1: 41.
30   Lowe 2002: 1.

In taking my leave of this station I cannot but express my feelings. Few have entered the Colony more desirous of a sphere of usefulness than me and my affectionate partner. However unsuccessful we may have been, few have endeavoured more to accomplish that for which we were engaged. I think I may venture to assert that none who have entered Australia have gone through greater hardships and suffering than myself, nor has my partner been without her trials, myself ever wandering while she has been unprotected, and with scarce a covering to shelter her, and just as a comfortable place was ready, for her to be informed that she was not to enter it. The failing of that station may be attributed to many issues, tho' its proximity to Melbourne may be considered primary, yet there are others. The Protector has no power to relieve the wants of Aborigines unless sick – I used a discretionary power once and succeeded at Arthurs Seat.[31]

The last word is reserved for the Bonurong themselves, out of the mouth of Yankee Yankee, quoted in full, in its context, in Chapter 11. Reminding Thomas that the Bonurong had stopped with him at Tubberubbabel, and worked, and wanted to sow potatoes, and obtain Kullurk as their reserve, they accused him of letting them down and going away. We must be careful not to read too much into this evidence of Bonurong agreement with Thomas' plan, but there can be no doubt of the *fact* of agreement, and to that extent, Thomas was entitled to claim that his plan was a success.

---

31   Thomas Journal, CY 2605, item 5, frame 282, ML.

2. The Context

The Port Phillip Protectorate lasted from 1839 to 1849, one of a number of European policy initiatives directed towards the traditional owners of the land: these included the Yarra Mission (1837–1839) on the site of the present botanical gardens on the south bank of the Yarra River; the Native Police Corps (1837–1853) at what is now Police Paddocks, Stud Road Dandenong, subsequently re-located to Merri Creek in what is now Yarra Bend Park; and the Baptist Aboriginal School (1845–1850), also at Merri Creek.

The Protectorate was a British idea, an earnest attempt to prevent in the Port Phillip District of New South Wales a repeat of what happened in Van Diemen's Land – the virtual destruction of the original inhabitants. Only 59 or so Tasmanian Aborigines were still alive in 1839, most of them confined at Wybelena on Flinders Island and expected then to die out as a people.

The man who rounded up these Van Diemen's Land (VDL) people in his so-called Friendly Mission in the 1830s, and subsequently became their Commandant at Wybelena, was George Augustus Robinson, now appointed by London to be the Chief Protector of the Aborigines of Port Phillip on the grounds of his prior experience in VDL. He was an unsuitable appointment for Port Phillip being vain and mean and more concerned with increasing his fortune[1] than with his charges: he was appointed just before his fraud at Wybelena was recognised by the authorities in VDL. He lived off his reputation as the sole instrument of black co-operation in VDL and was a poor manager of his staff in Port Phillip, in fact a bully.[2] It is alleged that he used Trucaninni as his mistress;[3] he brought a group of eight Aborigines to Port Phillip at government expense, and more came later with his wife,[4] but in the end, he turned them loose when the

---

1   He speculated in land from shortly after his arrival in Melbourne, and later, he speculated in gold, purchasing in small lots, building them up to 1000 oz lots and consigning them to an agent in London, see Appendix 1: 31 'Gold purchased by G.A. Robinson in Victoria' in Clark 2000, vol 6: 133. Shortly after La Trobe's arrival, Robinson requested that Langhorne's mission be turned over to the Protectorate allegedly for an infants school. La Trobe made a marginal note in his journal 'Set up a *stock yard* for *his son's cattle* in the mean time!' (La Trobe's exclamation mark), *HRV*, vol 7: 282.

2   Though there has been some recent revision of Robinson's VDL activities (Johnston and Rolls 2008), his actions in Port Phillip merit in my view, a harsher summary even than that given above. Thomas' son, himself undeniably a partisan reporter, is on record as saying that Robinson was a proven liar. According to WJ Thomas, Robinson gave the four assistant protectors a lecture on his arrival in Port Phillip about the VDL Aborigines at Wybelena – that they were civilised and sincere Christians, whereas the truth was, according to Thomas, he had trapped them into coming in by wholesale lying and was afraid of them, needing a body of police on Wybelena where he ruled them with a rod of iron and that they 'held him no good will' (CY 3106, frames 43–54, ML).

3   Rae-Ellis 1988.

4   *HRV*, vol 2B: 393.

government refused to keep them on rations.[5] One of these ten was a 12 year old boy named Ben Lomand, cast out to fend for himself; two of them were hanged, while Trucaninni escaped conviction and was sent back to VDL.[6]

Though there is no doubting Robinson's altruistic motives in attempting his Friendly Mission to the VDL Aborigines in the first place, by the end of 1836 he was soured by the failure of the authorities to reward him financially for the job he had done. The following lengthy quotation indicates his feelings, and goes some way to explain why he was out to feather his nest in Port Phillip:

> After near nine years service in one of the greatest enterprises ever achieved of its kind, after the most signal advantages gained by my successful endeavours in the security of life and property, in the increased value of land consequent upon the removal of the aborigines by my exertions and that of my family, after being the instrument of restoring peace and tranquillity to the colony at large, in being the means of saving the lives of numbers both black and white, after having thereby ameliorated the condition of the original occupants of the soil, after all these and numerous other and great advantages, myself to be refused land and refused a pension, and my sons also to have nothing, although they and I were unanimously recommended by a board of officers and by the Council, and not only not reward us but heap insult upon ingratitude by telling us it is enough to be employed, to tell me that had I fallen a sacrifice my family would have been abandoned without provision, what I would ask is all this but insult added to the basest ingratitude, ingratitude of the worst kind.[7]

To help Robinson the British government appointed four assistants, of whom three were Methodist schoolteachers, James Dredge, William Parker and William Thomas, while the fourth, Charles Sievwright, was an ex Army officer who arrived with serious problems.[8] These four arrived in Port Phillip in January 1839, from England via Sydney: they all had wives and they had 22 children between them. They arrived with expectations[9] but found no accommodation

---

5   The governor in Sydney retrospectively absolved Robinson from responsibility authorising La Trobe 'to release Mr Robinson from any further necessity of maintaining these persons, and at the same time to request that you will report whether they cannot in some advantageous manner be disposed of at Port Phillip, as there will be probably considerable difficulty in returning the Blacks to Flinders Island as proposed by Mr Robinson', (Col Sec to Superintendent, 2 October 1840, VPRS 10, unit 2/1069, PROV).

6   Two of these people Smallboy and Tunnerminnerwate, known in Port Phillip as Bob and Jack, were hanged in the first public execution in Port Phillip in 1842, after killing two whalers at Westernport. Trucaninni, Matilda and Fanny who were with them, were found not guilty and sent back to Van Diemen's Land; see *HRV*, vol 2B: 393; Macfarlane 1984.

7   Robinson Journal, 7 October 1836, in Plomley 1987: 386.

8   His financial troubles are discussed by Cannon in Chapter 14 of *HRV*, vol 2B: 365; he became unduly attached to Mrs Parker on the voyage out to New South Wales; Robinson told Dredge in an interview on 2 September 1842 that Sievwright was dismissed on the grounds of 'general immorality', (Dredge Diary, 1839–1843, Ms 5244: 264, SLV).

9   James Dredge, the assistant protector for the Goulburn, had a delicate wife, and he wrote that 'one object of my removal to this country was the benefit of my family', *HRV*, vol 2B: 433. Elsewhere he wrote that to relieve her of even the necessity of

(they had to live in tents), no organisation of their duties, no knowledge of their charges or their languages, and a penny-pinching government in Sydney which was almost bankrupt, and, as a consequence, failed to grant them what they needed for their jobs. One example will suffice; they were supposed to be given four bullocks each to cart to their districts all their supplies for the Aborigines, as well as all their tents and personal baggage and families, prior to commencing their duties. Though Governor Gipps directed from Sydney that they be supplied with four bullocks, Captain Lonsdale in Melbourne interpreted the direction as meaning one bullock each:[10] one bullock could not pull a loaded dray. So they remained in Melbourne for months.

William Thomas was given the 'Westernport or Melbourne District' defined as 'Bounded on the south by the coast; on the north by the Australian Alps; on the west by Port Phillip; the eastern boundary undefined': the Yarra and Port Phillip and Western Port blacks became his responsibility.[11] The Yarra blacks, the Warworong, owned the Yarra drainage basin – all that country from the dividing ranges south to the Bolin swamp,[12] that flows into the Yarra or Paarran. The Port Phillip and Western Port blacks, the Bonurong, owned all the coastal drainage basin, all the land from Werribee to Wilson's Promontory which was drained by the waterways that flow into Port Phillip and Western Port, including the lower reaches of the Yarra. The Yarra River is the exception to the principle of watercourses falling into the sea, according to Thomas.[13]

William Thomas was the standout assistant protector, in terms of intimacy with his people. He was a man of religious conviction who sacrificed himself and his family life in order to do his job. He led a deeply spiritual interior life, undoubtedly the source of his concern for the injustice of government policy:

> to infringe on which [their land] without remuneration is an injustice
> not consonant to humanity and repugnant to Christian feelings.[14]

Actually, the injustice was consonant not with British policy, but with the way that policy was interpreted in New South Wales.

Once Thomas almost put a curse on the land: he was speaking about Gippsland, but it is a measure of how much he identified with Aboriginal thinking that he used Aboriginal language as well as his own:

---

superintending servants doing the domestic work was one object he sought in coming to Port Phillip, see *HRV*, vol 2B: 428.

10   William Jackson Thomas, CY 3106, frame 57, ML.

11   *HRV*, vol 2B: 452.

12   Thomas Journal, Boundary South of the Yarra Blacks Country, CY 2984: 535, ML.

13   Thomas Miscellaneous Papers, CY 2984: 92, ML.

14   Thomas First Periodical Report, *HRV*, vol 2B: 622.

and what has the poor creatures for their country – not a *sou* ... can heavenly father look down with any degree of pleasure on a country located on such terms. Such injustice is of itself enough to prompt God from his place to visit with Murrain Mildew, catter pillar and pestilence.[15]

His religious conviction is probably too, the bedrock of his courage in standing up to the Chief Protector, and pressing the case for justice to the Superintendent of the Port Phillip District, Charles Joseph La Trobe, and to the Governor of New South Wales, Sir George Gipps.

Thomas asked first in 1839 that the proceeds from the sale of the 895 acres which is now South Yarra and Toorak, including the site of the Botanical Gardens, be given to the Port Phillip and Western Port blacks so that they could purchase cattle for themselves. This old 1837 mission site was their former reserve, granted by Sir Richard Bourke, and it was being measured for sale in ten acre allotments. Thomas respectfully requested Sir George Gipps to give them another reserve more in the interior, and with the cattle purchased from the sale proceeds, they could form their own agricultural and cattle station.[16] But his petition fell on deaf ears: the authorities did not see it as Thomas did, as a justice issue. They saw revenue.

Thomas' second petition to Gipps requests a whole raft of changes to what he considered to be unjust government policy:

- let them have firearms
- do not let settlers take them out of their own country because they are assassinated in the new country
- do not sell any more Special Surveys because the three that have been sold – Dendy's at Brighton, Unwin's at Bulleen and Jamieson's at Mt Martha – were all favoured fishing places of the natives
- do not make them work for their rations but feed them at the same generous scale as Robinson's VDL blacks receive without having to work[17]
- allow Aboriginal evidence to be given in court
- finally, as the Bonurong refuse to settle at Nerre Nerre Warren with the Warworong or Yarra blacks, give them what they want – a reserve for themselves between Sandy Point and Cape Schanck 'with the grand object likely to be attained of keeping the Aborigines in one place and securing the rising generation'.[18]

---

15   Thomas Journal, Monday 24 February 1845, CY 2606, item 3, frame 263, ML.
16   Thomas to Gipps, 20 December 1839, VPRS 10, unit 1, 1839/336, PROV.
17   Daily, 1 lb of meat fresh or salt, one and a half lbs of flour, 3 oz sugar, one quarter of an ounce of tea, 1 oz soap, half an ounce of salt.
18   Thomas' petition to Gipps, 23 June 1841, enc with VPRS 10, unit 3, 1841/909, PROV.

Thomas discussed this petition with La Trobe on 28 July 1841: La Trobe objected to some clauses and had not yet sent it to Sydney, a month after receiving it. Thomas learned that it was rejected by Gipps on 11 October 1841.

Thomas' third petition puts the case bluntly – the settlers' sheep and cattle eat the roots and herbs which were formerly devoured by the kangaroos, emus etc and the result is a scarcity of the means of subsistence for the Aborigines.[19]

The account that follows is about the minutiae of daily living for the Bonurong – it is an account of only one year. Perhaps therefore, a broadbrush impression of the wider context will be helpful in placing these daily living records in context – the British government expectations, the character of the squatters on the Mornington Peninsula, and the state of the Bonurong when Thomas arrived in 1839.

The model of the Protectorate

At the highest level of reality, the British government policy guidelines, the following is a fair summation of expectations of the Protectorate:

> The duties of the Protectors of the Aborigines in New Holland should consist first, in cultivating a personal knowledge of the natives, and a personal intercourse with them; and with that view these officers should be expected to acquire an adequate familiarity with the native language. To facilitate the growth of confidence, the Protectors should be furnished with some means of making to the tribes occasional presents of articles either of use or ornament, of course abstaining from the gift of liquors. The Protectors should ascertain what is that species of industry which is least foreign to the habits and disposition of the objects of their care, and should be provided with all the necessary means of supplying them with such employment. Especially should they claim for the maintenance of the Aborigines such land as may be necessary for their support. So long as agriculture shall be distasteful to them, they should be provided with the means of pursuing the chase without molestation.[20]

This is neither a noble nor a realistic set of guidelines, but it does at least presume that the Aborigines can continue to move freely about their land.

The Aborigines were to have the same rights as other British subjects:

---

19   Byrt 2004, CD WT 3126P.DOC.
20   Report from the Select Committee on Aborigines, House of Commons, 26 June 1837, *HRV*, vol 2A: 68.

> To regard them as aliens, with whom a war can exist, and against whom Her Majesty's troops may exercise belligerent rights, is to deny that protection to which they derive the highest possible claim from the sovereignty which has been assumed over the whole of their ancient possessions.[21]

There is confusion here – sovereignty is claimed but dispossession is not foreseen.

In passing, it must be said that there was no legal mechanism on the ground, so to speak, by which the Aborigines actually lost their rights to country, to their way of life. *Terra nullius* has nothing to do with what happened on the ground. Under the 'Squatting Act' of 1836, one of the functions of the Commissioners of Crown Land together with their Border Police was to protect the rights of Aborigines in distant parts of the country: half the expense of the Border Police was considered to be incurred on behalf of the Aborigines.[22] This Act assumes that Aborigines were free to move about their country.

Even ten years later, when the licence system for squatting was about to be replaced by the lease system, the British government was still insisting that the Aborigines were entitled to their traditional way of living:

> The Government must prevent the Aborigines being altogether excluded ... it is essential it be understood that leases granted ... give grantees only an exclusive[23] right of pasturage for their cattle and of cultivating fenced land ... these leases are not intended to deprive the natives of their former right to hunt or ... from the spontaneous produce of the soil.[24]

The actual mechanics of dispossession – keeping them out of town, off stations, off water supplies, killing their dogs, the replacement of game by flocks and herds – none of these were done by legal means, but rather, by administrative fiat and settlers' will.[25] Foxcroft's 1940 summary statement 'that the NSW Protectorate was an example of the application of will without knowledge to native problems' is accurate.[26]

---

21 Lord Glenelg to the Governor of NSW, Sir Richard Bourke, 26 July 1837, *HRV*, vol 2A: 69.

22 William Lithgow, Auditor General 'Return of the Expenses defrayed from the Colonial Treasury of NSW... [on] Aborigines', *NSW Legislative Council Votes & Proceedings*, 1843.

23 Exclusive against other squatters, not exclusive against the Aborigines.

24 Earl Grey to Governor Fitzroy, 11 February 1848, *HRA*, series 1, vol 26: 225.

25 In *That's my country belonging to me*, Clark (1998b) devotes Chapter 7 to the mechanics of dispossession, namely squatters who prohibited access, actions aimed to intimidate Aboriginal people, Aborigines kept out of townships, and architectural and locational adjustments.

26 Foxcroft 1940–1941 pt I: 77.

The character of the squatters on the Mornington Peninsula

It was a fact that the Aborigines of the Port Phillip District, the Bonurong and the Warworong were attracted to, and actually cultivated, high status Europeans – gentlemen – and that they despised convicts.[27] From the vantage point of a meritocracy such as our own society, it requires a real effort to understand how taken-for-granted were the manners, mores and attitudes of a class-based society. It so happens that most of the names of squatters on the Mornington Peninsula in 1839–40, who feature in Thomas' journals, also appear in Paul de Serville's appendixes of Gentlemen by Birth (titled, landed or armigerous families), Gentlemen in Society (profession, commission and upbringing) or Colonists claiming gentle birth and accepted by other gentlemen as gentlemen.[28] Edward Hobson and his brother, Dr Edmund Hobson (Kangerong), the brothers Archibald, Hugh and Thomas Bushby Jamieson[29] (Kangerong Special Survey), Robert Jamieson (Cape Schanck), Samuel Rawson (Kunnung with Robert Jamieson), Captain Reid (Tichingurook), Captain Baxter (Carup Carup), Alfred and Maurice Meyrick (Boniong), Henry Howard Meyrick (Coolart), the Barker brothers (Barrabong and Cape Schanck), and George Smith (Turtgoorook) living with a woman believed by Melbourne society to be a niece by marriage of the great Captain William Hobson RN, were all gentlemen in terms of one or other of de Serville's categories.

The Western Port squatters impressed Richard Howitt on a walk to Western Port and return to Melbourne in 1843:

> On this occasion as on others, my opinion was strengthened that the squatters, most of them the younger branches of wealthy and respectable English and Scotch families, are on the whole an intelligent and gentlemanly race.[30]

Two things matter about these gentlemen: as de Serville says, 'gentlemen approached the exotic flora and fauna and the black race with the curiosity of the Romantic amateur'.[31] Hence the corroborees which all Melbourne polite society attended, the collection of artefacts, the adoption of black children, the name exchanges, the genuine friendships between some gentlemen and high status Aboriginal men, such as that between the young Henry Howard Meyrick of Coolart, and Yal Yal, the young son of Bobbinary, the co-owner of the whole of the Mornington Peninsula including of course Coolart.

---

27 The evidence for this is to be found in Fels 1988: 90 ff 'Real Black Gentlemen'.
28 de Serville 1980, Appendixes 1, 2 and 3.
29 There was a Bonurong man, Trooper Bushby Jamieson, who served in Commandant Henry Dana's 1842 Native Police Corps.
30 Howitt 1845: 150.
31 de Serville 1980: 36.

If we ever knew it or noticed it, we have lost sight of a second fact – that the Mornington Peninsula squatters from the earliest period were so young – like overgrown schoolboys seems to be Dr Edmond Hobson's view. He was himself only 25 when he came down here to convalesce, and he wrote thus to his wife:

> I have not at all fallen in love with the Arthurs Seat society. The young ones are in conversation coarse and beastly; for example Mr Barker arrived here [Kangerong] yesterday from town, on his way called at Major Fraser's station [Mordialloc] where he saw Miss F in the bush, indecently exposed. This was the first topic and I suppose ere this everyone in the district knows he has seen Miss Fraser's naked bottom.[32]

Edward Hobson was 22; Henry Howard Meyrick was 17; brother Alfred was 19; cousin Maurice 20 (and Maurice was said to be an initiated man[33]); Samuel Rawson was 19; George Desailley was 17; his brother Francis junior 19; the Barker brothers were 22 and 24; the Jamieson brothers were in their twenties; only the two military men, Captain Reid and Captain Baxter, and George Smith were mature adults.[34] And contrary to what is commonly believed,[35] George Smith came down to the Mornington Peninsula not to Rye initially, but to Buckkermitterwarrer and Kangerong, and when he came, it was with a solid three year relationship of reciprocity already built up with Benbow, father of Mary, father also of Yankee Yankee.

The state of the Bonurong

Thomas wrote a thumbnail sketch of their social organisation thus:

> Their Government is patriarchal. They have a Chief to each tribe and a few Priests, Doctors, Enchanters, Dreamers etc who form a kind of Privy Council and Aristocracy. Their form of government however, is no burden to the State – the Chief governs, Priests advise, Doctors and Enchanters cure, Warriors fight, but each and all *gratis*, equally plying for their daily food.[36]

The first fact to be noted is that two of the Western Port clan heads, Budgery Tom and Kollorlock signed Batman's treaty: Thomas lists the signatories thus:

32   Hobson Papers, Ms 8457, Box 865/2, B, undated, SLV; de Serville makes the same point in his statement that 'Until the 1842 depression at least, the atmosphere in the settlement often resembled that of an un-reformed public school [in England] before the tone had been elevated by a middle-class Arnold', de Serville 1980: 37; Gunson makes a similar point, Gunson 1968: 40.
33   Webb 1996: 12.
34   This factor of youth in the squatters appears to be true of the western district as well. George Russell states that the majority were young – he mentions Armytage and Ricketts being not yet 20, and he says that the only mature man was Captain Foster Fyans appointed with judicial authority to prevent collisions with the natives, who was twice the squatters' age (Brown 1941-1971, vol 2: 57).
35   Hollinshed, undated, 'A local History of the Mornington Peninsula to 1900', TS, p. 80.
36   Thomas Miscellaneous Papers, CY 2984: 90, ML.

Billibellary — Chief Yarra

Moone Moonie — Ditto Land [illegible, looks like Marg]

Koolloorlook — Ditto Western Port

Metturandanuk — Ditto Ditto.[37]

It does not matter at the time, that the authorities subsequently repudiated it. On the ground, in face to face relationships where it did matter, the reciprocal obligation worked much like a rental agreement.[38] Batman fed them[39] and they expected it, and they were free to congregate in Melbourne. They referred back subsequently to Batman's time as the good times compared with life under the Protectorate. Billibellary made the first recorded protest about Protectorate stinginess and the governor's policy of exclusion from Melbourne at the end of 1839:

> **Why you want Black Fellows away? Plenty long time ago Meregeek[40] Batman come here. Black Fellows stop long long time. All Black Fellows plenty bread, plenty sugar, etc etc.[41]**

It was definitely not just a whim of La Trobe's that the blacks were to be excluded from congregating in Melbourne — the explicit directive came from Sydney:

> I have to acquaint you that His Excellency the Governor and His Honour the Superintendent have directed that no Aboriginal Blacks of this District are to visit the Township of Melbourne under any pretext whatever. You will therefore adopt the requisite measures for their so doing.[42]

Much later, Hugh McCrae added an editorial insert into that part of Georgiana's narrative in which she records that she crossed the Yarra in a punt, with two natives and a gin. Hugh says that natives on the outward journey from Melbourne were exempt from payment for the crossing.[43]

---

37   CY 2606, item 1, ML.
38   Batman called it 'the annual tribute to those who are the real owners of the soil', John Batman to Sir George Arthur, 25 June 1835, *HRV*, vol 1: 9.
39   This is but one piece of evidence — a systematic search would reveal the total amount of expenditure on food for the natives. The financial statements for the period 8 May to 8 July 1835 in the Port Phillip Association Papers list 43 pounds, 18 shillings and 2 pence as the amount spent on goods for the natives of Port Phillip (Ms 11230, SLV).
40   *Meregeek* means very good.
41   Billibellary's quoted words in Thomas to Robinson, 1 January 1840, CY 2946, item 2, ML. Billibellary was the most important clan head of the Warworong. There were 300 blacks in Melbourne including Goulburns who had come down to Melbourne to see La Trobe and participate in the feasting, and who remained at the invitation of the Warworong and Bonurong to fight the Barrabools. Thomas, at La Trobe's instigation was charged with getting them all out of town. Billibellary's argument was that in Batman's time they were allowed to stay in Melbourne and had plenty to eat. For another account of the same argument, see also Thomas Journal, 31 December 1839, CY 2604, item 4, ML.
42   Robinson to Thomas, 12 September 1840, enc to VPRS 10, unit 2, 1840/931, PROV.
43   McCrae 1966: 43.

Secondly, there was an influenza outbreak in Port Phillip in the first three months of 1839, just as the protectors arrived, and it is quite likely that Robinson and his VDL family brought it: he and his VDL family were already ill with it when they arrived at Port Phillip.[44] There was dysentery as well. So early in the job, the protectors had only a rudimentary understanding of tribes and country, and still less knowledge of the people as individuals. So the records do not enable us to determine how badly the Bonurong suffered as distinct from the other tribes. But Melbourne was their country – they were congregating there – it would be remarkable if they escaped the illness and the deaths. There was also 'the venereal'. Dr Cussen, who was called in by the protectors, said that he had never seen the people in such a distressed state.[45] Thomas made a list of families whom he was treating in Melbourne in April 1840 for the 'Bad Disorder': it includes some Bonurong.[46]

Thirdly they were hungry when they were in Melbourne.[47] Their pre-European pattern of living included regular congregating in what is now the city of Melbourne – all five of the Kulin nations – but for a short time only, for business and ceremony: local food resources could cope with large numbers for a short time. The arrival of the protectors with their goods and their promises, followed by the arrival of La Trobe in September 1839 attracted hundreds of the five tribes to Melbourne, expecting largesse. They stayed in the summer of 1839 for months, and came back in the spring, and they were hungry, denied access to European enclosures, forbidden to cut bark for miams for shelter, and with kangaroos scarce around what are now the suburbs of Melbourne: Thomas recorded in this period that he rode for 20 miles on the south of the Yarra and did not see one kangaroo.

By the time the protectors arrived, getting a living around Melbourne was hard – there were already 6000 whites in Port Phillip,[48] almost the same number as the protectors' estimation of the total native population for the whole of Victoria, and hundreds of thousands of sheep, not to mention the cattle.[49] In 1839 well over 200 ships arrived in Port Phillip bringing settlers and their livestock. An early Aboriginal response to this influx was given in evidence at the trial of ten Goulburn blacks in 1841: the settler quoted Windberry, a

---

44 An influenza epidemic raged in Hobart for months at the end of 1838 and the beginning of 1839. Two government vessels, the *Tamar* and the *Vansittart* brought it to Flinders Island in February 1839 and Robinson recorded that 'three parts' of the natives had contracted the illness, some 'very bad'; this happened as the cutter was loading for Port Phillip to bring Robinson and his VDL 'family', Plomley 1987: 616, 617.

45 *HRV*, vol 2B: 523–524.

46 'Families bad dis[order]', Thomas Journal, 12 April 1840, CY 2605, item 1, ML.

47 'Starving' according to *HRV*, vol 2B: 517.

48 Shaw 1989–90: 30.

49 I am not aware of any study of the effects of rotational stock grazing of sheep on *murnong* and the grasslands, nor of set-stock grazing of cattle. There is plenty of evidence that the stock did well in the early years, but I have not seen evidence or research on how the native pastures fared, except for the fact that game became scarce, presumably because of overgrazing.

Yarra black as asking for sheep, and when refused by the settler saying **'The sheep eat the grass belonging to his kangaroo, and what for no give him sheep?'**[50]

And it needs to be remembered that 1837–1840 was a major drought episode (a general fast was observed in Port Phillip on 2 November 1838 on account of the long-continued drought).[51] Some of the well known squatters who appear in this narrative were part of a joint stock venture to supply fresh water to Melbourne – Frederick Manton (Manton's Creek), Andrew McCrae (Arthur's Seat), Benjamin Baxter (Carup Carup), Alfred and George Langhorne (Dandenong), James Clow (Corhanwarrabul).[52] As a consequence of this long drought, the *murnong* or daisy yam, a tuberous root and a major vegetable and carbohydrate source, disappeared from the baked and dusty soil – cropped by sheep to the point where it could not be located underground. Though a settler told Thomas that you could actually dig and find *murnong* within enclosed sheep yards, where not a blade of green could be seen on top of the ground, that was not an option generally available to the Bonurong who were not allowed to enter enclosed or fenced land.[53]

But by far the most important thing to be noted is that they were still free to move about their country when the Protectorate was established. The fact has escaped our notice that it was a full three years, 1835–1838, before there was *any* squatting on the Mornington Peninsula, and when Thomas made his first visit to the Mornington Peninsula in 1839 there were only four European stations – Frazer at Mordialloc, Hobson at Dromana, Meyrick at Boneo and Jamieson at Cape Schanck. There were no boundaries between them, no perimeter fencing.[54]

The original owners of the soil (Batman's phrase) had made tactful and intelligent accommodations to white sensibilities. Thomas noted that they did not camp in stock paddocks, and they always camped on water a few hundred yards away from the squatters' huts.[55] This was partly because of their dogs (one time later in the 1840s the blacks between them had 900 dogs with them in Melbourne), and partly because Europeans thought they smelled.

---

50   'Report of Trial of Aborigines, Mr Barry defending', *Port Phillip Gazette*, 16 January 1841.

51   Gurner 1978[1876]: 43.

52   Sullivan 1985: 65.

53   Thomas to Robinson, 28 July 1839, *HRV*, vol 7: 332.

54   No map of Pastoral Runs is reproduced in this book, because the period under examination, 1839–1840 pre-dates the formal organisation of pastoral runs, and in the absence of boundaries any image would be misleading, just a guess.

55   Thomas Journal, 17 March 1840, CY 2605, item 1, ML. It is noteworthy though that in his summary retrospective for this March, 1840, he recorded that at Munnup near Dandenong on the trek back from Kunnung, the native dogs begin to give offence, all prepare to shift. Both observations are true, I suspect.

The arrival of La Trobe as Superintendent may be seen with hindsight to be the trigger that caused the collapse of Bonurong and Warworong society. Our local landowners did not die from the gun: on the contrary no Aboriginal person was killed by guns on the Mornington Peninsula. Equally, if not more importantly, because it was one of their own proud boasts, and the source of feelings of ingratitude and injustice, they not only did not kill any Europeans, they defended and helped them. Thomas confirmed it.

> Of all the tribes in Australia Felix only the Melbourne tribes have not stained the ground with white man's blood. They have peaceably given way to our intrusion … but for them, Melbourne might have been a sepulchre instead of a town.[56]

The protest against the white men's injustice and ingratitude, and assertion of ownership of the country, which first appeared in the records with Billibellary's objection quoted above on the last day of 1839, is more firmly expressed a few months later in Melbourne in April 1840, after La Trobe ordered the removal of their guns; their response was the logical rhetorical one of:

> **'What for white man guns? Big one hungry. Black fellows by & by – no kangaroo – white man take away black Fellows Country, now gun. By & by all dead poor blackfellow'**. They were very insolent for the rest of the day, Thomas wrote and he quoted them again as saying **'Yangelly, Yangelly** [be off with you][57] **bloody white man.**[58]

The protest is repeated in September when Benbow and Ben Benger related all their past good services to the white people then concluded with:

> **Now many white people come and turn Black fellows away – why white man Pilmularly [steal][59] ground? And no let good white fellows give poor Black fellows bread.**[60]

They were still asserting their claim two days later **'Deny white men's right to the land'**[61] is Thomas' marginal note. Benbow, clanhead of the Werribee River section related the story of how he and other Port Phillip blacks went after the Barabool blacks who had killed Charles Franks[62] and **booed**[63] them; he was

---

56 Thomas Periodical Report, 1 September 1843 to 1 December 1843, VPRS 4410, unit 3/78, PROV.
57 *Yangelly* means be off, see Thomas 'Leading sentences, vocab', CY 2605, item 1, ML.
58 Thomas Journal, CY 2605, item 1, ML.
59 *Pilmerlarle* means steal see Robinson, GA, Port Phillip vocab, in Plomley 1987: 672.
60 Thomas Journal, Sunday 13 September 1840, CY 2604, item 3, ML.
61 Bain Attwood has named Coranderrk as the first example of sustained protest in Australia, Attwood 2003: 6. Had the evidence presented here been available to him he may well have commenced his history with the Bonurong and Warworong protest from 1839.
62 Charles Franks and his convict servant Flinders were killed at Mt Cotterill north-west of Melbourne in 1836: Franks was killed for not paying the rent, see *HRV*, vol 2A: 40–41.
63 *Boo* means shoot, Thomas to Robinson, 10 July 1839, in *HRV*, vol 7: 328. 'Billy Lonsdale, Turnbull, Derrimut, Bangan, Mur re mu ram bin, Mr King and Burrenul [Mr Dredge] with arms and ammunition have

almost crying, Thomas wrote, as he told how he booed his own wife's mother – all for the sake of the whites. '**Now, go away, go away, soldiers say, no good that**'. Thomas explained that they 'make willums on white man's ground, and cut down Trees, & cut off bark, make white man sulky'. They replied '**Not white man's ground, black mans**'. Thomas found himself unable to refute that logic, and they went further, defied the rules, and scored a point against the soldiers. Immediately following the '**Not white man's ground, black mans**', he wrote:

> I found it a hard lesson to reason. I then showed them that there was a Rail paddock where they were Quomb'd. They (I could not help laughing) said **Marnameek Narlumbannun here no Horse soldiers Kimbarly**.[64]

They were still saying it a year later:

> The blacks very dissatisfied this morning and talk much about **no good white man, take away country, no good bush; All white men sit down, gogo kangaroo. Then Black fellows come to Melbourne and white men sulky. No good that. No Black fellows sulky when few white men here and Woodulyul Black**. This is not the first time they have reasoned in this manner.[65]

And they said it again in 1842. The testimony appears in the government enquiry into the Aborigines of 1858–59 and it came from Derrimut, a Bonurong, via the magistrate William Hull. Hull testified that in 1842, he saw a procession of 20 or 30 blacks walking the boundaries of Melbourne. He joined them – they were bewailing the occupation of this place by the white man, singing low and plaintive songs. He went on to tell the story of how he met Derrimut in Melbourne nearly opposite the Bank of Victoria and Derrimut asked him for a shilling. Hull refused to give him the shilling but said he would buy Derrimut bread:

> then he pointed with a plaintive manner which they can effect to the Bank of Victoria. He said '**You see, Mr Hull, Bank of Victoria, all this mine, all along here Derrimut's once; no matter now, me soon tumble down**'. I said '**Have you no children?**' and he flew into a passion immediately, '**Why me have lubra? Why me picaninny?**

---

left Melbourne for Geelong to boo emus at Bar ra bul.' Thomas wrote that the jealousy if not enmity between the Barrabool tribe and those who have gone *booi*ng is great, that he fears it is not only emus that they have gone to *boo*. Even so, it needs to be mentioned that *boo* has multiple meanings; the same word covered two other situations – shooting at some thing or someone and not killing, plus the further meaning of shooting up in the air in high spirits.

64   Thomas Journal, CY 2604, item 3, frame 195, ML.

65   Thomas Journal, Friday 17 September 1841, CY 2604, item 3, ML. I do not know as yet what *Woodulyul* means.

You have all this place, no good have children, no good have lubra, me tumble down and die very soon now'. They are very sensitive and they are all destroying their children now.[66]

They were acting out their protest by 1843. The following, with no editorial amendments, is from Thomas' Journal of Proceedings which he submitted to Robinson, the official version:

I have a long conversation with Billibellary, Chief of the Yarra tribe, on my belief that the blacks killed their infants he acknowledged that they did so and named who had had children since I had been among them, 8 in number (two only are living) he said they had two ways of doing so one by twisting a cord several times around their necks the other by putting a Koogra (opossum rug) over their heads, he said that the lubras made away with them that Blackfellows all about say, **'that no good have them Pickaninneys now, no country for Blackfellows like long time ago'**.

Thomas pointed out how wicked it was, that God when they died would ask all those lubras where those children were that were killed. Thomas further told Billibellary that there was country enough for black and white people if they would but stop in one place. Billibellary responded that if Yarra Blackfellows had a country on the Yarra they would stop on it and cultivate the ground. He said that there were three lubras who would soon have Pickaninneys and he would see that they did not kill them.[67]

Another version from his field journal for 7 October 1843 is as follows, again presented with no editorial amendments:

I have a long conversation this day with Billi Bellary on the subject of killing there Infants when born, he acknowledged it was so, I named those who had had children since I had been among them <u>8 in my tribes only</u>, and only his Suzanna alive – he said they done it with a cord Generally – but sometimes by putting a Koogra all round its head – he said that Black Lubra's say now **no good children, Black fellows say no country now for them, very good We kill & no more come up Pickaniny** – I pointed out to him the wickedness of the practice that God would ask all those Lubras when they died where those children

---

66 Testimony of William Hull Esq. JP, 9 November 1858, in 'Report of the Select Committee on the Aborigines', *Victoria, Legislative Council Votes & Proceedings*, 1859.
67 Thomas Journal of Proceedings for the period 1 September 1843 to 1 December 1843, VPRS 4410, unit 3/78, PROV.

were that they killed – Billybellary promised that he would endeavour to make them let their children live – he said there were 3 who would soon have pickaninys, marry.[68]

Thomas did record though, somewhat more understanding in his marginal comments on the births and deaths list for June to November 1844: noting that infanticide is on the increase, he added 'their argument has some reason, **no good pickaninnys now no country'**.[69]

It is fundamentally true to say that they died because they lost their land. Official policy from the first was to get them out of Melbourne where up until La Trobe's arrival they had been camping in their usual spots, South Melbourne by the Yarra falls, Botanical Gardens,[70] eastern hill, Richmond paddocks near the Melbourne Cricket Ground, Abbotsford, South Yarra, Toorak, Bulleen swamp, Merri Creek, Moonee Ponds, North Melbourne, Port Melbourne, when they needed or wanted to. The meetings of the confederacy of Kulin like the last huge one in 1844 when upwards of 800 were present, including Dana's Native Police in full uniform, were held at Merri Creek. This particular full and formal meeting concerned the Bonurong and Warworong – two of the leading men and greatest warriors Poleorong/Billy Lonsdale, a Bonurong, and Warwordo/Lively, a Warworong, underwent ritual spearing for killing Mr Manton's black, a Wooralim, at Tooradin.[71]

It seems that only then, when they were refused their rights to live and congregate in Melbourne that they recognised they had lost their rights to country, as compared with the continuing rights they maintained under the reciprocal rental agreement that they had with Batman. It is frightening to read in the records how quickly they moved from the position of freedom to move about their country, to regret and protest, and prediction that they would all die out. This bitter realisation first appears in the records in 1840, and it coincides with not permitting babies born to live. The conclusion seems inescapable, that when they realised that they had lost their country a meaningful future went too. It seems life itself could not be led as 'real' Bonurong, could not be imagined, without their country for their future children. This is not merely a matter of dispiritedness, or dejection or depression. It is a positive choice about identity and the essence of being Bonurong – who they were. In the western cultural tradition people who lay down their lives for an idea of the good are seen as martyrs, heroes, saints; they claim our reverence and respect. There is

---

68   Thomas Journal, CY 2606, item 2, ML. Note that the journal for October has been microfilmed backwards (frame 99).
69   Thomas Journal, CY 2604, item 5, frame 284, ML.
70   The Western Port tribes' camping place was 'where the Governor-General's residence now stands' according to 'Reminiscences from 1841 of William Kyle, a Pioneer', *Victorian Historical Magazine* (*VHM*) 10(3), June 1925: 164.
71   Thomas to Robinson, 13 February 1844, VPRS 11, unit 8/469, PROV.

a difference, it is true, between laying down one's own life, and taking that of one's child, but there is room for thought as to how great or how small that difference might be.

It is quite clear that both Robinson and Thomas' minds were attuned to the possibility of extinction by 1845. Part of the job description suggested by the House of Commons Select Committee on Aborigines (British Settlements) specifically urged the collection of accurate statistical information, the reason being:

> It is probable that the depopulation and decay of many tribes which, in different parts of the world, have sunk under European encroachments would have been arrested in its course, if the progress of the calamity had from time to time been brought distinctly under the notice of any authority competent to redress the wrong. In many cases, the first distinct apprehension of the reality and magnitude of the evil has not been acquired until it was ascertained that some uncivilized nation had ceased to exist.[72]

In answer to a request from Robinson for a report on the number of half-caste children, Thomas wrote bluntly 'I beg to state that there are none in either of the tribes in my district'. He went on 'The youngest child in my tribes is near five years old, which will shew the probable speedy extinction of these tribes'.[73] This child was Suzannah, Billibellary's daughter, born 7 November 1839 in the encampment by the Yarra.[74] On Thomas' Family Connections Census of 1846, the youngest Bonurong child is eight, a girl called Borut, the child of Old Doctor and his wife Boorowrook.[75] The oldest Warworong child is seven years old; little Suzannah's name is absent though Billibellary's six other children are listed. It seems that the Bonurong and the Warworong meant what they said – no child had survived since the beginning of 1840. In 1847 Thomas wrote that it was a strange thing that but one child is in existence of the Melbourne tribes of age since the date of the Colony.

---

72 *HRV*, vol 2A: 69.
73 Thomas to Robinson, 2 January 1845, CY 2606, item 3.
74 *HRV*, vol 2B: 603.
75 Thomas Papers, CY 3083, ML.

Fig 2. 'Billibellary's Young Lubra with infant on back'

Reproduced from the RB Smyth Papers with the permission of the State Library of Victoria.

Suzannah

20 November 1839, female baby born in encampment by the Yarra, 13 Days old, part of Billibellary's family (VPRS 10, unit 1/242, PROV); Sketch of her in *Historical Records of Victoria (HRV)*, vol 2B: 556, named after Mrs Thomas; 27 July 1842 – rations have been issued for her [allegedly as the wife of a serving Native Police man, but actually daughter of the high status chief, an example of Commandant Henry Dana's cooking the books in order to please Billibellary] since 1 May, on the same scale as the surveyors (Dana to La Trobe, enc to 42/1143, VPRS 19, Box 30, PROV); 31 July 1842 – Little Suzannah (Bergyunuk) female, aged 2, disease Pseudo Syphilis, treatment Licquor Arsenic plus aperients and copper sulphate washes (Medical Report of Henry Jones Dispenser to the Aboriginal Natives, Melbourne or Westernport District, from 1 July 1842 to 31 July 1842, VPRS 4410, unit 2, item 49, PROV); 15 Nov 1845 – Susanna, died at encampment east of Melbourne, aged 8, female, Yarra tribe, single (Thomas Return, Appendix D to Governor's Despatches, April–June 1846, A 1240, vol 51, ML). The *Port Phillip Patriot* of 10 October 1845 notes 'the fearful ravages' of an outbreak of whooping cough in Melbourne – it is possible that little Suzanna succumbed to this disease.

Thomas' retrospective (1857) view on the subject of infanticide[76]

Infanticide has existed among them – I do not think that it owing to want of food, or affection on the mother's part to a certain extent I attribute it more to the releasing them of the trouble in rearing their offspring. When I came among them in 1839 I soon found Infanticide existed, and in very urgent language got the Chief of the Yarra tribe to use his influence in stopping it. The Chief had a large family of his own and was in the strictest sense of the word a kind, good and sensible black. He arraigned the tribes at night upon the subject, and in foreceable language, and I was in hopes that he had succeeded, but a few months after I had reason to believe another had been made away with, and again urged the Chief when he frankly acknowledged that he could not stop it *'that the blacks said they had no country now and no good have em picckaninnies'*. I am fully persuaded that they do not commit infanticide upon any superstitious grounds. My impression is that it is

---

76   Response to Question 18, CY 2984, frames 48–49, ML.

about the 21ˢᵗ day after the birth that they are put out of the way. The mother's lamentation is affecting during the operation. I never had but one (almost evident) case of infanticide under my observation. I was far away on the track to Gippsland. At daybreak I heard the lamentation of death. I awoke my Government Servant and went direct to the lubra who had had an infant about three weeks.[77] She was in great (apparent) anguish but no babe. I insisted on seeing it when she pointed to a little fire about 30 yards off, and there sat the old woman who had been the nurse, with the little innocent wrapped over and over again, and corded up for internment. I with my knife cut the cords. The child was still warm but life had gone, smothering, (as no marks of violence was on the body) is in my opinion the way they despatch them. I may here remark that tho' I feel persuaded almost all since I have been among them have been made away with, yet such is their knowledge of my abhorrence, that when the infant is 14 or 15 days old will with a few others leave the encampment & return in about a fortnight invariable without their babe, their faces in deep morning [mourning].

77   Quondum, see Chapter 3.

3. The record of observation

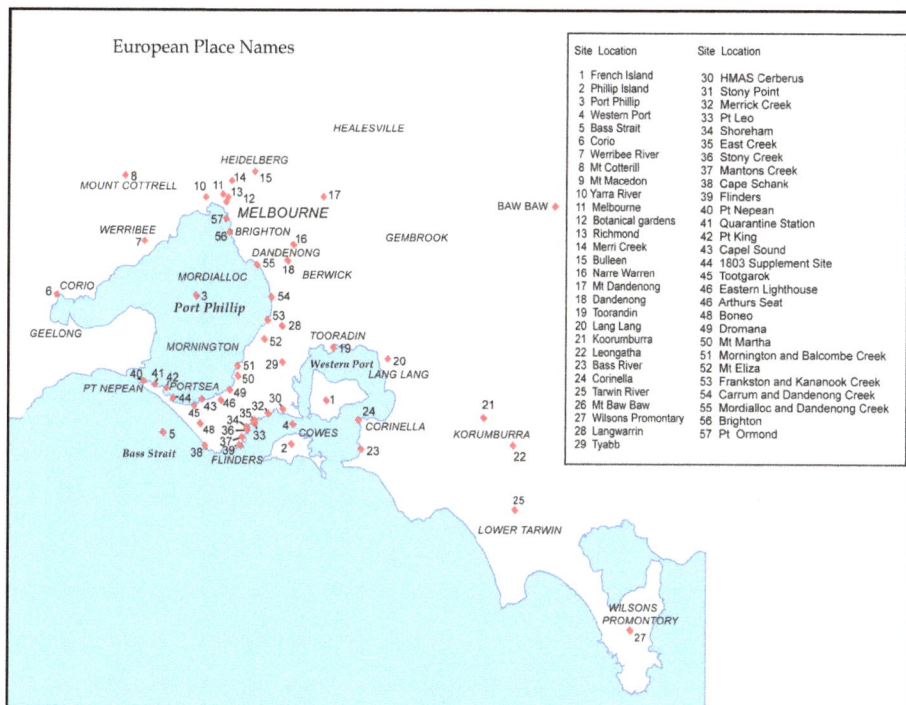

Fig 3. 'European placenames mentioned in text'

Phil Hughes, GIS department, Mornington Peninsula Shire, reproduced with permission.

This chronology is selective for the periods when the Bonurong were in Melbourne, noting only those events which I consider to be of significance or interest specifically to them. When they moved back into their own country, this chronology records incidents of significance on a daily basis – the fundamental criteria for selection being the aim of introducing the reader to the terms and conditions of daily living – what life was like, as well as getting the names of the people into the public record so that we can begin to see the original owners of the peninsula as people, not as the category 'The Aborigines'.

3 January 1839

The four Assistant Protectors, Edward Stone Parker, James Dredge, Charles Wightman Sievwright and William Thomas arrived in Melbourne from England via Sydney, all with wives and with 22 children between them.[1]

---

1   *HRV,* vol 2B: 419. Robinson told Dredge on 2 September 1842 that Sievwright was dismissed for 'general immorality' (not involving Aborigines), Dredge Diary 1839–1843, MS 5244, SLV; Dredge resigned early and was replaced by Le Souef who was also dismissed.

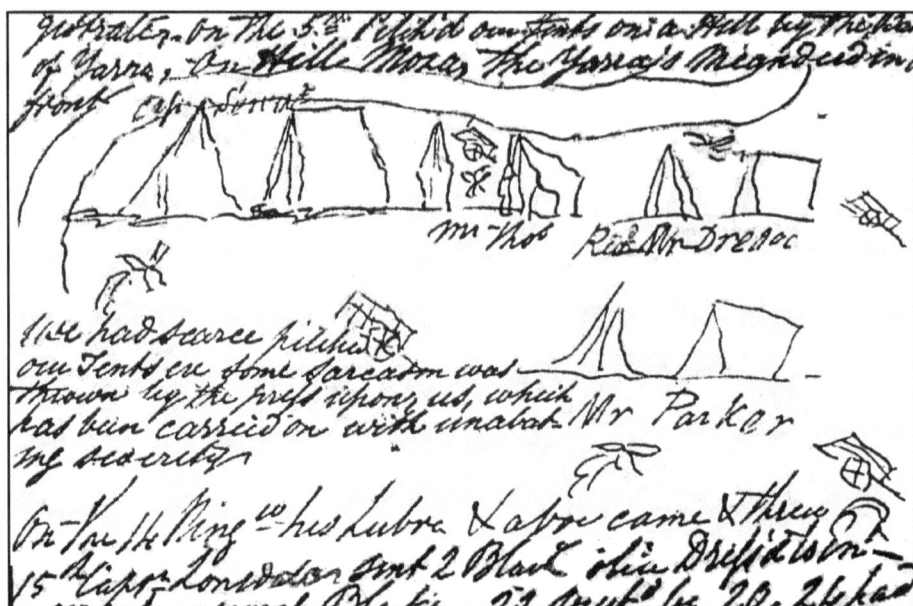

Fig 4. 'Assistant Protectors' tents at bend in Yarra'

Thomas sketch, from the William Thomas papers, 1834–1868, 1902, Mitchell Library, reproduced with the permission of the State Library of New South Wales.

14 January 1839

Ningerranow, a fine Aborigine and his wife and two boys aged about nine and 11 visited Thomas on the banks of the Yarra and demonstrated throwing a boomerang. The woman was dressed 'comfortable' wearing a fine opossum skin cloak and appeared very different to the naked wretches Thomas had seen at Sydney.[2]

12 February 1839

An old Bonurong woman named Dindo and her two sons Derremot and Ningerranow with their families were the first people to come in to the protectors presenting with the symptoms of influenza, which was to sweep through the blacks. Thomas consulted Assistant Protector Sievwright who had some medical knowledge as a consequence of his army service, and between their efforts and those of Mrs Thomas who sent a quart of tea plus bread to them every morning, they nursed this particular family back to health. Thomas was usually the bearer of the bread and tea, and he took his children with him, specifically 'in order to bring them into sympathy with these poor people'.[3]

---

2 Thomas Journal, CY 2604, item 3, frame 73, ML.
3 Thomas Journal, CY 2604, item 3, ML.

28 March 1839

'A Grand Feast to introduce the Protectors and convince the Blacks that the Protectors were their friends'.

> Friendly Blackfellows were despatched in all directions to sound the call among the more distant tribes. Arrangements were made with the Government to supply provisions, firewood, cooking utensils etc. Notice given in the two newspapers of the Grand Feast inviting the public to attend. The Protectors had borrowed a large marquee from the Survey Department, and provided at their own expense, lunch and liquid refreshment for the elite of Melbourne. The locality selected was on the Eastern Hill somewhere about the junction of Collins and Russell Streets.
>
> There on Thursday 28 March 1839 assembled more than 500 Blackfellows. A large fire was made with certain iron arrangements for spits, where whole quarters of beef and whole sheep were roasted. Men with choppers and knives on by blocks divided and distributed to the Blacks. By boilers in which Tea was made and served out in great pannicans. Altogether that day was consumed and carried away – for what they could not eat was given them to take away – 600lbs of beef, 200 lbs Mutton, 500 lbs Bread, 100 lbs Rice, 50 lbs Sugar, 7 lbs Tea.
>
> Mr Sievwright had charge of the Refreshment tent where a large number of Ladies and Gentlemen partook of the hospitality and thoroughly enjoyed the day. The other Protectors busily engaged serving the blacks.
>
> In the afternoon sports were held. Racing. They were divided into Groups. Two tomahawks stuck into a tree. 150 yards measured, Two Groups off. The first two in the race secured a Tomahawk each. Then other groups took their place, until a good many Tomahawks had been won. Then throwing the spear for various prizes, and the way those fellows would split a board one and a half inches thick was something to look at. Then throwing the reed spear at hats thrown into the air. Then wrestling, but they were not good at that, their greasy bodies not affording good hold. Climbing poles and throwing the Boomerang concluded the day. Care was taken that the Blacks should not get a drop of liquor.
>
> The whole passed off splendidly, everyone was pleased and the black Lubras carried off a good deal of tucker. The two assigned servants, who had assisted as waiters in the refreshment tent during the day, were found at night to be helplessly drunk and were turned into Government.[4]

---

4   William Jackson Thomas, 'Reminiscences', CY 3106, frames 54–55, ML.

1 April 1839

The Assistant Protectors were allocated their districts and ordered into the field, excepting Thomas, whose district was 'the Melbourne or Westernport District' and who was ordered to remain in Melbourne because so many Aborigines of his district were congregated there. He was also to act as the Chief Protector's scribe and clerk.[5]

6 May 1839

Thomas records the distressed and diseased state of the natives; in the opinion of Dr Cussen who was called to attend to them:

> In the whole of his experience of 18 months (and he has had occasion to attend many) that he never visited them in such a diseased and wretched state of want and disease, and that five or six more are at the verge of death, and that unless something is done to relieve their wants, speedy extinction must soon take place.[6]

He also corroborates Mr Sievwright's account of the awful prevalence of the venereal disease, and states further that 'they feel truly sensitive and grateful for any the smallest attention being paid to their condition'.[7]

The venereal

This is not a simple observation and it has to be carefully considered. Dr Cussen was horrified at 'the venereal'. Note that the observation refers to 'the natives' – it is not an observation about the Bonurong specifically but about people from all districts congregated in Melbourne. A secondary source has quoted Thomas as saying that 9/10 of the Bonurong were labouring with the Venereal Disease,[8] but this is a result of misreading the original source.

The original record is a quote with quotation marks included by Thomas in his journal for 5 May 1839, and repeated as a quote with quotation marks in his monthly summary of events:[9] it is from another Assistant Protector's report – Sievwright, just before the four assistant protectors were forced out of Melbourne by Robinson to their respective districts.

---

5   *HRV*, vol 2B: 451–452.
6   In the original Ms, Thomas calls this man Dr Cousins (Thomas Journal, Monday 6 May 1839, CY 2604, frame 82, ML). Dr Patrick Cussen was the Colonial Surgeon: Thomas often calls him Dr Cousins.
7   *HRV*, vol 2B: 524.
8   Sullivan 1981: 17.
9   CY 2604, item 1, frame 49 and frame 82, ML.

Mr S – report has this affecting sentence, 9/10 of these poor creatures are labouring under the Venereal Disease, which is not confined to age or sex, the Infant at the breast, as well as the aged & infirm are infected with it.

The observation refers to blacks congregating in Melbourne, not only the Bonurong; there had been blacks from Geelong, Mt Macedon, the Loddon River and the Goulburn River in town, as well as the Yarra and Western Port blacks. The observation doubtless includes Bonurong, but the flat assertion as it stands is simply wrong: it is not Thomas speaking, and it is not about the Bonurong exclusively. There is a section on the evidence for syphilis which questions the diagnosis itself, later in this chapter.

Thomas recorded their state as appalling (5 May); their sufferings were exacerbated by a period of extreme cold weather (bitter night 3 May, piercing cold 5 May). He wrote that he felt himself honoured to be able to assist a lubra to get her dying husband off the ground to attend to what nature required. He was very old, and blind, and his legs were paralysed, and once she had got him up clutching her digging stick, she had to move his legs one at a time. Her tenderness impressed him (19 May).[10] In another version of the same period Thomas records the word for cold:

> not a blanket to cover them and we their Protectors had not a single Blanket at our disposal for these poor creatures. St James the Apostle should have been here. Could the British Parliament or His Excellency have felt our feelings they could certainly never have placed us in such a position without means. They did not however in vain call out **dinke** – cold – I and my colleagues gave them blankets from our own beds.[11]

4 July 1839

Thomas receives his orders from the Chief Protector to depart for Western Port.[12]

13 July 1839

Thomas, still in Melbourne, decided to sleep with the blacks at their encampment, though his two servants refused. He had a tent, but no food or water, no bed and no pannican or billy. Two Bonurong men, Poleorong (Billy Lonsdale) and Munnmunngeen made up a big fire as close to Thomas' tent as was safe, and then slept outside his tent flap. In the morning before full daylight Poleorong peeped in when Thomas was reading his morning psalms. 'No bread you, no lay down you, no good that no bread' was Poleorong's response.

---

10   *HRV*, vol 2B: 522, 523, 525.
11   Thomas Journal, 5 May 1839, CY 2604, item 3, frame 82, ML.
12   *HRV*, vol 2B: 531.

Poleorong went and got him some fire, and some bread, sugar and tea saying **'white man give me, me give you'**. Thomas thanked him but sent the bread back and gave Poleorong the tea and sugar and half a crown. But Poleorong insisted **'No me give you'**. Thomas forced him to take the money but asked for water and a pannican which Poleorong brought to him. Thomas' stomach 'eaved' at the blacks' pannican and the blacks' water but he was so thirsty that he was glad of it.[13]

Poleorong/Polleorong/Billy Lonsdale

His father is Nomminditolong who died about 2 December 1839 after leaving the encampment at Moody Yallock (Thomas Journal, CY 2604, item 4, ML); his brother is Buller Bullup; Poleorong was a person analogous to a wizard, dreaded by strangers (Thomas Notebook in Brough Smyth Papers, SLV); his Aboriginal name Poleeorong alludes to the cherry tree where his mother brought him forth (Thomas, 17 August 1863 in Smyth 1878, vol 2: 91).

1837 — According to Brough Smyth quoting Thomas' notes, it was Governor Sir Richard Bourke who conferred on Poleorrong the name Billy Lonsdale after Captain Lonsdale, the first Police Magistrate in Port Phillip (Smyth 1972, vol 1: 82).

22 Jan 1839 — 'Saw one particularly fine young man as I was going to Melbourne. He was leaning against the post of a hut door. In his clean blanket down to his legs he had a majestic appearance. Nothing of the savage appeared in him. His countenance was dignified and frank. He surpassed all that I had yet seen. I went up to him. His speech was remarkable. Soft, in fact more like that of a female. He spoke English well, that is to say what he spoke was correct in pronunciation. He said **"You go to Melbourne"**. I said yes. He said to the brick-maker whose hut he was at **"Good bye"**. He asked me my name and told me his, he said Captain Lonsdale was his brother. I walked with him. He called a boat, we crossed the Yarra together. He was particular in telling me the names of the trees, ground, grass, water, dogs etc', (*HRV*, vol 2B: 436); 5 Jun 1839 — Billy Lonsdale and Turnbull brought to Robinson buttons and cloth for Native Police uniforms, from Captain Lonsdale (Robinson in Clark 1998, vol 1: 50); 11 Jun 1839 — Robinson purchased two blankets at eight shillings each for Turnbull and Billy Lonsdale (Robinson in Clark 1998, vol 1: 50); Jul 1839 — Poo-le-o-rong, name taken in encampment (Thomas 'A' diary, set 214, item 1, ML); 15 Jul 1839 — My first night sleeping with the blacks, Billy Lonsdale and Murrumban slept by my door. Poleorong brought Thomas food and water

13   Thomas Abstract for July 1839, CY 2604, item 2, frame 59, ML.

(Thomas 'A' diary, set 214/1, ML); 17 Jul 1839 – Ballaymoro alias Billy Lonsdale, he and six named others arrived at Geelong (Sievwright to CP, 39/10217 in 4/2471, AO of NSW); 17 Sep 1839 – Old Morragine told the story and Ningolobin confirmed it that Poleorong, Talliorang and Derrimut, with Kulpendure's help, killed Peter, Mr Langhorne's Murrumbidgee boy at Western Port. Next day, the culprits asked Thomas **'What for sulky?', 'No good that blackfellow, no his country this and no good you'** (Thomas Journal, 1839–40, uncat MSS set 214, box 1, ML); 17 Sep 1839 – same facts are recorded in Robinson (Clark 1998, vol 1: 83); 17 Nov 1839 – Billy Lonsdale called on Robinson and gave him a necklace of kangaroo teeth, for which Robinson gave in exchange a rug, knife and rice; Billy Lonsdale gave Robinson much info about the blacks, which Robinson says 'is entered' (Robinson in Clark 1998, vol 1: 344); 22 Nov 1839 – Poolirong, male aged 24, Bunurong tribe (Thomas census, VPRS 10, unit 1, PROV).

No date but early – At the brickworks at Princes Bridge, Thomas was with the Western Port black Billy Lonsdale who said, watching a man smooth clay, **Pundgyl make em Koolins – Pundgyl worked up the clay with his big one knife and when all soft commenced to make Man, beginning at the feet and the legs and so on upwards, he made a man on each piece of bark when he had made them he looked at them a long while was pleased danced round them he then got some stringy bark made hair of it and put on their heads once straight and the other he curled, Pundgyl was big one pleased and danced round them he gave each a name** (Byrt 2004, CY 3131, T DOC).

1840 – Thomas' half yearly report states that Poleorong and Buller Bullup left for Lake Colac without telling him (40/12629 in 4.2512/1, AO of NSW); 1840 – Listed with de Villiers and Kollorllok as a party of three in a large group of 57 present at Arthurs Seat and determined to go to Western Port (Thomas Journal, CY 2605, frame 8, ML); 1840 – Poleorong's name is on a list of single men (Thomas Journal, CY 2605, frame 23, ML); 7 Jun 1840 – in Melbourne Billy Lonsdale gave GA Robinson a list of 24 names of those Western Ports presently at Tubberubbabel (Clark 1998, vol 1: 344).

8 July 1841 – Dredge was at Geelong to preach and saw two Boonworong, Billy Lonsdale and Mr de Villiers (Dredge Diary 1839–1843, Ms 5244: 199, SLV).

5 Dec 1843 – Two blacks came to Thomas' tent at Merri Creek and said that he was 'no good' for writing a letter to La Trobe to put Billy Lonsdale and d'Villiers in gaol (VPRS 4410, unit 3/79: 2, PROV).

> 13 Feb 1844 – great gathering of the tribes, nearly 700, to witness judicial proceedings against Poleorong (Thomas to Robinson, VPRS 11, unit 8, PROV); no date – in his later remarks, Thomas says upwards of 800 were present and that Poleorong and Warardor were two of the leading men and greatest warriors in the Western Port tribe (Thomas in Bride 1969: 433); 7 Apr 1844 – Yankee Yankee brought before the Bench for obstructing the Chief Constable in his attempt to arrest Poleorong for the murder of the young Aboriginal boy in the service of Mr Manton at Western Port (Smyth 1972, vol 1: 81 quoting a colonial magistrate).
>
> 1846 or 1847 – CCL Tyers said that Billy Lonsdale and Yal Yal led a party from Melbourne who killed 30 of the Corner Inlet blacks between Tarwin and Corner Inlet (Governor's Despatches, January–December 1853, pp. 1649–1654, A 2342, ML).
>
> 13 Mar 1848 – Complaint by Poleorong about his employer Mr Glass; Billy Lonsdale does not wish me to stir further in it, he states that next season he will see that no blacks work for Glass (Thomas to Robinson, VPRS 11, box 11/691, PROV); 4 Sep 1848 – Commandant HEP Dana lists Billy Lonsdale among a number of Western Port men armed, and seeking revenge in Gippsland (La Trobe to Col Sec 19 September 1848, 48/10473 in Port Phillip Part 3, 4/2824, AO of NSW); 12 Sep 1848 – Thomas reports that when he was last at Western Port, quite a few Western Port men were in Gippsland to seduce or barter for women, including Billy Lonsdale, due back at the end of September (VPRS 11, Box 11/701, PROV).
>
> Jan 1852 – A Bacchus Marsh black 'killed Buller Bullup (Western Port Tribe and brother to Billy Lonsdale)' (Thomas Journal, Byrt 2004: 171).

16 August 1839

Thomas started for Arthurs Seat[14] having sent off his men and his cart earlier.[15] Robinson had suggested to him two days earlier that somewhere near Arthurs Seat would be preferable to the Western Port coast as a central situation for his district.[16]

17 August 1839

Thomas arrived at Edward Hobson's station, Kangerong, near Mt Martha on the Mornington Peninsula: there were about 36 natives there.[17]

---

14   *HRV*, vol 2B: 535.
15   Thomas Journal, Summary of Proceedings for August 1839, CY 3082, ML.
16   Thomas Journal, Summary of Proceedings for August 1839, CY 3082, ML.
17   *HRV*, vol 2B: 536. Note that Byrt annotates 'My first Journey with the blacks', as an 1839 document (Byrt 2004: 20). This is correct because Thomas himself has inserted 1839 at a later date, when he was writing up

18 August 1839

Thomas took the names and number of the blacks and commenced a vocabulary at Hobson's.[18] Apart from one old man[19] they all seemed perfectly well and happy.[20]

19 August 1839

Hobson showed Thomas his six work agreements with blacks lately in the service of Mr Batman.[21] Thomas informed the blacks living at Hobson's that he was going to live among them and make a miam for his lubra.[22] Next day when he visited the encampment he found six families preparing to go hunting for five days; they invited him to come too, and he would have gone with them, except that he had no provisions and he did not wish to start his 'career' with them by depending on their bounty. Several women and children went fishing, to be back in three days.[23]

Exploration on foot of the southern peninsula

20–25 August 1839

Thomas passed Meyricks' Station.[24] About six miles beyond Arthurs Seat, en route to Point Nepean, and about a furlong inland from the beach, he came upon several miams where there were vast quantities of oyster shells.[25] He spent the night at Desailley's station.[26]

He then 'imprudently' proceeded to Cape Schanck without compass or map, to visit Robert Jamieson who had been a fellow passenger on the ship out from England, but he did not call in at the station because he met Jamieson on the

---

his papers. But the document itself narrates the events of January and February 1840, when Billibellary in Melbourne exhorted the Bonurong to go to Arthurs Seat, then tried hard to prevent Thomas accompanying the Western Port blacks on their raid, on the grounds that he would be killed. When Thomas alludes to his first journey he is meaning the first journey to Western Port and beyond which took place in February 1840, see later in this chapter.

18   *HRV*, vol 2B: 536.

19   Thomas has scratched out something and there is an inkblot, so his text cannot be read with absolute confidence, but this old man is almost certainly Bunggane, male, Bonurong, aged 60, an elder, husband of Tuaningrook, who died at Arthurs Seat in August 1839, see Thomas Return of Births and Deaths, 1 April 1839 – 29 February 1840, VPRS 4410, unit 3/66, PROV. Bunggane was the father of Poleorong.

20   Thomas Journal, Summary of Proceedings for August 1839, CY 3082, ML.

21   Thomas Journal, set 214, item 1, ML. These men were Pigeon, Joseph and an unnamed man. The work agreements set out the work to be done and the wages paid. Hobson's three blacks received the same pay as a white man – 12 pounds, 14 shillings to 16 pounds plus board and lodging (*HRV*, vol 2B: 766).

22   Thomas Journal, Summary of Proceedings for August 1839, CY 3082, ML.

23   Thomas Journal, Summary of Proceedings for August 1839, CY 3082, ML.

24   *HRV*, vol 2B: 536. Boniong on the Old Cape Schanck road.

25   Thomas Journal, Summary of Proceedings for August 1839, CY 3082, ML.

26   The Desailley brothers' station was Tondomohuc: on Thomas' map he locates it at the back of Rosebud between Boniong and Port Phillip.

road. He filled his pockets with little fish like cockles from the beach, and traced minutely from Cape Schanck to Point Nepean but could not find the least appearance of a native encampment. He got to Point Nepean, then went back to Observation Point on the Western Port side, finding two faint tracks only. He crossed again to Point King where he passed several kangaroo tracks as plain as cattle tracks, and saw several flocks of boomer kangaroos, 50 or more depasturing together. He ran down the kangaroo tracks but could not find water, spending two days and a night without it, till it rained and he was able to catch water in a handkerchief which he sucked.[27] He was dive-bombed by an immense sea eagle, took fright and ran, came to a rise and saw Port Phillip, and was able to navigate his way back to the native encampment and his quarters at 4 pm on 25 August.[28] Next day he selected his head station Tubberubbabel, see Chapter 4.

On the inside cardboard front cover of Thomas' 'A' Diary, he wrote a description of what he saw on this first exploratory visit. It is reproduced here in full because of the value of the information – he gives the name of the mollusc, **Yearl Yearl**, from whence the people became known as the Yal Yals, corrupted later by misreading to Tal Tals, and he indicates clearly that the lime industry began with the destruction of middens, and there is an early mention of the First Settlement site at Sullivan's bay.

> Pt Nepean – the fragment of Old Settlement, the foundations of large house or building still remain, surely by the appearance a settlement was intended, though could any thought be so [one word illegible]. I have travelled here for miles in all Directions, in search of water (& now winter), but in vain, not even a puddle. About 1/2 Mile or More beyond Arthur's Seat & 1/4 mile from beech in reeds, a fine rivulet of water running rapid (now Winter) – beyond this on the way to Pt Nepean, thirteen miles from the coast, an agricultural and lime Establishment. 6 men are employed. All seem friendly to the blacks. Shells are here in abundance – may be gathered as fast as you can load (comparatively speaking). The Men informed me that they had a wonderful supply of good and excellent water. They have often shifted their huts and never failed of good supply of water by digging 20–30 feet. They had lately discovered some limestone. They dug by it and found water in abundance of the purest kind issuing from springs [two words illegible]. Agriculture they say pays wonderfully. I think I understand that this Establishment belongs to Mr Saul___. From Cape Schanck to Pt Nepean

---

27 This description of the kangaroo walk near or at Point King resonates with John Murray's 1802 description of the country about Point King having no water, several hundred acres recently burnt, large trees well spaced, no brush, altogether reminding him of Greenwich Park (Murray 2001: 66–67).
28 *HRV*, vol 2B: 537; Thomas Journal, Summary of Proceedings for August 1839, CY 3082, ML.

is the most dangerous coast I ever saw; rocks not only stretching into the sea, but separate from the Beech, in the sea, & almost the whole Beech is a strand of irregular rock, thousands of adhering fish, the likes of the cockle[29] kind, but much larger and fatter. The natives call them **Yearl Yearl.** I lived on these for 4 days, filling both my large pockets, so that I might prosecute my journey. Thro' some of these rocks I crept thro' that were on the beech, there was one huge rock about 90 or 100 feet high that had an opening like an archway wide enough for a dray or two to pass through. I slept on the top of the Mountain 2 nights and the sound of the sea most terrific as the waves struck the rocks in the sea like cannons going off, and that continually while the continued beating of the sea on the rock shore was like continuous thunder. The trees on the top of these mountains grows horizontal thus >>>>, large as well as small. I slept one night on an horizontal myrtle group which inclined with my weight like a bed and these trees are in good wholesome condition, and large as well, if not finer than any I have ever seen in the Colony. All of the bush kinds. I cannot account for this in no other way than the power of forces of SW winds forcing them in this oblique direction while young, and yet they are stronger in the earth, I do think, than those in the usual position. I saw but few, very few trees that had fallen tho' the wind here is enough to blow even rocks to pieces.

On the shore between Cape Schanck and Nepean Pt are many curious specimens of the growth of seaweed to rock. I do think that the muck of weed, seashell etc has formed if not the large rock on this coast, the rocky strand. I examined several portions of weed some with fish that had become that hard that I could not make an impression with my fingers, only pressing very hard with my stick, could then just imprint, and so as not to return to its former state – the seaweed, muck and sand, shellfish. I doubt not with the great powerful force of the SW wind have formed the heterogenous mass of Rocky Beech from Cape Schanck to Pt Nepean, and to establish my theory still more, the beech from Pt Nepean to Arthur's Seat is quite the reverse – seaweed soft and natural, and nature resumes in growth of trees etc etc. A clear flat sandy Beech presents itself, and uninterrupted by Rock etc, save just at the turn of Pt Nepean and at the base and peak of Arthur's Seat.

I traversed for four days almost every Mountain hill and dale from Pt Nepean to Cape Schanck – 1 day coasting only on the Beech,

---

29 Cockle is the common name for a group of (mostly) small, edible, saltwater clams, marine bi-valve molluscs in the family Cardiidae. There are more than 200 species of cockles with many more fossil forms.

1 day crossing from Cape Schanck to about 5 miles W of Arthur's Seat and about 1 and ½ miles from the coast to within 4 or 5 miles again off Pt Nepean, and 1 in crossing the tongue of land from the Arthur's Seat coast to the C Schanck coast, and then taking a central course by a diagonal direction between the two shores, coming within 3 miles of Arthur's Seat and then making for the Beech.

I saw 1 or 2 native paths in that tongue of land in the whole, about 50 kangaroo tracks, almost as large and as trodden down by foot of man. I saw, I should suppose, 500 at least and often 40 or 50 in a drove. They run an eminence size near Pt Nepean.[30] The country is rich and good, and if water was plentiful, doubt not but squatters would soon find their way hither. I could not find the least appearance of water in the whole rout till within a mile of Cape Schanck, and that I did not discover till the third day, when I drank to excess. About 2 miles further than Arthur's Seat were 12 huts most substantially built which I doubt not in their periodical fishing excursions they return to, & from appearances they return to and inhabit their own individual huts.

I should have stated on C Schanck and Nepean Pt is the fragments I should think of wreck – Cask, Hatchway [illegible] surely not the [illegible].[31]

8 September 1839

Thomas departed for Melbourne in response to an order from the Chief Protector.[32]

9 October 1839

Thomas departed from Melbourne with his wife and children for Arthurs Seat, a difficult journey with his wife sick, the creeks flooded (Mordialloc, Kannanook, Balcombe), the bullocks becoming stuck in mud with much unloading and reloading of the dray.[33] They arrived back at his hut at Tubberubbabel on 12 October and the lubras and children were pleased to greet him.[34]

14 October 1839

Robinson ordered Thomas straight back to Melbourne and the blacks were very dissatisfied, said **'Big one lie. You tell blackfellows to come to you and then you no stop'**.[35]

---

30 This is a puzzle – big kangaroos near Point Nepean; Robinson notes the same thing – big kangaroos, boomers, he calls them, at Point King. Why the kangaroos were so large as to be remarkable in this small area is the puzzle.
31 Thomas Journal, CY 2604, frame 1, ML. Even the original is difficult as the cardboard edge is deteriorating.
32 *HRV*, vol 2B: 542.
33 *HRV*, vol 2B: 551.
34 *HRV*, vol 2B: 552.
35 *HRV*, vol 2B: 552.

While in Melbourne, the most significant event appears to involve Billibellary's lubras. Robinson ordered Thomas to enquire into the circumstances of an attack on them by a butcher's dog. It was not an accident. Two eyewitnesses, Mr McArthur and Mr Henty actually saw the butcher, Thomas Whitehead, set his dog on the women and Thomas escorted the women, the witnesses and Billibellary to the Chief Magistrate, who refused to hear the case, and further, refused to grant a constable to bring the butcher to the court. Thomas issued a summons himself, exercising his power as a Justice of the Peace, and the next day, Saturday 19 October, prepared a tent in order to hear the case himself. The two witnesses attended, and Thomas took their depositions, and they all waited till midday but the accused did not appear. Thomas then waited on the chairman of Quarter Sessions and the Crown Prosecutor who 'refused to give any advice, the least ever, in Aboriginal matters'. In his account of this matter Thomas wrote in the margin:

> Is it possible when the powers that be are against the blacks any good will be done for them.[36]

21 October 1839

Thomas left Melbourne again for Arthurs Seat, meeting 54 blacks who were on their way to Tubberubbabel; he had another awful journey, wading through Mordialloc Creek up to his waist, nearly drowning his bullocks in a rising tide at a creek eight miles further on (Konigo, now Frankston); then further on he had another drama when his milking cow's calf swam back over another creek (between Frankston and Mt Martha, Smythe lists the following creeks, in order going south from Frankston, Narringulling, Ballar, Kackerabooite, Gunyung and Caarrar) the cow followed her calf, then the four hobbled bullocks followed the cow and her calf: everyone survived, and he got back to Tubberubbabel at sunset.[37]

26 October 1839

Thomas persuaded all the blacks at Hobson's to come to him at Tubberubbabel, and outlined his plan to them for manufactured goods – see Chapter 9. Then a black messenger arrived from Melbourne summoning all the blacks to Melbourne. Next morning, a Sunday, he had to cut short Divine Service so he could feed them before they set off. Only five remained – women and children.[38]

---

36   CY 2604, item 3, frame 112, ML.

37   *HRV*, vol 2B: 553–554.

38   *HRV*, vol 2B: 555. This census is an enclosure at Thomas to Robinson at VPRS 10, unit1/242, PROV. It is also on CY 3082, ML.

4 November 1839

Thomas received another summons from the Crown Prosecutor; he left Tubberubbabel for Melbourne, travelling 27 miles before stopping overnight at Mr Newton's station at Mordialloc where he met up with 17 of his blacks already en route back to Tubberubbabel. He wrote in his journal 'This makes the fourth time I have been ordered to return to Melbourne since I had orders to proceed to my district. Can any good result from such a system?'[39]

5 November 1839

He arrived Melbourne 1 pm and next day took a 'more correct census'.[40]

12 November 1839

With exquisite political sensibility reflecting the relative numerical strength of his two tribes (Waworong just over 120, Bonurong just over 80), Thomas selected his five Native Police, including two Bonurong, Buller Buller aged 20, who was Poleorong/Billy Lonsdale's brother, and Tulemlgate aged 24, who I suspect is Burrenum/Mr Dredge's brother, and three Warworong. Unlike the later 1842 Native Police Corps, the protectors' domestic police were supposed to keep order within the tribe.[41]

20 November 1839

Thomas Census: he submitted this more correct census to the Crown Prosecutor with a covering letter stating that the 83 Bonurong are practically the whole of the tribe, and while there may be about 20 more Warworong than the 124 whom he named, the combined total would not be more than 230 people.[42]

4 December 1839

Thomas received word in Melbourne about noon that his wife was very ill and not expected to live. He applied to Robinson for leave to go to Tuerong[43] but Robinson made him investigate an alleged assault first. He left at 6.30 pm and rode till 10 pm before camping because his horse was lame.[44]

---

39 *HRV*, vol 2B: 556.
40 *HRV*, vol 2B: 557.
41 All the recovered details of the 1839 Domestic Police have been included in Fels 1988, chapter 3.
42 There are two microfilmed copies of this census, one at Thomas to Robinson, 20 November 1839, VPRS 10, unit 1/242, PROV which is printable but faded. The other copy is at CY 3082, frames 47–50, ML, clear and legible, but unable to be printed due to the large paper size Thomas used. Taken together, these two versions produce accurate spellings of the names, with no possibilities of error in transcription.
43 Tuerong is the station being established by his son William Jackson Thomas; the same place, on the Old Moorooduc road near Balnarring road has been well known to peninsula residents as 'Tuerong Park', a Limousin and Murray Grey stud run by the late Dr John Stubbe, a descendant of William Thomas. *Tuerong* means laughing jackass, Thomas Vocab, CY 2984: 112, and was known as 'the bushman's timepiece', CY 2984, frame 124, ML.
44 VPRS 11, unit 7/289, PROV.

5 December 1839

He arrived at Tubberubbabel, not Tuerong, to find Mrs Thomas seriously ill there: 26 blacks there too.[45]

10 December 1839

Thomas departed Tubberubbabel with his wife for Melbourne: they arrived the same night with Thomas a casualty on the cart too, having been injured in a dray accident.[46]

15 December 1839

Thomas submitted to La Trobe his first petition for land, for a reservation for his blacks: La Trobe agreed to forward it to Sydney, and then spoke about the necessity of getting the blacks out of Melbourne. Thomas told the blacks that the governor was 'big one sulky' with them, and so was Captain Lonsdale and so were the soldiers.[47]

1 January 1840

In Melbourne, Billibellary made his comparison between the largesse under Batman and the stinginess of the Protectorate, and Thomas made his first request for an agricultural and cattle station for his blacks. Thomas' draft petition is addressed to Sir George Gipps, and he states that he has heard that the Aborigines' reserve, '895 acres of highly valuable land' near Melbourne has been surveyed and partitioned for sale, and that he has not heard of 'any reserve or remuneration in lieu of this land being in contemplation'.[48]

2 January 1840

Three Western Port men, D'Villiers, Mr Young (Nerreninnen) and Budgery Tom, plus six named Goulburn blacks depart 'after a Council of the ancients 11 in number' on an expedition to avenge two recent deaths. Thomas wrote a footnote 'Strange superstition that death is occasioned by another strange black cutting open the side while asleep and taking out the kidney which cannot be seen but by the doctors'.[49]

---

45 CY 2604, item 3, frame 131, ML.
46 *HRV*, vol 2B: 572.
47 Thomas Journal, CY 2604, item 4, ML. Item 4 is a fragment of Journal covering the period 8 December 1839 to January 1840, A marginal note indicates that it is a first draft which Thomas intended to re-write later. It contains the important information from Surveyor Smythe, lately at the Swan River, regarding the three named Bonurong women abducted from Western Port by the master of the *George* in 1834, presently at King Georges Sound and wanting to return to see their friends at Western Port, see Chapter 11.
48 The draft letter is at CY 3082: 57, ML and the version he actually sent is at VPRS 11, unit 7/292, PROV.
49 Thomas Journal, CY 2604, item 3, frame 136, ML.

Budgery Tom

Western Port chief, listed, with his mark, as a signatory to Batman's treaty.

His real name was Mooderrogar; his wife was Narrugrook and his two sons, both of whom distinguished themselves in the 1842 Native Police Corps were Buckup and Munnite (Thomas Family Connections census, CY 3083, ML). He was the senior owner of the country from Ruffy's station Mayune, north of Tooradin, to Narre Warren (Thomas Miscellaneous, CY 3130, ML).

No date, Budgery Tom, Chief Western Port (Byrt 2004, CD 214. 23 BO.DOC: 64, frame 31); No date – 'When white people had regularly made a footing at Port Phillip, one Budgery Tom was noted for giving names to European things and animals. These names are mostly of his giving' (Smyth 1876 quoting Thomas, vol 2: 124); No date – Budgery Tom's name is listed first on the list of the Principal Families who own the country of Mahun from Ruffy's station to Nerre Nerre Warren (Thomas CY 3130, ML).

21 Dec 1837 – The Native Police are doing well with the exception of the two men Tom and Nanupton whom has [sic] left the station without my knowledge. Tom's behaviour has been desperate bad (de Villiers to Police Magistrate Lonsdale, VPRS 4, unit 3, 37/174, PROV).

20 Mar 1839 – Mooduringu/Budgery Tom, age 30, (Dredge census, Robinson Papers, vol 54: 17, A 7075, ML); same date – Budgeree Tom, Waworong tribe, aged 30, listed on Dredge's census of Aborigines in vicinity of Melbourne as unmarried male whose family is not ascertained (Robinson Papers, vol 54, ML); 17 Dec 1839 – Budgery Tom severely wounded, not expected to live in a fight with Derrimut and Mr King who came to the encampment at Melbourne drunk, and Budgery Tom threw a wonguim at them, all the tribe up in arms enraged at Budgery Tom's wounds (Thomas Journal, CY 2604, item 3, ML); 17 Dec 1839 – Budgery Tom, Chief of the Western Port blacks (Thomas 'A' Diary, set 214, item 1, ML).

21 Jun 1840 – A rumour had reported that Budgery Tom and Kollorluk had been killed by Two Fold Bay blacks, but this day Thomas recorded that he was safe (Thomas Journal, CY 2604, item 3, ML); Feb 1840 – Budgery Tom, one lubra and two piccaninnies are listed on a list of 44 persons at Arthurs Seat determined to go to Western Port (Thomas

Journal, set 214/1, item 1, frame 8, CY 2605, ML); 24 Jul 1840 – All working well at Tubberubbabel, Budgery Tom acts as foreman and appears proud of it (Thomas Journal, CY 2604, item 3, ML); 27 Jul 1840 – Budjerre Tom, a male Aborigine going to Melbourne with the cart with Thomas' permission (Robinson Journal in Clark 1998, vol 1); 27 Jul 1840 – Budgery Tom's lubra made a basket of superior work for His Honor's Lady (Thomas Journal, CY 2604, item 3, ML); 2 Sep 1840 – Budgery Tom on being shown a map where Koran Warrabin range is,[I] described by consent of the others where good land is, the blacks all look upon Tom with the deepest attention … they had a short debate, deputed 5 young men to show me where the spot is (Thomas Journal, set 214, ML); 11 Oct 1840 – Pudg.ger.re Tom is recorded by Robinson as being one of those who gave the alarm when the armed party attacked an encampment on 'the Heidelburgh rode' (Clark 1998, vol 2: 9); 7 Nov 1840 – Budgery Tom described as one the Heads who made a fair map of the country on the ground then pointed to a place with a stick, and after warm debate the decision was made to choose Nerre Nerre Warren as the Protectorate site (Thomas Second Periodical Report, VPRS 4410, unit 1/67, PROV).

10 Jun 1841 – with pleasure I have often heard Billibellary and Budgery Tom give charge to the young men on going to Melbourne not to get drunk (Thomas to La Trobe, VPRS 10, unit 3, PROV); 1841 – Budgery Tom with Thomas, Beruke and Billibellary up Yarra River (VPRS 11, unit 7, PROV); Budgery Tom/Metterrandanuk, a signatory to Batman's treaty (Thomas Journal, 'Extracts from journal Oct.-Nov.', set 214, item 3, ML); 23 Aug 1841 – at Nerre Nerre Warren Thomas made a stand on principle about clothing for the children. He was making a serious attempt to establish the school and had given 15 new dresses to the girls and 15 new shirts to the boys, and the children had had their hair cut and were clean. Now the people determined on going away from the station. Thomas said give back the clothing, the blacks said take it:

> After a few altercatory words, Budgery Tom who was the principal spokesman and who wished to inform me that the lubras and Koolin Bopups[II] must have 2 fires, a fire for each as males never sit at same fire as females. A marginal note inserted here reads 'Female children are not allowed to sit in the absence of their parents at same fires with female children.[III] It was further urged that if they slept in the schoolroom, Wild Blackfellows could come. It was however, apparently settled that they should sleep

I. The Dandenong Ranges.

II. Children.

III. This seems a mistake as Thomas means the opposite.

in Mr Wilson's hut.[IV] Budgery Tom, who had all along said he would not go, said he was going. I was much surprised in fact Tom has often as well as Billibellary shown his prevaricating conduct. Tom asks if I will not come with Blackfellows. I state no unless Mr Robinson or Mr La Trobe with me. I want to see paddock round Wheat – but that when His Honor came home, I would come and see them. Tom describes on ground where each night sleep,[V] 1. Nerre Nerre Warren, 2. Monorer near Mr Napier's hut, 3. Nanmerparren, a waterhole near Mr Wright's and 4. Metpelling-Kunnung, near Mr Broomfield's station near Yarra. At Metpelling the Yarrat blacks to stop and send messengers go and fetch Goulbourn Blacks, have a Grand Corrob[r] and return at full moon. On return to hut much amused by seeing 3 Boys who had made Bark Canoes on a kind of Basin in creek' (Thomas Journal, CY 2605, item 5, frames 334–336, ML).[VI]

14 Jan 1842 – Thomas took Budgery Tom to Kangerong (Byrt 2004: 74); 23 Mar 1842 – Budgery Tom excites the blacks to have the Goulburn and other blacks sent for. I and Captain Dana threaten the blacks and all ends quietly (CY 732, item 5(e), ML).

23 Feb 1844 – Budgeree Tom and others of his tribe arrived from Gippsland at Halfway Flat near No Good Damper Inn at Dandenong where Georgiana McCrae was staying (McCrae 1966: 129).

April 1847 – Benbow told Robinson that Kar.ding.gor.oke/Karn.jin. goroke[VII] was Budgery Tom's wife (Clark 2002: 121).

6 Mar 1848 – Budgery Tom died on the station [Native Police HQ], buried (VPRS 90, PROV).

IV. Wilson was the teacher.

V. Mudmap shows a journey in the direction of north up the Yarra.

VI. 100 or so blacks departed, including Budgery Tom but leaving behind his lubra, and they did in fact take all the girls with them, and they did leave the dresses in the schoolroom, but the boys remained behind plus a number of adults, male and female totalling 48.

VII. One of the women abducted from the beach between Arthurs Seat and Portsea before white settlement, see Chapter 11.

3 January 1840

This revenge party returned because one of the men cut his foot and that was regarded as a bad omen. Thomas informed Robinson that another Council took place of 35, the greatest number he had ever known in Council, of both tribes, lasting for nearly two hours.[50] The upshot was that the blacks decide to leave Melbourne, and most did so within an hour – the Waworong in six divisions to the mountains, and the Bonurong to Arthurs Seat.[51] Most significantly, Billibellary, the Yarra chief, told Thomas that he had 'sent' the Bonurong to the Mornington Peninsula; he and his family departed Melbourne on Monday 6 January, not for his own country with the rest of his tribe, but for Arthurs Seat.[52] In his other journal covering the same period, Thomas recorded the names of those who remained in Melbourne, including Billibellary and his family, listed first, then Mingaragon who is Old Mr Man, and his family comprised of his three wives Togerurrook, Tugerurrook and Lagarook, plus his children 'Mungerer c, Lillerenook c, Lillerook c, Maryagrook l, Waregull l, one family'.[53]

7 January 1840

There are only 13 Aborigines in Melbourne including children and they have 'got a ride on a kindly settler's dray going to Arthurs Seat'.[54]

8 January 1840

Thomas left Melbourne late in the day and travelled only ten miles before camping; He committed himself to God and thought how different things were from what Sir George Arthur had stated; on 9 January he had another difficult day with his bowels very bad from drinking polluted water, and as well, the tide was in when he got to Mordialloc so he camped. The nine mile beach from Mordialloc to Frankston was called **Nerrimbekuk Keruk**: this beach was unusual in the size of its large honeysuckle trees, called *Worruk* or *Barbuntuno*. Thomas wrote that 'This tree generally is but of small height and width, but on this 9 Mile Beech is near equal to a large gum'.[55] He woke up in the night and looked at the sea but it was higher than the night before; he crossed at 8 am and caught up with 12 at the first encampment (probably Poliorong at the back of Mt Eliza), then collected another 65 'from the suburbs of Tubbarubbabel', which were Kangerong and Buckkermitterwarrer, and arrived at Tubberubbabel. They all remained till evening then apparently went back to their suburbs.[56]

---

50 Thomas to Robinson, 3 January 1840, enclosure with 40/2215 in 4/1135.1, AO of NSW.
51 Thomas First Periodical Report, August 1839 to 29 February 1840, *HRV*, vol 2B: 620.
52 Thomas Journal, CY 2604, item 3, frame 137, ML. Billibellary and his family, the only blacks left in Melbourne attended Divine Service with Thomas on the Sunday before he left.
53 CY 2605, item 1, frame 30, ML. 'c' represents coolin (male), 'l' represents lubra, in this case female children.
54 Thomas to Robinson, CY 2946, item 2, ML.
55 CY 2606, frame 18, ML: the honeysuckle is the term used generally in early writings to describe the coast Banksia.
56 Thomas Journal, CY 2605, item 1, ML.

15 January 1840

All the Bonurong collected together remained at Tubberubbabel for ten days.[57] (All the events and activities at Tubberubbabel are documented separately in Chapter 4.)

25 January 1840

Having cleared the country of food around Tubberubbabel and being unsuccessful at the hunt for two successive days, they moved to Tuerong.[58]

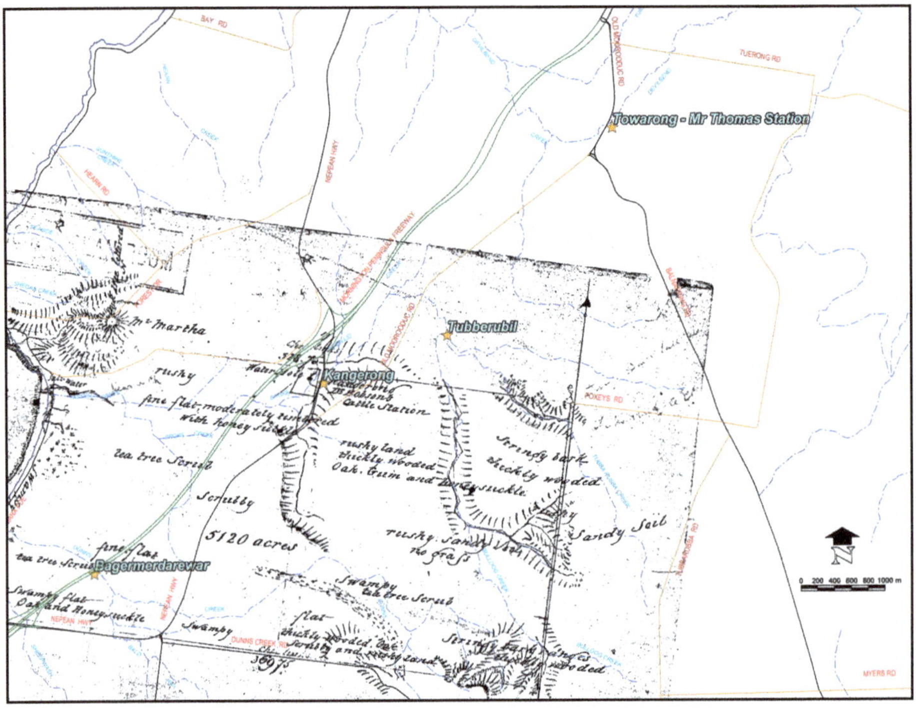

Fig 5. 'Official Protectorate Stations plus Thomas family home, 1839 – 1840'

Fels/Hughes Composite Map, based on Smythe 1841 and Nutt 1841, showing the three protectorate stations plus Thomas' own family station. The two base maps are © Crown (State of Victoria), 2010, all rights reserved, reproduced with the permission of the Surveyor General of Victoria.

1 February 1840

Quondum had a lubra piccaninny at Tuerong.[59]

---

57   *HRV*, vol 2B: 621.

58   Thomas Journal, CY 2605, item 1, ML.

59   Thomas Journal, CY 2605, item 1, ML. Quondom was the girl carried to Melbourne on her parents' backs, shot by wattlebark strippers prior to Batman's arrival. Her story and her baby's death are to be found later in this chapter. Quondum died in 1848, Thomas 'Return of Deaths', CY 3084, ML.

4 February 1840

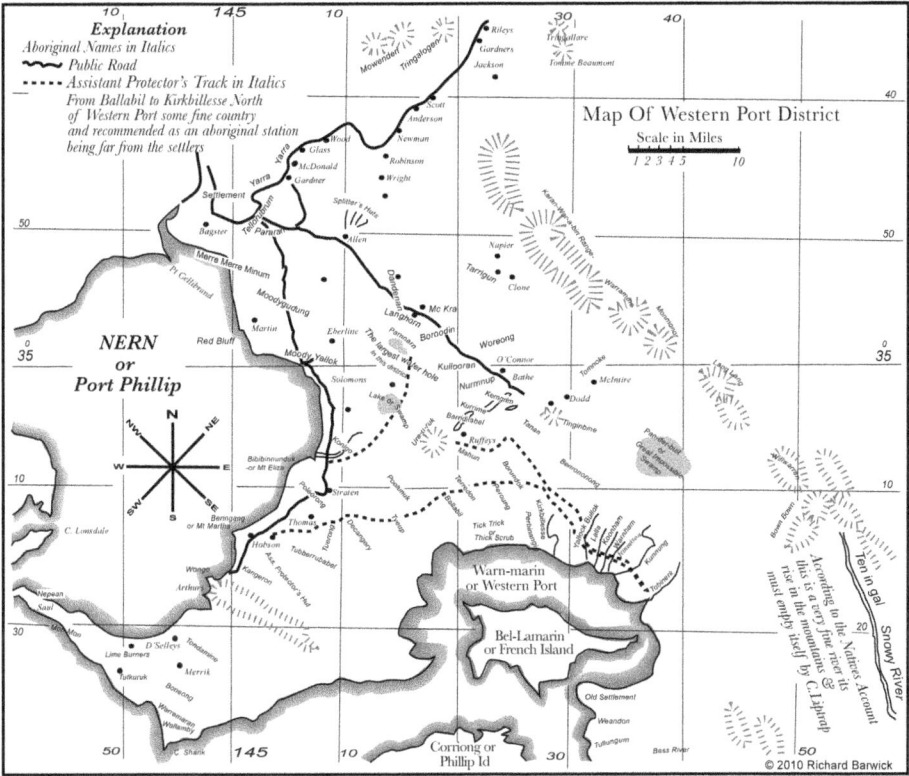

Map legend text:

Explanation
Aboriginal Names in Italics
~~ *Public Road*
---- *Assistant Protector's Track in Italics*
From Ballabil to Kirkbillesse North
of Western Port some fine country
and recommended as an aboriginal station
being far from the settlers

Map Of Western Port District
Scale in Miles

NERN
or
Port Phillip

Warn-marin
or Western Port

Bel-Lamarin
or French Island

Corriong or
Phillip Id

© 2010 Richard Barwick

Fig 6. 'Journey to Western Port, February 1840'

William Thomas, redrawn by Richard Barwick, VPRS 4410, unit 3/67, reproduced with the permission of the Keeper of Public Records, PROV, Australia.

The blacks held another Council and decided to split up, with 57 determined to go to Western Port, allegedly to go on then to Gippsland to get *Bullen Bullen* (lyrebird tails), but in fact, unknown to Thomas at the time, to conduct a revenge raid. The 57 were listed thus:

- Budgery Tom, 1 lubra and 2 pick (4)
- Jacky Jacky, 2 lubras and 4 pick (7)
- Lummer Lummer, 1 lubra and 2 pick (4)
- Kurboro, 2 lubras (3)
- Jackia, 2 pick (3)
- Jack Weatherly, 1 lubra, 1 pick (3)
- Burrenun, 1 lubra (2)
- Barberring, 1 lubra 3 pick (5)
- Old Devilliers, 2 lubras (3)

- Jack [illegible], 2 pick (3)
- Billy Lonsdale, Devilliers, Kollorlook (3)
- Mr Young, Pinterginner, Munmunginna (3)
- Mumbo, Munite, Bowrup (3)
- Wigegal, Tullurulgate, Turren (3)
- Billy Lonsdale's mother and Old Jack Weatherly (2)

The 44 who stayed gave Thomas to understand that they were going to divide into five parties headed by Jacky Jacky (definitely the Waworong clanhead Billibellary, even though it was not his country), Bogy Bogy/Pereuk (biographical details in Chapter 10), Old Mr Man (biographical details in Chapter 6), Big Benbow and Captain Turnbull (Ningolobin of the Mt Macedon clan of the Waworong). This is how Thomas listed the 44 who stayed at Arthurs Seat:

- Jacky Jacky and 2 lubras and children (10)
- Old Mr Man and his family (8)
- Captain Turnbull and lubra (2)
- Bogy Bogy and lubra and two children (4)
- Buller Bullup (1)
- Big Benbow, Little Benbow and lubra (3)
- Mr King [Tallon] and lubra
- Bondut and lubra
- Nerimbinek and lubra and child (3)
- Moolmungo, Toby, Henry and Benger
- The Old Doctor and his family (5) departed for Moody Yallok.[60]

In accord with his specific instructions from the Chief Protector, Thomas was obliged to accompany the larger party to Western Port, though they did not want him to.[61]

Munnite/Monite/Man.nite

Younger son of clan–head Budgery Tom, brother of Buckup

Feb 1840 – his name is on the list of 57 people at Arthurs Seat who are going on the raid to Gippsland (Thomas Journal, CY 2605, frame 8 ff, ML); 13 Feb 1840 – his name is on the list of the boys undergoing the 'Probity' ceremony at Kunnung (Thomas Journal, CY 2605, item 1, ML).

---

60   CY 2605, item 1, frame 8, ML.
61   Thomas to Robinson, 27 February 1840, CY 2946, item 2, ML. The map of this journey is at VPRS 4410, unit 3, item 67, PROV.

7 Jun 1841 – his name is on a list of blacks presently at Tubberubbabel given to Robinson in Melbourne by Billy Lonsdale (Clark 1998b: 344).

1842 – Munite's name is on a list of pupils presently attending school at Nerre Nerre Warren (VPRS 26, PROV).

1846 – Munite is on Thomas' Family Connections Census as 10 year old son of Budgery Tom (CY 3083, ML); 1 Apr 1846 – Munite's name is second on the list supplied by Mr Peacock of pupils attending the Merri Creek school for March but absent after that in the lists up to August. Thomas says that they get three good meals a day of the best food, that he examined the children and could not have supposed that so much could have been accomplished in such a short time; all the children can read one or two syllables in their lesson books; one advanced pupil could read a portion of Our Lord's parables; the children especially the boys are always clean; some occasionally sleep at the school; 'coercion cannot be adopted (the blacks never correcting their own offspring would not suffer whites to chastise them)', (Thomas Papers, set 214, item 10: 25–39, ML); 13 Oct 1846 – Munite is reported murdered and his kidney fat taken (Thomas Journal, CY 2606, ML); Thomas investigated, report was false (Thomas Journal, CY 2606, ML).

1 Mar 1847 – Manite, boy, recruit with 3rd Division of the Native Police Corps at Nerre Nerre Warren. Date of enlistment Jan. 1845 (Commandant Return, VPRS 19, Box 97, 47/1861, PROV); 7 Jul 1847 – Trooper Munite on list recommended for gratuity (La Trobe to Col Sec 47/5497 in box 4/2782, AO of NSW); Christmas Day 1847 – Troopers Charlie and Munite in confinement for creating disturbance and imbibing rum (Dandenong Daybook, VPRS 90, PROV).

24 Feb 1848 – Trooper Munite received gratuity five shillings, made X his mark (VPRS 90, PROV); 4 Aug 1848 – Troopers Tallboy and Munite arrived from Portland Bay with despatches; 8 Sep 1848 – Sergeant McLelland and Munite started for Mt Eckersley (VPRS 90, PROV).

22 Dec 1849 – Trooper Munite in town after stray horses (VPRS 90, PROV).

1 Jan 1850 – Trooper Munite in town, returned with 2 stray Mounted Police horses, and other stray troop horses (VPRS 90, PROV); 28 Jan 1850 – Troopers Munite and Andrew in Melbourne with 2 troop horses, Gruck and Bolivar, delivered over to Mr Sturt; Troopers Munite and Warremelpass in town with 3 troop horses to be shod; 30 Mar 1850 – Trooper Munite arrived from Gippsland; 15 Apr 1850 –

The weekly report delivered from the constables at Dandenong; Commandant, Toner and Trooper Munite in town; 24 Oct 1850 – His Honor arrived from Melbourne with Lady, attended by Trooper Marmbool. Commandant attended by Trooper Munite met them at the South Yarra pound; 20 Nov 1850 – Corporal O'Bryan and troopers Loughman and Munite left for Melbourne to do duty with His Honor (VPRS 90, PROV); Dec 1850 – William Strutt, artist, painted Tom Munight, Black Trooper, Melbourne tribe, at the Black Troopers Barracks, Richmond Paddocks, Melbourne.

12 Apr 1851 – Trooper Munite returned from patrolling after bushrangers escaped from Pentridge Stockade, unsuccessful; 1–31 May 1851, Manite on pay abstract receiving a pennyhalfpenny a day, four shillings for the month (VPRS 29, vol 55: 127, PROV); 3 May 1851 – whole force attended quarters parade and received pay; 25 May 1851 – Inspection of clothing of troops about to proceed to Gippsland viz Gellibrand, Tallboy, Charlie, Jack, Munite and Peter; 30 May 1851 – Gippsland party started, one officer, one sergeant, one European trooper and six native troopers including Munite; 17 Oct 1851 – Gippsland party arrived back; 29 Oct 1851 – Sergeant O'Brien, Corporal Hannan and Troopers Robinson, Billy and Munite left for Mt Alexander goldfields, Sergeant Major in Melbourne to equip them (VPRS 90, PROV).

25 Mar 1852 – Mr Langley with Corporal Brayshaw and Troopers Johnny, Condine and Munight left with 7 days rations for Point Nepean to assist in salvage of *Isabella Watson* wrecked on 21st; 31 Mar 1852 – Troopers Munight and Condine arrived at HQ having left Mr Langley at Pt Nepean without leave; 13 Apr 1852 – Mr Langley and party arrive from Pt Nepean; 28 Apr 1852 – Trooper Munite to town en route to Cape Otway with despatches; 7 Jun 1852 – Sergeant Williams to town en route to Murray District with Troopers Ridout, Munite, Marambool and Heister, and horses Spode, Fireater, Count Peter and Unknown, plus pack horse Clifton (VPRS 90, PROV).

c1863 – William Strutt used Munite as a character in his story *Cooey or the Trackers of Glenferrie* (Ms 5985, NLA).

Fig 7. 'Tom/Munight', 1850, William Strutt

Reproduced with the permission of the Parliamentary Library of Victoria.

Baddourup/Baddoorup/Poor-Tow-Rup/ Por.de.weer.rap/Big Benbow/Mr Smith

Boonoorung or coast tribe, George Smith's blackfellow; wife, Barbunggrook/Old Maria, Western Port tribe died between 30 Jun 1851 and 31 Dec 1851 (Thomas census, set 214, item 12: 143, ML); mother and father of Mary (died 15 April 1852).

29 Sep 1838 – George Smith complains of unwarrantable interference by Christiaan Ludolph Johannes de Villers in attempting to recruit this man Boudeor and wife and family from Smith for the Native Police; Smith has clothed and fed him for upwards of two years and he has lately become very useful (Smith to Police Magistrate Melbourne, VPRS 4, Box 5, 38/207, PROV, reproduced in *HRV*, vol 2A: 267).

> 19 May 1839 – Por.de.weer.rap, alias Mr Smith, country Wed.de.be.yal.loke, Par.dow.we.rap speaks good English, brother to Benbo (Robinson in Clark 2000: 16); Jul 1839 – Poor-tow-rup aka Mr Smith (Thomas census CY 2604, item 1, frame 31, ML).
>
> 17 Apr 1840 – Big Benbow, his confiscated gun was given to him by Mr Smith Lamb Inn (CY 2605, item 1, ML); 1840 – Big Benbow plus Little Benbow and his lubra are listed as at Arthurs Seat but not among the party going to Western Port; Big Benbow is going to lead a small group on the Port Phillip side (CY 2605, frame 8, ML).
>
> 19 Jul 1845 – George Smith's blackfellow en route with Mrs Smith's bag from Mr Walpole's (McCrae 1966: 197).
>
> 31 Dec 1847 – Big Benbow complained to Thomas that his lubra and daughter would not come with him from Liardet's; Thomas said that was because he gets drunk and beats them (CY 2606, frame 476, ML).
>
> 12 Sep 1848 – Benbow is with Western Port blacks in Gippsland, due back by the end of September; Dana says they are all armed and bent on revenge (both letters with La Trobe to Col Sec, 19 September 1848, 48/10473, in 4/2824, AO of NSW).
>
> 5 Jul 1849 – George Smith at the encampment on south side of Yarra saw Bondeon or Big Benbow diseased; he wrote to Robinson and said he would take care of him, defray his medical expenses (Robinson Papers, vol 57A: 499, ML).
>
> 10 Apr 1850 – Thomas records Old Benbow Boodurup as receiving rations (CY 3127, ML); 5 Aug 1850 – On Thomas' census of 26 Boonerong still alive, Buddorup is listed with his daughter Mary as a group of 2 (CY 3127, ML).

They camped on the first night out at Deangerong, north north-east of Tuerong; the water was bad, the scrub six feet high and the people had to hold up high branches above the scrub so Thomas could follow with his dray. Next night they camped at Tyerup 12 miles further on; again the water was bad but Pinterginner caught a kangaroo. The next named place on his map is Ballabil, where they camped on 6 February on a small hill without a water hole, though they got water by scraping. They passed Terredon (Tooradin). At Peorung the natives insisted on stopping for two days and Thomas was glad of it for the sake of the poor bullocks: he did paperwork. On the night of Saturday 8 February he records the fact that there were 20 men who divided up the days' catch of fish to their families just like Billingsgate fishmongers.

The next day being a Sunday, it was against Thomas' conscience to travel, but he over-ruled it in obedience to his orders to stick with them. It must have been an extraordinary day, as they pushed through seven miles of swamp with mud and water up to the axles, the bullocks so exhausted that their tongues were hanging out. The main body of blacks went on ahead and made a fire on a little rise at the end of the swamp as a signal, while another scouted ahead of Thomas' cart to find a way through the firmest mud. Then they had to outrun a bushfire. They made Kirkbillesse in the end, a small and beautiful flat by the first river where, in dykes as wide as the Yarra they caught 500 eels, two or three inches thick in half an hour.[62]

9 February 1840

It was here that Thomas learned the details of what he annotated in the margin as 'The fray at Western Port when 1ˢᵗ Tent pitched': it related to an event that happened just after white settlement at Melbourne.

Shooting at Western Port by visiting ship's crew in early 1836

The Port Phillip Association's JH Wedge reported this shooting to the Colonial Secretary in Sydney in March 1836,[63] nine months after Batman's treaty. William Buckley had heard a few weeks prior that a party of wattlebark strippers had surrounded a sleeping encampment of natives shortly after sunrise at Western Port and shot several. Buckley despatched messengers to request that the wounded natives be brought up to the settlement at Melbourne. Wedge visited them there and found that four had received gunshot wounds. Particularly mentioned by Wedge was a 13 year old girl wounded in both her legs by ball shot which passed through, grazing the bone: though she lived, the girl was not expected to gain the use of her legs again. Her parents carried her on their backs all the way from Western Port to Melbourne.

In response to Wedge's letter Governor Bourke sent down Police Magistrate George Stewart to investigate the outrage. The perpetrators were not settlers – they were known, though they are not named, and known as well, to be at Portland Bay for the whaling season: it was expected that they would be apprehended in the next whaling off-season when they would return to Western Port for more wattlebark. There is no record that this happened, but formal government of Melbourne was a consequence of Stewart's report, with the subsequent arrival of Captain William Lonsdale and some redcoats.

---

62   Thomas Journal, CY 2605, item 1, ML.
63   *HRV*, vol 1: 34–35.

Thomas heard the full story when he visited the young mother Quondum who had given birth to the baby girl at Tuerong the previous week, to give her some refreshment. He noticed a large scar on her arm, assumed it was a spear injury, and asked her when she was speared. Her response was **'long time ago me Pickaniny – White Man plenty shoot me – all Black Fellows pull away'**.[64] She showed Thomas all three wounds, two shots, large like buckshot, which had completely gone through the parts, one through the arm, and the other through the thigh. Upon further enquiry Thomas found that three others had been shot, Trinderlook, Koonmurong's lubra and Buller Bullup's lubra.[65]

He recorded their story thus:

> that a Gentleman whose name they think is Manborough from VDL pitched a double tent like mine. The blacks being in the neighbourhood, they came up but were ordered off. Not going off, they fired on them, the first time that they had seen or knew the effect of guns – they flew away – they were followed and at last got into the scrub. They secreted their woman two mornings, and afterwards 7 came down before daylight, listened, and cut open front of tent – Billy Lonsdale and D' Villers, while Kurborough, Budgery Tom, Jack Cloe,[66] Old George (dead) and two others came up and speared the men who were laying in the outer compartment and a female, instantly. Gentleman had his gun at hand, fired off but the shot went through the top of the tent and never hurt them. They flew to the bush and so the affair ended. They heard afterwards none had died of their spear wounds, save one who was speared at Port Phillip.[67]

10 February 1840

On this morning the tide was up so Thomas could not get the dray across the creek. He penned a note to Jamieson asking for a rope and the blacks took it to deliver. They crossed the creek and remained on the other side inviting him to join them but he would not leave the dray. The lubras were crying, and three swam back to him to escort him across. He made them some tea and bid them return. Then he had a good night's sleep alone under his cart, and sketched his situation.[68]

---

64 Thomas Journal CY 2605, item 1, frame 53, ML.
65 JP Fawkner gives 9 March 1836 as the date that the news of this shooting reached Melbourne (Billot 1982: 49).
66 There is no Mr Cloe mentioned anywhere but Bobbinnary's name is given once, in an early census, as Mr Clow.
67 Thomas Journal, CY 2604, item 3, ML.
68 Thomas Journal, CY 2605, item 1, frame 53, ML.

Fig 8. 'A singular appearance', men riding on the dray spears up

William Thomas, February 1840.

11 February 1840

This might have been the worst days' travel of Thomas' whole journey. Most of his blacks left him stranded; a letter to Jamieson asking for rope was not delivered; only some women and Martin and Pinterginner (Mr Hyatt) helped him by loading and unloading the dray three times to cross three rivers: at each crossing, Thomas expected his poor bullocks to be smothered in the mud. When he got to the encampment at Kunnung Creek, he rewarded the five women who helped him with gifts of tomahawks and plenty of rice and sugar, plus a knife and fork, then went to every miam and ticked off the men, telling them that he was plenty sulky with them, and so would the governor be if he knew what they had done. He refused to give them rations and he left them without wishing them goodnight.[69]

Thomas noted this day that blacks swim differently – 'they work the hands under their Bellies like ducks', not spreading out like 'we' do, and he could not see their legs while they were swimming. They do not dive, he said, but walk into the water and then swim.[70]

12 February 1840

Taking his compass Thomas walked down the Kunnung Creek from Jamieson's hut and the native encampment to the mudflats of Western Port opposite French Island and sketched the scene. He saw 'some thousands of swans black and white', and Pinterginner gave him a demonstration of the walking-tree method

69   Thomas Journal, CY 2605, item 1, frame 54, ML. There is an internal inconsistency in this day's entry, because in spite of his naming and rewarding those who helped him, Thomas also said that he had to bribe the men to help load and unload the dray for the river crossings, by allowing them to ride on the cart through the beautiful country, and he made a drawing of their singular appearance, sitting on the cart with spears raised.
70   Thomas Journal, CY 2605, item 1, frames 53–54, ML.

of stalking swans.[71] Elsewhere Thomas records the Aboriginal name of the swan as **Kon-wor-ror**.[72] Pinterginner climbed a high tree and observed exactly where the swans were, then loaded his own double-barrelled gun, and crept so slowly towards the swans that Thomas could not detect his movement. When Pinterginner fired, the noise was like the shaking of sails. Pinterginner actually missed, but was unconcerned saying **'plenty pull away but come back bye & bye'**.[73]

Fig 9. 'Natives crouching emu'

Sketch by ST Gill illustrating the walking tree method of hunting emu, Mitchell Library, reproduced with the permission of the State Library of New South Wales.

Thomas measured the mudflats opposite French Island as the tide went out – about a mile and a half – and decided that his idea of snowshoes for crossing them would never work. It was here that he asked the blacks if they ever went to French Island.[74]

French Island[75]

Pinterginner told him the story of 11 named men – himself, Billy Lonsdale, Nerenuner, Munmanginer, Buller Bullup, Mr King, Lively, Devilliers, Burenun, Bobinerring and Mr Hill who once, only once, a long time ago before the white men came, made a bark canoe that apparently fell to pieces:

---

71   Simon Wonga and two other young athletic blacks demonstrated this same walking tree method of hunting kangaroos to William Jackson Thomas on the Mornington Peninsula (CY 3106, frame 62, ML).
72   CY 2984: 112, ML.
73   Thomas Journal, CY 2605, item 1, frame 55, ML.
74   Thomas Journal, CY 2605, item 1, frames 55–56, ML.
75   A recently published history, *Frontier French Island* (Gooch 2006) contains much information.

Cut plenty bark and made boat went over only once plenty tumble to pieces; plenty of swans, kangaroo rats, but no Kangaroos or Oppossum. They were he said plenty frightened.[76]

It was here too, pointing to the mountains, that Pinterginner told Thomas that all the blacks from Kirkbillesse and Perrong to Wilson's Promontory were now dead, killed by the Two Fold Bay blacks a long time ago. All this country where we now were, were dead, not one left, **'Two Fold Black fellows long time ago killed many many, rest all dead'**. And it was here, in the evening that they made up their minds to depart. All the males[77] except two (Bobbinary and Old Tuart) departed eastwards, ostensibly on a five day expedition to hunt *bullen bullen* for their tail feathers. A lubra however told Thomas that they were going to kill wild black fellows, and by pointing to the thick part of her legs and then to her arm, indicated they were going to eat them.

Thomas worked himself up till he was regularly out of temper, talking to them on the theme of one Great Father who made all of us – '2 Fold Bay Black Fellows, Western Port Black Fellows, Barrabool, Golborn, white man this country, white man that country' – and offered to go with them and stand between them and the Two Fold black fellows if they were attacked, so that they would have to spear Thomas before they speared the Two Fold black fellows. They placated him with repeated promises of **'No kill Black Fellows. Lubra Bungarlurly** [wrong, stupid]', The old woman shook her head in anger, and that gesture convinced Thomas that she was right in what she said. He pretended to calm down, then decided to let his man Ross go with them: Ross was a 'steady' man whom he could safely trust, and his job was to watch their every movement.[78]

13 February 1840

Thomas woke early to the voices of lamentation: Quondom's baby, female, named Lowungrook, aged 12 days, born at Tuerong on 13 February had died just before dawn:[79] though her body was quite warm, the grandmother would not let Thomas unwrap it completely. The father was standing by naked because his blanket was on the baby. Thomas tried to shed a tear but could not, and told them that Bulito Marminarta had taken the Pickaniny and it would cry no more. With difficulty, Thomas persuaded them to allow the baby to be

---

76   Thomas Journal CY 2605, item 1, frame 56, ML. Elsewhere, in describing 'the social compact' that existed between the Goulburn, Barrabool, Devil's River, Yarra and Western Port tribes, and noting that they do not have intercourse by sea with other countries, Thomas recorded that 'the Coast tribe however used in former times to make very large canoes and go over to French Island at a certain season after eggs', Thomas Papers, CY 2984, frame 55, ML.

77   In his retrospective summary for February Thomas says 21 men left and intended to be away till the new moon.

78   Thomas Journal, CY 2605, item 1, frame 56, ML. James Ross is listed as an assigned servant on Thomas' Return to 1 April 1840, CY 2946, frame 44, ML.

79   Thomas Return of Births and Deaths, 29 February 1840, *HRV*, vol 2A: 626.

buried in a box which his man Ross made, and Thomas took off his hat and said a prayer. Thomas then cut the cape off his own travelling cloak and gave to the father who would be cold on the proposed hunting trip. 'Ridiculous', Thomas wrote in his margin, 'that some people say they kill and eat the first child or burn it'.[80]

Fig 10. 'Thomas' travelling cloak from which he cut the cape for Nerrinninen'

Reproduced with the permission of the State Library of Victoria.

---

80 Thomas Journal CY 2605, item 1, frames 56–57, ML.

The ceremony of 'installing the youths to probity'[81]

Thomas went on to describe this ceremony for the following boys, some of whom are Waworong and some Bonurong.

- Bowup
- Mumbo [brother of Nunuptune/Mr Langhorne, son of Tuvelau/Old George the king]
- Monite
- Wigegal
- Tullerulgate
- Turrunberin.

Lively (Warwardor) who was a Waworong, Burrenun (Mr Dredge) who was a Bonurong, and Nerreninen (Mr Young), also a Bonurong, officiated.

Fig 11. 'Nerenunnin'

William Thomas, in the RB Smyth Collection, reproduced with the permission of the State Library of Victoria.

---

81 Byrt has transcribed this, to be found on the CD ROM, WT 2605, Ceremony.DOC.

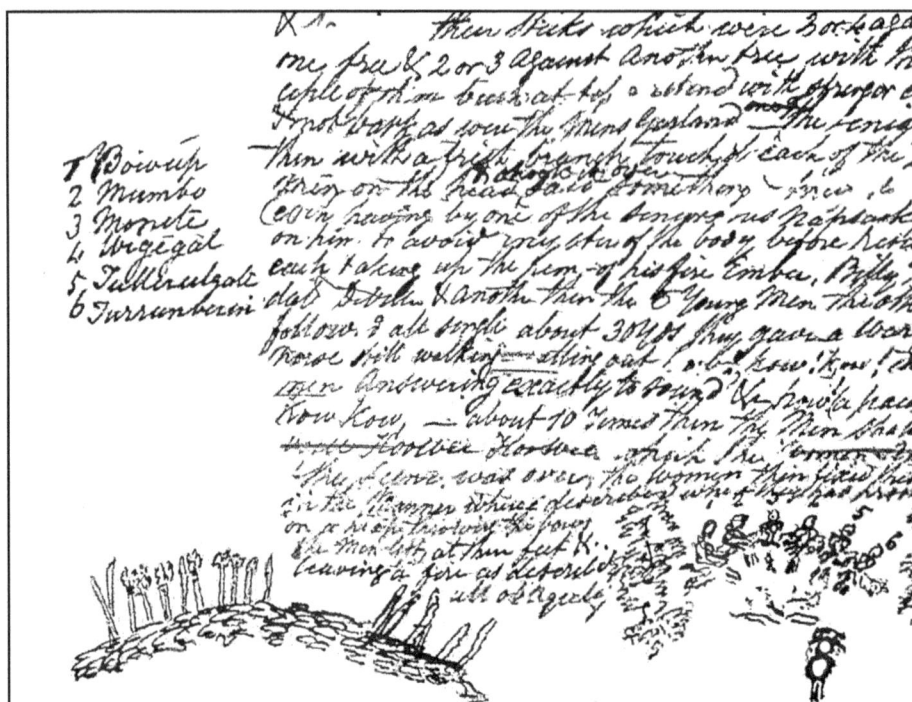

Fig 12. 'Sketch of Probity ceremony'

From the William Thomas papers, 1834–1868, 1902, Mitchell Library, reproduced with the permission of the State Library of New South Wales.

Thomas said that he was not aware before this of any ceremony taking place prior to going hunting or shooting. The ceremony consisted of cutting the boys hair with kangaroo teeth, burning it, greasing their bodies and garlanding them 'like a horse collar', while all the time the boys had their eyes turned to the earth, while the men brushed flies off their greased backs so there would be no movement on the boys' part. Then the elders took each a brush, held it before them and stripped naked and walked to where the lubras were about 50 yards away. The lubras had apparently disappeared, but in fact, they were all kneeling face to face huddled on the ground covered with blankets so that it looked just like bundles of clothes on the ground. The men threw their bushes at the lubras and not till they rose did Thomas have the least idea that what he saw was them. The women's faces were all blacked from eyes to chin. Thomas does not mention the departure in this journal entry, but he does in the summary of February. 21 men left, ostensibly to return at the new moon. Besides the six boys, the party included these men:

- Jack Weatherly
- Billy Lonsdale
- Mr de Villiers

- Quantom
- Budgery Tom
- Burrenum
- Lively
- Nerrebrenin
- Pinteginner
- Kollorlook
- Munmunginna
- Five men remain unidentified as yet.[82]

Ross did go, but turned back the day after they had spent all night making spears. He arrived back at Kunnung five days later exhausted, escorted by Kollorlook. Ross told of difficulty and privation and assured Thomas that he had seen enough to convince him that the boys 'were used for unnatural purposes'.[83]

The women went eeling, and on return were very forward in their Koolins' absence, 'licensus', according to Thomas; he had enough to do 'to keep them anyways in decorum', and had to reprove them for exposing their nakedness. They danced and appeared to forget their Koolings. Three or four of the young ones wanted to sleep in his tent. It shocked him that the recently bereaved young mother was as forward as the rest.[84]

17 February 1840

Ross returned, escorted by Kullorlook, and gave an account of his journey.[85] Four lubras were employed at Mr Jamieson's place[86] this day – Wigal (Burrenum's wife), Quondum (Nerrebrunin's wife), Jack Weatherly's lubra (Nulnulook) and Quondom's sister. Jamieson rewarded them with blankets and food. But the rest of the women had a poor day hunting and eeling and informed Thomas that they must move to another waterhole for eels and opossums: he agreed.

18 February 1840

Thomas distributed knives and forks to the lubras and Old Tuart, Kollorlook and Bobbinary. Wigal, Maria and Quondom's sister went again to Jamieson's station to work and got plenty of rice, sugar etc. There was a fight between the women this day, over a spear borrowed from an old man and returned to him, broken. Pretty soon the whole encampment, all female, was in arms. Thomas

---

82 That Mr de Villiers was a participant is attested to by another participant who told the story to Lavinia Hasell Brodribb Bennett in 1846 (see Chapter 8).
83 Monday 17 February 1840, CY 2605, item 1.
84 Thomas Journal, CY 2605, item 1, ML.
85 Transcribed by Byrt in her *Index*, on the CD ROM as WT 2605, Ross.DOC.
86 A later map, Coastal Survey CS 15A, shows the location of Jamieson's station, his stockyards, Tobinerk (by this time a station held by Samuel [Septimus] Martin), and the river Yallock Bulloc (VPRS 8168, PROV).

wrote that in general, he ignored fights because they were soon over with a few knocks of sticks, but he tried to intervene in this one, found he could not, and restricted himself to watching for fair play. But when they started pointing their sticks he put his foot down. No damage was done, he said – the lubras took different sides. But one women kept **wa wa wa**'ing till 11 pm, and three took themselves off into the bush to sleep.[87]

19 February 1840

There was another dispute between 'Old Mr Young's lubra and Maria. It appears that Young's lubra had said in Passion that Maria had not been working but with white men. I could not reconcile them'. After a stay of eight days they left Kunnung i.e. all the women and children plus one old and ill man rode on the bullock cart with 18 dogs.[88] One of Jamieson's bridges had been burned in a bushfire and an old man gave Thomas a lesson in building a proper bridge, and Thomas drew what the old man said, showing a semicircle upwards to horizontal as the correct way, and an inverted semicircle as the state of the existing improper bridge. Thomas 'burst out laughing in his face, patted him on his shoulder, said Marnameek'. They had 'horrible rough travel' over ten miles of burnt country and it was raining; they passed an old burial ground which he sketched – it was three feet high, with about 50 sticks laid horizontal and a burnt tree trunk at the end.[89] They camped at Tobinerk Creek and the women hunted and killed a kangaroo without assistance.[90]

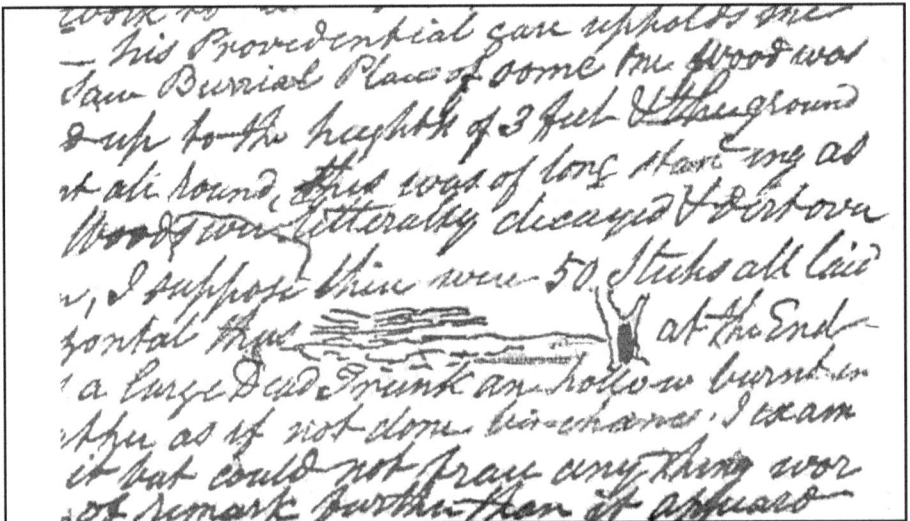

Fig 13. 'Native burial, near Tobinerk, 50 sticks piled up to height of 3 ft'

From the William Thomas papers, 1834–1868, 1902, Mitchell Library, reproduced with the permission of the State Library of New South Wales.

87 Thomas Journal, CY 2605, item 1, ML.
88 Thomas Journal, CY 2605, item 1, frame 62, ML.
89 Thomas Journal, CY 2605, item 1, frame 63, ML.
90 Thomas Journal, CY 2605, item 1, ML. Tobinerk Creek is the Lang Lang River.

20 February 1840

The women killed two kangaroos today, and three large wandeets like hares, plus they got eels and gum, and Thomas distributed more knives and forks and tomahawks. Thomas commenced teaching lessons 'in the native language' and in the evening they had a service: three children, one of whom had been at Langhorne's mission 'almost' were able to sing the hymn and the Doxology. Then the women had a corroboree, but it was a bitter cold night and Maria had not re-joined the encampment, and Thomas worried.[91]

21 February 1840

The natives are well, he wrote, 'with plenty of eels and gum, and they caught six bears, two opossums, and one large beast like our hares'. Eight children attended lessons and he rewarded them with sugar.

22 February 1840

Soon after sunrise the women went spearing eels; they did tolerably well, and got as well, four bears, two opossums, an abundance of gum, a quart or two of currobs, and about a quart of currants, 'both smaller than the English fruits but equally as delicious'. About two hours after sunset, the lubras whose koolins were away went about 50 yards from his tent and all as though one voice gave a shout which made the woods ring: they repeated it six times.[92]

23 February 1840

Though it was against Thomas' principles to travel on a Sunday, the women were insistent, so they packed up and left; the wheel of the cart went over a concealed log and seven were thrown from the dray but thanks to providence they landed in high grass and were uninjured, jumped up laughing, and arrived safely back at Kunnung.[93]

24 February 1840

Three lubras, two old men and five children left for three days and Thomas had six pupils for lessons in the morning, even more in the afternoon; one Kalkullo[94] could say the alphabet and spell simple words.[95] Their dogs killed some chickens and Samuel Rawson was enraged because it was the third time the hen had been foiled from raising her chickens; he shot one of the blacks' dogs, but then seemed uncertain that it was the right dog, and was all for shooting more, but Thomas dissuaded him. The women dug a grave three feet deep for the dog and

---

91   Thomas Journal, CY 2605, item 1, frame 63, ML.
92   Thomas Journal, CY 2605, item 1, ML.
93   Thomas Journal, CY 2605, item 1, ML.
94   See biographical details; he was later a member of Dana's 1842 Native Police Corps.
95   Thomas Journal, CY 2605, item 1, ML.

lined it with a waistcoat and a piece of green baize and a petticoat; they placed the dog in a sleeping position in the grave, surrounded the body with grass, 'patting it comfortable', then filled it in with pieces of bark. Robert Jamieson was impressed with the respect they paid the dog[96] and expressed himself sorry that he had killed the wrong one. He invited its owner (unnamed) and others to his hut and gave them gifts. That night however, the dogs killed more chickens – there was no recorded response from the Europeans.[97]

25 February 1840

The blacks' response was to leave this morning but the yoke was broken on Thomas' cart and he was able to persuade them to stay another day.

26 February 1840

The whole encampment moved about one mile down the creek. After a corroboree the seven women whose husbands were out on the expedition gave seven double shouts and scraped their feet on the ground then retired to rest.[98]

27 February 1840

Thomas' man Davis was sick and requested a pass to go to Melbourne to the hospital. Thomas agreed, and Kollorlook undertook to escort Davis as far as the first station, ie the furthest station from Melbourne, probably Ruffy's. Kollorlook gave Thomas his pet *Waller Wallert* (brush tailed possum) to mind, with instructions to lock it up in the box, and he showed Thomas how to turn the key.[99] But next day, Kollorlook disappointed Thomas by absconding with six others and not returning. Jamieson lent his boat and escorted Thomas and Davis out, but Thomas does not record whereto.

2 March 1840

The women had expected the men to have returned in the last two days, either to Kunnung or to Tobinerk.[100] For the first time, they left their children with him in his tent, for lessons. Rawson and some of the men from Jamieson's visited and complained that the blacks had set fire to the bush all round, and 200 cattle had strayed.

---

96   Jamieson saw it as respect but it was more than that. The relationship that women had with their dogs contains elements similar to those profound, best friend, best mate, male Australian relationship seen in the ABC's 'Working Dog Stories', and to the dog as substitute child in contemporary Australia. Tombocco (Henry) resigned from the Native Police over an argument with Commandant Henry Dana about Tomboco's wife's dog at Native Police Headquarters.
97   Thomas Journal, CY 2605, item 1, frame 65, ML.
98   Thomas Journal, CY 2605, item 1, ML.
99   Thomas Journal, CY 2605, item 1, frame 66, ML.
100   Thomas Journal, CY 2605, item 1, ML.

Tobinerk

This was a place Thomas described seven months later when he was in this district again, tracking the Gippsland blacks who had raided Jamieson's station. It was not 70 yards from where he pitched his tent in February. It was clearly a place of significance, the site of the Gippsland blacks' earlier massacre of Bonurong that is usually described as having taken place at Jamieson's, one creek away. It makes sense, as Jamieson's station is the only referent of observation at the time, and his run included both creeks. Thomas described and drew a sketch of a monument, an arched grove, extending 14 yards, comprised of gum saplings and tea tree, with nine dead stumps let into the ground close to each other like pillars, and raised ten feet from the ground against the centre stump were two old pieces of bark about two feet six inches long.[101]

4 March 1840

The women gave their six shouts again.[102]

6 March 1840

Old Tuat set fire to the bush to such an extent that it looked to Thomas like a wall of fire; he had been told not to. When the fire died down, Thomas could see all the native paths of a race 'all dead that had owned this spot'; he inserted 'murdered' above the word 'dead'.[103] 'They were deeply bedded in the earth'. 'No white molested them'.[104]

8 March 1840

This was a Sunday and all the lubras but three left early to hunt for kangaroos and opossums: only the youth and two old men were present for morning service. The women returned early, by three o'clock, with three kangaroos and nine possums, and in the evening Thomas had a comfortable service with all the women except two, all the children, the three old men, plus Rawson and five of his men. The scene was imposing, Thomas wrote, with the lubras inside his tent, Thomas at the door of the tent and all the males outside the tent.[105]

9 March 1840

Before dawn Thomas was wakened by the lubras making a hoop – they had heard their husbands hooping from afar. Bobbinaren with all the necklaces of reeds led the welcome party followed by the lubras then the children. The

---

101   Thomas Journal, undated, just before the entry for Sunday 11 October 1840, CY 2605, items 2–3, ML. The account of the deaths associated with this war cemetery as it has been called is given in Chapter 8.
102   Thomas Journal, CY 2605, item 1, ML.
103   Thomas Journal, CY 2605, item 1, ML.
104   Thomas Journal, CY 2605, item 1, ML.
105   Thomas Journal, CY 2605, item 1, frame 72, ML.

lubras placed the necklaces around the men's necks, and the children followed after the men who came in single, while the lubras brought up the rear. The lubras left the men about 50 yards from the encampment and the men squatted down. 'After a moment', Thomas went and greeted them with handshakes and tobacco and pipes. Three of the men were very bad with the rheumatics – Billy Lonsdale, Quandom and Budgery Tom.[106] Thomas had to nurse them, see Chapter 8. His summary of proceedings for March adds the detail that he heard the echoing of voices before daybreak and that the Koolins returned about 8 am.

11 March 1840

Having moved the mile closer to Western Port the previous day, where Quondom 'paid a departing respect to her departed Infant by lighting a large fire by at the east side of the Grave',[107] today they departed the district at daybreak in order to be with the tide. They got over the first river (Warnham) with difficulty, almost losing a bullock; the second river (Koorham) was no easier – one of Rawson's men who was helping was badly injured. At the third river (Balla), Thomas was pushing the cart through it when he lost his footing, fell in out of his depth and then got stuck in the mud with the tide rising rapidly; the blacks came to his assistance and he was able to swim to shore. They seemed in great consternation for his well being and he quoted them as saying **black fellows all plenty cry for Marminartra.** Night was coming on and the bullocks were exhausted so they camped right there on the bank of the river.

At the fourth river (Yallok Ballok) Thomas pushed the cart in water up to his chin while his man Ross, who could not swim, rode on the cart. But the blacks insisted that Thomas get out of the water in case he got stuck again in the mud, and seeing this, Ross got out of the cart out of his depth, went under and stayed under water for some time before Jack Weatherly jumped in and with difficulty got Ross' head above water and pulled him to the bank: a marginal note states that Ross actually drowned.

Thomas insisted on resuscitation according to the Humane Society of England principles, not the Aboriginal method of resuscitation – they would have laid him on his side on the river bank, almost upright:[108] it was 20 minutes before Ross could speak. The blacks insisted on pushing on though they had to stop three times because Ross was so ill, and they made camp at Tooradin where there was supposed to be water. But there was no water, and the bullocks were suffering on their third day without it.

---

106   Thomas Journal, CY 2605, item 1, ML.
107   Thomas added a marginal note that this was a general rule – fires lit out of respect for the dead are made to the east of the grave, Thomas Journal, CY 2605, item 1, frame 73, ML.
108   Thomas Journal, CY 2605, item 1, ML. William Jackson Thomas wrote that his father's only recreations were sailing, rowing and swimming; this would account for Thomas' up to date knowledge of lifesaving methods (CY 3106, frame 54, ML).

On 13 March it rained in torrents, and Thomas and Ross were both unwell, but the blacks insisted on continuing to the place where they planned to stop for three days, which was Ruffy's station called Mahun/Mayune. They were well received, and Thomas planned to make a sketch of the mountains, but 'all of a sudden' they decided to leave with three men going on Ruffy's dray to Melbourne, and the rest moving to O'Connor's station, where they were again kindly received. The blacks started splitting up – Kullorlook went out working with the sheep; Poleorong, Budgery Tom, Worwodor, Burrenum and Yal Yal got a lift in a settler's dray to Melbourne.[109]

They left O'Connor's on the 17 March, crossed the bridge at Dandenong, then camped in a spot chosen by the blacks, whereupon a pastoral licensee of the crown (un-named) abused them and told them to move on. 'We were very unwelcome guests' is how Thomas puts it: 'The poor Aborigines have come to a fine pitch' was his marginal note. He went on to record that the blacks are always very careful not to give offence by camping a long way from huts and never near stock. This time, they camped in a nook of the creek quite out of the way of cattle, and a good half mile from the huts of the squatter.[110] But unfortunately the place they chose ('the first station where we have been ill-received'[111]) was technically a paddock, though Thomas did not know it at the time: the paddock was perhaps a mile in extent with not more than a dozen cattle in it. He made a marginal query in his journal which seems to be about the blacks' rights to freedom of movement around their country. He asked himself:

> Query. Should a Paddock run on each side of a Public Road, & that of near a mile in extent, along a creek which at certain seasons of year is for 2 or 3 miles dry???.

With hindsight, it sounds as though this paddock was not fenced off from the road, though it must have had some method of confining the cattle.

More blacks left him to go to Melbourne, Pinterginner, Henry (Tombocco), Toby, Wigeal, Mumbo and Buller Bullup. Lummer Lummer had a 'most awful' fight with his wife.

They then travelled then to a lake called Parnhun,[112] a word that Thomas recorded he could not pronounce properly, being unable to get the twang at the end of it: the blacks kept saying **'Bungarly'** – wrong/stupid. They got to

---

109   Thomas Journal, CY 2605, item 1, frame 74, ML.
110   Thomas Journal, Tuesday 17 March 1840, CY 2605, item 1, ML.
111   Thomas Journal, CY 2605, item 1, frame 75, ML.
112   Langhorne's station.

Konagen on 22 March where they eeled,[113] then finally he was home next day to embrace his dear family at Tuerong, they and the blacks having moved from Tubberubbabel for safety while he was away.[114]

24 March 1840

Thomas went to Meyrick's station Boniong to investigate a report which turned out to be false, that there had been a robbery there. In fact, a party of his blacks had been encamped there for three weeks working at fencing for Maurice and Alfred Meyrick. He returned to Tuerong to find a message from Robinson demanding his presence in Melbourne.[115] In his second periodical report he states that the report was without any the least foundation; the party of blacks encamped at Mr 'Merricks' for three weeks had rendered 'Mr Merrick much acceptable service'.[116]

Rumour

The place of rumour in the often quoted hostility of settlers towards Aboriginal people has never been examined. La Trobe thought that the newspapers of Port Phillip at the time were the dregs of the earth, and it was the newspapers which published consistently negative information about the blacks. It is a horse and cart situation really – were the newspapers publishing stories that the editor knew his readers wanted to read, or did the newspapers shape squatters' opinion or both? And who spread the rumours that were published? And whose interests were served?

Assistant Protector Sievwright has recorded one group whose interests were served by the spreading of misinformation about the blacks – the pastoral workers. Sievwright explained how the system worked:

> The promulgation of the tales of horror, by the initiated to the newly arrived servants is a matter of policy as well as of amusement for with them, it continues a system, which it is expedient to uphold with the masters, by which a ready excuse is obtained (as easily made as difficult to gainsay) for their own – negligence or delinquency by imputing to a foraging party of the natives, every loss they sustain, and every misfortune that happens.[117]

If Sievwright is correct, then blaming the blacks was the stock response of servants to masters.

---

113 Frankston.
114 Monday 23 March 1840, Thomas Journal, CY 2605, item 1, ML.
115 Thomas Second Periodical Report, 7 November 1840, VPRS 4410, unit 3/67, PROV.
116 VPRS 4410, unit 3, item 67: 3, PROV.
117 Report March to August 1839, *HRV*, vol 7: 344.

The Chief Protector did not point the finger at anyone in his letter to the Colonial Secretary in Sydney, in which he said that:

> the depredations alleged to have been committed by the Aborigines at Mt Piper ... ascertained to be without the slightest foundation whatever ... numerous other cases of a similar nature ... produced to prejudice settlers against Aborigines generally.[118]

The *Port Phillip Gazette* was edited by George Arden, another 18 year old, a cadet of an ancient family but of unstable nature, twice imprisoned for libel.[119] The newspaper reported court proceedings and shipping arrivals, and quoted excerpts from foreign newspapers, and government proclamations etc, and there is no quarrel with any of that. But its Domestic Intelligence from rural Port Phillip seems to have relied on travellers' tales: newspapers in Port Phillip at this time need to be read with caution, as an indicator that something might have happened, but they cannot be relied upon. Mrs Madeleine Scott's letter to the editor, published 13 March 1841 is a good example.[120] She wrote that the newspaper had published an account the previous week stating that the blacks had set fire to her property: in fact, they were helping her to put the fire out. This is a similar experience to Thomas' at Meyrick's.[121]

Robinson did point the finger squarely at pastoralists themselves in a later observation. They spread rumours about native outrages in order to deter new squatters from settling in their districts and claiming some of country hitherto theirs to use. It worked like this: after the NSW Order in Council of 7 October 1847 anyone who could find a bit of country situated between neighbours who had to be five miles from where you proposed to sit down, could simply squat and pay the annual licence fee to the Commissioner of Crown Lands when he

---

118 22 March 1839, 39/4186 in 4/2471, AO of NSW.

119 Billot 1970: 77.

120 She is another who was 'favourably disposed towards the blacks' and was apparently liked in return. When someone's station is on their regular routes, it is likely to be because the property was already a regular encampment, was on water, and was pointed out to the squatter by its original owner. Scott's husband died after taking up the run Bushy Park at Dandenong, and she managed it alone for more than ten years.

121 Other examples include Lonsdale, April 1837, as usual a number of extraordinary stories and reports are circulated (*HRV*, vol 1: 121); Thomas puts little credit in newspapers ... mere hearsay (Thomas to CP, 2 Jan 1843, VPRS 11, Box 10, item 576, PROV); Police Magistrate Blair, Portland Bay, to La Trobe, 15 January 1842, there seems to be an unfortunate taste with some persons to exaggerate or mis-state every circumstance connected with the Aborigines (VPRS 19, Box 27, 42/534, PROV); Thomas rebutting diabolical murder by blacks report in *Port Phillip Patriot*, 29 July 1844, from previous experience many such rumours are groundless (VPRS 16, Box 61, 44/1308, PROV); Report of Manton killed by Aborigines on the Murray not true, OIC Native Police to La Trobe, 10 December 1845 (VPRS 19, Box 77, 45/2045, PROV); false report of a native attack on sheep not true, shepherd lost them, Commandant Dana to La Trobe, 20 August 1843, VPRS 19, Box 49, 43/2189, PROV; outrage by blacks at Whiteheads ... shepherd concocted story, Mr Whitehead says he regrets his letter of 23 July 1839, it was written under great excitement (Assistant Protector Dredge to CP, 12 August 1839 in 4/2471, AO of NSW).

called annually to assess and collect the fee, which was ten pounds for the licence, and so much per head for stock. Robinson recorded that it was 'common practice to raise cry against the blacks to keep people from country'.[122]

From 26 March to 30 April, Robinson kept Thomas in Melbourne dealing with the large numbers of blacks in town (496), including the Barrabools from Geelong, the Mt Macedons and the Goulburns.

12 April 1840

Thomas attended to the sick, 'very many what I call comfortable families has the Bad Disorder'. He names these families in the margin, 'Jackia Jackia, Old Doctor, Kurboro, Jacka (Wybo), Yal Yal, Bondite, Wiagal, McNole'.[123] Almost all the men, women and children went to collect mussels, quite an uncommon occurrence, Thomas noted, for men to go; they complain of being **'plenty hungry'**.[124]

'The Bad Disorder'

The bad disorder is the venereal. This issue really requires forensic investigation by a medically qualified person, and it requires that all the evidence from the whole of the Protectorate be considered, 1839–1849, not just the evidence from these earliest years. In fact a systematic search will be needed from 1835 on: seventeen months after Batman and Fawkner arrived, Robinson, on his first visit recorded that:

> the Aborigines on the settlement [Melbourne] are dreadfully afflicted with venereal … Some of the children are afflicted by it and the old persons can hardly walk.[125]

He heard three variant views on causation; the first was Lonsdale's opinion that 'the natives had this disorder among themselves, and a cure for it'. The second view was that 'this awful malady has been imported to them by the depraved whites, so Dr Cotter and H. Batman told me'. And William Buckley said 'they had no such disorder'.[126]

It will be necessary to collect every one of Thomas' six-monthly returns of births and deaths, with names, ages, tribal affiliation, place of death and cause of death. The raw numbers have been collated and enumerated for deaths, but not

---

122   Clark 2000, vol 5, 15 May 1847.
123   Thomas Journal CY 2605, item 1, frame 88, ML.
124   Thomas Journal, CY 2605, item 1, ML.
125   Plomley 1987: 408.
126   Plomley 1987: 410, 31 December 1836.

the individual's data. When this is done, it will be possible to see the morbidity from syphilis, and perhaps it will shed light on the question of the diagnosis, syphilis or pseudo syphilis or both.

It was not just a Bonurong issue: the Protectorate records for the stations to the west, to the north, and to the north-west demonstrate that this particular health problem was widespread.

In her article on later population changes and causes of death, Barwick identifies syphilis as 'the major single disease suffered by the Aborigines down to 1848'[127] at the Protectorate station at Mt Rouse in the western district.

There is an additional wealth of information to be gained from the records of the medical officers at the Goulburn Protectorate station near Seymour. These medical officers, Dr Baylie followed by Dr Neil Campbell, reported on the diseases and treatment of both the Goulburn River people from Dredge's Protectorate station near Seymour, (the Taungaurong), and the Loddon River people from Parker's protectorate station at Franklinford (the Djadjaworong). Overwhelmingly, Dr Neil Campbell's Goulburn River patients were being treated for syphilis, excrescences, ulcers of the penis and ulcers of the vagina.[128] Dr Baylie's report to La Trobe on the health of the Loddon River people stated that he found the people 'in a most painful condition labouring under the disease called Execrecence, improperly called venereal by the whites, a disease almost peculiar to themselves, and Gonorrhea'.[129]

Then there is the evidence from Henry Jones, medical dispenser at the central Protectorate station at Nerre Nerre Warren, evidence related to Thomas' people. Henry Jones is interesting on two grounds; he is not a doctor, and he names the disease he is treating as 'Pseudo Syphilis'. Further, he is treating pseudo syphilis internally with 'Liq Arsenic and aperients', and externally with 'Cupric Sulphate wash'.[130] Anyone who googles 'Syphilis and arsenic' will discover quickly that the use of arsenic as a treatment for syphilis became standard medical practice from 1910 on.[131] But the doctors at the Goulburn were not using arsenic – they were using silver nitrate, magnesium sulphate and copper sulphate. The question then becomes who was Henry Jones and how did he acquire his advanced medical knowledge? And further, was there, as has been

---

127 Barwick 1971: 307–308.
128 VPRS 4410, unit 1, items 1–45, medical reports to the Chief Protector 1841–45, plus more in unit 2, PROV.
129 27 December 1841, VPRS 4410, unit 1, item 4, PROV.
130 VPRS 4410, unit 2, items 48–51, PROV.
131 In 1870, mercury was an accepted treatment, see CE Reeves, *The cure of stricture by a new mode of dilatation and the on the injection of the preparations of mercury under the skin in syphilis*, Melbourne, 1870, SLV, and Anon, *The guide to health–an essay on all the impediments which blight the prospects of single and married life, and for the restoration and cure of which simple, safe and permanent remedies have been discovered*, Melbourne, 187?, SLV.

suggested, a native disease which he and Dr Baylie recognised but which was truly different to syphilis? And are we in the presence of the western diseases gonorrhoea and syphilis, and at the same time, the native disease called pseudo syphilis or 'execrecence'?

Bubrum

Thomas gives two descriptions or definitions or diagnoses of this:

> *Bubbarum* or *Bubbrum*. This is not like the itch which affects the whites, but is brought on no doubt from the same cause – it is a kind of leprocy [sic] affecting the legs, thighs, arms. They and their dogs are alike afflicted. & their cats to [sic]. They cure it by extracting oil from the feet of opossums. They run over the whole body but more especially the parts affected. They mix some weerup a fine red ochre in a little oil and rub the invalid both night and morning.[132]

> *Bubbrum*, a kind of leprosy or itch when very bad will night and morning grease the body particularly the parts most affected. If they have emu oil that is used. After remaining so for sometime to dry in, will rub the body over with Weerup mixed with a decoction of wattle bark.[133]

The relationship between excrescences and the native disease *buburum* needs to be investigated: there is one clear record of Aboriginal women making an association between '*bubrum*' and dogs. It was in May 1845 and there were 397 blacks from five tribes in Melbourne, plus their '900 at least dogs'. Apparently the police had orders to shoot dogs which were diseased. The evidence of the relationship came from the lubras who showed Thomas the warm body of a recently killed dog and said that it did not have the **Bubrum**. Thomas recorded in his journal that the body was that of a European dog, not a native dog. Four days later, Europeans killed five dogs and the blacks left Melbourne straight away.[134]

Origins of diseases

Under a heading 'Aboriginal diseases' Thomas recorded the following evidence of native attribution of origin:

> **Geagorry or Kor-o-gy** is a term used for diseases generally when above common cases a **Culmul**. They say that the **Bubrum** or smallpox[v] came

---

132 Undated, Thomas does not close his bracket, CY 3130, frame 94, ML.
133 Thomas Papers, CY 2984, frame 158, ML.
134 Thomas Papers, 17 and 21 August 1845, MSS 214/3, item 3, ML.

from NE – that the eruption like leprosy from the NE. Kind of itch came from the same quarter. **Calmal** a bloody flux NE. **Coor Coor** (Arero Boreus) lights SE by E. **Kurbull** (a fabulous fear) Gipps E. **Myndie** (a kind of Colerra) NW.

Thomas' insertion [v] above the word smallpox is as follows:

Mr Parker has this **Myndie** and I heard a black that come from the North call it as such, but my blacks affirm that **Myndie** is quite different that there is no eruption of the skin.[135]

Much later, Thomas treated a lubra 'awfully bad with a peculiar bubrum' by 'administer very cautiously the poisonous powder given me by Mr Long'.[136] In another instance the Bubberum resulted in swollen legs like gout.[137] Thomas recorded that 'the blacks say that the Warragle lubras have given them this rank species of bubrum'.[138] Elsewhere he wrote 'There is one [disease] which scarcely a black is free from, a kind of itch or leprosy'.[139] In an undated vocabulary, Thomas made this entry, '**Neuternin** – sores like Leprosy (not Bubrub)'.[140] These diseases are a complex issue, a major subject for suitably qualified medical investigators.

From Henry Jones' lists, some names of sufferers in addition to Thomas' list above can be recognised:

Yankee Yankee whose recovered biographical details are to be found in Chapter 11; he was for a long time on the sick list but showed 'considerable improvement', then, after three weeks on an excursion around his country with Thomas, came back 'perfectly recovered'.[141]

Little Suzannah aged two, Billibelary's daughter mentioned in Chapter 2, is listed in June 1842.[142]

Burruke/Gellibrand, aged 26.

Poky Poky, aged 35, Johnnie's father, whose biographical details are given in Chapter 10, is also on the June 1842 list.[143]

Ten other names are listed in July 1842 of whom:

---

135 Undated but followed by an observation dated 28 September 1844, CY 2606, frame 43, ML.
136 CY 2606, frame 500, ML.
137 Thomas, 16 June 1844, CY 2606, item 3, ML.
138 Saturday, 2 April 1848, CY 2606, frame 502, ML. He made a marginal note 'To be particularly noticed'.
139 Thomas Papers, CY 2984, frame 51, ML.
140 Thomas, Miscellaneous Papers, CY 3130, frame 104, ML.
141 Result or Remarks column in VPRS 4410, unit 2, item 50, PROV.
142 VPRS 4410, unit 2, item 48, PROV.
143 VPRS 4410, unit 2, item 49, PROV.

- Murrum/Charlotte, female aged 20 is a Waworong;

The others are not yet identified with certainty but they are:

- Burdeguruck, male, aged 8 years
- Worrungrook, female, aged 18 years
- Mendulnook, female, aged 17 years
- Babyhook/Mary, female, aged 17 years
- Mourkeek, female, aged 16 years
- Murrundurin/Maria, female, aged 20 years
- Tolimberick, male, aged 7 years
- Beuoreen, male, aged 19 years
- Murruny/Fanny, female, aged 20 years.[144]

Thomas believed that the Aborigines got the disease from the Europeans, but that their own cultural practices spread it:

> That virulent Disease which Civilized Man spreads from shore to shore has already thinn'd the number of Aborigines in Australia Felix and has every prospect of still carrying on its destruction, this disease is confined not to the young, the venerable in age and the infant at the Breast is alike affected – the awful depraved habits of themselves adds much to put a barrier to arrest its progress. There is but one family in my opinion among the Two Tribes I have under my charge but are more or less affected by it. I see no prospect whatever from the state of disease at present of any more births among them save in the Murry family, and in a few years unless this disease is arrested and the Lubras kept from intercourse with White Men the total Defunct of the Whole. I ground my opinion from experience. I find that the youths in fact while in their almost boyhood have access to the Lubras and imbibe the disease.[145]

Many years later, towards the end of his career, his opinion remained the same. This is his written response to question 12 Venereal, in a questionnaire from the Central Board regarding the diseases most common to the Aborigines and the mortality associated with them:

> Though this disease in the first instance must have been contracted from the whites, the native doctors have prescribed a cure which though simple has proved efficacious: they boil the wattle bark till it becomes very strong, and use it as a lotion to the parts affected. I can state from my own personal knowledge of three Goulburn blacks, having this

144   VPRS 4410, unit 2, item 48, PROV.
145   VPRS 4410, unit 3/67: 22, PROV.

disease so deeply rooted in them, that the then Colonial Surgeon, Dr Cousins, on examining them said life could not be saved unless they entered the Hospital and an operation performed, which they would not consent to; after eighteen months these three blacks returned to Melbourne among the tribes (two were young and the other middle-aged) perfectly cured, and the blacks assured me that they had only used the wattle bark lotion. Dr Wilmot, out late coroner, also saw these three blacks whilst in this state, and after their soundness, and in his report upon the Aborigines stated: 'However violent the disease may appear among aborigines that it could not enter into their system, as it did in European constitutions'.[146]

Presumably, by this last observation the coroner's experience was that the secondary and tertiary consequences of syphilis did not manifest themselves in the Aborigines. If this is so, then it seems to me to support Dr Baylie's opinion that there was a native disease as well as the western disease, especially as wattle bark was an attested cure: moreover, the native disease was benign in its long term consequences, compared with the western disease. And Yankee Yankee's cure from a native disease by means of the western treatment of arsenic requires explanation. And was the wattle bark distillation a pre-contact remedy for a pre-contact disease or was it an adaptation of traditional medical knowledge to a new problem? It must be said that it is hard to see how pre-contact technology could have been used to boil wattle bark for the length of time required to reduce the volume of water to a concentrated solution: perhaps the method of concentration was by evaporation in pre-contact times, and boiling was a post contact adaptation.[147]

These cases are undoubtedly the same as those mentioned by William Hull JP in his evidence to the 1858 Select Committee; they were so symptomatic that it was confidently predicted that they would die. They did not die, and Hull for one, concluded that there was a native disease resembling the venereal which was indigenous.[148]

---

146   Thomas, 8 November 1860, Appendix No 3, to the 'First Report of the Central Board appointed to watch over the interests of the Aborigines in the Colony of Victoria', *Victoria Legislative Council Votes & Proceedings*, 1861.

147   Thomas' drawing of a wooden water vessel that he said women carried at all times is reproduced in this book.

148   Evidence given Tuesday, 9 November 1858, in Victoria. *Victoria Legislative Council Votes & Proceedings*, 1859, Report p. 8.

A childhood observation of Barak

In an undated estray, Thomas recorded the beliefs of two children thus. They were cousins, both Warworong, both subsequently to serve long term in the Native Police.

> The black boys Kallkalla and Bearack[149] informed me today that the curlew which is [illegible] apparently in many parts of New South Wales, and which he called **Wellrook** has a note the <u>mournful</u> sound it emits no good to blackfellows. I understood the child to say it brought in sickness – another instance mentioned to me leads me to think that they pay considerable attention [ink blot obscures two words] of birds under the superstitious feeling of their good and evil tendency.[150]

'Medical Cures, Wonderful Instances of Venereal Disease'[151]

Under this heading, Thomas describes in detail the illnesses of three blacks, one an influential Yarra black named Wun Parn,[152] aged about 40 years and the other two unnamed young men from the Goulburn tribe. It is a lengthy account, full of detail about the symptoms of disease, the devotion of his friends in carrying him on a sheet of bark when he was beyond walking, and the efforts made by Thomas to assist him. Initially Wun Parn refused the help of the medical dispenser at Nerre Nerre Warren, but accepted help from Thomas with treatment prescribed by Henry Jones. This was bluestone plus lotion as strong as could be. Thomas doesn't mince words – 'the man's privates were a mass of corruption as were his nose and his ears', and he was near death according to Dr Cousen. But the Goulburn blacks smuggled him out of Melbourne and carried him at least 150 miles over the Mogulumbeek ranges to the north-east of Melbourne.

18 months later, the Goulburns re-appeared in Melbourne and:

> to my astonishment, he was as sound and healthy as ever … and by his own account had done nothing more than wash himself with decoction of wattle bark which I have seen them make for the like purpose but made very strong.[153]

---

149   The fact that both Thomas and Dana wrote Barak's name as Bearak or Bearack, together with the fact that some Europeans did too, eg Howitt, suggests that his name was pronounced not as in Barak Obama but as in bear.

150   10 December, no year, CY 2984, frame 12, ML.

151   CY 2984, frame 155, ML.

152   Thomas uses three different spellings for this man's name over two pages, and because in the same two pages he is frequently using 'Venereal' and 'Warren', it is simple to compare his pen strokes. The initial capital of this man's name looks like a V twice, and like a W once. But because V is not apparently used in Bonurong speech, it is rendered here as a W.

153   CY 2984, frame 157, ML.

The story of the cure of the two Goulburn men is similar in the description of the symptoms. Both less than 20 years of age, they appeared in Melbourne for the meeting of the tribes in 1840, and Dr Cussen was 'horrified', 'privates partly eaten away, nose and ears was truly awfully affected, even their mouths'. When they left to return to their own country, Thomas gave them a good quantity of bluestone, and according to their story, they used only his treatment. When he saw them next in Melbourne nine months later they were as sound as ever.[154]

Both native medicine and western medicine clearly worked: but what disease or diseases they worked on remains unclear. This is a serious issue which requires specialist medical knowledge and much more research to reach a full understanding of 'the bad disorder' and its consequences.

13 April 1840

This was a Monday. The Barrabools and Mt Macedons decided to shift encampment to the north side of the Yarra. Thomas advised his own blacks not to follow, and listed them as remaining on the south side with him – they are mostly Bonurong:

- Old Doctor (6)
- Bogy Bogy (3)
- Burrenum (4)
- Budgery Tom (5)
- Captain Turnbull (3)
- Mr Hill (4)
- D'Villiers (3)
- Old Jack (2)
- Mr King (2)
- Lummer Lummer (1), Munmunginna (1), Yal Yal (1), Kollorlook (1),
- Mr Hill and lubra (2),
- Billy Lonsdale and lubras (5)
- Buller Bullett's lubra (1), Lively (1), Dollar (1), Tearem (1), Tunmile (1), Bugup (1), Tarem (1).[155]

14 April 1840

In the morning Thomas received a communication from La Trobe telling him to move the blacks from the north side of the Yarra: 'His Honor is a strange man',

---

154   CY 2984, frame 157, ML.
155   Thomas Journal, CY 2605, item 1, frame 89, ML.

Thomas wrote, 'he thinks the blacks can be led about as a pack of children'.[156] La Trobe and Lonsdale visited the blacks' encampment for an hour, then decided that they could stay one night more and depart next day. At 4 pm the Goulburns came and there was a 'most desperate fight' during which one of his blacks received a wound from a glass-barbed spear through the thigh which gushed as though it had been from an animal killed. Thomas mentions '3 Goldborne blacks literally wrotten with Venereal Disease'.[157]

17 April 1840

La Trobe visited for a discussion about firearms, then sent two white constables to collect the firearms the blacks owned. There was much dissatisfaction and Thomas was forced to protect the constables. Thomas quoted the blacks' objection:

> **Their cry was what for White Man Guns? – Big one hungry – Black Fellows by and by – no kangaroo – White Man take away Black Fellows country, now gun. By and by all dead poor Black fellows.** The blacks were very insolent for the rest of the day, would not let white man be near them. **Yangally Yangally bloody white man.**[158]

Seven guns were taken from them, listed as follows:

- Mr King's given to him by Mr Batman
- Boggy Boggy's given to him by Mr Chuckman before settlement
- Big Benbow's given to him by Mr Smith of the Lamb Inn
- McNole's given to him by Rev. Mr Clow
- Davy/Mr Parker's gun given to him by Mr Thurnel
- Billy/Mr Mair's gun given to him by Mr Main
- Billy's gun given to him also by Mr Main
- Mr Hill's double barrelled gun given to him by Mr Smythe the Surveyor.[159]

In his second periodical report there is more detail: Thomas is defending himself, for the record, against La Trobe's perception that he was refusing to co-operate. Thomas told La Trobe that they often put their firearms in his tent at night for safekeeping, and La Trobe responded:

> that he considered it weakness in me not immediately seizing them. My answer was that it was not weakness but I could not consistently seize what had been forced on me as a trust, that His Honor would take into consideration my position among them, that they should be seized by the

---

156 Thomas Journal, CY 2605, item 1, frame 90, ML.
157 Thomas Journal, CY 2605, item 1, frame 91, ML.
158 Thomas Journal, CY 2605, item 1, frame 93, ML.
84   159 Thomas Journal, CY 2605, item 1, frame 92, ML.

authorities, & that I had on a former occasion given every opportunity of taking away a great stand of Fire Arms. His Honor replied that 'he would remove that unpleasant part of the business from me', and in a few hours sent a constable with the order. The Chief Protector has annotated this report, 'It was decidedly wrong of Mr Thomas to accept such a trust'.[160]

Later in this year Thomas recorded that it was the women who obtained powder and shot from settlers and conveyed it to the men.[161]

19 April 1840

Thomas received orders to break up the encampments on account of a diseased emigrant ship having arrived, the *Glenhuntly*[162] anchored off Point Ormond, Elwood: the ship was placed in quarantine near where the Aboriginal women went three times a week to get mussels. He could not convince the natives of the humane intentions of His Honor: they argued **'white men only would die'**.[163]

Encampments

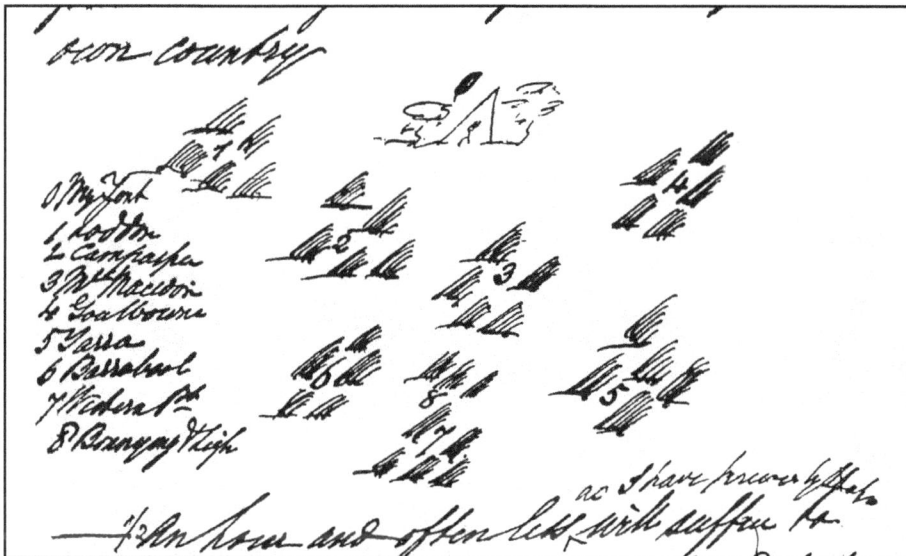

Fig 14. 'Sketch of relationship of encampments'

From the William Thomas papers, 1834–1868, 1902, Mitchell Library, reproduced with the permission of the State Library of New South Wales.

---

160   VPRS 4410, unit 3, item 67: 6–7, PROV.
161   Thomas to Robinson, 17 July 1840, VPRS 11, unit 7/317, PROV.
162   Brown says that the *Glen Huntly* expected from Greenock with 200 highlanders entered Port Phillip on 17 April flying the yellow flag of typhus, and was ordered into quarantine at the Red Bluff where her surviving passengers were detained from 1 to 20 June depending on their condition (Brown 1941–1971, vol 2: 344).
163   VPRS 4410, unit 3, item 67: 8, PROV.

Encampments were formally organised places. When the Bonurong were in Melbourne encamped with other 'tribes', their position in relation to the other groups was always closest to their own country, so that a diagram of the groups of their miams on the ground was an image of a birds eye view of the spatial relationship of their countries on the ground. Thomas drew a plan of this on the occasion of the greatest number of the tribes ever to be assembled in Melbourne in recorded times.[164] The occasion was the ritual spearing of two Western Port men, Billy Lonsdale and Lively over the killing at Western Port of the Wooralim boy at Mr Manton's at Western Port.

20 April 1840

Their departure from Melbourne was dramatic. Thomas had just received a large amount of food for the blacks, including 1200 pounds of flour, 500 pounds of rice plus sugar, tea, soap, tobacco, blankets and frocks. The blacks did not want to leave, and the argument for going or staying raged back and forth. In the end, Thomas put a stop to discussion: he put his fingers in his ears and said 'All gammon my blackfellows, all bungarly', threatened to re-load all the stores and send them back to La Trobe. They caved in and set fire to all the miams. He begged the punt[165] man to cease taking European drays across the Yarra in order to let the blacks cross. The punt man acquiesced, and in one crossing there were 187 men, women and children. La Trobe came down from his office to see the sight and bid Thomas tell them 'no angry only bullito[166] Barnbun weakun Kolin' and that soon he would come and see them in their own country.[167] The blacks set off for Arthurs Seat with Thomas to follow later. En route, about five miles from Melbourne (Elsternwick junction) Thomas met up with his blacks sitting down holding a Council. Two white men had told them that if they went to Arthurs Seat, they would all be killed by the Twofold Bay blacks. They were too frightened to move he wrote; they said that **'long long time ago Twofold Black fellows kill at night almost all Black Port Phillip'**.[168] They all went back to Melbourne.

Twofold Bay blacks

Twofold Bay blacks have been identified by Wesson in her *Historical Atlas*. They are the people who belonged to the south coast of New South Wales extending from the Burrill Lake in the north possibly as far south as Mallacoota in Victoria

---

164   Thomas Journal, CY 2606, item1, frame 57, ML.

165   The punt in 1839 was where the Swan Street Bridge was (WJ Thomas, CY 3106, frame 50, ML).

166   An examination of Thomas' translation of the first chapter of Genesis (see Chapter 12) reveals that the word *bullito* carries a significance of greatness. I do not understand what these quoted words of La Trobe mean, but maybe *bullito* refers to La Trobe's ultimate authority.

167   Thomas Journal, CY 2605, frames 95–96, ML.

168   21 April 1840, Thomas Journal, CY 2605, item 1, ML. There is more detail about this in Chapter 8.

and extending inland to the foothills of the Alps. Even a cursory glance at her map shows that the boundary of the country of these people was organised along the same principle as the Bonurong – drainage basins. They were a fishing people and their country was the drainage basins of all the south coast rivers. Their combined country boundaries lay in the space between the headwaters of the rivers that flowed east to the sea and the headwaters of the rivers that flowed west to join up with the Murray system.

Twofold Bay was an early descriptive term which had fallen out of use by the time the professional anthropologists started their research in the 1880s.[169] Their names for themselves and their language reflected their different way of getting a living. Their forest neighbours ate possum, koala and wombat and swamp wallaby, but not kangaroo, because the forest was too dense for kangaroo till cleared by European loggers. Their next neighbours on the Monaro plateau were in the country of the eastern grey kangaroo which subsequently abandoned the Monaro following the arrival of the squatters' cattle. In Wesson's view 'Twofold Bay blacks' appears to have been used, post contact, as a general term describing anyone east of 'us' in the context of 'those we fear'. There is no record of the Nallerkor mitter or Weecoon people of Twofold Bay raiding in west Gippsland'.[170] Twofold Bay blacks was a metaphor of the time for the Bonurong enemies.

In fact the Bonurong enemies were the Kurnai/Ganai of Gippsland, but Gippsland was not yet opened up from Melbourne, let alone named, so the Europeans of the early 1840s had no precise language to describe it. Common sense suggests that the Bonurong had an indigenous descriptor for their Kurnai/Ganai enemies before Europeans came, but if so, I have not found it. There was plenty of Bonurong information however, about named physical features in Gippsland. Thomas records Meruck as the name of a mountain between Western Port and Two Fold Bay, Bore Bore, the name of a large mountain some distance east of Western Port ... 'finds Snow River, and Woollom, a water that falls into Cape Liptrap'.[171]

There is a long coast line between Mallacoota, which Wesson suggests is the southern limit of the Twofold Bay blacks, and Wilson's Promontory, which almost all authorities agree is the eastern boundary of the Bonurong: it was rich in food resources, and subsequently found to be well populated, and the Bonurong knew the country. So the question remains unanswered as to how and why the Bonurong described their enemies as Twofold Bay blacks.

---

169   Wesson 2000: 151 ff.
170   Wesson 2000: 18.
171   Thomas List of Place Names, Y 2605, item 1, frame 26, ML.

26 April 1840

A young man named Rubertmuning[172] died in the night, a Goulburn youth who was speared by a Barrabool; he had been attended by Dr Wilkie whom Thomas goes out of his way to praise, and was expected to die in the night. Men had worked hard to cut a grave out of the ground with tomahawks (drought, hard clay), and the dying young man was moved out of his miam close to the grave. Thomas made a marginal note about his doubts – he had attended many deaths and had never actually seen the breath leaving the body, as he put it: he suspected that the practice was to tie up and wrap the person before they were actually dead. Thomas watched 'narrowly' all night, never leaving for more than five minutes. The young man was attended by a venerable man shedding tears over him, and as death approached, the young man pulled the blanket up over his head on three occasions. But the venerable man, who is never named, uncovered it each time. Towards morning, Dr Baily was present, and having examined the young man stepped eight yards away to another patient in another miam, and Thomas followed. Within two minutes at most, he said, he came back to find the young man completely trussed up with a cord around his neck plus his blanket – **gone dead**, said the venerable man. Thomas tried to get the young man untied but in vain; he wrote that he believed they bandaged up before death, and that the young man's action in pulling the blanket up over his head was an attempt to prevent Thomas from seeing the first cord drawn. The doctor said that it was not possible for the young man to have died in the two minutes since he last saw him. He was buried in the daylight, in a shield-shaped grave with no ceremony; Thomas spoke at the burial of the Resurrection. He was surprised to find that the blacks don't move encampment or have a discussion when they know the cause of death.[173]

In his 27 page formal account of 'Burial of the Dead' Thomas refers to this issue of the moment of death:

> The moment before the breath is out of the body (if not before*) his attendant raises his body, throws the pall over his head and shoulders and immediately he is lightly corded around the neck two or three times, his knees brought up to his breast.

Thomas' footnote* says the following:

> There is not a man in these Colonies who has been at the death of more Aborigines than myself. Yet I never saw one die tho' I have watched most carefully to satisfy myself on this point but always have been thwarted.[174]

---

172 'Rubertmuning, male, Goldborn, aged 18, single, speared by Eberbol a Barabool blak while corrob', Thomas Return of Births and Deaths, 29 February to 31 August 1840, VPRS 4410, unit 3, item 67, PROV.
173 Thomas Journal, CY 2604, item 3, frame 138, ML.
174 ML MSS C 339 (CY 3695).

In his second account of this death, which says that Rubertenning died at quarter to four on Saturday afternoon, 25 April, Thomas gives further detail but does not even mention his suspicions. He recorded that Rubertenning's pulse was low, and that he gave him a drink of tea which Rubertenning seemed to enjoy, that 'Dr Baylie was exceedingly kind', that the venerable aged kin came and comforted the dying man. Then Thomas quotes the venerable aged kin in the comforting:

> I could just comprehend that **he would soon be at Van Diemen's Land and come back again**. The poor fellow asked for the **Yan Yan**. One came. All began to cry. These people are very, very affectionate. About 1 hour before he died, they removed him about 10 yards from where he lay. He got weaker and weaker. They breathed etc etc in his navel, and in a moment or two he drew the blanket over his head assisted by his brother and the work of bandaging him commenced. He was put in three bandages.

Thomas then described the digging of the grave – his men helped. He recorded the fact that they do not bury just before or after sunset, so the young man was not interred till next day, and the whole of his chattels were as usual, buried with him, that 'the lamentations of the lubras was distressing, while the men in silence wept around the grave'. He ended his account with the summary statement:

> Many visitors were present & the Colonial Surgeon & however these people may be despised & unjustly their characters drawn, they have the tender sympathies of nature surpassing Civilized man.[175]

A few whites were present while the deep grave was being cut out of the hard clay, but the blacks begged that Thomas would send them away, which he did, and then took the opportunity to discuss views of life after death:

> I while in the preparation talk'd to them of a resurrection and they seem'd to have some knowledge. They talked about VDL which I stated 'Bungarly'.[176]

28 April 1840

La Trobe summoned Thomas and told him that if he could not succeed in breaking up the encampment himself, then La Trobe would send Captain Russell of the Mounted Police to do the job. Captain Russell arrived but did nothing, saying he would be back the next day if Thomas could not manage the job. A

175 Thomas Journal, Saturday 25 April 1840, and Sunday 26 April 1840, CY 2605, item 1, frames 98–99, ML.
176 Sunday 26 April 1840, CY 2605, item 1, frame 100, ML. VDL refers to the then-current belief that after they died, they would go to VDL: it was this belief that Thomas called *bungarly*, wrong or stupid.

'villain' told the blacks that the soldiers would come in the night and shoot them all. They were much alarmed, and though Thomas assured them that they would have to move next morning, he would 'protect them from all danger'. They said **Mareguk Mareguk Marminartar**[177] but he still had to promise to walk all night around the encampment to keep guard 'like a watchman' before they would be pacified and settle to sleep.[178]

29 April 1840

Thomas sent a message to La Trobe saying how distressed the encampment was last night, begging that the police not be sent, and received an answer from La Trobe and Captain Russell saying 'no force will be used'.[179]

30 April 1840

Thomas waited on La Trobe who told him that it was no use ploughing up ground at Tubberubbabel until Mr Robinson decided on a reserve, and bid him make the blacks useful, even if they had to work on Thomas' son's station at Tuerong. After 49 days, he finally left Melbourne with 77 Western Ports and 35 strangers as he called them, who were Barabools and Mt Macedons, camping the first night at Ewroruk (unidentified); then they stayed three days at Moody Yallock where other groups of Western Ports joined them; then travelled to Tuerong where more joined them from Poleorong (Mr Hyatt's station at the back of Mt Eliza)[180] and Tantine (Mr Stratton's sheep station at Mt Martha). They left the cart at Mordialloc with the bullocks.[181]

3 May 1840

Thomas' man Davis fell ill at Konigo (Frankston) and Thomas left him with Billy Lonsdale and proceeded to Tuerong.[182] He visited Tubberubbabel and 'had a good rummage around'.[183] Over the next two days, he met up with Billy Lonsdale,

177   Mareguk is usually written as *Merrijig* meaning very good. Marminarta is the combined tribes' word for Thomas, meaning good father.
178   Thomas Journal, CY 2605, item 1, ML.
179   Thomas Journal, CY 2605, item 1, frame 101, ML.
180   There is no person's name with this spelling in the pastoral records. This man might be William Highett, Manager of the branch opened on 17 October 1838 of the Union Bank of Australia (Gurner 1978[1876]: 43). Ian Clark suggests so. But I believe it is more likely to be his younger brother John, a squatter at Geelong (Brown 1941–1971, vol 2: 441). Another possibility is the Mr Hyatt from the Tamar River, Launceston, in partnership with Captain Ritchie, whom Robinson met in 1836 at the Saltwater River 12 miles from Melbourne (Plomley 1987: 409).
181   Thomas Journal, CY 2604, item 3, and CY 2605, item 1, ML.
182   Thomas Journal, CY 2604, item 3, ML. Thomas' man was the convicted man Thomas Davis, 'ship *Exmouth*, arrived 1831, sentence life, about 35 yo, 5 ft 6 in, dark complexion' (CY 2946, item 2, ML). He was punished early on for insolence to Robinson (*HRV*, vol 2B: 426 and index), but as will be seen, he does engage in Bonurong life, and they take sides with him against Thomas at one stage. However, in Thomas' Return of 1 April 1840, he lists Ross as James Ross (CY 2946, frame 44, ML).
183   Thomas Journal, CY 2605, item 1, ML.

Bobbinary and family, Lummer Lummer, Bob,[184] Marnmargina, Turnbull and lubra, Derremot, Ningolobin and lubra, and Dindoo who was Derrimut's mother. More unnamed blacks came from Poleorong and Tontine.[185]

Fig 15. 'Derrimut', 1837, by Benjamin Duttereau

Mitchell Library, reproduced with the permission of the State Library of New South Wales.

---

184   This Bob is possibly the VDL Aboriginal person whom Robinson worked with in his Friendly Mission.
185   Thomas Journal, CY 2604, item 3, ML. Stratton's Old Sheep Station, on a creek about 2.5 miles inland from Mornington beach (Survey the Coast from the mouth of Tangenong Creek to Arthurs Seat, George D Smythe, 13 November 1841, VPRS 8168/P 1, CS 81A, PROV). Thomas scribbled on a memo listing stations and their squatters in the early 1840s that the blacks say that Narren Gullen Creek at the back of Mt Eliza burst from an earthquake between there and Dandine (Tontine) see CY 2984: 543, ML.

Bobbinary/Pubbernarring/Bobbinnara/Bobinnary/ Bobbinnarree/Barberring

Co-owner with Burrenum (Mr Dredge) of the southern peninsula, specialist charmer

No date – we have in the Westernport tribe a celebrated charmer away of rain, old Bobbinary (Thomas in Bride 1969: 428); Bobbinary – a great charmer (Thomas CY 2606, item 1, ML).

Jul 1839 – name taken while in encampment, Bar-bun-a-ring/Mr Clow (Thomas A Diary, January to July 1839, set 214, unit 1, ML); 20 Nov 1839 – On Thomas' Census of Bonurong, male aged 40, wife Bindergrook aged 32, son Yal Yal aged 18 (Thomas to Robinson, VPRS 10, unit 1/242, PROV).

Feb 1840 – Barberring, wife and 3 pick are on the list of names of those determined to go to Western Port on the raid (Thomas Journal, CY 2605, item 1, ML); Feb 1840 – Bobbinarren sick at Kunnung (Thomas Journal, CY 2605, item 1, ML); 13 May 1840 – Thomas sent his cart to Boniong for potatoes for his family: Mr Man and family, and Bobinnary and family plus six children rode in the cart (Thomas Journal, CY 2604, item 3, ML); 22 May 1840 – Bobinnary and Burrenum set off for Kermitterwarer from Tubbarubbabel with supplies, the others to follow in 7 days (Thomas Journal, CY 2604, item 3, ML); 7 Jun 1840 – his name is on a list of blacks presently at Tubberubbabel, given to Robinson in Melbourne by Billy Lonsdale (Clark 1998b: 344); 12 Jun 1840 – Bobinarey and lubra and 2 children were in the party out on a ramble when the others including Thomas caught up with them at the encampment near Kullurk (Thomas Journal, CY 2604, item 3, ML); 13 Jun 1840 – Bobinary and lubra are in the party departing for game; left child with Thomas: on return, instead of travelling Kokobul to Tuerong, they will turn right and go to Mahun: will be absent 11 days (Thomas Journal, CY 2604, item 3, ML); 30 Jul 1840 – Bobbinary and lubra and Munmungina leave Tuerong for the coast (Thomas Journal, CY 2604, item 3, ML); 16 Sep 1840 – Bobinnary engaged with Jack Weatherly in a debate whether to move encampment from north bank of Yarra to the south bank: makes an impassioned speech taking opposite view to Jack Weatherley: encampment divides, 100 to go to north side of Yarra, 130 to stay on south side (Thomas, set 214, ML); 9 Dec 1840 – Bobbinary, Bogy Bogy, Lummer Lummer and a few others come to Nerre Nerre Warren, the blacks in a regular bustle; I shake hands & congratulate them, they say the Weston Port blacks **soon all come** (Thomas Journal, CY 2605, frame 202, ML).

5 Mar 1841 – from a camp about 30 miles up the Yarra Thomas reports that Bobbinary, Old Jack and Lummer Lummer go off for 3 days (Byrt 2004: 55); 23 Mar 1841 – Budgery Tom, Bobinnary and others left Nerre Nerre Warren again (Byrt 2004: 56).

28 Feb 1842 – Bobbinary and his lubra (unnamed) left Nerre Nerre Warren for Western Port (Byrt 2004: 76); 24 Mar 1842 – 2 families of Goulbourne blacks and 1 Pangerang family having arrived the previous day, Bobbinary and Lummer Lummer endeavour to use some persuasion to separate the blacks (Thomas Journal, CY 2605, item 5, ML).

30 Jul 1844 – acting on Benbow's information, Thomas went to the Western Port encampment by the beach at Melbourne, woke up Bobbinary and without questioning him about the murder of the Barabool black, asked Bobbinnara to show him the grave of Jack knocked down by a Goulburn black and his kidney fat taken; Bobbinnara did so – the grave was fenced around and a fire still smouldering to the east: Bobbinary said he had been ill 2 days and had been buried 9 days (Thomas to La Trobe, VPRS 19, Box 61, 44/1308, PROV).

Jan 1846 – on Family Connections census as Bobbinary, male, widower, son Yal Yal male, aged 20, daughter Boyyerup female aged 23: his country is Kangerong and these 3 people are the only ones in this section (Thomas, CY 3083, ML); 16 Feb 1846 – Bup.in.nar.ing, a young man of the Bur.in.yung bulluk, belonging about Pt Nepean, Yal Yal is his son (GA Robinson, Vocabulary Papers, quoted in Clark 2002: 220); 21 May 1846, Bobinarrey's name is on a list of Western Port blacks gone to Gippsland with murderous intent to catch wild blackfellows (Thomas Journal, CY 2606, ML).

13 Jul 1849 – died, belonging to Western Port tribe, male, aged 50, a widower (Thomas Return, VPRS 10, unit 11, 50/55, PROV); Bobbinary died at Muneep (CY 2606, frame 598, ML).

5 May 1840

Thomas sent his son and his son's man to Mordialloc to bring on the cart and the bullocks; they got back to Tuerong next day with the bullocks knocked up having travelled 67 miles in three days. The bullocks strayed from Tuerong and could not be found. Thomas got the 'house etc' swept out at Tubberubbabel. Many more blacks came to Tuerong.[186]

---

186   Thomas Journal, CY 2605, item 1, ML.

7 May 1840

By this date, the whole of the blacks (122) had gathered at the encampment at Tuerong and 'all selected a singular place for an encampment, a very high hill north of Tuerong waterholes – they appear a fine village'.[187] Thomas began to 'relieve' them, ie to distribute rations, but he had an altercation with the Bonurong about distributing rations to the strangers with them.[188] Next day Thomas, and his son searched all day for the bullocks: they found them at Tubberubbabel.[189]

9 May 1840

Thomas recorded that the blacks were happy and satisfied; there were 139 encamped with him at Tuerong, and another 23 at Hobson's farm (Buckkermitterwarrer) and Merricks Station, and that after **'three more sleeps to gogo Tubbarubbabel'**.[190]

10 May 1840

This was a Sunday, and after Divine Service Thomas distributed rations and there was a 'grand altercation'. Ningolobin (Captain Turnbull, Mt Macedon clan head) and Poleorong (Billy Lonsdale) wanted the rations placed before them so that they themselves could do the distributing. They were very insolent, he wrote:

> Captain comes – **give me** – holds up finger – Flour, Tea, Su, Rice, Tobac & soap – the Government sent Black fellows, threatens to go to Governor.

Thomas bid him go and tell the Governor to come and 'serve them Himself', and refused to give to him any rations on account of his insolence.[191]

Mt Macedon section

Thomas was in the wrong in this argument. Ningolobin was a Waworong and entitled to the rations, as Thomas was supposed to be looking after the two tribes Waworong and Bonurong. By taking the rations into Bonurong heartland, and by labelling Ningolobin as a stranger, Thomas was favouring the Bonurong, and may even have believed that his responsibilities lay only towards the Port Phillip and Western Port blacks, what he called the coast tribes. He was soon to be disabused of this notion and hauled back to Melbourne by Robinson who reminded him of his obligations to both tribes.

---

187 Thomas Journal, CY 2604, item 3, frame 140, ML.
188 Thomas Journal, CY 2604, item 3, ML.
189 Thomas Journal, CY 2605, item 1, ML.
190 Thomas Journal, CY 2605, item 1, frame 104, ML.
191 Thomas Journal, CY 2604, item 3, frame 141, ML.

Thomas appears later to have changed his mind about these Mt Macedon people: in his census of 1846, he listed them as the second of eight sections of the Boongurong:

- Werrerby Yallook
- Mt Macedon Boon
- Moody Yallock
- Konniga & Bush
- Kangerong
- Mahun by Western port
- Dandenong – all dead
- Western Port – ditto.[192]

In the afternoon, Poleorong and Ningolobin came to Thomas and begged him to shake hands. He did so, but still refused to give Ningolobin rations. But Mrs Thomas and William Jackson Thomas took Ningolobin and Poleorong and a few others into the house and gave them tea etc. Poleorong said to Mrs Thomas, very innocently, according to Thomas '**Me plenty Bungerly war war good Marminarta'**.[193] In his other journal recounting the same events Thomas wrote that:

> I was forc'd to be very sulky & continued so till night, when they one after another of the principals came in to pacify me. I said all gone sulky and shook hands.[194]

In the evening, at ten or half past ten, Mr Hobson and Merrik arrived having ridden seven miles in the dark from Buckkermitterwarrer to report the 'gross outrage' of the attempted assault on Barebun also known as Mary, Benbow's daughter, who was living with Mr and Mrs Smith and visiting Edward Hobson.[195] Old Mr Man and family, Old Doctor and family, Yal Yal, Bogup and Dollar left for Kangerong.[196]

---

192 Family Connections Census, January 1846, CY 3083, ML. At the beginning of his 1840 notebook, Thomas describes the last listed group/groups as the Bonkolwool, 'inhabit about Western Port & Dangernong, all extinct' (CY 2605, item 1, frame 26, ML). Taken in conjunction with the evidence of Barrabool and Mt Macedon relationships on 13 April, 17 May, 17 June as well as Thomas' map of relationships when encamped, plus the evidence of Barrabool relationships with Bonurong in the matter of the killing of Franks and his shepherd at Mt Cotterill, this listing of Mt Macedon people within a list of Bonurong clans might need to be taken more seriously.

193 *War War/Wa Wa* means fight: Poleorong felt it necessary or expedient to say that he was very stupid for fighting with his good father. There is emotional blackmail going on here, on both sides.

194 Thomas Journal, CY 2605, item 1, frame 104, ML.

195 For the details and depositions of this assault see Chapter 6. Elsewhere Thomas describes it as an 'attempted violation'.

196 Thomas Journal, CY 2604, item 3, frame 141, ML.

11 May 1840

At daybreak Thomas rode from Tuerong to Buckkermitterwarrer to take the depositions from Mary and from the witnesses regarding the gross outrage. He visited the native encampment at Buckkermitterwarrer and found about 24 people there, men women and children. He was much pleased at seeing two lubras wash as good as any London laundress, and the men and boys at work fencing. 'Stations of this kind are a benefit to the Aborigines'. When he got back to Tuerong, he found that the whole encampment had shifted to Kangerong, about five miles west of Tuerong. He told them not to camp in or near a brush paddock of Mr Hobson.[197] When he got back to Tuerong, he made preparations for his tent to camp with the blacks.[198] His other journal covering the same period states that all the blacks (122) went to Kangerong. Next day Big Benbow, Dermot, Mr Man and Benger were sick. Thomas invited the two encampments at Kangerong and Buckkermitterwarrer to come to Tubberubbabel.

12 May 1840

This was a Tuesday and Thomas visited the blacks at Kangerong to persuade them to come to Tubberubbabel.[199] Big Benbow, Deremot, Mr Mann and Benger were still sick.[200]

13 May 1840

Thomas sent his cart to Poniong for potatoes for his family. Mr Man and family, and Bobbinary and his family, plus six children rode in the cart, but there was an accident going round and over Arthurs Seat and it was reported that two boys were killed.[201] Some blacks persisted in remaining at Kangerong but Thomas would not take the rations to them there.[202]

14 May 1840

Thomas visited the blacks at the two encampments Buckkermitterwarrer and Kangerong. At the latter, the blacks told him that his dray had broken down at Kermitterrewarrer.[203] He rode there to check the truth of the matter and returned to Tuerong by way of Tubberubbabel to check on things. He sent his son to Boniong to fix and bring back the dray. Big Benbow (Baddourup, Mary's father) was seriously ill and Thomas gave him medicine.[204]

---

197   The brush fence enclosed the Kangerong waterhole and may be clearly seen on the survey plan of Jamieson's Special Survey, VPRS 8168, P/1, file 5A, PROV.
198   Thomas Journal CY 2605, item 1, ML.
199   Thomas Journal CY 2605, item 1, frame 103, ML.
200   Thomas Journal, CY 2604, frame 141, ML.
201   Thomas Journal CY 2604 item 3, frame ML. At the time, there were two tracks around Arthurs Seat, see Chapter 10.
202   Thomas Journal CY 2605, item 1, frame 105, ML.
203   Thomas Journal CY 2605, item 1, frame 105, ML. In his marginal note Thomas notes that the dray actually broke down at Poliong. This is definitely Boneong, Meyrick's station, where they went for the potatoes.
204   Thomas Journal CY 2605, item 1, ML; CY 2604, item 3, ML.

16 May 1840

After going back and forth to Tubberubbabel, Kangerong and Buckkermitterwarrer for two days, Thomas learned that the damage to the dray was serious, that it was almost in pieces, but that the two boys were seriously hurt, not killed. Surveyor Smythe 'inhumanely' refused assistance, and Mr Hobson's dray retrieved the situation. This day, Thomas moved permanently to Tubberubbabel.[205] He invited everyone at Buckkermitterwarrer and Kangerong to come to Tubberubbabel, and they agreed to come tomorrow to hear him '**big one talk**' meaning Divine Service. The Doctor (Wongara) and his family except for one youth who was very ill, left Buckkermitterwarrer for the limeburners.[206]

17 May 1840

This was a Sunday and Thomas found it 'an imposing sight' that all his own people were seated in five family groups, and the 'strangers' as he called them – the Barrabools and Mt Macedons – were seated all together but apart, for the distribution of rations at Tubberubbabel. They seemed to know now what Sunday meant, he wrote.[207] In this journal entry, Thomas merely states that he had conducted part of his service in their language. But in his periodical report he states that this was the first attempt to speak to them in their own tongue, as previously:

> I had before only spoke upon a God in my own Tongue English. We sang and went to prayers. I distributed flour and rice to them it being Sunday, and promised to distribute on the morrow Blankets and Shirts as far as they went.[208]

18 May 1840

Everyone shifted to Tubberubbabel and Thomas distributed flour to everyone, and explained his manufacturing policy.[209]

24 May 1840

Thomas extracted from the blacks their confession about the massacre of the Twofold Bay blacks near Wilson's promontory in February.[210] They then left Tubberubbabel, spent some days at Kangerong, then Buckkermitterwarrer, then went on a triangular journey around their country to Sandy Point, having given Thomas a mudmap of the route and a firm indication of how many days

---

205 Thomas Journal CY 2605, item 1, ML. Thomas Journal ends abruptly here and is followed by pages of vocabulary. When this version of his journal resumes, it is September.

206 Thomas Journal, CY 2604, item 3, frame 141, ML. Old Doctor had three children but one has been gravely ill for some time. They left the sick one with Thomas. Smythe's coastal survey shows the location of the named limeburners from White Cliffs to Point Nepean.

207 Thomas Journal, CY 2604, item 3, ML.

208 Thomas Second periodical Report, 7 November 1840, VPRS 4410, unit 3/67, PROV.

209 Thomas Journal, CY 2604, frame 142, ML. The details of daily living, work done, names etc will be found in Chapter 4 on Tubberubbabel, and Chapter 9 on manufacturing industry.

210 See Chapter 8.

they would encamp at each place.[211] On Tuesday 2 June he rode out around Arthurs Seat and along the coast, looking for smoke, for a sign of them, then he remembered that the proposed return journey was not on the Port Phillip side of the peninsula but across from Western Port, from Somers to Dromana.[212]

5 June 1840

Thomas rode out in the opposite direction to meet his returning blacks and fell in with some of the principal Western Port people: Derremut, Ningernow (Derrimut's brother) and his lubra, Dindo (Derrimut's mother), Budgery Tom and family, Burrenum (Mr Dredge) and lubra and two brothers, and Munmungina.[213]

6 June 1840

These 13 people departed from Tubberubbabel to move in to the encampment just beyond Kangerong (Buckkermitterwarrer). There were 55 people there all told.[214]

7 June 1840

82 blacks attended Divine Service: Thomas fed 42 men, 17 lubras, 19 children and four sick, but they returned to the encampment by Kangerong to sleep.[215]

8 June 1840

To Thomas' great surprise, three blacks left for Melbourne in Mr Martin's boat – Poleorong and Buller Bullet, but he does not name the third. The blacks came back to Tubberubbabel and encamped by his hut.[216]

13 June 1840

Saturday. Thomas' man Ross arrives at Tubberubbabel from Melbourne with an 'Official' which was a copy of the approval from the governor in Sydney via La Trobe and Robinson for a reserve for the blacks.[217]

15 June 1840

Monday. Thomas started with a party of the natives of Western Port tribe, and two Mt Macedons with their lubras towards that '**Good country**' that they described to Thomas and said that they wanted for their reserve; they gave him a map and a compass bearing which was accurate. Thomas mentioned this

---

211 Thomas Journal, CY 2604, frame 144, ML. This mudmap includes as number 3 stopping place Willamarang Cape Schanck. This is close to Bungil's Cave on the cliff face at Cape Schanck, which has now been placed on the Register by AAV as a result of research done by Fels and a group from the Flinders District Historical Society in 2005.
212 Thomas Journal, CY 2604, frame 145, ML.
213 Thomas Journal, CY 2604, item 3, ML.
214 Thomas Journal, CY 2604, item 3, ML.
215 Thomas Journal, CY 2604, item 3, ML.
216 Thomas Journal, CY 2604, item 3, ML.
217 Thomas Journal, CY 2604, item 3, ML.

accuracy to Budgery Tom who 'laughed and considered me stupid that I did not know that from the description they had before given me on parting'.[218] They camped at Kunnundrum on route but there was no water: Thomas' waterbag had just enough for a cup of tea for himself and the blacks.[219]

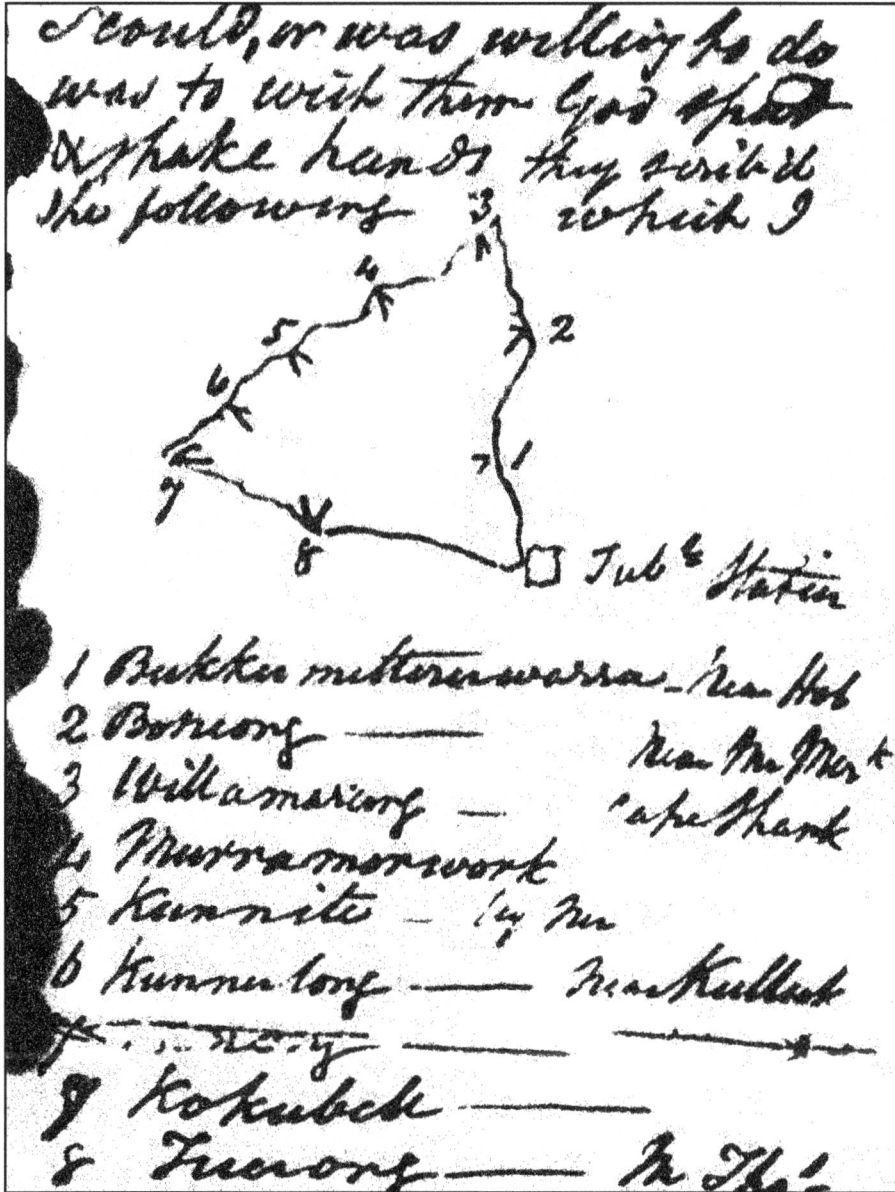

Fig 16. 'Mudmap of route around Mornington Peninsula'

Thomas sketch, from the William Thomas papers, 1834–1868, 1902, Mitchell Library, reproduced with the permission of the State Library of New South Wales.

218   Thomas Journal, CY 2604, frame 148, ML.
219   Thomas Journal, CY 2604, item 3, frame 148, ML.

In what may or may not be a co-incidence, though there is no evidence to interpret the events, in the same week that the majority of the Western Port blacks took Thomas to Kulluk and pointed out their choice for a reserve with some solemnity, Yal Yal, the co-owner of that same land took Henry Howard Meyrick to the same general place Coolourt and pointed it out to him as a run.

16 June 1840

The party proceeded to the chosen place Kulluk, and Thomas was much gratified by it … they encamped about one mile from Kulluk.[220]

17 June 1840

The Mt Macedon clanhead Ningolobin (Captain Turnbull) assaulted his wife.

18 June 1840

Ningolobin departed for Nunnup, then returned in:

> a violent rage, throws his powerful spears promiscuously in the Encampment. One hit the cart just where I was holding, and another almost hit my man Davis. Budgery Tom and he has a regular set to.

They left Kulluk after a ceremony and returned to Tubberubbabel. The breaking up of the encampment one mile from Kulluk had a pleasing appearance as they descended down hill one by one, the women at some distance, also one by one, but in another direction. They encamped on the journey back to Tubberubbabel at a miserable place called Nermoin by Kokubel.[221]

19 June 1840

Arrived at Tubberubbabel safe about 11 o'clock.[222]

20 June 1840

At Tubberubbabel the whole encampment was excited by a rumour that the Two Fold Bay blacks had killed Old Kullorluk (senior clan-head, signatory to Batman's treaty), and Young Budgery Tom (another clan-head, also a signatory). Mr Hobson visited to complain that the blacks' dogs had rushed his sheep, but after discussion, concluded it was a tale of his shepherd. Thomas took a good view, a sketch, of the encampment.[223]

---

220 Thomas Journal, CY 2604, item 3, frame 148, ML. For all the information collected about their proposed reserve, Kullurk/Kulluk/Coolart, see Chapter 7.
221 Thomas Journal, CY 2604, item 3, frame 149, ML. Kokubel was one of their regular encampments on their route around the peninsula, see Thomas diagram in Journal 12 July 1840, CY 2604, item 3, ML.
222 Thomas Journal, CY 2604, item 3, ML.
223 Thomas Journal, CY 2604, item 3, ML.

12 July 1840

For the three weeks since June 20, they have been at Tubberubbabel, with small parties coming and going, giving Thomas their route, and a mudmap which he copied, and their estimation of days away; they were at pains to tell him that they were not going to Melbourne, and Thomas was gratified that they were going by choice and not from necessity.[224] He also gave them their 'stipend', ie their rations, before they went off.[225]

14 July 1840

Thomas' gratification was short-lived – on this day, they told him that they had to move encampment because there were no kangaroo. 'This convinced me', he wrote:

> that the Blacks perambulate as much from necessity as choice, and, to use a colonial Phrase, it is necessary in order to give that part of Blacks run a spell.[226]

Thomas seems to be describing Indigenous paddock rotation.

15 July 1840

This was a very wet and windy day, fortunately for the poor blacks for game, he recorded. They wanted to go to Melbourne but he encouraged them to move encampment instead.[227]

19 July 1840

Finally, the natives shifted encampment to a flat by Tuerong. They were off in 'five minutes', so quickly that they could not have Divine Service. As they, 'I knew, shifted from dire necessity, I could not say nay'. But as usual, Thomas would not permit his dray to travel on a Sunday: as they were no great distance from his son's station, he ordered Mrs Thomas to give them 24 pounds of potatoes and six pounds of rice.[228]

20 July 1840

As soon as Thomas could find his bullocks he shifted his tent and took it to the native encampment, by Tuerong, taking supplies with him, and relieved all who applied.[229]

---

224 Thomas Journal, CY 2604, item 3, ML.
225 See entry for Saturday 11 July 1840, CY 2604, item 3, ML.
226 Thomas Journal, CY 2604, item 3, ML.
227 Thomas Journal, CY 2604, item 3, ML.
228 Thomas Journal, CY 2604, item 3, frame 161, ML.
229 Thomas Journal, CY 2604, item 3, ML.

21 July 1840

The blacks were still unsuccessful in hunting game, though at a new place, and complained of not having any wax to stick glass on their spears.[230] The lubras were not inclined to make baskets, except two who sat down by Mrs Thomas and made six watch pockets; the blacks were all bent on getting to Melbourne – nothing but Melbourne will do.[231]

22 July 1840

The blacks give Thomas to understand that the parties away from the encampment will not come in unless ordered to, and that they had been away from the tribe too long. So Thomas got on his horse and went looking for them where the blacks said they would be. He visited Buckkermitterwarrer and found Old Mr Man and family, Old Billy, Dollar and Lively. They told Thomas to write a letter and they would take it to the blackfellows out perambulating. He did so, in their language. They all read it, and Old Mr Man held it carefully up to dry, as though it were a draft for 1000 pounds. Thomas addressed it to the Koolin and gave it to them to deliver, then returned to Tuerong.[232]

23 July 1840

Thomas went to Poleorong to look for another party but they had left three nights ago, so he went onto Tantine, but they had left there one night ago. On his return he found Nuluptune advising the encampment to leave and go to Melbourne, but Thomas argued that they could not unless the Robinson and the Governor[233] ordered such a move. They wanted a letter for Melbourne, ie a pass. Thomas refused.

They then had an argument about the work/rations issue. The blacks said that they would get plenty to eat in Melbourne **'Merregeek white men, plenty bungarly Thomas'**. He responded by recalling the goodness of the Governor, what a large amount of white paper money the food cost, and how few skins and baskets they had brought him lately. He showed them 'more than ordinary displeasure'; they said he was **'big one sulky'**; they said **'we all gogo no work'**. He fed them and at the last serving out, he threw the pannican down in anger saying 'no good my blackfellows'. They went off for a long discussion by the fire, and Thomas ostentatiously took the crosscut saw and got his eldest daughter to help him cut down two trees. This shamed them, and Bob came and

---

230   Thomas' drawing of spears, including the formidable glass-tipped spear, is reproduced as Fig 23.
231   Thomas Journal, CY 2604, item 3, ML.
232   Thomas Journal, CY 2604, item 3, ML.
233   La Trobe's official title all through the 1840s, until Glorious Separation of the Colony of Victoria, was Superintendent of the Port Phillip District of New South Wales. But the blacks always refer to him as the Governor, or the big one Governor, and Thomas uses their language of description.

took the saw out of the girl's hand and he and Thomas cut down two more trees. Then they all went back to work and worked hard till the evening. Thomas' son rewarded them for the work, and they replied **'all gone sulky'**.[234]

25 July 1840

They were 'somewhat more satisfied' this day, and actually asked for work; Thomas lists the fetching of wood and water, harrowing, cross-cut sawing, chopping, as work done: two people brought in skins. Budgery Tom acted as foreman and appeared proud of it. Mr Hyatt called and said that he didn't know what Thomas had done with the blacks, but whenever they come now (to Tontine) they are always willing to work.[235]

27 July 1840

Thomas sent his cart off from Tuerong to Melbourne for supplies, taking the work of the blacks – seven fruit baskets, eight strong fruit baskets, 35 various mats, 54 kangaroo skins, 46 *Tuans*, 12 *Bemen*, 12 opossum. The Chief Protector arrived at Tuerong and found fault with everything; he told Thomas to collect all his blacks, go to Melbourne, meet up with Yarra blacks, order provisions and get the combined tribes to select a suitable spot for a location.[236]

28 July 1840

Robinson and Thomas visited Tubberubbabel, Kangerong and Buckker-mitterwarrer, Thomas' three Protectorate stations.[237]

4 to 5 August 1840

Thomas, guided by Budgery Tom and Bogy Bogy, walked from Tuerong to Sandy Point to Kunnite (either East Creek or Stony Creek, unidentified positively as yet) and back again to Tuerong by compass bearing given by blacks. They were looking to round up Western Port blacks out hunting, in order for the whole tribe to go to Melbourne according to Robinson's instructions, to select a place for a reserve.[238]

Transcription 4 and 5 August 1840

Wednesday 4 August 1840

am determined to go myself. The blacks try to persuade me off, by telling me they are on the mountain and **too much wood and no gogo**

---

234   Thomas Journal, CY 2604, item 3, ML.
235   Thomas Journal, CY 2604, item 3, frame 164, ML.
236   Thomas Journal, CY 2604, item 3, ML.
237   Thomas Journal, CY 2604, item 3, frame 165, ML. Robinson's record is in Clark 1998, vol 1: 356–359.
238   Thomas Journal, CY 2604, item 3, ML.

Yarraman [can't ride a horse] I say me no frightened, me walk. They say **plenty break foot.** But I was determined saying Mr Robinson say me big one lazy. Finding me resolute, bedding one mark on the ground[239] the direction they were through the bush taking my compass, till debating the matter. At last they said **you be kill'd by wild black fellows, no Marminarta then Western Port blackfellows.** Me said no mind. 2* [marginal note says Budgery Tom and Bogy Bogy] stepp'd forward and said **no long way, 2 sleep and nerlingo** [come back], **no you go alone, we go with Marminarta. I** said well Marnameck. Took damper in my pocket to last for 4 days, compass and chart. Made the poor blacks work hard till 4 o'clock. One of my blacks explains by Sandy Point. Made pot of tea and begg'd they wld proceed to next bearing towards direction of Cape Schank. The 2 blacks felt much surprised at not meeting their tracks and talked to each other. They both had firearms. We went on till sunset but without discovering any tracks of them and encamp'd at a place called Kannite* where is some fine water in deep gullies like a creek spring from must be a portion of the Wongo Range, and made its way when full into the sea, tho at this time of the year the sand was perfect by the beech. Yet about 200 yds from was a bank of salt water of great size lock'd in by drifting up of sand, and must be at the wet season a formidable inlet of the sea I believe, little if at all known [Stony Creek or East Creek]. Some pretty pathes here and there of good feed in the Ranges and many stray'd cattle appear, 36 or 38 came pass'd our sleeping place at night to drink. I slep soundly under a gum tree with 2 armed savages about me, I am sorry to say with more apparent safety than with 2 of my own colour so armed promiscuously in the Bush.

Wednesday 5 August 1840 [should be Thursday]

The two blacks give me to understand that the blacks not being there or at the other place [Sandy Point] – are among the ranges 3 sleeps more & vouch that they would be sure & bring them in, no good me going, I should break my legs – I at first insist in going but knowing what hungry fellows I had about me after a few miles walking, agree to leave them on a perfect understanding that they bring in the blacks. They unreasonably begg'd me damper, tea and sugar. I was not pleased as I fully expected a night in the Bush. However on the faith their bringing in the blacks cut off what I thought I should eat another meal & taking a pannican and bit of sugar gave them the rest. Begg'd of them a good guide [compass bearing] never mind what in the way. They say **no go strait.** I say Yes you tell me. They directed me a strait line very carefully. I took the bearing, shook hands and started. I passed over some queer

---

239 Mudmap.

country [grass trees ?] and thickly and thickly timbered ranges, but kept my course, and making Ner Ner [Port Phillip] which I did in 3 hours. Made a fire, a pot of tea, smok'd my pipe, read a small portion of Scriptures and proceeded. Such was the accuracy of the blacks direction & I must take some little credit in my own direction in stearing to correct and determination to pass if possible in a direct course that by 4 o'clock I came withing 600 yards of my son's hut [Tuerong], out of my course to the west only that space*.

Thomas' PS to this day's entry states 'Blacks much surprised at my finding my way'.

10 August 1840

Thomas and blacks departed Tuerong after a stay of 21 days for Melbourne, summoned by Robinson; they encamped at Poleorongon one night, then Konigo one night, then Moody Yallock two nights en route. The party was short of food and Thomas' dray was filled with the blacks' baggage.[240]

15 August 1840

Thomas and the blacks bypassed Melbourne; the whole of the Western Port blacks, except Dr and family who are at Point Nepean, arrived at Kurruk (Toorak) where the Yarra blacks are on a pretty north-facing rise by Yarra, 215 in all.[241]

19 August 1840

Old Kollorlok makes an noble and powerful speech, which much surprised me, so fluent that he would not let another put a word in edgeways. The purport of his speech was to pacify the blacks, that **before white man came no flour, that Black fellows got drunk and made big one Governor at Melbourne sulky, that bye and bye have a Pickaniny** [little or small] **Melbourne; no** [not] **white fellows Melbourne,** [but] **Blackfellows' Melbourne; Bulganna** [bullock/ beef] **no** [not] **White Mans** [but] **black Mans; potatoes no** [not] **white mans** [but] **black mans.** This was all alluding to the station about to be formed, and he concluded by saying **white fellows come to black fellows Melbourne, only Marminarta, Bob, Jemmy, bad Davy say Yangelly, Yangelly** [go away]; **Black Police turn them away.** The concluding part of Kollorluk's speech had a wonderful effect, all through the encampment, **Ah, Ah, Ah, Ah** which in general and in this case meant yes. They were pretty peaceable after this.[242]

---

240   Thomas Journal, CY 2604, item 3, ML.
241   Thomas Journal, CY 2604, item 3, ML.
242   Thomas Journal, CY 2604, item 3, ML.

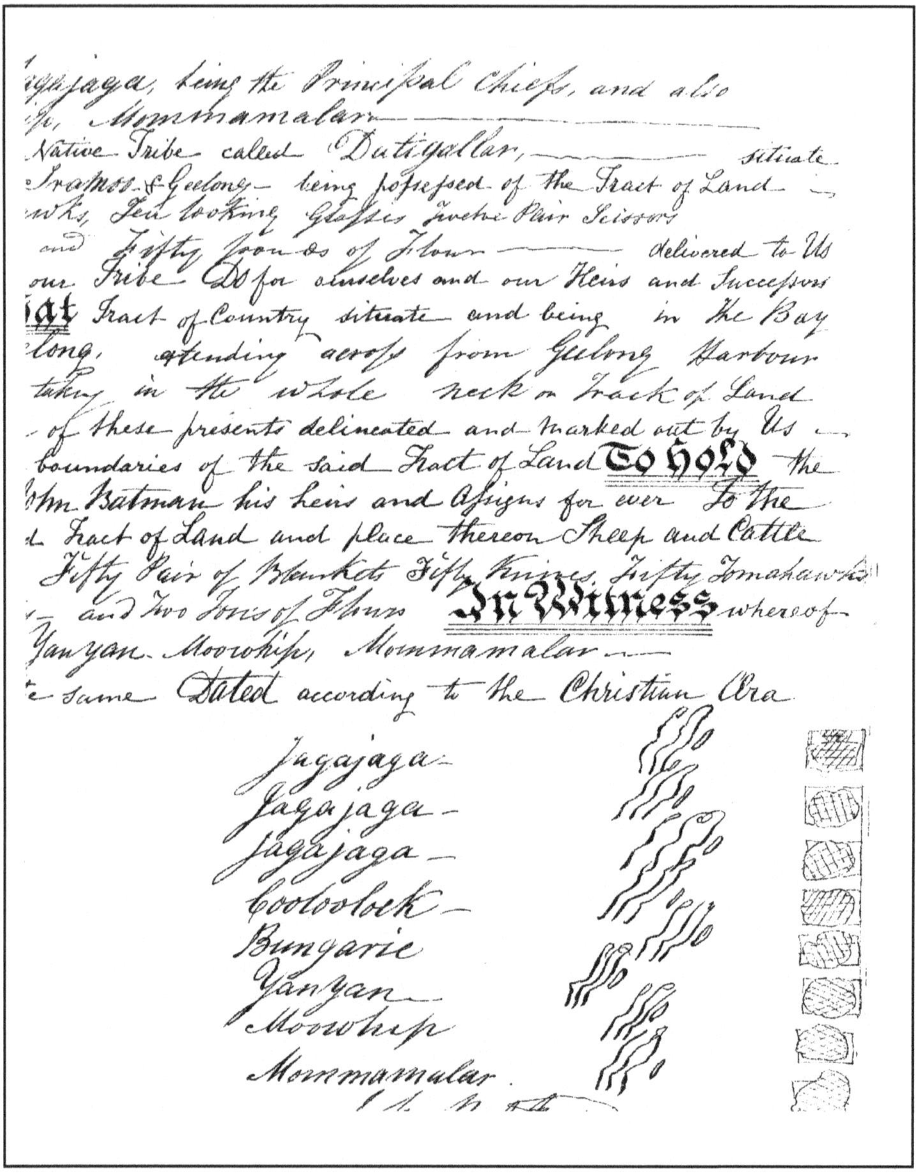

...jaga, being the Principal Chiefs, and also
...Mommamalar ——
Native Tribe called Dutigallar, —— situate
Iramoo & Geelong — being possessed of the Tract of Land —
...ks, Ten looking Glasses Twelve Pair Scissors
and Fifty Pounds of Flour —— delivered to Us
our Tribe Do for ourselves and our Heirs and Successors
hat Tract of Country situate and being in the Bay
...long, extending across from Geelong Harbour
taking in the whole neck or Tract of Land
of these presents delineated and marked out by Us
boundaries of the said Tract of Land To Hold the
John Batman his heirs and Assigns for ever To the
d Tract of Land and place thereon Sheep and Cattle
Fifty Pair of Blankets Fifty Knives, Fifty Tomahawks
and Two Tons of Flour In Witness whereof
Yanyan Moowhip, Mommamalar —
e same Dated according to the Christian Era

Jagajaga
Jagajaga
Jagajaga
Cooloolock
Bungarie
Yanyan
Moowhip
Mommamalar

Fig 17A. and B. 'Marks made by Budgery Tom and Kollorlook on the Geelong and Melbourne Treaties'

The Geelong signatures reproduced from the facsimile edition of James Dawson's Australian Aborigines, and the Melbourne signatures from the front and back of the Melbourne document, reproduced with the permission of the State Library of Victoria.

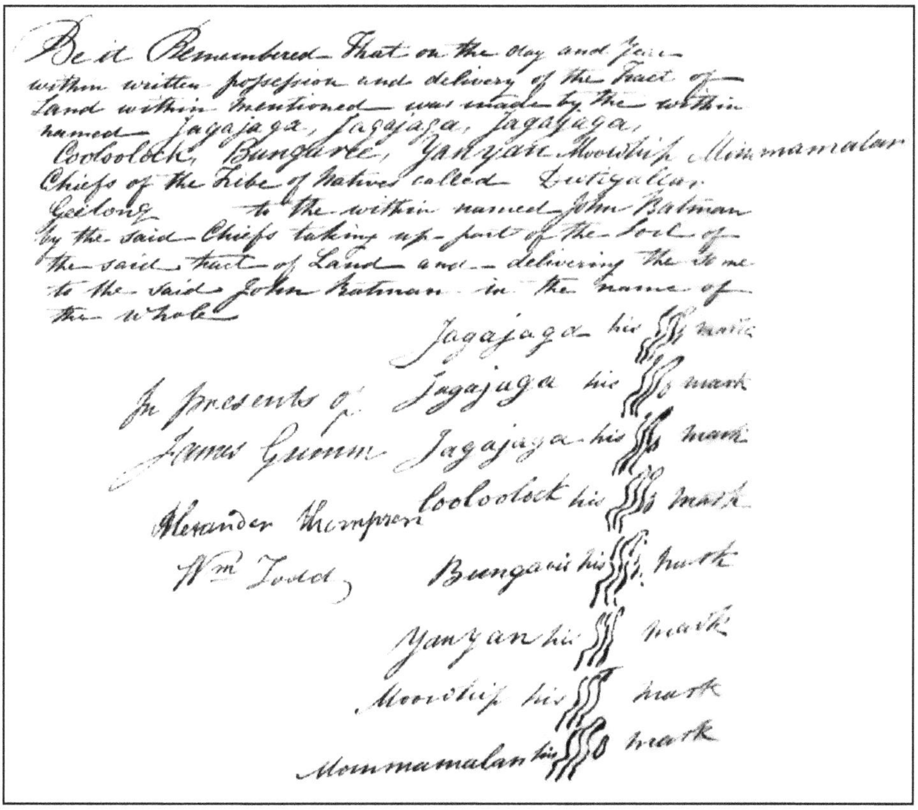

Be it Remembered That on the day and Year within written possession and delivery of the Tract of Land within mentioned was made by the within named Jagajaga, Jagajaga, Jagajaga, Cooloolock, Bungaree, Yanyan Moowhip Mommamalar Chiefs of the Tribe of Natives called Dutigallar Geelong to the within named John Batman by the said Chiefs taking up part of the Soil of the said tract of Land and delivering the same to the said John Batman in the name of the whole

Jagajaga his mark

In presents of Jagajaga his mark

James Gumm Jagajaga his mark

Alexander Thompson Cooloolock his mark

Wm Todd Bungarie his mark

Yanyan his mark

Moowhip his mark

Mommamalan his mark

Fig 17B.

The Geelong signatures reproduced from the facsimile edition of James Dawson's Australian Aborigines, and the Melbourne signatures from the front and back of the Melbourne document, reproduced with the permission of the State Library of Victoria.

Kollorlook/Cooloolock/Koolerook/Coolorlock/ Koolooloook/Collerlook/Kollorluk/Colorlok

Western Port Bonurong 'Chief', listed, with his mark, as a signatory to Batman's treaty, senior owner of country at the top of Western Port including Mahun.

6 Jun 1835 – Cooloolock's name on Batman's treaty (SLV); Coolorlock – his mark recorded along with other signatories to Batman's treaty (Howitt Papers, Box 9, Folder 4, Paper 4, Museum of Victoria).

20 Mar 1839 – On Assistant Protector James Dredge's first census as Koolerook, Waworong tribe, aged 40, unmarried, family not ascertained (Robinson Papers, vol 54, ML); 18 Sep 1839 – Old man; Thomas was remonstrating against the killing of Peter, Mr Langhorne's Murrumbidgee boy, by local men. Blacks reacted **'What for sulky. No good that blackfellow, no his country and no good you'**. Old Collorlook got very angry and protected Thomas (Thomas Journal, set 214, box 1, ML).

1840 – Kollorlook has done the duties of a shepherd for 6 months (Thomas Periodical Report, VPRS 4410, unit 3, no 67, p. 23, PROV); 1840 – Kollorlook – listed with Billy Lonsdale and d'Villiers in a group of three at Arthurs Seat who are determined to go to Westernport (Thomas Journal, CY 2605, frame 8, ML); 28 Feb 1840 – Kullerlook leaves Thomas at Kunnung at Western Port and with several others plus Thomas' man Ross, goes to Melbourne (CY 2605, item 1, ML); 15 Mar 1840 – at O'Connors station near Dandenong en the way back from the raid into Gippsland, Kullorlook stayed and went out with O'Connor's sheep (CY 2605, item 1, ML); 7 Apr 1840 – Collerlook is one of a Council of six Port Phillip and Barabool blacks held by the side of Thomas' tent (CY 2605, frame 67, ML); 13 Apr 1840 – Kollorlook listed among the families shifting encampment in Melbourne (CY 2605, item 1, ML); 17 May 1840 – Thomas gave Kollorlock a red blanket with which he was most pleased (CY 2604, item 3, ML); 21 June 1840 – a rumour had reported that Kullorluk and Budgery Tom (the two 'chiefs') had been killed by the Twofold Bay blacks, and Thomas was pleased to record today that they were safe (CY 2604, item 3, ML); 17 Aug 1840 – Old Kollorluk makes what Thomas calls the noble and powerful speech about the past and the proposed future (CY 2604, item 3, ML); Oct 1840 – 'Old Koolooloook, veteran, still hale and hearty, but his hoary head and white beard, his scars tell of many years of the rude buffeting of savage life'; he was the sage of the tribe, when he spoke in Council all listened with the most respectful attention, his long experience in all the feints, 'manoevers', deceptions and expedients of blackfellows, and his ready means of circumventing them, rendered him almost indispensable to the tracking party, 'a perfect Hawk-eye and Leather stocking' (WJ Thomas, describing him at the time he joined the search party to track the Gippsland blacks who raided Jamieson's station, CY 3106, frame 106, ML).

25 Jan 1840 – Billy Lonsdale and most of the Western Port blacks visited Nerre Nerre Warren and chatted with Thomas, Old Kollorlook had a bad spear wound in his side (Byrt 2004: 53).

11 Feb 1841 – On a journey with the blacks from Nerre Nerre Warren north-east by north over the ranges, Old Kollorlook's athletic and tracking skills were much appreciated (Byrt 2004: 53); Kollorlook with Yal Yal, Yanki Yanki and Beruke alias Gellibrand gave Thomas information about the murder by the Goulburn blacks of the Adelaide black Jemmy at Whitehead's station not 15 miles from Melbourne (Thomas to Robinson, VPRS 11, unit 8/417, PROV).

Jan 1846 – Listed on Thomas Family Connections census as Kollorlook, Western Port, belonging to the section that claims the country of Mahun near Western Port, a widower (CY 3083, ML).

1 May 1848 – Kollorlook has a violent cold like influenza; Thomas gave him Dover powder; 2 May 1848 – Old Kollorlook looked 'very weak, he says that he can scarce see, he does not complain of any pain. I make him take some tea and some sugar. He says his new wife has gone away to Geelong. His pulse weak but regular'; 3 May 1848 – 'Kollorlook still weak but would not take a gentle dose of rhubarb – but takes 2 pills to ease the phlegm, after very great pressing and giving him some sugar and pence – he says **he no take physic for some wild black had taken his fat*. Blacks say no use physic when fat is gone.** Nor could I make any impression on him or the Old D^{rs} about him – to the contrary. This man like others must take his chance. Oh God, when will these poor dark creatures eyes be opened'. [*Thomas' marginal note says that the old people after this idea has seized them cannot be induced unless in great pain to take any medicine] (CY 2606, frame 507, ML); Koollorlook' obituary: 'a Western Port black, died 5 May 1848. He was the last living who signed the Deed with the VDL adventurers in 1835. A fine black & faithful to the last to the whites. He oftern Piloted me thro' the Ranges, no fear of water when Kollorlook led the party, but once in the Koronwarrable Ranges he was out. We Encamped by the side of a creek, tho' very deep no water. We were all jaded. Poor Koolloluk said **never before big one seen & no water here, his words.** Were in a great strait, about 3 blks, myself & 2 men, who were stating

they were sure if not killed that we should die by hunger & thirst following these wretches. We had loosed our bullocks. Kooloorlook left us for an hour and returned saying no water. All of a sudden he said **No Bungerellarly get em water for** [illegible] & **banban oram Yannanna** – we always travelled with 2 2 gallon casks to fill when we left. He led my two men follow him, watch the bullocks. He went and about half a mile by men's account in a scrub was a tremendous hollow gum tree, must have lain there for years, which had a quantity of water in which they filled the 2 Kegs which we quombad in our tent for fear of loosing it. The lubras just got enough from the tree to supply the wants of the encampment, but the poor bullocks was forc'd to be chained to a tree all night. Koolloorlook was a great man. When not in the Bush would settle down with Mr Ruffy or Mr O'Connor shepherding. He was with Mr O'Connor a month or two constantly for 2 years and never was know to lose a sheep. I have seen him on a cold black Winter's day enduring hail and rain in the Western Port Plains. A shepherd on O'Connor's station one evening came home with many sheep short. This was a fine joak for Kulloorluck, he said **stupid white man no stupid Black Shepherd.** He started by daybreak in the morning and got in all the lost sheep. He was much opposed to the formation of the Native Police & no sooner did any of the Coast Tribe enter than he by enveigling them got them to desert. He came one day to Nerre Nerre Warren and got two of the finest Blacks who labor'd away, for two months the police was never sent out on a bush duty. I do think Mr La Trobe's fine feelings tho' they were formed was afraid of their destroying other blacks,, but they used for 2 hours March Backwards and forward from 1 tree to a certain distance as in direction of Captain Dana. Old Kollorlook watched this small duty & said to 2 fine Working blacks who were grubbing trees **big one stupid you, see Lazy fellows there only Yangan pickaning wages these blacks. Me work Get Damper, tea, meat Tobacco etc.** They entered into his feelings and cut work.' (Thomas Journal, CY 2606, item 1, frame 63, ML).

Koolloorlook, Western Port tribe, male, aged 56, widower, died south of the Yarra (Thomas Return, set 214, item 11, ML); Kollorlook had a son of the same name who was mentioned in the first report of the Central Board in 1861 as having been shepherding for 18 months and never lost a sheep (1861: 17).

27 August 1840

At Bolin (Bulleen) the Western Port blacks feel themselves that they have made 'a sorry choice' to join with Yarra blacks and settle. Yarra blacks say **good country this.**[243]

2 September 1840

Thomas had a regular set to with the blacks. The Western Port blacks again want to go to Gam Grim (between Carrum swamp and Dandenong), which Thomas opposes on the grounds that there are too many white people there. Thomas threatens to leave them and return to England. They try to pacify him and at length both tribes agree to settle by the Koran Warabin Range (Dandenongs). Robinson arrived and placed a map before them and Budgery Tom 'by consent of the others' agrees that it is good land.[244]

5 September 1840

Thomas is guided by blacks from the Yarra and Western Port tribe to a spot called Nerre Nerre Warren in the Corrhanwarrabul Ranges and decides that it is a suitable place for a reserve for the two tribes.[245]

This is the effective end of the Protectorate on the Mornington Peninsula, though there are frequent mentions in Thomas' journal subsequently of visits to the Mornington Peninsula checking all the encampments, looking for the Western Port people who refused to stay at the new protectorate station Nerre Nerre Warren.

It was uncharacteristic of Thomas to mock Budgery Tom for pretending to map-read. In his second periodical report Thomas describes what happened. He and the Chief Protector showed Budgery Tom a map of the district. Budgery Tom then made a 'fair' map on the ground and pointed with a stick to the place which he believed suitable. It was a sophisticated choice being on the margin of Bonurong and Waworong land: Tangenong (Dandenong) creek flowed into Port Phillip and was thus clearly Bonurong. North of Dandenong creek was Warworong. The creek itself is not the boundary, but rising ground somewhere to the north of it would have been the no-man's land where both groups could hunt but not camp, and the route by which messengers travelled.

Thomas set off for this place with five men, two of them Bonurong, and three of them Waworong, reflecting precisely the relative numerical strengths of the two tribes, similar to the selection of the five domestic police. Then he came back to

---

243   Thomas Journal, CY 2604, item 3, ML.
244   Thomas Journal, CY 2604, item 3, frame 189, ML.
245   Thomas Journal, CY 2604, item 3, ML.

Melbourne to gather all the people up and move them. There were 200. But they refused to go, calling Thomas a spy[246] and not a friend, blaming him as the cause of the authorities' removing them from Melbourne.

Robinson threatened 'coercive measures for their removal'[247] and Thomas found himself arguing that such would be against the whole protectorate charter which was 'to protect'. He said that the only effective way to get them to move would be to provide them with a homestead. La Trobe agreed and approved the place Nerre Nerre Warren.

When Thomas reported this to the two tribes, they received it with 'particular satisfaction'[248] but stayed put until they actually saw the flour and the rest of the stores. Thomas went on to say that he thought that the news of the proposed homestead which he thought would have filled their minds with gladness had no effect on them, because they were 'literally glutted'[249] with provisions from the town of Melbourne.

24 September 1840

'The fact is that the blacks are so bountifully supplied by Melbournians that they not only get lazy but dainty, no longer begging bullocks' heads, sheep heads etc to encampment'.[250] He went on to relate the example of one of Mr Walpole's bullocks. It was injured, and it was a long time before it was put out of its misery. But in the end 'the blacks refused to catch as it was not fresh'. Thomas must mean that the head and other off-cuts were the payment the blacks received for helping to catch and kill a beast. In this case the poor beast had lingered too long and the blacks did not regard the meat as good and so they refused it.[251]

25 September 1840

Bogy Bogy and his party came in to the encampment on the Yarra with news. Thomas wrote that they don't know just how much of their talk that he understood. But they did: the whole of the blacks moved across to the other side of the Yarra to get away from him **'for one night to plenty talk'**.[252]

---

246   CY 2604, frame 192, ML.
247   Thomas Third Periodical Report, VPRS 4410, unit 3, item 68: 2, PROV. In his monthly summary for September, Thomas quotes Robinson 'The Chief Protector states if I cannot persuade them there is force at my demand. I strongly object to it and propose resignation rather than use force' (Thomas Journal, set 214/2, item 5(b): 11, ML).
248   Thomas Third Periodical Report, VPRS 4410, unit 3, item 68: 3, PROV.
249   Thomas Third Periodical Report, VPRS 4410, unit 3, item 68: 3, PROV.
250   Thomas Journal, CY 2604, frame 205, ML.
251   This discriminating judgment of what constitutes good food stands in marked contrast to what Robinson recorded the previous year 'bullocks that were drowned, tho in a fetid state, afforded ample food for the Natives', 15 March 1839 (Clark 1998b: 16).
252   CY 2605, frame 133, ML.

Their proposed expulsion from the town had heightened the generosity of the settlers who planted in their minds the view that **'that place no good Blackfellows, too much work there'**. Thomas again raised with Robinson the issue of their future support, that is, giving them rations: partly, he was afraid of not being reimbursed if he fed them out of his own stores as he had done at Tubberubbabel.

As matters turned out, the delay proved to have awful consequences to everyone, as Major Lettsom arrived in town. While the blacks stayed put in Melbourne waiting for assurances about future food, they had sent messengers to the Goulburns asking them to come down to Melbourne: Major Lettsom followed them down to Melbourne. Lettsom had a list of Aborigines wanted by the authorities as 'objectionable characters' including two of Thomas' blacks. Lettsom said that if he could not get those on the list he would take others as hostages.[253]

Thomas went into familiar defence mode on behalf of his blacks: there was no charge against the Aborigines; there was no recognised authority ie a constable, to exercise the warrant; he would not comply, as compliance would mean going against his instructions from the British government. If hostages were taken, he predicted, 'the whole colony might become a scene of carnage'.

Thursday 1 October 1840

This is <u>not</u> the day of the well known roundup by Major Lettsom. When the well known roundup occurred, Thomas was with Nunuptune and Mumbo tracking the Kurnai who raided Jamieson's (see Chapter 8). On this day Thomas had a discussion with the Bonurong and asked them if the soldiers had taken any of their Koolings and they said:

> no, that they had swum the river & some had got up the trees, but that many of them were further on at Mr Smythe's.[254]

He left this group and went to George Smith's where:

> the men women and children flocked around me. I pacified them as well as I could. One Old Man Moragine said **'me no go to Nerer Nere Warren, bye & bye big Wild Soldier come there, me stop here, die here'**. I stopp'd about them some hours trying to pacify them, had their fears of coming to Nere Nere Warren, said **'we gogo bush first and then when all gone wild soldiers, come Nere Nere Warren, and no**

---

253   One copy of the list is an estray at CY 2605, items 2–3, frame 129, ML.
254   That is further on than Merri Creek, not with the big encampment, at Surveyor Smythe's. This makes sense; later this month Thomas records that the whole of the Western Ports moved because they were afraid of the Goulburn blacks, CY 2605, frame 169, ML.

more come to Port Phillip. Why white man big one frighten Black fellow?' I endeavoured to persuade them that the cause originated in Black Fellows killing White men, & that Governor in Sydney sent soldiers to catch Black fellows. They said 'plenty Bungarlarly Big one wild soldiers, no Port Phillip Black Fellow kill White man'. I left them a little pacified but their revenge not satisfied. Some said they would go and get plenty Goldbourn and Barrabool Black fellows to come and be sulky with white men. I returned to my dray and proceeded towards Nere Nere Warren.[255]

Major Lettsom's roundup

Major Lettsom's well known roundup, the 'carnage at Hydleburg' happened on Sunday 11 October 1840, a Sunday according to Thomas, but he is wrong about this, as it happened the day before.[256] In one account that he wrote, Thomas mentions Major Newman, Lt Russell and 11 mounted redcoats 'Karbines etc glaringly presenting themselves' galloping at 6.30 am to surround the sleeping blacks on the Heidleberg road, 'the earth shook under them'.[257]

They shot dead the famous, respected and admired Winberri while he was in the act of raising a waddy against an officer, and they rounded up and marched into the barracks at Melbourne between 200 and 400 people of the Thongworong, Waworong, Wooralim and Boonworong tribes. Winberri was aged 23, brother of Nerimbineck, son of old Ningologin, a Yarra black.[258] Winberri was by family connection able to pass safely through distant remote tribes,[259] a man with a 'noble spirit' according to Thomas who wrote a three page description of the unusual mourning ritual for Winberri carried out morning and evening by his aged father and his only sister.[260]

Robinson's account of the aftermath of Major Lettsom's roundup

This account has been transcribed and published, but is accessible only in libraries. It is reproduced here in full, except for the list of Goulburn blacks and Yarra blacks who were arrested. According to Robinson, no Bonurong people were incarcerated in gaol, though some were injured.

---

255 Thomas Journal, CY 2605, frame 143, undated estray, ML.
256 Thomas Journal, CY 2605, frame 171, ML.
257 Thomas Journal, October-December 1840, set 214/2 (c), ML.
258 First report of raid in Dredge Diary, Ms 5244: 173, SLV; circumstances of raid in La Trobe to Col Sec enc No 2, 46/598; Winberri a Yarra black stirring up Goulburn blacks, Peter Snodgrass to La Trobe, 30 March 1840, VPRS 19, box 4, 40/237, PROV; death, Thomas Return of Births and Deaths, VPRS 4410, unit 3, PROV.
259 Thomas in Bride 1969[1898]: 408.
260 Papers sent to Mr Duffy, 1858, CY 3131, frames 79–81, ML.

Sunday 11 October 1840

About 9am His Honor and Major Lettsom called at my office to report that the three tribes, Boongerongs, Waverongs and Tar.doon.gerongs had been surrounded by the military and police force and were all lodged in the stockade at the prison barracks and that Windberri who had resisted the authorities had been shot dead. See evidence and depositions. His Honor gave me an order to get supplies from the contractor Craig for the natives. He said women and children all had been taken and that they were drafting out the worst characters. I said I would immediately go to them. Mr Lilly called soon after and said Mr Parker had sent him to inform of what had arrived. I said I had been apprized. Parker he said was with them. Rode into town. Mounted Robert on a horse of my own to attend me. Found about 300 natives men women and children in the stockade huddled together. They were picking out the accused by the whites. Snodgrass was very conspicuous and busy. There was crowd of white people at the barracks. The natives were pleased to see me. Gave them a supply of food. Thirty five men and boys were chained, two by two, and separated from the rest. Their wives and children and mothers were there and witnessed a harsh and heart rending scene and I may add illegal proceeding. Mr Wilkinson said he witnessed the bringing in of the natives and said he was shocked by the cruelty of the military and police. If the women, many of whom had young children, happened to be behind as also the old and infirm, they were goaded with bayonets by the soldiers and hit with the but end of their muskets or cut with the sabre of the native police [there was no Native Police Corps in existence at the time; this puzzling reference must refer to the same kind of sabres that had been issued to the 1837 Native Police Corps under de Villiers]. This I heard from several respectable individuals and which was too clearly born out by the wounds on the persons of the natives I myself saw their scars and subsequently mentioned it to His Honor. One man had a piece cut out of his cheek, some said it was by the bullet that killed Winberri, another old man, Bor.run.up.ton, I saw with a cut on the crown of his head. Mr Le Souef reported that a man who had escaped and come to his station had a bruise on the ear. Several of the women showed me the injuries they had received from the military and police sent to apprehend them. Was in communication with His Honor the greater part of today. His Honor read me a letter he'd addressed to Major Lettsom relative to the subject of the previous day's meeting and averting to my sentiments and also the way the natives were to be apprehended etc. The undermined Aboriginal natives were chained by the leg, two together, and lodged in gaol [here follows the list of names of Yarra and Goulburn blacks].

In the afternoon rode out with Mr Simpson and Yaldwin to where the natives had encamped, which was about two miles on the Heidelburgh rode. The day was fine and we overtook Mr Hobson and with a few native men who were going out to their place of encampment at the verge of the new town to the run of Captain Lonsdale near the remains of a small camp. The fires were burning at the large camp which occupied a large space of open ground and clear. The native's utensils lay scattered about in every possible direction: spears, broken rope and different articles of clothing. It grieved me to see such which to the natives these articles are of value as much or more so than our fine habiliments for a greater amount of labour has been expended upon them. Articles of some kinds lay scattered along the line of [...]. A vast number of dogs had also been shot, not as was stated by order of Mr La Trobe, but by some malicious and evil disposed white persons. I found Mr Parker t the camp with some blacks whom I had ordered there for the purpose of collecting the articles belonging to the natives. On my arrival Ningkallerbil and Little Benbow went missing with all speed and shouting for help before a mounted policeman who was galloping after them. I reprehended his conduct. Some of the white ruffians had stolen and taken away a variety of articles belonging to the natives. There was no merit in attacking the natives they were encamped on open ground and contiguous to Melbourne. All the troops [...] and mounted and border police surrounded them and all mill round. The Port Phillip natives made no resistance. One man Pudg. ger.re Tom saw the armed party approach first and gave the alarm. The troops surrounded the native camp and commenced breaking the spears of the natives. At first the Goulburn blacks took up their weapons, fear or custom might have induced that. The Port Phillip natives told them to lay them down again, which they did. Ningkallerbell, Pardeweerap [this is Poor.tow.rup/Baddorup/Big Benbow/Mr Smith/George Smith's blackfellow, Yankee Yankee's father, Barebun/Mary's father] and some others of the Boongerongs pointed out the Goulburn blacks and others that were wanted to the soldiers. Ningkallerbell told me this. For further particulars of capture refer to comment next book. Men, women and children, old and young invalids and others were all huddled away together like a drove of cattle or sheep. Women with young children, if unable to keep up with the rest were struck. Old men, several as well as young, had sabre cuts some on their heads and on other parts of the body. I was told by Mr Wilkinson and other respectable persons it was a melancholy sight: the natives crying and making a noise at the camp. Windberry was pointed out by a rascally white man Bill, who has associated with the blacks from the commencement of the settlement and who had been for a length of time cohabiting with Borremun's wife, alias Dredge, wife's name Mary Ann. I rode out with Yaldwin and saw the camp and the body of Winberri who was shot. This was a melancholy business, he was shot by Sergeant Leary, see evidence, in the act as they say of striking Vignoller. Afternoon went and saw the black buried outside the burying ground. A coffin had been made. After the natives see list had been drafted out, about 22 in all, they were iron and handcuffed and put in gaol and the Port Phillip men women and children were liberated. I sent them over the water with Parker.[261]

According to Thomas, in timing this 'unconstitutional' roundup, Major Lettsom specifically took advantage of Thomas' absence tracking the Gippsland blacks who raided Jamieson's. Many people bore to their graves the scars of the wounds they received that day of Lettsom's roundup.[262] One of these was the Bonurong chief Mingaragon/Old Mr Man whose biographical entry is in chapter 6.

---

261   Clark 1998, vol 2: 7–10.
262   Papers sent to Mr Duffy, 1858, CY 3131, frames 79–81, ML.

4. Tubberubbabel, Protectorate head station

> Tubberubbabel/Tubberrubabel/Tub er rub ber bil/ Tubburub*
> Aborig Station/Mr Thomas' First Station/Tubberrubbabil/
> Tuberubbabel/Tubbarubbabel/Terabbabl

Tubberubbabel is the Protectorate head station, shown to Thomas by the owner Burrenum (Mr Dredge) who was born there. It is Bonurong heartland where the 100 huts were found by Gellibrand's party in 1836. It is also the place where the Bonurong accepted Thomas' proposals for a future. The intimacies of daily interaction at the site are presented here, and in Chapter 9 the issues are examined surrounding the paid work done at this place by the Bonurong: at the end of this chapter is the Bonurong retrospective view of it all.

Its location has been identified by the following steps. Kangerong's position is located precisely on Surveyor Nutt's map of Jamieson's Special Survey of 1840. Thomas, who navigated his way round the bush with a compass and Aboriginal mudmaps, locates Tubberubbabel one mile north-east of Kangerong, and Robinson's description agrees: Tubberubbabel is one mile from Kangerong. After Gellibrand's party landed on the beach near Sandy Point, they walked for nine miles in a north-westerly direction heading for Port Phillip: this party also had compasses. After nine miles walking, followed by a pause because Gellibrand was ill and they were out of water, they sent out scouts who found water. The whole party then tracked the scouts' path and came upon the waterholes and the 100 huts, within a quarter of an hour.

Overlaying the cadastre and the topographic maps on Smythe's 1841 map,[1] Hughes drew a circle of one mile radius around Kangerong, and in the direction of north-east from Kangerong, this circle intersects Tubbarubba Creek near its junction both with Bulldog Creek, and with a tributary of Tubbarubba Creek. Using Gellibrand's information to check this identification, a back bearing of nine miles south-east from this place ends in the middle of the sandy Somers beach, which must be presumed as Gellibrand's starting point, as, even though he uses the only descriptor available to him at the time, Sandy Point, seamen do not anchor or disembark at actual points or promontories where currents swirl, especially when there is a gentle sloping sandy beach a stone's throw away:[2] somewhere on what we now know as Somers beach would have been the

---

1 Smythe was found to be astonishingly accurate.
2 The final version of these working maps is P Hughes, 'Location of Protectorate stations and Tuerong, 1 September 2009'.

departure point for the walk across the peninsula. William Jackson Thomas' mileage and distance estimates agree with this identification: his mileage estimates in two directions, from Arthurs Seat to Tubberubbabel, and from Port Phillip to Tubberubbabel are out by only 0.6 miles. In February 2010, as this book was going to the editor, by courtesy of the Surveyor General's office, I saw Smythe's field notebooks: they confirm the location.

Fig 18. 'Location of Protectorate Station'

© Phil Hughes, 2010, Mornington Peninsula Shire.

It is now private property, near the Old Moorooduc road, and is thus inaccessible to the public: its address cannot be given for reasons of privacy. Aboriginal Affairs Victoria has been notified in line with the legal obligation under the *Aboriginal Heritage Act 2006* of any person who finds an Aboriginal site, and AAV will contact the owners. Though the site is effectively lost to the public, here, for a short time, there was optimism, and for that reason alone it needs to be remembered.

There is an undated sketch of an encampment included in the papers which Thomas sent to Mr Duffy for publication many years later of a corroboree at an encampment. Thomas has written across the bottom 'Let me have this again:

I lay great value on young productions'. Young means early in this context, so it is possible, or even likely, that this sketch showing his tent is done at Tubberubbabel.[3]

It needs to be remembered that at the time these records were made, the only referents of observation for the Mornington Peninsula were Cape Schanck, Point Nepean, Arthurs Seat and Sandy Point, all places known to everyone, having been named more than 30 years earlier by the navigators, charting from the sea. Much of Thomas' correspondence with Robinson and La Trobe in Melbourne is sent from Arthurs Seat when his journal indicates he was living at Tubberubbabel.

In this chapter all the recorded mentions of Tubberubbabel which I have found in the various primary records are presented chronologically, including the lengthy quotation from William Jackson Thomas who recorded more detail than did his father: he, and Thomas' assigned convict servants, and the Bonurong levelled the ground, built several buildings, one 30 feet by ten feet with sashed windows, plastered with lime from the limeburners at Point Nepean, plus a good stockyard for the bullocks, a fenced garden, and a bridge over the creek: these several buildings, and the bridge may well have left physical traces, not yet found because prior to this, we have not known where to look. Surveyor Smythe's field notes show a road, which is the road from Hobson's station at Kangerong, shown also on one of Thomas' undated maps.[4] Thomas mentions once in his journal the desirability of cutting a road from Tubberubbabel straight across to Mt Martha, thus cutting a triangle off the route that his supplies had to take from Melbourne, that is from Melbourne to Hobson's, then up and across to Tubberubbabel. There are three burials here, Kurnboro/Old Maria, Bunggame who was Mr King's father, and Old Morragine.

27 January 1836

Joseph Tice Gellibrand was a passenger in the *Norval*, a vessel chartered by the Port Phillip Association to bring 1000 sheep from VDL to Port Phillip. Bad weather forced the ship instead into Western Port and the sheep were landed near Corinella: most perished. Intending to get help from the settlement at Melbourne, Gellibrand led a party which was taken across Western Port in a boat and dropped off at Sandy Point with the intention of walking overland to Melbourne.

Gellibrand's party walked about nine miles north-west from Sandy Point. Then he collapsed, and some members of the party went in search of water. They returned over an hour later 'with the intelligence that they had fallen in with about 100 native huts and near the huts had discovered water'. When Gellibrand

---

3   CY 2984: 555, ML.
4   CY 2984, frame 300, ML.

recovered, they 'packed up our things and proceeded on our course and in about a quarter of an hour, came to a few waterholes surrounded with a thick scrub'.[5] The name of these waterholes, with the 100 huts nearby is Tubbarubbabel.[6]

26 August 1839

Having arrived on the Mornington Peninsula on 17 August 1839, and having spent the next nine days visiting his people at their encampments at the settlers' stations and exploring the country south of Arthurs Seat, looking for a place where the natives congregated, on this day Thomas selected the site for his station where Burrenun (Mr Dredge)[7] said he was born: it was opposite to a series of waterholes called by the natives Tubbarubbabel.[8]

Burrenum/Bore.rer.num/Booronung/Booronung/ Boorunun/Borremum/Bun.Ranrung/Mr Dredge/Jack

Burrunun is the name of a large jew fish of the porpoise kind (CY 3130, frame 93, ML).

Co—owner with Bobbinary of the southern peninsula.

Burenum/Jack/Mr Dredge – influential healer, married to Wigal a daughter of Billibellary. Burenum was a brother to Munmunginna/ Dr Bailey, had recognised authority, but not named as chief (Barwick 1984: 117).

20 Mar 1839 – Booronung alias Jack, age 30, Boonworong tribe, wife Wyulk alias Mary Ann aged 18 (Dredge Census in Robinson Papers, vol 54, ML); 24 Mar 1839 – One ... a Boonworong who calls himself my brother and names himself as Mitter Dredge received a severe contusion to the right temple at a fight between Waworong and Tonguerong tribes (Assistant Protector James Dredge, Journal No 2, Box 16, SLV); Jul 1839 – Burenum/Mr Dredge, name taken in encampment

---

5   Joseph Tice Gellibrand, 'Memorandum of a trip to Port Phillip' in Bride 1983[1898]: 11.

6   The identification was made thus: Kangerong's position is located precisely on Surveyor Nutt's map of Jamieson's Special Survey of 1840. Thomas, who navigated his way round the bush with a compass and Aboriginal mudmaps, locates Tubbarubbabel one mile north-east of Kangerong. Phil Hughes of the MPS GIS department has pinpointed this spot. Gellibrand's party landed on the beach near Sandy Point and walked for nine miles in a north-westerly direction headed for Port Phillip: this party also had compasses. After nine miles walking, they came upon the waterholes and the 100 huts within a further quarter of an hour. A back bearing from Tubbarubbabel in a south-east direction, extended for nine miles, ends on Somers beach.

7   26 August 1839 in Thomas Summary of Proceedings during August 1839, CY 3082, ML; Byrt 2004, CD WT 3082S.DOC.

8   Thomas Summary of Proceedings during August 1839, CY 3082, ML. Byrt 2004, CD WT 3082S.DOC. From 4 June 1839 – 3 October 1839, Thomas Journal CY 2604, item 3 is indecipherable because the ink is so faded. The record of observation presented here is constructed from this summary of August, together with the published version in HRV. There is often a difference of one day between the two versions.

(Thomas 'A' diary, set 214, item 1, ML); 13 Jul 1839 – Fell from a tree, arm swelled (Thomas Journal 1839–40, set 214, item 1, ML); 17 Jul 1839 – Bun-ranrung and six other named blacks arrived at Geelong (Assistant Protector Sievwright to Robinson, enc with 39/10217 in 4/2471, AO of NSW); Jul 1839 – Burrenum in a sad state – appears as if his arm will never get better from a burn – treated it for two days then Burrenum, one of the greatest ramblers in the whole tribe, was off (CY 2604, item 2, ML); 26 Aug 1839 – Burrenum, Tubberubbabel is his birthplace (CY 3082 S DOC); 27 Aug 1839 – Burrenum alias Mr Dredge cut bark for Thomas' hut roof at Tubberubbabel (Thomas Journal, set 214, item 1, ML); 4 Sep 1839, Thomas visited Burrenum's miam at Tubberubbabel – it was like a butcher's shop with legs and parts of kangaroo hung all around (*HRV*, vol 2B: 541); 27 Sep 1839 – Burrenum Western Port doctor called in to officiate on an old man, the first Thomas knew that he was a doctor (*HRV*, vol 2B: 547); 4 Nov 1839 – Wigul at Tubberubbabel making a fine basket (*HRV*, vol 2B: 555).

23 Jan 1840 – Yal Yal and Burrenum return to the encampment at Tubberubbabel with plenty of fowl, enough for the whole encampment (Thomas Journal, CY 2605, item 1); Feb 1840 – Burrenum and his lubra, a party of two, are listed at Arthurs Seat as among those determined to go to Western Port [on the Gippsland raid] (Thomas Journal, CY 2605, frame 8, ML); 5 Jun 1840 – Thomas rode out from Tubberubbabel to look for the returning party from Western Port; he fell in Burrenum and his two brothers and his lubra (CY 2604, item 3, ML); Jun 1840 – Bore.rer.num, his name is on a list of those presently at Arthurs Seat given to Robinson in Melbourne by Billy Lonsdale (Robinson in Clark 1998b: 344); 11 Oct 1840 – Borremum alias Dredge, his wife Mary Anne has been co-habiting with white man, rascally, called Bill (Robinson in Clark 1998, vol 2: 344).

5 Dec 1842 – He always knows where his wife is with Europeans; merely by fits and starts he requires her; he is a wandering unsettled black, she is the reverse (Thomas to Robinson, VPRS 11, unit 8, PROV).

1846 – Burrunun, male aged 25 and his lubra Wigal aged 20, and Tilberburnin, a male aged 11, all Western Port are on Thomas' Family Connections census. Burrenun's own country is Moody Yallock [though Thomas lists him as well as owner of the Mornington Peninsula, his birthplace]. His name is listed immediately after that of the principal owner Old Doctor (CY 3083, ML).

5 Aug 1850 – On a list of the number of Bonurong and Waworong tribes left [26 of the former all named, 38 of the latter all named] Thomas lists Burrenun and Wigal as a group of two (CY 3127, ML).

13 Dec 1851 – Boorunun alias Jack, male Boonoorong tribe, has 2 lubras Wigul alias Christianna and Mynggrook [inserted later by Thomas Mynggrook dead (1852)] (Thomas census, set 214, item 12: 143, ML).

William Jackson Thomas' description of the establishment of the Protectorate station

At length after some weeks[9] pleasantly travelling [with the Bonurong] we came to a creek about six miles NE of Arthurs Seat and about the same distance from the Bay – here the blacks wanted the station to be located.[10] It was a pleasant enough place, the mountains at the back, splendid light wood flats, well grassed hills, creek with large permanent waterholes. We camped and took some time looking around before determining to make it a permanent station. About four miles distant at Kangerong we found a cattle station occupied by Mr Hobson (brother of Dr Hobson a celebrated medico in those days). He had always been on friendly terms with the natives and had no objection to their proximity. So after due consideration we decided to remain here. A gentle rise was selected for the house, a sort of table land well out of reach of the floods, the blacks showing us by the marks on the trees to what heights the floods sometimes rise; the ground [was] cleared of trees and undergrowth, and levelled. Now I wonder if it is worthwhile to tell you how we built a house, wind and weather tight, warm and comfortable out of materials altogether found on the ground. Perhaps it will for it will show you some of the work of the early pioneers of the Colony.

The first thing was to mark out the house 30 feet by 12 feet wide, divided into three rooms each 10 feet. Then collect sufficient saplings which when barked would be 5 inches in diameter. A dozen blacks with the men soon brought in loads. The stay at home blacks quickly barked them. These were then cut to 9 feet lengths for standards. Thicker wood was required for the wall plates. These were adzed flat on both sides so as to rest fair on the posts to which they were spiked. The work of

---

9   The Bonurong, with Thomas' son plus the bullocks and cart, set off at least a week before Thomas, camping at Brighton, Mordialloc and Frankston along the way (CY 3106, frame 59, ML).
10   The location of Tubbarubbabel, identified by the shire's GIS is 6.6 miles: William Jackson Thomas' estimate agrees well.

digging holes was done by the men. I superintended the carpentering, or rather, did most myself. The posts [were] erected all 7 ft 6 ins from the ground, wall plates in and spiked, the corners and joints halved.

Then came the process of wattling, for the structure was to be what is called Wattle and Daub. The standards were spaced to leave openings of 3 or 4 feet. A thin sapling was nailed on each side of the standard, a center one stuck in the ground midway between the standards as under –

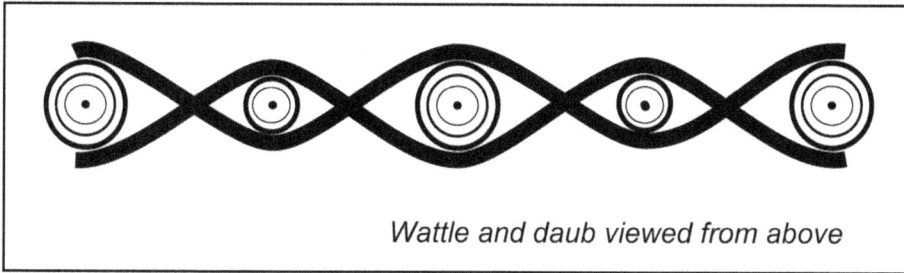

Wattle and daub viewed from above

Fig 19. 'Wattle and daub construction'

Sketch, © Richard Barwick, 2010, based on a sketch by William Jackson Thomas, in the William Thomas Papers, Mitchell Library.

Ti tree was cut the required lengths, and this kind of basket work carried from ground to wall plates. A large quantity of mortar [was] made with loam chopped from and a little lime which latter was got from the lime burners at Point Nepean. Then the work of plastering laid on, on both sides simultaneously, one man inside and me outside. The roof was of saplings, rafters, ridge, the whole covered by sheets of stringy bark for which we had to send several miles into the mountains. The chimney of sods, with a flour barrel on the top.[11] The whole was completed in a fortnight and habitable in three weeks, it took time for the plaster to dry. Doors, table and bunks were made of boards from Mr Hobson at Kangerong. The blacks worked very well. Father made it an invariable practice to pay them for their work, rewarding them with Tea, Sugar, Flour or Tobacco. Our house being completed we took a good rest and time to look round. We had encamped near us about 130 natives. These took something to feed. Daily a large number went out in the morning and generally brought back a full bag. The game is plentiful. There were lots of women who went out with their Merriny sticks to dig roots, and a good many children romping about. I have arranged to accompany them in a Kangaroo hunt Native fashion.[12]

---

11   Robinson later described this building as an old wattle and daub hut in the Tower of Peiza style, at least two feet out of perpendicular, see 27 July 1840 ff.
12   CY 3106, frames 60–62, ML.

Having described his days' hunting, and the walking tree method of stalking kangaroos, William Jackson Thomas went on to add further detail about the buildings at Tubberubbabel:

Time went on, other rooms were added to the house. Glazed sashes were provided from the Settlement. Hobson had sawyers in the forest: from him we [obtained] floor boards which were to floor the house. Canvas [was] nailed up for ceiling. Out buildings erected and at length when all was ready Mother and my sisters arrived. In the mean time, I had by riding about become well acquainted with the Country many miles around. And discovered a tract of land which I considered would make a First Class cattle station, well grassed, permanent water, and a clear run of good country for five miles around in every direction. So after due consideration I determined to at once secure the run. I went to town, applied to and obtained license for a Squatting Run 'Touerng', about four miles east of the northern point of Mt Martha, engaged two men, borrowed father's small tent until we had huts built ... borrowed father's bullocks ... soon I had a good slab hut, and a comfortable hut for the men, strong stock and milking yards and Dairy were gradually added. The house and station buildings were erected on the flat top of a rise from the creek, the large Waterhole in front, to the right hand run a tributary stream ... our buildings were thatched with reeds got from a swamp nearby ... soon year after year more runs were taken up – Dr Barker and John Barker took up Cape Schanck, Maurice Meyrick took a sheep station between Cape Schanck and Arthur's Seat, Cap^n Reid dropped on a station down to the point of Mt Martha, Tom Goring a sheep station about four miles from Tuerong in the Melbourne road, and Stratton on the beach between Mount Martha and Mount Eliza. We were all very good friends, visited each other and exchanged many little neighbourly services. The one thing we were combined about was to prevent any other squatters dropping down between us. Intruders were respectfully warned off, but if that was ineffectual, the services of the Crown Lands Comm. were called in ... I was the first in the district to make cheese [description follows] ... after a time it was found that the position of 'Terubbabl' was unsuited for a permanent Aboriginal Station. A site was selected on the Dandenong Creek ... I used frequently to ride over to see Father and the family, the distance was about 30 miles. Although a large number of blacks migrated with Father to the new station, a good few remained at my station not liking the strict regulation of the issue of stores etc. About this time, the descent of the Gipps Land Blacks upon the station of my friend Mr Jamieson and the plunder and destruction of his property took place. The part I took in the pursuit is fully told in another place. We will now pass over some years during which I had disposed of the Station and removed to land my Father had purchased at Coburg (then called Pentridge). We had then somewhere about 100 acres...[13]

27 August 1839

Thomas was at his quarters at Tubberubbabel with 15 blacks about his tent before breakfast: they appeared delighted to see Thomas' lubra's miam in the process of construction. Burrenum got his tomahawk and cut bark for the roof of Mrs Thomas' hut. Thomas gave breakfast to Burrenum and three unnamed lubras, who then went with Thomas' son to cut tea-tree. One of the lubras was an old woman and Thomas and his son tried to persuade her not to go out cutting down tea-tree but she insisted, and Thomas' son said at the end of the day that she had cut as much as any of the young ones. The rest of his 15 visitors lay idling by the fire all day, and the whole party from Kangerong except the old man paid a visit.[14]

28 August 1839

While he was on his way from Tubberubbabel to Kangerong, Thomas met a party of lubras coming to Tubberubbabel with tomahawks to cut tea-tree for his house. Thomas gave them a note to his son, authorising the payment in tea and flour for their work. They worked well according to Thomas' son, and when he returned Thomas gave them all a good feed. They lay down to sleep till evening and he gave them more flour and sugar to take away.[15] In his summary version Thomas adds the fact that an old woman insisted on going with the younger lubras to cut tea tree, and though he and his son tried to persuade her not to as she was so old, she cut as much as any of the young ones.[16]

---

13   CY 3106, frames 62–65, ML. For those interested in European history, WT Jackson gives an account of the Barker/Meyrick duel, which was occasioned according to Thomas, by Barker's cutting down a magnificent oak tree, the first in the district, in the dry creek which was the boundary between the two runs, an oak tree which Meyrick painted, the painting being sent home to England. Dr Barker was a stutterer; the account casts him in an unfavorable light.

14   *HRV,* vol 2B: 538–539, and 'Summary of Proceedings during August 1839', CY 3082, ML. The old man (unnamed), three lubras and four children had arrived at Kangerong on 18 August in 'a very distressed state'. It is almost certain, that this is Old Mr Man – this is the exact structure of his family, and there is no other Bonurong family with one old man, three lubras and four children, but why he should arrive distressed is not recorded.

15   *HRV,* vol 2B: 539.

16   Thomas Summary of Proceedings during August 1839, CY 3082, ML. Byrt 2004, CD WT 3082S.DOC.

29 August 1839

The blacks came in numbers to his tent, and Thomas gave beads to an attractive widow (unnamed) and her three children: he put a double row on her, and a single row on each of her children, all girls, as fine children as he had ever seen Black or White.[17] He also gave five knives to five men, and a hank of twine to be shared. They wanted as well, thread and needles but he had none. Even so, they must have been cheerful – they were 'all on the *qui vive*' he wrote. But all the stores for them were finished, except for tea, and he had to feed them from his own private supplies – a sheep, 27 pounds of flour, seven pounds of sugar, one and a half pounds of tea and a pound of tobacco. It is 'unmerciful and inconsistent' he wrote, that he was sent to civilise and protect them, and see that their wants are supplied, but he has not been given the means to do so.[18]

30 August 1839

More people visited him, including a man with a fine gun, and a fresh family introduced by the widow to whom he gave the beads the previous day; Thomas fed them all, but he had so little food that he was glad when they all left that night so that he himself could have a bite to eat.[19]

31 August 1839

Overnight there was heavy rain, 'dreadful' Thomas called it, 'torrents': it continued all day and flooded his tent: the flats were under water, and even the blacks had to shift to higher ground. Thomas could not light a fire so some of the blacks swam the creek with firesticks in their mouth and he was grateful for their thoughtfulness. Because of the rain he had few visitors and was glad, as all his provisions were gone.[20]

Bunggane/Bungumm

Married man, aged 60, Bunggane died at Arthurs Seat, August 1839; he was Tuaningrook's Kolin, an elder (Return of Births and Deaths, 1 April 1839 to 29 February 1840, VPRS 4410, unit 3, PROV); Bunggane, married, Mr King's father, died at Arthur's Seat after leaving the encampment S of the Yarra (CY 2604, item 4, ML); Bunggum, male Bonurong, 60, a man of influence died at Arthur's Seat in August 1839 (CY 2946, item 2, ML).

---

17 Thomas Summary of Proceedings during August 1839, CY 3082, ML. Byrt 2004, CD WT 3082S.DOC.
18 *HRV*, vol 2B: 539–540.
19 *HRV*, vol 2B: 540.
20 *HRV*, vol 2B: 540; Thomas Summary of Proceedings during August 1839, CY 3082, ML. Byrt 2004, CD WT 3082S.DOC.

1 September 1839

Thomas was reduced to feeding the people out of his own family supplies. The lubras came with their children and watched Thomas shave. His man Ross gave them a brush and comb and soap, and they washed and combed the children and everyone looked 'smart'. It was a Sunday so he held two Divine Services, am and pm, and boiled a leg of mutton for dinner. This, with some kangaroo they had, 'filled their bellies'.[21]

2 September 1839

Thomas sent his dray to Melbourne for supplies; he confided again to his journal that sending him to his people without provisions was 'truly uncharitable'. He was afraid to visit the encampment because 'the poor creatures' would want food. Only three blacks visited his tent.[22]

3 September 1839

This day he did visit their encampment but found only the old sick man and six others. They told him **'Black fellows go another white man's miam. You no flour'**. He tried to placate them by assuring them that he would soon have provisions, and stayed the day with them. In the evening he was amused that the lubras made their fires and prepared for the return of the men just like careful domesticated wives in England, getting a clean hearth and a good fire going before the return of their husbands from their labour.[23]

4 September 1839

Thomas visited Burrenum's miam – it was like a butcher's shop with legs and parts of kangaroo hung all around. He and two other men had returned the previous night heavily laden. Thomas gave beads to two lubras and others followed him back to his tent. He gave them all the mutton he had left over, and a trifle of flour which he could ill spare being short himself.[24]

5 September 1839

When he visited this day Thomas found that they had a great abundance of meat, enough for a week. Nevertheless some followed him back to his tent, hoping. He had nothing to give but what he had borrowed from his son at Tuerong.[25] The blacks fetched him three pails full of mud for the wattle and daub hut he was building and Thomas paid them wages for the labour.[26]

---

21   *HRV*, vol 2B: 540.
22   *HRV*, vol 2B: 540.
23   *HRV*, vol 2B: 540.
24   *HRV*, vol 2B: 541.
25   This observation challenges William Jackson Thomas' Reminiscences. WJ Thomas recorded that the building of Thomas' house at Tubbarubbabel took two weeks, plus a week for the plaster to dry. Then WJ Thomas took a rest, then selected Tuerong. But this observation of William Thomas places his son at Tuerong earlier. WJ Thomas's Reminiscences were written in the twentieth century, so it is his estimate of elapsed time which is more likely to be at fault: the sequence is clear – first they built Tubberubbabel, then he selected Tuerong as his own station.
26   *HRV*, vol 2B: 541. He paid wages not in money but in food.

6 September 1839

A large party of blacks came to Thomas' tent and he gave them all tomahawks, for which they sat down and started making handles, complaining about the poor quality of the eyes of the tomahawks, which Thomas agreed, were certainly the worst that he had ever seen.[27] He lent them an iron pot and got them to boil some mutton and kangaroo tails, but he was critical of their manners and their impatience. Burrenum was 'a little my confidant'. They sat around, sang and slept for the rest of the day and he wished he had some employment for them.[28]

Fig 20. 'Trade tomahawk of the 1830s', the quality of which the Bonurong men criticised

From the Wilson P Evans Collection, State Library of Victoria.

7 September 1839

There were 36 in the encampment, anxious to know when Thomas' dray would return from Melbourne. It arrived in the afternoon with ten letters from Robinson, critical of Thomas and demanding his immediate return to Melbourne. Thomas was anguished; he could not find the words to tell his people he had to leave them, and when he did they were not happy. He quoted them as saying **'Black fellows no more sit down here'**.

---

27   An illustration of a tomahawk from this period is reproduced as Fig 20.
28   *HRV*, vol 2B: 541.

Thomas departed Tubberubbabel at sunrise, calming his spirits with the biblical quotation 'Even so seems it good in Thy sight'. In Melbourne, he found that the Chief Protector had been harassing Mrs Thomas, threatening Thomas' dismissal for not answering correspondence which he had not even received while at Tubberubbabel.[29]

23 September 1839

Thomas, still in Melbourne, despatched his son William Jackson Thomas and his servant to Tubberubbabel to continue the building work.[30]

His Honour the Superintendent of the Port Phillip District, Charles Joseph La Trobe arrived in Melbourne on 30 September 1839 and the blacks started to talk of the feast that would follow (similar to the feast which the protectors had put on in March). On 2 October Thomas recorded that he must go to Tubberubbabel; also that the blacks 'have it in their head that they are all going to be supplied with everything'. On 3 October he had to unpack the dray as the order to depart for Tubberubbabel was rescinded. On 8 October, Thomas finally received permission from the Chief Protector to take his family to Tubberubbabel but to return immediately to Melbourne.[31]

12 October 1839

Thomas and his family arrived at Tubberubbabel from Melbourne after a difficult journey – the cart was up to its axles in mud and the bullocks up to their bellies; they got stuck at Moody Yallock and had to unload everything; Mrs Thomas was unwell and their little children were screaming; they spent a night in a swamp on the south side of what is now Frankston after trying for three hours in darkness to get the cart unstuck. The lubras and their children were pleased to see Mrs Thomas and the Thomas children. He issued rice to them, and a blanket to an old man. After dinner, he visited the encampment, obliged to tell the people that he was under orders to return immediately to Melbourne; they were 'very dissatisfied, say **"big one lie. You tell blackfellows to come to you and then you no stop"**'. Thomas felt the truth of their remark and felt sure that 'such duplicity would not succeed but disgust them, but orders must be obeyed'. Next day he held a prayer service not at his tent, but at the native encampment 200 yards away, then he left for Melbourne, leaving Mrs Thomas and the children at his tent.[32]

---

29   *HRV*, vol 2B: 541–542.
30   *HRV*, vol 2B: 546.
31   *HRV*, vol 2B: 548, 549, 551.
32   *HRV*, vol 2B: 552.

21 October 1839[33]

After a week in Melbourne, Thomas told Robinson that most of his blacks had left Melbourne for the Arthurs Seat district and requested permission to follow. He despatched his son and his servant with the cart and followed himself later in the day with the dray and his other man.[34] On the same day, Thomas wrote another letter to Robinson in which he states that Tubberubbabel is a place much frequented and never deserted.[35]

22 October 1839

Again, the dray got stuck crossing Moody Yallock Creek – they waded across up to their middles in water unloading it, then borrowed two more bullocks from Mr Newton's station and got the dray free. Two miles after the creek they fell in with 54 blacks en route to Thomas' hut at Tubberubbabel.[36]

24 October 1839

Thomas had another arduous and dramatic day. They broke camp early because they had to make Konnigo Creek (Kannanook) at what is now Frankston, before high tide. But the dray got stuck in the creek anyway, and a bullock turned sulky and lay down and nearly drowned. Then in the evening when they were encamped, something spooked his milk cow who broke loose and swam the creek to head back to Melbourne; she was followed by her calf, then by the four bullocks who were hobbled, thus could not swim, and were in danger of drowning. Thomas' man, who was a good swimmer,[37] plunged in and they were all rescued. That night, while Thomas was on watch, he dropped off to sleep and the bullocks strayed and had to be caught again in the moonlight. Next day, at the last creek (Balcombe) they had to do it all over again, but some of the blacks came and helped them and they made Tubberubbabel at sunset. He saw his dear wife and children and had a comfortable tea with the blacks all around him and he thanked God for all His mercies.[38]

---

33   In his Letter book for this date Thomas wrote a memo suggesting that since Tubbarubbabel was 48 miles away, by cutting a cross road from the main road, he could reduce the journey by three to four miles, giving a good direction and thus make it easier for people to find him (CY 2946, ML). There is no listing in PROV of this letter being sent to the Chief Protector.

34   *HRV*, vol 2B: 553. Ross and Bob Davis were the two men. Ross (no given name) was discharged from servitude to the Protector of the Aborigines in May 1839 (*HRV*, vol 3: 264).

35   Thomas to Robinson, 21 October 1839, enc with 40/2215 in 4/1135.1, AO of NSW.

36   Thomas Journal, CY 2604, item 3, ML.

37   This man must have been his man Bob Davis as his other man Ross could not swim, see 11 March 1840 in Chapter 3.

38   Thomas Journal, CY 2604, item 3, frame 114, ML.

25 October 1839

Up early, he distributed rice and sugar and proposed a spot for those presently with Mr Hobson at Kangerong to erect their miams at Tubberubbabel and they promised to do so the next day.

26 October 1839

Thomas went early to Kangerong 'their principal encampment'; the people broke up their encampment, said good-bye to Mr Hobson and followed him to his hut at Tubberubbabel. He then outlined his proposal for a manufacturing industry – the women would make baskets, Thomas' daughters would teach them how to make hats, and the men were to skin the kangaroos. In return, Thomas would give them the worth of the goods in flour, tomahawks etc: the goods would be sent to Melbourne to be sold.[39] Thomas did not record their response. But to his 'great surprise', just before sunset, the lubras presented him with two baskets they had just made for Thomas' two eldest girls. He offered to pay for them in rice and send them to Melbourne but they were insistent that these particular baskets were a gift. He quoted them as saying **'make em plenty by and bye for Melbourne. Your Pickaninys them'**. Thomas 'obeyed' them and gave them a reciprocal gift of flour and sugar from his own store. Then, with a timing that was wretched for him and his proposal for a manufacturing industry, a messenger (unnamed) arrived from Melbourne summoning them all, and there was much excitement.[40]

27 October 1839

Thomas was up early and walked around the encampment, stopping to rub Old Jack and Morragine's feet with emu oil. He 'mustered' everyone after breakfast – family, servants and blacks for the first of Sunday's two Divine Services, but had to cut the service short because the messenger was urging them to go now: 'What restraint they must be under when summoned', he recorded. He distributed rice and sugar to them and they were off, even Morragine whose foot was so bad that Thomas bandaged it for him for the walk. 'To comfort' Thomas, they left lots of spears and some bags, saying they had to go, but they would soon return. 61 people departed and five remained at Tubberubbabel.[41]

---

39 This is all he wrote in his journal on this day; how it worked out in practice is discussed in Chapter 9 on manufacturing industry, food policy and theories of civilising.

40 Thomas Journal, CY 2604, item 3, frame 114, ML.

41 Thomas Journal, CY 2604, item 3, ML.

Morragine

20 Nov 1839 – In Thomas' census of the Bonurong, Morragan is described as male, Bonurong, aged 32, has lost the use of his legs and is under the charge of Mr Thomas at Arthurs Seat (VPRS 10, unit 1/242, PROV). He was attended by the Aboriginal doctor in Melbourne on 4 October 1839 (*HRV*, vol 2B: 550) and is possibly the old man who was attended by the doctor Burrenum (Mr Dredge); this was the first time that Thomas knew Burrenum was a doctor (*HRV*, vol 2B: 547). Thomas' son found Morragen dead at Tubberubbabel on 19 December 1839 (CY 2604, item 4). He was Tarlongrook's husband (Thomas Return, VPRS 4410, unit 3). His European name was Jack Lope (Names Taken in Encampment, July 1839, CY 2604, item 1, ML).

It is apparent from his journal that the five who remained were two women and three children. They lived together for the next nine days 'as family', being rationed by Thomas as well as being fed, sometimes from his table, making baskets, learning to read, paying 'astonishing' attention to Divine Service. 'They assure me **that no long time and all my blacks come back and set down by me**'. He mentions only one by name, Wigal, the wife of Burrenum the owner of the country,[42] who made a fine basket for Thomas to send to Melbourne to get flour for the black lubras. On 4 November Thomas' cart arrived from Melbourne with a summons from Robinson to return immediately – the fourth time he had been called back from his district. He left immediately and en route met 17 of his blacks at Mr Newton's station at Mordialloc, already on their way back to Tubberubbabel.

Except for a there and back journey to Tubberubbabel from 3 to 10 December to bring his seriously ill wife to Melbourne, Thomas remained in Melbourne doing work for Robinson until January 1840. On his flying visit to Tubberubbabel he found 27 still living there but he mentions only one by name, Old Maria who wept bitterly and clung to the cart on Mrs Thomas' departure. During this period in Melbourne, on 12 November, he selected his five Native Police, three from the Warworong and two from the Bonurong – Buller Bullut aged 20, and Tulemlgate aged 24.[43]

The first fortnight in December was characterised by much fighting with the Barrabools who came en masse to Melbourne. Thomas submitted his first petition for land to La Trobe who agreed to forward it to Sydney and who

---

42   One wonders if she was the responsible person left behind to keep an eye on things.
43   Unlike the successful 1842 Native Police Corps, the protectors' domestic police were supposed to keep order within the tribe, in effect, to be put in a compromised position, caught between age-old law and custom and the new imperative, European law and custom. All the recovered details of the 1839 Domestic Police have been included in Chapter 3 of Fels 1988.

spoke about the necessity of getting the blacks out of Melbourne.[44] Thomas told the people that the Governor was 'plenty sulky' with them, as were Captain Lonsdale and the soldiers: it was the women who started packing up on hearing this. But the men refused to leave, harking back again to the time of plenty they experienced with Mr Batman. Some pages are cut out of Thomas' journal, and when it resumes with a list of deaths from April to December, the next entry is 1 January 1840 and the encampment at Melbourne is deserted except for a few.

8 January 1840

By this date all Thomas' blacks had left Melbourne and Thomas took his requisition for stores, already signed by Robinson, to La Trobe for approval. To his dismay, La Trobe reprimanded him for being still in Melbourne and refused to give permission for the stores: as he confided to his journal, he had nearly 200 blacks anticipating these stores, and it was a far cry from what was promised: he got on his horse and set off for Tubberubbabel travelling ten miles before camping under a gum tree and committing himself to God.[45]

10 January 1840

Thomas arrived at Tubberubbabel; some blacks were ready to pull him off his horse and shake hands; the lubras and children in the bush under the trees were 'hollowing out' long before he saw them. 65 people were there and he went from group to group 'pacifying' them, assuring them that his wheelbarrow would arrive soon with supplies. 'Truly this is bad work' he wrote 'if ever any department was despised and had obstacles thrown in the way, we have. Could the Home Government see my situation now, they would order things different'.[46]

11 January 1840

Six children attended lessons but showed very little anxiety to learn their letters; some could repeat the alphabet but not recognise the letters when shown. Three people were ill requiring treatment – Old Maria, and Mr King's mother, and Kurblening, a youth aged 11 who was Old Doctor's son and whose health was in serious decline.[47]

---

44   Thomas Journal, CY 2604, item 4, ML. Item 4 is a fragment of Journal covering the period 8 December 1839 to January 1840, A marginal note indicates that it is a first draft which Thomas intended to re-write later. It contains the important information from Surveyor Smythe, lately at the Swan River, regarding the three named Bonurong women abducted from Western Port by the master of the *George* in 1834, presently at King Georges Sound and wanting to return to see their friends at Western Port.
45   CY 2605, item 1, frame 31, ML.
46   Thomas Journal CY 2605, item 1, frame 31, ML.
47   Thomas Journal CY 2605, item 1, ML.

12 January 1840

At Divine Service the people were 'remarkably attentive' at the singing[48] and seemed 'delighted' with Thomas' son's flute-playing.[49] Burrenum (Mr Dredge), D'Villiers, Nerreninnen (Mr Young), Poleorong (Billy Lonsdale) and Ningolobin (Captain John Bull) left on a four day emu hunt,[50] Thomas having given them sugar and rice. In the afternoon a native arrived with news of the cart on the way being filled with plenty of Yellowniboy, Nerong, Caom, Bulganner etc and Thomas concluded that His Honour had reconsidered the case of the poor blacks. At 11.30 pm Budgery Tom came and said that there were wild black fellows in the bush, whereupon he, Jackia Jackia, Thomas, and three other unnamed men set off into the bush to search. They found no-one and Thomas laughed at their folly.[51]

13 January 1840

By this date, Thomas had succeeded in collecting all the blacks from the five different encampments[52] on the Mornington Peninsula where he found them on 9 January, and 'they all encamped together on the north and south sides of a creek called Tubberrubabel, my tent in the midst where we erected a shed of some length for teaching the children and to be used as a place of worship'.[53] Thomas' large tent was erected this day.[54]

Thomas' description of an encampment

> Their habitation is frail but answers well their purpose, a few sheets of bark cut in a few minutes and erected is their habitation. These sheets of bark are about six feet long, oblique raised to the angle of about 90 degrees windward, every alternate sheet is reversed so that no rain can enter. The sides are filled up with short pieces of bark and brush and a sheet of bark at the top thus ////. A good miam or hut will hold 2 adults and 3 children – they are not permanent, are knocked down or burnt on breaking up the encampment – they consist of one apartment only.
>
> In a large encampment they are divided into hamlets – some influential black taking charge of six or eight miams & so on, say 5 hamlets. These hamlets are 50 yards or more from each other while the miams in a single hamlet is not more than 3 or 4 yards apart, merely sufficient to avoid

---

48 It remains to be discovered whether the Bonurong were different in their enjoyment of music. In 1844 when Thomas gave a service at Merri Creek for the Loddon River blacks, he noted that 'They paid great attention but would not sing like my blacks' (ML MSS 214/3, 1 September 1844).

49 Thomas Journal CY 2605, item 1, ML.

50 The Balnarring racecourse in Coolart road is called Emu Plains.

51 Thomas Journal CY 2605, item 1, frame 32, ML.

52 In his journal he calls these encampments 'suburbs of Tubberubbabel', CY 2605, item 1, ML.

53 First Periodical Report, *HRV*, vol 2B; 621.

54 Thomas' large tent was double, bell shaped.

danger from each others fires. The head of each hamlet keeps order, settles all grievances. But the Chief of the tribe governs all their movements. I should have stated that in wet weather a trench is dug with a tomahawk round the back and sides of their miams to let off the water.[55]

When the Bonurong were encamped by themselves, the encampment would have followed the general principles explained to AW Howitt by Barak[56] – a favourable position relative to the weather, and in many cases facing the rising sun. The relationship of miams on the ground depended on the relationship of any individual or group with the important clan heads and principal families. Thomas drew this too, from Barak's information which would have been as true for the Bonurong as for the Waworong. Barak put himself at the centre of the diagram for illustrative purposes.[57] He and his wife and child were number one; his brother and wife and child were number two close to him; Barak's father and mother were number three, double the distance away and in another direction; Barak's wife's mother and father were even further away in the same direction and screened from Barak's sight; the young men's miams were the furthest away from Barak, and lastly Bonurong visitors were the same distance away from Barak as his own mother and father, but in a different direction. When Thomas camped with them, he situated his tent so that its flap or opening faced their miams.

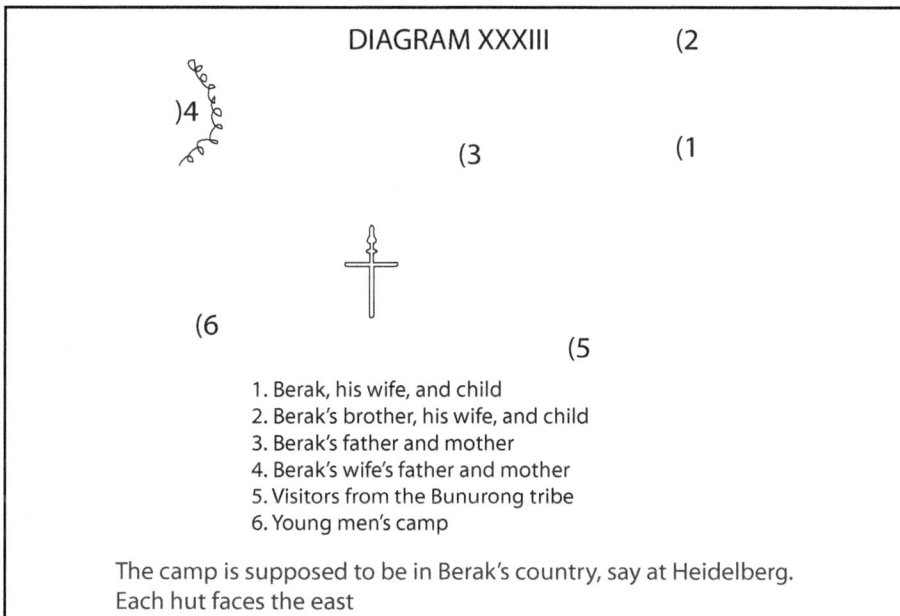

Fig 21. 'William Barak's mudmap of an encampment'

Reproduced from Howitt 1904: 775.

---

55   William Thomas Miscellaneous Papers, CY 2984, frame 52, ML.
56   Howitt 1904: 775.
57   Barak's drawing is reproduced as Fig 21.

14 January 1840

The blacks were restless and 'very disappointed' at the non-arrival of the stores and refused to help in the construction of a hut.[58]

15 January 1840

One of the blacks went to Bob Davis who was sick in bed and said **'all bungarly you'** whereupon Davis leaped from his bed 'like a madman' and threatened Thomas' life. Then Davis absconded with two blacks and the rest were sulky and called Thomas **'plenty sulky with Maregii Davis'**. Thomas had ten children at school learning with wooden letters, but one by one they all went off to bathe.[59]

16 January 1840

'At Tubberubbabel native encampment there are about 90 natives and 23 miams'. In this letter Thomas adds the further detail that it is a series of waterholes, and it is his large tent that is pitched in the midst of them. He goes on to say that they are not merely disappointed at the non-arrival of the stores, they feel 'deceived' and he pleads yet again that La Trobe would condescend to grant supplies to these people – the most peaceable and the least troublesome to the settlers, more than any other district.[60]

17 January 1840

Surveyor Smythe and some of the blacks went hunting;[61] other blacks showed 'great anger' with Thomas' treatment of Davis and threatened to leave Tubberubbabel if Thomas would not have him back. Thomas was copying his letters into his letter book when he was interrupted five or six times by emissaries acting like 'aidecamps' from Davis in the bush: in the end Davis came back penitent, saying that he had misunderstood the blacks – it was Smythe the surveyor who did not like Davis, not Thomas. All the blacks were at Tubberubbabel except Bogy Bogy and Mr Man. Thomas put a stop to Mr Mann's going to VDL,[62] and called on Mr Hobson who was out. Thomas made a place for public worship and put a looking glass in a tree 'for the coming Sabbath'. The people came and looked into the glass highly pleased.[63]

---

58   Thomas Journal CY 2605, item 1, ML.
59   Thomas Journal CY 2605, item 1, frame 33, ML.
60   VPRS 11, unit 7/299, PROV.
61   Surveyor George Douglas Smythe was called by the Bonurong 'Mamghie' and his brother Henry Hutchinson Smythe 'Dareem' (McCrae 1934: 100).
62   It has to be asked, though I cannot answer it, why were they going to VDL? Thomas stopped Old Mr Mann this time, but Pinterginner went a couple of months later, and on his return he brought back Mary from George Smith's place.
63   Thomas Journal CY 2605, item 1, ML.

18 January 1840

This was a Saturday and Thomas recorded that he 'amused' himself with the blacks: amusements for Thomas means playing games. It is about this time at Tubberubbabel that he recorded the vocabulary for ball games including wicket and ball, his named informant being the Western Port chief Budgery Tom.[64]

As this is probably the first ever record of the Indigenous ball game believed by many in Victoria to be a forerunner of the high kicking game, Australian Rules football, Thomas' later description of it is given here.

Marngrook

The Marngrook (or the ball) is a favourite game with boys and men. A party assemble; one makes a ball of opossum skin or whatnot of a good size. The ball is kicked up and not thrown by the hand as white boys do. The ball is kicked into the air not along the ground. There is a general scramble to catch it in the air. The tall blackfellows stand the best chance. When caught it is again kicked up in the air with great force and ascends straight up and as high as when thrown by the hand. They will play at this game for hours and fine exercise it is for adults or youths. The girls play at Marngrook but throw it up as white children.[65]

19 January 1840

Thomas was 'much hurt' to discover that though it was the Sabbath, Munmunginner and seven others, unnamed, intended to go hunting with spears.[66]

20 January 1840

Thomas had 14 children at school – he made a twig alphabet which failed, then wrote large capital letters on bark. He got the children to say as far as G: he put the letters up in the following order A C F D E B. He gave sugar to those who did not attend school in order to encourage them. In a marginal note, Thomas records that Yal Yal, Mr Young (Nerreninnen), Pinterginner, Karlmile, and Burrenum left on Sunday.[67]

---

64 See Chapter 12.
65 Aborigines: Amusements and War Implements, 15 June 1858, CY 3131, frames 37–38, ML.
66 Thomas Journal, CY 2605, item 1, frame 35, ML.
67 Thomas Journal, CY 2605, item 1, ML.

Yal Yal/Mr Meyrick – Bonurong – son and heir of Bobbinary, co-owner of the southern peninsula

Yal Yal, heir to Bobbinnary, clan head (Barwick 1984: 117); no date – Henry Meyrick found in him a friend on whose loyalty and affection he could always rely (Meyrick 1939: 142).

20 Mar 1839 – Yal Yal aka Dr Ewen, male aged 14 of Boonworong tribe whose family is not ascertained (Protector James Dredge's Census in Robinson Papers, vol 54, ML); Jul 1839 – Yal Yal's name taken on a census of Bonurong in the encampment (Thomas 'A' diary, January – July 1839, set 214, item 1, ML); 20 Nov 1839 – Yal Yal, Bonurong tribe, male aged 18, listed on census taken by Protector William Thomas at the encampment on the banks of the Yarra (VPRS 10, unit 1/242).

1840 – Burrenum and Yal Yal return with plenty of fowl etc etc, enough for the whole encampment at Tubberubbabel (Thomas Journal, CY 2605, item 1, ML); Yal Yal's name is on a list of single men taken by Protector Thomas (Thomas Journal, CY 2605, set 214/2, item 1, frame 23, ML); 14 March 1840 – Yal Yal was one of a group of five leading men who got a lift to Melbourne in a dray from O'Connor's station about 30 miles east of Melbourne: the others were Poleorong, Budgery Tom, Worwodor and Burrenum (CY 2605, item 1, ML); 7 Apr 1840 – in Melbourne for a great meeting of the tribes, young Yal Yal is mentioned as a participant in a Council of six Port Phillip blacks; the others were Collerlook, D'Villiers, Toltoy's brother, Old Jack Weatherly and Billy Lonsdale (CY 2605, item 1, ML); 12 Apr 1840 – Yal Yal has the bad disorder (CY 2605, item 1, ML); 10 Dec 1840 – Yal Yal was among a party of Western Port Aborigines who came to the new Protectorate station at Nerre Nerre Warren, all wanting food and blankets even though they had their own possum skin rugs. They were trying to entice the others to leave Nerre Nerre Warren (Byrt 2004: 44). Yal Yal's father Bobbinary was one who had come in to Nerre Nerre Warren the previous day (Byrt 2004: 44).

8 Jun 1841 – Yal Yal murdered Bareing, a Yarra black at Mr Ruffy's station at Mahun in Westernport. Nerre Ninnon was with him. (Protector Thomas 'List of murders in the vicinity of Melbourne by Aborigines on Aborigines', set 214, item 9, Corr. Returns etc 1835–1845, ML); 14 Sep 1841 – Yal Yal's mother intervened on his behalf when he and Nerreninnon were undergoing Aboriginal judicial proceedings over the boy they murdered (Thomas Papers, set 214/2, item 5, Transcription[I] CY 2605, frame 348, ML);

I. There is an amazing amount of detail in Thomas' account of this ritual spearing. It has been transcribed by Pauline Byrt

19 Dec 1841 – Yal Yal's recent murdering of the boy has encouraged the blacks to believe that no punishment awaits such deeds (Thomas to Robinson, VPRS 11, unit 8/417, PROV); 21 Dec 1841 – Yal Yal is an informant, with Kollorlook, Yanki Yanki and Beruke alias Gellibrand regarding the murder of the Adelaide black Jemmy at Whitehead's station, by the Goulburn blacks (Thomas to Robinson, VPRS 11, unit 8/418, PROV).

6 Jan 1842 – Yal Yal and party were at Captain Reid's station[II] (Byrt 2004: 74); 24 Feb 1842 – Yal Yal received blankets, clothing and equipment; enrolled in the Native Police and made his mark; deserted a few days after enlistment; since wished to return, but in the meantime Commandant Henry Edmund Pulteney Dana had received orders from Superintendent Charles La Trobe to limit the Native Police Corps to 20 men, so Dana refused to have him back (Dana to Superintendent, 31 March 1842, VPRS 19, Box 28, 42/674, PROV); 31 Aug 1842 – on Medical Dispenser's list suffering from Pseudo Syphilis, treatment Liq Arsenic and aperients internally and Blackwash externally (Henry Jones to Chief Protector, VPRS 4410, unit 2, item 50, PROV).

1844 – Yal Yal accompanied Henry Meyrick who left his station Boniong on the Mornington Peninsula, driving 2000 sheep for 10 weeks on a trek to a new station on the Thomson River in Gippsland (Meyrick 1939: 171).

Mar 1845 – Ninggolobin told Thomas that Yal Yal shot Pinterginner (Byrt 2004: 99); 30 Apr 1845 – Thomas to Latrobe regarding the report of the Native Police and the Westernport blacks killing Gippsland blacks – the report was fabricated to account for Pinterginner's death at the hands of Yal Yal. Two reliable informants Moody Warrin (Mt Macedon) and Bon John (Barrabool) said that Yal Yal had often threatened to kill Pinterginner and did so, and fabricated the story. (VPRS 19, Box 70, 45/759, PROV); 18 Aug 1845 – there is a report that Yal Yal is about to lead to the hymeneal altar – the fair Puppa-co-ran-go-rook, only daughter of Brikko-Mirring, or the one-eyed (Hales and Le Cheminant 1997: 27); same date – in his letter to Mama from the Prince of Wales hotel in Melbourne, Henry H Meyrick writes that Yal Yal who is with him particularly desires to be remembered to her, or in his own words, he wishes that I would write his name very big on the paper (Ms 7959, Box 654: 15, SLV).

II. Now The Briars.

Jan 1846 – Yal Yal is listed in Thomas' criticism of the Native Police Corps as one of the Melbourne tribes who joined the Native Police and then deserted (Thomas Quarterly Report, enc to 46/3341 in 4/2745.1, AO of NSW); Jan 1846 – Yal Yal is listed on Thomas Family Connections census, as Kangerong section of the Bonurong, male aged 20, father Bobbinary a widower, sister Boyyeup aged 23 (CY 3083, ML); 3 Feb 1846 – Yal Yal en route again with Meyrick's party for Gippsland (Meyrick 1939: 193); 13 Feb 1846 – Yal Yal named the creek the party crossed to get onto the Wild Cattle Run, then armed with Alfred Meyrick's rifle helped to hunt and shoot a wild bull (Hales and Le Cheminant 1997: 36); 16 Feb 1846 – listed by Robinson as son of Bup.in.nar.ing, of the Bur.in.yung balluk belonging about Pt Nepean, presently stopping with Mr Merrik (GA Robinson, Vocabulary Papers, quoted in Clark 2002: 220); 19 Apr 1846 – Yal Yal's name is on a list of blacks which La Trobe requested to go to King's Island following the wrecking of the ship *Cataraqui* (Thomas Journal CY 2606, ML); 21 May 1846 – Yal Yal's name is on a list of Western Port blacks gone with murderous intent to catch wild blackfellows (Thomas Journal CY 2606, ML); 9 Sep 1846 – Yal Yal and other Westernport blacks were examined by the committee in charge of the search for the alleged white woman in Gippsland; Yal Yal was supposed to have seen her; not so; Yal Yal got the story from a Gippsland black (Thomas Quarterly Report, enc to 46/9277 in 4/2745.1, AO of NSW); 9 Sep 1846 – Yal Yal avoids Thomas who believes that the blacks are telling the truth as they know it, but that they are mislead by certain parties (Thomas Journal, CY 2606, ML); Sep 1846 – in his monthly report for 1 – 30 September 1846, Thomas expresses doubts about the evidence the committee has gathered. 'Even Yal Yal says "another one blackfellow in Gippsland say so"' (set 214, item 10: 67, ML); 14 Sep 1846 – Thomas writes that Yal Yal and two other blacks will not come near him because they know that Thomas fears that not everything they have said is the truth (Thomas to Chief Protector, set 214, item 10: 61, ML); 20 Oct 1846 – Thomas farewelled the party who were going to search for the white woman – they were 10 in number, all excited, looking clean and comfortable; they left with Mr de Villiers on the steamer *Shamrock*. The party included Little Benbow (Boollut), Lively (Warwado), Yal Yal, Charley (Lillero), Tearram, Toby (Talleorong), Nowrrup, Minghim and Dollar (Nerretnunin) (Thomas Monthly Report for October 1846, set 214, item 10: 79ff, ML). In his journal of this date Thomas notes that they were all armed and well turned out in new clothing (CY 2606, ML); Dec 1846 – Yal Yal is mentioned as one of the people Thomas has closely examined and on whose word much reliance has been placed regarding the white woman (Thomas Quarterly Report, 1 September–30 November 1846, enc with Lonsdale to Col Sec 46/9277 in 4/2745.1, AO of NSW).

Jan 1847 – Yal Yal alias Mr Meyrick was cool and deliberate with Christiaan de Villiers on the expedition in search of the alleged white woman in Gippsland (*Port Phillip Patriot*, 10 February 1847); 6 Apr 1847 – Yal Yal – a black with Tommy, Toby and Jack a wadden, in the boat crew under Mr McLeod and Mr Hill, setting off today in another search for the white woman (Commissioner of Crown Landers Tyers to LaTrobe, VPRS 19, Box 92, 47/701, PROV); 22 Apr 1847 – Yal Yal is mentioned as one of the search party in Tyers' instructions for the search (enc to VPRS 19, Box 92, 47/907, PROV); 22 Nov 1847 – in a letter to Mama Henry Meyrick quoted Yal Yal's mode of expressing tiredness 'me plenty leepy' (Hales and Le Cheminant 1997: 40).

5 Aug 1850 – Yal Yal and his lubra Kikerterbruk are on a census of names of all the remaining Bonurong and Waworong taken by Thomas in Melbourne on this day (Thomas Journal, CY 3127, ML).

26 Mar 1852 – Yal Yal alias Mr Meyrick, male of the Boonoorong tribe was killed on this day. He had 2 lubras who were Lurkerbruck, and Wyoorung alias Judy (Thomas Census, in set 214, item 12: 143, ML). According to George Gordon McCrae, 'Yal Yal died off the road between Mordialloc and Brighton. He fell in single combat with another man of his tribe known to us as Williamstown. He was buried where he fell, with his right arm projecting from the soil' (George Gordon McCrae, Reminiscences, vol 4, 2523/5 d, SLV).

21 January 1840

This day he had only five at school for whom he made a large alphabet on cartridge paper which seemed to please them very much.[68]

Death of Kurnboro/Old Maria

Old Maria was very ill with brain fever, out of her senses, jumping into the water. Thomas was sure she was deranged and consulted surveyor Smythe. They agreed that bleeding was necessary but they could not prevail on the native doctors to do it. But the native doctors did agree to have four leeches put on her temple (there were leeches in part of the creek, they said). Maria's

---

68   Thomas Journal, CY 2605, item 1, ML.

daughter went to fetch leeches but did not return till the afternoon, without the leeches. Maria became 'frantic': Thomas prevented her on several occasions from throwing herself into the creek, though the others about her seemed unconcerned. Benbow arrived from Melbourne with a rumour about a collision which excited everyone, and by the time Thomas turned to check on Maria, she was absent, with her husband Doctor sitting alone by his fire. Thomas immediately made them light a bush to go and seek her, and they found Maria in the creek 'near drownded, lost all strength and just the top of her head was seen'. They pulled her out by her arms, and after a quarter of an hour, she a little recovered, her frantic fits returned. Thomas and Smythe remained with her till 1 am. When Thomas checked on her again at 5.30 am he 'found her still alive, but her feet dead, the rattles was in her throat'. He made her some tea and got the husband to try her with a spoon, and the tea went down but with difficulty. At 8 am he had just left her, but Mr Smyth was still present, when all life departed. She was bound up precisely as men but without half attention.[69] In his Return of Births and Deaths for the period, Thomas names her as Kurnboro, a Bonurong, aged 41, much attached to whites.[70]

23 January 1840

Burrenum and Yal Yal etc etc who left on 20 January returned with plenty of fowl, ten kangaroos, 14 opossum and swans, enough for the whole encampment; Burrenum much concerned about Maria.[71]

25 January 1840

After leaving Tubberubbabel on 25 January because they had not caught any food for two days, they encamped at Tuerong about five miles SE from Mt Martha where they remained ten days. The whole party was 101 people. They then split into smaller groups in order to procure food, and Thomas accompanied the largest group of 57 to cross the country to the east side of Western Port. 44 remained in the vicinity of Arthurs Seat.[72]

February 1840

Thomas' party camped at 11 places all of which are marked on his map of 29 February 1840. This is the famous raid on their enemies in Gippsland, the events of which were outlined in Chapter 3, and the context and consequences of which form Chapter 8. Then they returned to Melbourne via Dandenong at the end of March. Thomas was in Melbourne for all of April, the encampment at one stage consisting of 496 people – 203 Waworong and Bonurong, 87 Mt

69   Thomas Journal, CY 2605, item 1, frames 36–37, ML.
70   VPRS 4410, unit 3/66, PROV.
71   Thomas Journal, CY 2605, item 1, ML. Burrenum/Mr Dredge was a doctor: Old Maria may have been his wife, but this is not confirmed as yet.
72   Thomas First Periodical Report, *HRV*, vol 2B; 621.

Macedon, 95 Barrabool and 111 Goulburn.[73] Thomas and all the blacks left Melbourne on 29 April after a stay of 49 days and by 6 May everyone was south of Moody Yallock.[74]

17 May 1840

Thomas having issued an invitation to the two encampments at Kangerong and Buckkermitterwarrer to visit him at Tubberubbabel, 66 people arrived, and sat down in five groups according to their family connections, with 'the strangers, Mt Macedons and Barrabools 1 [separate party]', an 'imposing' sight. He distributed rations, gave Kollorlock a red shirt 'with which he was much pleased', then read Divine Service. They departed in the afternoon, promising him that 'all' would return next day.[75]

18 May 1840

All the blacks (122) came and encamped opposite Thomas' hut at Tubberubbabel. He distributed flour to the people he considered to be his own blacks, and he gave blankets to the old, but to the Mt Macedon blacks who were with his Western Port blacks he gave only a 'trifle' of flour, and even then he emphasised that they (Mt Macedons) had to bring him skins in return for rations.[76]

19 May 1840

Thomas distributed 48 blankets and 15 shirts to the whole of his Western Port blacks, cutting blankets in half for the children, giving the shirts to those who had opossum skin cloaks, so that by the end, everyone was well-clad. Thomas made a marginal note 'except the Dr and his family – his son ill had one'. The blacks cut bark for Thomas' hut, made a good brush stockyard for the bullocks, and made a fence for Thomas' garden.[77]

20 May 1840

This day they wanted flour, but Thomas wanted work in exchange. They threatened to go to the Governor: Burrenum and the Mt Macedon man Captain Turnbull were 'very sausy', so Thomas locked the store and retired to his tent to write. They came and apologised, and set to work to cut bark for his house. 12 of them worked hard, he wrote. He gave to each of the 12 workers one and a half pounds of flour, plus two pounds of sugar to be shared between them. Several lubras walked to Tuerong to work for his son, as did some of the Barrabools and Mt Macedons, and were rewarded, but in addition, to encourage them, Thomas

---

73   Thomas Journal, 11 April 1840, CY 2605, item 1, frame 95, ML.
74   Thomas Journal, CY 2604, item 3, frame 140, ML.
75   Thomas Journal, CY 2604, item 3, frame 142, ML.
76   Thomas Journal, CY 2604, item 3, frame 142, ML.
77   Thomas Journal, CY 2604, item 3, ML.

gave more flour and rice on their return to Tubberubbabel. There were still 122 people at Tubberubbabel. Thomas has 'perished in the nights with cold' because his hut has been almost un-roofed.[78]

21 May 1840

'The blacks again work hard at my hut, re-cover it'; his last sentence for this days' entry is 'natives finish my hut': Derrimut's mother Dindow and another lubra made three baskets which Thomas promised to send to the Governor for sale. They talk of taking a circuit round to Point Nepean to Sandy Point then back to Tubberubbabel. Thomas decided that if they take the lubras with them, he will not follow them, but if they leave the lubras behind, he will follow them 'as then only is their time of destruction'. Thomas recorded his scale of payment for manufactured goods – two cups of flour and a small amount of sugar for each basket; two cups of rice and a bit of sugar for every two skins; three cups of rice for four skins etc.[79]

22 May 1840

From Tubberubbabel Thomas forwarded items manufactured by the Aborigines to Mr Lilly.[80] Items included seven baskets, four opossum skins, one kangaroo skin, and one dozen squirrel skins. Thomas says they have many more, and only in the last few days has he made them aware of the benefits they might derive from their labour; he estimated production at two dozen of each, weekly.[81]

On the same day, Burrenum and Bobbinary left for Kermitterrewarrer[82] ahead of the others who will follow in seven days; they took supplies of seven pounds of flour and two pounds of sugar.[83]

24 May 1840

Sunday. This was the day Thomas 'extorted' from the blacks the confession of the killing of the Two Fold Bay men, women and children on their February excursion. He made them bring to him the souvenirs they still had in their possession. He preached on the commandment 'Thou shalt do no murder' and explained the difference between wilful murder and accidental killing (Chapter 8).[84]

---

78   Thomas Journal, CY 2604, item 3, ML.
79   Thomas Journal, CY 2604, item 3, frame 143–144, ML. He had learned from the experience of February when they successfully deceived him regarding their intention to go to Gippsland to kill their enemies the Two Fold Bay blacks.
80   George Lilly is the Melbourne merchant who 'volunteered to act gratuitously as agent in all matters where the private property of the natives are concerned, to receive monies when due and deposit the same in the Melbourne Savings Bank in accordance with the terms of the Agreements entered into', *HRV*, vol 2B: 766.
81   VPRS 11, unit 7/309, PROV.
82   Both Georgiana and George Gordon McCrae mention the Aboriginal encampment below their house, which I believe is Kermitterrewarrer (see Chapter 10). Much later settler accounts mention Chinaman's creek at Rosebud as an encampment. By then the old wooden lighthouse and the keeper's cottages would have been built at McCrae below the old homestead. The possibility exists that they shifted their traditional encamping place because of the European intrusion.
83   Thomas Journal, CY 2604, item 3, ML.
84   Thomas Journal, CY 2604, item 3, frame 144, ML.

25 May 1840

The whole of the blacks leave 'Tubberub' after a stay of seven days. Thomas was very ill from sleeping in a faulty tent and asks his son to go look for them at Buckkermitterwarrer. Some return asking if he was angry.[85] He asked them what route they intended to take, and they made a mudmap on the ground. He shook hands with them and they left. There were still 122 people in the encampment before this dispersal. Then, to his 'great surprise' Nuluptune returned and stayed the night with him, 'pretends he will go no more with his Blackfellows'.[86]

26 May 1840

Poleorong returned to 'chat' with Nuluptune and Thomas watched the latter 'very closely'. He gave them both flour.[87]

They went first to Kangerong, then Buckkermitterwarrer, then around their country on a triangular route ending at Sandy Point. Thomas went looking for signs of their return each day from 1 June to Arthurs Seat and along the coast of Port Phillip, but then remembered from the map that they were intending to return from the Western Port coast; he met up with the principal men of the Western Ports on 5 June – Derremut, Ningenow and lubra, Dindoo, Budgery Tom and family, Burrenun and lubra and Burrenun's two brothers, and Munmanginna. These 13 stayed one night at Tubberubbabel then shifted encampment to join the others just beyond Kangerong.[88]

6 June 1840

Saturday. Thomas proposed the work for the following week to be building a bridge across the creek at Tubberubbabel, two doors for the store, and if possible begin splitting.[89]

7 June 1840

This was a Sunday and 82 blacks came to Tubberubbabel for the service but they returned to their encampment by Kangerong to sleep. He gives the structure of this population according to how many mouths he fed: 42 men, 17 lubras, 19 male children, four female children.[90]

---

85   It seems that when Thomas retires to his tent, they interpret that as sulkiness.
86   Thomas Journal, CY 2604, item 3, frame 144, ML. Nuluptune would have been deputised to keep a watching brief on Thomas.
87   Thomas Journal, CY 2604, item 3, frame 144, ML.
88   Thomas Journal, CY 2604, item 3, ML.
89   Thomas Journal, CY 2604, item 3, ML.
90   Thomas Journal, CY 2604, item 3, ML.

8 June 1840

To Thomas' great surprise, three blacks left in Mr Martin's boat for Melbourne, the brothers Poleorong and Buller Bullup, and an unnamed person, the only three absent from his tribe (tribe, singular), all of whom were encamped by his hut.[91]

Also on this day, Poleorong, having arrived in Melbourne gave the following list of people presently at 'Tubberrubbabil' to the Chief Protector:

- Derremart
- Pardynup
- Niggerenaul
- Pubbernarrin–Bobbinary
- Neer.re.min.min alias Mr Young
- Lum.mare.rer–Nern Nern, alias Old Man Billy
- Man.nite
- Murn
- Ningcallerbel–alias Captain Turnbull
- Nunupton–Billy Langhorne
- Hill–Murremmurrembean
- Bore.rer.num–Mr Dredge
- Wore.rer.gor.uc
- Tallun–Mr King
- Ly.bil.ly
- Bee.her.rac–Bearack
- Pen.dug.ge.min
- Wor.ro.gope
- Mr Man, old 30–Mingarer
- Young Mr Man
- Car.per.re–Kurburo
- Doctor, Tare.im
- Nar.ner.ring
- Um.mer.gil.pow.[92]

---

91   Thomas Journal, CY 2604, item 3, frame 145, ML.
92   Clark 1988, vol 1: 344.

Mr Man/Mangerer/Mungarer/Mingerer

Son of Old Mr Man, the venerable chief; his sister is Maryagrook; he is the younger brother of both King Benbow and Big Benbow; he is not to be confused with Old Mr Man the chief who bears the same name.

3 Jan 1840 – In names taken in encampment Mangerer is son of Chief Mingearagon, listed with four siblings (Thomas CY 2605, item 1, ML).

Jan 1846 – Old Mr Man plus 2 Benbows plus Derrimut are listed as Weeriby Yallok section of the Boonurong tribe; Mangerer, male aged 18 is listed still with his father, a widower, and his sisters, his father's name having been overwritten (Family Connections census, CY 3083, ML).

31 Dec 1847 – Near Brighton Thomas: 'saw the graves of Old Mr Man alias [blank] & Dindoo the two oldest in the tribes, buried in at present an unenclosed spot about 3 chains from the road. Poor Old Dindoos seemed a careless grave but [blank] seemed to have some pains taken with it. Its enclosure was in the form of a heptagon thus & seven wattle saplings making the figure lay horisontally on the ground. On enquiry, as I had never seen one of this horizontal form before, I was led to understand that it was to show their fast defuncation, that but 7 remained of his tribe. A bit of fern had sprung up over his mortal remains which I drew out, and left the spot full of reflection on the mysterious dealings of providence, as finite mortal unable to unravel the mystery of the rapid decrease of these people, apparently diminished (tho the idea is uncharitable) to make room for a more intelligent race, for I must bear testimony for the last 10 years that the tribes to which he belonged have never been (save in Major Lettsom's cruel mission) injured by white men but always welcome visitors at stations, nor have any been before our courts but for the crime of drunkenness. I was much pleased on my return to Melbourne to see the son of this Old Man basking under a tree with 6 white men resting at mid-day from the toils of the field. I heard of him a good character. I told him I had been thinking over the grave of his father & hoped that he would keep from drink & live happy with the whites.' (Thomas, CY 2606, frame 476, ML). (This son of Old Mr Man, the recently deceased Chief Mingaragon, is Mangerer).

5 Aug 1850 – On Thomas' census of 26 Boonurong still alive, Mr Man and his sister Maryagrook as a 2 person group (CY 3127, ML).

13 Dec 1851 – On Thomas' census as Myngerra, male Mr Man, no lubra (Thomas Papers, set 214, item 12: 143, ML).

25 Oct 1853 – On Thomas' census of Boonoorong as male no lubra (ML MSS set 214/13: 141).

1 Sep 1863 – On Thomas' census as Mon-ga-ra, Mr Man (CRS B 312, item no 9, AA).

9 June 1840

Tuesday. Blacks begin the bridge across the creek.[93] On this same day, Thomas wrote directly to La Trobe enquiring if the skins were saleable, noting that if so, the money could go towards defraying the cost of supplies. He also said that among his 122 people were 35 'strangers', which means in effect, confirmation of his Bonurong population as 87.

10 June 1840

The blacks just going to work at the bridge when Budgery Tom, Bobbinary and Burrenum urge them to stop the work – they propose all at once to shift off, in five mins confusion, debate, cabal. Part agree to go, part to stop. I upbraid those who are going as I give them their portion of flour. Burrenum in sulks would not wait for his. This is a [illegible] wanderer. Those who left were Burrenun and family, Turndine and family, Bobinnary and family, Mr King and family, Budgery Tom and family, Devillers and family, Turnbull and lubra, and young and old Kolorlok.[94]

That evening, after an altercation, two people drew a very correct chart of where the departed party were going – both charts tallied and there were 100 people left after the departures.

11 June 1840

Old Mr Man at Buckkermitterwarrer is accused of taking away a Mt Macedon lubra. Jack goes off with three large glass spears to kill her and Mr Man. Thomas went to Buckkermitterwarrer to investigate but the tale was false. Bridge finished.[95]

12 June 1840

It rained in torrents this day. Some women made baskets and some went for grass for basket making; some men stretched skins 'got overnight', while some

---

93 Thomas Journal, CY 2604, item 3, frame 146, ML.
94 Thomas Journal, CY 2604, item 3, frame 146, ML.
95 Thomas Journal, CY 2604, item 3, ML. There is still a bridge across the creek at the site of the old protectorate station, near Old Moorooduc Road.

cut wood. 'Old Dindow [this is not a male, she is Derrimut's mother] shows that Wooden Pickaxe better than Iron one, by with dexterity making some holes for rails before house'. Thomas took an account of where all his blacks were:

AT ABORIGINAL STATION

Kurboro, 2 lubras and Old Tuat — 4

Murrunbean and 2 lubras — 3

Budgery Tom, lubra and 1 picks — 3

Ning lubra and Dindow — 3

Big Benbow and lubra — 2

6 Western Port children left.

TOTAL 21

BARABOOLS ETC (ALSO AT ABORIGINAL STATION)

Linnaret and lubra and child TowangKurran — 3

Korun, lubra and child — 3

Balladul and two children — 3

Wondut and lubra — 2

Merridut, lubra and two children — 4

Tugal, lubra and pick — 3

Welgromin, lubra and Pick — 3

Golan and lubra — 2

Karngedon and lubra — 2

Turrin, lubra and child — 3

Gorreker, lubra and child — 3

Torungerong, Torrederrebun, Gungangrun, Bollute, Bokatungamun, Torrenbaltum, Morum, Torrenwakun, Moodewarren — all young men

---

TOTAL AT STATION 61

AT BUCKKAMITTORWARRA

Old Mr Man and family — 8

Binbangrook and lubra — 2

Winnunning lubra — 1

Bagumbaboot lubra — 1

Young men — Dollar, Lillero, Tamarabun, Tarem, Lillyrook, Mingar — 6

TOTAL 18

AT TURTGURUK
Old Doctor and family – 6
Bogy Bogy, 2 lubras and 2 pick – 5
Little Benbow and lubra – 2
Ben Benger and lubra – 2
Lummer Lummer, lubra and child – 3
Kulkulbulluk and lubra – 2
Wallan and lubra – 2

TOTAL 22

AT PORT PHILLIP
Young men – Lively, Bullut Bullut, Poleorong, Nunuptune

TOTAL 4

OUT ON RAMBLE
Burrenum and lubra – 2
King and lubra – 2
Turnbull and lubra – 2
Bobinnary one lubra and 2 children – 4
Turtgurruk or Nern Nern and lubra – 2
Young men – Nerreminen, Yal Yal, Toby, Warranditolong, Lutguderwrungun, Mumbo, Minnen, Boronmoto, Nerimbineck or Young Winberry – 9

TOTAL 21*

* Thomas Journal, CY 2604, item 3, frames 146–147, ML.

13 June 1840

Ningeranown came in with 'a very long tale about the Governor sending Billy Lonsdale and the blacks out of Melbourne'. Thomas' man Ross arrived from Melbourne with an official letter approving a grant of land for a reserve, and Thomas broached to them the subject of 'Good Land' they talked of.[96]

The next day was a Sunday and Thomas would not make elective journeys on the Sabbath. On Monday 15 June they set off for the good country of the Western Port blacks' choice, Kullurk [Coolart]. They returned to Tubberubbabel on 19 June.[97]

---

96 Thomas Journal, CY 2604, item 3, frame 148, ML.
97 Thomas Journal, CY 2604, item 3, ML.

20 June 1840

Pinterginner returns from VDL and brings with him Mary from Mr Smiths.[98] Mr Hobson made a complaint about the blacks' dogs rushing his sheep, but after a bit, considered it a tale of his shepherds. Thomas took a 'good view' of the station.[99] The encampment was excited about a report of Budgery Tom's son and Old Kullorluk being killed by 'wild black fellows'; there was much howling. In a letter to Robinson Thomas states that he has 89 people at Tubberubbabel and 42 at the stations of settlers around him.[100]

21 June 1840

'2 Settlers come at night in consequence vile report of a surveyor – that I had begged of Government to make Kangeron a settlement and with intent to [illegible]'. His marginal note, as always emphasising highlights, reads 'vile report of settlers by Smythe'. Thomas brought into the encampment three Yarra blacks named Worworong, Palangoon and Paladary, whom he found in the bush a few miles from Tubberubbabel, and learned from them that Kullorluk and the youth (Budgery Tom's son, unnamed, either Buckup or Munite) are safe: he gave them each a red shirt. 43 men attended Divine Service but not the women, they being too far off to hear. Hobson called again and said that the report about the blacks' dogs rushing his sheep was false, that the shepherd had left his flock and they had scattered, and the shepherd made up the story.[101]

23 June 1840

> All peaceable, sparingly with supplies – gave liberally to three lubras who brought baskets – all on a sudden a Council sits. The result was that Encamp* was to shift. When I enquired were [sic] I was much disappointed – it was not 500 yards from my hut. They made pretence wood got short, but I was given to understand afterwards that they feared the Governor would come and see me and be sulky with them. Mr Hobson comes to inform me that 2 VDL lubras was in the District, run away from Mr Robinson.[102]

---

98   Thomas Journal, CY 2604, item 3, ML. The fact that Thomas links these two facts – of Pinterginner's return from VDL and his removing Mary from the Smiths – suggests to me that he had been on an embassy to Mary's mother. Four vessels arrived from Launceston in the week prior to this journal observation, the *Elizabeth, Pickwick, Enterprise* and *Sir John Franklin*.

99   Thomas Journal, CY 2604, item 3, frame 149, ML. I have searched, so far unsuccessfully for this sketch.

100   Thomas to Robinson, 20 June 1840, VPRS 11, unit 7/311, PROV.

101   Thomas Journal, CY 2604, item 3, frame 150, ML. The explanation of the vile report comes in the journal six days later: it is a report which Thomas regards as a slander on him, that Smythe had told settlers that Thomas was pressing the government for Edward Hobson's run Kangerong as a reserve for the blacks (Thomas Journal, Saturday 27 June 1840, CY 2604, item 3, ML).

102   Thomas Journal, CY 2604, item 3, ML.

These women are Trucaninni and Charlotte who was Johnny Franklin's mother. Charlotte/Sarah/Kalloongoo was not a native of VDL but a Kaurna woman taken by sealers from Kangaroo Island to Bass Strait.[103] It was because she came to Port Phillip as part of Robinson's black 'family' that Thomas described her as being from VDL.

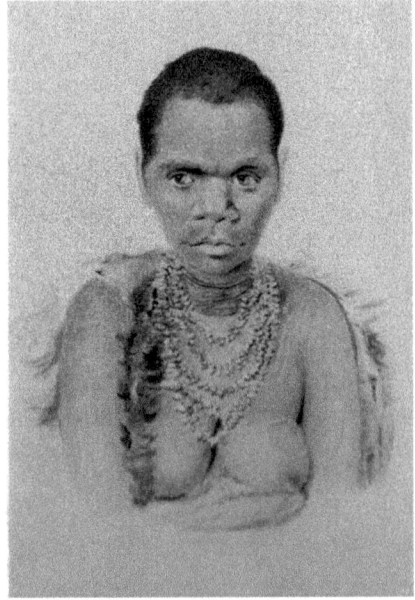

Fig 22. 'Trucanini'

Reproduced from James Fenton's *A History of Tasmania from its Discovery in 1642 to the Present Time*, J Walch, Hobart, 1884.

24 June 1840

The whole of the blacks are in the encampment except Old Doctor and his three children, and Kullorluk and Budgery Tom's son. Mr Mann again disturbs the encampment because he wants a lubra (he has three wives at this time) but all ends in talk. Thomas' stores were all gone so some lubras went to Mrs Thomas at Tuerong and she fed them, presumably according to her husband's instructions which were to feed the lubras 'sparingly' but to 'fully relieve three old lubras and four children'.[104]

25 June 1840

Food is short. Over two days, Murrumbein and his family, and Poleorong, and six Mt Macedon blacks, and Bob and three others shift to Poleorongon, Mr Hyatt's

---

103   Amery 1996: 42.
104   Thomas Journal, CY 2604, item 3, frame 150, ML.

station where surveyor Smythe has his tents. Thomas 'appeases' the blacks by feeding them from his private store. The Chief Protector's son arrived looking for Trucannini and Charlotte, and Thomas told him where they were, but he returned that night saying he could not find them. The blacks are anxiously awaiting the arrival of the dray with the stores.[105]

25 June 1840

In Melbourne, Robinson took delivery from Assistant Protector Thomas' station the following articles: 11 buckets, two table mats, 25 kangaroo skins, 23 opossum skins, 65 squirrel skins and 25 basins.[106] Thomas had sent this consignment off three days earlier, recording that it was 13 baskets, two mats, 75 *Tuins* (Flying squirrel), 55 *Bemins*, 14 *Wallert*s (possum), 24 *Koem* (Kangaroo).

26 June 1840

The lubras made baskets but Thomas told them to keep them until the dray returns. Lummer Lummer, Old George's lubra and Tuat are very sick, and Thomas fed them and gave them medicine. Ningolobin and his lubra left for surveyor Smythe's encampment, and Thomas learned that Smythe proposed to take three Western Port blacks plus the Mt Macedon blacks to Melbourne. There were 100 people at Tubberubbabel.[107]

27 June 1840

At daybreak Thomas went to Poleorongong at the back of Mt Eliza and confronted Smythe who said that he was not intending to take the three Western Port blacks to Melbourne, only the Mt Macedon blacks. Then Thomas fronted him about the report Thomas heard from the two settlers,[108] regarding Thomas allegedly wanting Kangerong for a reserve; Smythe said it was 'a d--- lie'. Robinson's son arrived back having found Trucaninni and Charlotte and they stayed overnight. The Mt Macedon blacks left Poleorongong and returned to Tubberubbabel, making 112 people in the encampment. In the margin Thomas wrote that he warned his Western Port blacks 'not to go to Melbourne without a note from me'.[109]

---

105   Thomas Journal, CY 2604, item 3, frame 150, ML. I cannot identify Bob with certainty. It is possible but unlikely, that it is Ben Benger whose European name was Robert Webb, unlikely because Ben Benger was well known in Melbourne society under his real name, not his exchanged name; it could be a diminutive of Bobbinary, but when Thomas' pen is flying and he abbreviates, he usually writes Bob plus a superscript squiggle, and though it may be suspected that he means Bobbinary, such observations have not been included in the biographical details: they are not certain. This reference to plain Bob is most likely to refer to either Robert Bullet or Robert Allen, two of Batman's VDL blacks who signed work agreements with Mr ET Newton at Mordialloc, Thomas Journal, 9/10 June 1839, CY 3082: 11, ML. One of these men married into the Bonurong.
106   Clark 1988, vol 1: 347.
107   Thomas Journal, CY 2604, item 3, frame 151, ML.
108   The two settlers are Edward Hobson and Robert Jamieson.
109   Thomas Journal, CY 2604, item 3, frame 151, ML.

28 June 1840

Sunday. It rained in torrents and Thomas held Divine Service in the hut but only four attended. Robinson junior, Trucaninni and Charlotte departed for Melbourne via Tuerong where they received supplies from Mrs Thomas, and Nuluptune brings a report that the cart has broken down at Poleorongong. Mrs Thomas complains of the demands made on her by the blacks.[110]

29 June 1840

Two Yarra blacks, Old Mr Murry and Young Murry arrived with the news that Billibellary was ill at Clow's station near Nerre Nerre Warren, and four young men, Woranditalong, Munmunginna, Turnmile and Willu departed immediately with a gift from Thomas of a red shirt, plus an invitation to bring all the Yarra blacks down to Tubberubbabel. Ross returned from Mr Hyatt's with the news that it was untrue that the dray had broken down, and he brought with him flour from Hyatt's, repayment of a loan from Thomas' store. Nuluptune was reported to have stolen something from Mr White, but on enquiry Thomas learned that some flour was found in a shirt by him in the hut. There are 119 people in the encampment.[111]

30 June 1840

Several of the lubras went to Tuerong to obtain potatoes from Mrs Thomas. The stores finally arrived − 1000 lbs of flour, 400 lbs of sugar, 600 lbs of rice and eight lbs of tobacco, together with a gratifying communication from La Trobe, for which Thomas thanked God, plus what looks to be a personal present from La Trobe for the Aborigines − two dozen 'Tommyhawks', two dozen knives, four dozen hooks, nine balls of string, four dozen needles and one bundle of thread. Thomas repaid to his son William Jackson Thomas the rations which were advanced for the blacks out of private stores held by Thomas junior, and re-iterates that food obtained from Thomas junior must be paid for with labour by the blacks. 'Gave Nuluptune a lecture on Mr Stratton's concern[112] and threaten to send him to jail. Nul seems very careless; however he and his brother Mumbo start about an hour later for the Yarra'.[113]

1 July 1840

Thomas received three good baskets from lubras and paid one of them three pounds of flour, and the other two a tomahawk each which much pleased them all. The Mt Macedon blacks importune him much for the same privileges as his

---

110   Thomas Journal, CY 2604, item 3, frame 151, ML.
111   Thomas Journal, CY 2604, item 3, frame 152, ML.
112   Mr Stratton's station is shown on Thomas' map at Poleorongon, on the Nepean Highway between Mt Eliza and Mt Martha.
113   Thomas Journal, CY 2604, item 3, frame 152, ML.

Western Port blacks, but Thomas says they have to go to their own country as they have been down here for a long time. Two Mt Macedons work and Thomas rewards them. 'They form a deputation and beg of me a letter to pass them through to their own country in case Governor or others should stop them'. Three strange blacks arrived and claimed kinship with Thomas' blacks: he was suspicious, but Benbow, Derrimut and Moragine identified them as Murronban (Barabool), Turrenbulkon (Barabool), and Mulgum (Mt Macedon), with two lubras and one child. The blacks one after another come from Tuerong and tell Thomas that his wife is very ill.[114]

2 July 1840

At daybreak Thomas returned to Tubberubbabel, to find that the strangers importune to stop ten days more, but Thomas does not encourage them. The blacks held a two hour council by Thomas' hut which finally produced the decision that the Mt Macedon blacks would go home, but only if Thomas gave them a letter. This he did, writing a large letter with all their names in the margin, which seemed to comfort them. But he had to hold his pen in the air for five minutes, pointing at the date on the letter, till at last they said 'tomorrow'. Thomas shook hands with everyone, telling them not to rob etc on the way, and they left stopping one night at Tuerong. Thomas visited them at Tuerong and gave each departing family from Mrs Thomas' store flour and rice, and before they left the lubras said goodbye to good Mrs Thomas. Thomas did not record how many people were left but he noted that:

- 4 gone to Mr Hobson's [Buckkermitterwarrer]
- 4 gone to see Billibellary [Nerre Nerre Warren]
- 2 gone to Mr O'Connor's [south-east of Dandenong]
- 2 gone a little way with Surveyor Smythe [from the back of Mt Eliza]
- Dr, wife and child and Captain Turnbull to Mt Macedon.[115]

3 July 1840

Thomas visited Tuerong and found the Mt Macedon's not inclined to leave, though he noted that it certainly was a cold and frosty morning: he suspected that his blacks were pressing them to stay. They eventually left in the afternoon and encamped at Poleorongon. At Tubberubbabel, Derrimut and his family pressed Thomas for a letter to go to Melbourne.[116]

---

114 Thomas Journal, CY 2604, item 3, ML.
115 Thomas Journal, CY 2604, item 3, frame 153, ML.
116 Thomas Journal, CY 2604, item 3, frame 154, ML.

4 July 1840

The blacks are beginning to experience a shortage of 'provender game', and Old Tuat and Young Murry depart for Mr Ruffy's station (Cranbourne), intending to continue on from there to Mr Ryrie's on the upper Yarra. Thomas encourages the blacks to persevere because he expects Robinson soon, to approve of their chosen place, Kullurk, as their reserve. There are still 98 people at Tubberubbabel, with only a few out at known places. Thomas gave tomahawks to Tuat, Bogy Bogy and Wigal who wished to leave, and they changed their minds and stayed.[117]

5 July 1840

This was a Sunday. Thomas' men reported that some blacks who slept in the men's hut (the European men's hut) stole seven pounds of meat: the blacks were Murrum, Burrenum and Moragin and son, Davy and Borunmolook[118] who was supposed to be the thief. 'Much angry feelings' Thomas recorded, but he gives no indication whether the men were angry, or the blacks were angry, or both groups.

Alleged theft by Toby's brother

With this modest report commences a lengthy and stubborn stand off between the blacks and Thomas' men. In the evening Thomas' men asked to question Toby's brother, but it was Thomas who questioned 'the young youth'. Thomas thought he heard an Aboriginal voice saying 'must not tell' and that, in turn made Thomas 'very angry'. Whereupon Toby jumped up and threw three wonguims at the men's hut, breaking a corner of it. Thomas ran towards Toby who whipped out a gun and pointed it at Thomas. Thomas seized the gun and gave it to his man Davis to put away in Thomas' hut and secure the door. But on the way to the hut Burrenum stopped Davis and said that the gun was his, that he had only lent it to the young man to get kangaroo, half of which Toby would give to Burrenum in exchange for the loan.

'The whole camp was in confusion, the aged came about me to see if I was hurt'. Thomas insisted on not issuing the rations until the robber was discovered. 'The blacks insisted it was a dog that stole it, the men the reverse'. Then Thomas 'very solemnly charge[d] the men what the result was likely to be [hungry blacks]. They wish me to look over it [Thomas means overlook] & appeared sorry that they had made any stir about it. I said no, they never had committed a robbery till now and I was determined to shew my determination to punish'.

---

117 Ruffy's, O'Connor's and Clow's stations are between the top of Western Port and Dandenong.
118 Toby/Borunmoolin, male, Westernport, aged 20 is listed on the 1846 Family Connections census as a young man, an orphan; his brother is also named Toby-Nerrimnundock male orphan, aged 15 (CY 3083, ML). This would make them respectively 14 years old and nine years old in 1840.

Thomas questioned the men again: the verisimilitude that Thomas' men provided was that the trunk where the meat was kept was tied with bands of strong string around the lid, twisted around about three inches below the lid and the ends of the string were interwoven into the bands: it was exactly as they left it when they woke up in the morning. 'On the finding the string so twisted hung the certainty of the theft'.

The blacks again denied the theft, asserting that it must have been the dogs, and as Thomas wrote, if they did indeed steal the meat then it would be the very first instance of theft and he would not stand for it: in his heart though, he was inclined to believe them. They were insistent that two or three times in the night the dogs came into the men's tent and had to be driven out.

Thomas retired to his hut having told the blacks that neither he nor his men could tell who did it but that God knew and one day would tell. The old men spent another hour trying to get the truth. In the end the blacks all thronged into Thomas' hut, and crowded the passage outside and protested their innocence. They said '**no we sulky you, know give flour, good you, no you sulky**'. The anxiety of the whole to appease him touched Thomas and he assured them that he was not sulky – he just wanted them to tell him who did it. They all declared that they could not tell him who did it, that it must have been the dogs as they would have found out who did it. 'I could not help in my mind believing them' wrote Thomas.

Then they went further and explained that Toby was not sulky with Thomas, only generally sulky because Thomas' men claimed that his brother stole the meat, and that when Toby shot off the gun, he was not aiming at Thomas but at his own dog. 'All entreated that he [Toby] might come to me, stating **Toby big one cry**'.

Thomas consented to a formal interview with a little preliminary scene setting: he built up his fire and lit a candle. Escorted by Burrenum, Mr King and d' Villiers, Toby entered the hut and 'rushed' to Thomas, took hold of his hand and shook it for a 'long time'. Then he sat down on the flour and said '**me plenty tell you**' in English and his own tongue. His story was as follows.

Toby's testimony

That 'in morning Man Davis tell me [my] Brother steal meat. [My] Brother say no [not] me steal Bulgana – [then] me and brother gogo kangaroo – When me get in Bush, me make Brother stop & say why you steal meat. Me take Wonguin tilbert Brother, Brother big one cry, no me steal meat, me sleep – Me [Toby] said you now tell me lie. Brother [said] no lie, me tell you no lie, no lie. Then me

> and Brother gogo nangheit Koen [kangaroo] Boo [shoot]. **We both
> sat down, make fire, eat no me, let my brother eat. Me say no – me
> plenty tilbert you, no you, you tell me big one lie. You steal man
> Marminarta meat. My Brother Big Big Big one cry – no me steal
> meat, no you kill me, no me meat Pilmerlaly** [take or steal]**, no me
> see meat, me sleep. Me** [Toby] **Big one cry then, me tell my Brother
> no more you cry, big one Bungarly** [stupid] **Davy.**

> **Me make my brother eat & me wipe my brothers face, say no more
> cry you, big lie Davy – Brother eat Pikaniny** [small]**, then me and
> brother nerlingo** [come back] **Your Miam. When sit down, Davy
> come, say your Brother stole meat – me say you lie and me big
> one sulky, threw wonguim – then you** [Thomas] **come and tell me
> what for you do that? – me take up Tranbullabil** [gun] **and shoot
> my dog, no me shoot at Marminarta, no, no, no, plenty sleeps you
> Marminarta** [ie Thomas will not be dead] **no me boo** [shoot] **you, me
> boo wonguim, me warmbil sulky.**

Thomas goes on to say that he had called both his men in prior to permitting Toby to speak, and without making any comment on Toby's narrative, Thomas questioned the men yet again. Ross was not so sure but he stuck to his story. Then Thomas had a brainwave – he asked if anything else was in the box, only to find that there was half a cooked damper.

Thomas knew immediately that the blacks had not stolen the meat – no black would take salt beef when damper was available, and perhaps the men read his face because they in their turn 'straight away seemed most anxious to drop the matter'. Thomas recorded 'After this, for my part, I believe the box was neither fastened at night nor found so in the morning'. He took the opportunity, missed in the morning because of the 'cabal', to hold a Divine Service and preached on the topic of 'Thou God seeist me'. He does not record whether he said out loud that the blacks had told the truth and his men had lied.

Thomas made a marginal note as follows:

> When a black is sulky, he will throw wonguims, spears or anything
> promiscuously in the encampment. The blacks never chastise him for so
> doing, but avoid the danger, and when all thrown, men of importance
> will scold him and make him desist.[119]

6 July 1840

Next morning they were all about him early, with skins, anxious to see if he had forgotten the anger of yesterday. Wollum, a Mt Macedon black slightly

---

119   Sunday, 5 July 1840, CY 2604, item 3, frames 154–157, ML.

speared his lubra for not getting him water. Thomas categorises this action as disobedience by the lubra, explicable because Wollum had another lubra in his miam at the time: he punished Wollum by not buying his skins from him. Thomas set the blacks to cutting wood and paid them as workers and then ordered them to make *benaks* for two days. The four people returned who had gone in the boat to Melbourne saying '**No Captain Lonsdale but Governor big one sulky.** Benbow return and say **No sulky. Governor say come to Mr Thomas**'.[120]

7 July 1840

Blacks importune him to go to Melbourne and take them. Murrumbean brings a report that two Mounted Police are at Mr Hyatt's station. 'I ascertain that they are not, and appease the encampment'.[121]

8 July 1840

The blacks appear very satisfied with their rewards for skins and *benaks*. It is reported that two Yarra blacks are on the way here on an embassy. The encampment is peaceable, but over-anxious to see Melbourne and not very industrious.[122]

9 July 1840

Thomas received two officials (letters) and as he opened them, the blacks were anxious to know if Mr Robinson is coming and whether or not the Governor is sulky. They bring in a tale that two white men say that they are to go to Melbourne – plenty to eat there. He received so many skins and *benaks* that he put them in the store without counting them.[123]

10 and 11 July 1840

The blacks' anxiety to go to Melbourne is increasing daily, but the women continue to make their baskets. Thomas spends his time walking round the encampment and encouraging them, and he shows them much satisfaction at their efforts. 'Some blacks after receiving their stipend go they say for a few days. They begin to enquire when Chief Protector will come and **find out country**'.[124]

12 July 1840

This was a Sunday and Thomas had 32 at a comfortable service 'all males, the females are not allowed to attend'.[125] (Later this year, on 15 November 1840 at

120 Thomas Journal, CY 2604, item 3, ML.
121 Thomas Journal, CY 2604, item 3, frame 157, ML.
122 Thomas Journal, CY 2604, item 3, frame 157, ML.
123 Thomas Journal, CY 2604, item 3, frame 157–158, ML.
124 Thomas Journal, CY 2604, item 3, frame 158, ML.
125 Thomas Journal, CY 2604, item 3, ML.

Nerre Nerre Warren, Thomas made a point of recording the very first time that
he ever knew the females to attend Divine Service with the males.)[126] The subject
of his sermon was the Goodness of God in day by day giving his creatures
food. Many people wanted to bring him skins and baskets but he would not
accept them on the Sabbath. Some asked him for knives – he refused 'No give
only Tungang on Sunday. One said **No you sulky me gogo**. I said no sulky
but why you gogo leave Marminarta? They said **only little way** and gave me a
full direction of where going'. He said the reason was that they have no *wuller
wullert* (possum); they were sick of kangaroo and they loved *wuller wullert*.
Thomas wished them God speed and shook hands and they scribed a map of
their route which was a triangle:

- To Bukkermitterwarra near Hobson's
- Then Boneong near Mr Merricks
- Then Willarmarang, Cape Schanck
- Then Kunnite by Ner
- Then Kunnulong near Kullurk
- Then Kokubell
- Then Tuerong, Mr Thomas
- Then Tubrub Station.

Then they left saying **'Bengaro'** four times then **'Nerlingo'** which Thomas
translated as '8 sleeps then come back'.[127]

Those who left on the ramble were:

- Ben Benger and lubra – 2
- Mr King and lubra – 2
- Burrenum, lubra and brother – 3
- Morragen – 1
- Toby and brother – 2
- Nerreninen and Toranbilgum – 2.

13 July 1840

Next day four more blacks tell Thomas that they are departing on the same
route, but instead of returning to Tuerong from Kokobul, they will turn right
and go to Mahun and will be away 11 days. This group consists of:

---

126 Thomas Journal, CY 2605, item 1, frame 186, ML. Much later, on 23 April 1848 in Melbourne, Thomas
had a Divine Service at an encampment of 18 women and five children in the morning, then in the afternoon,
found that eight men and a boy had prepared for Divine Service, made up a seat for him etc. '[I] apologize for
speaking to the lubras and children first, but tho they did not like the preference, they shook hands and said
"**never mind, no sulky us**" [Thomas' quotation marks]', CY 2606, frame 505, ML).
127 Thomas Journal, CY 2604, item 3, frame 159, ML.

- Lummer Lummer and lubra – 2
- Nern Nern and lubra – 2
- Bobinnary and lubra, leaving children behind – 2
- Waworong – 1
- TOTAL – 7.

The lubras also departed to get grass for baskets, and Thomas gave them six pounds of flour and six pounds of rice in case of emergency, as the encampment had caught only one kangaroo. The fact is, he said, that they must leave this district for a time. They call out **'plenty hungry'**.

14 July 1840

Two messengers arrived from the Yarra blacks in Melbourne saying **'plenty to eat, plenty bungerlarly'** and Thomas' blacks are all agog to go to Melbourne; he could not get a word in edgeways, he wrote. In the evening they came to him and said they must leave Tubberubbabel as there no kangaroo to be got. There have been but two kangaroo and opossums got in the last two days, he wrote, and what is that among so many? He found it necessary to give extra this day, besides what Mrs Thomas has given them. He fed 42 people – 20 men, five lubras, eight boys and nine girls.[128]

15 July 1840

Thomas recorded that it was very wet and windy, and this was fortunate for the poor blacks for game. The women must be back from getting grass because he feeds 12 lubras, but the men are very dissatisfied with their ill success in game.[129]

Wind and hunting

The necessity of wind for successful hunting is mentioned again on 31 July. The men have not been successful at hunting, and Thomas suspects that their failure is organised by them in order to put pressure on him to allow them to go to Melbourne. 'It is singular if game was rare a fortnight back, that they find no difficulty now. I state my suspicions to them – they say **now plenty of wind.** The last few days certainly was windy'.[130]

One of the songs that Betbenjee taught the young George Gordon McCrae at Arthurs Seat was a 'song for raising the wind', presumably for hunting.[131]

17 July 1840

The men are idle, Thomas recorded but he received two baskets 'in fact men make women work or they would be starving'. He received a 'very superior

---

128 Thomas Journal, CY 2604, item 3, ML.
129 Thomas Journal, CY 2604, item 3, frame 160, ML.
130 Thomas Journal, CY 2604, item 3, frame 166, ML.
131 George Gordon McCrae, 'Reminiscences not exploits', vol 4, Ms 2523/5(d), SLV.

basket' for which he gave 'most liberal' but the 'rogue of a husband' took it and would not let the lubra have a bit, so he gave the unnamed woman some bread, and gave her husband a 'good scolding'.[132]

18 July 1840

The youngest Murry, one of the Yarra blacks who arrived on 14 July departed with two warm red shirts, one for Billibellary and one for Old Murry (also known as Tuart, also known as Old Jack Weatherly), and a message to the Yarra blacks not to gogo Melbourne but to come down here to Tubberubbabel.[133]

19 July 1840

The blacks all moved to Tuerong, so early that Thomas could not have his service. It being a Sunday, he could not follow them so he gave instructions to Mrs Thomas to give them 24 pounds of potatoes and six pounds of rice.

20 July 1840

Thomas caught the bullocks, loaded the dray with his tent and followed them to Tuerong, but they were not happy with the hunt – they had no wax to stick the glass on their spears.[134]

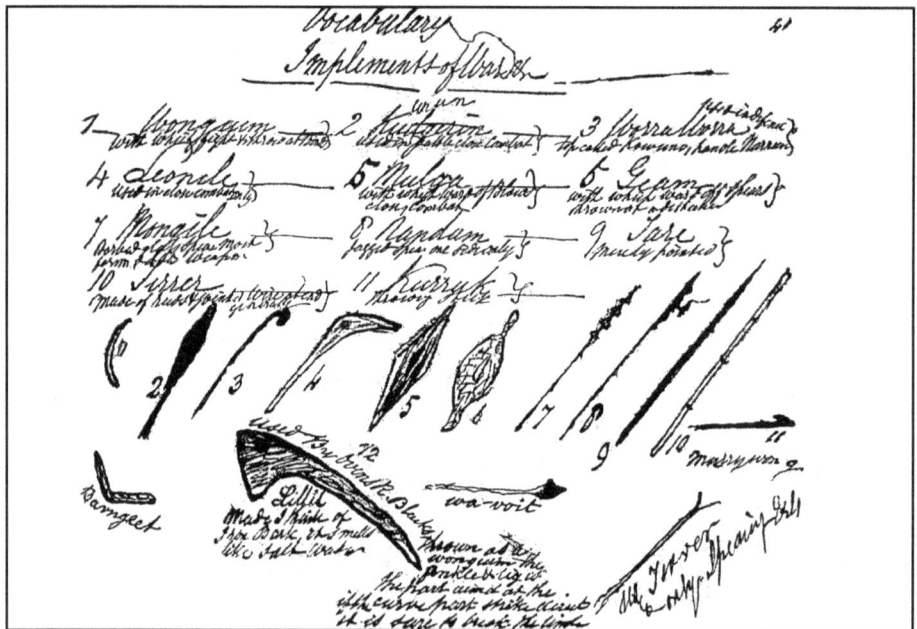

Fig 23. 'Implements of War'

Thomas sketch showing barbed glass spear, from the William Thomas papers, 1834–1868, 1902, Mitchell Library, reproduced with the permission of the State Library of New South Wales.

132 Thomas Journal, CY 2604, item 3, ML.
133 Thomas Journal, CY 2604, item 3, ML.
164 134 Thomas Journal, CY 2604, item 3, ML.

21 July 1840

The blacks gave Thomas to understand that it was 'no good' that the rambling parties were still away, and further, that the rambling parties would not come in unless told to. So he went to Buckkermitterwarrer, Poleorongong and Tontine looking for them. Bob, Nuluptune and Bogy Bogy returned next day.

23 July 1840

The people are anxious to go to Melbourne '**Merygeek** [very good] **white man say plenty Bungarly** [stupid] **Mr Thomas.**' Thomas viewed this attitude as ingratitude and reminded them of the goodness of the Governor, what a large amount of white and paper money (**Noogra**) that flour and rice and sugar cost. He pointed out that he was receiving few skins and showed 'more than ordinary displeasure'. They said '**Marminartra big one sulky**'. Nevertheless he gave them their allowance, whereupon they said '**we all gogo no work**'. He lost his temper and 'threw the panican as I gave the last into the bag, and said no good my blackfellows'. They went off and had a long discussion by the fire, while he with his eldest daughter ostentatiously took the crosscut saw and cut down two trees. This was too much for Bob[135] who came over and took the saw out of Thomas' daughter's hand, and he and Thomas cut down two more trees. They all came back to work and continued till the evening, whereupon Thomas' son fed them as the work had been done on his property. The day finished with the blacks saying '**all gone sulky**'.[136]

24 July 1840

Before even he had a chance to wish the people good morning, the cry went up '**gogo Melbourne**'. Two more blacks came in, and one of them, the Yarra black Mr Murry, left again without saying goodbye, 'at which I am angry'. They were still 'unfortunate' in game and Thomas felt sorry for them.[137]

25 July 1840

They appeared more satisfied this day and all worked well getting wood and water so there would be no need to work on the Sunday. They also harrowed. Budgery Tom acted as foreman and appeared proud of it. A settler, Mr Hyatt[138] called, and said he did not know what Thomas had done with the blacks, but

135 Unidentified.
136 Thomas Journal, CY 2604, item 3, ML.
137 Thomas Journal, CY 2604, item 3, ML.
138 From Poleorongong on the Nepean Highway between Mt Eliza and Mt Martha. John Highett was thought to be the first person who crossed Dandenong creek taking his stock to the neighbourhood of Frankston (Sutherland 1888).

whenever they come now they are always willing to work. The lubras came at the end of the day to say **'tomorrow big one Sunday no work'**. Thomas relieved (ie fed) 53 persons: 20 men, 17 women, nine boys and seven girls.[139]

26 July 1840

Thomas had a comfortable service with his natives, his family also present. Three 'poor' lubras brought him baskets which he refused to accept because it was Sunday and he went on to make the observation that they are learning to observe the Sabbath and he has already noticed a difference – 'an extra streak [of ochre] of the face or clean shirt'.[140]

Ochre

Bright red ochre is a sign of joy and mirth; white ochre is a sign of death and grief; yellow ochre and brown ochre are used in corroborees. Mt Eliza abounds with almost all kinds of clay.[141] The extra streak to mark the Sabbath would have been red ochre.

27 July 1840

Thomas wrote again to La Trobe, copying it to Robinson, requesting La Trobe 'when his weighty duties would permit' to select the reserve for his blacks. Budgery Tom's lubra made a 'basket of superior work' as a gift to Mrs La Trobe. Thomas then went to Poleorongong and Tontine looking for parties of his blacks but they had departed towards Konigo (Frankston): when he returned to Tuerong he found that Robinson had arrived.[142]

27 July 1840

The Chief Protector visited 'Tub.er.rub.ber.bil', two and a half miles from Thomas Junior's station (Tuerong) and one mile from 'Gan.jer.ong [Kangerong]' Thomas Senior's second station.

> Here was an old wattle and daub hut in the Tower of Peiza style, at least two feet out of perpendicular, it was shored up and thatched with grass. This part of the country is hilly and thickly wooded. There is an abundance of grass.[143]

In his entry for this same day, Thomas notes that Robinson criticised him severely for writing to La Trobe without going through Robinson, for neglecting half his

---

139   Thomas Journal, CY 2604, item 3, ML.
140   Thomas Journal, CY 2604, item 3, frame 164, ML.
141   Thomas Papers, CY 2984: 111, ML.
142   Thomas Journal, CY 2604, item 3, frame 165, ML.
143   Clark 1988, vol 1: 357.

duties ie the Yarra blacks, and generally found fault with him. Robinson simply refused to speak about a reserve for the Bonurong, and Thomas could get no instructions, which Thomas experienced as 'unjust and unkind'. Robinson was prepared to leave without giving Thomas any orders: it was only on the road back to Melbourne when Thomas accompanied Robinson for some miles that Robinson opened up and told Thomas to collect all his blacks together, bring them to Melbourne, find the Yarra blacks and together settle on a reserve for both tribes then order blankets and supplies.[144]

1 August 1840

Thomas sent a party off to bring in the blacks who were down towards Point Nepean, and he made up his last returns of stores. In the 30 days since the stores arrived on 30 June, he had distributed to his people 796 pounds of flour, all of the rice which was 600 pounds, 373 pounds of sugar, six pounds of tobacco. His stock on hand was 204 pounds of flour, nil rice, 36 pounds sugar, eight pounds of soap, seven pounds of tea, and one and a half pounds of tobacco.[145]

4 August 1840

Mr Man and his family came in and upon questioning him Thomas found that only the blacks at Buckkermitterwarrer intended to follow. There were other parties out who had failed to return. Thomas decided to go and bring these parties in himself, but the people demurred by telling him that the absent ones were on the mountain (Arthurs Seat) and **'too much wood no gogo Yarraman'** ie the forest was too dense for Thomas to ride his horse. Thomas said he would walk instead of riding his horse, to which their response was that he would **'plenty break foot'**. Thomas reminded them that Robinson had said he (Thomas) was 'big one lazy', and that persuaded them that he really was determined to go. So they made a mudmap on the ground of where the absent parties were, and he took compass bearings from it. Then they had a full debate about the wisdom of his going off by himself and informed him that **'you be kill'd by Wild Black Fellows, no Marminarta then'**. Thomas said 'no mind'. Then Budgery Tom and Bogy Bogy stepped forward and said **'no long way – two sleeps and nerlingo** [come back]**, no you go alone we go with Marminarta'**.[146]

Thomas took his compass and four days supply of damper plus his tea making gear; they had firearms. They walked first to one of the blacks' encampment places by Sandy Point, arriving at 4 pm and making tea. Finding no one there, they turned south in the direction of Cape Schanck, and walked till sunset when they were at an encampment called Kunnite where there was fine water in deep

144   29 July 1840, CY 2604, item 3, frame 165, ML.
145   Thomas Journal, CY 2604, item 3, ML.
146   Thomas Journal, CY 2604, item 3, frames 167–168, ML.

gullies like a creek issuing from the Wonga range (Arthurs Seat).[147] Thomas was taken by this place noting that at this time of the year the beach was unbroken, and there was a great sized lake about 200 yards from the beach of salt water locked in by the drifting up of sand; he thought that it must be a formidable inlet of the sea in the wet season, little, if at all known.[148] There were some pretty patches of good feed, and during the night about 40 cattle passed them on the way to drink. He noted that 'I slept soundly under a gum tree here with 2 armed savages about me, I am sorry to say with more apparent safety that with 2 of my own colour so arm'd promiscuously in the Bush'.[149]

Next morning, Budgery Tom and Bogy Bogy informed him that not having found the absent parties at the two encampments, they must be on the mountain, and that Thomas could not go on the mountain because he would break his legs. They said that they would bring them in, and Thomas reluctantly agreed, giving them most of his supplies. They gave him another compass bearing, a straight line from Kunnite to Tuerong; they wanted to give him an easier route but he was adamant – a straight line was what he wanted. They parted and he passed over some 'queer' country (possibly grasstree country), slept another night in the bush and got back safely to Tuerong, their compass bearing bringing him out within 600 yards of his son's hut.

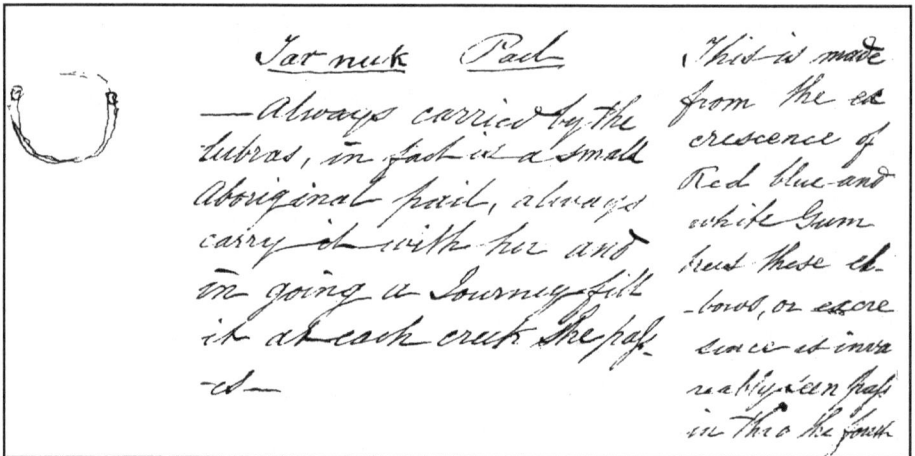

Fig 24. 'Tarnuck', vessel for carrying water

Thomas sketch, from the William Thomas papers, 1834–1868, 1902, Mitchell Library, reproduced with the permission of the State Library of New South Wales.

---

147 Kunnite is unidentified as yet, but it must be either Stony creek at Shoreham or East creek at Point Leo.
148 There are two creeks which rise near the top of Arthurs Seat, East Creek emerging at Point Leo beach and Stony Creek emerging at Pines beach Shoreham. Each of these two creeks blocks up with sand according to wind and tide conditions. The Kunnite encampment is at one of them, not yet identified.
149 Thomas Journal, CY 2604, item 3, frame 168, ML.

When he arrived back at the encampment, it was in 'a cabal' because Kurboro (Mr Ruffy) had speared his lubra for not getting water.[150] Kurboro came to him and told him his tale **'she no fetch me water and I big one sulky, plenty sorry me, plenty cry, big one sulky Marminarta'**. Thomas, 'knowing that such is their custom' reproved him, dressed his wife's wound, and noted that they both seemed sorry. The supplies are all gone, he wrote, so he gave to the aged from his own private store. Next day he expressed his anger that the absent parties had not come in, and announced that he was leaving the following Monday whether they were all with him or not. On Sunday he had to break his rule about not travelling on the Sabbath because a report came in that a black had attacked Hobson's dray en route Buckkermitterwarrer to Kangerong.

They finally departed on Monday 10 August after 21 days at Tuerong, with the dray overloaded with the blacks' luggage; they encamped at the usual places, Poleorongong, Konigo, Moody Yallock, then with Nulupton as guide, struck off the usual route to the east, finally camping in a miserable swamp not three miles south-east of Melbourne. Thomas had been worried – it was a dull day, no sun, his compass was on the dray, the bullocks were knocked up and they had no food. They finally arrived at Kurruk, a very pretty encampment on a north rise where the Yarra blacks were, and that night, Thomas had nearly all his charges in the one place – 215 of both tribes.

Thomas' summary half-yearly report for the period 29 February 1840 to 31 August 1840 states that he is preaching to the Western Port blacks at Tubberubbabel in their own language; that the women make baskets for three to four hours daily; that the men instead of throwing the animal whole on the fire carefully skin the animal and present the skins for a cup or two of flour or sugar; that in July a total of:

- 79 kangaroo skins
- 41 opossum skins
- 50 *bimen*
- 151 flying squirrels
- 69 baskets
- 5 mats
- 6 watch pockets

---

150 Kurboro's biographical details are in Chapter 7.

were forwarded to Melbourne; that the blacks had constructed a good bridge over Tubberubbabel Creek; that the blacks had done much good work for his son and other settlers including fencing for Meyricks at Boniong; most of the blacks can handle a cross-cut saw as well as any white man; and finally, that there are many good shearers and dressers of sheep among them, one having been a shepherd for six months.[151]

Bonurong retrospective on Tubberubbabel

3 September 1844

Tuesday. Thomas told Yankee Yankee that great good might be done if he would prevail upon the Western Port blacks to settle down and cultivate the ground. His answer was:[152]

> **Where it [illegible] Black Fellows want Kulluck and white man would not let them have it. You know when you was at Tubbarubbabel Black fellows stopped with you and worked and wanted to sow potatoes but you go away and go to the Yarra blacks.** These observations were so [illegible]. I am so often upbraided by the Western Port tribe for removing from them that it is useless arguing with them when I know I have not the power to accede were they so disposed.[153]

No date but after 1845

There used to be close to the Jamiesons at Kangerong an Aboriginal Mission Station called Terubbabel, a name gradually improved upon by the Darkies till it found itself in Tubberubbabel ... the Tubberubbabel waterhole actually figuring on the map of the period, a well established rendezvous also for men making out for cattle during the dry season.[154]

---

151   The shepherd is Kolorlook; Thomas, enc to La Trobe to Col Sec 3 December 1840, 40/12629 in Port Phillip 1840, 4.2512/1, AO of NSW.
152   Thomas used quotation marks, unusual for him: he must have regarded Yankee's comment as important.
153   Thomas Journal, CY 2606, item 3.
154   George Gordon McCrae, 'Experiences not exploits', vol 3, Ms 2523/4/c, SLV.

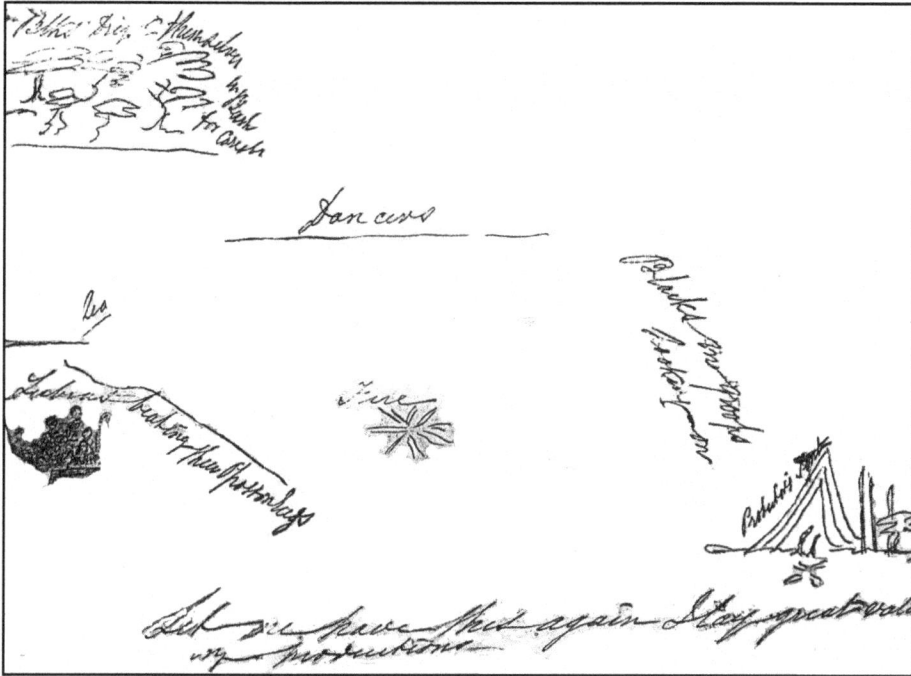

Fig 25. 'Sketch of Corroboree'

Thomas sketch which he has labelled 'early work' so is possibly done at Tubberubbabel, from the William Thomas papers, 1834–1868, 1902, Mitchell Library, reproduced with the permission of the State Library of New South Wales.

5. Kangerong, Protectorate second station

Kangerong/Kangeron/Kangerrong/Canjeerung/Gan.jer.rong/
Karangarong/The Principal Encampment/Mr Hobson's Station/
Kangerong – Mr Hob* Station/The Survey/Hugh Jamieson's Special
Survey/Kangerong House

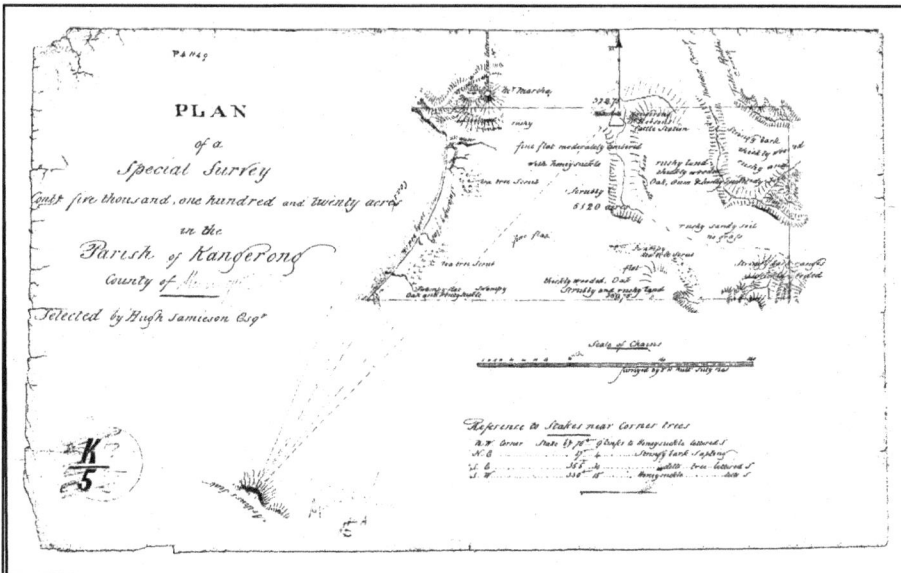

Fig 26. 'Plan of Special Survey of Kangerong', SS 5A

Kangerong is the Aboriginal name for the place occupied as a pastoral run by Edward William Hobson who took it up in the middle of 1838 but was subsequently forced off it by Hugh Jamieson's purchase of it in 1841 as a Special Survey.

Assistant Protector William Thomas described Kangerong, meaning the run, as the principal encampment of the Bonurong on the Mornington Peninsula. But Hobson's run, Kangerong, actually included all three Protectorate stations. It is marked on two plans, that of Nutt 1841 and Smythe 1841, on the lower south-east slopes of Mt Martha within the Brokil Creek drainage system, near Ellerina Road; it is marked also on four different maps drawn by the Assistant Protector William Thomas.

The Bonurong encampment Kangerong has been identified as the rising ground near the roundabout where the Nepean Highway crosses over the Moorooduc Freeway. The Brokil Creek drainage system shown on Smythe's map has been altered over the course of time by road construction works, and the actual site of the encampment has been destroyed in the construction of the freeway and its ramps, plus the Nepean Highway overpass. The identification was made in a manner similar to the identification of Tubberubbabel. The encampment at Kangerong was 'within quarter of a mile'[1] of Hobson's. Doubtless on the advice of the Bonurong, Hobson's house was situated on rising ground; it was 50 yards to the east of the waterhole belonging to the Bonurong, now fenced.[2] Their own encampment would have been on rising ground also, 'the blacks showing us by the marks on the trees to what heights the floods sometimes rise'.[3] Circles of a quarter of a mile in radius drawn around Hobson's, and around the waterhole, quickly reveal that the encampment would not have been on the low-lying floodplain of Brokil Creek in the south-west quadrant of the circle. Nor would it have been on the hilly country to the south-east, because if it was, then Hobson's house would have stood between the Aboriginal encampment and their water. The north-east quadrant of these circles is also the low-lying floodplain of the junction of Tassel's Creek and Brokil Creek. It is the north-west quadrant of these circles that satisfies all the conditions for a typical encampment, closest to their former waterhole, on rising ground, away from the European, and still close to Brokil Creek after its junction with Tassel's Creek. The two circles in fact intersect here.

Nutt's map of his survey throws up an ambiguous gap in the fencing around the waterhole. It is possible that this gap is an artefact of the production process of the map, a mistake, but it is at least possible that there actually was a gap in the fence around the waterhole, and that its purpose was to allow the Bonurong free access to their water while keeping out the sheep. It will be noticed below that Thomas told the people not to camp within the fence.

Whenever Kangerong is mentioned, it needs to be asked from the context – is it Hobson's run that is meant, or the actual place where he lived at this time, which was Buckkermitterwarrer near the drive-in, or the hut where his shepherd lived on the run Kangerong and where Kangerong House was being built, or the Aboriginal encampment called Kangerong, a short distance from the waterhole, the shepherd's hut and the new house being built? Sometimes, it is not possible to be sure.

There was nothing here at Kangerong belonging to the Protectorate, no buildings, no equipment, no supplies. The simple fact is that the Bonurong were already living here in two separate encampments on their own land on which Hobson 'dropped', to use the language of Samuel Jackson Thomas.[4] In my view,

---

1   *HRV*, vol 2B: 536.
2   George D Smythe, 1841, CS 81A, PROV.
3   William Jackson Thomas, CY 3106, frame 61, ML.
174   4   CY 3106, frame 63, ML.

it is most likely that the Bonurong showed Edward Hobson and/or George Smith this land, in the same manner as they pointed out Tubberubbabel to Thomas, and Kullurk to Henry Howard Meyrick, and Carup Carup to Captain Baxter. If so, their reasoning does not appear to have been recorded, but it is likely to be along the lines which the historian Jan Penney described in her PhD thesis on the explorer Charles Sturt and his boat journey down the Murray. Penney describes various Indigenous groups attempting to entice Sturt to settle down with them so that they could access the material goods which he carried, and they wanted. The recovered biographical details of the Europeans George Smith and Edward Hobson are presented in this chapter and the next chapter because they are crucial in understanding the good relationships that existed.

29 January 1836

Joseph Tice Gellibrand's party including Mr Gardiner, Mr Robertson and Mr Leake, having walked from Sandy Point, found water near the 100 huts now identified as Tubberubbabel, camped, walked further, altered their line of march a point or two more west, then:

> came upon a salt water Creek which led to Port Phillip Bay. We found a fire burning at two native huts and every appearance of their having been occupied the previous night, and on the Beach we found tracks of natives proceeding to Arthur's Seat.[5]

This party, having altered the direction of its line of march by a few points westward after Tubberubbabel, would have walked through Kangerong en route to the mouth of Brokil Creek.

1838

Edward William Hobson settled at Kangerong.[6]

The Hobson family

Edward William Hobson and his brother Edmund Hobson are said to have been born in New South Wales:[7] they were baptised in VDL:[8] their father, also named Edward, was a schoolmaster in the VDL district of Clarence Plains.[9] Edward William was a seaman in his youth in the coastal trade around Australia and New Zealand, with his mother's family the Lutterells. He arrived in Port Phillip in 1837, taking up his first station on the Plenty River.

---

5   Bride 1983[1898]: 11–12. This is the mouth of Tassel's or Brokil Creek, now developed as a marina.
6   Billis and Kenyon 1974[1932]: 83.
7   'Hobson, Edward William (1816 – 1890?)', *Australian Dictionary of Biography*, vol 1: 544.
8   Register of Births, Deaths, Marriages, Archives Office of Tasmania.
9   Clark 2000, vol 5: 246.

Edmund, the much loved and respected doctor, was an heir to his grandfather, Dr Lutterell, and was sent to Europe to obtain his medical qualification. He accompanied Lady Jane Franklin on her overland journey from Port Phillip to Sydney in 1839, and while on a stopover at Port Phillip, he visited Kangerong. In 1840 he returned permanently to Port Phillip with his wife Margaret, spending time at Kangerong while he was convalescing from pulmonary disease. While at Kangerong he travelled by gig to Wul-wul-a-bulluk, the station at Capel Sound, for which he held the licence with his brother, and the place where a substantial house was built by the time the McCrae family took up their run at Arthurs Seat.[10] The Index to Depasturing Licences, 1840 to 1851, shows him to have taken out some licences in his own name, as well as other licences with his brother Edward, and with Dr James Agnew, another connection from VDL, in both the Western Port and Gippsland squatting districts.[11]

Robinson's journal for 1847 records numerous mentions of visiting Dr Hobson, taking tea with him, dining with him, showing interest in the fossil specimens which Edmund, a distinguished naturalist, collected, and corresponding with him while Robinson was away on field trips. When Robinson's wife Maria lay dying in the winter of 1848, Robinson sent a dozen roses to Mrs Hobson which resulted in Mrs Hobson calling the next day: separately, Edmund Hobson called and offered to pray for Mrs Robinson, an offer rejected by Robinson (Dr Godfrey Howitt was Mrs Robinson's physician, not Dr Edmund Hobson).[12]

The mother of Edmund and Edward Hobson, Melvina Hobson nee Lutterell, was known in Port Phillip as George Smith's wife, though exhaustive searches in Tasmanian, New South Wales and Victorian archives reveal no marriage, and she was not buried as Melvina Smith but as Melvina Hobson, widow. She lived with George Smith at Dr Edmond Hobson's Melbourne house Carrencurrenalk, on the south side of the Yarra, near the McCraes at Mayfield, opposite what is now the Studley Park golf course. They had a house as well at Capel Sound.

George Smith had a son known in the records only as Mr Smith Junior (no given name is ever mentioned), and it is not known whether he was Melvina Hobson's son by George Smith or George Smith's son by a previous marriage.[13] Edward Hobson was the first squatter on the Mornington Peninsula, and the extended families, together with their connections, were deeply engaged with the Bonurong.

---

10   Edmund Hobson to Margaret Hobson Ms 8457, Box 865/2B, SLV. This letter is undated but is possibly 1843 as Edmund enquires after 'little Jack'. Edmund and Margaret Hobson had twin boys born Melbourne 1843, one of whom John, died aged five in 1848 the same year as his father. This child is presumably little Jack, see Pioneer Index, Victoria, 1836–1888. In the same year 1848, Margaret Hobson had another set of twins.
11   Button Index, GMF 92/Box 38, SLV; Jane Franklin, GH, Hobart 18 February 1841 to my dear Dr Hobson, Ms 8457, Box 865/1/c, SLV.
12   Clark 2000, vol 5: 205. Mrs Robinson died on 10 August 1848.
13   For George Smith's wife/Melvina/mother of Edward and Edmond, see George Gordon McCrae, Ms 2523/4/c, SLV; for Carrencurrenalk, see Kerr's *Melbourne Almanac* for 1841.

Kangerong was the principal encampment on the Mornington Peninsula and the run functioned for Europeans as well, as the hub of the district. Edward Hobson was helpful to the new chums Alfred and Maurice Meyrick at Boniong; later, he facilitated their brother and cousin Henry Howard Meyrick onto Colourt. Edward Hobson is the pivotal figure in the early history, and it is highly likely that this Bonurong speaking young man, with his good relations with the Bonurong, together with George Smith, his mother's partner, set the tone of the peaceful interactions on the Mornington Peninsula. It is fatuous to dismiss these good relationships as attributable to the fact that the Bonurong were a mild and inoffensive race (a judgement sourced from Henry Howard Meyrick and repeated endlessly in local histories). The Bonurong were no different from any other nation in the Kulin Confederacy in terms of their culture and lifestyle. That there was no conflict at all on the Mornington Peninsula is to be explained in the same terms as conflict is explained in other regions of Victoria, that is, in terms of individual leaders, of social and political agendas of groups, of the tone of relationships both Indigenous and European. It is patronising to label such powerful and distinguished leaders as Old Mr Mann, Koolloorlook, Kurborough, Old Doctor, Bobbinary, Budgery Tom, to name but a few, as 'a mild and inoffensive race'.

Fig 27. 'Tommy Hobson'

Carl Walter photograph, 1866, at Coranderrk; *possibly* related to Edward Hobson's Tommy. Reproduced with the permission of the State Library of Victoria.

As can be seen from the records of their relationships with the Bonurong in this chapter and in the next, Edward Hobson and George Smith seemed genuinely to like them and to respect them; more importantly, these day-to-day records demonstrate that the Bonurong men and women observed Europeans keenly, interpreted European reactions accurately, judged them, criticised them, defied them, manipulated them to get what they wanted, all the while giving precedence in their decision making to their prior tribal relationships: they also retained their freedom of movement throughout their country (except Melbourne).

no date

Kangerong is on a Thomas map which he has annotated 'these places are not put down upon any scale merely [illegible] to show watercourses, names and position regarding the coast'.[14] This map is undated and located now in a miscellaneous collection of equally undated material. But it probably dates from 1839, at the time of Thomas' first walk around the peninsula, and subsequent selection of Tubberubbabel, as he specifically relates the Aboriginal camping places to the creeks they are on, and states that beyond Arthurs Seat there is no creek of any importance, and this latter conclusion was the prime reason for selecting Tubberubbabel.

At the beginning of 1839

'Between my run[15] [Jamieson, at Cape Schanck] and Melbourne, a distance of about 70 miles, there was but one settler Mr Edward Hobson, located at Kangerong at the base of Arthurs Seat'.[16]

4–6 April 1839

Dr Edmund Hobson, who had arrived in Port Phillip with Lady Franklin's party from VDL, en route overland to Sydney, visited his brother Edward at Kangerong. Edmund recorded that he met a very intelligent native at Kangerong, from whom his brother had received great assistance, and who was somewhat of a traveller, having visited VDL and Flinders Island.[17] This man gave him

---

14   Thomas Papers set 214, item 22: 529, ML.

15   The writer is Robert Jamieson at Cape Schanck (Bride 1983[1898]: 90).

16   It was actually Hobson's farm station that was situated at the base of Arthurs Seat, his hut and his cattle paddocks; his other station Kangerong where his sheep were was situated on the lower slopes of Mt Martha. See Map 'Jamieson's Special Survey', SS 5A, 8081, VPRS 8168, PROV.

17   JP Fawkner brought three natives of Port Phillip to VDL in September 1836; one named Dallah Kalkeith returned to Port Phillip from Circular Head (Billot 1982: 95). The other two were Derrimut and Betbenjee, see Plomley 1987: 655. But there is no mention of their going to Flinders Island. William Buckley moved permanently to VDL in 1837. The two Bonurong men who fit this description of having visited Flinders Island and VDL before 1839 are Derrimut and Ben Benger. Ben Benger/Bait Banger/Bedbenji/Ner-rong-er/Nerongho/ Robert Webb/Captain Good, age about 25 in 1839, wife Lygil/Ligee/Lizzie, age 17 in 1839, visited Tasmania with William Buckley in 1836. Ben Benger was a clan head whose country was the Werribee River. He died between June and December 1851. Thomas used him as an example of deep and abiding love in answer to a question on chastity in an enquiry – he and his wife were seldom parted. The other person whom it could have been is Derrimut, but I think this unlikely as Derrimut was known as 'Fawkner's civilised black', and I think it likely that he would have been so described if it were he: future work may make this identification

information about the egg sacks of stingrays and sharks among other things.[18] When the brothers returned to Melbourne for Edmund to resume his escort duties with Lady Franklin, they found that her party had left, but they caught up with them at Craigieburn, and Lady Franklin recorded in her own journal:

> Dr Hobson's brother speaks their language well and has a very intelligent native – his brother is 22 and has 700 or 1000 sheep and 150 cattle – is steady and active – has love of literature.[19]

Later, in 1847, Edmund Hobson operated on the young Bonurong man, Corporal Buckup of the Native Police, an amputation of a leg under ether which saved Buckup's life.[20] Buckup was a son of the Bonurong clanhead Budgery Tom, mentioned so frequently in these early protectorate records, the owner of all the country around Carrum swamp and across to the Western Port Highway.

21 June 1839

In a letter to Robinson of this date Thomas notes that the former natives of John Batman, Bull, Pigeon and Joe the marine have been engaged or decoyed in the service of Mr Smith Junior, son of Mr Smith of the Lamb Inn and are now at Arthurs Seat about 50 miles from Melbourne. They went in a boat.[21]

John Batman's VDL natives

By the time the Sydney Aboriginal men known as John Batman's natives turn up on the Mornington Peninsula, they have a vast amount of experience in dealing with Europeans and Aborigines both in VDL and at Port Phillip and in Pigeon's case, Western Australia. The names by which they were listed on vessels to Port Phillip are as follows – Jno Pigeon, Martin, Bill Bullets, Joe Bangett, Jno Stewart, Old Bull, and Chief Mackey.[22] Batman also brought over two young Tasmanian boys, John Allen and Ben Lomand. Some of these men had been with Batman in his conciliation efforts with the Tasmanian Aborigines; two of them

---

certain. Considering that Robinson stated subsequently, in 1838 before he arrived in Port Phillip as Chief Protector, that his VDL blacks were very friendly with the blacks at Port Phillip (see Chapter 11), the travels of Derrimut and Betbenjee, and the relationship in general, require further research.

18   EC Hobson, 'Diary of a Journey overland from Melbourne to the Hume River with Lady Franklin's party April 1839', Ms 383/09, Box 25/1, SLV.

19   Russell 2002: 38.

20   Chief Protector's report for 1847, Robinson Papers, vol 61: 40, ML. Buckup's biographical details are in Chapter 7.

21   CY 3082, ML. In the next letter of 22 June, Thomas gives details of the following: Robert Bullett and Robert Allen in the service of Mr Newton at Mordialloc; Thomas Warton, ten years old, of Port Phillip living with Mrs Warton; Jack eight years old, living with Mr Arden editor of the *Port Phillip Gazette*, and going to school; Mr Batman's black Jack who went with the dray to supply forage for the horse police and was left at the Goulburn; Bungat removed to Baxter's station at the Goulburn; Sam, removed to Dixon's station at the Goulburn; Pigeon taken by young Smith to Arthur's Seat; Ben Loman at a station at Gellibrand's point, Williamstown; John Allen and Old Bull at Batman's sheep station; Cook was dead, and Pigeon had been given a grant of land in VDL.

22   Plomley 1966: 474.

had received land grants of 100 acres from Governor Arthur; Pigeon had been with the sealers in Bass Strait and was a crewman on board the *Hunter* in 1826; he was left at the Recherche Archipelago and made his way to King George's Sound[23] where he was employed by the first commandant Major Lockyer;[24] he possibly knew, or knew of Bonurong women. All the Sydney blacks of John Batman could speak English and were considered 'civilised'; some of them were present with the Bonurong men Budgery Tom and Kollorlook at the signing of the treaty;[25] some went with Benbow and the other Bonurong men in the parties who went after the men who killed Franks and Flinders; some lived at Batman's hill where the cauldron of rice and jam was kept going round the clock for feeding the Port Phillip people.

Ten of Batman's blacks were present with about 50 Port Phillip Aborigines on Batman's hill at the first public religious service conducted in Port Phillip in April 1836, a Church of England service conducted by the Reverend Joseph Orton.[26] According to the minister, the Aborigines were:

> the largest portion of my congregation … who sat very quietly during the time of service, and seemed particularly interested by the singing.[27]

Of this largest portion of the congregation, Aborigines, Orton went on to describe Batman's Sydney blacks in particular:

> smart, intelligent looking fellows, dressed in red shirts and white trousers, with black handkerchiefs about their necks. The chief of the party was decorated with a full military suit presented to him by Governor Arthur which he wore with ease and grace.

It was a Colonel's uniform, in excellent condition, with the cocked hat and feathers forming the crowning ornament.[28] This uniform was presented honourably to the recipient, a formal recognition of services rendered – not a joke. Neither

---

23   Plomley and Henley 1990: 7; Cumpston 1970: 87.

24   *HRA*, 3rd series, vol vi: 469.

25   One of Batman's initial party, William Todd remained at Indented Head when Batman went back to Tasmania and kept a journal which has survived. He mentions the Sydney blacks Pigeon, Joe and Bull, and says that the local Aborigines' 'joy was beyond anything when they saw them'; Todd also says that the local Aborigines sang the same song at the corroboree that night as the Sydney blacks (William Todd, 'Journal June to November 1835 at Indented Head', Ms 7692, Box 28/11, SLV).

26   Bonwick 1856: 133. Bonwick's informant was an eyewitness, Mr William Willoughby who purchased the Cape Schanck run from Robert Jamieson and later settled at Langwarrin. He was the father of the lost child thought, *wrongly*, to be taken by the Bonurong in 1846. It is still repeated in local histories that the Bonurong took her. In fact at least three children went missing in Bonurong country, the others that I know of being pound-keeper Atkinson's child in 1846 (for whom the Native Police searched), and a child from Barker's station at Cape Schanck in 1850 about whom Jamieson told the McCraes that a sock had been found half a mile from where the child went missing, and they were not going to tell the father of this distressing fact. The myth about Willoughby's child being abducted probably gained credence because, as Thomas noted, Old Maria was known to be very much attached to the child.

27   Rev Joseph Orton's memorandum quoted in Symons 1870: 136–137; Campbell n.d.:165.

28   Bonwick 1856: 133.

Orton nor Bonwick offer any evidence to suggest why the Bonurong and Waworong attended, or what they made of the featured procession of the ten strikingly dressed foreign Aborigines.

When Robinson uses the term 'decoyed' it is more likely to be sour grapes than to reflect the reality of an informed engagement of these men to work at Kangerong.

July 1839

Edward Hobson, Robert Jamieson and George Desailley:

> together with three aboriginal natives [unnamed] carted a whaleboat from Kangerong to Western Port for the purpose of exploring the country in the neighbourhood of that bay[29] ... Mr Hobson's station was on what is now[30] the Point Nepean Road.

George Desailley

George Desailley was another youngster, just 17 years old when he crossed over from VDL. His father was Dr Francis Desailley and his brother was Francis Junior. They arrived in the ill-fated *Britannia* on 1 April 1839: the father went to the Glenelg River, then to Gippsland. The two young brothers went to Edward Hobson's Kangerong station and seemingly formed an outstation for Hobson, marked on Smythe's 1841 map as Tondanue at the back of Rosebud, en route to Boniong. The connection was a family one; Edward Hobson's grandfather, Dr Lutterell, was a friend of both Dr Francis and Dr TA Desailley. The Desailley brothers ended up in the Riverina holding 2,000,000 acres – the largest landholding in New South Wales.[31] Desailley's hut is shown near Tondanue at the back of present Rosebud on a Thomas map.[32]

no date but before August 1839

A work agreement was entered into between Edward William Hobson and three of John Batman's Sydney natives,[33] Pigeon, Joseph and Unnamed. The salaries were 12 pounds 14 shillings and 16 pounds plus board and lodging.[34]

---

29   Bride 1983[1898]: 90.

30   1853.

31   Kenyon, AS Ms 7597, Box 502/7, SLV.

32   VPRS 4410, unit 3/67, PROV.

33   Batman had died in May.

34   *HRV,* vol 2B: 744, 766. There is a large file with documents that show that Robinson's blacks cut adrift, including little Johnny Franklin, the New Holland native from South Australia who came over with his mother Charlotte/Sarah, were also engaged under work agreements which included housing, board, clothing and monthly cash, at VPRS 10, unit 1/334, PROV. Johnny Franklin was put with settler David Hill for no money but instruction in reading and writing plus board, lodging and clothing (*HRV,* vol 2B: 748).

August 1839

Thomas on his first journey to the Mornington Peninsula wrote that:

> A chop tree was the only guide to Arthur's Seat which Mr Hobson with the assistance of the Western Port blacks had marked.

It was a heathy country, he said, between Melbourne and Arthurs Seat, ie sandy, so that though the dray had been there twice, it had not left a track.[35]

17 August 1839

About 2 pm on this day Thomas and his son:

> arrived at the first station, Mr Hobson's, 48 miles from Melbourne ... Mr H made us very comfortable. After taking refreshment we went to the blacks, who were within quarter of a mile.[36]

On 18 August he spent most of the day with the Bonurong and was much surprised to see how comfortable they were compared to what they are when in Melbourne. There was one old man about whom he wrote a comment which is indecipherable, but he said the rest seemed well and happy.[37] A family arrived in 'a very distressed state', consisting of an old man, three lubras and four children.[38] He took a census of the blacks and commenced a vocabulary. On 19 August Thomas saw the signed work agreement papers of the above-mentioned three natives[39] at Hobson's and was 'most pleased to find the straightforward conduct of this settler'.[40]

In his summary of proceedings for August, Thomas adds the further detail that there were 36 in the whole encampment at Kangerong and that he stayed with them till night, and informed them that he was going to live among them and make a miam for his lubra.[41] They were preparing to leave on a five day excursion around their country and they invited him to go with them, and he said he would have accepted the invitation except that his cart had not arrived from Melbourne and he had no provisions and did not want to 'depend on their bounty' at the start of his 'career' among them.

He accompanied the men on their excursion for a while, and then turned back to Hobson's where he found the women and children preparing to depart on a

---

35   Byrt 2004, CD WT 2606 F.DOC.
36   *HRV*, vol 2B: 536. It needs to be noted that Thomas' dates differ by a day in his Summary of Proceedings for August.
37   Thomas Summary of Proceedings for August 1839, CY 3082, ML. Bunggame mentioned in Chapter 3.
38   *HRV*, vol 2B: 536. There is only one family in the records with this structure, the family of the Bonurong chief Old Mr Man.
39   In a draft letter to Robinson, Thomas names the third man as Joe the Marine (CY 3082, ML).
40   Thomas Summary of Proceedings for August 1839, CY 3082, ML.
41   Thomas Summary of Proceedings for August 1839, CY 3082, ML.

three day fishing expedition.[42] Thomas then made his first exploratory journey on foot around the Mornington Peninsula from 21 August to 25 August 'to ascertain the probable resort of the blacks'. He arrived back at Hobson's on 26 August and, presumably on the basis of not finding any other evidence of favourite congregating spots on his five day exploration, nor water, he selected 'the site of my hut where Burrenum [Mr Dredge] said he was born, opposite to a series of waterholes called by the natives Tubberubbabel'.

26 August 1839

Thomas visited the blacks' encampment at Kangerong and was:

> much struck with two blacks cleaning their guns. They had screwdrivers and took the lock to pieces, cleaning the barrel and touch hole as carefully as any white man. Others were employed in sewing skins with sinews of kangaroo, others in stretching skins out on pieces of bark.

Thomas stayed with them till evening.[43]

27 August 1839

Thomas was at his quarters at Tubberubbabel when 'the whole party from Kangerong except the old man pay me a visit'. He wrote that they were 'delighted' to see construction begun on his lubra's miam.[44]

28 August 1839

Thomas visited them early in the day at Kangerong, and on the way he met a party of lubras who were coming to Tubberubbabel to cut bark and tea-tree for him for the construction of his house. He returned to Tubberubbabel at 2 pm to find that his son spoke well of their work and said that they had cut nearly enough bark and tea-tree. Thomas gave them a good feed and they lay down and slept till evening when he sent them home to Kangerong with more flour and sugar.[45]

24 October 1839

After a hazardous journey from Melbourne to Tubberubbabel (bullock dray got stuck several times, his cow got loose and swam a flooded Creek, then her calf followed, then the hobbled bullocks followed and nearly drowned), Thomas got safe to Tubberubbabel at sunset.[46] The next day he visited the natives early at Kangerong, gave them rice and sugar and proposed a spot for them to erect their miams 'of which they promise to do the following morning'. Next day,

---

42   Thomas Summary of Proceedings for August 1839, CY 3082, ML.
43   Thomas Journal, *HRV*, vol 2B: 538.
44   Thomas Journal, *HRV*, vol 2B: 538.
45   Thomas Journal, *HRV*, vol 2B: 539.
46   Thomas Journal, *HRV*, vol 2B: 554.

26 October 1839, he visited early 'the natives' principal encampment about 1 mile southwest of my hut'. The principal encampment is Kangerong: his hut, the site for his Protectorate station, is Tubberubbabel. The natives 'break their encampment with Mr Hobson, said goodbye' and all followed him to Tubberubbabel by noon.[47]

They agreed to move to Tubberubbabel because Thomas told them the government would ration them there. But the rations were meagre, and they complained that it was not like the good rations they received from Batman and Fawkner. Thomas was repeatedly called back to Melbourne by the Chief Protector, and though he left his wife and children at Tubberubbabel, and his son William Jackson Thomas squatted at Tuerong, and though Thomas and Mrs Thomas and their son often distributed personal supplies to the blacks, there was seldom enough to feed everybody.

1840

On a list of placenames 'Kangerong – Mr Hobson's Station'.[48]

11 January 1840

Thomas visited Kangerong; there were 19 natives there, two of whom were ill. He bid them come to Tubberubbabel and attempted to teach six children their letters, but they showed very little anxiety to learn: they can repeat the letters by heart, but do not recognise them when shown. A marginal note records that the sick people at Kangerong were Maria who was Mr King's mother, and Kurblene aged 11 years who was one of the sons of Old Doctor and who appeared to be in a decline.[49]

Old Doctor/Won-go-no/Wonggonar/Wongoro/ Wongona/Wongurn

His country was Kurrun, the flat country from Moody Yallock to Konnigo, including Horsfold's and the great Marsh [Carrum swamp] (Principal families and the countries they claim, CY 3130, frame 32).

Jul 1839 – Doctor/WON-GO-NO (Name taken in encampment, Thomas 'A' Diary, set 214, item 1, ML).

11 Jan 1840 – Thomas visited Kangerong and attended to those who were ill; Kurblening a youth aged 11, Old Doctor's son appeared to

47 Thomas Journal, *HRV*, vol 2B: 554.
48 Thomas Papers set 214/2, item 1, ML; Byrt 2004, CD WT 2605 N.DOC.
49 CY 2605, item 1, ML.

be in a decline (CY 2605, item 1, ML); Feb 1840 – On Thomas' list of those not going to Western Port on the raid is Dr and his family who are going to Moody Yallock, a party of 5 (Thomas 2605, frame 8, ML); 13 Apr 1840 – Prior to the fight, still encamped on South side of river, Old Doctor and 6 of his family (CY 2605, item 1, ML); 22 Apr 1840 – Thomas and the Bonurong were camped at Moody Yallock en route to Tubbarubbabel, and Doctor and his family joined us (CY 2604, item 3, ML); 16 May 1840 – The Doctor and family except one youth very ill leave Buckermittawarra for the limeburners (CY 2604, item 3, ML); 12 Jun 1840 – Old Doctor and family, six persons in all are at Turtgurruk (CY 2604, ML); 24 Jun 1840 – Doctor has three children (CY 2604, item 3, ML); 9 Aug 1840 – Described by Hobson's drayman as a tall man, known to be well disposed (CY 2604, ML); 15 Aug 1840 – Saturday, the whole of the Western Port blacks are at Melbourne except Doctor and his family who are at Pt Nepean (CY 2604, item 3, ML); on a list from 1840 of Principal Families is Old Doctor Wongurn c. and Beurar l. bracketed together as a couple, parents, plus their children Morap c. Kurberener c. Pourrut l. and Wilwilrup l. (CY 2605, item 1, ML); Doctor and his family were one of four families staying with Henry Howard Meyrick at Narren–Gullen station at the back of Mt Eliza towards the end of 1840; Doctor performed an operation on Cognamine Wongill alias Lively, who was sick with a pain in the breast. Doctor placed the patient on his back, knelt at his side and pummelled his chest 'most unmercifully'. All of a sudden Doctor jumped up and showed the onlookers a large nail which he said he pulled out of the chest of the patient; he started singing, threw the nail into the sea and stated that he had cured the patient; and he had – next day Lively went kangarooing with Meyrick (HH Meyrick in Hales and Le Cheminant 1997: 14).

7 Jul 1842 – WONGGONAR, male, aged 60, married, died at Mahun Western Port, most celebrated Doctor (CY 3082, first doc on reel, ML).

1846 – On 'Family Connections Census' are Old Doctor's widow, Boorowrook and her two daughters, Wilwilrook aged 10 and Borut aged 8 (CY 3083, ML).

1861 – In an estray dated 1861, Thomas lists a Boorut, a female, lubra of Andrew a Gippsland man, with two children who are a male aged six years named Wandum, and a half caste aged two years, all of whom are with Mr Green at Coranderrk (CY 2984: 235, ML).

17 January 1840

Thomas visited Hobson but he was out. Thomas took the opportunity to reprimand Pigeon for making free with the lubras.[50]

28 January 1840

Police Magistrate Captain William Lonsdale wants to know from Thomas whether there are any new Aborigines at Kangerong.[51]

9 May 1840

Thomas recorded 23 Aborigines at Hobson's and Merricks.[52]

11 May 1840

Thomas found the whole of the blacks at Kangerong, 122 of them.[53]

13 May 1840

Thomas gave further details of the encampment at Kangerong described as 'about 5 miles W of Tuerong. Give them charge not to Encamp or near in a brush paddock of Mr Hobson at Kangerong'.[54] In a report to Robinson, Thomas noted that they were camped 'on a rise by Kangerong by Mt Martha'.[55]

16 May 1840

Mr Man and family and the young men return to Kangerong.[56]

27 May 1840

Thomas, sick from an illness he attributes to his leaky tent roof, learned from his son that the blacks who left Tubberubbabel on Monday 25 May are at Kangerong. Thomas visited and found 104.[57]

29 May 1840

Thomas visited the blacks' encampment at Kangerong only to find they had shifted to Bukkumetterawarra by Arthurs Seat.[58]

---

50   CY 2605, item 1, frame 35, ML.
51   Thomas Journal CY 2605, item 1, ML.
52   Thomas Journal, CY 2605, item 1, ML.
53   Thomas Journal, CY 2604, item 3, ML.
54   Thomas Journal, CY 2605, item 1, ML.
55   Thomas Second Periodical Report, 7 November 1840, VPRS 4410, unit 3/67, PROV.
56   Thomas Journal, CY 2604 item 3, ML.
57   Thomas Journal, CY 2604, item 3, ML.
58   Thomas Journal, CY 2604, item 3, ML.

27 July 1840

Ganjerong is Mr Thomas Senior's second station, one mile from Tubberubberbil. Robinson visited 'Gan.jer.rong' with Thomas the next day and recorded the added information that Thomas' third station was called 'Bag.her.me.dare. re.wur.er'.[59]

9 August 1840

This is a Sunday, and Thomas normally does not travel but he has gone to Buckkermitterrwarrer to investigate an alleged assault on Hobson's dray travelling the road between Buckkermitterwarrer and Kangerong. The assault took place within 400 yards of the hut at Kangerong, and Thomas records that there are 11 hands with the carpenters living there at Kangerong.[60]

August 1840

Superintendent La Trobe made a four day visit to Arthurs Seat and Cape Schanck but made no mention of Aborigines.

August 30

With Elliot Herriot, he having taken up a run at Cape Schanck adjacent to James Thomson's. A long ride. The last part in the dark to Hobson's. Very little of the intervening country taken.

August 31

Up. Camp the second night on the shore of Capel Sound. Explore the country towards the Schanck on one hand, and towards Pt Nepean on the other. Visit the site of Collins Settlement (1802). Greatly struck with the character of the long point separating the Bay and the Schanck and terminating in Pt Nepean – Sand dunes – The oak forest – & "cups and saucers". Failed to reach the Point. No station at Arthur's Seat till long after this, nor on the point beyond a few limeburners who may have been already there.

September 1

Camp at Creek

September 2

Hobson's

---

59   Clark 1988, vol 1: 356, 357.
60   Thomas Journal, CY 2604, item 3, ML.

September 3

Return home.[61]

1840 or 1841

Hobson's and Kangerong are both marked on a Thomas map of the Western Port District.[62]

29 January 1841

Hobson's station is shown on another Thomas map of the Western Port District.[63]

22 May 1841

Thomas visited Tubberubbabel, Kangerong, Bukkerrmerderra and Deangeong only to find all the Aborigines had gone to Melbourne. Slept at his son's station at Tuerong.[64]

1841

Description of Hugh Jamieson's Survey 'County of [blank on original], parish of Kangerong near Mt Martha. Bounded on the west by Port Phillip Bay, on the north by a line about 10 chains south of Mt Martha bearing East 328 chains 75 links, on the East by a line bearing South 160 chains and on the South by a line bearing West 369 chains 75 links'.[65]

23 June 1841

Assistant Protector William Thomas in a formal petition to the Governor of New South Wales Sir George Gipps:

> prays that no more Special Surveys be disposed of in his District without the Protector being consulted whether or not the Aborigines can dispense with the same ... there are four blocks already disposed of in Your Petitioner's District, three of the four are a serious loss to the Aborigines, viz that block by the coast by the Red Bluff [Henry Dendy's Special Survey, 5180 acres at Brighton and Moorabbin, which Liardet painted],[66] that block by Mt Martha [Hugh Jamieson's Special Survey of

---

61   Charles Joseph La Trobe, Australian Notes 1839–1854, Dates of Journeys etc, Ms 130003, vol 4, SLV.
62   VPRS 4410, PO unit 3, item 67, PROV.
63   This map was formerly located with its correspondence at VPRS 11, Box 7, no 365, but has been re-located to VPRS 6760/PO unit 1, item 1, PROV. It is also reproduced in *HRV*, vol 2B: 578–579.
64   Thomas Journal, CY 2605, item 5, ML.
65   VPRS 14152/P 0001, unit 000001, PROV.
66   *HRV*, vol 6: 380. The fourth Special Survey which was not mentioned as a site of importance for fishing was Henry Elgar's Special Survey of 5180 acres at Boroondara and Nunawading.

5180 acres including Kangarong, Tubberubbabel and Bukkerrmerderra], and the splendid swamp by the Yarra [Frederick Wright Unwin's Special Survey of 5180 acres at Bulleen], all favourable fishing places.[67]

July 1841

Kangerong, Dr Hobson's cattle station is shown as a rectangle with a waterhole on Thomas H Nutt's 'Plan of a Special Survey containing five thousand one hundred and twenty acres selected by Hugh Jamieson Esq in the Parish of Kangerong County of [blank on original]'[68] Mornington filled in by another hand subsequently.

no date but probably July 1841

Hobson's is marked on a third Thomas map.[69]

13 November 1841

Canjerung – the rectangular homestead site including a water pool is marked on George D Smythe's 'Survey the Coast of Port Phillip from the Mouth of Tangenong Creek to Arthur's Seat'.[70]

14 January 1842

Thomas took Budgery Tom to Kangerong.[71]

8 September 1843

Thomas in Melbourne was concerned for the welfare of his blacks and went to enquire along the beach. He called at a number of native encampments for which he gave the native name, and in the margin, the squatter occupying the run. These places were Boollerim – Mr Shannessey, Binningean – Captain Baxter[72] and Ballewrungan – Mr Gorringe[73] where he stopped the night having travelled 43 miles on horseback. He found no blacks. Next day he visited Tuerong then Kangerong and heard at Kangerong that the blacks were at Kulluck. The next day was a Sunday; even so, he rode from Tuerong to Kulluk and found the blacks. They then came to Tuerong and encamped by a Creek, about 30 of them, all Western Ports except one Barrabool lubra and her child. 'The poor children and lubras look very sadly', he wrote ' – poor creatures'.[74]

---

67 Enclosure to VPRS 10, unit 3, 1841/909, PROV.

68 Special Survey 5, VPRS 8168, P/1, PROV.

69 Thomas uncat Ms set 214, item 22: 547, ML.

70 CS 81a, VPRS 8168, P/1, PROV.

71 Thomas Journal, CY 2605, item 5, ML.

72 We know this as the run Carup Carup.

73 Ballewrungan is Poleorongong, the important encampment at the back of Mt Eliza.

74 Thomas Journal, CY 2606, item 2, ML. Thomas crossed out another sentence in this days' entry for which the verb cannot be read. It looks like a matter of regret for the station they once had.

17 January 1844

Mortgagee's Sale advertised in the *Sydney Morning Herald*, of Jamieson's Special Survey, 5120 acres plus a cottage on the estate, and other improvements, to be held in Sydney on 8 February.[75]

15 February 1844

Georgiana McCrae recorded that Captain and Mrs Reid, Mr Jamieson, Mr McCrae and 'myself' went on horseback to inspect the Survey. Alighted at Kangerong House.

19 April 1844

Mr McCrae and Mr Jamieson started for Kangerong.

11 June 1845

Mr Russell (government surveyor) and party arrive for the survey of 6000 acres.[76]

11 July 1845

Mr McCrae leaves tomorrow for Kangerong, to ride with Mr Jamieson for Melbourne.[77]

1 November 1845

Superintendent La Trobe and Commandant Henry Dana of the Native Police visited Mt Eliza, Karangerong, Arthurs Seat, Cape Schanck and the Pulpit Rock. Next day La Trobe noted 'the fine wild view' and had a long ride after kangaroo with Barker and Dana on the western side of the peninsula. On the following day he started before breakfast and rode to Arthurs Seat, thence to town, leaving Dana at the end of the Long Beach. He arrived back in his Melbourne office at 1 pm.[78]

no date but after 1845

'Not far from our old Devonian neighbours lived the holders of the Kangerong Special Survey, three brothers, gentlemen by birth, breeding and education, capital horsemen and the best of neighbours. Their weatherboard house an unpretending structure well finished with nooks, stockwhips and branding irons, sufficiently spoke to its owners — one a bit of a dandy, another a reading man and the third like each of the others, an out and out bushman'.[79] The three Jamieson brothers were Bushby, Hugh J and Archibald J.[80]

---

75   *Sydney Morning Herald*, Wednesday 17 January 1844: 4.
76   Weber 2001: 546.
77   McCrae 1966: 127, 137, 195.
78   Charles Joseph La Trobe, 'Memoranda of Journeys...', vol 1, no 37, Ms 130003, Box 79/1, safe, SLV.
79   George Gordon McCrae, 'Experiences not exploits', vol 3, Ms 2523/4/c, SLV. These are the Jamieson brothers.
80   McCrae 1987: 62.

Bush/Bushby/Busby/Busby Jamieson/ Trooper Bushby Jamieson

He came from the Vale of Tempe cattle station, owned by the Jamieson brothers, purchased by William Kyle's father, renamed Tarcomb: it was west of the Tallarook ranges, over the Goulburn River. This black in particular was always ready to help us, taught us tracking, knowledge of distances, of direction for travelling, the necessity of caution. He would say 'plenty wild blackfellows alonga there' … very intelligent and useful, afterwards joined the Mounted Police under Captain Dana and Lt Walsh.[I]

13 Sep 1845 – Trooper Bush arrived with troop horse Panekin and very insolent.

4 Jul 1850 – Trooper Bushby returned from Melbourne [to Native Police Corps HQ at Nerre Nerre Warren] bringing the two horses belonging to Mr Powlett; 28 Aug 1850 – Trooper Bushby arrived from Melbourne with despatches to send Corporal O/Bryan and a trooper to escort a prisoner from Mt Macedon; 29 Aug 1850 – Corporal Gellibrand and Trooper Bushby left for Melbourne; 17 Oct 1850 – Trooper Bushby arrived from Melbourne with letters for the Commandant; 19 Oct 1850 – His Honor left the station accompanied by Troopers Marambool [Warworong man] and Bushby; 25 Oct 1840 – Troopers Bushby and Tommy in Melbourne; 14/15 Nov 1850 – Troopers Bushby and Condine are to attend drill [the day after the opening of Princes Bridge which the Corps attended]; 24 Dec 1850 – Trooper Bushby left for Melbourne with letters from the Commandant.

9 Apr 1851 – Trooper Bushby arrived from Melbourne with despatches; 10 Apr 1851 – he departed; 24 Apr 1851 – Trooper Bushby arrived from Melbourne; 2 May 1851 – Corporal Cohen and Troopers Souwester [Port Fairy], Robinson, Isaacs relieved Bushby, Peter and Condine who returned to station; 3 May 1851 – parade and pay; 14 May 1851 – Troopers Bushby and Condine to stockade [the Native Police Corps were the first guards at Pentridge]; 19 Jul 1851 – Troopers Paddy and Murray left for Pentridge to replace Troopers Bushby and Sam deserted (all 'Dandenong Daybook', VPRS 90, PROV). 1 to 31 May 1851 – Trooper Bushby, pay abstract, receiving one and a half pence per day, three shillings and ten and a half pence per month (VPRS 29, vol 55: 127, PROV).

I. 'Reminiscences of William Kyle', Victorian Historical Magazine 10(3), June 1925: 160.

January 1846

On Thomas' 'Boongurong Family Connections Port' census of this date, he lists the sections of the Boonwurrong, the places they belong to, the names, sex and age of the people. Kangerong is a section. It has only three people – Bobbinary, male, widower; Yal Yal, male 20 and Boyyerup, female 23.[81]

Disappearance of Willoughby's child

Even today, secondary sources are on our library shelves which state that the Bonurong stole this child. They did not. Because the alleged perpetrators ended up at Kangerong, the recovered evidence is presented here. I regard the Aboriginal evidence as truthful: Billy Lonsdale himself organised the checking, and the women would not lie to him.

6 March 1846

The Chief Protector having ordered Thomas to Western Port to investigate the disappearance of Mr Willoughby's child, Thomas was at Willoughby's station (Lang Warren) helping to search for the child who had gone missing from the No Good Damper Inn. At Ruffy's station (Mahun) he learned that Lummer Lummer, Nerreninen, Worrakup, Korrabak and Old Maria happened to be passing at about the time the child wandered off, and everyone knew that 'This lubra [Maria] had previously shewn a favourable fond disposition for the child'.

Next day, Thomas accompanied Mr Willoughby six miles to Mrs Martha King's station on Kings Creek at present Hastings, where Mr Sage (Captain Baxter's future son-in-law, later of Sage's cottage) and Mr Meyrick (Henry Howard of Coolart) assured him that Old Maria was at the Heads on the day that the child disappeared. Thomas and Willoughby walked back to Lang Warren and Thomas insisted that the pond be drained. No body was found. Then he went back to Mr Ruffy's only to find that there had been a mistake in the earlier evidence – Old Maria was confirmed as not being with the four male Bonurong when the little girl wandered off. Thomas then learned the details at the No Good Damper Inn.

The mother of the child had recently been confined of another child at the No Good Damper Inn. The little girl, about four years old, followed her father to the stockyards about 100 yards away. While they were at the stockyard, a boy in charge of some cattle came and told Mr Willoughby that the cattle were lost. Mr Willoughby promptly left, believing as he said, that the child would go back the 100 yards to the No Good Damper Inn. After about an hour, the father returned from the lost cattle and discovered that the child was missing.

---

81   Thomas Papers, Family Connections Census, CY 3083, ML.

Immediate searches proved fruitless, and the child's body, mangled by native cats, was not found till three weeks later, less than one and a quarter to one and a half miles away.

A fortnight after the child went missing, but before the body was found, Billy Lonsdale told Thomas that on hearing of the disappearance of the child and the rumour, he (Billy Lonsdale) sent a young man to Point Nepean to check on Old Billy's lubra and Jack's lubra, and that they did not have the child, nor had they seen it. They were now at Kangerong.[82]

Undated but between 7 May 1847 and 6 September 1848

In Georgiana's own account of young Myrnong hiding in the chimney of Georgiana's bedroom to escape from her husband, she recorded that Myrnong escaped to Kangerong where she was waddied (Hugh Gordon's edition states that she escaped to the Survey).[83]

1848

Liardet would like to lease portion of Jamieson's Survey and have a boat and seine net … would be a pleasant neighbour.[84]

21 December 1852

Superintendent La Trobe, having gone down from Melbourne to Point Lonsdale in the pilot boat, crossed the bay to look at the *Ticonderoga* moored off the Quarantine Station, then rode to Settlement Point, then to the Burrell's at Arthurs Seat, then to 'the Survey' and on to Balcombe's and Melbourne.[85]

---

82   Thomas Journal, CY 2606, frames 338–342, ML.
83   Weber 2001: 610.
84   McCrae 1966: 255.
85   Charles Joseph La Trobe, 'Memoranda of Journeys…', vol 2, no 83, Ms 130003, Box 79/1, safe, SLV.

6. Buckkermitterwarrer, Protectorate third station

> Buckkermitterwarer/Buckkermitterwarrer/Bukkumitterar/
> Bagermedarewurerer/Bag er me dare re wur er/Bakmedarroway
> Creek/ Backerrmarderrewarra/Baggamahjarrawah/
> Buckkamitterrawar/ Bukkumetterawarra/Bukkermitterawarrar/
> Buckemerdurra/Bagometerorer Mr Hobson's Farm Station/
> Buckkumitterawarra/Buckkermitterwarer/Bogometerorer Mr
> Hob* Farm Station/ Packomedurrawurra/Bag.er.me.dare.re.wur.
> rer – Mr Thomas Senior's third station/Buckermerderra Warra/
> Buckermerderwarra/Packomedurrawurra/Bukkumitterar/ BUKKU^AI

I. The above names are the various spellings as they appear in the records.

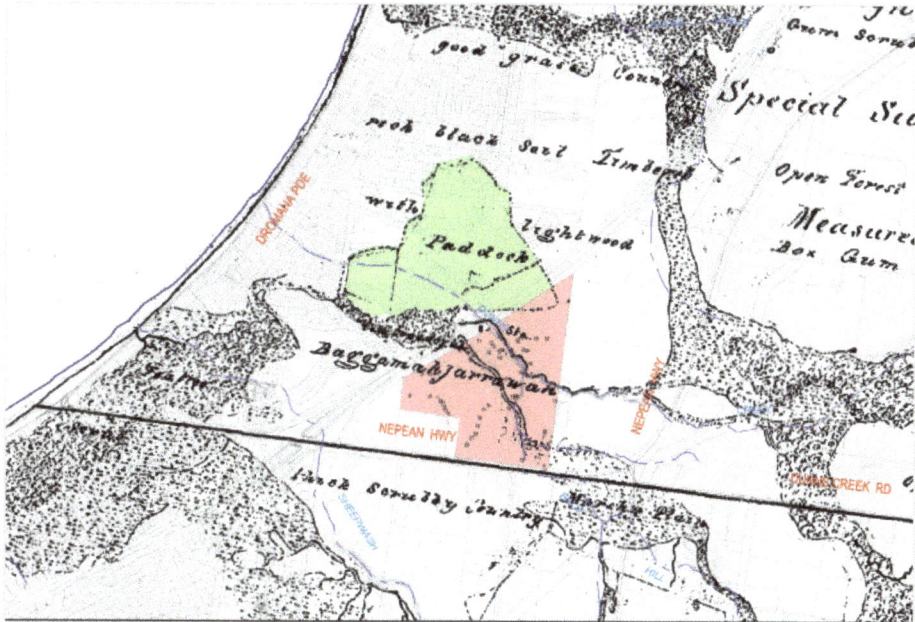

Fig 28. 'Fels/Hughes Composite Map',

Cadastral overlay on Smythe 1841 and Nutt 1841, showing Edward Hobson's fenced paddocks, the location of his hut marked *Sta, and the proposed development. The two base maps are © Crown (State of Victoria), 2010, all rights reserved, reproduced with the permission of the Surveyor General of Victoria.

Buckkermitterwarrer, the third Protectorate station was where Edward William Hobson actually lived (see map). La Trobe camped here on 30 August 1840.

It has links with the distant past as the site of the pre-contact massacre when almost half the Bonurong were killed in a dawn raid by their traditional enemies the Kurnai of Gippsland (see Chapter 8).

It has links with the colonial past – it was the place where the young girl named Barebun also known as Mary, who was both daughter of the Bonurong chief Benbow and wife of the Waworong chief Billibellary, was assaulted: from here two gentlemen, Mr Hobson and Mr Meyrick caught and saddled their horses at 10 pm on a cold Sunday night in May and rode seven miles to the Assistant Protector to report the assault – an expression of concern unseen anywhere else in the ethnographic literature.

It was Barebun/Mary's brother, Yankee Yankee, also known as Robert Cunningham, who was the boy abducted off the beach in 1833 who subsequently turned up at the encampment at Merri Creek in Melbourne in 1841 with such an astonishing story that Thomas was at first disbelieving. He had been taken in the kidnappers' ship to Preservation Island in Bass Strait, then made his way to Launceston, then to the Swan River settlement where he worked for two years; he then took passage to Adelaide where he worked a further two years for two masters. He then took ship for Melbourne (see Chapter 11). Yankee Yankee was the Bonurong man who subsequently accused Thomas of bad faith in promising the Bonurong the place known as Kullurk/Coolart as their reserve, and then not delivering on the promise (see Chapter 7).

The site may have a link with Coranderrk. The Mr Tommy known as Hobson's black, who went to Gippsland with him, is more than likely to be the Tommy who went to California with George Smith, and may be the same Tommy Hobson who ended up at Coranderrk where he was photographed prior to 1866: more research is needed.

Thomas described Buckkermitterwarrer as a model station, good for the blacks: it seems that there was scarcely a day when some Bonurong were not there. He called it a dormitory suburb of the head Protectorate station Tubberubbabel. All the references to the place are presented here in chronological order.

It has significance in the present: it has an extension to 2013 of a valid planning permit granted by the Victorian Civil and Administrative Tribunal, to start to build 'a Holiday Resort incorporating a winery, a function centre, a restaurant, a residential hotel, a caravan and camping park and a golf driving range'.[1] Its initial Cultural Management Plan was rejected by Aboriginal Affairs Victoria, but after archaeological excavations the developer has submitted another which has been approved. Archaeological excavations have demonstrated extensive use of the site, with one sample dated to 6000 BP. It is in the Green Wedge Zone.

---

1   VCAT reference no P1025/2006; Permit application no P05/2642; VCAT Extension reference P1942/2009.

Buckkermitterwarrer is virtually unknown, not featuring in any of our histories, but it should be there. The following chapter is a chronological record of observations about the site.

no date

Bagometterorer, Mr Hobson's Farm Station, is on a list of Aboriginal placenames which Thomas recorded in his journal.[2]

no date

'Backerrmadderrewaarra, inland from Arthur's Seat'.[3]

no date

'Buckermerderra Warra is two miles from Kangerong. A Tea Tree creek empties itself into arm of the swamp between Bukermerderwarra and the Coast'.[4]

no date

Shown as Buckerrmorderrewarra on a creek line on Thomas' map entitled Tuerong and surrounds.[5]

17 August 1835

The settlers on board Fawkner's *Enterprise* commanded by Captain Lancey landed at Arthurs Seat and returned to the ship in the evening.[6]

March 1836

John Aitken's brig the *Chile*, bringing stock from VDL, ran aground near Dromana and he was forced to unload the sheep at Arthurs Seat. He described his contact with the Bonurong thus: 'With reference to the natives – On landing at Arthur's Seat, they were most friendly, assisting me to land my sheep, etc. About 80 was the number I then saw, being the Western Port tribe, some of whom accompanied me in my journey round the Bay to Melbourne'.[7]

June 1839

Thomas reports that three of John Batman's VDL blacks, named Bull, Pigeon and Joe, have been engaged or decoyed in the service of Mr Smith Junior, son of Mr George Smith of the Lamb Inn Melbourne, at Arthurs Seat, about 50 miles from Melbourne: they went in a boat.[8]

---

2 Thomas Journal, CY 2605, item 1, ML.
3 Thomas Journal, CY 2984, ML.
4 Thomas Journal, CY 2984, Map p. 543, ML.
5 Thomas Papers, set 214/22: 529, ML.
6 Billot 1982: 5.
7 Bride 1983[1898]: 49.
8 Thomas to Robinson, CY 3082: 7, 13, ML. Edward Hobson transported stores and people from Melbourne to Dromana by ship, and thence by dray via Buckkermitterwarrer to Kangerong. It is believed that he and his

17 August 1839

About 2 pm on this day Thomas and his son 'arrived at the first station, Mr Hobson's, 48 miles from Melbourne ... Mr H made us very comfortable. After taking refreshment we went to the blacks, who were within quarter of a mile'.[9] On 18 August he spent most of the day with them and was much surprised to see how comfortable they were compared to what they are when in Melbourne. There was one old man about whom he wrote a comment which is indecipherable, but he said the rest seemed well and happy. He took a census of the blacks. On 19 August Thomas saw the signed work agreement papers of the above-mentioned three natives[10] at Hobson's and was 'most pleased to find the straightforward conduct of this settler'.[11]

25 December 1939

Samuel Rawson returned with his business partner Robert Jamieson to Edward Hobson's hospitable hut at Arthurs Seat to celebrate Christmas with Hobson, Mr and Mrs Smith, the Meyrick cousins Alfred and Maurice, and George Desailley. He described the hut as having walls full of holes, a roof covered with bark through the crevices of which a person might have crept with the greatest ease, and an earth floor,[12] situated in the middle of the eternal forest when till 18 months before a white man had never trod.[13]

Robert Jamieson

Samuel Rawson and Robert Jamieson were fellow cabin passengers in the *Florentia* on the voyage out to New South Wales in 1838. Jamieson bought the Cape Schanck run for just under 4000 pounds sterling, including 750 cattle, drays, horses, six months stores and the station. He bought it on terms with three years to pay off, and Rawson bought in for 1000 pounds, which was the amount of Jamieson's second term payment due 1 January 1840. At this time, they were in the process of moving the whole enterprise to better grazing land at the head of Western Port, the pastoral runs Tobinerk and Yallock. They did well initially in the highly speculative market; Rawson informed his father in England at the end of 1840 that the station and stock at Western Port were worth just over 8000 pounds. But then came the economic crash.

---

brother Dr Edmund Hobson owned the *Rosebud* after which the town is named (Cole 1984: 82). This could not have been Hobson's first boat, a mere dinghy capable of being carried by two people across the beach, see Samuel Rawson's Journal, November 1839, 204/1, NLA.

9   *HRV*, vol 2B: 536. It needs to be noted that Thomas' dates differ by a day in his Summary of Proceedings for August.

10   In a draft letter to Robinson, Thomas names the third man as Joe the Marine (CY 3082, ML).

11   Thomas Summary of Proceedings for August 1839, CY 3082, ML.

12   Rawson Papers, Ms 204/1, NLA.

13   This suggests a mid-1838 occupation by Hobson.

Samuel Rawson

Samuel Rawson was just 20 years old at this time, having arrived from England in the *Florentia*. He had family capital to invest, but was himself ambivalent about a career in the army, or life as a squatter. He did both, first trying the squatting then accepting a commission in the 28th Regiment, which left Sydney for India in 1842. The National Library has a large collection of his papers, including journals and letters, of which the most valuable for present purposes are his 'Journal from 1839 kept while forming a new station at Western Port on the southern coast of New Holland' and 'Journal of an expedition after some VDL blacks'.[14]

This latter expedition in November 1841, to apprehend Bob and Jack, Trucaninni, Fanny and Matilda who killed the two whalers named William Cook and The Yankee in the vicinity of the coal mines at Cape Paterson, had all the elements of an impending disaster – a classic massacre: there was a large party of armed Europeans including government officials, Commissioner of Crown Lands Powlett, Assistant Protector Thomas, Lt Vignolles and eight of his soldiers, settlers including Jamieson, Hobson, Rawson, Mundy, plus eight Bonurong and Waworong trackers including Warwardor (Lively), Billy Langhorne (Nunuptune), Warrengitalong, Poky Poky (Johnny's father see Chapter 10), Beruke (Gellibrand), Buller Bullup (Mr McArthur) and Buckup (Budgery Tom's son), plus Pigeon, the VDL black formerly with Batman, but now with Hobson.

But *nothing happened* – the party simply captured the five VDL blacks. This expedition requires a fresh look, a comparison with later similar expeditions into Gippsland and the western district which did end in massacres, in an effort to discover what made the difference.

10 January 1840

The blacks having left Melbourne on 6 January,[15] Thomas arrived in his district and collected 65 from the 'suburbs' of Tubberubbabel which were Buckkermitterwarrer and Kangerong. They remained all day with him then went back to their suburbs.[16]

---

14 Rawson, Ms 204/1, NLA. Included are some accounts made out to Rawson by George Smith of the Lamb Inn Melbourne, for a stay from 25–27 March 1839, breakfast 2/6, dinner 2/6, bed 2/6, horse stabling and feed 6/- (Ms 204/9, folder 3, NLA).
15 Thomas Journal, CY 2604, item 3, ML.
16 Thomas Journal, CY 2605, item 1, ML.

First week in May 1840

With Maurice and Alfred Meyrick, and Messers Hobson and Brodribb, Henry Howard Meyrick, just arrived from England, rode from Melbourne down to Packomedurrawurra which is the name of Hobson's Station.[17]

9 May 1840

23 blacks were encamped at Hobson's farm.[18]

10 May 1840

At 10 pm on this Sunday night, two gentlemen, Hobson and Meyrick, rode from Buckkermitterwarrer (near Dromana drive-in) to Thomas's son's station at Tuerong (near the intersection of Balnarring Road with Old Moorooduc Road) where Thomas and the Bonurong were encamped. The gentlemen informed Thomas of a 'gross outrage' on an Aboriginal girl called Mary at Mr Hobson's farm station at Buckkermitterrwarrer, seven miles away to the south, near Arthurs Seat. Thomas could not catch his horse in the dark, probably because he had no night paddock or yards, but the gentlemen assured him that the girl was safe in the house with the gentry.[19]

Thomas owned a pretty little Arabian mare named Bess, for whom he paid £60.[20] (When she later took ill and collapsed under him while he was riding her, he wept, and stayed out in the bush with her all night with no food, and no matches to light a fire; he was forced to leave her next day by a creek but she was caught subsequently, and brought home, and she recovered.)[21] But at this time she was heavily in foal, as well as having a colt running at foot. Robinson noted this in his journal, criticising Thomas because he was still drawing forage at two shillings and sixpence per day for the mare.[22] Presumably, Robinson thought she should be turned out on pasture, not working, in which case Thomas would not be eligible for the forage allowance. It was one of Robinson's numerous criticisms of Thomas when in fact it was Robinson who was to line his pockets in a big way in land and gold speculation.

11 May 1840

At daybreak Thomas rode to Buckkermitterwarrer, Mr Hobson's farm station, and took the sworn depositions of Mr Smith and two of Hobson's men: he also took a deposition from the Aboriginal girl. He then 'Visited the natives

---

17   Hales and Le Cheminant 1997: 10.
18   Thomas Journal, CY 2605, item 1, ML.
19   Thomas to Robinson, VPRS 11, unit 7, item 307, PROV; Thomas Report, 7 November 1840, enc to 40/12629 in 4/2512.1, AO of NSW; CY 2604, item 3, and CY 2605, item 1, ML; also Byrt 2004, CD WT 2946, 11 May DOC.
20   She carried him through all his bush journeyings (William Jackson Thomas, CY 3106, frame 60, ML).
21   Thomas Journal, 11, 12 and 19 March 1841, CY 2605, item 5, ML.
22   Clark 1998, vol 1: 358.

encampment at Bukker about 24 men women and children, was much pleased at seeing 2 Lubras wash as well and handy as a Laundress in London. Men and boys making fence, in fact Stations of this kind are a benefit to the Aborigines'.[23]

The gross outrage on Mary

Her real name was Barebun. She was not just an ordinary girl: she was a high-status individual being a daughter of Baddourup/Big Benbow,[24] who was a son of the most influential clan head of the Bonurong, and who was also a brother to King Benbow. Mary's mother was Barbungrook/Old Maria, and her brother was Yankee Yankee/Robert Cunningham, who was abducted as a young boy off the beach at Point King by sealers about 1834, and walked back into the Bonurong encampment in Melbourne in 1841 after seven years working at the Swan River and Adelaide.[25] Mary had been given in marriage to Billibellary, the Waworong chief, in November 1839, but she ran away from the marriage back to her father Benbow. Billibellary had woken up in the morning to find her missing, so he went to Benbow's miam with a tomahawk, cut her head and dragged her back by the hair to his own miam.[26] Thomas scolded Billibellary regarding his cruelty to his new young wife. But then her father waddied her because she would not stay with Billibellary and Thomas took her to the colonial surgeon because he thought her arm was broken.[27]

Clearly with the knowledge of the protector,[28] she was living as a companion/servant/adoptee/protégé of Mr and Mrs George Smith. Thomas wrote to Robinson that she had made herself very useful to the Smiths, having been with them for some time. She slept in the same apartment with them (by that, the very proper Thomas meant that she slept in the house, not the servants' hut), and travelled with the Smiths wherever they go; she spoke English well, and Mr Smith proposed teaching her to read. She was very desirous of conforming

---

23   Thomas Journal, CY 2605, item 1, ML.

24   Thomas Family Connections Census, January 1846, CY 3083, ML. Mary is also listed as daughter of Buddorup, in a group of two on a list of 26 Bonurong and 38 Waworong in Melbourne on Monday 5 August 1850, CY 3127, and on the Census of 13 December 1851, in Thomas Papers, set 214, item 12: 143, ML. Thomas revisited this 1851 census, updating it with subsequent deaths. As it was his practice to link married couples on his censuses, and Mary is still listed with her parents, the presumption is that she did not marry again. She died 15 June 1852.

25   See his recovered biographical details in Chapter 9.

26   *HRV*, vol 2B: 567.

27   Marriage and Thomas scolding Billibellary, 25 and 26 November 1839, Thomas Papers, uncat Ms set 214, box 1, ML; Taking Mary to surgeon, 2 December 1839, *HRV*, vol 2B: 571.

28   I suspect that Mary's mother, Big Benbow/Baddourup's wife was one of the women abducted off the beach, and that is the reason she was living with Baddourup's friend George Smith.

to the habits of civilised life, and though the blacks have decoyed her away sometimes, she has always returned to the Smiths. She had come with Mr and Mrs Smith to Buckkermitterrwarrer about a fortnight previously on a visit.[29]

George Smith[30]

This man has a long history of good relationships with the Bonurong, documented from 1836 to 1850. Robinson described him as 'an encourager' of the blacks,[31] and Thomas described him as 'Mr Smith, the late publican of the Lamb Inn ... is very kind and liberal to the Aborigines, they camp near him'.[32] In fact Robinson records that George Smith, unlike other settlers, allowed the natives to camp *inside* his paddock fences.[33] In a letter to La Trobe in 1840, responding to a note directing Robinson to move the blacks out of town, Robinson said they were encamped next to Mr Smith's and added a PS to his letter:

> Mr Thomas informs me that Mr Smith is very kind to the Blacks and rewards them liberally for any little service they perform. It is therefore not surprising the Blacks should take up their Station near to Mr Smiths when he affords them such liberal encouragement.[34]

He arrived from VDL in 1836,[35] initially as manager of Charles Franks' sheep station at Mt Cotterill, near Werribee. In his testimony regarding the killing of Franks and his shepherd by the blacks, George Smith showed that he understood the reciprocity involved in Batman's treaty. He said that Franks 'had a great aversion to the native blacks, and would not give them food, thinking it the best way to prevent them from frequenting the station'[36] Franks would not meet the reciprocal obligation. Notwithstanding the facts that Batman's treaty was rejected subsequently by the authorities as illegal, and that the Aboriginal signatories must have had a less than perfect understanding of it (simply because Batman's Sydney blacks' language was foreign to the locals), it

---

29 Thomas to Robinson, from Tubbarubbabel, 11 May 1840, VPRS 11, unit 7/307, PROV.

30 I am more than usually grateful to the State Library of Victoria, in particular Jane Miller, who, recognising the importance of George Smith to Aboriginal settler relationships went to extraordinary lengths to search for him in records far and wide.

31 Clark 1998, vol 1: 369.

32 Thomas to Robinson, enc with Lettsom to Thomas, 24 September 1840, 40/10673 in 4/2511, Port Phillip 1840 (2), AO of NSW.

33 Clark 2000, vol 6: 87.

34 Robinson to La Trobe, 16 September 1840, VPRS 10, unit 2, 1840/909, PROV.

35 Billis and Kenyon (1974[1930]: 42) give his arrival date as 25 May 1836, with 500 sheep owned by the executors of Charles Franks.

36 Sworn deposition, 21 October 1836, *HRV*, vol 2A: 43 ff. All the letters, depositions and sworn witness statements related to the killing of Charles Franks and his shepherd Flinders alias Hindes comprise most of Chapter 2.

nevertheless functioned on the ground as a reciprocal obligation – the local Port Phillip Aborigines expected to be fed, and were fed. But not by Franks and he was killed.

The killing of Charles Franks and his convict shepherd

A recently published book makes a mocking and scornful judgement on George Smith and accuses him of vigilantism.[37] Powerfully written by an Indigenous author, it specifically states in the title pages that 'This is not history, it's an incitement': under these circumstances a critic is discomfited. But Pascoe's account is simply deceitful in that it leaves out of the narrative the significant fact that it was a joint European/Aboriginal party.

The Aborigines they were tracking were not Goulburn men as Pascoe asserts, but Waudthourong (to be fair to Pascoe, he is only following the editor of *Historical Records of Victoria* in asserting that Callen and Dundom were Goulburn blacks – that they were Waudthourong has only come to light in this current research via Benbow's testimony). The most serious mistake that Pascoe makes is listing 23 names of 'heavily armed volunteers' who go out 'not involved in casual reprisal but a calculated vigilante campaign' without telling the reader that seven of those names were the names of Aboriginal men.

In listing these 23 names Pascoe does not tell the reader that Benbow, the clanhead so prominent in this story of the Bonurong, was an Aboriginal member of the so-called vigilante party, as were the well known Derrimut, Baitlange (usually spelled in the records as Ben Benger, chief of the district adjoining the Werribee River; he was Georgiana McCrae's friend and her portrait of him is well known) and Ballyan. Nor does Pascoe tell the reader that the killing of Franks by the Aborigines happened on Benbow's own land 'near Mt Cotterill on the Werribee River'. Nor does Pascoe inform the reader that another three of the so-called vigilante party were John Batman's Sydney blacks – Bullett, Stewart and Joe the marine. Had Pascoe told the reader that seven of the 23 were Aboriginal men, including the real owners of the land, a thoughtful reader might just have wondered about the flat statement that it was a vigilante raid. In this case, Pascoe has not allowed the facts to get in the way of a good polemic.

Even so, the evidence which it seems that Pascoe has not seen, reveals a situation of greater complexity than simple vigilantism, a situation that Clark has pointed to in his biography of Derrimut: Clark has sub-titled this article 'traitor, saviour or a man of his people?'[38] According to John Pascoe Fawkner's journal, the Europeans at the settlement when the news arrived of the killing of Franks and his shepherd:

---

37 Pascoe 2007: 6.
38 Clark 2005.

'I Succeeded Once'

enlisted as many Natives as would consent to go & agreed to send them out to deal with the Murderers as they think according to their Rules they should be treated. [They were] well armed and provided. I furnished Provisions, Arms & Ammunition for our party.[39]

This is a painful record to read now: it has already been seen in Chapter 1 how painful it was at the time – Benbow owned his own actions, acknowledged that he had done a hard thing, was almost crying when he reminded Thomas of all the good services which he and the Bonurong had rendered; 'booing' the Wathaurung was one of those 'good services' he recollected.

Judgement of the Europeans' action is easy – devious, manipulative Europeans who sent the Aborigines off to do the dirty work. But this is a simplistic view, implying as it does, that the Aborigines were without volition, mere tools of a white agenda, and mere objects at the disposal of the Europeans. It is an outdated way of looking at the past – good and simple Aborigines and awful Europeans. We know that situations were more complex than that, and we have learned to look for, and respect, evidence of Aboriginal volition. We are in the presence here of mature adults, intelligent men, black and white, with their own agendas. My best understanding is along the lines of 'my friend's enemy is mine own enemy'. I suspect that if the killers of Franks and Flinders were, for whatever reason, at odds with Benbow, Derrimut, Ben Benger and Ballyan, then it might have been a case of their own agenda corresponding with the European's agenda. If this is not true, the motives of those four who elected to throw in their lot with the Europeans, and the motives of those natives who were asked to but refused, remain unknowable on the available evidence.

Betbenjee/Bedbenje/Bet Bengai/Besberger/ Besbenger/Baitbanger/Ben-Benjie/Baitlainge/ Betbenji/Ben Benger/Nerrongho-Ben Benger/ Ner-rong-er/Robert Webb/Captain Good

Kurung-Jang-Balluk clan headman, country at Werribee River, on margins of two Bunurong clans, two Wathourarung clans and two Woiwuorung clans, born around 1814 or 1815, died July 1847 [this is incorrect, see below] (Barwick 1984, part 2: 121).

Visited Tasmania in 1836 with Buckley and Derrimut; Prince or Chief of district adjoining Werribbee district; got drunk on arrival in Tasmania and was so heartily disgusted that he could never be induced to touch spirits since (Bunce 1857: 60).

---

39   Billot 1982.

16 Nov 1835 – with Dallah Kal Keith and another black, Bait Bainger is guiding Fawkner's party (Billot 1982: 15).

6 Mar 1836 – with JP Fawkner down the river a-pleasuring (Billot 1982: 48); 23 to 25 Mar 1836 – hunting and fishing for Fawkner; 27 Mar 1836 – Bait banger refused to carry a sail to the boat for Fawkner, and Fawkner 'turned him adrift to learn better manners' (Billot 1982: 53); 13 Jul 1836 – with Mr John Woods party en route to the property of Charles Franks lately murdered (*HRV*, vol 2A: 47); 28 Oct 1836 – now with Derrymock in VDL (*HRV*, vol 2A: 47).

10 Dec 1837 – Besbenger with whom I have sent in the prisoner Smith to the doctor (de Villiers [Native Police Commandant] to Lonsdale, VPRS 4, unit 3, 37/167, PROV).

16 May 1838 – de Villiers' testimony that Bet Bengai and Derrimut and Dela Kal Keith gave him an account of the sheep stealing to the westwards by the Aborigines now in gaol (*HRV*, vol 2A: 299–301).

20 Mar 1839 – Bedbenje/Robert Webb, Watowrong tribe, aged 25, wife Ligu/Eliza aged 17, on Dredge's census of Aborigines in the vicinity of Melbourne (Robinson Papers, vol 54, ML); July 1839 – Ben Benger/Ner-rong-or/Cap Good, alternative names recorded in encampment, also wife's name Lodiget (Thomas A Diary, set 214, unit 1, ML); 17 Jul 1839 – arrived at Geelong with party from the Yarra Ningolobin, Derrimut, Billy Lonsdale, Murra Murrabine, Warwordor alias Mr King, Burran rung (Sievwright to Robinson, enc with 39/10217 in 4/2471, AO of NSW); Nov 1839 – Thomas' 'more correct' census of this month lists Neronger, male aged 24 years with wife Ligu aged 18 years (CY 3082, frame 50, ML). (There is another copy of this at VPRS 10, unit 1/242, and a corrupt and incomplete version published at *HRV*, vol 2B: 603–607).

1840 – His name is the list in a group of four including Moolmungo, Henry and Toby, at Arthurs Seat, not going to Westernport (Thomas Journal, CY 2605, frame 8, ML).

18 Jul 1845 – Bentbenjie and Eliza and her brother Charlie came to quamby (Georgiana McCrae in Weber 2000: 564); 18 Jul 1845 – in Hugh McCrae's published version, he has added another name, that of Sally, and he has altered the Charlie of the original to George so that the public record of Georgiana McCrae states that Ben Benjie, Eliza, Sally with her brother George came to quamby for the night (McCrae 1966: 196).

1846 – On Thomas Family Connections census as Nerrongho/Ben Benger, male, wife Lygee (CY 3083, ML); 28 Dec 1845 – at Arthur's Seat, Ben-Benjie went out with the gun in search of ducks; throwing his boomerangs (McCrae 1966: 240); 29 Dec 1845 – he was spearing fish (McCrae 1966: 241); 30 Dec – Ben-Benjie gave me three bommerings, one *leanquil* (waddy), one fishing spear and a woomera, and to Sandy a *mulka* (shield) to keep for him as he went to Devine's [a lime burner] this morning (McCrae 1966: 241).

4 Jul 1847 – Vile murder … A girl, Lygu, lubra of Ben Benger a Western Port black was stolen or decoyed away by Nerreninnen alias Mr Young, tracked by Ben Benger, Nerreninnen had a gun and shot Ben Benger beyond Arthurs Seat (Thomas to Robinson, VPRS 11, Box 10/665, PROV); 7 Jul 1847 – Thomas discovers that Ben Benger was not killed at Pt Nepean, the report came from King Benbow and others: a footnote states that Ben Benger and four others saved Melbourne in the early days (Thomas Quarterly Report, June–August 1847, 47/7444 in 4/2783, AO of NSW);

After June 1851 – Ben Benger died, a Western Port [This is incorrect (Thomas census, 13 December 1851, CY 3127: 143, ML).

25 Oct 1853 – Ben Benger, male, no lubra, on Thomas census of Boonorong tribe. In pencil against Ben Benger's name is written 'At Mr Balcombe's' (Thomas set 214/13: 141, ML).

No date – Ben Benger and his wife were an inseparable couple, seldom parted (Thomas, in answer to a question on Chastity, CY 2984: 82, ML).

No date – Then there was Benjy, the black fellow, friend of the McCrae children, and later of the growing Balcombe's, who eventually gravitated to The Briars, and whose grave is under a big gum tree near the homestead (Brookes 1956: 30).

1860s – 'Lady Murphy would journey from The Briars to visit her friends at McCrae [Burrell family]. On her carriage sat a black man in green livery' (McLear 2006: 34). It can only be hoped that this liveried servant was not the distinguished Betbenjee, but the observation is inserted here for the sake of future researchers.

There is no doubt that George Smith arrived with Franks' sheep and managed them, and subsequently sold them to Edward Hobson who did very well out of them, but he was actually the agent for the brothers Charles and John Franks according to the editor of the *Clyde Company Papers*, and the accounts rendered to him by the Clyde Company are made out to George Smith and Co.[40]

George Smith became a publican, obtaining a liquor licence quite early, in 1836, by virtue of his good reputation in VDL,[41] and developed the business from a rented cottage of Fawkner's to the substantial 31 roomed Lamb Inn with cellars and stables by 1839.[42] At the first land sales he purchased the freehold of the land on which it was situated in Collins Street, later to become Scott's Hotel, and he held as well a depasturing licence for his 1200 sheep and 20 cattle on the north side of the Yarra not far from Melbourne.[43] He was free, Protestant and married, four persons in his household, all above the age of 12, one of whom was a female: this census information suggests a family, but the most exhaustive efforts by the Tasmanian Archive and Heritage Office have not been able to discover his wife's name or the names of his children, nor when and in what ship he came to Australia or even if he was native born, though I am now fairly sure that he belongs to the family of Thomas Smith and Co, shipbuilders and merchants, of Pyrmont, Sydney.

George Smith was clearly a man of means for in addition to owning the Lamb Inn he owned property described thus in his insolvency proceedings:

> That beautiful and truly valuable suburban section No 61 belonging to the said estate [George Smith] situated on the Yarra Yarra about one and a half miles from town. The property consists of 25 acres the greater part of which is in cultivation, a large portion of it being laid out a garden in the highest state of improvement and filled with the choicest fruit trees. There is on the ground a neat cottage with stable and other outhouses.[44]

The description could have added the vegetable garden – there is a news item in the *Port Phillip Herald* of 28 February 1840 that George Smith cut from his garden a pumpkin weighing 38 lbs with a girth of 54 inches which was available for viewing at the house in Collins Street which he lately purchased from Mr Greiner. George Smith is listed in Kerr's *Melbourne Almanac* in 1841 as living at Carrencurrenalk, South Yarra, which was also Dr Edmund Hobson's address. Carran-Carranulk, as Georgiana McCrae spells it, named after the *carran* or

---

40   Brown 1941–1971, 1836 vol: 40–41.
41   *HRV*, vol 4: 396–397.
42   *HRV*, vol 4: 465. PL Brown states that at the time when the Lamb Inn was advertised for sale in January 1840, its relatively large public rooms. Cellars, stone foundation, stables and outhouses could justify its use as the general meeting place for professional and business men, for an increasing group of suburban satellites and less frequently for squatters from the bush (Brown 1941–1971, vol 2: 303).
43   *HRV*, vol 6: 136–137, 153, 186. His run was said to be at Bundoora see Billis and Kenyon 1974[1932]: 141. Kenyon's Card Index at SLV records that Smith's sheep were on Keelbundora at Preston, Sections 11 and 19.
44   *Port Phillip Herald,* 29 July 1842: 1.

prickly myrtle, is shown on Fawkner's 1841 Plan of Town of Melbourne[45] on the north side of what is now Victoria Street, Abbotsford, near Church Street: on Fawkner's map. It is opposite Edward Curr's property, St Helliers, which became in later years the Good Shepherd convent site and is now a community arts centre and the Collingwood children's farm.

George Smith sold the Lamb Inn in 1840 to a Mr Watson[46] then became insolvent in February 1842,[47] probably because Watson failed to pay. Niel Black described in his journal the system operating in a cashless Port Phillip in 1840:

> everything is done by bills at six months and twelve months, and to enable the party to meet his bills he disposes of the property ere the end of that term and takes bills of the same date which he discounts and pays off his own bills when due. In this way business is carried on to a fearful and dangerous extent.[48]

In the newspaper account of George Smith's application to the Insolvency Court to be discharged from insolvency, Judge Croke, in granting the application, is quoted as saying 'he believed the applicant to be a very deserving person and that the depression of the times only had compelled him to go to the Insolvent Court'.[49]

Contrary to what is widely asserted, he did *not* hold a licence for Wul-Wul-a-Bulluk on the Mornington Peninsula: a thorough search of the original Pastoral Run Papers produced no papers for Wul-Wul-a-Bulluk in the box which holds all the original 'W' Pastoral Run Papers.[50] Wul-Wul-a-Bulluk is not a pastoral run; it is the name of the house at Capel Sound where he lived in the 1840s.[51]

He *did* hold the licence for Tootgarook through the late 1840s,[52] and he is on Commissioner of Crown Lands Edward Grimes' list for 1848 of people who have not paid their licence fee.[53] George Gordon McCrae described him as a 'settler' whose 'little station' was seven miles from Arthurs Seat, the first establishment

---

45 McCrae 1934: 51 map-endpapers, description.
46 MacKellar 2008: 154–155 (Niel Black's Journal 5 February 1840).
47 Kenyon Card Index, Ms, SLV. George Smith is also mentioned in the Clyde Company's Papers, listing articles purchased by him shortly after his arrival in 1836.
48 MacKellar 2008: 154–155 (Niel Black's Journal 3 December 1839).
49 *Port Phillip Herald*, 4 November 1942: 2.
50 PROV. I am grateful for the opportunity to search the original files.
51 It was situated opposite the Cameron's Bight jetty, within the triangle bounded by Cameron's Close, Morotai Street and the beach.
52 Marion Button 'Depasturing Licence Index, 1840–1851 from *Port Phillip Herald* and *Argus*', CMF 92, Box 38, SLV.
53 Letters received Treasury, January 47 to December 49, VPRS 7, P0000, item 2: 88, 159, PROV. On the same list were the Wedge brothers of Ballymarang, Henry Tuck of Manton's Creek, Thomas Russel of Mt Martha, Andrew McCrae of Arthur's Seat, William Dawson of Tewrong, George Playne of Tanti, James Davey of Ballyrungan.

past the Old Settlement site when travelling towards Arthurs Seat from Point Nepean. It was 'called by the natives Wul-wul-buluk', and it was a little to the south of what used to be called the Big Swamp.[54] George D Smythe's 1841 'Survey of the coast from the west side of Port Phillip to Western Port'[55] locates the first establishment past the old settlement site when travelling towards Melbourne as Dr Hobson's sheep station. It is perhaps a quarter of a mile from the eastern sister on the track to Arthurs Seat and Melbourne, with Cameron's station a little further on, about midway around Cameron's Bight.[56] Smythe's map also locates Tootgarook but he records it as a place or an area with a native name, not as a run; in fact he makes three of his characteristic dots for locations of settlers, only one of whom he names, Freeman (Thomas records Freeman as running sheep).

The simple, though for the time, extraordinary explanation is that George Smith lived with Malvina Hobson nee Lutterell, mother of Edward and Edmund at Capel Sound. George Gordon McCrae devotes pages to describing their lovely house and garden and view, and Mrs Smith's culinary achievements and her kindness to the McCrae boys. But there is no record of a divorce from Edward Hobson senior and she died as Malvina Hobson, as indicated earlier.

The biographer of the Lutterell family[57] tells an amazing story of Malvina's life. Baptised in Tonbridge Kent in 1799, one of ten children in the family, she was brought to New South Wales by her father Dr Edward Luttrell who received a land grant and an appointment as assistant colonial surgeon at Parramatta. She was married as a child-bride to Edward Hobson senior in 1813, and produced her two sons Edmund and Edward quite quickly. They are alleged to have been born in Parramatta, but New South Wales has no record of this and their baptisms are recorded in VDL, and Edmund at least was raised by his grandparents in Hobart. Edward Hobson senior is last picked up in the records running a school in Clarence Plains, VDL.

By 1823 Malvina was living openly with a convicted man named Bartholomew Broughton: Broughton's offence is unspecified but he was a gentleman, formerly a lieutenant in the Royal Navy. Malvina's parents must have approved of Broughton because when he died, he was buried with Dr Lutterell in the Lutterell family vault. But Dr Lutterell definitely did not approve of Malvina – in his will, in which he left his estate to his sons and to his dearly beloved grandson Edmund, he noted that Edmund was a poor unfortunate orphan whose parents did not love him and who left him without any provision or patrimony.

---

54   McCrae 1987: 58.
55   CS 17a, VPRS 8168, PROV.
56   Cameron's on Smythe's map is probably Henry Garvis Cameron, listed by Billis and Kenyon as being at Point Nepean from 1840–1857 onwards, and as being the author of an 1840 report on coal in Victoria (Billis and Kenyon 1974[1932]: 39).
57   In 1992.

Malvina Lutterell/Hobson/Broughton/Smith was a practical woman it seems. In 1844, when Sarah Anne Cain, a lime burner's four year old daughter was found, exhausted, keeping crows off her face with her hand, having been missing for four days and five nights, it was Mrs Smith who had the knowledge and the presence of mind to put the child in a warm bath, then feed her a teaspoon of food at a time until the little girl recovered.[58] She was generous as well. In the winter of 1845 Georgiana McCrae sent one of the men working for the McCraes to Mrs Smith to borrow some beef because the McCraes had run out, and the contract with their workers Henry Tuck and Lanty Cheney specified a ration of ten lbs of beef per week; Mrs Smith sent back not only the requested beef but a ham and greens as well.[59]

The Smiths were living at Capel Sound in July 1846 when George Smith's blackfellows called in en route from Melbourne with the bag which Georgiana McCrae's servant raided for onions, but which contained daffodil bulbs.[60] The McCrae's tutor Mr John McLure was a visitor to George Smith's station along the beach in 1848, as was Mr Liardet.[61] However they managed it, Mrs Smith was acknowledged in polite society, and George Smith remained connected to her sons and grandsons, though not to her. She was buried in Brighton after her death in 1866 with a neighbour as informant, ignorant of her living son's name and whereabouts, aware only that she had a son who was a doctor.[62] There is a letter in the Hobson Papers from George Smith by this time, 1867, resident in Sydney, addressed to Dr Hobson's son, dealing with the issue of 125 acres of land in Sydney granted to Malvina Luttrell the mother of Edward and Edmund Hobson.[63]

It was George Smith and Edward Hobson who established the fame of the cups country for horse breeding, not James Purves who purchased the run as a going concern with an already established reputation. George Gordon McCrae mentions Smith's horses well before Purves came to the district, 'It was always a pleasant tramp for us from Arthur's Seat [to Boniong] through Hobson's flat with its little knots of horses and browsing cows'.[64]

In 1849, George Smith purchased shares in a joint venture company, set up by the Sydney firm of Thomas Smith and Company, which built and fitted out the brigantine *Sea Gull*, 62 tons, 66 feet long, copper bottomed, with a spacious 12 berth cabin for the gentry and a smaller cabin for the crew. The prospectus was

---

58   McCrae 1934: 140.
59   McCrae 1934: 170.
60   McCrae 1966: 197.
61   McCrae 1966: 236.
62   Death certificate, Registry of Births, Deaths, Marriages, Victoria.
63   'Luttrell, Edward (1756 – 1824)', *Australian Dictionary of Biography*, vol 2: 139.
64   Noted horse breeder – PL Brown in Brown 1941–1971; horses and cattle on flats – GG McCrae, 'Experiences not exploits', vol 3, Ms 12018, SLV.

for a commercial profit making visit to the California goldfields, and it stated that two Aboriginals would be among those sailing as crew, to receive a bonus (unspecified). Thomas Smith, the head of the Sydney shipping firm of Thomas Smith and Co, Western Lea, Pyrmont was the owner of the vessel, and he sailed with three sons – GFC Smith, WH Smith and FM Smith. But in the newspaper account, George Smith's name on the passenger list is inserted between the names of the father Thomas and those of his three sons.[65] To me, this suggests that George Smith was family, possibly a brother of the shipping owner Thomas, possibly but less likely, the eldest son.[66]

The Captain was Richard Henry Alexander Napper who married Emma Lutterell, sister of Malvina. Captain Napper and Mrs Edmund Hobson are often mentioned in George Augustus Robinson's journal in the late 1840s engaged in reciprocal visiting and social and scientific discussions with Dr Godfrey Howitt. A daughter of the Napper/Lutterell marriage, named Marie Ann Martha Celine Helena Napper subsequently married her cousin Edward Hobson, brother of Edmund and son of Malvina and Edward Hobson senior.

The *Sea Gull* sailed from Sydney on 17 December 1849, with the two Bonurong young men, Pokey's son named Johnny, and Tommy (almost certainly Tommy Hobson), and arrived in San Francisco via Tahiti on 1 April 1850, 105 days out from Sydney. The *Sea Gull* was sold in California three weeks later by Robert Campbell's agent.[67] In San Francisco, George Smith (and presumably Johnny and Tommy) lived in a weatherboard house constructed on piles built out over the water near the dock. It is not generally known that there was a rush of Victorian settlers to the California goldfields before gold was found in Australia, and the index of these people lists a Mr Smith as arriving back in Melbourne per the ship *J Merithew*, master Captain Abbott,[68] and this is probably George Smith as the date of arrival (5 October 1850) corresponds with the date on which Thomas saw Johnnie and Tommy back in Melbourne. Johnny's subsequent death and burial near the lighthouse is the subject of Chapter 10.

George Smith's relationships with the Bonurong

Back in 1838 George Smith wrote, from his Collins Street address, a letter of protest to Police Magistrate William Lonsdale complaining that Mr Christiaan de Villiers was endeavouring by threats and every other means in his power

---

65 *The Maitland Mercury and Hunter River General Advertizer*, Saturday 22 December 1849: 2.
66 Genealogists may be more successful in identifying George Smith. My difficulty has been that entering George Smith, post 1788 into the NSW Register of Births Deaths and Marriages gives a zero result: there is no other certain fact regarding his mother's name or father's name, or child's name, or date or place of birth or death, or place where such was registered, so there is nothing for the computer to sort.
67 Bateson 1963: 91–94.
68 McLeod 2006.

to induce two of his blacks to join the Native Police. They are mentioned by name – Bondeom whom George Smith has fed and clothed for upwards of two years, and Mr Mann to whom Smith had paid a great deal of attention and who was now exceedingly handy with habits of industry and who goes out to work with the white men who are employed 'down' on Smith's station. It is wrong, he wrote, to entice blacks already partly civilised at considerable expense and trouble, and he requested that Lonsdale tell de Villiers to desist.[69] Bondeom is securely identified as Big Benbow/Old Benbow/Baddourup, Mary's father. Spelled as Poor-tow-rup, Baddourup/Benbow is on the July 1839 census of the Bonurong as having the exchanged or conferred name of Mr Smith.[70]

Only a month before the assault on Mary, Thomas had been forced by La Trobe (in his turn acting on a specific directive from the Governor in Sydney) to confiscate guns from the Bonurong. Thomas knew that it was perfectly safe for them to have the guns, that they needed the guns now that game was so scarce, that they did not use the guns on each other, or on whites. But La Trobe went by the book: he was mindful that official policy towards Aborigines specifically warned against settlers giving the natives guns. The guns were given to the Bonurong men by European men with whom they had reciprocal relationships, and one of them was Benbow's gun, given to him by George Smith.[71]

Big Benbow was known as one of George Smith's blackfellows, and it was an enduring friendship: ten years later, when Big Benbow's health was failing, George Smith wrote to the Chief Protector stating that he would take care of him, and defray all his medical expenses.[72] Big Benbow's wife Barbungrook/Old Maria became a close friend of Thomas' wife, and appears often in the records of the Protectorate. One of Benbow's wives was one of the women abducted off the beach between Arthurs Seat and Point Nepean in 1834.

Mary's situation with Mr and Mrs Smith is interesting. Thomas expressed the opinion that Aboriginal children living with Europeans were placed there by their relatives as spies. This is a partial truth. Aboriginal children were left in school at the 1837 Mission in the care of George Langhorne in exchange for food for their parents. Aboriginal children were also frequently left with Thomas as a signifier that their parents would return. There is always an element of reciprocal obligation in the placement of these children, even when Europeans think that they have adopted them permanently. Always and inevitably, the children were removed from Europeans when they reached puberty. These children[73] were at risk in ways which were not appreciated at first, but which

---

69   George Smith to Lonsdale, 29 September 1838, VPRS 4, box 5, 38/207, PROV.
70   CY 2604, item 1, ML.
71   Thomas Journal, Friday 17 April 1840, CY 2605, item 1, ML.
72   George Smith to Robinson, 5 July 1849, Robinson Papers, vol 57A: 499, ML.
73   This subject does not appear to have been researched anywhere. I have about 50 cards of individual children 'adopted' by Europeans. There is much more to be understood about the nature of this relationship.

Thomas came to recognise. Their European masters/guardians/adoptive parents took the children with them when they travelled, and the children, being in other people's country, not properly introduced and properly sponsored, were sometimes killed (Thomas uses the word assassinated). This is what happened to Peter, the Murrumbidgee boy adopted by George Langhorne, the missionary. He was killed by the Bonurong men Derrimut and Poleorong (Billy Lonsdale) and Tallon (Mr King): the blacks said to Thomas **'no good that blackfellow, no his country'**.[74]

Mary's situation with the Smiths raises even more questions than usual. Was she there of her own choice? Seemingly yes is the answer. Did her father place her there? Did Thomas place her there as a rescue, in light of the fact that she had been injured by both her father and her husband? What was Billibellary's attitude? She did after all belong to him by law.

Whether the gentlemen went to the trouble they did because they were gentlemen, or whether it is an example of George Smith's good relationships, or whether the respect they paid Mary was due to her high status, is not made clear in the records. But for two European gentlemen to catch and saddle their horses, then ride seven miles in the cold and dark of a May Sunday night on the Mornington Peninsula to report to the Protector, is a demonstration of concern unprecedented in the records of the Protectorate.

Mary's deposition

> Mary alias Barebun stated, me by water butt for water. Bullock driver red shirt pulled her away. She said You Blackguard. Bullock driver put hand on mouth, and hand on back, pulled me to ground. Me got hand away from mouth and plenty cry out. Bullock driver pull away, and white man, cook, brought me to Mrs Smith. Bullock driver no hurt me, only knocked me down, and make nose and mouth bleed.[75]

The three other depositions from the Europeans add further facts. William Smith, an agricultural labourer in the employment of Mr Hobson at Buckkermitterwarrer, heard screaming in the dark at about seven o'clock at night. He went towards the sound and found Mrs Smith's house maid crying, next to a tree about 30 yards from the hut. She said that a white man **'been beating her, White Man Kimbarly bullocks today'**. That was all he knew.

---

74 18 September 1839, Thomas Papers, uncat Mss, set 214, ML.

75 Thomas Letterbook, draft letter, CY 2946, frames 51–52, ML. The official letter reporting the outrage and enclosing copies of the depositions is Thomas to Robinson, 11 May 1840, VPRS 11, unit 7/307, PROV.

Anthony Thompson was hut keeper to Mr Hobson at Buckkermitterwarrer. He gave the same bare outline, adding the details that 'she was crying, her nose was bleeding and she seemed stupefied'. He asked her what the matter was and she did not answer, so he took her to Mrs Smith.

George Smith confirmed that about seven o'clock the previous night, Thompson had brought Mary to the hut, bleeding at the nose. She said that the bullock driver with the red shirt had struck her. This was Pierce Dunfield, about six foot tall, with dark hair and high cheekbones, about 40 years of age. Smith sent for him but the men said that he was already in bed. Nevertheless he turned up, with 'trowzers' on and the red shirt. Smith told him to leave the premises immediately; he enquired what for, and George Smith replied that he knew well what for, and Smith would say it again before Captain Lonsdale. Smith then sent Meyrick and Hobson to the Protector. About an hour later, when the girl was washed and calm and collected, Smith asked her for more details. She said that she was standing by the water cask when Pierce Dunfield took her by the arm and forced her away. When she resisted, and told him he was a blackguard, and he had better be off, he replied that if she called him that name,[76] he would knock her down. Mary said **'very well, you knock me down'**. He then put his hand over her mouth and nose, and she struggled and fell. He put his knee or foot on her breast and she cried out, and then heard the Europeans calling for her. George Smith concluded his testimony by saying that there was no other man on the premises who wore a red shirt but Pierce Dunfield, and that Dunfield cleared off as soon as Smith sent for the Protector.

If that is all that happened, then by modern standards, the assault would not be described as 'a gross outrage'. Dunfield's intent was probably sexual gratification[77] but Mary stood up to him. Her use of the word 'blackguard' placed him in an inferior position in the social scale, and seems to have enraged him. It didn't help her in the short term to the extent she was slightly injured physically, but where it matters, in her nerve and her self-possession, Mary won the encounter.

14 and 15 May 1840

Thomas visited the blacks at Buckkermitterwarrer; the blacks told him 'a strange story' that two boys had been killed in a dray accident in going round Arthurs Seat. The day before, 13 May, he had sent the dray from Tuerong to the

---

76   Blackguard was a demeaning insult in polite society of the time; according to the Oxford dictionary it carries connotations of inferiority, an insult handed out to a menial. It is interesting that a bullock driver objected so vehemently to it coming from an Aboriginal girl.
77   Thomas calls it an 'attempted assault' in CY 2604, item 3, ML. and in another version an 'attempted violation'.

Meyricks' station at Boniong to obtain potatoes of which they were very fond.[78] In fact the boys were not killed but there had been an accident and two were injured.[79]

On Monday 15 May 1840 all the blacks left the two encampments at Buckkermitterwarrer and Kangerong and shifted to the head protectorate station Tubberubbabel where they remained for a week. On Sunday 24 May 1840, Thomas extracted from the blacks their confession to the massacre and they all promptly left Tubberubbabel.

26 May 1840

Thomas was very ill this day, he suspected through sleeping in a leaky tent, so he sent his son to Buckkermitterwarrer to look for the blacks.[80]

29 May 1840

Thomas visited the encampment at Kangerong and found it had shifted to Buckkermitterwarrer by Arthurs Seat. Next day he rode there but they had all gone on their journey around the country to Sandy Point.[81]

5 June 1840

Thomas rode out to meet the returning blacks, and fell in with some of the principal Western Port blacks – Derrimut, Derrimut's brother Ningnow and his lubra, Derrimut's mother Dindoo, Budgery Tom and his family, Burrenum (Mr Dredge) and his lubra and his two brothers, and Munmungina, 13 persons in all. They stayed one night with him at Tubberubbabel and moved the next day to join the others 'just beyond Kangerong where they were encamped'. There were 55 in all.[82]

11 June 1840

Old Mr Man at Bukkumitterar is accused of taking away a Mt Macedon lubra, Jacks, who goes off with three large glass spears to kill her and Mr Man. Me and my men pacify him by stating that I will go following morning to Bukku & if Mr Man has, to bring her home – I however went that even and saw & found old tale false – return – Jack immediately leaves, says to me **bungarlarly**…[83]

---

78   Missionary Langhorne, *HRV*, vol 2A: 174.
79   Thomas Journal, CY 2604, item 3, ML.
80   Thomas Journal, CY 2604, item 3, ML.
81   Thomas Journal, CY 2604, item 3, ML. For Sandy Point see entry for 2 June.
82   Thomas Journal, CY 2604, item 3, ML.
83   Thomas Journal, CY 2604, item 3, ML.

Mingaragon/Old Mr Man/Mr Mann/Mingal-gur-rer/ Min.gare.rer

Jul 1839 – Name taken in encampment, Mingal-gur-rer, European name Mr Man (Thomas 'A' diary, January-July 1839, set 214, unit 1, ML); 18 Aug 1839 – A family arrived in 'a very distressed state', consisting of an old man, three lubras and four children (*HRV*, vol 2B: 536. There is only one Bonurong family with this structure.); 20 Nov 1839 – On Thomas' census as Mingaragon, male, aged 68, with three wives, Togerrook aged 50, another Togerrook aged 46, Lagerrook aged 29, and five children, Yellerrook, female aged 8, Yit Yit female aged 4, Maryagrook female aged 6, Waregulk female aged 4, and Lellerbook male aged 2. Described as a man of some importance has three wives and all are sisters. He seldom visits the settlers unless something of importance is going on that requires the whole of the tribe (Thomas, VPRS 10, unit1/242, PROV).[I]

3 Jan 1840 – Names taken in encampment, Chief Mingaragon, his three lubras Togerurrook, Tugerurrook and Lagurook, and his children Mungerer c,[II] Lillerenook c, Lillerook c, Maryagrook l,[III] Waregull l (Thomas, CY 2605, item 1, ML); Feb 1840 – Old Mr Man and his family, eight persons in all are at Arthurs Seat, not going to Gippsland, and Old Mr Man is to head up one of the five parties remaining (Thomas, CY 2605, frame 8, ML); 11 Jun 1840 – At Bukkermitterar Old Mr Man is accused falsely of taking a Mt Macedon lubra (Thomas, CY 2604, item3, ML); 12 Jun 1840 – At Buckkumittorwarra, are Old Mr Man and his family, 8 in all (Thomas, CY 2604, item3, ML); 22 Jun 1840 – At Tubberubbabel, Old Mr Man makes a disturbance, wishes another lubra he having three already (Thomas CY 2604, ML); 30 Sep 1840 – Jack Weatherley came pm and reported that Min.gare.rer alias Mr Man had been taken to jail by the constables … Mr Man is a Yalloger (Robinson in Clark 1998, vol 1: 376).

Aug 1842 – Minkerra – Mr Man, on medical dispenser's list at Nerre Nerre Warren being treated for Psora, treatment being magnesium sulphate etc (Henry Jones, VPRS 4410, unit 2, item 50, PROV).

28 Nov 1843 – The Chief of the Western Port blacks, Old Mr Man's lubra dies near Punt road, named Lundum Merneeyowrook, aged 40 (Thomas, CY 2606, item 2: 21, ML).

I. Thomas meant that Old Mr Man seldom visits the settlement of Melbourne.

II. In a list of names like this 'c' does not represent child but coolin, ie male child, boy.

III. In a list of names like this, after the adults have been named, Thomas uses l to represent female child, girl.

Sep 1844 – 'Old Mr Man gives me a sad account of the loss of his three wives' (Thomas, CY 2606, item 3, ML); 30 Nov 1844 – Thomas list of births and deaths for the six month period shows that Mr Man's three wives died one after the other as follows – 15 Jun, Largarook, aged 38, WP, died in the bush south of the Yarra; 9 Aug, Toogoorook, aged 44, WP, died in the bush south of Yarra; and 12 Aug Toogoorook, aged 25, WP, died in the bush south of Yarra, three lubras one family (CY 2604, item 5, frame 264, ML).

Jan 1846 – Family Connections census, Old Mr Man, 2 Benbows and Derrimut are listed as one section, Werrerby Yallook. On the list of names Thomas has overwritten and the name appears to be Wombungnurlook, male widower, his children being Mangerer male 18, Lillerrook 13, Dit Dit 10 and Warregulk 11, 5 persons in the family (Thomas, CY 3083, ML).

31 Dec 1847 – Near Brighton Thomas saw the graves of Old Mr Man alias [blank] & Dindoo the two oldest in the tribes, buried in at present an unenclosed spot about 3 chains from the road. Poor Old Dindoos seemed a careless grave but [blank] seemed to have some pains taken with it. Its enclosure was in the form of a heptagon thus[IV] & seven wattle saplings making the figure lay horisontally on the ground. On enquiry, as I had never seen one of this horizontal form before, I was led to understand that it was to show their fast defuncation, that but 7 remained of his tribe. A bit of fern had sprung up over his mortal remains which I drew out, and left the spot full of reflection on the mysterious dealings of providence, as finite mortal unable to unravel the mystery of the rapid decrease of these people, apparently Minishid (tho the idea is uncharitable) to make room for a more intelligent race, for I must bear testimony for the last 10 years that the tribes to which he belonged have never been (save in Major Lettsom's cruel mission) injured by white men but always welcome visitors at stations, nor have any been before our courts but for the crime of drunkenness. I was much pleased on my return to Melbourne to see the son of this Old Man basking under a tree with 6 white men resting at mid-day from the toils of the field. I heard of him a good character. I told him I had been thinking over the grave of his father & hoped that he would keep from drink & live happy with the whites (Thomas, CY 2606, frame 476, ML).

IV. Thomas' sketch is reproduced as Fig 29.

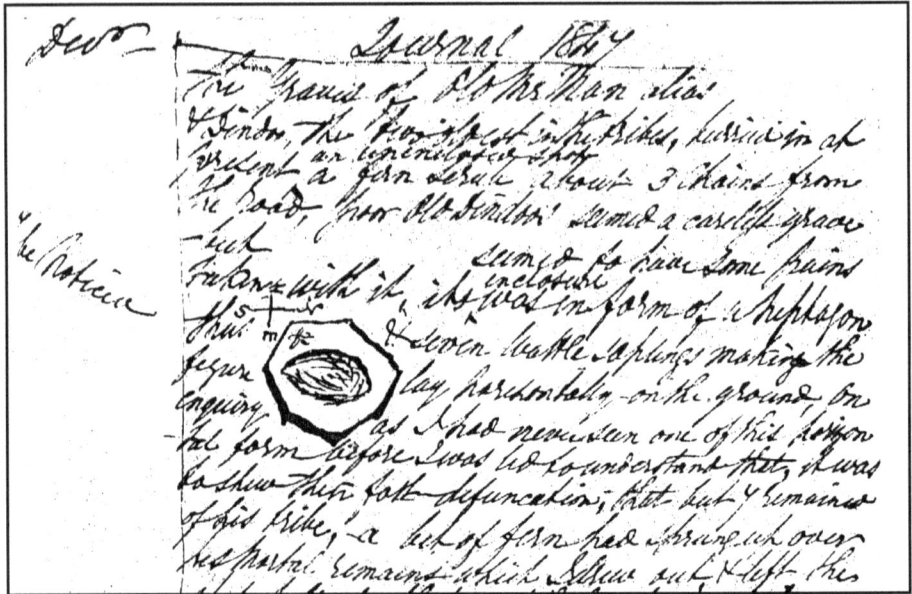

Fig 29. 'Old Mr Mann's unusual hexagon-shaped grave'

Thomas sketch, from the William Thomas papers, 1834–1868, 1902, Mitchell Library, reproduced with the permission of the State Library of New South Wales.

16 June 1840

Three black guides (unnamed) took Henry Howard Meyrick from Packomedurrawurra to Boniong then showed him Colourt which he described as having a splendid salt water river running through it.[84]

2 July 1840

Four blacks are at Hobson's.[85]

22 July 1840

The blacks at Tubbarubbabel were concerned that some small parties had been away for too long, and said to Thomas that they would not return unless ordered. Thomas visited Buckkermitterwarrer and found Old Mr Man and family, Old Billy, Dollar and Lively there. Old Mr Man asked Thomas to write a letter telling the absent ones to come back – *nerlingo*. Thomas wrote the letter in their own language and addressed it to the Koolins, and Old Mr Man carefully held it up to dry as if it had been a cheque for 1000 pounds; they all read the letter.[86]

---

84   Henry Howard Meyrick, Letters, Ms 7959, Box 654, SLV.
85   Thomas Journal, CY 2604, item 3, ML.
86   Thomas Journal, CY 2604, item 3, ML.

27 July 1840

The Chief Protector visited and recorded 'Bag.er.me.dare.re.wur.rer', alternative phonetic Bag.ger.me.dare.re.wur.rer. 'This is Mr Thomas Senior's third station, one and a half miles from Gan.jer.rong. From here to Bor.ny.yong, Merrick's Station is 12 miles'.[87]

28 July 1840

This day the Chief Protector rode over the country between Hobson's first station (Kangerong) where he had a fine view of the heads to Wongo (Arthurs Seat):

> Rode over some flat country resembling the American prairies. Level as water and green as an emerald and studded with clumps of casuarina and cherry trees and mimosa or silver wattle and small clumps of tea tree. Saw a party of natives at Hobson's fetching water and getting wood' [Hobson's farm station Bag.er.me.dare.re.wur.rer].[88]

4 August 1840

Thomas had received instructions to round up all the blacks and bring them to Melbourne to select a reserve. Mr Man and his family arrived this day at Tubberubbabel, only to inform him that the blacks were not on their way in, only those whom Thomas had seen a few days previously at Buckkermitterwarrer, plus those on the mountain (Arthurs Seat). Thomas was angry and said he would go and fetch them himself, but they said '**too much wood – no gogo Yarraman**' meaning Thomas could not ride his horse because the mountain was too timbered.[89]

9 August 1840

Thomas at Tuerong got word that there had been an Aboriginal attack on Hobson's dray laden with stores that had arrived by boat, travelling on the road from Buckkermitterwarrer to Kangerong. Thomas inspected the spot on the road where the event happened, within 400 yards of Kangerong, and the tree behind which the attacker hid; the road was muddy and there were signs of a scuffle. The dray driver was back at Buckkermitterwarrer, but the overseer, Mr Atkins, described the man as being very big and tall and strong, as tall as, if not taller than the Old Doctor. Atkins said that the dray driver knew the Old Doctor and it was not him; the dray driver knew that the Old Doctor and his family were far away down towards Point Nepean, and besides, the Old Doctor was 'well disposed'.

---

87   Clark 1988, vol 1: 356.
88   Clark 1988, vol 1: 357.
89   Thomas Journal, CY 2604, item 3, ML.

Thomas went to Buckkermitterwarrer and interviewed Hobson and the dray man. The dray driver's story was that he was driving along the road nearly at Kangerong when he heard a black say **give bread** and the next minute the black had jumped into the back of the dray. The dray driver cooeed to the men at the hut at Kangerong but they did not hear. He wrestled with the black and the dray man had tufts of the black's hair and tufts from his opossum skin cloak as evidence. The black got away from him in the greasy conditions, in the direction of Mt Martha. As a strange black had been seen on Mt Martha over the previous days, Thomas went to look for him but found no evidence.[90]

30 August 1840

Superintendent La Trobe and Eliot Heriot, who had taken up a run at Cape Schanck adjacent to James Thomson, rode from Melbourne to Arthurs Seat 'a long ride, the last part in the dark to Hobson's'. La Trobe calls the run 'Karangarong', and records that they camped at 'the Creek' for two nights, then on the shore at Capel Sound where he saw the remains of 'Collins Settlement (1802)' (La Trobe was mistaken in the year) then back to Hobson's and returned to Melbourne on 3 September.[91] This creek is the same one on which the Bonurong camped but La Trobe makes no mention of Aborigines.

14 December 1840

By this date the Central Protectorate Station for the Yarra and Westernport blacks had been established at Nerre Nerre Warren and La Trobe had inspected it and approved. But the Western Port blacks did not like it, and kept coming and going to their own country. On this date Thomas rode in search of them and went to Buckkermitterwarrer where Mr King (Tallon) indicated that they were at Tuerong.[92]

16 May 1841

Hobson is sold out by one of these villainous special surveys.[93]

22 May 1841

Thomas visited Tubberubbabel, Kangerong, Bukkerrmerderra and Deangeong only to find all the Aborigines had gone to Melbourne. Old Doctor and his family had been at Buckkermitterwarrer. Slept at his son's station at Tuerong.[94]

---

90   Thomas Journal, CY 2604, item 3, ML.
91   La Trobe, Memoranda No 4 in Australian Notes, 1839–1854, MSM 541, safe, SLV.
92   Thomas Journal, CY 2605, items 2–3, ML.
93   Hales and Le Cheminant 1997: 20. Hugh Jamieson had made his 'Special Survey' purchase of 5120 acres bounded by Dromana beach, Ellerina Road and Nepean Highway. It included both encampments Buckkermitterwarrer and Kangerong (and both Hobson's sheep station and farm station).
94   Thomas Journal, CY 2605, item 5, ML.

18 November 1841

Shown as Baggamahjarrawah with fenced paddocks and a mark to indicate the location of the homestead on George D Smythe's map.[95]

No date but between 1840 when he arrived, and prior to the birth of his twins in 1843.

Dr Edmund Hobson was at Buckkermitterwarrer convalescing from serious illness. He wrote to his wife at Yarra Yarra care of the Post Office in Melbourne that the 'blacks celebrated my arrival by dancing the Corobbara in fancy dress'. He also said that the men are splitting timber for the dairy.[96] In another letter a week later he wrote that the house (this could be Kangerong House or the house at Capel Sound) is coming on, and he looks forward to dear Margaret's joining him because it is more salubrious and beautiful and interesting country. He sends a kiss to his little son Jack and regards to his mother (Malvina).[97]

15 February 1844

Georgiana McCrae and her husband were house guests of Captain and Mrs Reid at Tichingorourke (Reid's station, now The Briars). These two couples, together with Hugh Jamieson, rode to inspect Jamieson's Survey. After calling first at Kangarong House, where they saw a Mrs Newby and her two girls,[98] Captain Reid took Georgiana to see his standby station on Bakmadarroway Creek. After leaving the Survey they came upon the Commissioner of Crown Lands Powlett who had suggested to Georgiana's husband as a possible run, the land subsequently taken up by Andrew McCrae called Arthur's Seat.[99]

No date but between 1844 and 1851

Jamieson's Survey – fine flat green country the good quality of the soil being evidenced by the beautiful blackwood trees dotted all over it.[100]

No date but between 1844 and 1851

'During the winter months with the big creeks running bankers, the Cananuke and the Mordialloc, and the flat land north–easterly of what is now Dromana a bog', the McCrae family used lime boats to get to Melbourne during the 1840s.[101]

---

95   'Survey the Coast of Port Phillip from the Mouth of Tangenong Creek to Arthur's Seat with internal features', CS 81A, PROV.

96   Edmund Hobson to Margaret Hobson, in Hobson Papers, Ms 8457, Box 865/2B, SLV.

97   Edmund Hobson to Margaret Hobson, in Hobson Papers, Ms 8457, Box 865/2B, SLV.

98   Mrs Newby was a survivor of a ship lost in a storm in Port Phillip, with her husband the Captain going down, as well as other children including her son.

99   McCrae 1966: 127.

100   McCrae 1911: 20.

101   McCrae 1911: 17.

1850s

'In the early years emus were plentiful … during the 1850s Bill, George, John and Tom McLear would visit the aborigines who had their kitchen middens among the honeysuckles (banksias) on the sand rise by the mouth of Dunn's Creek'.[102]

---

102   McLear 2006: 97.

7. Kullurk, the Bonurong choice for a reserve

Kullurk/Kulluck/Kulluk/Kullurt/Callert/Colourt/Coolert/Coollourt/
Coolurt/Sandy Point/Tulum/Yellodungo/Yellodungho

The named place Kullurk, this general area around Sandy Point, was the Bonurong choice for a reserve, and it was the place to which they looked back to Thomas, accusingly, when they did not get it. Many Europeans walked across it and described the land as fine open country, which means that it was burned regularly as a kangaroo run by the Bonurong. Some described huts and signs of habitation. It is more prominent in the early records than either Point Nepean or Cape Schanck as a resort of the blacks. Point Nepean has claimed our attention because of the public fight to save it. But I suspect that there has been some inflation of importance used in the arguments to save it: Thomas does not mention it as a place of special significance – it is Kullurk which he mentions more frequently, and which they visited more frequently, and where Thomas mentions the solemnity of women acting separately from men (see 18 June 1840 below).

Coolart is now in public ownership, managed by Parks Victoria, with a substantial and impressive building, built by Frederick Grimwade in 1895, and grounds used now as a sanctuary for native wildlife from the time of its purchase by Thomas Luxton in 1937. Every scrap of information that I have been able to find from the earliest use of this land has been brought together here for consideration. By virtue of being the Bonurong choice for a reserve in 1840, a fact apparently not noticed since then, it merits its place in our recollection, and in our understanding of how the Bonurong regarded their country.

Thomas marked on some of his maps a rectangle immediately to the north of the site occupied now by the naval base HMAS *Cerberus*.[1] Smythe marked it as Callert, Merricks Station, at almost exactly the place that Coolart now occupies,[2] and Smythe also labelled Tarrnuck as the head of Hann's Inlet.[3] Thomas' full description of it is reproduced. The most southerly extent of mangrove association vegetation occurs about one kilometre north of Sandy Point.[4]

---

1   CY 2984, frame 300, ML.
2   CS 17A, 1841, PROV.
3   Smythe, 1842 Survey of the Islands of Western Port, accompanying Mr Hoddle's letter of 1 May, PROV.
4   Gordon 1997: 157.

1804

Lt Charles Robbins described the west coast of Western Port 'all the way down [travelling south] to the sandy point [Sandy Point] abreast the west point [Tortoise Head] of the Western island [French Island] a miserable low and swampy country for three or four miles in'.[5]

1825–1826

For a whole year, a party of Europeans camped at Western Port rebuilding a ship. The account of this prolonged stay entered the records via a report from Captain Whyte of the VDL government vessel, the brig *Duke of York*. Whyte had been commissioned to scour the Bass Strait islands for runaways, which he did, capturing 17 named convicts. He then poked his nose into Western Port, where he picked up John Scott who had lived there with a black woman, a Tasmanian, by whom he had three children, and discovered as well, Mr James Smith, his son Marmaduke and the vessel *Caledonia*, whom he escorted back under guard to Hobart. Mr Smith's story was checked by the authorities and accepted as truthful.[6] 'The gentleman, on investigating the circumstances, was more to be pitied than blamed'.[7]

Smith had purchased the *Caledonia*, apparently without a marine survey, and finding himself in Western Port with the sloop so infirm as to be sinking, he rebuilt it. He was skilled at shipbuilding, had plenty of provisions, and managed to convert the *Caledonia* 'into a handsome schooner of double the tonnage', an improbable achievement as Valda Cole commented, but that is what the records say. While at Western Port, he explored the Mornington Peninsula and hunted across it.

> Proceeding up the western channel, and opposite the second island [French] is another large tributary stream [? Merricks Creek], flowing through a level country of fine pasture land, lightly wooded and formed into a peninsula by Port Phillip about 15 or 20 miles to the west. Mr Smith met with a fine lagoon [? Tootgarook Swamp] in the centre of this tract, while hunting kangaroo which he found very numerous. Both the islands consist of good land, but the upper one is rather thickly wooded. The soil in general of the whole country is a deep vegetable mould, resting on a stratum of clay or fuller's earth, and appears to be the deposit which this valuable river (as yet but partially explored) has washed down from higher ground.[8]

---

5   Labilliere 1878, vol 1: 176.
6   Mr Smith does not have a given name in these accounts but Valda Cole has kindly identified them for me: they left Hobart on 19 January 1825 and returned 16 February 1826 (pers comm 27 November 2009).
7   *Hobart Town Gazette*, Saturday 13 May 1826: 2.
8   Article headed 'Western Port' in *Hobart Town Gazette*, Saturday 20 May 1826: 3.

James Smith met blacks whom he described as 'a stately, healthy race easy to be civilised', 'their huts form villages of 40 to 50', but there is an imprecision in the newspaper account which suggests to me that he *could* have been describing people he met on the east coast of Western Port, not on the Mornington Peninsula. On the other hand, if he did not meet any blacks on the Mornington Peninsula, he would have been just about the only European party in the early records who did not, so it is more likely that the imprecision comes from how the newspaper reporter understood the story.

17 November 1826

Dumont D'Urville's party explored the area around Sandy Point. They:

> went all over this tongue of land ... applied themselves to hunting kangaroos ... came upon a watercourse which seemed to belong to a river, although the water was still brackish, and he [Gaimard] noted recent traces of the presence of natives ... the open terrain is delightfully undulating. Here there are fine stands of trees easy to get through, there are vast grass-covered clearings, with well defined paths and linked by other tracks so regular and well-marked that it is hard to conceive how these could have happened without the hand of man.[9]

The French were correct – this was firestick-farmed country, frequently visited.

February 1827

The explorer William Hovell walking south from the vicinity of Melbourne said that:

> There appears to be but little good Land ... until we arrive at a Creek which comes out at Sandy Point, Western Port; from that Southwardly in the direction of Cape Schanck is good open forest Land, grass thick, and a good quality.[10]

28 January 1836

Joseph Tice Gellibrand and his party landed at Sandy Point (after the disastrous loss of over 1000 sheep at Corinella) and saw 'many tracks of the Natives upon the Beach'.[11]

---

9   Cole 1984: 50–51.
10 *Historical Records of Australia*, series 3, vol 5: 856.
11 Bride 1983[1898]: 10–11.

March 1836

George Russell and George Mackillop, anxious to find if sheep could be landed at Sandy Point and driven to Melbourne, camped at Sandy Point on the site of an old native encampment which had not been used by the natives for some months previous. Their two native guides slept in an old mia mia.[12]

July 1839

Edward Hobson, Robert Jamieson and George Desailley together with three Aboriginal natives (unnamed) carted a whaleboat from Kangerong to Western Port for the purpose of exploring the country in the neighbourhood of that bay.[13] 'Mr Hobson's station was on what is now[14] the Point Nepean Road'.

Edward Hobson's hut at that time was at Buckkermitterwarrer, by the Dromana Drive-in, and the boat landed supplies from Melbourne on Dromana beach, so the most logical route, the shortest and the easiest, would have followed the old Bittern-Dromana Road up over the escarpment and down towards Western Port: either Somers beach or Balnarring beach would be the departure point for the sea exploration of Western Port – either departure point would have taken them through the country the Aborigines named as Kullurk.

23 December 1839

Thomas' Memorial to the Governor of New South Wales, Sir George Gipps reminding the governor that his predecessor Sir Richard Bourke had approved a reserve for the blacks of 895 acres on the Yarra at Melbourne, that it was now very valuable and Thomas has heard that the government intends to sell; Thomas asks for land in his district of Western Port, exact location unspecified, for the use and benefit of his Aborigines as an agricultural and cattle establishment.[15]

29 February 1840

In remarks following his first periodical report of this date, Thomas explains why his people are in such need for a reserve:

> The Aborigines in my district have not, like in other districts, back country to fly to: the ocean on the south and west, the Yarra and Melbourne to the north.

---

12   Brown 1935: 87–89.
13   Bride 1983[1898]: 90.
14   1853.
15   VPRS 10, unit 1, 39/336, PROV.

And how it will be used:

> an agricultural and cattle station … an asylum … an Establishment in my District where the infirm may find shelter, the young education, and the industrious employment.[16]

28 April 1840

The Colonial Secretary informed La Trobe that the Governor approved of one square mile for each protector as an inner permanent reserve for cultivation, with an outer temporary reserve of five miles radius for hunting for the Aborigines.[17]

May 1840

Henry Howard Meyrick's letter home to 'dear Mama' in which he gives the detail of his selection of Coolourt is dated 16 June 1840, but the events occurred in the second week in May:

> I left the ship for good on the first of May … and after settling my business, rode down with Hobson, Maurice, Alfred and Mr Brodribb (of whom more anon) to Packomedurrawurra which is the name of Hobson's station. I stayed there one day and then Maurice, Alfred and myself, walked (ten miles) to Boniong, where we shot kangaroos and minded the sheep for a week, and then started on our first expedition into the bush to explore a run about 36 miles from Boniong called Colourt. We took no provisions with us, trusting to our guns for food, our black guides were excellent hands at stalking kangaroo, which we cut up and eat half raw, nothing like walking in the bush for an appetite. We found an excellent run, but we shall have to clear away a marsh to get water; there is a splendid river running thro' the middle of it but unfortunately it is salt, it is however full of fish and covered with ducks. We slept there under a miah–miah which the guides knocked up: we went however supperless to bed, as the kangaroos disappeared at sundown, and the next morning started for home and thence to Melbourne.[18]

21 May 1840

At Tubberubbabel, the Western Port blacks talk of taking a circuit to Point Nepean then to Sandy Point and back to the station at Tubberubbabel.[19]

---

16 *HRV,* vol 2B: 625.
17 VPRS 10, unit 2, 1840/395, PROV.
18 Hales and Le Cheminant 1997: 10.
19 Thomas Journal, CY 2604, item 3, ML.

25 May 1840

Thomas insists on knowing the route they will take and they made him a mudmap with the number of nights they would *quamba* at each place. A later mudmap of a similar circuit shows Kullurk as near Kunnerlong.

2 June 1840

Thomas went looking for his blacks along the coast of Port Phillip from Arthurs Seat to Point Nepean, but could not see any smoke; he returned and checked his paper (his copy of their mudmap) and found that they proposed to return by Sandy Point: they had gone to Cape Schanck via Arthurs Seat and were to return along the Western Port coast.[20]

5 June 1840

Thomas rode out from Tubberubbabel in the direction of Sandy Point and fell in with some of the principal Western Port blacks who were returning home viz Derremut, Ningeranow (Derrimut's brother), Dindoo (their mother), Budgery Tom and family, Burrenum, his two brothers and his lubra, and Munmunginna.[21]

11 June 1840

In Melbourne, 'Governor approved of a reserve of 10 square miles of land for each of the assistant protectors'.[22]

Selection of Kullurk, 'the good land they talk of'

13 June 1840

Thomas' man Ross arrived at Tubberubbabel from Melbourne with the official notification of the grant of land. Thomas broached to them the subject of 'the good land they talk of'.

15 June 1840

Started with a part of the Natives of Western Port Tribe & 2 Mt Macedons with their lubras toward that Good country ... encamp at Kunnundrum. After encamping took my compass imagining that I was not far from course and plan of the rambling party out.[23] After going half a mile or more saw smoke. Returned, mentioned to Budgery Tom who laughed

---

20   Thomas Journal, CY 2604, item 3, ML.
21   Thomas Journal, CY 2604, item 3, ML.
22   Robinson Journal, Clark 1998, vol 1: 345.
23   There were 21 named people out on the ramble, having left Tubberubbabel on 10 June.

and considered me stupid that I did not know that from the description they had before given me on parting. No water had just enough in bag for tea for self and blacks.[24]

16 June 1840

Early start without breakfast, no water. After going about 3 miles come up to water, had breakfast and give bullocks water. About 11 o'clock came up to the Blacks Encampment. I give them a cordial shake hands, commend them for giving me such a correct chart, and after an hour or so delay they take me to Kulluk. I am well satisfied with it. Encampment about 1 mile from Kulluk. [His marginal note says] Visit Kulluk, much gratified with it.

There are 36 people encamped. [In his second periodical report, Thomas notes that] with the exception of one family and two individuals, the whole of the Boonorong tribe were encamped & made choice of Kullock as their Locating Place.[25]

17 June 1840

Thomas took Ross' spade, tried the soil in several places and found it good. He noted though that it had no standing water but a large bed of reeds.[26] He also identified one of the Mt Macedon blacks as Captain Turnbull who assaulted his wife.

18 June 1840

Captain Turnbull starts for Nunnup.[27] Broke up the encampment, proceeded accompanied by whole to Tubberubbabel. I should have stated just before starting while putting bullocks in dray, Captain Turnbull returns in a violent rage, throws his powerful spears promiscuously into the encampment. One hit the cart just where I was holding and another almost hit my man Davis. Budgery Tom and he has a regular set to. He starts. The breaking up of the encampment had a pleasing appearance. As they descended down the hill one by one, the women at some distance one by one in another direction. Encamped at a miserable place called Nermoin by Kokobul.[28]

---

24 Thomas Journal, CY 2604, item 3, frame 148, ML.
25 VPRS 4410, unit 3, item 67: 16, PROV.
26 Thomas Journal, CY 2604, item 3, ML.
27 This is the native name for O'Connor's station near Dandenong (Thomas map, VPRS 4410, unit 3/67, PROV).
28 Thomas Journal, CY 2604, item 3, frame 149, ML.

Thomas locates Kulluk on his maps as a square on Hann's Inlet which is now HMAS *Cerberus*. The encampment one mile away on a hill may be Tower Hill at Somers. Henry Meyrick's run Colourt is shown from the earliest government survey of the peninsula to be where Coolart homestead is now.

19 June 1840

Friday. Arrived at Tubberubbabel safe about 11 o'clock. Captain Turnbull went off in earnest, and Thomas discovered that 'The blacks this trip made me opossum cloak and my two men'.[29]

20 June 1840

Thomas wrote to Robinson describing the place the Bonurong selected:

> I have the honour to acknowledge receipt of your communication of the 11th inst. In which His Excellency the Governor has been pleased to grant one square mile in behalf of the Aborigines of my District, and as an homestead for myself and family.
>
> Accompanied by the Western Port Natives, I visited a part much spoken of by them as a good country. After two days journey they brought me to the country they had spoken of called Kullurk.
>
> Kullurk is situated west of Western Port. I have well examined this spot. There is abundance of Game of all descriptions, about six or seven hundred acres of good land well adapted for cultivation. The surrounding country is barren, woody and worthless to the settler but of infinite value to the Aborigine.
>
> I stop'd two days there. I examined the soil at different [sic] & in general it is 18 inches & two feet of dark good soil.
>
> It has the sea to the East, a Salt Water Creek from the sea running inland about three miles forms a boundary to the Southward.[30]
>
> This country is of the Natives own choosing, is far away from settlers. I do not know that a single settler will be disturbed. Another recommendation is that the Yarra blacks are said to be fond of this part of the country & will no doubt avail themselves of its advantages.
>
> There are no line [sic] of road to the spot. In the map accompanying my report will be found the road mark. The nighest I should say is the Arthurs Seat Road.

---

29 Thomas Journal, CY 2604, item 3, ML.
30 Merricks Creek.

I have the honour to be your most obedient servant, Wm Thomas, Asst. Prot. Aborg. Western Port District.[31]

In his second periodical report, Thomas reiterates that it was 'a spot I often heard them talk about'.[32]

20 June 1840

The native dogs are so numerous at Colourt that it would be nigh impossible to run sheep.[33]

26 June 1840

In Melbourne, the Chief Protector called on His Honour who approved of Robinson's going to Thomas' district to select a reserve of land.[34]

28 July 1840

The Chief Protector's assessment was as follows:

> The situation chosen by Mr Thomas on the sea coast [Kullurk] was the worst that could be selected ... I told the natives that the Waverong were under Mr Thomas' care as well as themselves – the Boongerongs, and that they would have to occupy some land intermediate between the two districts and have a town of their own which would supersede the necessity of their coming to Melbourne.[35]

4 August 1840

Thomas was edgy about his blacks still out on a ramble while he had received an instruction from the Chief Protector to round them up and bring them to Melbourne to join the Yarra blacks and select a joint reserve. Budgery Tom and Bogy Bogy took him looking for some of the blacks to an encampment by Sandy Point.[36]

21 September 1840

Assistant Protector William Thomas' map of Part of Western Port District shows the head stations of the settlers, the new proposed Protectorate site at Narre Narre Warren and the previously approved site as a rectangle labelled 'Kulluk' on the northern side of Sandy Point.[37]

---

31 VPRS 11, unit 7/312, PROV.
32 7 November 1840, VPRS 4410, unit 3/67, PROV.
33 Henry Howard Meyrick, Letters, Ms 7959, Box 654, SLV.
34 Clark 1998, vol 1: 347.
35 Clark 1998, vol 1: 358.
36 Thomas Journal, CY 2604, item 3, ML.
37 Enclosure with VPRS 11, unit 7/330, PROV.

23 November 1840

After the conclusion of a ceremony at Nerre Nerre Warren, the following Western Port blacks left for Toolum, Kornwarra and eel-catching at Kirkbillesse. Those who departed were Kurboro and two lubras, Nern Nern, Beruke, Nuluptune, Burburo Burboro, Worrunditolong, Poligerry, Pickaninny Tommy, Turnmile, Bugup, Kullorluk, Jack Weatherley and lubra plus two unnamed youths. They came and wished Thomas goodbye and asked if he was angry at their going. He said no, and they told him that they would return after five night's *quamba*.[38]

Buckup/Buggup – Bonurong – elder son of Budgery Tom

Heir to Budgery Tom, clan head Mayone-Bulluk, whose country was around Carrum swamp (Barwick 1984: 117); A fine-looking fellow, six feet high, broad-shouldered, well-proportioned, with a bold, open cast of countenance, set off with well-trimmed whiskers and moustache ... a crack hand with the gloves ... good wrestler ... calm and lofty expression (R Boldrewood, 1899: 81).

1840 – His name is on a list of single Bonurong men (Thomas Journal, no date, CY 2605, item 1, ML); on a list of principal families, father Budgery Tom, brother Munite, (Thomas Journal, no date, CY 2605, item 1, ML); Feb 1840 – his father Budgery Tom is listed with wife and 2 pick as among those determined to go to Western Port on the raid (Thomas Journal, CY 2605, item 1); 13 Apr 1840 – on a list of families shifting encampment in Melbourne (Thomas Journal, CY 2605, item 1, ML).

2 Dec 1841 – One of seven men of the Waworong and Bonurong groups who volunteered to assist the authorities to capture the five Van Diemen's Land Aborigines who killed two whalers at Western Port in October 1841; all seven men joined the 1842 native police on its formation two months later; as a gratuity for capturing the Van Diemen's Land people, Buckup and the others asked for and received 1 blanket, 1 shirt, 1 pair of trousers, a leather belt with a buckle, a neck handkerchief and a straw hat; they asked also for a gun, but in vain (Thomas to Robinson, VPRS 11, Unit 8, PROV).

24 Feb 1842 – Enrolled in the native police and made his mark; received blankets, clothing and equipment, drilled twice daily (Dana to La Trobe, 31 March 1842, VPRS 19, Box 28, 42/674, PROV); 27 Jul 1842 – Rations have been issued to Buckup since 1 Feb last; a member of the 1st division;

---

38   Thomas Journal, CY 2605, item 2 and 3, frame 193, ML.

went to the westward [ie to the Western District on the first experimental excursion in the winter of 1842] (Dana to La Trobe, VPRS 19, Box 31, enc with 42/1143); 13 Sep 1842 – Buckup, mounted on Punch, one of the nine troopers who accompanied Dana on the first experimental journey to the Portland Bay district in the winter of 1842. On arrival at The Grange, Dana recorded the following, 'I have particularly to bring under your [La Trobe's] notice the good conduct of Yupton and Buckup during the march from Melbourne. The good care they took of their horses and their cleanly and orderly conduct. I have not one cause of complaint against one of the men. All obeying orders cheerfully and endeavouring to please me as much as possible' (Dana, Diary, in T O'Callaghan, SLV); 21 Sep 1842 – Buckup and Nerimbineck on duty at Mr Hunter's station; 27 Sep – 1 Oct 1842 – tracking the depredators and the 200 sheep taken from Desailley's station; 10 Oct 1842 – Buckup, Gellibrand, Nerimbineck and Yupton started with Dana for the Hopkins River to call at all stations along the way; 27 Oct 1842 – Buckup left at Rickett's station after travelling over 300 miles, he having caught a severe cold from the constant wet; 1 Nov 1842 – Buckup and Nerimbineck dragged the unconscious Dana from the flooded Wannon River after Dana nearly drowned trying to swim his horse across (Dana, Diary, in T O'Callaghan, SLV); 22 Nov 1842 – Commandant commends Buckup and Yupton who gallantly rescued him from drowning while Dana was trying to swim the flooded Wannon River; Buckup in particular deserves every praise for his conduct, he being only a few days off duty during the whole time the Corps was in the Western District (VPRS 19, Box 38, 42/2153, PROV); 5 Dec 1842 – Dana and the police arrived back in Melbourne from Portland Bay; Dana left the same day, taking Buckup and four other native police to join Commissioner Powlett at Westernport; 6 Dec 1842 – Dana left three of his police on duty with Powlett, taking Buckup and Gellibrand by boat to Jamieson's station at Westernport, and thence to check on the limeburners at Pt Nepean, and stations on the Mornington Peninsula (Dana, Diary, in T O'Callaghan, SLV); 1842 – aged 18, single, no children, never punished; on duty with Commissioner Powlett in May in pursuit of bushrangers; on duty three months with officers in Westernport District; several times handed drunken men [Europeans] over to the police in Melbourne; on duty in the Portland Bay District, often took and had charge of prisoners, conducted himself exceedingly well in many trying and dangerous circumstances; took four absconders at the Wannon and brought them to gaol; general conduct extremely good, obedient, quiet, anxious to perform his duty well and to improve (Dana, Return, for the year 1842 in *NSW Legislative Council Votes & Proceedings*, 1844).

4 Jan 1843 – Buckup warned Thomas, working in the garden at Nerre Nerre Warren of the presence of four suspicious characters, who turned out to be runaway sailors from the *Thomas Hughes*, a ship in port; they were four of the tallest, stoutest sailors Thomas ever saw; four native police took them into custody and escorted them to gaol at Melbourne [Thomas said two would have been enough, but they had no handcuffs] (Thomas, Quarterly Report, *NSW Legislative Council Votes & Proceedings*, 1843); 29 Sep 1843 – Buckup on duty in Portland Bay District since 27 June (Dana to La Trobe, enc with 43/7302 in 4/1135.1, AO of NSW); Jul to Aug 1843 – On the road to Portland; carrying despatches from The Grange to Mt Eckersley; pursuing the murderers of Mr Ward's child, captured on suspicion; Sep 1843 – Seeking Ward's child, tracking Bassett's murderers, severely wounded; Oct 1843 – Escorting prisoners, to the Protector's station, with despatches to Melbourne (Dana, Return, 30 June 1844, enc with 42/8217 in 4/1135.1, AO of NSW); 28 Oct 1843 – his name is on Thomas' list of men in the Native Police (CY 2606, item 1, ML); 3 Nov 1843 – Buckup and Henry returned from Portland Bay with despatches (Thomas, Journal, uncat Ms, set 214, item 3, ML); 11 Nov 1843 – Thomas recorded the story from the native police gathered around his fire at Merri Creek, of their exploits including the killing of 17 Aborigines, of whom Buggup shot 2 (Thomas, Journal, uncat Ms, set 214, item 3, ML); 30 Nov 1843 – Authority from the Col Sec to pay Buckup and Yupton, two of the best men who acted as Corporals, at the rate of threepence a day (VPRS 29, vol 13); Dec 1843 – To Mt Macedon (Dana, Return, 30 June 1844, enc with 42/8217 in 4/1135.1, AO of NSW).

1 to 31 Jan 1844 – Corporal Buckup receiving pay at the rate of threepence a day (VPRS 29, vol 18, PROV); Jan 1844 – At H.Q., assisting in the capture of an illicit still; Feb 1844 – With Commissioner Powlett to Gippsland (Dana, Return, 30 June 1844 – enc with 42/8217 in 4/1135.1, AO of NSW); 8 Feb 1844 – Buckup's absence in Gippsland noted by Thomas in his account of the native police present at the great gathering of tribes for judicial proceedings at Merri Creek (Thomas to Robinson, VPRS 11, unit 8, PROV); Mar 1844 – Returned from Gippsland with the Commissioner; Apr 1844 – Westernport and the bush; May 1844 – With Commissioner Powlett, collision at the Pyrenees; Jun 1844 – At H.Q., Conduct report, Corporal at threepence a day, conduct uniformly good (Dana Return, 30 June 1844, enc with 42/8217 in 4/1135.1, AO of NSW); No date, but either 1844 or 1845 – TA Browne records the arrival of a detachment of native police at his property Squattlesea Mere in the Portland Bay District: The Corporal

[Buckup] rode slightly in front, the others following in line ... Buckup saluted, 'We have been sent up by Mr Dana, Sir, to stop at this station a bit. Believe the blacks have been very bad about here' (TA Browne, 1899: 80–81).

Feb 1845 – Buckup was one of four native police with Sergeant Bennett who captured Wandilla, the Buninyong Aborigine who speared Booby, a young Aboriginal boy in the company of a European, on 12 December 1844 on the Keilor Rd (Dana to La Trobe, VPRS 19, Box 70, 45/714, PROV); on or about 2 Nov 1845 – Corporal Buckup involved in the shooting in self-defence of two Gippsland Aborigines at Robert Thompson's station Clydebank (Tyers' Deposition, enc with 46/1288, VPRS 19, Box 84, PROV); 27 Nov 1845 – General Muster, Commandant presented natives with money from His Honour for good conduct (VPRS 90, PROV); Corporal Buckup and another Native Trooper set off for Cape Otway with La Trobe and Sergeant McGregor (VPRS 90, PROV); 29 Nov 1845 – At Dana's request, have sanctioned pay of ten shillings each to troopers of the Corps as an approval of their uniform good conduct at Gippsland and the Wimmera last winter (La Trobe to Col Sec, 45/8847 in 4/2704, AO of NSW); Dec 1845 – Corporal Buckup has been receiving pay at threepence a day [separate from gratuity] (VPRS 29, vol 18, PROV); 21 Dec 1845 – Buckup, Native Place Yarra Yarra, enlisted Feb 1842, length of service 3 years 11 months (Dana, Return, VPRS 19, Box 77, 45/2179, PROV).

Jan 1846 – On Thomas' Family Connections census with his father Mooderrogar (Budgery Tom), mother Narragrook, Buggup male aged 20, brother Munnite, male aged 10 (Thomas CY 3083, ML); 16 Jan 1846 – Issued with the following articles prior to departure for duty at the Murray River with the 2nd division under Mr WAP Dana, saddle complete, 2 jackets, 2 pair duck trousers, 1 pair moleskins, 1 red shirt, 2 regatta shirts, new boots and spurs, sword and new carabine and cap, kit complete (VPRS 90, PROV); Jan 1846 – Listed as one of the Melbourne tribes still in the Corps on Thomas criticism of the native police (Thomas, Quarterly Report, December 1845–March 1846, enc with 46/3341 in 44/2745.1, AO of NSW); 1–31 Dec 1846 – Corporal Buckup receiving threepence a day (VPRS 29, vol 24, PROV).

1 Mar 1847 – Corporal Buckup, 2nd division, date of enlistment January 1842, horses name Surrey, aged but fit for duty (Dana, Return, VPRS 19, Box 97, 47/1861, PROV); 12 Apr 1847 – Buckup one of the native police in encampment at Merri Creek, having come down from

Nerre Nerre Warren for duty at the race meeting in Melbourne; 'Something amiss with the native police', wrote Thomas; they all sent their police uniforms back to Nerre Nerre Warren with a boy on horseback and refused to go themselves, except for Buckup, who accompanied the boy (Thomas to Robinson, VPRS 10, Box 8, 47/561, PROV); 5 Jul 1847 – Buckup one of 26 troopers approved by La Trobe for gratuity of five shillings (Dana to La Trobe, VPRS 19, Box 94, 47/1225, PROV); 15 Nov 1847 – Sergeant McGregor went with Corporal Buckup and placed him under the care of Dr Hobson (VPRS 90, PROV); 22 Nov 1847 – Buggup has had his left thigh amputated under ether at the residence of Dr Hobson on the banks of the Yarra (Thomas, Quarterly Report, September – November 1847, enc with 47/9842 in 4/2784, AO of NSW); 24 November 1847 – Robinson visited Buckup who has had his leg amputated at Dr Hobson's (Clark 2000, vol 5: 189); no date - Surgeon's bill, Dr Hobson for Buckup, ten pounds (Robinson Papers, vol 57A, ML); 1847 – A successful operation under the influence of ether was performed by Dr Hobson on Buckup, a domesticated Aboriginal of the Yarra tribe; the patient had suffered for a considerable time from a white swelling in the knee and was gradually sinking. A few days would have closed his existence. The limb was removed above the knee, and the patient recovered and is now well (Robinson, Annual Report for 1847, Papers, vol 61: 40, ML); 31 Dec 1847 – Corporal Buckup has been receiving pay at threepence a day (VPRS 29, vols 27 and 28, PROV).

21 Jan 1848 – Native Corporal Buckup returned from Dr Hobson's (VPRS 90, PROV); 2 Oct 1848 – Corporal Buckup died; 3 Oct 1848 – Corporal Buckup buried with military honours; 4 Oct 1848 – Men employed in fencing in grave (VPRS 90, PROV); 12 Oct 1848 – Dana reported to La Trobe Buckup's death; he was quite recovered from the effects of the operation, Dana said, but died from a violent cold and inflammation [others were sick at the time]; he was one of four Corporals being paid at the rate of threepence a day for steadiness and good conduct. Minuted by La Trobe, poor Buckup (Dana to La Trobe, VPRS 19, Box 111, 48/2169, PROV); 22 Dec 1848 – Thomas visited Nerre Nerre Warren to enquire into the deaths of Corporal Buckup and Bungaleena; found they had been carefully attended to, visited by the Colonial Surgeon twice (VPRS 11, Box 11/710, PROV).

26 Nov 1851 – Author of a letter to the editor praising the native police cites Buckup some years ago at the Gippsland races admonishing another unnamed native policeman **'Get out of that you drunken brute, you are a disgrace to the b… Corps'** (*Argus*, 26 November 1851).

> A fine intelligent man; after two expeditions he was made Corporal and received pay; he continued in the police until his death; had been on much arduous duty; from the effect of one very long day's ride, somehow his ankle was hurt by the stirrup iron, which was not considered of any consequence; however, after some months, it so affected his leg then his thigh, that to save his life amputation was required which he consented to. He was one of the first in the colony who underwent an operation under the influence of ether; the operation was performed by Doctors Hobson, Thomas and Barker. He lived a year after the operation making himself useful at the police barracks till his death on 2 September 1848 after nearly six years service (Thomas in Bride 1983[1898]: 405).

1841

'Callert' Merricks Cattle Station is shown on George D Smythe's map 'Survey the Coast from the West side of Port Phillip to Western Port with internal features'. Callert is located virtually on the coast of Western Port quite some distance from and south of Sandy Point: Smythe's map commences at Sandy Point, and is 'stretched' between what is now Somers and Balnarring. Callert would be almost exactly where Coolart is located now.[39]

29 January 1841

'Kulluk' is shown located north of Sandy Point on Thomas' map accompanying his letter to the Chief Protector of this date.[40]

no date

Yet another Thomas map annotated 'Not having my papers and instruments could not give a better sketch' shows Kulluk as a square, the Protector's hut at Tubberubbabel and Nerre Nerre Warren, also as a square.[41]

20 March 1841

'Alfred is now erecting huts on the shores of Western Port at Sandy Point the native name thereof being Colourt ... where we have found an abundance of fresh water'.[42]

---

39   VPRS 8168, P 1/12, file CS 17A, PROV.
40   VPRS 11, unit 7/365. The map has been separated from the correspondence and is now located at VPRS 6760, P O unit 1, file no 1, PROV. It is reproduced in Coutts 1983: 55; *HRV*, vol 2B: 578.
41   William Thomas Miscellaneous Papers, 1838–1868, CY 2984, frame 300, ML.
42   Letters of Henry Howard Meyrick, Ms 7959, Box 654, SLV.

16 May 1841

'Alfred has been all this time at Colourt, making preparations, building huts etc … cattle go to Colourt on Thursday'.[43]

23 June 1841

In a formal Petition to the Governor of New South Wales Sir George Gipps, Assistant Protector William Thomas 'prays that a Block of land equal in size to that of Narre Narre Warren be reserved between Sandy Point and Cape Schanck for the Aborigines of the Boonwurrung or Coast Tribe, and another station formed there on the scale and in every respect as the Central Stations'. Thomas gives as the reason 'the total failure of uniting the two tribes' at Narre Narre Warren – the Coast Tribe will not stay there out of their own country. They have 'occasionally visited it, but their visits have been but transient'.

In fact 'I believe that the friendship of the two tribes have suffered thereby, so much that the Coast tribe prefer the distant tribe of the Barrabools to their near neighbours, and continually are sallying forth to and fro to that District, and often upbraid your Petitioner for not coming and living among them'.[44]

10 September 1841

Letter to his mama from Henry Howard Meyrick at Colourt, giving his news – that he is bullock driving and cultivating, has sown two acres of wheat and one acre of oats, and that as soon as the rain finishes, he will plant an acre of potatoes.[45]

25 November 1841

Letter to his mama from Henry Howard Meyrick at Colourt saying that the economic crisis at Melbourne is fast approaching – no credit – not a single merchant in Melbourne can take up bills, and the consequence is that no one can get a farthing for their produce. But the Meyricks have cash and are not suffering. The whole neighbourhood has been thrown into the utmost confusion by the actions of the three VDL blacks' murder and robbery.[46]

24 March 1842

The encampment is at Turruk in Melbourne (Toorak). Two families of Goulburns and one Pangerang had arrived the previous day, and Budgery Tom excited the people to have other groups sent for. Captain Dana and Thomas had to use

---

43   Letters of Henry Howard Meyrick, Ms 7959, Box 654, SLV.
44   The formal petition is an enclosure in Thomas to La Trobe, VPRS 10, unit 3, 1841/909, PROV.
45   Letters of Henry Howard Meyrick, Ms 7959, Box 654, SLV.
46   Letters of Henry Howard Meyrick, Ms 7959, Box 654, SLV.

threats and all ended quietly. But this day, Lummer Lummer and Bobbinary endeavour to use some persuasion to separate the blacks at the encampment at Turruk. 'I interfere and Lummer Lummer states his determination to leave for Kulluk'.[47]

8 September 1843

Thomas in Melbourne was concerned for the welfare of his blacks and went to enquire along the beach. He called at a number of native encampments for which he gave the native name, and in the margin, the squatter occupying the run. These places were, Boollerim – Mr Shannessey, Binningean – Captain Baxter[48] and Ballewrungan – Mr Gorringe[49] where he stopped the night having travelled 43 miles on horseback. He found no blacks. Next day he visited Tuerong then Kangerong and heard at Kangerong that the blacks were at Kulluck. The next day was a Sunday but even so he rode from Tuerong to Kulluk and found the blacks. They then came to Tuerong and encamped by a creek, about 30 of them, all Western Ports except one Barrabool lubra and her child. 'The poor children and lubras look very sadly', he wrote, ' – poor creatures'.[50]

3 September 1844

Tuesday. Thomas told Yankee Yankee in Melbourne that great good might be done if he would prevail upon the Western Port blacks to settle down and cultivate the ground. His answer was:

> **Where it [illegible] Black Fellows want Kulluck and white man would not let them have it. You know when you was at Tubbarubbabel Black fellows stopped with you and worked and wanted to sow potatoes but you go away and go to the Yarra blacks.** These observations were so [illegible]. I am so often upbraided by the Western Port tribe for removing from them that it is useless arguing with them when I know I have not the power to accede were they so disposed.[51]

15 January 1845

Letter to his sister Susan from Henry Howard Meyrick at Colourt, relating the death of poor little Hamilton at Baillie's station 90 miles from Melbourne on the Gippsland Road. Alfred was there when the accident happened and gives all the details.[52]

---

47   Thomas Journal, CY 2605, item 5, frame 397, ML.
48   We know this as the run Carup Carup.
49   Ballewrungan is Poleorongong, the important encampment at the back of Mt Eliza.
50   Thomas Journal, CY 2606, item 2, ML. Thomas crossed out another sentence in this days' entry for which the verb cannot be read. It looks like a matter of regret for the station they once had.
51   Thomas Journal, CY 2606, item 3, ML.
52   Letters of Henry Howard Meyrick, Ms 7959, Box 654, SLV.

18 August 1845

The blacks are very fast disappearing from the face of the earth … of 'our' tribe of blacks there are only eight men and children and one woman … Yal Yal is about to marry Puppa-co-ran-go-rok only daughter of Brikko Morning or the one-eyed.[53]

11 April 1846

Alfred has sold Colourt for 90 pounds.

17 April 1847

Henry Meyrick's summary for his mother of his life so far in Port Phillip says that he went to Colourt, commenced to form a station, and after spending 60 pounds was obliged to leave it, then went to Narren Gullen a place where nothing can possibly thrive and purchased cattle from one whom he esteemed a friend but was not. The cattle were wild, and many of them got away and the others did no good, so he moved back to Coolourt. The cattle did not do much better at Colourt, so, after some years hard work at the dairy he and cousin Alfred found themselves in the hard times of the general financial collapse in Port Phillip. They tried sheep but sheep did not do any better, and because they were scabby the only place they could travel them to was Gippsland. Byrne, the man to whom they sold Colourt, did no better with the land.[54]

1849

Thomas went looking for the Western Port blacks, by this time with their numbers augmented with Gippsland wives. There were none at the nine mile beach (Boolerum), none down Arthurs Seat way, and none on the Western Port coast. Mr Mantuan from Kullert between the Point[55] and Sandy Point told Thomas that there were no Aborigines in that district.[56]

27 February 1849

His name means bear. Thomas heard this day from a settler in Melbourne that Kurbooro had died at Kulluk.[57]

---

53   Letters of Henry Howard Meyrick, Ms 7959, Box 654, SLV.
54   Hales and Le Cheminant 1997: 42–43.
55   Now Pt Leo, but known then as Bobbinaring (various spellings) Point.
56   Thomas Weekly Report, 20–27 July 1849, CY 2606, item 3–8, ML.
57   Thomas Journal, 20–28 February 1849, CY 2606, frame 570, ML.

Kur.bo.roo/Kar.bor.er/Car.per.rer/Carborer/Kurboro/ Kurburu/Kurburra/Kaborer/Kurboror alias Mr Ruffy

His country was the Yallok Bulluk, from Mantuans to Jamiesons along the four muddy rivers at Western Port (Thomas Miscellaneous Information, CY 3130, ML).

Undated – 'Seasons as given by black, Kurboro, WP, summer – Woodin, winter – Pereen, spring – Perripe, autumn – Pilligerin' (CY 3126, frame 160, ML).

1839 – On Thomas' more correct census as Kubburrough, male 42 years, with two lubras, Kurundum aged 20 and Bowyeup aged 16 (CY 3082, frame 51, ML).

1840 – Undated – Kurboro with 2 lubras and 2 pickaninnys is listed at Arthurs Seat among the 57 determined to go on the revenge raid to Western Port (CY 2605, frame 8, ML); 7 Jun 1840 – Car-per-rer's name is on a list of blacks presently at Tubberubbabel given to Robinson in Melbourne by Billy Lonsdale (Clark 1998, vol 1: 344); 12 Jun 1840 – Kurburo with two lubras and Old Tuart is at Tubberubbabel (CY 2604, item 3, ML); in August 1840 he speared his wife and was most distressed afterwards as has been seen in Chapter 4.

1841 – In the afternoon of Wednesday 31 March 1841, Kurboro's lubra Quondom struck Mrs Wilson [manager's wife] at Nerre Nerre Warren because Mrs Wilson would not give Quondom water, on the grounds that she could not spare it. Quondom snatched some water and threw it on Mrs Wilson's face, then struck her. Thomas broke and burned Quondom's digging stick in front of her as a punishment. Then Kurboro speared Quondum in the arm. Then Thomas recorded 'I was much displeased with Kurboro who was also in tears. I showed great sorrow & spirted water from my mouth for some time on the wound, pretended to mourn' (Thomas, CY 2605, item 5, frame 256, ML).

1842 – On Wednesday 17 February, at Nerre Nerre Warren Thomas recorded 'a cruel punishment and fight' – 'a lubra from her brother Kurboro is most seriously maltreated – for marrying herself without consent of her Brother' (Byrt 2004: 76); 28 Feb 1842 – Kurboro and his family plus other named blacks left Nerre Nerre Warren for Western Port (Byrt 2004: 76).

1 Jul 1844 – Carborer, now at Narre Narre Warren is a Yowenjerrie, alive, the latter speaks the language of the Gippsland tribes (Clark 1998, vol 4: 120); He and Munmunginna are the only two people living of the Yowenjerry (Clark 1998, vol 4: 120).

1846 – Kurboror is listed on the Family Connections census with his wife Quondom, but no children (CY 3083, ML).

Kurburu's song – the words and the tune in the key of B minor are reproduced in *Native Tribes of South-East Australia*.[1] The information came from Barack, and Howitt's understanding was that it was composed and sung by a bard called Kurburu who lived during the early settlement of the country by the whites near where the town of Berwick now stands. He was supposed to have killed a native bear, and being possessed by its *Murup* or spirit, thenceforth sang its song.

Kurburu's Song.

Sounded as if in the key of B minor.

Tempo moderato. M ♩ = 100.

ē - - na gur - é - a   nung ngal - úr - ma   bá - reng

gūr - - uk ba   mirnín   mirnín   nge bŭrun   bángan   bŏdha[1]

e - lḗ - re   mŭr - ingå̄ : ē   yam-yam mŭdhan guru bai wĩrge ngū-ràk.

Fig 30. 'Words and Music of Kurburu's song'

Reproduced from Howitt 1904: 420.

'I was not able to get a verbatim translation of it, but Berak gave me the following free translation:

You cut across my track

You spilled my blood

And you broke your tomahawk on my head.

1. Howitt 1904: 420–422.

Kurboro a well known Western Port black, and held in high esteem as a sorcerer, a dreamer and diviner, was named "The Bear" under the following circumstances. Kur.bo.roo was born at the foot of a tree, and during his mother's trouble a bear in the tree growled and grunted until Kur.bo.roo was born, when he eased his noise. By this, it was said, the bear intended to show that the male child born at the foot of the tree should have the privilege of consulting the bear, and the child was called Kur.bo.roo. Kur.bo.roo attained to some excellence in his profession and was regarded by all as a very wise man and a doctor. When a black dreams of bears it is a sad omen. All the people are afraid when anyone dreams of bears. One time when there were about 200 blacks at Nerre Nerre Warren, including about 18 at the school, Kur.bo.roo had a dream. He dreamed that he was surrounded by bears. He awoke in a great fright about one o'clock in the morning, and at once aroused the whole encampment. It was half an hour or more before I could discover the cause of the great excitement everywhere apparent. Fires were suddenly set ablaze. The young blacks climbed the trees, cut down boughs and fed the fires. The men women and children rushed hither and thither displaying the greatest terror. I reasoned with them, sought to soothe them, endeavoured to control them, but all my efforts were useless. They fled from the spot where they had so long lived in comfort. By eight o'clock in the morning, the forest was a solitude – not a soul remained; and all because of a dream of Kur.bo.roo'.[II]

Again, Thomas wrote of being out with a celebrated Western Port black, tracking five other blacks. They lost the tracks, then passed a tree where a bear made a noise as they passed.

'The black stopped and a parley commenced. I stood alternately gazing at the black and the bear. At length my black came to me and said **Me big one stupid; bear tell me you no you go that way**. We immediately crossed the creek, and took a different tack. Strange as it may appear, we had not altered our course above one and a half miles before we came upon the tracks of the five blacks and never lost them thereafter'.[III]

Thomas also wrote about a transgression of cultural norms regarding the bear: it was permissible to cook and eat the bear, but not to skin it. Thomas 'sadly wanted a bear's skin to make a cap but I could never get it'. One day he importuned a Yarra black who had brought in a

II. Quotation from Thomas in Smyth 1876, vol 1: 447–448.

III. Thomas in Bride 1983[1898]: 427.

bear before the rest had returned from hunting, to skin it. Initially he refused, but at length after bribing from Thomas, and assurances that the sorcerers and other chiefs were absent and would never know about it, the young man skinned the bear and Thomas took the skin to his tent. But the man grew anxious and remorse overtook him. He said **'Poor blacks lose 'em all water now'**, and he became so alarmed, and exhibited such terror that the old doctors came to enquire into the cause. He told all. Much excitement followed, but Thomas laughed at their fears. At length though, he was obliged to return the skin to them, and the skin and the bear were buried in the same manner as a black man is buried. 'Though the bear was actually roasting' Thomas wrote, 'his body was taken away and buried with the skin. This ceremony they all believed would propitiate the bears, and avert the calamity of a loss of water'.[IV]

Thomas recorded too, the belief system underpinning this behaviour regarding the bear:

'The bear too, must not be skinned. The blacks have a strange tale of the bears having stolen all their *tarnuk* (buckets) and drained a creek of water, and so bewildered the blacks that Karakarook came down, and it was settled by Karakarook, on the part of the blacks, that they would no more take the skins from the bears bodies, and on the part of the bears, that they would no more in any way molest the blacks in supply of water or vessel.'[V]

Brough Smyth offers two more elaborate versions of the story, and of the belief, as well as the large statement that 'The Native Bear, Kur-bo-roo, is the sage counsellor of the Aborigines in all their difficulties'. In the Upper Yarra version, not only could the bear not be skinned, his bones could not be broken either, and 'No one has roasted Koob-borr without his skin or broken his bones in killing him since the law was made'.[VI] Wesson has identified Karborer as the author of the views of the mountains taken from Yerring station (Smyth 2002: 16–17).

IV. Quotation from Thomas in Smyth 1876, vol 1: 447.

V. Thomas in Bride 1983[1898]: 427.

VI. Smyth 1876, vol 1: 446–449.

King Benbow's request for land

20 March 1849

The occasion was the formal visit from New South Wales of Governor Fitzroy. The Aborigines arrived in Melbourne on 17 March having been told that His Excellency would give them a feast. On this day, Benbow said that he was going to see the governor. In the afternoon, well equipped in his Commissariat uniform, he waited at the entrance to the Royal hotel for his turn to be introduced to the governor. He said that:

> **he had sent up his brass plate like white man's letter** [Thomas inserted "meaning card" in brackets] **and that bye and bye he was to see the governor** … he had been duped by the white men … his object … to ask the governor for a country for the Western Port blackfellows.[58]

27 July 1849

Thomas' weekly report states that he went looking for his Western Port blacks, and Mr Mantuan, from Kullert between Sandy Point and the Point told him that there were no Aborigines in that district.[59]

15 July 1850

In reply to a request from the Governor in Sydney via La Trobe asking where the reserve for the Bonurong should be located, Thomas wrote:

> It is with regret that I am not prepared to state precisely where the reserve of the Coast 'or Boonurong' tribe should be situated and that from their growing restless disposition which seems to increase upon them as their number awfully decrease – Since their friendly intercourse with some tribes in Gipps Land they may be said as a body to be more in that District than in their own. A few years back when shifting from Melbourne their regular route was natural, shifting gradually along the Coast to the nine mile beach, Mt Eliza, (Berringwallin) Mount Martha, (Nerngallin) Arthurs Seat, (Wongho) Point Nepean (Monmore) Cape Schank (Tuornangho) Sandy Point (Yollodunnho) then to the index & returning in land by Mahoon (Western Port plains) to Dandenong the whole circuitous route of their Country, but the last 2 or 3 years, from Melbourne they merely take a turn to the nine mile beach and make direct for the route to Gipps Land leaving the most valuable part of their country and lairs located regularly deserted. –

---

58   A contemporary sketch of King Benbow in his uniform wearing his brass plate is reproduced in *HRV*, vol 2B: 546. The written record is Thomas Half-yearly Report, 30 June 1849, at 4/2872, Pt 2, 1849 in AO of NSW.
59   CY 2606, item 3–8, ML.

Nor is this the only difficulty another arises which makes me Cautious ere I offer any fixed plan respecting them to Your Honor, which is the diminition of their numbers. Your Honors position among us must perceive to a considerable extent their decrease even had not my half yearly returns when Assistant Protector made such known to the Government, the last 6 months has as tho' to vie with former mortality shifted no small number from the ranks of the living to the dead, that what with those who have died by the visitation of God in a natural way (and many of these have through intemperate habits brought on premature death) and those in an unnatural way I may say by the visitation of the Devil, it is my firm impression & I think I am not overdrawing the mortality when I state the startling fact that not one-third of their number exist which at my first coming among them numbered but eighty-three, cannot leave more than twenty-eight. I fear there are less, and no children to fill up the ranks of the dead, points the dial of mortality to steadily to their speedy extinction – taking these considerations into account it would be useless sacrificing a great block of land for this tribe. I should say a regular section of 640 acres would suffice, but before even this is granted or any expense gone to by Government I should prefer taking a careful census of this minished tribe, & consult them that they might select the locality. Were I left to settle the spot it would be on the Coast near Mt Eliza or Sandy Point.[60]

1850

On a list of runs in the County Mornington and Intermediate Districts, along the coast from Mt Eliza to Bass River, Thomas lists as number 14 'Willm Payne, Coolert W Pt Bay, 19 square miles'.[61]

1850

An amended schedule for pastoral run Port Phillip No 147, submitted by William Payne corrects the information previously submitted regarding the run's southern boundary. On the previously submitted schedule he described Coollert's southern boundary as the run Cape Schanck, thus claiming all the land from Somers to West Head. On the amended schedule, he states the southern boundary is 'a bluff and camping ground about three miles on the coast towards Cape Schanck from Coolort'.[62] The other boundaries remain the same; the northern boundary is Warringite Creek which is halfway between Coollert and

60 Byrt 2004, CD CY 3084 B DOC.
61 Thomas Papers, CY 3127, ML.
62 VPRS 5920, jacket mf no 296, PROV. This fact will be important in the identification of Aboriginal encampments. Three miles from the homestead Coolart is Cliff Road, the high ground at Balnarring/Merricks beaches. The question is whether encampment refers to an Aboriginal place or a cattle camp. Encampment is not a bush word, not a usual word to describe a plain and simple cattle camp.

Mrs King's run, the eastern boundary is Western Port, the western boundary is the Arthurs Seat Ranges run.[63] This bluff and camping ground three miles from Coolourt would be Balnarring Heights.

10 January 1855

On Harry Drew's application to transfer the run Coolert Station to Joseph Hann, the Commissioner of Crown Lands has commented 'this is an original run – improvements considerable – good dwelling house, stockyards, cultivation paddocks – no road access near homestead, allowed 640 acres at upset price of 20 shillings per acre'.[64]

no date

On a list entitled 'Names of Places found afterwards' by Assistant Protector William Thomas is the following:

'Merarmile – A rise of springs about 10 miles NE of Arthur's Seat these springs feed Ner Ner, Kunnulong falls into the swamp at Kulluk from there to Nerwein into the sea by Sandy Point'.[65]

no date

'Yellodungoo – Sandy Point'.[66]

no date

'Sandy Point – Yellodungo'.[67]

1850s–1860s

Roll Plan 88 shows Coolort, 10,000 acres, extending from Warrangine Creek southwards to Merricks Creek during the occupancy of Joseph Hann.

1869

W Owens' map of Victoria with pastoral runs shows Coolurt as a district name for the country extending from Sandy Point to Tyabb.

63   VPRS 5920, jacket mf no 296, PROV.
64   Drew to CCL Barnard, 9 February 1854, 54/152, VPRS 5920, jacket mf no 296, PROV.
65   Byrt 2004, CD Language Files, 214. 23 BO. DOC, p. 71.
66   Byrt 2004, CD Language Files, 214. 23 BO. DOC, p. 70.
67   Byrt 2004, CD Language Files, 214. 22. DOC, frame 273, p. 523. This is annotated 'HMAS *Cerberus*, sdm', which is Dr Stephen Mayne, La Trobe University, who did the language transcriptions for Byrt.

8. The raid into Gippsland and the massacres remembered

The evidence for the pre-contact massacre which occurred between Kangerong and Arthurs Seat, at Buckkermitterwarrer, comes into the records in the context of the Bonurong raid into Gippsland in February 1840. Thomas was embarrassed that his blacks had deceived him – after this raid, he understood better the meanings of their actions; if they left the women and children behind, and took spears, it meant trouble for him. It is an interesting comment on how well they were reading power and authority at that time, that though they successfully kept knowledge of the purpose of the raid into Gippsland from Thomas, they had no qualms about being frank with the young Samuel Rawson who was told that it was a revenge raid,[1] while Thomas had to work it out for himself from behaviours.

After this raid Thomas obliged them to give him mudmaps of their proposed routes and estimations of their time away on their journeys. He was appalled that they brought back flesh, and he could scarcely credit that they exulted in the event. Bypassing the Chief Protector, he reported this raid directly to La Trobe. Then he set about investigating the raid by seemingly innocuous questions to various participants. It is only through this investigation that we can discover firm facts about the Two Fold Bay[2] tribe's earlier massacre of nearly half the Bonurong – men, women and children at Buckkermitterwarrer: two other raids, one at Brighton and one at Jamieson's at the Kunnung River are also recalled.

Thomas' painful duty

Thomas commences his June 1840 letter to La Trobe with a statement that it is his 'painful duty' to inform him that the Western Port blacks had deceived him in February, by leaving all the women and children and the old men with him at the river Kunnung at Western Port, and telling him that they were off to the east (Gippsland) for *bullen bullen* tails, whereas in fact they had gone with the specific intention of finding and killing Gippsland blacks, eating their flesh and bringing some back to Western Port.[3]

---

1   Samuel Rawson, 'Journal from November 1839 kept while forming a new station at Western Port on the southern coast of New Holland', 9 March 1840, Ms 204/1, NLA.

2   'Two Fold Bay' does not mean the place on the south coast of New South Wales, as explained in Chapter 3 with reference to Wesson's study. 'Two Fold Bay' is a descriptor of the Kurnai of Gippsland; but as 'Two Fold Bay' is the expression that the Bonurong and Thomas used consistently, I follow them here, as I do in their use of 'blacks'.

3   The draft version is in Thomas Papers, CY 2946, frames 53–56, ML; the final version is Thomas to La Trobe, 6 June 1840, VPRS 10, unit 2, 1840/569, PROV.

Thomas, in farewelling them on their journey into the country of their enemies warned them not to kill 'wild blacks' and even offered to accompany them and stand between them and the Two Fold Bay blacks and endure the spearings himself. He told them that if they did kill blacks, he would tell the governor. They were away far longer than they had planned[4] and Thomas feared they had fallen victim to their enemies. They arrived back weak with exhaustion, and he had to nurse them for three or four days; but he was suspicious of the time elapsed and searched their bags. He found nothing, and they assured him that everything was alright, so matters rested.

Then a settler from Westernport (Jamieson) arrived at the encampment at Kunnung and told Thomas that his blacks (Thomas') had shown 'my blacks' (Jamieson's) the flesh of a human body which they said was part of the body of a Two Fold Bay black. Thomas interviewed the 20 Bonurong and they denied it. Then three other settlers told him the same story – Thomas' blacks had shown 'their blacks' the flesh.

Thomas then devised what he called 'a cunning strategy' to determine the truth of the matter. He stated in his second periodical report that it was on the 24 May 1840, a Sunday, at Tubberubbabel that he finally got the truth.[5] Seemingly innocently, he questioned a youth who had been on the raid, and enquired where they had slept each night. He used his journal to check the number of nights they had been away. Then he confronted 'the principal actors'. He told them that he, Thomas, knew all about his blackfellows, and that God knows, sees, and hears all too. He then repeated back to the principal actors what he had learned from the youth – where and when they encamped each night on the raid. This unnerved them, and one of them began to cry. Then the whole story came out. They had followed tracks and come upon a sleeping encampment of 14 at Taringal by the Snowy River (it was actually the Tarwin River, but Snowy was what he wrote in his first report). They killed nine with spears and tomahawks, one man, two lubras and six children – the rest escaped. The bodies of two of the children were quartered and brought back to Kunnung. As well, the whole body of a little child was brought back and planted in the bush not 20 yards from where Thomas was camped at Tobinerk. They 'showed no remorse', in fact, 'exulted in their triumph' but were 'dreadfully frightened' of what La Trobe would do when Thomas reported.[6]

---

4   The hunting party was expected back on 29 inst, Thomas to Robinson from Kunnung, 27 February 1840, VPRS 11, unit 7/300, PROV.

5   VPRS 4410, unit 3/67, PROV.

6   Enlarged photocopy obtained from ML: Thomas Papers, CY 2946, frames 53, 54, 55, 56. This is the version in Thomas' Journal. The version that he actually sent to La Trobe is at VPRS 10, unit 2, 1840/569, PROV.

The eating of flesh

Samuel Rawson who was at Kunnung at the time recorded their return on 9 March 1840 'bringing immense quantities of human flesh with them; it seems they had come upon the tribe when the men were away hunting and killed ten, eight of whom were children'. After describing the fine river and the fine countryside around the victims' encampment, Rawson continued:

> the blacks on their return staid several days at the station and feasted with the women and children on the flesh they had brought back and seemed to enjoy it amazingly, and were much surprised that I would not join them. It had exactly the appearance of a piece of fat pork with a very thick skin.[7]

In an undated later record, Thomas said that they 'returned with pieces of mutilated bodies of their victims with them, arms, legs and pieces of flesh principally of female children eaten by them and friends'.[8] About the practices of the Bonurong enemies he wrote:

> The Gippsland blacks, Omeo and others are cannibals, so far as eating their enemies – all my blacks that they have killed they eat – and when capture any of another tribe at a distance if practicable bring them prisoner giving them food etc[9] till arrive at their tribe, when a Grand feed. They watch over him at night, making him sleep in the middle of them, some invariably watch at night – their victim was always killed by Tomahawk at back of the neck – married men and chiefs alone eat the manfood – single men, women and children don't partake.[10]

The Chief Protector himself was well aware of much of the detail of eating flesh: a number of Port Phillip men and a Port Phillip woman, including Mr King and Mr Murry produced flesh, including a child's head, hand and foot, and gave killing and cooking details over three days of interrogation by Robinson in September 1839,[11] long before this raid.

Robinson had encountered the practice as early as 1836 when he recorded the explanation offered by Buckley. The full quotation is as follows:

> A native boy from the Bar.ra.bal hills which Captain Robson had brought to the settlement from this station was killed by the Westernport Aborigines and the body was found in the river mutilated, parts skinned

---

7   Rawson, Journal, Ms 204/1, NLA.
8   Notebook, Brough Smyth Papers, Ms 8781, Box 1176/6(b), SLV.
9   Thomas inserts a superscript here which seems to read, 'like the American Ind'.
10   CY 2984: 220, ML.
11   The full story is in Clark 1998, vol 1: 79–82.

and pieces of flesh cut off, and the people at the settlement said it was cannibalism. I say not, I do not believe them cannibals. Buckley says not, says they sometimes eat for or out of revenge.[12]

George Henry Haydon saw human flesh in their possession on several occasions.[13]

They did not eat flesh indiscriminately – there were two categories of 'enemy'. Thomas recorded that:

> it cannot be denied that they are cannibals in the strictest sense of the Word, they eat the flesh and drink the blood of their enemies – not those with whom they occasionally carry on a Warfare, but with what they term Marnmate or wild Blacks, who are in the habit of [illegible] all who fall in their way.[14]

Clearly there is a world of meaning in the eating of flesh and these are only Thomas' and Robinson's initial encounters with that world:[15] from our stance in the twenty-first century it may be important to attempt to understand it, but not until all the evidence is considered, not merely the earliest.

Mummification

In any analysis of the treatment of the bodies of killed enemies, mummification needs to be mentioned as well. Thomas described briefly the process thus: the hand is placed between two flat stones which are slightly heated. The wrist is filled with red ochre till the hand is hard and dry. The stones are then removed and the hand is perfectly seasoned and not the least offensive in smell. Thomas saw such hands brought back from Gippsland by Port Phillip Aborigines in 1847, suspended round the neck held with great veneration.[16] Robinson recorded that Thomas told him of five mummified hands brought from Gippsland and worn as 'charms belonging to dead persons'.[17]

Another part of that world of meaning is the practice of not permitting children born to live. Quite early, in describing the grief of the young mother Quondum, whose baby had died from natural causes as he believed at the time, though subsequently he changed his mind, Thomas made a marginal note scorning the belief held by some Europeans that the Port Phillip people killed and ate

---

12   Robinson Journal, 29 December 1836, in Plomley 1987: 409.
13   Haydon 1846: 105.
14   Thomas Second Periodical Report, VPRS 4410, unit 3/67: 22, PROV.
15   Robinson learned subsequently of reports of cannibalism from other districts; for example, the reports for the Western District are mentioned in Critchett 1990.
16   Thomas Journal, 1 June 1847 to 31 August 1847, VPRS 4410, unit 4/99, PROV.
17   Clark 2000, vol 5: 171. An illustration of a 'dead hand' is to be found in Howitt 1904: 460.

their babies.[18] Nor have I seen any such evidence – the point that I am making is that their views on life and death demand more respect from us than the dismissive 'our lot were a peaceful lot' which denies them their rightful place in our histories.

Trophies

Thomas adds further detail of the raid into Gippsland in his journal record. He insisted that the blacks bring to him what they had left of trophies. They produced one man's cloak with 16 spear holes in it, one lubra's basket and a tomahawk. It was Burrenum who broke down and cried bitterly, but even so, none felt sorry for their actions. After showing his disapprobation, Thomas preached to them from the sixth commandment – thou shalt do no murder. He explained the difference between wilful murder and accidental killing.[19]

The route to Gippsland

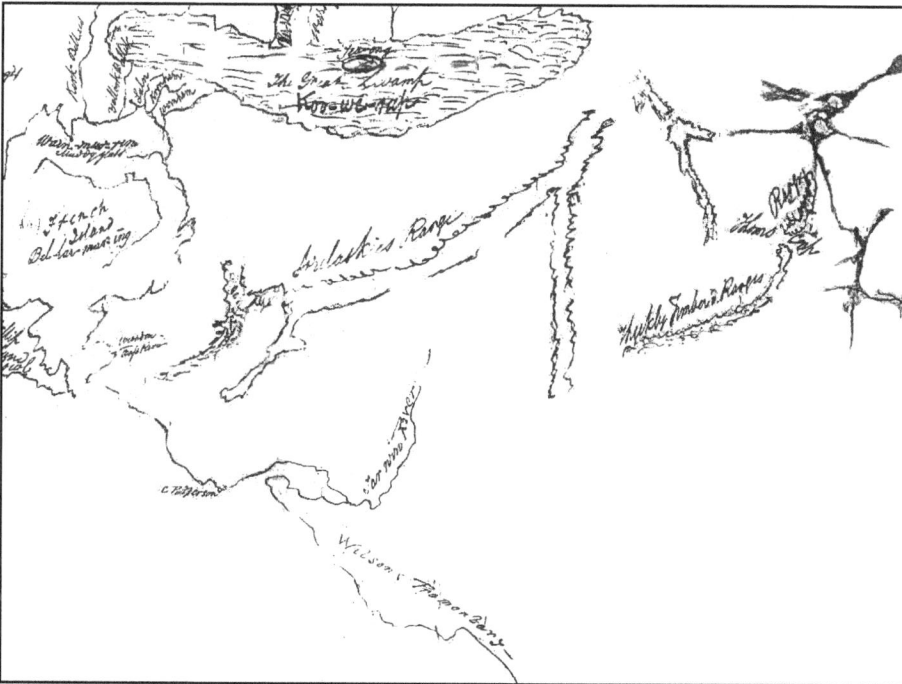

Fig 31. 'Physical features of country, showing departure point and destination of February 1840 raid'

Thomas sketch, from the William Thomas papers, 1834–1868, 1902, Mitchell Library, reproduced with the permission of the State Library of New South Wales.

---

18   13 February 1840, CY 2605, item 1, ML.
19   Thomas Journal, CY 2604, item 3, ML.

The camping places on the raid into Gippsland and the number of nights stopped were as follows:

- 1 night at Perumbo – water
- 2 nights at Langnun – ditto [possibly Lang Lang]
- 1 night at Tenden – ditto
- 4 nights at Barbinbulluk – ditto
- 2 nights at Mullum Mullum – ditto [bracketed with Tondubet]
- 3 nights at Kurlkunduk – ditto, very big *bullen bullen* [probably Kilcunda]
- 2 nights at Bunolm – ditto
- 1 night at Peandum – ditto
- 3 nights at Pulunuruk – ditto
- 3 nights at Boyup Boyup – ditto
- 1 night at Teremit – ditto
- 1 night at Tobinerk – ditto.[20]

The name of Dr Jamieson's station is Baggal-norruck.[21] The distance from the starting point near modern Koo-wee-rup to the Snowy River is 165 miles as the crow flies: there and back in 21 days always seemed unlikely considering the terrain. In his second periodical report Thomas gives the destination not as the Snowy River, but 'towards Wilson's promontory', ie the Tarwin River near the Bonurong boundary with the Kurnai, and this seems more likely.[22] It would have been from Tobinerk that they gave the great shout that the lubras heard and responded to at Kunnung, mentioned in Chapter 3.

Ross' testimony, as Thomas took it down, does not agree totally with the above. Ross said that there was no water at the first encampment, and that they managed by drinking about ten quarts of water from a hollow in a large dead tree on the ground. Longlun, where they stopped two nights was on a large body of water that goes to Mr Andersons.[23] The 16 February was the last night he encamped with them and they were up all night making spears: at that stage they were keeping to a course NE by N bearing to the E, and getting into country almost impassable, with no food but bears.[24]

To explain to La Trobe the deadly enmity that had existed for a very long time between the Bonurong and their eastern neighbours, Thomas went on to list the

---

20   CY 2605, item 1, with vocab, ML.
21   Thomas Miscellaneous Papers, CY 2984, frame 282, ML.
22   VPRS 4410, unit 3/67: 13, PROV.
23   Thomas Massie and Samuel Anderson were at the Bass River, the furthest station out from Melbourne in 1840, Thomas to Robinson, 27 February 1840, CY 2946, item 2, ML. According to Gunson they used bricks from the old 1826 settlement at Corinella in the construction of their first homestead, Gunson 1968: 19.
24   Thomas Journal, 17 February 1840, CY 2605, item 1, ML.

events in which the Bonurong had suffered at the hands of the Kurnai. Thomas was at pains to point out that he was not excusing or justifying their behaviour, and neither were they. Thomas explained to La Trobe that he had known about these historic events almost from when he arrived in Melbourne, and that they formed part of the Bonurong *singing*.[25]

The Bonurong suffering at the hands of the Two Fold Bay tribe[26]

'About four years ago [1836] 77 people were killed at Little Brighton not nine miles from Melbourne'.[27] Thomas' writing is not easy to read, though as scholars know, it is nowhere near as difficult as Robinson's, but Thomas' numbers are usually quite clear. In this case, he has used an upward sweep before the down stroke of the numeral. At first glance, the number here appears to be 77. But 77 is a very large number of people to be killed in a dawn raid by rushing a sleeping encampment which this event was. For a long time, I doubted the evidence of my own eyes and was inclined to believe that the number must be 11.

The high number though, was confirmed by Munmunginna to Robinson in 1844. A party of five Europeans including Robinson, Sergeant Windredge of the Native Police, George Henry Haydon, another policeman named Keef plus six Native Police including Munmunginna, were pushing into Gippsland in an attempt to open up a road for commerce. As they struggled through the country inland from Cape Liptrap, Robinson recorded that it belonged to the Yowwengerre section of the Boongerong, now extinct, extirpated by the Boro Boro Willum or Gippsland blacks.

> The chief or mor mun of the Yowengerre was Pur. Rine, native place Warmun, is dead. This tribe once powerful are defunct and the country in consequence is unburnt having no native inhabitants. This is the reason why the country is so scrubby. The natives of Gippsland visit the inlet at Pubin.borro and other inlets in the snowing season. There must have been an awful massacre of these natives. Mun mun jin ind's father

---

25   In his 1858 paper for Mr Duffy on Songs and Dances, Thomas distinguishes between 'sacred or profane' songs. Sacred and traditional songs are usually accompanied by 'effigys' which bear some resemblance to what they represent in song. The carved tree at Worawen and the monuments at Tobinerk would seem to fall into this category of effigies, with sacred songs attached to them (CY 3131, frame 18, ML).

26   Robinson recorded in September 1840 that the Waverong natives called all the Twofold Bay natives Tarn. dil or Bar.bar.ry (Clark 2000, vol 6: 87).

27   This was well known to early settlers, is mentioned in histories of Brighton, and pioneers' accounts – it was commonplace information in early Melbourne history. It happened in, or near, what is now Hurlingham park in East Brighton: the Aboriginal name for it was Worrowen meaning place of sorrow (Thomas Quarterly Report 1 July to 31 December 1849, Dixson Library), and the corroboree tree on which stick figures were incised detailing the events was still standing in the 1860s. It eventually fell after a lightning strike, according to early Brighton pioneers' accounts.

was a Yowengerre; Mun mun jin ind gave me an account of the natives of the country and also gave me the names. The natives of Gippsland have killed 70 of the Boongerong at Brighton.[28]

In a subsequent account Thomas gives more detail:

blacks remember the awful affair at Warrowen (place of sorrow) near where Brighton now stands, where in 1834 nearly a quarter of the Western Port blacks were massacred by the Gippsland blacks who stole up on them before dawn of day.[29]

In a later paper for Mr Duffy on monuments and inscriptions, Thomas gives further detail of this massacre in his description of an incised tree:

[They have] no monuments whatever further than devices on trees where any great calamity have befallen them. On a large gum tree in Brighton, on the estate of Mr McMillan was a host of blacks lying as dead carved on the trunk for a yard or two up. The spot was called Woorroowen or incessant weeping. Near this spot in the year 1833 or 4, the Gippsland blacks stole at night upon the Western Port or Coast tribe and killed 60 or 70 of them.[30]

My conclusion is that the high number killed at Little Brighton is correct, 77.

As well, it follows logically, that if the 70 people killed were 'nearly a quarter' of the Bonurong, then the total Bonurong population was of the order of 300 or so in the early 1830s. An early pioneers' history of Brighton states that the Aborigines told early settlers tales of a tradition which they had of a great tribal fight in the vicinity of Landcox Park, in which 'large numbers' were killed. In the early days, settlers found bones and evidences of camp fires having been numerous at the place pointed out as the scene of the fight.[31] Another pioneer's account mentions ploughing up bones by the earliest settler at Hurlingham Park.[32] These two parks are practically contiguous in East Brighton, in the triangle between the Nepean Highway, Hawthorn Road and North Road. Before being renamed separately by Europeans, they would have been the same place or space.

---

28   Clark 1998, vol 4: 49.
29   Thomas half-yearly report, 1 July to 31 December 1849, VPRS 10, unit 11, 1850/55, PROV.
30   William Thomas Miscellaneous Papers, CY 2984, frame 52, ML.
31   John B Cooper, 'The History of Brighton 1842–1925', Ms Typescript, Brighton City Library.
32   Cheeseman Family Papers, Brighton Historical Society.

Munmungina/Manmangina/Munmunginna/ Munmunginnong/Mun-mun-gin-non/Munmungeena/ Munmungena/Munmungin/Marnminginner/ Munonmungi/Mr Dun/Dr Bailey/Jack

Brother to Burrenum (Mr Dredge), recognised authority on the Mornington Peninsula but not a chief (Barwick 1984: 117).

Fine, faithful black, good disposition and temper. Out on three expeditions. Taken ill at the Wimmera and returned before his comrades. Black doctors recommended rambling through the district which he did to no effect. Died at Mahoon 16 August 1845 (Thomas in Bride 1969: 409).

20 Mar 1839 – Munmunginna, Jack, Boonorong tribe, age 18, unmarried male whose family is not ascertained (Dredge census, Robinson Papers, vol 54, ML); Jul 1839 – Mun-mun-gin-non, name taken in encampment (Thomas, set 214, unit 1, ML); 18 Nov 1839 – Munmungin beastly drunk, this youth till morning kept the encampment into excitement, gets the liquor from Mr Lee (Thomas in *HRV*, vol 2B: 558).

1840 – his name is on a list of single men grouped with Mr Young (Nerreninnen) and Pinterginner, determined to go on the raid to Gippsland (Thomas, CY 2605, frame 8, ML); 1840 – his name is on another list of single men who are part of the principal families (Thomas, CY 2605, frame 23, ML); 7 Feb 1840 – Marnminginner and Pinterginner come into the encampment near Tooradin at 11 pm from Mr O'Connors ... signalled with the call of a wild dog ... brought in plenty of damper, potatoes and flour which they got from an old shepherd working for Mr Devilliers (Thomas, CY 2605, item 1, ML); 12 Feb 1840 – Munmanginer was one of those who went to French Island long, long time ago before white man come (Thomas, CY 2605, item 1, ML); 13 Apr 1840 – Barrabools and Mt Macedons shift camp in Melbourne to north side of Yarra but Munmunginum is one of a large group mainly Bonurong who stay with Thomas (Thomas, CY 2605, item 1, ML); 24 Nov 1840 – From Nerre Nerre Warren Thomas sends his dray to Tuerong to bring Mrs Thomas, Munmunginna accompanies dray (Thomas, CY 2605, item 2, frame 192, ML); 26 Nov 1840 – Munmunginna among the party of Western Ports leaving Nerre Nerre Warren for 5 days to go to Korrwarra, Toolum [Balnarring] and Kirkbilesse [near Tooradin] for eels (Thomas, CY 2605, item 2, frame

193, ML); 11 Dec 1840 – At Nerre Nerre Warren after a dispute about work [the Western Ports want to leave, saying **no good work**], Munmunginna comes to Thomas and says Western Port blacks **all gogo me also go goodbye**. They have gone to Surveyor Smyth, have left the lubras behind and Thomas fears they are about to go on a bloody mission (Thomas, CY 2605, item 2, frame 204, ML).

24 Feb 1842 – Munmungina enrolled in Native Police Corps, received blankets and equipment; made his mark; remained at Nerre Nerre Warren till 28 March; Corps then left because of lack of water and marched in easy stages to Yarra Yarra and camped opposite surveyor's paddock (Dana to La Trobe, VPRS 19, box 28, 42/674, PROV); 27 Jul 1842 – 2nd Division to the westward including Munmunginna, rationed since 1 Feb (Commandant to La Trobe, VPRS 19, box 30, 42/1143, PROV); 2 Nov 1842 – 'It was at Mollisons that my black trooper Dr Bailey gave me a lesson about native names, **Mititern – Mimitedon – Momiteden – Momitaten – Momateden – Momatzeden – Monmacedon**' (La Trobe 'Memoranda of Journeys', Ms 130003, Box 79/1, safe, SLV); 1842 – Return of Corps for the year – Munonmungi or Dr Bailey, aged 20, single, no children, never punished, on duty at Western Port and for 4 months at Mt Macedon police station. General conduct very good, well disposed and obedient (*NSW Legislative Council Votes & Proceedings*, 1844).

20 Sep 1843 – Thomas visited encampment at Merri Creek, party of Native Police preparing to depart for Gippsland, Munmungina, Yummerbuk, Murrembean, Kunnunnnerbun, Kulpendure and Mumbo – 'some of the principal families but not a wimper or wild howling as heretofore, only shaking of hands like white peoples. The mother of Kulpendure [also known as Robin, Billibellary's own son] dropped a tear down her sable cheek, but Billibellary soon quiet'd it by saying **no gammon white man plenty come back 2 moons**. They left in good spirits promising not to kill Gippsland blacks only shake hands' (CY 2606, frame 108, ML); 29 Sep 1843 – Munmungina, Dr Bailey, on service sine 19 September in Gippsland (Dana Return, 43/7302 in 4/1135.1, AO of NSW); 20 Oct 1843 – Yankee Yankee, Ben Benger and a few other Western Ports came into the encampment at Merri Creek with some plan or news which caused the Native Police to be 'most trying' and Sergeant Bennett could do nothing with them, some feigning ill, others said direct they would not go. Finally 5 were made to go [off again to Gippsland], 2 currently serving Native Police, Mummungina and Charlie, 2 who had been dismissed Benbow and Poky Poky, and one who was a deserter Kulklo.

Two lubras cried bitterly, Munmunginna's mother and sister (CY 2606, frame 87, ML); Oct – Nov 1843 – With CCL Tyers endeavouring to get through to Gippsland. Back before 25 December 1843 (Dana Return, 43/7302 in 4/1135.1, AO of NSW).

Feb 1844 – Munmunginna is one of the named Native Police among 700 of the tribes assembled at Merri Creek to watch judicial proceedings (Thomas to CP, VPRS 11, unit 8/469); Apr 1844 – Munmunginna is with Sergeant Windredge, Robinson, Thomas and Haydon and five other named Native Police pushing through into Gippsland (Haydon 1846: 122); Jul 1844 – he comes from this country, Tobon.nur.rick, [Jamieson's station] (Robinson in Clark 1998, vol 4: 115); 27 Apr 1844 – Mun mun jin ind's father was a Yowengerre, from Warmun, now dead … tribe all extinct … this is why the country is so scrubby. He gave me an account of the natives of the country and also gave me the names. The natives of Gippsland have killed 70 of the Boongerong at Brighton (Robinson in Clark 1998, vol 4: 49); 27 May 1844 – Munmunginnong's conduct is not as good as Sergeant Windredge expected but he hopes that in a short time he can make Mumbo and Munmunginnong as good as the rest (Windredge to Dana, enc to 44/6172 in 4/2666, AO of NSW); 1 Jul 1843 – 30 Jun 1844, Munmungina's name is on a return of Native Police stating that he is obedient and willing (VPRS 19, Box 60, 44/1177 (a), PROV).

19 Feb 1845 – Munmungina is praised by CCL Tyers for his good conduct as one of the 4 Native Police on duty in Gippsland for last seven months (Tyers to La Trobe, VPRS 19, Box 68, 45/324, PROV); 23 Mar 1845 – With six other named Native Police Munmungina is given 3 days leave for good conduct to go to Merri Creek [from HQ at Nerre Nerre Warren] to attend a coroborree (VPRS 90, PROV); 10 Aug 1845 – Munmunginner died at Mahun, Western Port, aged 25, single, one of the NP (Thomas Return of deaths June 1845 – November 1845, in Governor's Despatches, vol 51, MLA 1240, ML); 21 Sep 1845 – Burrenum arrives at the encampment south of Melbourne and confirms the news that Munmunginna died about six weeks ago at Mahun. Much lamentation among lubras especially Billibellary's (CY 2606, item 3, ML).

Then Thomas gives the evidence for the next massacre in the sequence.

'About 9 years ago [about 1831]', 12 Bonurong were killed at the place in Westernport at which 20 Bonurong men left all their women and children and three old men in Thomas' care while they went to Gippsland to kill their enemies – this is the river Kunnung which flows into Western Port near modern Koo–wee–rup, referred to in the records as Jamieson's station.[33] The importance of this location has already been seen in the elaborate monuments that Thomas saw and described and which are reproduced in this book.

Another version of this massacre was recorded by James Maxwell Clow,[34] son of the Rev James Clow, and manager of his station, Tirhatuan, on Dandenong Creek:

> Previously to the country which lies on the western side of the bay of Western Port (between what was at one time Manton's, and Allan's run), being occupied by squatters in the year 1835, the Gippsland blacks attacked some five-and-twenty of the Western Port tribe in the gray of the morning, and cut off every one of them. Their tombs consist of many cairns plainly visible to this day. When I went to reside at Dandenong in 1838, the blacks told me of the occurrence, and that they never had been able to avenge the wrong.[35]

Then he gives the evidence for the massacre between Kangerong and Arthurs Seat: 'about 18 or 20 years back nearly half the tribe were killed between Kangerong and Arthur's Seat'.[36] Definitionally, for nearly half the Bonurong to be wiped out, they must have been surprised while asleep in a dawn raid by their enemies. This was the way Aboriginal groups destroyed their enemies when they meant business.[37]

An important cultural difference needs mention here. Aboriginal cultural practice was to settle matters of honour in large formal gatherings, with one to one combat by trial. When one of the warriors fell or was injured, that was enough; honour was satisfied. It is a very well adapted strategy for small populations. Knowledge of this puts the Gippsland raids into perspective.[38]

---

33   See Thomas 'Map of Western Port District', VPRS 4410, unit 3, item 67, PROV.

34   Bride 1983[1898]: 359. Ian D Clark has drawn attention to this reference, which does not seem to have been noticed previously, possibly because it is a footnote in James Maxwell Clow's account of his station in another squatting district, near Lake Hindmarsh in the Wimmera, and not in his father's account of Tirhatuan, the well known account.

35   In addition to their run Manton's Creek at Flinders, Charles and Frederick Manton held another run Tooradan, known as Manton's Heifer station at the top end of Western Port opposite the north-west point of French Island (VPRS 6168, CS 68, PROV); Robert Innes Allen held Balla Balla at Tooradin.

36   Thomas to La Trobe, 6 June 1840, from Arthur's Seat, Letter book 2, Thomas Papers, set 214/8, item 2, CY 2946, ML.

37   For the same reason, Standing Orders for the Native Police Corps of 1842 specifically prohibited surrounding a sleeping encampment and rushing it at dawn.

38   Europeans failed to see that this was an adaptive strategy well suited to small populations. They were inclined to contrast the failure to fight large battles with the cultural strategies of the Europeans' valiant foes the Maoris, who fought in serried ranks exactly as the British did at that time, see Fels 1988: 191.

The fact of the timing was confirmed to Thomas on 21 April 1840, when the Bonurong, fearful, would not continue on their planned route to Arthurs Seat – the massacre happened at night.[39]

Thomas recorded two aspects of routine group behaviour that lead us in the present to the conclusion that this encampment between Kangerong and Arthurs Seat would certainly have been Baggamahjarrawah/Buckkermitterwarrer. He recorded that 'Natives have their regular staying places':[40] these encampments are like train stations. Both the Bonurong and their enemies used the same encampments on the eastern side of Western Port, and anyone travelling to and from Melbourne, even though the route was outside their own country, for example Barrabools, Mt Macedons, Waworongs, all used the regular Bonurong encampments on their journeys, Elsternwick, Brighton, Mordialloc, Carrum, Frankston, Mt Eliza, Mt Martha, on the eastern coast of Port Phillip.

His second observation was that though they usually shifted encampment upon a death, when they knew the cause of death they did not bother, 'Natives do not shift Encampment when death is occasioned by accident or killing'.[41] The Bonurong continued to use the massacre site Worawen, the place of sorrow: Worrowurk, a Western Port black, aged 28 died on 4 August 1843 at Worawen.[42] They, and their enemies the Kurnai, continued to use the massacre site at Kunnung where the memorials were erected, and they continued to use Buckkermitterwarrer, the only encampment between Kangerong and Arthurs Seat.

This amphitheatre area from Mt Martha to Arthurs Seat appears to have been Bonurong heartland,[43] and the evidence from Thomas' papers suggests that some people were permanently in occupation. They were a fishing tribe according to George Gordon McCrae,[44] and the prime fishing spot was the mouth of Brokil Creek, a site which has now been destroyed, regrettably without archaeological investigation because its significance was not known, in the construction of the Martha Cove development.[45]

---

39 Thomas Journal, CY 2605, item 1, ML.

40 Thomas Journal 6 February 1840, Byrt 2004: 31.

41 Thomas Papers set 214/2, item 1, 26 April 1840, summary marginal note, CY 2605, ML.

42 Thomas Summary of Births and Deaths, 1 March to 1 December 1843, Y 2604, item 5, ML. Unusually, Thomas did not write a column for sex but that is a male name and this person is one of the D'Villiers brothers, Warrawaruk, Koolin, married, wife Maryagrook, a member of one of the Principal Families of the Bonurong (CY 2605, item 1, ML). These two men acquired their names from Christiaan Ludolph Johannes de Villiers who instituted the 1837 Native Police in Port Phillip. Note though, the inconsistency that the same person is listed exactly the same way on Thomas 'Family Connections' Census of 1846. There were two De Villiers brothers: one of these records is false. I suspect that it is this one, the wrong brother is listed. Warrawurk has 'a 22 yo son Lively' on the Family Connections census. The brother who died at Warrowen was only 28 at date of death.

43 Tubberubbabel, where Gellibrand's party found the 100 huts was 'never deserted'.

44 McCrae 1911: 19.

45 The author of the archaeological report on Martha Cove knew of the existence of the Protectorate, did not know that it was started on the Mornington Peninsula, and hopelessly confused stations established after

The massacres remembered

This massacre of 18–20 years ago was quoted as the reason for their refusal to go back to Arthurs Seat after the big tribal meeting in April 1840. After receiving his marching orders from La Trobe, Thomas managed with some difficulty to get all the five tribes on their way back to their various home countries. They burned all the encampments and the Bonurong set off for Arthurs Seat. Thomas himself set off next day and caught up with a large party of 87 Bonurong encamped by the track at present day Elsternwick. 26 of the men were sitting down in council, frightened – all would be killed if they went to Arthurs Seat. They had met two white men and a Sydney black travelling with a flock of sheep. The Sydney black told the Bonurong that 'plenty' Two Fold Bay tribe, together with the VDL black Ben Lomand, were on their way to kill all the Bonurong. Thomas was furious, and chased after this party, tracking them by their sheep. He hauled the Sydney black back to the Bonurong council, threatening him with jail, and obliged him to tell his story again to Thomas in front of the Bonurong council and 'all came out'. The Sydney black acknowledged that he had not seen this war party from Gippsland, that Ben Lomand and two white men had told him the story. But 'it was all to no avail. My blacks were too much frightened. They said **long, long time ago Twofold Blackfellow kill at night almost all Black Port Phillip**'.[46] Thomas was not able to persuade them to go on to the Arthurs Seat district, and he and they returned to Melbourne. Next day, he recorded meeting a black on horseback, Dalla[47] who told him that all the blacks were frightened and that even the white surveyor of the district, Smythe, was frightened of the wild blacks.

When the Bonurong finally got over their doubts about the wisdom of going back to the Arthurs Seat district, another spanner was thrown into the works by one of Robinson's VDL blacks, Isaac, who arrived in the Arthurs Seat district armed with a large musket. He said he was in search of two of Robinson's VDL lubras, Trucaninni and Charlotte, and attempted to ingratiate himself with the settlers by warning them that the Two Fold Bay blackfellows were 'coming down'. He 'bid them get plenty of guns ready'. Isaac then robbed Hyatt's station about 43 miles from Melbourne,[48] taking food, clothing, tobacco, rug and blankets, pannican, buckshot and about ten flints. Then he disappeared.[49]

1861 by the Board appointed to watch over the interests of the Aborigines, with the Protectorate of 20 years earlier.

46 Thomas Journal, 21 April 1840, CY 2605, set 214/2, item 1, ML.

47 Unidentified as yet. He could be Dalla Kal Keth, or he could be Talliorang (Dollar Dollar), a Western Port black, listed as aged 22, an unmarried man, an orphan, on Thomas Family Connections Census, 1846 (CY 3083, ML); he also appears on Thomas' 1840 list as an unmarried man.

48 Ian Clark identifies this person as John Highett of Pal.lay.rang.un station near Tuerong: it is the same place that Thomas inscribes as Poleorongong. It is the same place as Meyrick inscribes as Ballanarong south of Mt Eliza (Meyrick 1939: 171). The southern boundary of Ballmarang was the northern boundary of Tuerong (*Port Phillip Gazette*, 13 December 1848: 557). Gunson notes that John Highett was believed to be the first person to take stock over the Dandenong Creek, settling near Frankston (Gunson 1968: 19).

49 Thomas to Robinson from Tubberubbabel 14 May 1840, VPRS 11, unit 7/308, PROV.

William Buckley, the convict who escaped from Collins' settlement at Sorrento in 1803 and made his way round the bay where he was adopted by the Waudthourong at Indented Heads, also recounted the massacre, though, as with all of Buckley's recollections which can be checked, he got it partly wrong and partly right. He described the Bonurong as 'a small tribe ... greatly thinned in number by a cruel onslaught made on them in the night by the Waworongs, on which occasion they murdered men, women and children'.[50] In this instance, Buckley got the name of the perpetrators wrong.

On 12 February 1840, Pinterginner (Mr Hyatt) one of Thomas' Bonurong Native Police,[51] told Thomas that:

> **all the blacks from Wilson's Promontory ... to Kirkbillesse all this country where we now were dead, not one left. Two Fold Black fellows long time ago killed many, many, rest all dead.**[52]

George Gordon McCrae, writing of the period 1845–51 when his family was living at Arthurs Seat, lists among the three obsessions of the blacks dread of the 'Warrigal' or 'wild blackfellow'. When they were encamped in force, say 100 to 200 strong, he wrote, they encamped in the snug retreat in the bottom between the Cape Schanck Road and the bay, beneath the shadows of the great Coast Banksia, or in the aromatic covert of the *Bimbel* or beach tea tree, but when they arrived in straggling parties by twos and threes, or by the half-dozen, they infinitely preferred the protection of a three railed fence and as close to the house or huts as might be.[53]

At about the same time in Gippsland, Mr Tommy, a young Bonurong accompanying Edward Hobson's large party to Port Albert in 1844, 'took great pains to explain the whole affair' to Lavinia Brodribb Bennett when they passed the spot where the revenge party cut up some of the Kurnai bodies of those they killed in March 1840. He was present at the time, as well as Billy Lonsdale and de Villiers and two unnamed others. The occasion of telling the story, retrospectively, was the finding of a knife by Mr Sage, one of Edward Hobson's party. On finding the knife, Sage turned to Tommy and said 'dropped by a white man I believe'. But Tommy said '**Boruck** (which means in their language "No")' and went on to tell the story of the revenge raid and the killing of the nine men women and

---

50   *HRV*, vol 2A: 176.
51   Pinterginner/Bentagunen/Pen.dug.ge.min is a prominent Bonurong in the records of this period. His country was probably Mt Eliza.
52   Thomas Journal, CY 2605, frame 56, ML.
53   George Gordon McCrae, 'Reminiscences not exploits', vol 4, Ms 2523/5(d), SLV. The other two obsessive dreads were the spells of the cordage or magician/doctor, and of the evil spirit Gudyill-Gudyill.

children, the same story he told to Lavinia Brodribb Bennett: regrettably for us, avid for information, she says that 'I did not pay much attention to it at the time'.[54]

In 1846 Thomas questioned the absence of all the men from an encampment at Grim Grim; the women told him that they had gone to **'catch wild blackfellows'**, and after a 'little humouring' from Thomas the women gave the names of those gone on 'this murderous errand', 18 men from the Western Port, Mt Macedon, Yarra and Barabool tribes. The Western Port men were:

- Budgery Tom
- Worringittolong
- Worrunteorong
- Burrenun
- Poleorong
- Buller Bullup
- Bobbinary
- Lummer Lummer
- Yal Yal
- Nerreninnen.

The old man Berberry explained to Thomas that:

> **The Gippsland blacks are very bad men,[55] steal and kill white man's Bullocks and they gone to helpem white man too much frightened to gogo bush.[56]**

Even as late as July 1850, when Thomas consulted the Western Port blacks yet again on their preference for a reserve, they chose Moody Yallook on the grounds that there were plenty of eels there, but also because 'they should not feel safe at being further on the coast on account of the Gippsland blacks'.[57]

Many years later R Brough Smyth asked Thomas to make a careful estimate of the Aboriginal population of the whole of Victoria just prior to white settlement.

---

54   Lavinia Hasell Bennett, *Account of a Journey to Gippsland*, 7 May 1844, p. 182 and 26 May 1844, pp. 188–189, in Brodribb 1976. Note that the editor has done an excellent job in transcribing Lavinia's difficult writing, but is not an expert on Bonurong people. He has guessed Mr Jonny as the name of the Bonurong (fn 18, p. 182), the letter formation of the name being ambiguous. I believe that it is most likely that Hobson took 'his' black Tommy on this trip. But if the present whereabouts of this journal were known, and permission was given to read it, the identification might be clear. The other 'sable companion' on this trip with Hobson was Charlie Tara with whom Tommy was associated in the 1846 search for the alleged white woman. More research is needed.
55   Pinterginner/Bentagunen/Pen.dug.ge.min is a prominent Bonurong in the records of this period. His country was probably Mt Eliza.
56   Thomas Journal, Thursday 21 May 1846, CY 2606, frame 353, ML.
57   Thomas Journal, Friday 26 July 1850, CY 3127, ML.

The figure Thomas gave him was 'not less than 6000'. Of that number, Thomas' count of the Aborigines within the counties of Bourke, Evelyn and Mornington was 350. But Thomas went on to state that:

> one half at least of one of the tribes inhabiting these counties had perished in 1834 in a war with the Gippsland and Omeo blacks and that previous to the war the number was not less than 500.[58]

At roughly the same time that Brough Smyth was collecting his material but quite independently, a Western Port man named Peter (Tu-ar-dit on 1861 census) working for the McHaffies on Phillip Island, familiar with the traditions, told McHaffie of the almost complete annihilation of the Western Port blacks by the Cape Liptrap blacks.[59]

Gippsland blacks' recorded view of the Bonurong

> Those living in the Western Port district of Victoria they [the Kurnai] called Thurung or tiger-snakes because as I [Howitt] have heard them say, 'they came sneaking about to kill us'.[60] Howitt recorded also his understanding of the extent of Bonurong country: 'It may be mentioned that a strip of country from the mouth of the Werribee River, and including what is now Williamstown and the southern suburbs of Melbourne, belonged to the Bunurong, a coast tribe, which occupied the coast line from there around Hobson's Bay to Mordialloc, the whole of the Mornington Peninsula, and the coast from Westernport Bay to Anderson's Inlet'.[61] He also thought that 'Tradition and legend both point to the Bunurong or Wurunjeri being the parent stock [of the Kurnai]'.[62] Further, he stated that 'The Bonurong at Anderson's Inlet intermarried with the Jato-wara-wara division of the Brataua clan of the Kurnai, but I have no knowledge of how such marriages were arranged.[63]

---

58   Smyth 1972[1878], vol 1: 32. Brough Smyth inserted a footnote, 'I give this statement as it was given to me'. One wonders at that; it is almost a disclaimer. Note that this description, 'within the counties of Bourke, Evelyn and Mornington', roughly embraces the combined country of the Warworong and the Bonurong. The combined population was counted on the 1839 census, and amounted to a little over 200. Thomas is saying that more than half of the combined population of the two tribes had perished prior to contact.
59   McHaffie was told in 1870: Hardy 1942.
60   Howitt 1904: 41.
61   Howitt 1904: 71.
62   Howitt 1904: 134.
63   Howitt 1904: 257.

Payback, the retaliation raid by the Twofold Bay blacks

The Twofold Bay blacks did come after the Bonurong, on 3 October 1840, seven months after the Bonurong raid into their country. The Twofold Bay blacks got as far west as Jamieson's station on the river Kunnung but they contented themselves with trashing the huts and carrying off much European plunder.[64] Thomas' detailed account is very interesting because it tells of the remarkable monuments at encampments which were used, in turn, both by the Bonurong and their enemies.

Thomas was told to investigate the raid, and he left Nerre Nerre Warren for Jamieson's then Gippsland with the brothers Nuluptune and Mumbo.

Nunupton/Nunuptune/Nalnuptune/Nuluptune/ Nunnapoton/Nunupthen/Namapton/Billy Langhorne/ Mr Langhorne

A Bonurong man, according to Barwick, a son of Tuolwing/Old George the King who was clan head of the Ngaruk–Willam, whose country has not been determined with certainty: one primary source says Brighton and Mordialloc, another says from Gardiner's creek to south of Dandenong (Barwick 1984: 117). Thomas' 1846 census lists him and his brother Mumbo as Bonurong whose country is Mt Macedon, but on the Yarra blacks section of the census, Nunuptune and his brother Mumbo are listed again as young men principally orphans[I] (Thomas, CY 3083, ML).

Remained but a few months in the Native Police Corps. He was a good tempered fellow but as restless as a hyena in confinement. He was accused unjustly of taking Mr Willoughby's child at Western Port.[II] This so frightened him that for years he scarce rambled further than the coast from Mt Eliza to Pt Nepean (Thomas in Bride 1969: 408)

21 Dec 1837 – The Native Police are doing well with the exception of two men Tom and Namapton whom has left the station without my knowledge (CLJ de Villiers to PM Lonsdale, VPRS 4, unit 3, 37/174, PROV).

I. This discrepancy is of particular importance given the evidence presented earlier related to the long stay of the Mt Macedon blacks with the Bonurong at Tubberubbabel and the arguments about whether they were entitled to be rationed as Bonurong.

II. A rumour gained some credence that the blacks had taken the child from the co-incidence of the fact that a small party were in the district at the time, Lummer Lummer, Nerreninnen, Worrakup, Korrabuk and Old Maria, Joe's lubra: Old Maria was known to be very fond of the child. The child in fact wandered off from the No Good Damper Inn at Dandenong and was never found. This is only one of a number of lost in the bush events involving children: a child was lost from Barker's at Cape Schanck in 1850; Atkinson's child was lost from the Yarra pound in 1846 and the Native Police searched for it. There were others. The subject of lost in the bush children and Aborigines would make a good minor thesis or journal article.

64   VPRS 11, unit 7/336, PROV.

16 May 1838 – CLJ de Villiers testified that on a few weeks earlier, Bet Bengai had told him that Nunnapoton was concerned in the depredations on Clarke's, Jackson's and Clerk's stations and was present at Mr Atkins (*HRV*, vol 2A: 301); 20 Mar 1839 – Listed on Dredge's census as Nalnuptune, age 18, Waworong tribe, unmarried male whose family is not ascertained (Robinson Papers, vol 54, ML); 23 Apr 1839 – Disturbance in camp ... only Nunupton disappointed of a lubra firing off a gun ... he is a Western Port black, a laughing good tempered fellow, every day some new advice would be taken about his clothes (Thomas, uncat Ms set 214, item 14, ML); Jul 1839 – Nunupton/Mr Langhorne, name taken in encampment (Thomas CY 2604, item 1, frame 31, ML); 1 Sep 1839 – Nunupton returned from a war expedition because he was ill (Robinson in Clark 1998, vol 1: 77); 7 Sep 1839 – Nunupton set off with Robinson and some VDL aborigines plus Nunupton's father en route to Arthurs Seat. Nunupton abandoned the party (Robinson in Clark 1998, vol 1: 78); 18 Sep 1839 – drunk, described another murder [that of Tommy] (Thomas CY 2604, item 3, frame 105, ML); 3 Nov 1839 – Nunupton, Bilbilyerry and several other men and boys came to Robinson's quarters to tell him that Nunupton's father, Old George, had just died (Robinson in Clark 1998, vol 1: 101).

21 Feb 1840 – Two Jajoworung blacks who visited Robinson while he was in their country told him that the Port Phillip blacks were *very good* and said they knew Nunupton and Ningolobin [Captain Turnbull] (Robinson in Clark 1998, vol 1: 176); 7 Jun 1840 – his name is on a list of blacks presently at Tubberubbabel (Robinson in Clark 1998, vol 1: 344); 28 Jul 1840 – Nunupton travelled with us to Arthurs Seat on his way to Merricks to muster the Boongerong blacks (Robinson in Clark 1998, vol 1: 357); Aug 1840 – Listed on Parker's return as Konongwillam section of Waworong tribe inhabiting country of Mt Macedon (4/2512.1, AO of NSW); 15 Oct 1840 – Thomas left Nerre Nerre Warren accompanied by Mumbo and Nunuptune (VPRS 11, unit 8, PROV).

2 Dec 1841 – one of 7 blacks who assisted Thomas and CL Powlett in the capture of the VDL blacks Bob and Jack. As a reward they asked for 1 pr trousers, 1 shirt, 1 blanket, leather belt with buckle, neckhandkerhief, and a straw hat and a gun (Thomas to Robinson, VPRS 11, unit 8, PROV).

24 Feb 1842 – Received blankets, clothing and equipment, enrolled and made his mark in the new Native Police Corps at Nerre Nerre Warren; drilled twice daily; Corps remained at Nerre Nerre Warren till water supply failed then marched in easy stages to Yarra opposite surveyor's paddock (Commandant Dana to La Trobe, 31 March 1842, VPRS 19, box 28, 42/674, PROV); 11 Mar 1842 – Nuluptune in the night fires a gun at [blank] formerly a Goulburn black. Altercation. With assistance of Captain Dana settle the affair. Nuluptune strongly protested that he did not shoot at or to them. I take the gun away (Thomas CY 2605, item 5(e), frame 394, ML); 1842 – Nunupton is on the commandant's return for the year as aged 25, married with 1 wife and 2 children; punished occasionally – rations stopped, and confined. On duty at Nerre Nerre Warren in search of lost woman; often employed as a messenger; duty about the camp. General conduct good at first, fond of wandering, a pretty good messenger, likely to improve (*NSW Legislative Council Votes & Proceedings*, 1844); 27 Jul 1842 – Nulupton, 2nd division of Corps, remained at Merri Creek, rationed since 1 February (Dana Return, VPRS 19, box 30, 42/143, PROV).

1843 – Nunupthen/Mr Langhorne – on service in Gippsland since 19 Sep (La Trobe to Col Sec, 4/1135.1, AO of NSW); Nov 1843 – Nunupton has been in the bush for three months (Thomas Uncat Ms set 214, item 3, ML).

1844 – Nunupthen dismissed (Return of NPC, VPRS 19, Box 60, 44/1177 (a), PROV).

9 Sep 1845 – Nunupton's lubra Tuundergrookk, died at Grim Grim 2 weeks ago (Thomas, CY 2606, item 3, ML).

Jan 1846 – On Thomas' list of Native Police who deserted (Quarterly Report, enc to 46/3341 in 4/2745.1, AO of NSW).

11 Aug 1849 – Nunuptune, male aged 30, married, Yarra tribe, died at Mt Eliza (Return, VPRS 10, unit 11, 50/55, PROV).

Mumbo

Son of Tuolwing/Old George the King, and brother to Nunupton/Billy Langhorne.

1835 to 1837 – At some period between these two dates Mumbo was a pupil at George Langhorne's school on the Botanical Gardens site, and could read and answer questions from Dr Watts' catechism (Thomas Quarterly report, December 1846 to February 1847, set 214, item 6, ML).

1837 – Accompanied a party including Alfred Langhorne, one of the Hawdon brothers and Alick Cockburn to a waterhole seven miles from the Dandenong flat (J Bourke, Memoranda of the early days, Ms ML quoted in Hibbins 1984: 23); Quoted as the source of the name of the No Good Damper Inn; according to Bourke the spring was the colour of ink and the damper they baked was consequently black; according to Bourke when Mumbo got his share he said 'I believe no good damper this one' (Hibbins 1984: 25).

Jul 1839 – On Thomas' list of names taken in encampment as Bul-len-goong – Manbo (CY 2604, item 1, frame 31, ML).

3 Jan 1840 – Feb 1840 – Mumbo's name is on the list of those determined to go to Western Port on the raid to Gippsland (Thomas, CY 2605, frame 8, ML); 15 Oct 1840 – Thomas left Nerre Nerre Warren to go to Western Port to investigate raid on Jamiesons (VPRS 11, unit 8, PROV).

26 Sep 1843 – Recruited into Native Police Corps; Oct to Dec 1843 – with CCL Tyers in Gippsland; 25 Dec 1843 – returned to HQ (Dana Return, 4/1135.1, AO of NSW, and La Trobe to Col Sec 43/7302 in 4/1135.1, AO of NSW).

Apr 1844 – With Sergeant Windredge and five other Native Police accompanying Thomas, Robinson and Haydon through Western Port (Haydon 1846: 122); 27 May 1844 – Sergeant Windredge is optimistic Mumbo can be made as good as the others (Windredge to Dana, enc with 44/6172 in 4/2666, AO of NSW); 1 Jul 1843 – 30 Jun 1844 – Likely to prove one of the best men. Recruited end of September 1843 (VPRS 19, Box 60, 44/1177 (a), PROV).

19 Feb 1845 – Praised by CCL Tyers, one of 4 Native Police on duty in Gippsland for last 7 months (VPRS 19, Box 68, 45/324, PROV); 23 Mar 1845 – With 6 other named Native Police given permission for good conduct to go to Merri Creek on three days leave (VPRS 90, PROV); 29

> Dec 1845 – Native place Yarra Yarra, date of enlistment January 1843, length of service 3 years (Dana return, VPRS 19, Box 77, 45/2179, PROV); 8 Apr 1845 – Sergeant Bennett started with Mumbo and two other native troopers to join CCL Powlett's party (VPRS 90, PROV); 2 Sep 1845 – Mumbo returned to HQ and reported the death of his comrade Moonie Moonie after an absence of five months with Mr Powlett's party at the Wimmera (VPRS 90, PROV).
>
> Jan 1846 – On Thomas' list criticising the Native Police as one of the Melbourne tribes who deserted (Quarterly report, enc to 46/3341 in 4/2745.1, AO of NSW); 10 Dec 1846 – Constable Thornhill in Melbourne in charge of two native troopers Mumbo and Jackey which was sent to hospital for medical aid (VPRS 90, PROV). Dec 1846 – One of 2 Native Police admitted to hospital, both under 18 years of age. Thomas visited him in hospital, told him God knows all things and perhaps was afflicting him for aiding in killing a Loddon black some time previous. Mumbo got 'very wrath' said the Loddon blacks had killed all the native police and taken out his marmdulla. Mumbo staggered out to Thomas' horse, tried to mount, couldn't … sunken eyes, ghostly countenance … he died a few days later (Thomas Quarterly Report, December 1846 – February 1847, set 214, item 6, ML).

Thomas left Nerre Nerre Warren on 7 October 1840 with the two brothers, not telling them why he wanted them to accompany him. Just before the first muddy river,[65] they saw smoke of a large fire and the blacks climbed a tree and came down anxious – it was the smoke of the Two Fold Bay black fellows, they said. Thomas left Bob Davis and Mumbo and the cart here, to wait till he could arrange at Jamieson's to send a boat back for them, and he and Nuluptune swam the next four rivers.[66] When they got to Jamieson's, the station presented a 'doleful experience': three glazed windows in the house were demolished; watches, plate, china, glass, beds, bedding, wearing apparel, household utensils, tools, mill and plough were all destroyed.

Few stations, Thomas said, were better fitted up than Jamieson's and few had more property on them. Straps were cut from saddles and everything iron was either taken or cut off the leather. Feathers were turned out of pillows, and with sacks they stole, they carried off their plunder. A married couple just arrived from Scotland to work for Jamieson lost £300 worth of property and

---

65   Woollabin, according to his map of 13 Rivers or creeks flowing into the east side of Western Port, CY 3130, no pagination, after p. 107, before p. 111, ML.

66   Kirkbillase, Lalln, Kunun and Warmbrim, CY 3130, no pagination, after p. 107, before p. 111, ML.

an ex-convict lost his precious certificate of freedom. The raid had commenced before dawn, about quarter past five, and ended around 9 am, and the blacks left behind waddies, large shields and a few spears.

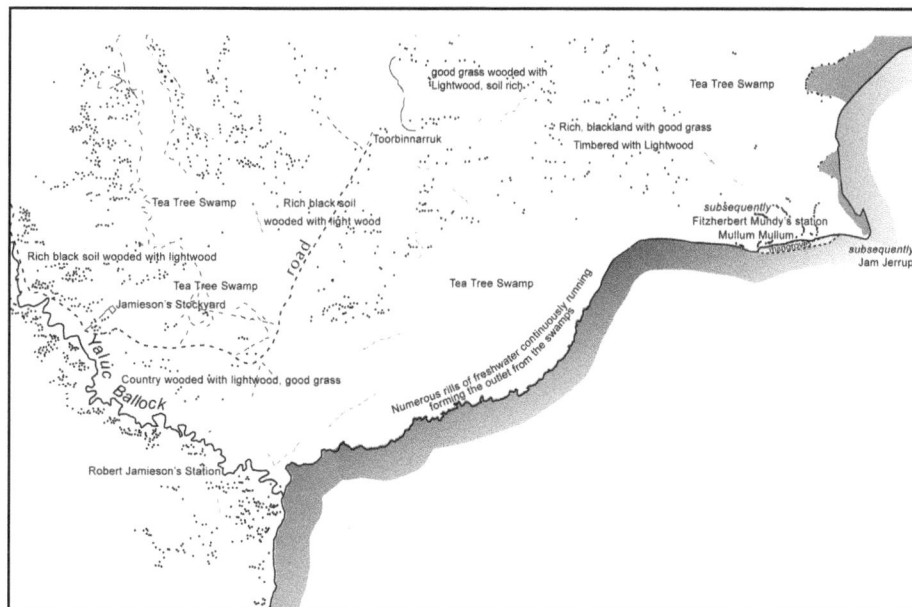

Fig 32. 'Jamieson's Station 1840'

Sketch, © Richard Barwick, 2010, based on George D Smythe's Coastal Survey 15A. This base map is © Crown (State of Victoria), 2010, all rights reserved, Surveyor General of Victoria.

In a second account of the same events, Thomas recorded that the Kurnai had also left behind 'part of a wallaby cloak rather badly formed'.[67] It was the sight of this cloak which seems to have upset Nunuptune and Mumbo to an extraordinary degree. They were 'terribly frightened', 'cowed', by nightfall, and it was all Thomas could do to keep up their spirits. They would not sleep under cover, and he was obliged to sit up with them keeping guard till midnight, when his man took over the watch. But they were in better spirits next day.

Thomas and Nuluptune and two of Jamieson's men followed the tracks of the departing raiders. About a quarter of a mile from Jamieson's, exactly where Thomas and the waiting Bonurong had camped in February was the spot where the Two Fold Bay blacks had encamped on the night before the raid. Nuluptune went carefully round the fires – there were 18 tiny fires of three sticks each, just enough to keep fire going, smaller than the palm of Thomas' hand. Nuluptune counted the number of blacks who had slept at each fire and notched a stick. The total was huge – 97 men.

---

67   Thomas Journal, CY 2605, frame 149, ML.

About another quarter of a mile along, again where Thomas and the Bonurong had encamped in January was the place where the Two Fold Bay blacks had encamped one night earlier than the night/morning of the raid. The fires here were larger. There were two devices which Thomas sketched and which Nuluptune could neither decipher nor explain; presumably they were Kurnai markings. They continued on the raiders' tracks to the next river[68] where the raiders had cut down saplings to carry their booty across. Here was another stoppage, and another formed arch.[69] Here, the raiders had repacked their plunder more carefully. Thomas found a large milk dish with the ironware wrenched out, a volume of *Dwight's Theology*, part of the back of a looking glass, tops of 'trowzers' cut off, and a quantity of newspapers and flour plus several shields.

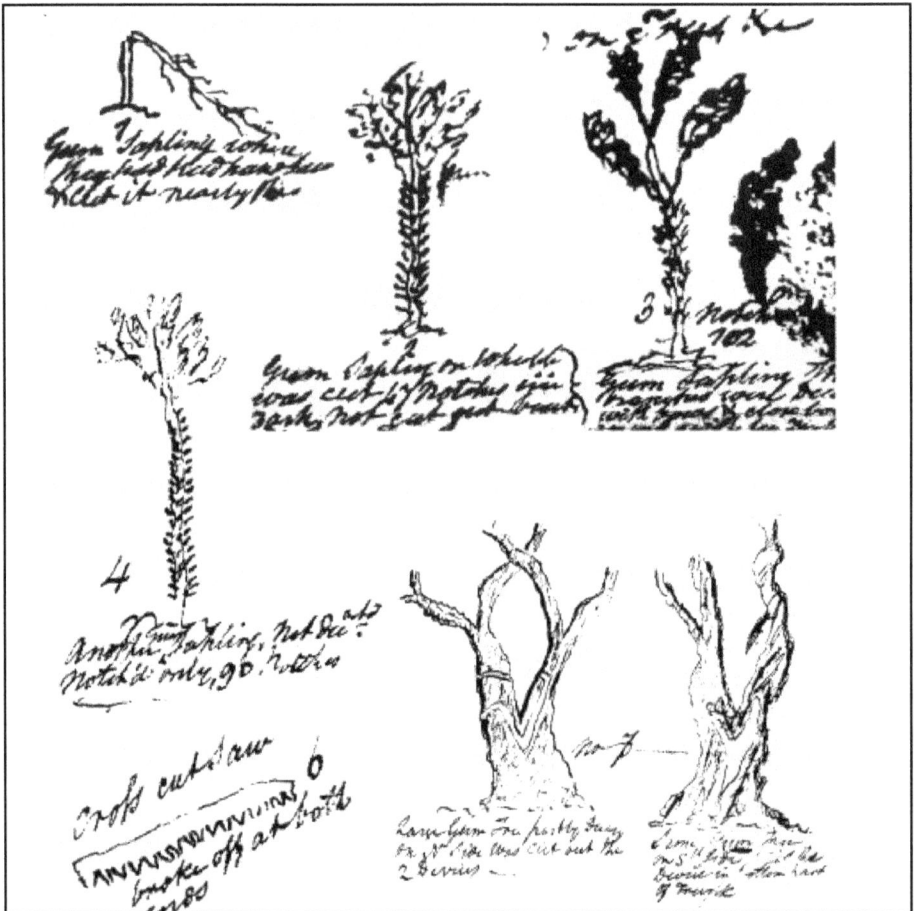

Fig 33. 'Six monuments to the dead, 10 October 1840'

Thomas sketch, from the William Thomas papers, 1834–1868, 1902, Mitchell Library, reproduced with the permission of the State Library of New South Wales.

---

68   Kunnung River.
69   Thomas had sketched this in February.

Fig 34. 'Monument at Tobinerk, 10 October 1840'

Thomas sketch, from the William Thomas papers, 1834–1868, 1902, Mitchell Library, reproduced with the permission of the State Library of New South Wales.

Nuluptune would go no further, not on any consideration. Thomas even offered to let him ride the horse while Thomas walked, but to no avail. Thomas was able to track them further because their tracks were very plain, as plain as cattle: the horses were often up to their bellies in water. They saw nothing but newspapers and broken china and a hat of Jamiesons, till they came to the river Tobinerk about three miles beyond Jamieson's station. Here they found a crosscut saw with the ends cut off, and the covers of *Chambers Edinburgh Journal*, fragments of other books, and seven singular devices on trees.[70] They could not cross the creek because it was too dangerous for the horses – the departing raiders had thrown in to the water so many stumps and trees. But Thomas and his mare did somehow, and on the other side the first thing that presented itself was the artificial arched grove of gum saplings and tea-tree extending over some yards. There was another large milk dish with the wire taken out, straps of stirrups, bullock and other chains, four shields, some fragments of books, more feathers and newspapers. Not four yards from where Thomas pitched his tent in February was a singular pillar of nine dead stumps let into the ground, standing perpendicularly ten feet high with two large pieces of bark standing up against the centre stump.

Thomas thought that the raiders had never seen a white man because they were ignorant of flour and sugar, and he did not think they were from Two Fold Bay because he suspected the existence of two or three large tribes in Gippsland. He returned to Jamieson's, thinking that it was a singular and pleasing feature of this Extensive Robbery that no personal violence was given on either side except in their attempt to walk off with Mrs Houlston. They gave her up without violence except for pulling out her earrings. A gun was fired up in the air but they just jumped and laughed. One of them was injured – the first who attempted the windows shoved his fist through and most dreadfully cut his arm and hand. They afterwards broke the windows with spears. Thomas concluded his account by noting that on their last visit they came within eight miles of Melbourne without ever meeting any civilisation because Jamieson's station was not there then.[71] Thomas expects that they will be back, and Jamieson's men fear it: 'I agree', wrote Thomas.[72]

Jamieson wrote to Samuel Rawson giving a graphic account of the raid and the damage, describing the attackers as 'mountain blacks … evidently in search of the Port Phillip tribe'. He gave the most powerful evidential detail in support of his observation that they were unacquainted with Europeans – the fact that they threw away damper, flour, tea and sugar. Jamieson fired one shot to which they paid not the slightest attention, 'I might as well have pointed a walking stick'. The attack went on for four hours, with Jamieson holed up in his hut, preventing their entry via the windows by using his gun 'club fashion'. In spite of his preventing them from entering the hut, they managed to hook out through the windows an 'immense amount of things including blankets, bedding, watch glass, brushes, razors etc'.[73] When Rawson wrote to his sister Elizabeth, he added the further detail that Jamieson was asleep when the raid

---

70 CY 2605, frames 149 and 150, ML.
71 The 1834 massacre at Little Brighton-Warowen.
72 Thomas to Robinson, 15 October 1840, VPRS 11, unit 7/336, PROV.
73 Rawson Papers, Ms 1029, folder 4, NLA.

started, that he was woken by a yell and rushed out of his hut, to find himself surrounded by 100 savages and seized: he knocked two down and got safely back to his hut.[74] He also told his sister that by this time, the date of his letter, the cattle were recovering from their fright.

A year later in 1841, when Commissioner of Crown Lands Powlett with police, plus Jamieson and Rawson, were tracking the VDL blacks who had killed the two men at Westernport, Powlett asked for military men to accompany the Port Phillip blacks who were tracking Bob and Jack, Trucaninni, Fanny and Matilda because the Port Phillip blacks were so scared of meeting the Gippsland blacks.[75]

This raid retaliatory at Jamieson's by the Gippsland blacks from the east was by any standard big, with 97 fighting men. If their raids in the pre-contact years were of the same magnitude, it is easy to see how they could have wiped out half the Bonurong at Buckkermitterwarrer, by surrounding a sleeping encampment and attacking at dawn, and, as well, killed 77 at Waraween in Brighton, and not difficult to understand why the Bonurong were so afraid of them. It is equally of significance that they camped at the same places where they had erected monuments in the past, and that the Bonurong used the same encampments. There is conservatism here, perhaps even a ritual significance.

The original cause of the feud

The root cause of all this death and destruction is as yet unknown, but from an outsiders' perspective now, trying to understand their reality then, the first possibilities to investigate are the common causes of conflict – blame attributed to an outside group for any Bonurong death which was not clearly an accident, dispute over resources, dispute over country and dispute over females.

The 'cup of iniquity'; the attribution of blame for a death to an external group[76]

Father's district was occupied by two tribes of Aborigines the 'Waverong' and the 'Boonwarong' – the Waverongs owning all land bounded in the North by the Yarra, the Bay in the West as far as Frankston – the Boonwarongs the southern part extending to Point Nepean, all round Weston Port Bay to the eastern ranges. These two tribes were on friendly terms and had as long as the memory of Blackfellows carried them, entered into a treaty offensive and defensive. [Marginal note is

---

74   Letter dated, 19 December 1840, Rawson Papers, Ms 1029, folder 4, NLA.
75   CCL FA Powlett to La Trobe, 16 November 1841, VPRS 19, Box 22, 41/1835, PROV.
76   William Jackson Thomas' explanation is reproduced here in full without comment, CY 3106, frames 56–58, ML.

as follows: against their mortal enemies the Gippsland Native, always designated the Wild Blackfellow]. These two tribes numbered about 450 all told, they were on cordial friendly relations with the settlers, and at the present day [1902] not one remains alive.

The cause of this hereditary enmity between the Weston Port Natives and the Gippsland Natives, I took some pains to search out. It appears according to the firm belief of all Blackfellows that death is in no case (except accident) the result of natural causes, but is always the work of an enemy, of some other tribes who cause the death by craft, charms or muttering some form of imprecation. On the death of any man of the tribe (for they never bother about the Women) – After this man is buried, a space of about one foot is cleared all around the grave, not a blade of grass left; made quite smooth – the graves are always round about four feet in diameter – The medicine men if there are more than one in the tribe, make a long and careful examination of the Ground so cleared, mumbling a monotonous sort of Chant all the time, at length they find or pretend to have found the direction of the Tribe, a member of which has caused the death.

The medicine men of the Western Port Tribe generally spot a member of the Gippsland tribes as the delinquent. This is noted as one against that tribe. After several deaths the cup of iniquity of the Gippsland tribes is supposed to be full, and calls for punishment. For the purpose of inflicting this punishment eight or ten young strong men are selected, who are to show their skill and bravery in an expeditionary raid near the borders of their enemy's country. When they near the borders of the enemy's country they divide into parties of two or three, advance in the most stealthily manner, being careful to leave as little trail as possible. At length they find a weak, detached little group. They wait until they see the young men depart to hunt, then they fall upon the unfortunate old men and women, all of which they ruthlessly murder. They then cut open the bodies, take out the kidney fat, and other portions, with which they return to their own country and exhibit as trophies of the success of their murderous expedition.

This [is] no one-sided affair, for the Gippsland natives act exactly on the same lines. The Western Port Natives tell of many fearful slaughters of their tribe by the Gippsland natives. This unsatisfactory state of the political relations between the several Tribes caused them to be in continual fear and ever watchful.

I have known long consultation among the sages of the Tribe about the fragment of a bone picked up from the ashes of a recent fire, a mile or two from the encampment. They knew that none of their tribe had lighted that fire, and they believed that the bone was that of a bird or beast from beyond the mountains, therefore their enemies were on the Warpath. The Warriors must be called together, scouts despatched in all directions to track out and expel the intruding blackfellows. I have known a whole encampment to be thrown into a state of panic by the note of a bird or the croak of a frog a little out of tune. The Natives while scouting in the bush signal their position to their company by imitating the note of a bird or some other bush sound previously agreed upon. So when they hear any familiar sound not quite correct, they jump to the conclusion Wild Blackfellows and prepare accordingly.

Dispute over resources as an explanation for the feud

The explanation that the origin of the feud was a dispute over resources is said to have come originally from Barak, the inheritor of the authority of Billibellary via his son Simon Wonga. But there are problems with it. The secondary source uses quotation marks for the following:

'long before the white men came to Melbourne' when 'Mordialloc people went down to the Tarwin to feast on native cabbage', they followed and killed some of the Port Albert Kurnai who had consumed this resource without permission. The Kurnai had raided Western Port to avenge these killings and 'the Gippsland and Westernport blacks were never friends after'.[77]

The problem is that I have not been able to find the original reference, which comes originally from the nineteenth century anthropologist Alfred Howitt. He was the Police Magistrate at Sale, and he was a good one, but his deep passion was for all things Aboriginal, and his own knowledge, together with information from correspondents, was vast.[78] He invited William Barak to come down to Sale from the Aboriginal Station Coranderrk at Healesville in 1884,[79] to participate in a revival of Kurnai initiation ceremonies, and as well, provide Howitt with information about the Yarra and Western Port blacks. Barak was willing, and the Central Board for the Protection of Aborigines provided a rail ticket.[80]

---

77 Barwick 1984, pt 2: 116. The reference given is 'Howitt Papers'.
78 There are large repositories of his papers and correspondence at both the State Library of Victoria and the Museum of Victoria. The Museum's papers are currently being digitised and are unavailable for six months.
79 Howitt's biographer states that he made 73 foolscap pages of notes from his conversations with Barak in 1882 and 1884 (Walker 1971: 305).
80 Mulvaney 1970: 205–217.

Unlike William Thomas and George Augustus Robinson, who lived day to day on terms of intimacy with the Aborigines, this was the only time Howitt spent with Barak, about a month. The doubt which must exist regarding the information arises from the descriptor 'the Mordialloc tribe'. The problem has been referred to earlier, the loss of the identity Bonurong, in favour of the European descriptor 'Mordialloc tribe'. It seems to boil down to the following logical possibilities – either Barak was getting old and had forgotten that the Bonurong were much greater than the Mordialloc remnants (it seems to me unlikely that he forgot, but possible that he had got used to the fact of the Bonurong being all gone) or Howitt interpreted Barak as saying Mordialloc tribe because everybody in the European world knew of the 'last of the Mordialloc tribe', or Howitt fed him the descriptor 'Mordialloc tribe' in the conversation. When the original reference is found, and read in its context, this problem may be solved.

The other disconcerting fact about Barak's explanation is that the native cabbage does not appear on the list of native foodstuffs eaten in Victoria, a list prepared for Brough Smyth, secretary to the Central Board by the then government botanist.[81] The list includes the leaves of the *Nasturtium terrestre,* and several species of *Cardimine* and *Lepidium* which were used for cress, and it is possible that 'native cabbage' is subsumed somewhere here. The list also includes the young top shoots of the cabbage palm *Livistonia australis,* another, but more remote possibility.

Then there is the belief to be found on the contemporary Wurundjeri website, which asserts that the dispute was over grass trees, not cabbage grass. The problem with this is that there were extensive grass tree areas on the Mornington Peninsula (Thomas' queer country), and remnants remain still on the walking track through the National Park between Baldry's Road and Cape Schanck. It is difficult to imagine a feud of such proportions over a resource which was plentiful in friends' country.

Dispute over ownership of country as an explanation for feud – 'debatable land'

The secretary of the Central Board was another person with a keen interest in collecting information about all matters to do with Aborigines, and he recorded versions of the myth about Loo-errn, a spirit believed by some Aboriginal groups to be good, and by others to be evil. Loo-errn had his home at Wilson's Promontory, and controlled the country between Hoddle's Creek and Wilson's

---

81   Smyth 1972[1878], vol 1: 212–214.

Promontory:[82] Smyth explained what the power of control meant – life or death: if anyone intruded into this country without authorisation, they would die at the end of their journey. This was believed. When the members of the Native Police Corps accompanied Robinson and Haydon on the well known 1844 journey, through Gippsland to Two Fold Bay, then across the Alps to Cooma, down to Albury and home, a six month excursion, they performed a ceremony when they got onto this country. Further on, when they came upon an old Kurnai encampment, they worked themselves up into a violent passion and destroyed it. These men were Tunmiel, Mumbo, Munmungina, Waworong, Poligerry and Moonee Moonee.[83]

Smyth called this land 'the debatable land' and he was led to believe by sources whom he does not name, that in former times it was 'held sometimes by the Western Port blacks and sometimes by the tribes inhabiting Western Gippsland'.[84]

Niel Gunson (with his map maker Keith Mitchell) went to considerable trouble to construct a map showing the tribal boundaries of the Bonurong and their neighbours, and as well, the early squatting stations, clearly showing the 'Debatable Land', between the Koo-wee-rup swamp and the Tarwin River.[85] This country was uninhabited by Aborigines at the time of contact with Europeans, but it was claimed as Bonurong under the following circumstances. In the course of the above-mentioned 1844 journey, when the party was in sight of Cape Liptrap, one of the Native Police, Munmungina, (brother of Burrenum/Mr Dredge), gave Robinson information. Munmungina said that all this country had belonged to the Bonurong who had all been exterminated by the Gippsland blacks except for two people of whom Munmungina was one. Munmungina told Robinson that his own country was Tobin.nur rick Creek and Koornong Creek, ie Manton's run and Jamieson's runs at Tooradin and Lang Lang. Munmungina's dead father was Pur.rine, chief of the Yowenjerre, and his country was Warm.mum or Wilson's Promontory.[86] The other Yowenjerre man who was still alive was Carborer (Kurboro).

Without exception, early observers noted and hated the dense, scrubby, almost impenetrable bush country to the south-east of Melbourne. The Native Police Corps made three attempts by different routes to get through to Gippsland in the early 1840s: in the end Commissioner of Crown Lands Tyers had to go by sea to take up his appointment.

---

82   Smyth 1972[1878], vol 1: 454.
83   Fels 1988: 173–174.
84   Smyth 1972[1878], vol 2: 14.
85   Gunson 1968: 15 for map.
86   Clark 1998, vol 4: 49, 115.

Gunson believes it very probable that this debatable land between the great swamp and the Tarwin River was never thickly populated, functioning as an Aboriginal 'no-man's land probably only visited at particular times of the year'.[87]

It was the Chief Protector's view that this country was in the state it was because it had not been burnt, all the owners who formerly cared for it, the Yowenjerre, now being dead: as Thomas put it, the tribe was extinct.

All these views have been reviewed recently by the historical geographer Ian Clark for the Native Title Unit of the Justice Department, released under Freedom of Information with considerable portions blacked out.[88] He believes that the Chief Protector was wrong in assuming that because the country was unburnt, therefore the original inhabitants must be dead: 'This deduction was based on a false analogy with examples of "unnatural ground" (his [Robinson's] term for the neglected estates of clans exterminated or driven elsewhere by squatters) seen on his 1841 tour of western Victoria'.[89]

Clark believes Brough Smyth was wrong too in his 'false conclusion that the area east of Western Port bay was "debatable ground" held sometimes by Kulin and sometimes by Kurnai'.[90] Clark says that while Howitt's book[91] left some things out, his 'notes proved that the Kulin-Kurnai boundary was clearly defined and that the reciprocal raiding of the 1830s and 1840s was not over land but a "blood feud"'.[92] Clark's major interest in this report seems to have been not the debatable land of Robinson and Smyth and Gunson, but the land further east between Anderson's Inlet and Wilson's Promontory.

Earthquakes as a factor in territorial ambiguity

My own view on all this is that one piece of possible evidence has been neglected – taking seriously the Bonurong evidence, and as a consequence, considering the shape and extent of Bonurong country prior to the earthquake which the Bonurong remembered as drowning Port Phillip and Western Port.

---

87   Gunson 1968: 3.
88   Clark 2002. I am grateful to Ruth Gooch for this report.
89   Clark 2002: 247.
90   Clark 2002: 248.
91   Howitt 1904.
92   Clark 2002: 248.

Georgiana McCrae's link between earthquakes and depopulation

Hugh McCrae actually *left out* of both of his editions of Georgiana's journal her final statement following her narrative of Johnny's death in Bogie's arms (Chapter 10):

> are these Aborigines of ours of the same race degenerated through the agency of earthquake, floods and famine?[93]

Georgiana herself recorded two earthquakes, the first on 30 May 1841 and a big one on 28 April 1847. Andrew McCrae was on top of Arthurs Seat for this second one that she recorded, and he said that besides the rumbling under his feet, there was a noise like that of a ship's gun at sea.[94] And when she was speculating after Johnny died, about similarity in burial customs, she used earthquakes as the first of three possible causes of degeneration, the other two being flood and famine.[95] From the juxtaposition in the text of Georgiana's account of Johnnie's death, and Bogie, and the speculation about earthquakes, flood and famine, I suspect that she heard the earthquake evidence from Bogie as well.

It *could* be the case that Georgiana was using the word degenerate with its contemporary meaning, ie degradation from type, but she was not a racist, not pejorative in her writing about her sable friends, and I think it is more likely that she was using the word in the sense of the primary Oxford English Dictionary meaning, ie having lost the qualities proper to its kind – in this case, population numbers. Throughout history, the sequence of events – weather event, flood, famine – is associated automatically with the consequences of death and de-population. This is how Georgiana's speculation reads, as an historical sequence.

Further earthquake evidence from Georgiana McCrae

> Mr Robert Russell tells me that Mr Cobb converses with the Aborigines in their own language – and believes the accounts they give him of the formation of Port Phillip bay – **'Plenty long ago – gago, gago, gago a long o' Corio'**, viz they could go across on foot from our side of the Bay to Geelong – They describe a Hurricane – trees bending to and fro and then the ground sank down – and the sea rushed in at the

---

93 Weber 2001, 5 October 1851: 654–659.
94 McCrae 1966[1934].
95 Georgiana McCrae's journal, 30 October 1850 in Weber 2001: 656. Hugh McCrae has left it out of his editing of Georgiana's journal.

Heads – and became broad and deep **'as today'**. M[r] La Trobe told me long ago that there is a tradition among the Western-port blacks[96] that – **'Plenty long – time ago'** the Yarra's course was along what is now the Carrum carrum swamp – and ran into the sea at Western Port – At Dight's falls on the Yarra, near Campbellfield are distant traces of some Earthquake, where the Darebin joins the Yarra – and to the North of this, the ground had evidently sunk down with the trees still standing on it – **some fifty** feet below the former height of the surface – from which it had now been rent.[97]

The Chief Protector's evidence

George Augustus Robinson recorded in his journal a detailed account of the big earthquake of 28 April 1847:

> At 34 minutes past 4 pm on Wednesday 28 April, I was sitting communicating with Mrs Robinson. The weather was calm, the day had been fine and pleasant. We had just parted with a visitor then crossing the river when suddenly the house shook and a loud noise like the noise of carriage running along the verandah and along the roof – the vibrations were short and rapid and lasted about two minutes. Mrs Robinson enquired what was that. I said at once shock of earthquake and the earth did literally quake. My servant cutting wood said he saw the stable shake, and the gardener saw the trees move and the ground under him. Captain Hove my neighbour came to ask my opinion about it. The mercury was below 60 degrees etc where it had been for two or three days proceeding.[98]

Reverend James Clow's evidence

The Rev James Clow at Tirhatuan near Dandenong recorded three separate subterranean events, one of which, in January 1850 was a significant noise experience, apparently without tremors.[99] It was a noise like that of an approaching bushfire, and Mrs Clow went outside repeatedly to look and smell for smoke, but the noise came from under the ground: the outstation workers at the mountain gap in the ranges behind Narre Narre Warren heard it too.

---

96   La Trobe's favourite black trooper was Munmunginna/Dr Bailey – probably the source of the report.
97   Georgiana McCrae's journal, 30 October 1850 in Weber 2001: 638–640.
98   Clark 2000, vol 5.
99   Bride 1983[1898]: 111.

The other two events were full earthquakes, one in February or March 1843, the other being the big one of 1847 recorded as well by Robinson and Georgiana McCrae. The 1843 earthquake occurred:

> at midnight, when the moon was full, the sky cloudless and the wind still. To me and others at Tirhatuan, the sound was as if a light conveyance, making a sharp rattling noise, had passed rapidly between the house and the kitchen – these buildings being about eight yards apart. The tremour, though distinctly felt, was not great; but at the outstation, near the base of the mountain [Mt Dandenong] both the shock and the noise were very considerable. The two men sleeping in the hut were instantly aroused, and ran out to ascertain what was the matter; but neither seeing nor hearing anything unusual, they conjectured what had happened; and as the shock was experienced in the same manner at Rourke's station, about five miles off, it would appear that it was severest along the base of the mountain.

> The second shock was felt in 1847, at the same season of the year. It occurred at four o'clock in the afternoon, and was experienced at the same time in Melbourne and other adjacent places. Those in the house at Tirhatuan, when they felt it moving, ran out in alarm, not doubting for a moment what it was. And a party that were out riding in the direction of the mountain heard it, and were struck with the noise as an extraordinary one, they thought it was caused by horses galloping in the bush.[100]

Then there is Thomas' evidence on his sketch of the stations between Narren Gullen (Mt Eliza) and Dandine (Tontine/Mt Martha) 'blacks say **burst from by earthquake between there and Dandine**'.[101] This is exactly where the Balcombe Fault is located on a map produced by the geologist RA Keble in 1951,[102] the basis of the Geological Survey Map of the Mornington Peninsula:[103] it is almost certainly Balcombe Creek to which the blacks referred.

To a non-geologist, another of Keble's maps is disconcerting to say the least: the coast lines of Port Phillip and Western Port are there, it is true, but one has to search to find them. This map collapses time; it is showing 'The stream systems of the Peninsula' but the time is not the present (the present coast lines are irrelevant); the map is showing the abiding stream systems before the

---

100   Bride 1983[1898]: 112.
101   CY 2984: 543, ML.
102   Keble 1968[1950]: 54, fig 49.
103   I am grateful to Colin Morissey for a copy of the large and valuable Geological Survey of Victoria maps, No 867, zone 7, which have been placed on the Mornington Peninsula Shire database.

uplift of the central escarpment, as they existed before uplift, and as they still exist today, obscured under the waters of Port Phillip and Western Port, deep water channels of navigation.

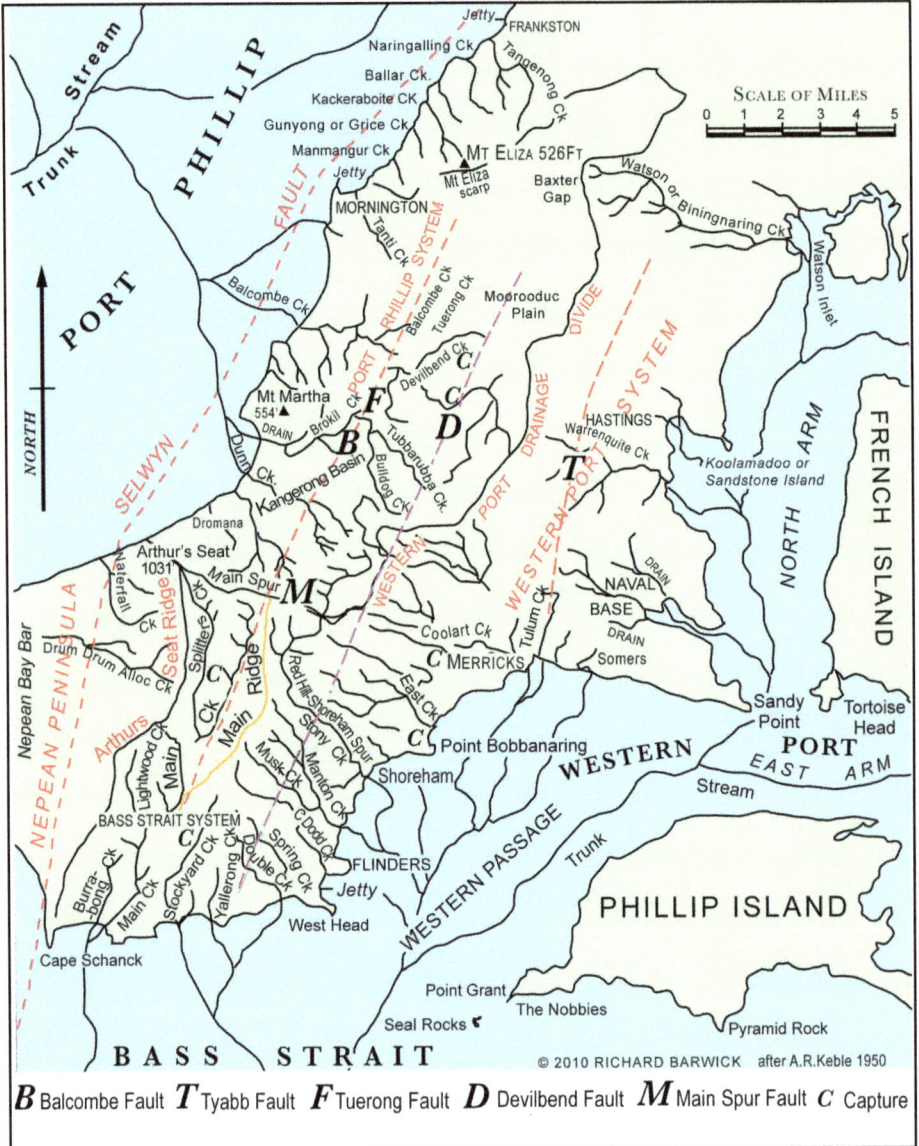

Fig 35 Keble's map 'Mornington Peninsula drainage'

Figure redrawn by Richard Barwick from original by AR Keble, 1950.

Bonurong evidence of earthquakes

Earthquakes were also on the Bonurong minds in the 1840s. There is Yankee Yankee's evidence to William Hull: though Yankee Yankee was long dead when the evidence was subsequently published, he must have given it in conversation with the magistrate Hull before his death in 1846. Hull testified thus:

> With regard to traditions, I may say it is not generally known that the blacks, – Cunningham [Yankee Yankee], Murray and Old Bembo, say that their grandfather, 'My uncle', as they call him – they do not know the word grandfather, my uncle is the term they use for all progenitors – recollected when Hobson's Bay was a kangaroo ground; they say **'Plenty catch kangaroo, and plenty catch opossum there'**; and Murray assured me that the passage up the bay through which the ships came, is the river Yarra, and that the river once went out the heads, but that the sea broke in, and that Hobson's Bay, which was once a hunting ground became what it is.[104]

Hull was cross examined on this in two follow up questions. The chairman, the Hon Thomas McCombie tried to get Hull to agree that the evidence on the ground suggested that the water in the bay had been *higher* once than it was now, and that this suggested a receding of the water rather than a rushing in. But Hull was obdurate; to each follow up question he said 'I only state what their tradition was'.

Recent sedimentary dating of cores from old mines department drilling in Port Phillip has resulted in evidence astonishing to non-scientists. Dr Guy Holdgate, Research Fellow in Geology at The University of Melbourne, has used these results, plus Port of Melbourne Corporation's dredging program multibeam survey results of the bay floor, plus sparker seismic results from his 1970s work with the Geological Survey of Victoria, to model bay water level changes in Port Phillip over the last 10,000 years.

In essence, he believes that climate change has resulted in Port Phillip periodically becoming a dry plain within the last 10,000 years, and most crucially from the point of view of assessing Bonurong evidence, Port Phillip was dry from around 1000 BP to around 3500 BP. The following summary was provided by Holdgate:

1. Port Phillip a dry glacial non-marine surface at 10,000 yrs BP.

2. Between 10,000 and ~7,000 yrs BP there is evidence for freshwater lakes, with marine outside the heads.

3. Marine waters enter the bay at ~7,000 and by 6,000 yrs BP flood to ~+2 to 3m above present reaching to Flemington.

---

104   Answer to Q. 213, Report of Select Committee, *Victoria, Legislative Council Votes & Proceedings*, 1859: 12.

4. Entrances then block with sand sometime after ~3,600 yrs BP.

5. Bay levels start to fall due to evaporation>River/rain input.

6. A still stand in Lake Phillip occurs at -20m below sea level.

7. Major desiccation to -25m below sea level.

8. A hiatus occurs in bay sedimentation between ~3,600 and ~1,000 yrs BP when no sedimentation took place.

9. The bay entrances unblock at around 1,000 yrs BP.

10. Modern bay levels reached shortly thereafter, and open marine sedimentation in the bay resumes.[105]

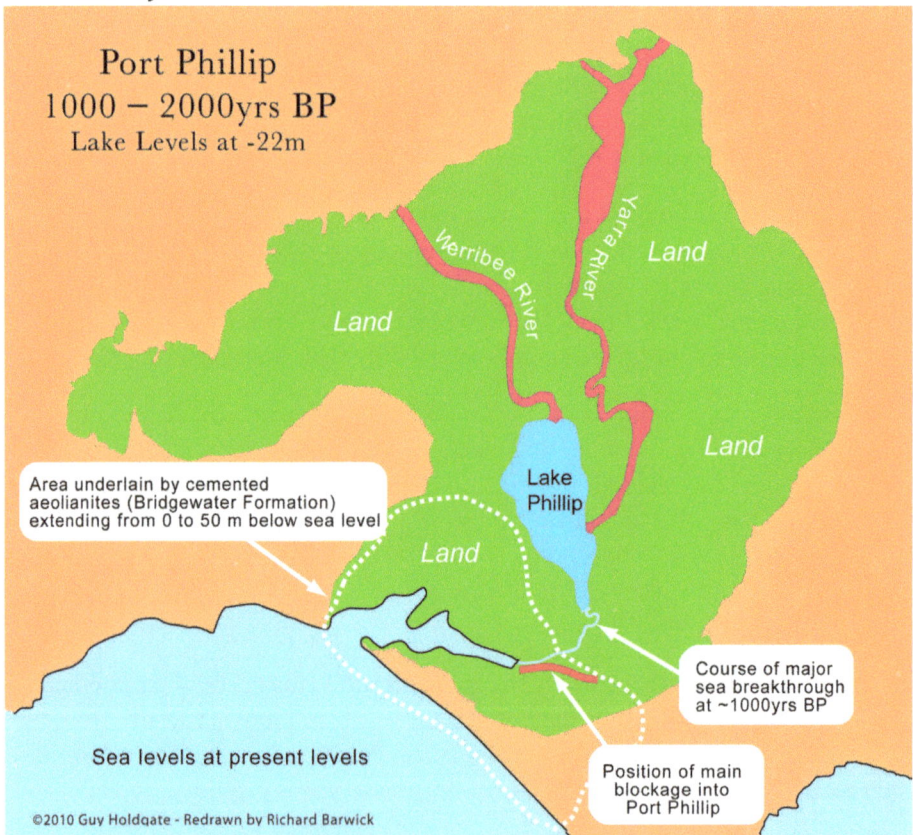

Fig 36. Map of Port Phillip Bay area during the drying period 1000-2000 years BP when the South Channel was blocked

Figure modified from Holdgate et al (2010) in preparation, © Dr Guy Holdgate, 2010.

---

105   G Holdgate, Seminar, 15 May 2009, Monash University.

Holdgate's explanation is that Port Phillip is mostly shallow, and in extended dry periods the evaporation rate exceeds the infill of water flowing into the bay via the Yarra from its catchment area: parts of the South Channel become blocked with sand. Holdgate's evidence supports Aboriginal evidence that they used to walk across dry hunting land to Corio: 1000 years is a credible span of time for an oral culture to transmit important information from generation to generation.

What the scientific evidence does not do is support the Aboriginal testimony of an earthquake unblocking the Rip with the consequent flooding of Port Phillip from Bass Strait, ie the hurricane and earthquake evidence from Georgiana's journal. Nevertheless, it is still possible to imagine a reconciliation of the oral tradition with the scientific findings. Suppose for example, a Bonurong group were encamped on the deep waterhole near the South Channel, and an earthquake along the Selwyn fault broached the sand banked Rip. It could have flooded this particular encampment and killed everyone even though it did not flood Port Phillip.

It is only fair to state that geological opinion is sceptical about this speculation, and the reason turns on earthquake magnitude. The personal narratives of Clow, McCrae and Robinson are suggestive of an earthquake of around 4 to 5 on the Richter scale. Reading the evidence on the ground of the Selwyn fault, the geologists know that there must have been earthquakes of the magnitude of 5 or 6 on the Richter scale. But an earthquake conforming to the Aboriginal testimony would be around 8 on the scale, and earthquakes of such magnitude are unknown in Australia, though common in New Zealand and other places. Holdgate does not dismiss the Aboriginal testimony out of hand, and can even suggest 'a likely blockage area in Port Phillip where the five fathom contour lines nearly come together just north of Capel Sound'.[106] It is where he believes that the breakthrough occurred of the waters of Bass Strait onto the dry plain around 1000 BP.[107]

Undoubtedly there is more to be learned about these processes of drying and flooding and their potential effects on Bonurong lifestyle and population: Aboriginal oral tradition of the sea rushing in cannot be dismissed out of hand.

It seems to me to be impossible that such a catastrophic event as Bonurong loss of the major hunting grounds of Port Phillip and Western Port (though as Holdgate points out, the loss would be slow, over an extended period of time) would not have had some effect on relationships with their contiguous

---

106   Guy Holdgate, pers comm 28 July 2009. Holdgate has subsequently modified his view on the rapidity of flooding, see *The Age*, 8 May 2011.
107   Enlargement of detail showing choke point north of Capel Sound, reproduced with the kind permission of Dr Holdgate and the Port of Melbourne Corporation.

neighbours. To me, the cabbage grass hypothesis as an explanation for the Bonurong/Kurnai feud is not compelling. Change in Western Port possibly requires more research.

Theft of women as an explanation for feud

The third possible explanation, that females were at the heart of the feud, rests on just a little evidence collected in passing, but whether cause or consequence is problematic. The Gippsland 'Chief' Bungaleena/Bun-je-leene was captured with his two wives and three children by the expedition party in search of the alleged white woman in Gippsland. Commissioner of Crown Lands Tyers wrote that he was a 'wily black who has duped us all'.[108] He and his family were taken to the headquarters of the Native Police Corps at Nerre Nerre Warren where he was confined in a hut with the door open, but guarded. Commandant Dana wrote of him that 'the poor old man was one of the least troublesome and showed more intelligence than any of the old natives who have ever been on this station'.[109]

While he was in confinement, Robinson visited him:

> inquiring into the nature and fact of the Western Port lubra which was formely [sic] stolen by Bungaleena and is now in his possession'.[110]

The woman's name had been given by Bungaleena at the time of his capture as Lundagun.[111] After questioning Bungaleena, Robinson recorded that she was said to be the daughter of the Western Port man Nerm Nerm also known as Old Man Billy.[112] Nerm Nerm will be met with again in Chapter 11 as the father of the young man Poligerry, and a principal in the serious dispute about marriage rules, involving Benbow and Kitty. Two weeks after Robinson recorded his information from Bungaleena, Narm Narm/Old Man Billy visited Robinson in his office at Melbourne: Narm Narm was a Boonwrong native, 56 years old, father of Perredit who was a wife of Bungallena. Perredit was a native of Palawrone creek at Mr Horsfold's (Horsfold's station was east of Carrum swamp, roughly on the present Western Port Highway). She was stolen when a girl from Baw Baw[113] at Tarnjil.[114]

---

108 CCL to La Trobe, 24 April 1847, 47/789, enc to VPRS 19, Box 92, 47/907, PROV.
109 Dana to La Trobe, VPRS 19, Box 113, 48/2429, PROV.
110 Dandenong Daybook, 14 July 1847, VPRS 90, PROV.
111 Sergeant McLelland to Commandant, 21 February 1847, enc to VPRS 19, Box 90, 47/436, PROV.
112 Clark 2000, vol 5: 163.
113 In discussing the high country and the watershed of the Yarra, William Jackson Thomas mentions a defined Aboriginal track on a spur above Alderman's Creek leading down from Baw Baw, the mere fact of which suggests regular use (CY 3106, frame 90, ML).
114 Clark 2000, vol 5: 165.

Nern Nern/Narm Narm/Murn Murn/Nerm Nerm/ Nannano/Old Man Billy

Nerm Nerm (Old Billy) appears on Thomas' 1846 census at the head of the listing of Western Port families as a widow, wife Kurdergoorook, sons Polligerry aged 20 and Tareremo aged 18, whose country is Konniga and the beach [ie Frankston and the 9 mile beach between it and Mordialloc] (Thomas, CY 3083, ML).

1840 – Nerm Nerm is on a list of principal families with his lubra Nerven Nerven and his male child Tareum; he is Mr Hill's father,[I] (Thomas Papers, CY 2605, item 1); 12 June 1840 – Nerm Nerm/Turtgurrook – his name is on a list with his lubra (unnamed), no children, out on a ramble (Thomas Journal, CY 2604, item 3, ML); 26 April 1841 – Kurdogrook, Western Port, wife of Koolin Nerm Nerm died at Mr Horsfold's this day (Thomas Journal, CY 2605, item 5, ML); 5 May 1841 – Thomas records her death again, this time writing that she was 58 years old, a Western Port woman, was the wife of Nerm Nerm and mother of Billibellary's wife, and that she died at Polionerrang (Thomas Journal, CY 2605, item 5, ML); before her marriage to Nerm Nerm, Kurdogrook was already the widow of Tuolwing (Old George the King), and the mother of Nunupton (Billy Langhorne) and Mumbo; 24 July 1847 – Thomas informs Robinson that he has made diligent enquiries regarding the Aboriginal native of the Boonurron tribe named Old Man Charlie alias Nannanno … presumes he is Old Man Billy alias Nern Nern … he is still out in the bush but expected to come to Melbourne soon (Thomas to Robinson, VPRS 11, Box 10/667, PROV); 28 July 1847 – Narm Narm, Old Man Billy, a Boonwrong native, 56, father of Perredit who is the wife of Bungaleena now at Narre Narre Warreen, came to the office with Mr Murray. She is native of Palawrone creek at Mr Horsfolds, Karome [Carrum] name of big swamp. She was stolen when a girl from Baw Baw at Tarnjil. Old Man Billy is named after Port Phillip which is called Narm Narm (Robinson Journal, 28 July 1847); 29 June 1849 – Nerm Nerm alias Billy died during the night (VPRS 11, Box 11/718, PROV).

I. Mr Hill is Murrum Murrum Bean, a member of the 1842 Native Police Corps.

The stealing in pre-contact time, of the child who was Nerm Nerm's daughter, from Mt Baw Baw, must be accepted as fact, as it came from Nerm Nerm; the presumption is that the child was at Mt Baw Baw with her parents. Mt Baw Baw is one of the highest peaks lying roughly on the boundary of Boonwurrung and Kurnai country, with drainage from its slopes flowing both south-west to the Yarra system and south-east to the Gippsland river system. This tiny piece of evidence could support an hypothesis that the feud was over country, or it could posit an hypothesis that the feud was about females, especially in light of the fact that on the very first time that the natives who accompanied the official expedition in search of the alleged white woman in Gippsland returned to Melbourne they brought back with them 'five girls, children from Gippsland'.[115]

It is regrettable though, that the origins of a feud with such consequences remain still, a puzzle.

---

115   Clark 2000, vol 5: 171.

9. Manufacturing industry on the Mornington Peninsula, 'the successful plan at Arthurs Seat'

Thomas proposed that instead of throwing whole bodies of animals in the fire to cook, the Bonurong could skin them and sell the skins, and the women could sell their baskets, plus hats plus watch pockets for which Mrs Thomas would supply a pattern: this was what he called his 'successful plan at Arthurs Seat'. This plan was in accordance with the Protectors' instructions from England quoted earlier – the Protectors should ascertain what is that species of industry which is least foreign to the habits and disposition of the objects of their care, and should be provided with all the necessary means of supplying them with such employment.

The Bonurong took to the plan with enthusiasm, and within a short time, adapted it. When the Protectorate shifted from the Mornington Peninsula to Nerre Nerre Warren late in 1840, and they didn't like Nerre Nerre Warren, and walked away from being under the control of the Protectorate, they bypassed the Protectorate's middleman role, and sold their skins directly in Melbourne for cash, in order to purchase what they wanted – powder and shot:[1] but the long-term consequences were such misery from being cold that Thomas begged them to go back to sewing cloaks.[2]

On 22 May 1840, Thomas forwarded to Melbourne from Tubberubbabel the 'first fruits of Aboriginal manufacturing' – 17 skins and seven baskets:[3] the consignment of skins comprised four opossum, one kangaroo and a dozen 'squirrels'.[4] As he said to the Chief Protector, it was only in May when they all settled down at Tubberubbabel that he had made them sensible of the benefits they might derive from labour. He predicted that he could send a great quantity of skins to Melbourne, and if they were saleable, then he felt sure that the money earned would defray a great part, if not all, of 'the supplies granted to them from time to time'.[5] He was very pleased about this consignment, the first

---

1   Thomas Petition to Gipps, VPRS 10, unit 3, 1841/909, PROV.
2   The phenomenon known as 'blanketisation', that is, the substitution of traditional waterproof garments for European blankets, which absorbed water, constituted a health hazard when worn in the same way as the former waterproof garments.
3   Thomas Second Periodical Report, VPRS 4410, unit 3/67, PROV.
4   What Thomas calls a squirrel is probably what we know as a ring-tail possum, a member of the family Phalangeridae, arboreal, nocturnal, with prehensile tail.
5   VPRS 11, unit 7/309, PROV.

of several such, and subsequently looked back a year later from Nerre Nerre Warren, where almost all was going wrong, at both his success at Arthurs Seat and the reason for it.

Thomas' successful plan – feed the people and reward additionally for labour

He gave a simple description of the plan when he looked back on it in a later plea to Robinson to sanction rations:

> I would most earnestly solicit through your influence with His Honour the permission of adopting at the Central Aboriginal Station Nerre Nerre Warren, the plan I pursued at Arthurs Seat ... the plan adopted at Arthurs Seat was to give all adults on the station one pint of flour or rice daily, and about 2 oz of sugar, rewarding those who laboured extra. This plan secured almost immediate order and satisfaction. The native women might be seen daily occupying themselves in making baskets, while the men were careful in procuring skins.[6]

But though Thomas received a 'gratifying communication from His Honour the Superintendent touching his Pleasure and approbation of the Application of the Aborigines',[7] La Trobe never did sanction feeding everyone; at best Thomas received supplies for the old and infirm, and for the young children, and for those who would attend Divine Service on Sundays.[8] What he did at Arthurs Seat was off his own bat, so to speak, and it amounted to misappropriation of public funds. La Trobe observed to Robinson that Mr Thomas issued indiscriminately rations to the natives, and said he did it on his own responsibility.[9]

In their refusal to feed the people, La Trobe and Robinson acted contrary to what the British government expected. In what should have been experienced by them as a stinging rebuke from the Secretary of State for War and the Colonies, Lord Grey wrote the following to Sir George Gipps:

> I cannot conceal from myself that the failure of the system of Protectors has been at least as complete as that of the missions. I have no doubt that a portion of this ill-success, perhaps a large portion, is attributable to the want of some judgement and zealous activity on the part of the Assistant-Protectors. Thus the habit of collecting large bodies of natives

---

6   VPRS 11, unit 8/392, PROV.
7   Application means work.
8   When the Sabbath flour was 'no good' in their opinion, they refused to attend Divine Service at Nerre Nerre Warren, see Fels 1988: 51.
9   Clark 1988, vol 2: 29.

in one spot, and in the immediate vicinity of the settlers, without any previous provision for subsistence or employment, was a proceeding of singular indiscretion.[10]

This judgement was not fair on Thomas, though it ought to have been sheeted home to Robinson. Thomas did issue rations on his own responsibility, contrary to orders, and got into trouble for it: his logic was quite in line with the thinking of those who sent him out from England. For the year 1840, the total list of supplies from the contractor Manton's, for Mr Thomas' station, is as follows:

Flour	15300 lbs	£167 - 6 -10
Meat	5000 lbs	£82 - 0 - 7
Tea	198 lbs	£33 - 0 - 0
Sugar	2300 lbs	£38 - 6 - 8
Tobacco	63 lbs	£5- 15 - 6
Soap	154 lbs	£3 - 4 - 2
Salt	1000 lbs	£4 - 3 - 4
Rice	1200 lbs	£12- 10 - 0
Total		£346 - 7 - 1

He probably got away with it because of the isolation of Tubberubbabel which has been noted – only four stations between Cape Schanck and Melbourne in 1839, twelve, a year later. He does not appear to have defied policy in the matter of rations again, and in fact, was dobbed in by Robinson to La Trobe and called in for an explanation of why he distributed rations 'indiscriminately' to the people in his care when the rations were meant only for the sick and the aged and for orphan children. A filled in *pro forma* from the days immediately after they abandoned the protectorate on the Mornington Peninsula to re-locate at Nerre Nerre Warren indicates that his largesse, besides getting him into trouble with his superiors, may not have been in the best interests of the health of his people. The Bonurong no sooner helped to select Nerre Nerre Warren than most of them decamped, and for most of September Thomas was feeding only five people, to whom he gave daily, to share between them, four pounds of flour, two ounces of tea and one and a half pounds of sugar.[11]

---

10 Despatch no 225, 20 December 1842, enc no 10, in *NSW Legislative Council Votes & Proceedings*, 1843.
11 Enc. with Robinson to La Trobe, 14 November 1840, VPRS 10, unit 2, 1840/1143, PROV.

Comparison of ration scales

To get an idea of how that scale compared with others on the public purse, Ration No 2 for gaol attendants, witnesses and persons awaiting bail, consisted of 20 ounces of wheat bread, eight ounces of maize, 16 ounces of fresh beef, a quarter of an ounce of salt, one ounce of sugar and a quarter of an ounce of soap. Ration No 9, for prisoners confined to gaol was 12 ounces of wheat bread, 12 ounces of maize meal, four ounces of fresh beef, eight ounces of vegetables, half an ounce of salt and half an ounce of soap. Ration No 10, for the children of female prisoners confined to gaol was eight ounces of wheat bread, four ounces of fresh beef, one pint of milk and one quarter of an ounce of yellow soap.[12]

For an idea of appropriate rations for the 1839 Protector's Police, La Trobe took a retrospective view of what was issued to the 1837 de Villiers' Corps of Native Police and thought it a bit generous 'My impression is that reduction might be made in this without injury'. This daily ration was one and a half pounds of flour, one pound of beef or ten ounces of salt pork, two and a half ounces of sugar, one ounce of tea, a quarter of an ounce of soap and a half ounce of salt.[13]

But in the early days on the Mornington Peninsula, he had enough supplies to use food as a reward for the children at school and as a part of the reward for work done by adults, in addition to the daily supply of flour or rice plus sugar that he distributed.

The following vocabulary which he recorded, probably in May 1840 at Tubberubbabel when they were building a bridge across the 'Tubbarubbabel creek', gives a glimpse of his successful plan. The fact that he recorded dialogue seeking information about intended destinations, about lessons to the children, about construction work, but not about manufacturing, doubtless means he had nothing to tell them about skinning. They were already skilled in manufacturing opossum cloaks: they merely extended the range of animals they skinned. For construction work, for going to school and learning the alphabet, for manufactured goods, the Bonurong were paid in trifles of flour, rice etc in addition to the daily illegal ration that Thomas distributed.

The vocabulary of work

Come my blackfellows, work a little then big one eat – *Murrumbick Koolin Mungear Wyebo Tanganan Bullibo.*

Who made this? – *Willaina Mongeol Kunne?*

---

12   Treasury Letters Received 1838–1846, VPRS 7/P 0000, unit 000001, PROV.
13   La Trobe to Robinson, 23 November 1839, 39/135, enc with La Trobe to Col Sec, 25 November 1839, 39/12991 in Port Phillip box 4/1135.1, AO of NSW.

Me made it – *Nunnnun Monguit*

Where work today? – *Winda Mongear Yelling…n*[14]

Work at fence – *Mongan Narlarguon*

Here hold up that – *Wa Koonark Nerrim Kulk*

Hold it upright – *Koonark Terremuk*

Ram down the earth – *Kullerbuk beck*

Lift it up a bit – *Tarnbuk Wyebo*

Cut or adze it – *Tarmuk nge* ·

Turn it over – *Wilgobuk turnit*

Put it down there, very good, no stupid you – *Marbugut nge Marnamukniar Nowlunnin Murrumbinna*

No lazy you like another blackfellow – *Utturp Tandoring mungo Koolin Murrumbinna Near Tarmdum*

Now, no more work, me give you dinner – *Nebbo Umanara Murrumbinna Tanganan Tinderbub Mongan*[15]

It is not the building works they did though, but the manufactured goods that are of present interest. On 20 June 1840 he forwarded from Tubberubbabel a much larger consignment comprised of 13 baskets, two mats, 75 *Tuan* skins, 24 opossum skins, 55 *Bemin*[16] skins and 24 kangaroo skins.[17] In July, the range of manufactured goods was extended by the addition of watch pockets. Watch pockets are interesting. They were made from small skins to a pattern cut out by Mrs Thomas, and put together by the women. It must have been the custom for settlers to hang up their watches by the fireplace in their huts, because that was the market they were aiming at.[18] Very handsome they were, said Thomas. Mrs Thomas found that she could not give the women as much attention as she would have liked because they insisted on working only in the open air and working outside was too cold for Mrs Thomas who had been dangerously ill a few months earlier, an illness brought on by living in the damp and leaking-

---

14 Ink blot on three letters – illegible.
15 Transcribed from Thomas 'Brief Vocabulary of the Aboriginal Language as spoken by the Boonurrong and Warvoorong tribe, District of Port Phillip', no date, but currently located next to the letter which describes the Boonurrong choice of Kullurk as their reserve, VPRS 11, unit 7, item 313, PROV.
16 *Bemin* is the ring-tailed possum; see 'Succinct Sketch of the Aboriginal Language' in *Victoria, Legislative Council Votes & Proceedings*, 1858–59: 91, Appendix D.
17 VPRS 11, unit 7/311, PROV.
18 Thomas to Robinson from Tubberubbabel, 9 July 1840, VPRS 11, unit 7/316, PROV.

roofed hut at Tuerong. There might also have not been much room in Thomas' hut; in July, he had so many manufactured goods in it that it gave the appearance of a 'rough store'.

Baskets are interesting too. The first mention of baskets is quite early in October 1839 at Tubberubbabel. The day after his arrival back from Melbourne when he outlined his plan to them, the women presented baskets to Thomas just before sunset, as gifts for his daughters: the women made it explicitly clear to Thomas that these baskets were not for sale, that they were a present – '**make em plenty by and bye for Melbourne. Your piccaninnies them'**. He had enough of an idea of correct behaviour to reciprocate with a gift of flour and sugar from his own private store.[19] Another set of baskets he took back with him to Melbourne for sale.

Nearly a year later Mrs Thomas extended the uses for the traditional skills. She designed and taught them how to do baskets for dogs, and baskets for fruit, and long oval flat baskets for clothes storage.[20] Flat mats were made which Robinson called table mats.[21]

Robinson's advice to the other protectors that their charges be encouraged to follow the example of Thomas' people on the Mornington Peninsula and go in for manufacturing bore fruit. Parker's Jajoworrung (Loddon River people) at 'Lar.ne.barramul' at Mt Franklin sent a considerable amount of manufactured goods to Melbourne in the year 1842. Assistant Protector Edward S Parker's 'Return of the number of hats, Baskets etc made by Aboriginal Women and Girls at the Station Lar.ne.barramul' lists 96 hats of various sizes, 70 baskets, 42 table mats and 11 nets.[22]

The skin industry was a group effort too. Thomas said that three months ago they did not skin animals, but threw them on the fire, turning them to singe off the fur, unless they very much needed a skin for a specific purpose. 'Now however, they are almost ashamed of throwing an unskinned animal on the fire, and the skins furnish them with what they consider to be the luxuries of life'.[23] Old men who were superannuated would stretch the skins. Thomas recorded one instance where 'the men stretched skins got overnight'.[24] Children made *mindermins* which were pegs hardened in fire, for use in stretching the skins.[25]

---

19   *HRV*, vol 2B: 554.
20   Thomas to Robinson, 9 July 1840 from Tubberubbabel, VPRS 11, unit 7/316, PROV. George Langhorne recorded from his mission experience 1835–37 that women already made neat oval baskets of grass tree neatly plaited, *HRV*, vol 2A: 177.
21   Flat mats: see Clark 1988, vol 2: 29.
22   Appendix No 8, enc. to La Trobe to Col Sec Sydney, 16 March 1843, no 43/398, in *NSW Legislative Council Votes & Proceedings*, 1843.
23   VPRS 11, unit 7/316, PROV.
24   Thomas Journal, 12 June 1840, CY 2604, item 3, frame 147, ML.
25   Second Periodical Report, 7 November 1840, VPRS 4410, unit 3/67, PROV.

One man would draw into fine threads the sinews of the kangaroo tails; another would pin and stretch the skins; another would sew the skins together as neat as any tailor would do a garment, pressing the skins down every three or four inches.[26] He mentions groups of six or seven stretching skins and eight women making baskets.

A later local record describes these pegs as wooden nails about three inches long. One man sits down on the ground and stretches the skin upon a piece of bark at its full length, then he nails one side of the skin and pulls the other side with all his might so as to make it a great deal wider, then he nails the first side down well with one nail and so on until he has finished the whole.[27] Thomas would not accept delivery of any manufactured items from the blacks on a Sunday, in order to show respect for the Sabbath.[28]

The following table of goods manufactured on the Mornington Peninsula was transcribed by Byrt.[29]

Skin	Kangaroo	Opossums	Bemin	Fly Squirrel	Baskets	Mats	Watch Pockets
May 22	1	4	0	12	7	0	0
June 9	0	11	3	18	2	0	0
June 22	24	14	35	75	13	2	0
July 27	54	12	12	46	47	3	6
	79	41	50	151	69	5	6

The articles for sale were taken in the cart by Thomas' assigned servant Davis, and delivered to Mr George Lilly, storekeeper at Melbourne, who did not charge a commission on his services, 'Mr Lilly is agent at Melbourne gratuitously'.[30] Some goods were sold at public auction, perhaps to establish prices. Lilly recorded the following prices for goods sold:

- Baskets – one shilling and sixpence
- Kangaroo skins – ten pence
- Opossum skins – four shillings for a dozen
- Native cat – tuppence halfpenny.

These goods were described as 'Account Sales, Skins and Baskets, for a/c and risk of the Aborigines Establishment'. Some cash went to Bullett, a Sydney

26 27 August 1839, 'Summary of Proceedings during August', Byrt 2004, CD CY 3082 S.DOC.
27 McCrae 1966: 252.
28 Thomas Journal, 12 July 1840, CY 2604, items 3 and 4, ML.
29 Byrt 2004, CD CY 3082, commencing frame 12.
30 Robinson to La Trobe, 21 August 1840, VPRS 10, unit 2, 1840/815, PROV.

native, formerly one of John Batman's blacks.[31] Thomas' plan was that the blacks who made the goods would be the ones to benefit from their labour, for luxuries, because their basic subsistence would be provided, but this document implies that the money received was to go to the Protectorate account with the Commissariat. It is important to bear in mind that everyone in Port Phillip on the government payroll received rations or money in lieu – soldiers, bureaucrats, convicts – under a finely graded remuneration system which took into account the quality of the rations provided. There were three or four grades of flour, and the same for tobacco.

To gain an idea of equivalent values, flour at that time was sixpence per pound weight, tea between two and three shillings per pound weight, salt sixpence per pound weight and sugar four pence per pound weight.[32] A kangaroo skin sold at ten pence in Melbourne would purchase one pound of flour plus a little tea and sugar: this is roughly the daily ration that he was distributing to his people at Tubberubbabel, quite against the proposed policy of the Chief Protector. Another comparison may be made with the work/ration scale adopted by the first missionary George Langhorne, at the botanical gardens mission – two hours labour was worth half a pound of bread; four hours labour was worth half a pound of bread plus four ounces of meat.[33]

The Chief Protector's policy on work

Robinson's policy was simply that the blacks should labour for their food: he thought that supplying rations induced 'vassalage'.[34] It is at least possible that his hardline view was based on his experience with his VDL blacks who were rationed at government expense with no work obligations required from them. Robinson had brought them as his 'family' from VDL but he was sick of them by now, and engaged at this time in arguing with the governor in Sydney about their rations: the government was soon to approve of Robinson's cutting them adrift. Thomas' petition to Gipps of 1841 specifically compares the VDL blacks 'no work obligation' with the obligation of the Port Phillip blacks to work for rations.

There does not appear to be evidence that the Chief Protector thought that any sort of compensation should be afforded 'the real owners of the soil' for the use of their land. What Robinson was concerned about was developing a scale of rations to be supplied in payment for work performed. He wrote to La

---

31 VPRS 11/P/0001, 1840, PROV. Bullett was indeed a Sydney black but he was much travelled, coming to Port Phillip from VDL as one of John Batman's blacks in 1835. To give Bullett cash from the Protectorate accounts was surely a misappropriation on Robinson's part.

32 *HRV*, vol 1: 178.

33 VPRS 4, Box 2, 37/90, PROV.

34 Chief Protector to La Trobe, 23 December 1839, VPRS 10, unit 1, 30/363, PROV.

Trobe in December 1839 on this subject, a letter that reads now as miserable and bureaucratic, showing him to be in almost complete opposition to his Assistant Protector philosophically and morally.

Europeans had been in Port Phillip for nearly four years when the protectors arrived, and for those four years Europeans had been distributing rations to the local Aboriginal groups under the terms of Batman's Treaty. It does not matter now, nor did it matter then to the Aborigines that the treaty was illegal – the fact was that the food was delivered. Batman called it 'the annual tribute to those who are the real owners of the soil'.[35] Food functioned as the rent paid for the use of the land as a sheep and cattle run. In addition many Aboriginal people worked for wages, what they called white money; in fencing, stock handling, shepherding, message carrying, washing clothes, guiding shooting parties, chopping wood, felling trees, stripping bark and so on. In an economy which was short of labour:

> Labouring hands are so scarce that the blacks are decoyed from one master to another, persons knowing that the Bench refuses to take recognizance of their agreement.[36]

They worked well, and Europeans relied on them, but what they would *not* do was work day in day out on a permanent basis all year round (see the first hand evidence from Kolloorlook and Yankee Yankee elsewhere in this story).

Where Thomas approved of cash wages being paid for labour, and the Aboriginal owners of the soil interpreted the rations given to them as rent money, Robinson laid out to La Trobe a plan whereby Aborigines would work for their rations. His attitude to work and food in itself probably crippled any good the Protectorate might have done. Set up in England with such earnest determination – that what happened in Tasmania would not be repeated in Port Phillip – the Protectorate needed a better man than Robinson showed himself to be.

The Chief Protector began his letter to La Trobe with a concession – that though ten hours a day was the standard for a white man, 'for a savage bred to war and the chase', the hours should not exceed six or possibly eight. He wrote that ten hours labour a day should be sufficient to pay for a man's needs, but if he had a wife and children who could not work, his needs would be greater: they would also need clothing. He went on to say that:

> the ration system is in my opinion totally unsuited to the state of savages, that is when taken in connection with their own civilization. It has a tendency to lower them rather than elevate them in the scale of humanity.

---

35   John Batman to Sir George Arthur, 25 June 1835, *HRV*, vol 1: 9.
36   *HRV*, vol 2B: 573.

The ration system is prejudicial to the interests of natives, whether it be given as a gratuity or in lieu of labour; in the former it induces to inactivity and in the latter to vassalage. They should be taught to know their want should fit their occupation. A desire for civilization, comfort and for the possession of property should be created, these principles being implanted. The [illegible] of the Assistant Protector should be to induce them to acquire property, by honest and persevering industry, and to protect them in its possession. The work of civilization has then commenced, erratic habits forsaken. The wandering Aboriginal turned settler, his life and property is secured, he is independent in character and appreciates the enjoyment of his improved condition.

Individual possession of property will do more to overcome their erratic habits than any other. It will be the duty of the Assistant Protector to point out to the Aboriginal Natives as opportunity offers the advantages and disadvantages emanating from these various modes of existence, and when the instructions already issued are fulfilled, and when they, the Assistant Protectors are prepared to guarantee that the Aboriginal Natives are ready and willing to settle down in one fixed abode, and not till then, shall I feel it my duty to recommend to the Government the immediate formation for the Assistant Protectors of fixed Establishments.

In the mean time, and until a more Systematic arrangement can be effected, every disposition to industry should be encouraged, and if gratuities of food and clothing are afforded, it ought in no case to be acted upon except for the Sick, Aged, Infirm, Young children and Mothers of Families. The Chief of Tribes should on political grounds[37] be exempt from labour.

If food and clothing are given as remuneration for labour, the scale of reward should be proportionate to the work done, and not to the time occupied. This can be effected, but then there are some kinds of labour that cannot be judged of by quality such as jobbing. This therefore must be regulated by time under the circumstances and for the present and later stated. I think a discretionary power should be vested in the Assistant Protectors permitting them to dispense rewards in food and clothing for the encouragement of industry and good conduct.

The young and hale of the Aboriginals ought not to receive provisions except as an equivalent for industry, for to give it as a gratuity would tend only to idleness, dissoluteness and mischief. Until fixed Establishments are formed the description of Labour for the employment of Aborigines

37 Later, when the Native Police Corps was established, the chief was similarly exempted from labour on similar grounds.

is a subject for consideration. As soon however as the Assistant Protector has selected a place in the Central parts of their Districts as a centre of operations and homestead for their families the Aborigines might be employed in gardening and Spade husbandry and fencing, as well as bullock drivers and messengers, instead of Crown prisoners as present.

The women ought to be employed in washing, sewing and other domestic labour. The females are frequently employed by persons in Town and Country in various kinds of industry, fetching water, chopping wood and in washing – it would be desirable to know how many Aboriginal natives are now employed at the Assistant Protectors Establishments, as also the number and names of the persons family engaged, with the description of labour they were engaged in lest my view and sentiment be mistaken.

I beg to remark that I am not one of those who suppose that the civilization of savages must precede their Evangelization for this would be contrary not only to the general order of things but civilization itself.[38] [three words illegible] also teacher, otherwise such a theory therefore if permitted would be mischievous in its tendency, and harmful to its results; if a man is Christianized he is sure to be civilized. Civilization follows, and does not precede Christianity, and if any lasting and real good is to be effected to the Australian Aborigines, Religion, and it alone must be the precursor in all its operations. The Superstitious prejudices of the natives have done more to retard their civilization than any other – months of hard labour and fatiguing service in quest of an Aboriginal tribe[39] has had its hopes and prospects suddenly blighted by the death of a leading member of their community, the cause of which, according to their superstitious faith was attributed to the white stranger.

Cottages also built and fitted up[40] for their occupation have, after the death of an individual been vacated and entirely abandoned, the death of [illegible] party having been attributed to an evil spirit who inhabited the Dwelling.

---

38   In espousing this view, Robinson placed himself in opposition to Governor Gipps, whose views were recorded in an interview in Sydney in late 1838 with the Assistant Protectors, and sent to Robinson in Hobart by William Thomas, 'he was most desirous that we should use our utmost exertion to civilize them before we attempted to evangelise them … he doubted very much if the New Hollanders would ever take the Scriptures … they seemed to have no curiosity or desire for the Bible or any book … he did think one of the greatest stimula was teaching them the value of money' (Thomas to Robinson, 27 November 1838, in Plomley 1987: 773).

39   His friendly mission in VDL.

40   At Wybelena on Flinders Island.

Numerous instances might be adduced to show that their superstitious prejudice militates against, stands in the way of their Civilization and which Christian instruction can only remove.[41]

In this letter to La Trobe, Robinson mentions almost all the issues which would confront Thomas in his efforts to set up the Protectorate – location (in the central part of the two tribes' district, rather than where the Bonurong wanted it), rations, employment, the necessity of a census. It was underpinned by the widely held contemporary view that Christianity must precede civilisation, and it was shot through with Robinson's personal conviction that the possession of private property would lead to a sedentary lifestyle.

Robinson's views prevailed, and he was sufficiently impressed by the manufacture of goods on the Mornington Peninsula that he wrote a circular letter to the other three protectors at the Goulburn and Loddon rivers and Geelong, encouraging them to follow Thomas' example:

> Mr Assistant Thomas having on several occasions remitted to Melbourne for sale several small articles of Aboriginal industry, His Honour the Superintendent desires that the same encouragement may be afforded to the Aboriginal natives of the other Districts.
>
> In order thereto, it is requested that a scale of prices be fixed for which the articles should be sold, for the natives to receive in provisions or useful articles the full value of the money realized. I have therefore to request that you will inform me what you deem a fair equivalent, when a form will be prepared and printed to enable you to keep account of the Articles received and those given in exchange clear and easy.
>
> His Honour is of the opinion that money on no account should be given to the natives.
>
> In fixing a scale of prices or equivalent, you will exercise your own judgement, as the prices heretofore realized cannot be any criterion; many of the trifles having been bought as mere curiosities, in the articles of skins also, the Markets fluctuate.
>
> Of course the agents will get the highest prices. The supplies will be placed to the credit of the natives (Mr Lilly is agent at Melbourne gratuitously), and no doubt some well-disposed person may be found who will undertake for the benefit of the Natives, a similar duty at [blank]. If not the articles can be forwarded to Mr Lilly at Melbourne.[42]

---

41   VPRS 10, unit 1, 1839/363, PROV.
42   Circular to assistant protectors, an enc. with Robinson to La Trobe, 21 August 1840, VPRS 10, unit 2/815, PROV.

Though later in his life Robinson underwent a conversion experience,[43] never, after Arthurs Seat, was Thomas free to distribute rations daily to all comers. The rations for work policy came to have unfortunate consequences in the end. It taught the hungry people to feign sickness in order to obtain food.[44] And it left them cold and exposed to bad weather because they sold their skins instead of making possum skin cloaks to keep them warm. In September 1843 Thomas in Melbourne was concerned for the welfare of his blacks, and went to enquire for them along the beach.

He called at a number of native encampments for which he gave the native name, and in the margin, the squatter occupying the run. These places were Boollerim, Mr Shannessey, Binningean, Captain Baxter[45] and Ballewrungan, Mr Gorringe[46] where he stopped the night having travelled 43 miles on horseback. He found no blacks. Next day he visited Tuerong, then Kangerong, and heard at Kangerong that the blacks were at Kulluck. The next day was a Sunday, and he must have been seriously concerned because he broke his own rule against travelling on a Sunday, and rode from Tuerong to Kulluck where he found them. They then came to Tuerong and encamped by a creek, about 30 of them, all Western Ports except one Barrabool lubra and her child. It was awful weather, wet and stormy, and the poor children and lubras look very sadly, 'poor creatures': he 'begged' them not to sell their skins to the whites but to make cloaks.[47]

Thomas can be left with the last word – 'I used a discretionary power once and succeeded at Arthurs Seat'.[48]

---

43   At the end of his time in Australia when his job had been abolished, he recorded in his journal the following 'The natives should be treated [as] men, they work as men and they should be treated same as men, a fair day's wage for a fair day's labour but this is never accorded them. It is thought that if they get food it is enough for blacks' (Monday 28 January 1850, in Clark 2000, vol 6: 16).

44   *HRV*, vol 2B: 547.

45   The run Carup Carup.

46   Ballewrungan is Poleorongong.

47   Thomas Journal, CY 2606, item 2, frame 113, ML. Thomas crossed out another sentence in this days' entry for which the verb cannot be read. It looks like a matter of regret for the station they once had.

48   Thomas Journal, CY 2604, item 5, frame 282, ML.

10. Death of Johnny and his burial on the foreshore at McCrae

Johnny's death and burial occurred in a later and different era, the gold rush period, 11 years after the Protectorate moved from the Mornington Peninsula. I came upon the location of his grave when seeking information from George Gordon McCrae's journal about George Smith. Then George Smith turned out to be the earliest legal licence holder of the foreshore where Johnny was buried. I was struck with the intimacy, the connectedness of these people, black and white, in those far-off days: here are the same people, Bogy Bogy/Pereuk and George Smith, first met with in the Protectorate era.

And when I went down to the lighthouse precinct to estimate what George Gordon McCrae might have meant by 'a little to the south of the present lighthouse', it seemed obvious that Johnny was buried either beneath a public car park or possibly beneath Point Nepean Road. We must walk unknowingly over Aboriginal graves on the Mornington Peninsula, but it is quite a different matter to park vehicles and trailers on a grave once we know it is there. This chapter brings together all the information gathered about Johnny's death and the location of his grave site. Aboriginal Affairs Victoria will act on the matter.

The most well-known account of Johnnie's death comes to us from the journal of Georgiana McCrae: it survived almost by accident, being included in a portion of Georgiana's diary 'Scrip scrap' which had become separated from the rest of her journals and was found damaged and disordered in her desk:[1] it is a brief and moving account.

But the editor of Georgiana's journal, her grandson Hugh, has been damningly criticised in a recent PhD thesis[2] for his prejudiced and manipulative changes to the original text, as well as his insertions, which, taken together, subvert Georgiana's meaning: so shocking are these changes which Hugh McCrae made to his grandmother's journal that Weber concluded:

> Once one has been made aware of the extent of the re-writing of Georgiana's journal the book can no longer be seen as the journal of Georgiana McCrae.[3]

---

1 McCrae 1966: 201.
2 Therese Weber, 'Port Phillip Papers: The Australian Journals of Georgiana McCrae' (Weber 2001). Mornington Peninsula Shire library has purchased a CD copy of this thesis now housed in its local history collection at Rosebud.
3 Weber 2001: 227.

My own comparisons of texts for those parts of Georgiana's story which I have used tend to confirm this strong statement, so the following account by Georgiana of Johnnie's death and burial is copied from Weber's manuscript.[4] On Weber's CD-ROM, she has reproduced a photographic image of Georgiana's text on one page, and Weber's own transcription on the page facing. The following journal extract commences on 1 October 1851. Note that the spelling of the name is not fixed – Georgiana calls him Johnnie, and her son George Gordon McCrae spells the name as Johnny.

Death of Johnnie

A cold and frosty morning – Poor Old 'Bogie' in great distress as his son is dying – George went to administer what comfort he could – but the poor fellow was scarcely able to swallow anything – liquid – The old man trying to revive him by breathing into his mouth, and instead of allowing the lad to breathe his last in peace and quiet – the old man kept him in his arms, singing into his ear, & from time to time pulling up his eyelids to let him see the light of the sun – About noon we heard a loud Wail from the Lubras, and (the party were Qambying at the foot of our paddock outside the fence & the Cape Shanck road) and we knew by this that poor 'Johnnie' had been released from his sufferings – An hour later 'Mrs Bogie' came up to say 'Bogie' wished to see George 'to speak to him' – On George's return we learnt that the old man wanted string or rope to bind the corpse hand and foot, – & to help dig the grave.

The body was wrapped in the blanket and opossum rug in a sitting position, with the elbows resting on the knees, the chin supported by the left hand – and the right one supporting the right angle of the jaw bone – The strings were tightly swathed around, and George having dug a grave breast high – The Father and the (5th) stepmother deposited the body in the sand. They then covered it with twigs – and then – after placing the last bottle of medicine I had sent him and a new pannickin beside the body, the sand was replaced and well trodden-down and before George had left them – Bogie had begun to fence the space around with branches thickly set – Bogie says, he being old, does not intend to kill a blackfellow to satisfy Johnnie's death –[5]

2nd The day following – George went down to fix a stout wood slab as a/Head/mark for poor Johnnie's grave. His name deeply cut in a piece

4   Weber 2001: 654–659.
5   This description of the burial of Johnnie conforms closely to the archetype recounted in Thomas' lengthy paper on 'Manners and Customs of the Aborigines: Burial of the Dead' in C 339, CY 3695, ML.

of soft deel thereon thus[6] – Bogie quite pleased to see his son's remains marked 'All the same 'as white – fellow'– To-morrow Bogie goes to the Bush 'to cry with others of his race[7] –

Fig 37. 'Memorial Cross'

George Gordon McCrae. Georgiana also sketched this cross but George Gordon's sketch is reproduced because he actually constructed the memorial for his friend. From the McCrae Papers reproduced with the permission of the State Library of Victoria.

3rd Bogie came up to ask me for a crepe hat-band similar to one on a Hat he pointed out to me so I had to take it off the Hat – & Bogie departed.

5th A taxed cart[8] drove up – & a nimble-footed blackfellow sprang from it – and went hurriedly towards Johnnie's grave, – and knelt down, thrust his hand into the mound of sand and inserted therein three or four gumleaves – and then returned to the cart – and went off towards the Green hills[9] – No doubt the youth had done the needful to appease the manes of his fellow man – for it seems their belief is, that those leaves

---

6   Georgiana has drawn in her text an illustration of Johnnie's memorial marker. Though Georgiana consistently spells the name as Johnnie in her own text, her drawing shows JOHNNY as does George Gordon's illustration.

7   Weber notes in her analysis the sometimes incoherent use Georgiana makes of quotation marks, frequently forgetting to close them.

8   Weber's footnote says that a taxed cart was a two-wheeled originally springless open cart used mainly for trade or agricultural purposes on which was charged only a reduced duty, removed entirely, in spite of the name, in the 1830s.

9   Colin McLear identifies the Green hills as either side of Purves Road on the eastern spine of Arthurs Seat (McLear 2006: 107).

will convey to the dead, the intelligence that his death had been avenged – What is remarkable is that some bodies found in Peru, enclosed in large earthern jars were in precisely the same attitude as that of Johnny – are these Aborigines of ours of the same race degenerated through the agency of earthquake, floods and famine?

5th This Johnny – had gone to California with Geo Smith – & on his return the camping out in Australia during the winter months had brought on Pthisis to which the natives are all more or less suspect, and a few months ago Johnny broke a blood vessel in his lungs – He was a very intelligent nice looking lad – probably 20 years of age – Before he went to California he had been an ally and Hunting companion of our boys – and his death has cast quite a shadow over them all.

George Gordon McCrae

George Gordon McCrae was Georgiana's eldest son, 18 years old at the time of Johnny's death.[10] His account is another first-hand participant narrative, written specifically to pass on information about the Bonurong, because they were all dead: this dates the account as post 1875. The account specifically mentions the present lighthouse which was commissioned in 1883, replacing the earlier one of 1854. George Gordon McCrae spoke to the infant Historical Society of Victoria twice in 1909, on recollections of Melbourne and Port Phillip in the 1840s, the articles being published subsequently in the *Victorian Historical Magazine* in 1911 and 1912, and republished in book form in 1987.[11] The text of the published articles follows closely the text of the reminiscences, and it is overwhelmingly likely that he wrote his reminiscences, gave his two addresses to the historical society, and published them, all around the same time, the early twentieth century.

George Gordon McCrae's description of Johnny's burial[12]

When Mr Smith sailed he took with him one of our young Aboriginals of whom further and later on … Johnny was put before the mast and soon became an adept at handling reefing, steering, indeed he might well have been rated able seaman after his two trans Pacific voyages. How long Mr Smith remained in California I forget. They returned apparently not much richer than when they started but brought with

---

10 'McCrae, George Gordon (1833 – 1927)', *Australian Dictionary of Biography*, vol 5: 136.
11 McCrae 1987.
12 George Gordon McCrae, 'Experiences not exploits', vol 3, Ms 2523/4/c, SLV.

them stories of huge fortunes made by others. Johnny on his return to us resumed the possum rug and tomahawk and became once more the companion of my shooting and fishing expeditions. To whatever cause it may have been due he fell into a galloping consumption of which he died, worn away to a shadow of his former self.

I myself carried his body on my shoulders to the grave prepared for him by his father and friends in the very heart of the bimbel[13] scrub in the 'bottom' close to the sea[14] and a little to the south of the position occupied by the iron lighthouse of today. I set up a little memorial tablet there; a square bit of hardwood planking on which I had chiselled the word JOHNNY. After having nailed which on to a stout upright at the head of the grave, I left regretting that it was out of my power to afford him anything more permanent. However, it lasted for years, an object of pride as well as veneration with his family and our blacks in general.[15]

The grave was not long and narrow but a bowl shaped excavation like on a very large scale the den of an ant-lion. This was in the first instance lined about the lower part with sheets of bark, which in turn were covered pretty thickly with leaves from the gum trees. This couch being sufficiently prepared, his people placing the body just before burial in a sitting position, tied the thumbs and great toes together, rolled it up in his rug and other wraps which being secured by stout ties, they lowered into the grave. Leaves were then carefully spread over it and packed in on either side above all a few sheets of bark were laid, on these further leaves and bark and lastly the sand filled in till it reached the level of the soil but without raising any mound. There was no ceremony, no talk that I can remember. All drew away from the grave decently and in silence.

This description of an aboriginal funeral as in our part of the country I have given believing that it acquires an additional interest from the fact that of Johnny's hunting and fishing tribe not a single individual survives to this day.[16]

In his published paper George Gordon McCrae uses practically the same language as he used in his journal to describe the burial, not as Johnny's, but as a typical burial in our district. The only detail which differs is that in the published version he states that a cord tightly joins the already tied great toes and the thumbs.[17]

---

13   Elsewhere in his Ms George Gordon McCrae defines the bimbel as 'beach tea tree'.
14   The 'bottom' was the foreshore, an Aboriginal encampment and a favourite place for cows with calves.
15   Fig 37.
16   George Gordon McCrae, 'Experiences not exploits', vol 3, Ms 2523/4/c, SLV.
17   McCrae 1911: 24.

Location of Johnnie/Johnny's grave

The first observation to be made about the location is that at the presumed time of George Gordon McCrae's description, the early twentieth century, lighthouses, and piers for the bay steamers, and roads for the summer 'season' were everyday topics of newspaper articles. For example, a lengthy article entitled *Round the Lighthouses* published in 1909 describes how the government vessel the *Lady Loch* made regular visits four times a year around all Victorian lighthouses 'carrying stores and transferring the staff from one lighthouse to another'. The first call on these quarterly runs was to Dromana, where the lighthouse keeper and his family (plus a hive of bees) embarked for Cape Everard.[18] Another 1909 article entitled *Seaside Motoring* suggests a Sunday drive to the Mornington Peninsula and assures the reader that 'the road is in good order between Dromana and Rosebud, it having lately been repaired'.[19] My own feeling is that if the road had been built over Johnny's grave, George McCrae would have said so at the time. As can be seen from the Rose postcards, dated 1940–1960, the road remained a single carriageway in both directions until it was widened: though this widening was done within living memory, I have been unable to discover exactly when it was done. The question becomes did the road widening extend over the grave, or is the grave still under the grassed area of the car park in front of the McCrae Yacht Club?

Taking George Gordon McCrae's account as truthful – he is not only an eyewitness but a participant, and given the close, though not total agreement with Georgiana's account, it is certain that the place of death was not exactly the place of burial.[20] George Gordon McCrae carried Johnnie's body from one place to the other. Johnny died in the encampment at the foot of the paddock outside the fence and outside the road, therefore close to the sea, and was buried at a place near which Bogie gathered branches from the scrub beside the road, therefore close to the road.

Fencing

Several lines of fencing are mentioned in the original sources, the first one being a sturdy three rail fence enclosing the whole of the ground which included the house, the tutor's hut, the kitchen and the cleared land in front of the house. This fence and these buildings are all shown in Georgiana's four watercolours of the

---

18   *Argus,* 13 February 1909: 4.
19   *Argus,* 29 November 1911: 10.
20   This agrees well with Thomas' account of traditional 'Burial of the dead' – the body is not buried where the person died but moved 100 yards or so away for burial. Thomas does not suggest a reason for this.

homestead.[21] The house is on the 16 metre contour line,[22] 'situated on a terrace of sandy soil two hundred yards up from the beach' according to Georgiana,[23] and 'less than an eighth of a mile from the sea' according to her son.[24]

The second line of fencing is equally clear from Georgiana's paintings. She valued her water view extending to the heads, and a large area in front of the house is depicted as cleared in her paintings. The little elevation or escarpment on which McCrae House stands, extends towards the sea to Burrell Street, which runs parallel to the sea. On the sea side of Burrell Street, the land falls away sharply; Georgiana would not have had her water view towards the heads were it not for this sharp fall away of the land: her front house paddock fence was probably aligned along Burrell Street, and it appears from her paintings to be a brush fence sufficient to keep animals from the cleared space in front of the house. In 1850 a new garden fence was commenced, made of vertical poles with tea tree stick wattling.[25]

The fence at the road

The third fence is what Georgiana calls the paddock fence, outside of which was the Cape Schanck road. This fence ran the whole length of the frontage of the property, as far as 'the creek'.[26] That this creek is Drum Drum Alloc Creek is evidenced by its description in Andrew Murison McCrae's application for lease of his run whose boundaries are as follows:

> On the north by Mr Jamieson's special survey 4 miles, on the west by the coast line of the bay to the nose of the mountain called St Anthony's Nose, from thence along the Cape Schanck road to the Drumdunnuallock creek being the boundary line with Mr Barker, and on the south by the creek to its source, thence by a line bearing east to a point where the continuation of the eastern boundary of the said special survey meets the said line, the large waterhole below the bald hill being in common with the Mt Martha run; also that piece of land between the Cape Schanck road and the sea, commencing near the rocks or the Point

---

21   There are four views of McCrae homestead by Georgiana, from the north, south, east and west which show the homestead buildings firmly enclosed by a three rail fence, and as well, a view of The Heads from below the House, which shows a brush fence (McCrae 1966: 168–169, 184–185).
22   Phil Hughes, Mornington Peninsula Shire, pers comm 8 October 2008.
23   McCrae 1966: 227.
24   McCrae 1911: 19.
25   Weber 2001, 13 October 1850: 638.
26   George Smith to La Trobe, 7 January 1848, 48/148, VPRS 5359/P/0000, unit 000010, PROV.

known as St Anthony's Nose, and ending at the creek at the junction of the Point Nepean and Cape Schanck roads, nearly opposite the end of the paddock fence.[27]

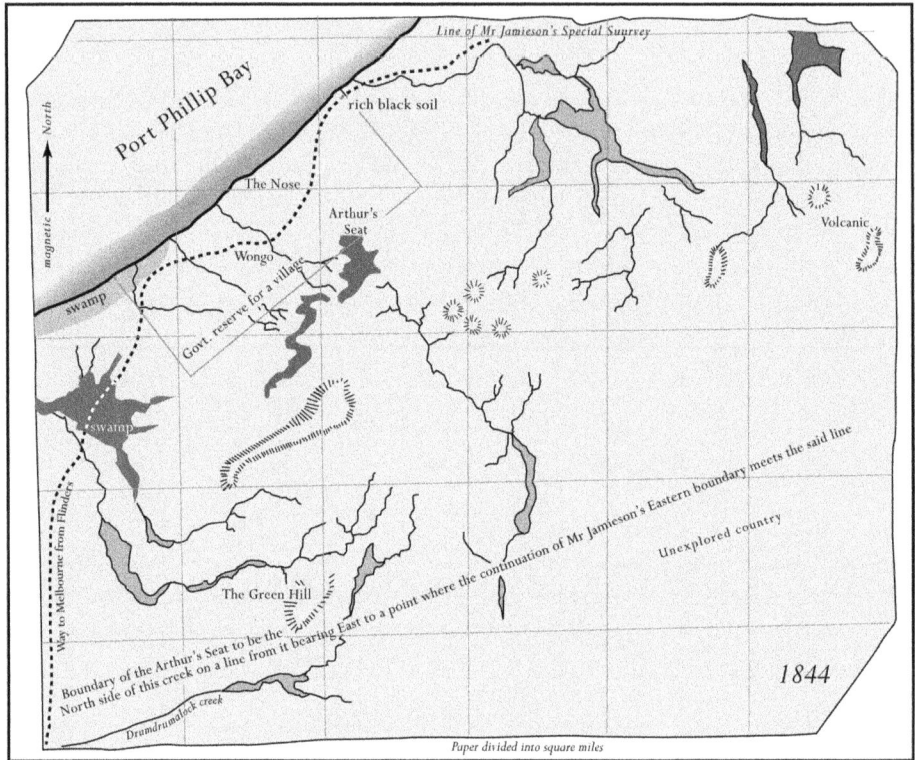

Fig 38. 'Plan of Arthur's Seat Run, 1844'

Andrew Murison McCrae, edited, reproduced with the permission of the National Trust of Australia (Victoria).

George Gordon McCrae confirms the lower line of fencing in his description of 'the bottom' which is 'the broad strip of land extending from high water mark to our lower level of fencing, well sheltered and densely wooded ... the forest was huge she-oaks'.[28] He writes that this coastal foreshore strip was 'for long a great camping ground of the blacks, as well as being the favourite resort of cows with young calves. It was called the bottom. The sheep yards were one mile from the house towards Cape Schanck.[29]

---

27 *Port Phillip Gazette*, 13 December 1848, 'Supplementary List of Claims to leases of Crown Lands beyond the settled districts'.
28 George Gordon McCrae, 'Experiences not exploits', vol 2, Ms 2523/4/c, SLV.
29 McCrae 1934: 167.

Coastal foreshore strip between high water and the Nepean Highway

Fig 39. 'Nepean Highway From The Rocks McCrae, Vic, 1950'

Image no: a00192, reproduced with the permission of the State Library of Victoria.

Fig 40. 'McCrae family boatshed showing large coastal banksia on foreshore'

George Gordon McCrae, reproduced with the permission of the State Library of Victoria.

Initially the McCraes did not have the use of this strip of land as their run did not extend from the house to the water. The 'belt of land' that ran between the beach and the road was one continuous forest of coast honeysuckle[30] from St Anthony's Nose almost to the White Cliff (Rye).[31] Andrew McCrae asked George Smith of Wul-Wul-a-Bulluk at Capel Sound to give him this coastal strip, and George Smith agreed. He requested La Trobe to alter the run description for Arthurs Seat:

> Having promised Mr McCrae the small piece of land opposite his residence at Arthurs Seat of which I now beg leave to give a description I request that it may be added to the lease about to be issued to him.

Smith described the strip as:

> the small piece of land between the Cape Schanck rd and the sea, commencing near the Rocks on the Point known as St Anthony's Nose and ending at the creek at the junction of the Point Nepean and Cape Schanck roads nearly opposite the end of Mr McCrae's paddock fence.[32]

Location of road

The question then becomes where was the lower fence and therefore the road in 1851? The information regarding the position of the road comes from three sources – the 1841 government survey done four years before the McCrae's took up their run,[33] the 1844 plan of the Arthurs Seat run, presumably by Andrew McCrae,[34] now in the ownership of the National Trust and hanging on the wall in the visitor centre attached to McCrae House, and the later survey done for Joseph Brooks Burrell's application for a pre-emptive right,[35] he having purchased from the McCraes on their return to Melbourne in 1851.

All three show what we now know as the Nepean Highway along the coastal foreshore, in 1841 and 1844 as a track, and in 1860 as a three chain road reservation, in its present position. In addition, the 1860 survey shows the lighthouse, the old wooden one erected in 1854. Both the later maps show another track which left the Nepean Highway and ended at the homestead (probably Burrell Street).

---

30 Thomas gives the name of the coastal honeysuckle as 'Worruk or Barbuntuno' (CY 2606, frame 18, ML). Honeysuckle was the name used by early colonial writers for Banksia, see Mclear 2006.
31 McCrae 1911: 20.
32 George Smith to La Trobe, 7 January 1848, 48/148, VPRS 5359/P/0000, unit 000010, PROV.
33 VPRS 8168/P 1, unit 12, file CS 17 A, PROV.
34 Fig 38.
35 M Callanan, 29 September 1860, no 60/394, A 10, SLV.

There were two options in 1841, still operating in 1845, for getting around Anthony's Nose. Wheeled vehicles went up and over the spur of Anthony's Nose at about the level on which the freeway is now built. Georgiana calls this the 'Mountain Road': the temporary huts built for Andrew McCrae, for the tutor Mr McLure, for the boys, for the workers Lanty and the Tuck family, all nestled close to the brush fence abutting this rear of the property road, higher up the mountain than the new house.[36]

This Mountain Road is the Old Cape Schanck road, veering off from the present Nepean Highway more or less at the position of the present freeway, proceeding along Bayview Road, passing the rear of the McCrae property and proceeding to Boneo, thence by Boneo Road to Cape Schanck. This agrees well with the road shown on Surveyor Smythe's map of the southern peninsula, dated 1841.[37] Foot traffic, mounted riders and driven stock went round Anthony's Nose at beach level. There are instances on record where a wheeled vehicle, Dr Hobson's gig, found the winding road round Arthurs Seat (the up and over route) so steep that he had to descend to the beach and go round by the sand, 'at a snail's gallop' as he described to his wife in a letter.[38]

Equally, there are instances when the surf pounding against Anthony's Nose left no beach and presumably, the stockman had to wait for the weather to improve or stock had to be driven up and over the spur. Georgiana records an instance of this when Mr Merrick knocked on the door and requested a bed for the night because he could not get his bullocks around Anthony's Nose.[39] Mr Merrick was in serious trouble on this occasion because not only could he not get his bullocks around the Nose because of the surf, but his dray was bogged on what Georgiana called 'the old mountain road', so that Henry Tuck and Lanty had to go and rescue him.[40]

On Smythe's very accurate Coastal Survey map of 1841, these two routes around Anthony's Nose converged somewhere near the present township of McCrae. Phil Hughes has overlaid the cadastre on Smythe's map and the divergence appears to be at the junction of what are now The Avenue, Wattle Place and Point Nepean Road at McCrae.[41] So that when George Gordon McCrae writes of 'our home lying on the road branching off to Cape Schanck, Western Port and the Heads' and the consequent constant hospitality they were called upon to extend to travellers, and when Georgiana writes of the Cape Schanck road in

---

36   McCrae 1934: 154.
37   George D Smythe, 'Survey the coast from the west side of Port Phillip to Western Port', CS 17A, VPRS 8168/P 1, unit 12, PROV; see also CS 68, VPRS 8168, PROV.
38   Edmund Hobson to Margaret Hobson, undated but early 1840s, Ms 8457, Box 865/2, B/2, SLV.
39   Weber 2001, 15 June 1845: 548.
40   Weber 2001, 17 June 1845: 548–550.
41   Phil Hughes, Mornington Peninsula Shire, pers comm 8 February 2010.

front of their house, they are referring to one track or road, now the present Point Nepean Road. The Parish Plan of Wannaeue shows that the Nepean Highway road reserve was a three chain road, gazetted 10 November 1863.[42]

Lighthouse

The present lighthouse, the iron one in existence at the time George Gordon wrote his reminiscences was built in England, dis-assembled, transported to Australia, re-built commencing in 1872 and turned on at its present site in 1883, replacing the earlier wooden one which was dismantled and carried to the top of Arthurs Seat to act as a viewing platform. There is a photo taken in the course of construction of the new iron lighthouse which shows clearly *both lighthouses* standing, the old wooden one directly behind the new one, that is closer to the sea. This is to be expected as the lighthouse formed part of a 'lights in line' system, keeping ships safe and steady on course in the south channel. Had the position of the lighthouse been changed appreciably, then all the channel markers would have required shifting. There are also photographs in the Rose series of Victorian postcards which show that the keepers' cottages, now demolished, were situated to the north and east of the iron lighthouse. The two acre reserve for the lighthouse was gazetted in 1872.[43] It is 250 feet wide measured from the sea to the road.[44]

Fig 41. 'Stereoscopic glass slide of old wooden lighthouse and present lighthouse (1883) in process of construction'

From the George Jones Collection, reproduced with the permission of Lighthouses of Australia.

---

42   820 Bje, 1837 Wannueue, 1863, Map Collection, SLV.
43   *Government Gazette*, 1872: 1784. Lands temporarily reserved from sale, Wannaeue near Dromana, two acres more or less, bearings and distances given.
44   820 Bje, 1837 Wannueue, Map Collection, SLV.

It is worth remembering that when the wooden lighthouse was built in 1854, Johnny's stout hardwood memorial cross would have been standing: it was an age which respected death – it would not have been vandalised, and it could not have deteriorated into decay in three years. And as George Gordon McCrae specifically stated, Johnnie's father was pleased with the memorial, and it lasted for years, an object of pride and veneration for his family and blacks alike.

Fig 42. 'South Channel Lighthouse showing relationship to keepers' cottages'

Image no rg001542, 1940–1960, reproduced with the permission of the State Library of Victoria.

Fig 43. 'South Channel Lighthouse', perspective showing that the lighthouse was constructed adjacent to, not behind, the keepers' cottages

Reproduced with the permission of Lighthouses of Australia.

Lighthouse keepers' cottages

The best Rose postcard of the keepers' cottages, shows them built very close to the road, on the Melbourne side of the lighthouse, that is, to the north-east, but the angle of the photo does not rule out the possibility that the cottages were built partly in front of the lighthouse. Another Rose postcard, this one with the image of the lighthouse taken from the beach makes it clear that this was not so: the cottages were not built in a direct line between the lighthouse and the road.

The Government Gazettes record the contracts entered into for the construction of the cottages. £2000 was spent in 1872 erecting the skeleton lighthouse, quarters etc near Arthurs Seat;[45] £294 was spent on the balance of the contract a few months later;[46] £160 was spent the following year on an oil store, fencing etc at the Lighthouse Station, Arthurs Seat;[47] in 1890, further additions to the Lighthouse quarters and painting etc cost £359.[48] Tenders were called in 1891 for cartage of furniture from Dromana pier to the lighthouse and for the supply of firewood cut to five foot lengths.[49] According to the Victorian Heritage database, these cottages were built at the foot of the lighthouse, and were demolished after World War II, apparently later than 1978,[50] but I have not been able to discover exactly when. A comparison of the physical features in the whole Rose post card series suggests as a working hypothesis that the front fence of the cottages was the limit of the road reservation.

Kermeterrewarrar

The 'great camping ground of the blacks' who were described as 'a hunting and fishing tribe' was occupied so long as fish and game were at their best. The people never numbered more than 200 in George Gordon McCrae's recollection, and at intervals they would strike camp and move in other directions but they always came back.[51]

The McCraes got their water from a good permanent spring of fine water welling up in the midst of a tea-tree scrub above the house and there was a waterhole below the house which they named St Anton's Well.[52] In addition, there were two small creeks that ran either side of the house, brackish and occasionally

---

45 *Government Gazette*, no 48, 19 July 1872: 1354.
46 *Government Gazette*, no 64, 20 September 1872: 1752.
47 *Government Gazette*, no 81, 14 November 1872: 2008.
48 *Government Gazette*, no 98, 24 October 1890: 4204.
49 *Argus*, 15 December 1891: 10.
50 Pers comm 21 February 2010, McCrae Yacht Club.
51 McCrae 1911: 21.
52 Weber 2001, July 1846: 586.

salt and their mouths generally silted up in summer.[53] One of them however, answered very well to keep the three McCrae boats in during the summer.[54] 'Our boatshed was on the beach below the house'.[55]

They had great assistance from the blacks in netting and line fishing, and the blacks taught them the exact bait for different fish, and how to spear them with good effect. All this information dates from January 1845 onwards, when the McCrae tutor Mr McLure, and the four McCrae boys moved permanently to Arthurs Seat, living in huts as they built the homestead: Georgiana and Andrew McCrae moved permanently to Arthurs Seat in June 1845.[56]

1845 is five years after the Protectorate moved from the Mornington Peninsula, and two years after the new Protectorate station Nerre Nerre Warren was given over to the Native Police, and Thomas relocated to Merri Creek. The Protectorate was still operating, but only children were more or less permanently at Merri Creek with the school master.

This land occupied by the McCraes was already an Aboriginal encampment known to the Assistant Protector William Thomas by the name of Kermitterrewarrer. It was to this encampment that Thomas went in order to discover the truth about the dray accident described earlier, and it was to this encampment that Bobbinary and Burrenum proceeded when they set off for the ramble earlier mentioned.

Pereuk/Poky Poky/Old Poky/Bogy Bogy/Old Bogie/ Bogie

Johnny's real name was recorded once by Thomas as Utrunbrook (Principal families, 1840, CY 2605, item 1, ML), and once by Robinson as Yar. er. en. bope (Johnny) name of Port Phillip Aborigine who went with L Smith to California, 13 December 1850 (Clark 2000, vol 6: 34). He was the son of a man whose real name was Pereuk/Bareuk, but who was mostly known in the records as Bogy Bogy or Poky Poky. Johnny's mother's name was Barebun. Johnny's father was probably but not certainly, one of George Smith's blackfellows (VPRS 4, Box 5, 38/207, PROV).

---

53 Only one of these creeks is locatable today, Coburn Creek which emerges into the bay east of the Lighthouse opposite Coburn Avenue (Hughes Map, McCrae burial, 19 September 2008). Coburn is a Scottish name which is mentioned in Georgiana's early journals or drawings.
54 There is a pen and ink drawing showing one boat with its mast stepped, moored in a creek, and another boat upended on stilts in a little boathouse on the shore (McCrae Papers, SLV): Fig 40.
55 George Gordon McCrae, 'Experiences not exploits', vol 2, Ms 2523/4/d, SLV.
56 Niall 1994.

Johnny's father, Peruek, was recorded for the first time by Assistant Protector Dredge in the encampment at Melbourne in March 1839, as 'Beera/Bogee Bogee, age 25, Waworong tribe [this is wrong – he was a Bonurong, but the protectors had been in Melbourne only two months; it is interesting that in their initial capturing of the people's names on paper, the protectors got the phonetics roughly correct, and mostly the correct number of syllables, but very often they got the initial consonant wrong. Thomas relates with regard to his first census that the people all lined up and filed past him, making a game of it, and rejoining the queue and giving a different name the second time round. It sounds as though the scribe might have been looking at his paper and not at the person giving the information as he wrote it down], with a wife Marburon known as Mary, and two children a boy Yadenbook aged three and a girl Wagul aged two' (Dredge Census, Robinson Papers, vol 54, ML). In July of that year Thomas recorded him as We–ur–ruk/Bogy Boge, and his wife as Barebun, an old woman (CY 2604, item 1, ML).

On 17 April 1840, Boggy Boggy was in possession of a firearm given to him by Mr Cheekman (Thomas Journal, CY 2605, item 1, ML). Bogy Bogy's name, as head of a party of five – himself, two wives and two pickaninnies, was on the list of those who chose to stay on the Mornington Peninsula and not go to Western Port on the revenge raid into Gippsland (CY 2605, frame 8, ML). In June 1840, when all the Bonurong were at Tubberubbabel, Bogy Bogy with two wives and two children was at Turtgurruk (CY 2604, item 3, ML).

In August of that year at Major Frazer's at Mordialloc, Bogy Bogy assaulted his wife very harshly because she was found hiding in the chimney of the hut on the property where Major Frazer's 16 year old son lived. His wife was clean and well dressed and concealing herself when sprung by Thomas who wrote that Bogy Bogy was normally the mildest and most inoffensive of men, and was distressed when his rage cooled and he realised how badly he had hurt his wife (CY 2604, item 3, frame 173, ML).

In 1841, Pureuk alias Poky Poky was one of the seven blacks who assisted Thomas and Commissioner of Crown Land Powlett in capturing the VDL blacks after they killed two Europeans at Western Port. For a reward, the seven asked for a blanket, shirt, trowzers, leather belt with buckle, neckerchief, straw hat and a gun (Thomas to Robinson, VPRS 11, unit 8/415, PROV). This success led directly to the establishment of the 1842 Native Police Corps under Commandant Henry Dana.

On 24 February 1842, Pereuk enrolled in Dana's Native Police Corps, and made his mark; he received blankets, clothing and equipment, and the Corps drilled twice daily till March when they had to abandon Nerre Nerre Warren because of the scarcity of water, and marched in easy stages to Merri Creek (Dana to La Trobe, 31 March 1842, VPRS 19, Box 28, 42/674, PROV). At the end of 1842, Pereuk was recorded as aged 35, married with one wife and two children, never punished, on duty for four months at the Mt Macedon police station. His general conduct was good, and he was said to do well about the camp, but was useless on duty (Dana Return, *NSW Legislative Council Votes & Proceedings*, 1844). He was in the second division of the NPC at Merri Creek (Dana Return, VPRS 19, Box 30, 42/1143, PROV) and had been rationed since 1 February 1842 (Dana Return, 27 July 1842, VPRS 19, Box 60, 42/1143, PROV); 31 Jul 1842 – Poky Poky is on the Medical Dispenser's list at Merri Creek being treated for the disease Pseudo Syphilis, the treatment being Liq Arsenic plus aperients internally and Blackwash externally (Henry Jones to Chief Protector, VPRS 4410, unit 2, item 49, PROV).

In 1844, Pereuk is on a return as dismissed from the Corps, and he may well be one of the two unnamed police who were dismissed in 1843 for being absent without leave (Dana Return, 21 September 1843, 4/1135.1, AO of NSW). In 1846 Poky Poky was listed in Thomas' criticism of the Corps as one of those who deserted (Thomas enc. to 46/3341 in 4/2745.1, AO of NSW).

20 Jan 1846 – Poky Poky voluntarily goes to the hospital (Thomas Journal, CY 2606, frame 330, ML); In 1846, Thomas recorded Peerup or Poky Poky on his Family Connections census as male, widower, with a son named Tareum aged 12 (this is Johnny under a different name) and a daughter Barut aged 10 (CY 3083, ML).

In 1848 Poky Poky's name was on a list of Western Port blacks gone to Gippsland, armed and bent on revenge (HEP Dana, 48/10473 in 4/2824, AO of NSW). Thomas said that Poky Poky was one of a number of Western Port men presently in Gippsland to barter for or seduce young lubras (VPRS 11, Box 11/701, PROV).

In his half-yearly return for July to December 1849, Thomas lists Johnny and Tommy, Pokey's sons as having gone to California with Mr Smith (CY 3127, ML). In his reminiscences[I] George Gordon McCrae recorded the

---

I. George Gordon McCrae, 'Experiences not exploits', vol 2, Ms 2523/4/c, SLV.

name of the ship as the *Sea Gull*, owner George Smith, master Captain Napper (Edward Hobson's father in law). The prospectus for the voyage states that the two Bonurong youths were to be paid as crew, but the amount was unspecified (Bateson). Johnny and Tommy were still away in August 1850, but had returned from California by 26 September 1850, and by 5 October when Thomas met him south of the Yarra, Johnny had discarded his European clothes and 'as filthy as ever' was proceeding to Western Port (all in Thomas Journal, CY 3127, ML). Tommy[II] though, in servitude to Mr Hobson for one year, he met with cattle from Gippsland on 28 October 1850 (Thomas Journal, CY 3127, ML).

Johnny's father Pereuk/Old Pokey/Bogie died at Western Port shortly after the death of his son, recorded by Thomas in his 1851 census, as dying in the same period (June to December 1851) as his son (Thomas Papers, set 214, item 12: 143, ML).

II. This person Tommy Hobson is possibly/probably the Tommy Hobson whose portrait was taken at Coranderrk in the 1860s though the notes accompanying the portrait identify him as Yarra. There is much more to be discovered about Tommy Hobson from the massive Gippsland records of the Commissioner of Crown Lands Tyers, related to the search for the alleged white woman.

It is this Johnny, son of Pereuk/Old Pokey/Bogie who is buried in a large deep grave just south of the lighthouse, by the Nepean Highway, probably under the public car park between the McCrae Yacht Club compound and Point Nepean Road.

11. The abduction between Arthurs Seat and Point Nepean, and Yankee Yankee's return

The account which follows considers the so far discovered information about eight females and a boy, those who were taken from Port Phillip 'about a year and a half ago' before John Helder Wedge reported the abduction in March 1836.[1] If Wedge's understanding of his Aboriginal informants was correct, that would place the abduction as occurring in the latter half of 1834. It is a remarkable fact that the abducted boy Yankee Yankee (Robert Cunningham) was the brother of Barebun (Mary) whose story was told in Chapter 6. It is equally remarkable that the VDL woman, Matilda, who originally decoyed the Bonurong women into captivity by the sealer George Meredith, came subsequently to Port Phillip as one of the Chief Protector's 'family', spent time with Trucaninni on the Mornington Peninsula, was charged with the murder of the two whalers at Western Port (for whose killing Bob and Jack were hanged) but like Trucaninni, was not convicted, and with her, was deported back to VDL. When she returned to Port Phillip with Robinson in 1839, she gave her account of her earlier complicity in the abduction of the eight females and a boy from under Point Nepean. She is a first hand participant witness, the type of source whom historians like, because though these witnesses seldom know the complexities of the whole event, what they do know can usually be relied upon.

Previous scholarly research

There are several accounts which examine aspects of the abduction, but only one of them is available in its entirety to the public, and one exists as yet in draft form only. Effectively inaccessible to readers outside universities, they are:

- Diane Barwick's 1985 work[2] which is used by the Boonwurrung Foundation in support of its claim that they are linked with the original owners via Louisa Briggs, and that they are the rightful inheritors now, of the Mornington Peninsula.

- The yet to be published 'The Problem with Louisa Briggs',[3] by Jacqueline D'Arcy, an historian who has been employed by the Bonurong Land Council Aboriginal Corporation, is critical of Barwick's 1985 work, and concludes

---

1 JH Wedge to VDL Col Sec Montague, 13 March 1836, *HRV*, vol 1: 35. It is important to note that the Police Magistrate's report records that it was 'upwards of' that is, more than 18 months ago.
2 'This most resolute lady: A biographical puzzle' (Barwick 1985).
3 Jacqueline D'Arcy, Draft Ms, The Problem with Louisa Briggs, 8 October 2009.

that Louisa Briggs is not the person whom the Boonwurrung Foundation believes her to be, and is in fact, a woman of Tasmanian descent.

- There is the 2002 study by Ian D Clark,[4] undertaken for the Department of Justice on behalf of Native Title claimants: like all Freedom of Information documents, this is available to the public for a fee, but with significant portions blacked out, including parts of the table of contents and the bibliography, as well as Clark's assessment.

- There are three Historical and Genealogical Reports dated 14 October 2005, 10 November 2005 and 8 September 2006, prepared for the Native Title Tribunal, which are not public documents, so the author's name is unknown.

- Finally there is Sue Wesson's report for the Victorian Aboriginal Heritage Council, also unavailable. The Victorian Aboriginal Heritage Council is the peak body which was established under the 2006 Aboriginal Heritage Act, responsible for deciding which groups in the Victorian Indigenous community have the right to speak for their country and thus be recognised in decision-making relative to their country.

That these reports are closed means that the following research cannot be concerned with claims – they are not available for public discourse so that claims cannot be assessed. But this chapter *can* present for the first time for the general reader as well as the broader Indigenous community, the primary evidence, and it *can* explore some internal inconsistencies in that evidence.

The following chronology is divided into three parts:

Part 1, the abduction from Port Phillip,

Part 2, the evidence for the possibly separate abduction from Western Port, and

Part 3, Yankee Yankee's return home to Victoria eight years after being abducted.

Part 1: the abduction between Arthurs Seat and Point Nepean

As will be seen, numbers are important. John Helder Wedge writing in March 1836 understood that four women were taken.[5] Robinson too, thought that there were four women abducted, but his exact words will be noted in the quotation below – he 'thought' he heard four: he was not sure. Yankee Yankee was himself a participant, whose journey took him from Port Phillip to the Bass Strait islands,

---

4 Clark 2002: 3. I am grateful to Ruth Gooch who obtained this report from the Department of Justice under FOI.

5 Wedge to Montague, *HRV*, vol 1: 35.

then to Launceston, King George's Sound, the Swan River and Adelaide, before he finally returned home after eight years: his version mentions eight females. Barwick believes that there were 11, 'In 1833 a sealing schooner made another raid near Arthurs Seat … Seven women, two young girls and two lads were taken to the Bass Strait islands'.[6] D'Arcy believes that there were nine. It is not possible to know Clark's opinion because it has been blacked out in his report. From this brief summary it is clear that there is as yet, no scholarly consensus on the facts.

The four females, whom Robinson recorded, about whom the Europeans were concerned in 1836, were the wives of distinguished Bonurong men: they were not 'ordinary' women, in so far as anyone is 'ordinary'. They were the wives of 'chiefs' Derrimut, Betbenjee, Budgery Tom, and by deduction, Big Benbow (because the child Yankee Yankee was taken 'with his lubra'; at aged six or eight years he was too young to have a lubra – presumably, he was with his mother, not with a wife, when they were taken. When he returned to the encampment on the south of the Yarra in June 1841, he slept the first night in his father's miam. Big Benbow was his father; therefore the lubra was Benbow's wife). A fifth named woman jumped overboard near Wilson's Promontory, swam to the beach and walked back to Port Phillip. The concerned Europeans did not mention the female children whom Robinson named in his journal: Robinson mentions two girls, and names them. To recapitulate, Yankee Yankee, the participant eye witness, mentions eight females plus himself. As the details of his first person narrative have been checked with shipping records, and are completely verified (see Part 3 of this chapter), I regard him as the most reliable and credible witness and I take it that there were eight females plus himself taken in the Meredith abduction.

The initial report of the c1834 abduction from under Point Nepean, and the follow–up

15 March 1836

It will be remembered that Batman and Fawkner arrived in mid-1835. Nine months later, the Port Phillip Association representative, JH Wedge wrote to John Montague, the colonial secretary of VDL, and reported the following:

> Since my late arrival at this place I have learned that a flagrant outrage has been committed upon the natives at Western Port by a party of men employed in collecting mimosa bark [this is the shooting and injury to Quondum described in Chapter 8], the details of which I feel called upon,

6   Barwick 1998: 20.

as one of the parties called upon for their protection, to communicate to you for the information of the Lieutenant Governor [Sir George Arthur in VDL], in the hope that His Excellency will recommend to the Governor in Chief [Sir Richard Bourke in Sydney] to take such steps as he may deem necessary to prevent a repetition of such acts of aggression on a harmless and unoffending race of men, who have evinced the most earnest desire since our intercourse with them (upwards of nine months) to maintain the friendly understanding that has been established ... a few weeks since four individuals had received gunshot wounds ... about a year and a half ago a similar attack was made upon the natives and four of their women were taken from them. It is to be lamented that the like outrages have been committed upon the Aborigines at Portland Bay and other whaling stations, and unless some measures be adopted to protect the natives, a spirit of hostility will be created against the whites, which in all probability will lead to a state of warfare between them and the Aborigines, which will only terminate when the black man will cease to exist.[7]

As a result of Wedge's letter, Governor Bourke sent down to Port Phillip George Stewart, the Police Magistrate of Campbelltown, to investigate: his report includes the following:

In obedience to the commands of His Excellency the Governor ... I embarked on board the revenue cutter *Prince George* ... for the purpose of proceeding to Port Phillip ... I have in the first place to report that the parties who are believed to have committed the two outrages at Westernport, one [the abduction] upwards of 18 months ago and the other in March last [the shooting of Quondom examined earlier in Chapter 3], have long since left the colony. The principal, accused of perpetrating the first, commanded a sealing vessel and was killed by the natives in the neighbourhood of Spencer's Gulf [this is George Meredith]. One of the females he carried from Westernport is reported to have been with him at the time he was killed. The perpetrator of the latter [this is the shooting of Quondom] is, I have every reason to believe, a half-caste named Tomlins, at present employed in a whaling establishment at Portland Bay. In the spring of the year, when the whaling season is over, it is the custom of the men belonging to the establishment to employ themselves in collecting mimosa bark, during which employment an attack was made upon a native family, in which two women were wounded. It is expected that next season they will again return to Westernport, when should the Government not deem it

---

7   JH Wedge to VDL Col Sec, 15 March 1836, *HRV*, vol 1: 34.

necessary to make any Police Establishment, I have every reason to hope that the delinquent and his accomplices, if any, will be apprehended by the residents at Port Phillip.[8]

Reading this today, it seems that with one perpetrator dead, and the other expected to be caught next bark harvesting season, the Police Magistrate's interest did not extend to recovering the abducted women.

8 October 1836

Six months after first notifying the authorities of the abduction, Port Phillip Association representative, Wedge, wrote again to the colonial secretary in Sydney requesting that he instruct the commandant of Flinders Island (George Augustus Robinson, soon to be Chief Protector at Port Phillip) to rescue some native women, four in number they believed, who had been abducted from the coast of New Holland by sealers, and were now believed to be on the islands in Bass Strait. Two of the women are wives of men who have been 'civilised' by Mr Fawkner and are friendly to the Port Phillip Association.[9] That is, two of the women are apparently the wives of Derrimut and Betbenjee.

11 October 1836

Robinson received a letter from the VDL Colonial Secretary 'relative to the four Port Phillip Aboriginal females'.[10]

24 November 1836

Wedge wrote again to the Colonial Secretary in VDL suggesting a plan whereby he, together with some natives from the tribe from whom the women were abducted would travel from Port Phillip in the VDL government vessel to the islands in Bass Strait and rescue the women. He has pledged it to the natives, he said.[11]

As a result of Wedge's reports and requests, the VDL government sent Robinson to Port Phillip with two instructions – to acquire information about the women abducted from that district, then to get them back from the sealers. The following are his journal entries leading up to, and including, that visit.

---

8   Police Magistrate George Stewart to Col Sec Sydney, *HRV*, vol 1: 39.

9   JH Wedge to VDL Col Sec, 8 October 1836, *HRV*, vol 2A: 52. Plomley accepts that there were four women abducted and gives the recipient number of Wedge's letter as CSO 5/19/384, AO of Tasmania (Plomley 1966: 938).

10   Plomley 1987: 398.

11   JH Wedge to VDL Col Sec, 24 November 1836, *HRV*, vol 2A: 53.

The Chief Protector's knowledge of the New Holland women in 1836

In March 1831 long before he came to Port Phillip, Robinson did a sweep through the islands of Bass Strait on behalf of the VDL government ordering the sealers to give up their native women and vacate the islands: in the course of this sweep, he recorded many names of both men and women.[12] 'New Holland women' are Aboriginal women from mainland Australia, from King George's Sound, Kangaroo Island and the south coast of South Australia, and from Port Phillip and Western Port. Whether abducted or in domestic/working relationships, their extensive travels were as part of the sealing, whaling and trading activities in these parts in the early nineteenth century.[13]

Five years later in 1836, while he was Commandant on Wybelena, the station on Flinders Island established for the remnants of the Tasmanian population who were still alive, Robinson collected more information about women still with sealers, including women from the mainland of Australia: this was three years *before* he came to Port Phillip as Chief Protector. He was already familiar with the environment and the population both European and Indigenous before he undertook this task. The following are his journal entries which mention the women abducted from Port Phillip.

12 January 1836

At Gun Carriage Island, there were six sealers, two Tasmanian females, three New Holland females and one Calcutta female. This information came from the surgeon on Flinders Island who had been sent there to make a report on the sealers and their women. Most of the sealers were away on the coast of New Holland. The surgeon was told that Munro (the sealer James Munro/Munroe) gave seven pounds for the New Holland woman he has named Emue.[14]

---

12   Plomley 1966: 325.

13   Lyndall Ryan asserts that there were about 50 sealers and 100 Aboriginal women and their part-Aboriginal children living in the islands in Bass Strait in 1820 (Ryan 1980: 69). The well known illustration of the sealers' hut at Western Port dating from Dumont d'Urville's stay in the *Astrolabe* in 1826, most recently reproduced in Gooch 2008: 31, is but one small piece of evidence of these sealers in Western Port.

14   This woman is identified as a Kaurna from Adelaide or the Adelaide Plains in Amery 1996: 39. When Robinson knew her 'she was the property of Abyssinia Jack', see Plomley 1987: 335–336. Emue known as Sarah, re-named by Robinson Charlotte when she was on Flinders Island, came to Port Phillip with Robinson and absconded with Trucaninni and lived for a while at Tootgoorook.

9 May 1836

William Proctor, sealer, told Robinson that the New Holland women were brought to the straits by George Meredith, that Munro has one,[15] Bailey[16] has one, and the other sealer the last.[17]

17 June 1836

Maria, subsequently known as Matilda, was landed by the sealers on Flinders Island and walked in to Wybelena; she had come from Gun Carriage Island. Another woman was also landed, but she was taken off by Abyssinia Jack (formerly of Kangaroo Island) who also had a New Holland woman.[18]

23 July 1836

Three sealers were on Gun Carriage Island with several New Holland women. In addition, Abyssinia Jack had other New Holland women stolen by George Meredith from their country adjacent to Kangaroo Island.[19]

9 August 1836

On Preservation Island, Dr Allen[20] spoke with Munro who had a native of New Holland with him, who had recently had a child; Smith was living with him and they had 'several' New Holland women.[21]

30 August 1836

The sealers Tucker, Beadon, Dobson, Abyssinia Jack and a half-caste youth belonging to Beadon, told Robinson that they had heard that there were several native women from Western Port and Port Phillip on Gun Carriage Island and on Clark Island; no names were recorded.[22]

---

15   Polly Munro was a New Hollander from Point Nepean; Samuel Blythe married her in 1845. In 1850 he was at the Victorian goldfields (Plomley and Henley 1990: 38). Margery Munro was brought from Point Nepean by George Meredith; she lived with James Munro. She had a son Robert Munro about 22 years old; she had a daughter Polly Bligh who herself had two half-caste children, girls about eight or ten on Walker Island (Plomley and Henley 1990: 48).

16   Thomas Bailey, convicted 1818, transported for seven years, arrived in Sydney in the *Atlas* in 1819, arrived in Hobart 1820, aged 36, born in Bath (Plomley and Henley 1990: 35).

17   Plomley 1987: 353.

18   Plomley 1987: 360. A drawing of Matilda is reproduced by Plomley on page 338. Elsewhere, in Plomley and Henley 1990: 115, Matilda's real name is given as MAY.TE.PUE.MIN.NER.

19   Plomley 1987: 366–367.

20   The medical officer, married to Robinson's daughter.

21   Plomley 1987: 373.

22   Plomley 1987: 379.

5 October 1836

George Augustus Robinson, in Hobart, met the two Port Phillip natives who informed him that the sealers had taken away their wives, and that the women were now with the sealers in the straits. Historian NJB Plomley has identified these men with John Pascoe Fawkner as the Bonurong men Derrimut and Betbenjee (Baitbanger).[23]

3 December 1836

An Aboriginal female of Westernport is staying with the respectable Dr Smith at George Town; this is *not* an abduction – Plomley annotates the event as an example of how many Aboriginal persons were travelling in colonial vessels in this early colonial period.[24]

15 December 1836

Captain Hurburgh arrived at Flinders Island in the schooner *Eliza* to take Robinson to Port Phillip to investigate the kidnapping of some Port Phillip women who had fallen into the hands of the sealers; these were the women removed by George Meredith. This matter had been brought to the attention of Lieutenant Governor Arthur by Fawkner when he was in Hobart Town in October.[25] It seems that Robinson was instructed in Hobart Town to try to obtain evidence of this kidnapping.[26]

22 December 1836

'H.M. Cruiser *Eliza* was dispatched for the purpose of emancipating the New Holland female natives of Port Phillip'.[27]

26 December 1836

At noon, the *Eliza* entered the heads of Port Phillip. Robinson was aboard, accompanied by some of his Aborigines from Flinders Island, including Matilda who had been the decoy who enticed the Port Phillip women aboard Meredith's vessel in the first place, thus enabling the abduction: the Master of the *Eliza* was Captain Hurburgh. The bush at Point Nepean was on fire.

---

23 Plomley 1987: 385, 655.
24 Plomley 1987: 397.
25 CSO 1/901/19140, Tasmanian Archives.
26 Plomley 1987: 670.
27 Plomley 1987: 404.

Robinson's journal record of Matilda's story

Matilda the VDL woman[28] pointed out the spot a few miles down the harbour at Point Nepean where she said George Meredith and his crew of sealers stole the native women. The men's names were Brown, Mr West the master of the schooner, a man named Billy. Said the schooner anchored off, the sealers went on shore. Said there were plenty of forest boomer kangaroos at the point. Said they deceived the people; gammoned them. Said the native men upset the boat and the men were all wet and fell into the water. Said there was plenty of blackfellows, some on the Port Phillip side, some outside, sea coast. Said the sealers were afraid of the Port Phillip natives. Said they employed her to entice them. George Meredith stole the, I think she said four women, took them in the schooner first to Kings Island and then to Hunter and Clarks and Gun Carriage Islands, and then sold them to the sealers there. I am informed that Munro bought one. She pointed out the small islands in the mid of the port soon after you enter and told me that the natives had killed two white men there; they found their bones and an iron pot and tomahawk. Kept the eastern channel on the Nepean side; Arthurs Seat ahead named after the hill of that name at Edinburgh, of which I conceive it bears no resemblance either in form or magnitude. Borrow the Australian Directory of Bass Strait and coasts of VDL as compiled from papers in the Hydrographical Office; it will be of great use in compiling my work. Bush on fire at Arthurs Seat. Heard the natives cooeeing and hallooing to us. Pursued our course along the shore. The land thinly covered with timber (sheoak), thinly wooded and grassy with undulating grassy hills. The woods may be termed open forest. On nearing the shore at Arthurs Seat, heard human voices cooeeing from the smoke and bushes which we took for natives. My natives saw some black swans flying and was much pleased on recognising the same birds as they had in their own country ... The natives are highly pleased with the country and want to leave Flinders and fix their abode in this country.[29]

---

28 Matilda, a VDL woman, was a well travelled woman whom Robinson used to find and identify women in Bass Strait (Plomley 1987: 695), and whom he brought subsequently to Port Phillip as part of his family (*HRV*, vol 2B: 417).
29 Robinson Journal, Monday 26 December 1836 in Plomley 1987: 405.

Plomley's incomplete quotation of the statement of Matilda

She had been for a long time living with the sealers; and was in Geo Meredith's schooner when he went to Port Phillip. The vessel anchored under Pt Nepean, where there was a tribe of natives. She, Maria, was forced to entice some of the best looking women and girls to the sealers, who seized and bound them, and took them on board the schooner. After a sealing voyage to King Island and the Hunter Islands, Meredith took the women to the Furneaux Islands and left them there.[30]

The complete statement of Matilda in Tasmanian Archives

'The Statement of [blank] alias Maria alias Matilda'

Says she has been for a long time with the Sealers. That she was in George Meredith's Schooner when he went to Port Phillip. That the Vessel anchored within the entrance of the Port under Point Nepean. That there was a tribe of Natives on the Point hunting kangaroo, that they the Sealer's Men went on Shore in their Boats and enticed the Natives, and told her to do the same. After fixing upon the best looking women and Girls did at a preconceived sign seize upon and tie them with cords, and then conveyed them on board the Schooner and proceeded on a Sealing Voyage to King's Island and the Hunter Islands and thence to the Furneaux Islands were [sic] they were left by Meredith. This woman having accompanied me to Port Phillip pointed out the spot and described these proceedings.[31]

27 December 1836

'Matilda said the sealers did not shoot the blacks, nor did the blacks spear the whites; both parties were afraid to commence hostilities; but the sealers tied the women's hands with rope and put them in the boat'.[32]

28 December 1836

Robinson held a conference 'with Buckley and the Port Phillip aborigines during the day'.[33]

---

30 Plomley 1987: 677.
31 Robinson to Col Sec VDL, 12 January 1837, AOT/CSO5/19/384: 171–196, State Library of Tasmania and Tasmanian Archive and Heritage Office.
32 Robinson Journal, Monday 26 December 1836 in Plomley 1987: 406.
33 Robinson Journal, Tuesday 28 December 1837 in Plomley 1987: 407.

30 December 1836

Robinson 'conferred with the natives today'.[34]

31 December 1836

In Melbourne, after several conferences between Robinson and the Port Phillip natives, and after the Commandant William Lonsdale expressed doubt that he could succeed in getting any natives to accompany Robinson, two Bonurong men, 'Dal.la.gal.reeth'[35] and Derremart, agreed to go with Robinson to the islands.[36] Note that it is not stated specifically that both these men had lost their wives to the sealers, but it is a reasonable presumption.

1 January 1837

'This morning left Port Phillip for the *Eliza* at 11 am. The Port Phillip natives refused to go with me'.[37]

3 January 1837

> Got the vessel off early this morning. Stood across to Arthur's Seat to get into the western channel ... The circumstances of the Port Phillip aborigines not accompanying us is their own fault. The schooner having come here for the purpose of doing an act of justice is a credit to the Van Diemen's Land government, and if the Port Phillip natives objected on the ground of their not liking to accompany strangers it would have been the duty of the government to have deputed Buckley or any other person in their service to have accompanied them; and if it was as the commandant [Captain William Lonsdale] and Buckley said, namely that they did not care about them, then no party was to blame. But this I feel assured is not the case. They like all savages have strong kindred affection. Theirs is not an outward emotion, they feel inwardly and strong natural affection. The fact is they are under the influence of the depraved whites, and those characters have told them they are not going to Launceston or Hobart but to Flinders Island and where they would be kept and would never be permitted to return to their own country. But the circumstance of Buckley having said they having been taken from them a long time and they have forgotten them is false, but it exonerates the VDL government from neglect or inattention to the cause of humanity.[38]

---

34 Robinson Journal, Tuesday 30 December 1837 in Plomley 1987: 410. It is important to note that contrary to Clark's citation, Derrimut was *not* recorded as an informant on this date (Clark 2002: 117).

35 Barwick identifies this man as Derrimut's sister's son in 'Mapping the past' (Barwick 1984: 119).

36 Plomley 1987: 410.

37 Robinson Journal, Tuesday 3 January 1837 in Plomley 1987: 412.

38 Robinson Journal, Tuesday 3 January 1837 in Plomley 1987: 412.

7 January 1837

Shortly after Robinson departed Port Phillip for Flinders Island, Police Magistrate Lonsdale wrote to inform Governor Sir Richard Bourke in Sydney that the VDL government schooner called into Port Phillip 'a week ago' for the purpose of procuring some natives to accompany Mr George Augustus Robinson to the islands in Bass Strait to bring the women back, but 'they refused saying it was so long since they went away that they did not care about their return'. 'The schooner therefore returned without the intended object being effected'.[39]

9 January 1837

Robinson, in the government schooner sailing back to Flinders Island recorded that he:

> Went on shore at Preservation Island with Captain Hurburgh ... found on shore James Monro who had a New Holland woman a native of Port Phillip. She was ill in bed. Had an infant child by some of the sealers; had also a daughter about 14 years of age that she had in her own country. This was an interesting girl and it grieved me to leave her in such hands for I felt persuaded she would be maltreated. Another daughter belonging to this woman was living with Strognal on Gun Carriage by whom she had two children; she was about 16 years of age ... There is positive proof that Munro bought the woman with whom he was co-habiting and it is currently reported that he gave 7 for her. He denies having given a consideration for her by her being old or as he said he supposed she would not have fallen to his share; but this is only evasive, there is positive proof that not only was a consideration given for this woman, but for every other woman brought from Port Phillip by George Meredith the original importer. The intention of visiting Preservation and the other islands was to endeavour to rescue the women native of Port Phillip from the sealers and to restore them to their own country, but against this measure they the sealers have taken every precaution to frustrate ... Acquainted Monro with the purpose of my visit and that it was the intention of the government to have the Port Phillip native women removed to their own country. He said the woman was ill in mind and that he would bring her to the settlement so soon as she recovered if it met by [sic] approbation. He was very civil but this was all duplicity. Kelly a sealer whom I had employed when at the Hunter Islands was also living with Monro ... Before quitting Preservation Island Richard Maynard a sealer came to Preservation Island from Clarks Island. He had with him a New Holland native of

---

39   Lonsdale to Col Sec Sydney, 7 January 1837, *HRV*, vol 2A: 54.

Port Phillip. She was far advanced in pregnancy. She was a fine looking woman. She was completely under the influence of the sealer Maynard and when asked whether she would like to go to her own country she replied **she would see me b___**. Captain Hurburgh was with me at the time. Poor creature, her case and that of the others is truly pitiable. The man was impertinent and I warned him to quit the islands. To some remarks from Captain H he replied that he knew she was stolen from her own country by G Meredith but with that he nothing to do.[40]

This is an important observation. On the one day, in 1837, Robinson can account for the four following Port Phillip females:

- Monro's sick and old Port Phillip woman together with her half-caste infant born in the straits
- Her 14 year old daughter born in Port Phillip, the 'interesting girl'
- Her 16 year old daughter born in Port Phillip, now living with Strugnell, a girl who has two half-caste children by Strugnell, born in the straits (without making unwarranted cultural assumptions about Aboriginal methods of birth control, or the effects of lactation on fertility, a crude guess would be that this girl had been in the straits for two years at least, more likely four)
- The pregnant Port Phillip woman who arrived on the island with Maynard while Robinson was there and to whom he spoke: possibly, but not certainly, this woman was pregnant to Maynard: all writers on the subject note that the sealers swapped or bartered the women, so that a chance observation may correctly or incorrectly attribute the parentage of a child to a certain European, but in reality, long-term relationship observations carry more weight as regards parentage.

12 January 1837

Robinson reported back by letter to the VDL Colonial Secretary on his trip to Port Phillip and his failure to recover the stolen Port Phillip women and he attached to his 25 page report the statement reproduced above, by the Tasmanian Aboriginal woman Maria, alias Matilda.[41] Surprisingly, there is more detail in the report than is contained in the journal. The following points are of interest:

- The meeting at Melbourne with the Port Phillip natives took place on 28 December with Buckley as interpreter.
- Most of the natives were away from the settlement hunting, and only one of the men who had been robbed of their wives was present; the total number

40 Robinson Journal, Monday 9 January 1837 in Plomley 1987: 415. Plomley offers a small biography of George Meredith, Plomley 1987: 964, and James Munroe, Plomley 1987: 965.
41 Robinson Journal, Tuesday 3 January 1837, Annotations, in Plomley 1987: 677.

of natives present was 20; both men and women were present and both sexes spoke.

- 'the whole of the natives bore testimony to the violent outrage that had been committed upon them. One aged woman had had two daughters forced from her and she by signs and gestures evinced the strongest possible feelings at their loss, pointed in the direction whence they were taken from at Point Nepean, the Head of the eastern entrance to Port Phillip, described the kind of vessel they were taken in as having two masts'.

- Because there were only 20 natives in the settlement it was thought advisable to send for the rest of the tribe, but having waited five days for them, Robinson decided to depart, on the stated ground that the Master of the *Eliza*, Hursbugh, had orders to return to Hobart without delay. On 9 January he went ashore at Preservation Island and found James Munro and another man named Kelly whom he had met previously at the Hunter Islands:

  There was also two Aboriginal female Natives of Port Phillip, a mother and daughter, the latter of whom a fine young Girl between 13 and 14 years of age. This woman was cohabiting with James Munro, and by whom she had a child which was then at the breast. She was afflicted and confined to her bed. There was also one VDL woman and several half caste Girls on the Islands, one of whom apparently about 14 years of age, the daughter of Scott, a sealer residing on King's Island. This girl was then living with Kelly.

- The mother of the baby was 'more aged than the rest' and in 'precarious' health, and Munro stated that it was because she was aged that he obtained her.

- Munro said that another of the Port Phillip women was on Clarke's Island cohabiting with a sealer named Maynard, on which island several other half-caste girls and VDL native women were staying. Maynard and the Port Phillip woman referred to came to Preservation Island – 'this woman appeared to be enceinte and I subsequently learned that she was far advanced in pregnancy … this individual as well as the other natives of Port Phillip were the finest I had yet seen. It is the practice of the sealers to select the finest women and Girls of this unfortunate race … Munro stated that one of the Women brought from Port Phillip had absconded from the Islanders* at a small inlet called Sealer's Cove on the South Coast of New Holland at Wilson's Promontory.' 'As I had no intimation from the Natives at Port Phillip that that this woman had returned I am fearfully apprehensive she was destroyed by these nefarious persons'.[42]

---

42 Robinson did not know it but Tootkuningrook did get back.

- Robinson's asterisk is a marginal note reading thus: 'A more appropriate name than sealers since it is a well known fact that these men have not lived by sealing alone for these many years past'.[43]

- Robinson went on to report on the sealers, singling out Stragnell as a man of 'most infamous description', but saw no more Port Phillip native women himself.

- Robinson left the vessel:

  sensing that my presence was wanted at the settlement [Wybelena] I did not visit the other islands. This duty therefore devolved upon the Master of the Schooner who reported as follows. That on proceeding to Woody Island he there found two men James [? Everett] and another alias Abyesinnia Jack with three New Holland women and five children, some of these women are from Spencer's Gulf, and with the exception of one woman said they had no wish to leave the sealers. Found 17 individuals residing on Gun Carriage, that is seven men, i.e. Tucker-Beedon-Riddell-Proctor-Dobson-Stragnell, and a man called Stonehurst, a runaway convict, together with five women – one a native of Port Phillip, an Indian, one half-caste, two VDL females and five children. The Port Phillip woman had two children and said she had no wish to go to her own country.

- Robinson's report concluded with a request for two strong whaleboats and a respectable experienced seaman, sworn in as a constable, to act as Superintendent to patrol the islands.[44]

18 February 1837

A letter from the Colonial Secretary in Sydney to Captain Lonsdale in Melbourne approved of the steps taken in the attempt to recover the abducted women: 'I am directed by His Excellency the Governor to inform you that in acting as you did, by endeavouring to persuade some of the natives to accompany Mr Robinson, you took a very proper view of the case'.[45]

27 March 1837

Strognall and a New Holland woman with two children were seen, allegedly on their way to the Kent Islands but Robinson believes that he was going to the

---

43   A recently published history by Ruth Gooch (2008), gives a more balanced view of sealers in that she considers as well, the evidence contrary to the received view; her conclusion is that in most cases, the women chose to stay with the sealers.

44   AOT/CSO5/19/384: 171–196.

45   Col Sec Sydney to Lonsdale, 18 February 1837, *HRV* vol 2A: 55.

Sisters to hunt. Mr Allen, sent on a mission to tell the sealers to quit this group of islands (because the Tasmanians from Wybelena hunted there) warned him not to go there.[46]

20 September 1837

> A sealer named Stragnel arrived at the settlement [Wybelena] and begged assistance to repair his boat … He had with him a female native of Port Phillip and two children that she had by this man. The woman did not appear more than 17 years of age and was daughter to the woman who was cohabiting with James Munro. She was one of those taken from her country by Meredith. Stragnel is a most notorious fellow.[47]

10 August 1838

There was 'sensation' on Flinders Island with the arrival of the *Hobart Town Gazette*, stating that it was the intention of the home government (Britain) to appoint Robinson as Protector of the Aborigines of Port Phillip, and that the Tasmanian Aborigines at present incarcerated on Flinders Island could accompany him if it pleased them to do so.[48]

Within eight days Robinson had sailed to Hobart and received the news officially from Sir George Arthur. Interestingly, the Governor indicated that previously he had been opposed to such a move of the Tasmanian Aborigines because it was his belief that the natives of Port Phillip would 'destroy them'.[49] Even more interestingly, considering the links Robinson made between ownership of private property, civilisation and Christianity, it was planned that these Tasmanian Aborigines would bring with them the 1300 sheep they owned, thus 'leading to the excitement in the former [the natives of Port Phillip], of the spirit of acquisition, and consequent civilisation'.[50]

Robinson then took ship for Sydney for an interview with the Governor of New South Wales. He visited the gaol on 3 September 1838, only to find that the eight Bonurong and Warworong men accused of sheep stealing and sent to Sydney for trial, had been liberated from gaol the previous week and sent to the Benevolent Asylum. From there, six had escaped,[51] and two 'were taken out and sent on board of the *Prince George* revenue cutter by the Governor's orders to make sailors of them, an absurd and unjust measure'.[52]

---

46   Plomley 1987: 435.
47   Robinson Journal, Wednesday 20 September 1837 in Plomley 1987: 478.
48   Robinson Journal, Plomley 1987: 576.
49   Robinson Journal, Plomley 1987: 578.
50   Robinson Journal, Plomley 1987: 581.
51   Moonee Moonee Senior, Bunia Logan, Mainger, Poen/Murray, Murrummurrumbeel/Mr Hill and Moragine/Jack Sloe (Fels 1986: 117). Georgiana McCrae's Moonie is the son of Moonee Moonee. He walked back to Port Phillip and arrived safely.
52   Robinson Journal, Plomley 1987: 582.

On his return to VDL to settle his affairs and prepare for departure to Port Phillip, Robinson was called to a meeting of the Executive Council of VDL, which was considering the issue of the VDL Aborigines' removal to Port Phillip: this was November 1838. The council had before it correspondence from the Colonial Secretary of New South Wales, vehemently opposing the move: Robinson responded with a plea for his 'special family' ie those who had been with him a long time. In this plea, he made the surprising statement that his special family consisted in total of 35 persons (out of a total population on Flinders Island of 78) and that there would be no trouble at Port Phillip: he added that these people were very friendly with the Port Phillip natives, so that no collisions were likely between them.[53]

This last observation cries out for an answer – by what means of communication were the VDL Aborigines at Wybelena 'very friendly' with the Port Phillip natives at home in Port Phillip in 1838?

28 February 1839

After a 48 hour voyage from Flinders Island, Robinson and his family of Aborigines arrived in Port Phillip, all sick with influenza; the natives went on shore the next day, and the four assistant protectors came on board the VDL cutter.[54]

Abduction location

'Under Point Nepean' was a specific descriptor of the nineteenth century. Sir Richard Bourke used it to describe the anchored position of HMS *Rattlesnake* when he visited Port Phillip with Captain Hobson in 1837. He described the vessel as being 'under Point Nepean' when it was moored four miles east of Point Nepean and three miles from Colonel Collins' settlement.[55] This position is Portsea Pier, Portsea Pub, and Point Franklin. The term 'under Point Nepean' was still in use in 1878, as for example when it was reported in a newspaper that it was not often that a boat can land under Point Nepean more especially at this time of the year (April).[56] This newspaper article was describing the difficulty of hauling guns weighing four tons up the 60 foot cliff at Fort Nepean. This descriptor at least tells us that the place of abduction was not near Arthurs Seat. Taking together the following pieces of evidence:

---

53   Robinson Journal, in Plomley 1987: 771.
54   Clark 1998, vol 1: 11, 13. A list of the natives is at Robinson to La Trobe, 18 December 1839, *HRV*, vol 2B: 417.
55   Boys 1935: 62–63.
56   *Argus*, 24 April 1878: 5.

- that Meredith's crew anchored 'under Point Nepean', a few miles down the harbour
- that several of the early navigators seem to have anchored at what is now Portsea beach, that is, that it was in general use as an anchorage
- that the tribe was hunting boomer kangaroos 'at the point'
- that Matilda drew Robinson's attention to 'the point' after they were inside the heads
- that Thomas saw the tracks of boomer kangaroo at Point King, and ran them down, and saw flocks of 50 or so
- that Thomas explored as far south as four to five miles from Point Nepean
- that Point Nepean itself was bush

I suggest that the place of abduction was in the vicinity of either Pt Franklin or Pt King.

Some comments on Robinson's record of the names of the abducted women

3 January 1837

In a list of this day's date, of vocabulary, plus names of natives, which he made on the ship back to Flinders Island, Robinson records the following names: they are published in Plomley's Journal Annotations.[57]

- DOOG.BY.ER.UM.BORE.OKE, the mother of the two girls stolen from Port Phillip
- NAY.NAR.GOR.ROTE, one of the girls names taken by the sealers
- BO.RO.DANG.ER.GOR.ROKE, another girl taken by the sealers
- NAN.DER.GOR.OKE, Derremart's wife who was taken by the sealers.

Barwick has identified NAN DER GOR OKE as Elizabeth Maynard and DOOG BY ER UM BORE OKE as Margery Munro, but without showing how the identification was made.[58] Clark also notes that the evidence is absent from Barwick's account of how she made the positive identification,[59] and D'Arcy discounts the putative identification. Plomley and Henley believed that the New Holland woman living with Munro in January 1837 was 'probably the Margery Munro who, with her daughter, had been abducted by George Meredith'.[60]

---

57 Robinson Journal, Tuesday 3 January 1837 in Plomley 1987: 675. Note that this account does not mention Yankee Yankee, the male child of Benbow's wife, who was abducted with his mother.
58 Barwick 1985: 227.
59 Clark 2002: 129.
60 Plomley and Henley 1990: 92.

It cannot however, be the case that DOOG.BY.ER.UM.BORE.OKE, the mother of the two girls stolen from Port Phillip, is Margery Munro, because Robinson clearly states in his report to the Colonial Secretary VDL that DOOG.BY.ER. UM.BORE.OKE is still at Port Phillip, still weeping for her two stolen girls, describing the ship, pointing to the heads, describing how her daughters were torn away from her: she was not abducted at all.

The misidentification of DOOG BY ER UM BORE OKE as Margery Munro is important because both the Boonwurrung Foundation and the Bonurong Land Council Aboriginal Corporation descent claims go back through Louisa Briggs to Polly Bligh and Polly Bligh's mother Margery Munro.

Taken together, Robinson's two records make plain that the abducted group included the two daughters of DOOG.BY.ER.UM.BORE.OKE (she herself being still in Melbourne), plus the aged woman living with James Monro, ill, and with a baby at the breast, as well as this aged woman's 14-year-old daughter, the interesting girl who was herself born in Port Phillip, plus her other daughter, 16 years old, also born in Port Phillip, and living now with Strugnall. These five are clearly separate individuals from two separate families at Port Phillip. There are two sets of sisters among the abductees.

The fine looking girl, advanced in pregnancy who was living with Richard Maynard, and the Port Phillip woman with two children who was living with Abysinnia Jack and did not wish to return to her own country, *could* have been the two daughters of DOOG.BY.ER.UM.BORE.OKE. But they are *not* the same people as the 14 year old and the 16 year old girls who have their own mother living in the Straits, not still back at Port Phillip. This identification has serious implications for the genealogical links between Louisa Briggs and Polly Bligh and the putative ancestor, wrongly identified as DOOG.BY.ER.UM.BORE.OKE.

The implication in the Boonwurrung statement to Parliament that a female child, her mother and her grandmother were at Point Nepean for women's secret business is not supported by the evidence, which clearly states that the tribe was there hunting kangaroo.

In another record of the names of the sealing men on different islands, Robinson writes that James Munro on Preservation Island has one New Holland woman, native of Port Phillip, and her daughter aged 14 also a native of Port Phillip, and a half-caste infant child belonging to the mother. Richard Maynard on Clarks Island had one Port Phillip woman.[61] The sealer, Munro, told Robinson that he was told that one woman from Port Phillip ran away from the sealers at Bay

---

61   Robinson Journal, Tuesday 3 January 1837 in Plomley 1987: 416.

and Back Cove at Wilson's Promontory.[62] YANKI YANKI, the boy, confirmed this when he returned to Port Phillip in 1841 (see later in this chapter). This woman's name was TOUTKUNINGROOK.[63]

There is another woman, TOOLOM, with a Western Port name, described only as a New Holland woman living with Isaac.[64] Clark has noted that there is no other information available about Toolom in the research of those who have constructed the genealogies of the Bass Strait islanders.[65] KAR.DING.GOR.OKE, living with Morgan in 1837,[66] was a young woman belonging to the Western Port chief, Budgery Tom.[67] This information was supplied ten years later to Robinson in Melbourne in 1847, as was the name of Meen.dut.Goroke.[68] NINJIT, who was living with Jack Williams, NEE.NUT.NOMY and WON.GOR.RUG are also names of New Holland women which Robinson recorded, and Clark lists them as such, but whether he regards them as originally from the Port Phillip or Western Port coasts is blacked out in his report. Their names come from Robinson's 1837 list constructed as he inspected the islands on his way back to VDL after his unsuccessful attempt to persuade the husbands of the women to help him rescue them. Then there is NAN.NERT.GOROKE whose name was supplied to Robinson by Benbow in 1847.[69]

It is crucial to both Indigenous groups' foundation narratives that Margery Munro be identified. As she is not DOOG.BY.ER.UM.BORE.OKE, as previously thought, then who is she? Circumstantial evidence suggests that we should at least ask the question, could she be the wife of Big Benbow/Baddourup whose biographical details were given in Chapter 3? The woman with Munro in 1837 was old, sick, with a newborn baby and her 14 and 16 year old daughters with her in the straits: she is the only abductee described as old, though of course 'old' is a relative term – both Indigenous and European persons described Aboriginal people as 'old' when they were around 40 years. Meredith's crew, as was noted above, made a positive selection for the best looking women and girls. In 1837, Barebun/Mary here in Port Phillip was 12 years old and without a mother – possibly the reason she was living with the Smiths, and possibly the reason why in all the tooing and froing related to her marriage with Billibellary, and her subsequent assault at Buckkermitterwarrer, her mother is never mentioned: her mother might have been in Bass Strait. Her brother Yankee Yankee, abducted

---

62 Robinson Journal, Tuesday 3 January 1837 in Plomley 1987: 415.
63 Thomas Miscellaneous Papers, CY 3130, frame 35, ML.
64 Robinson Journal, Tuesday 3 January 1837 in Plomley 1987: 416.
65 Clark 2002: 120.
66 Robinson Journal, Tuesday 3 January 1837 in Plomley 1987: 416.
67 Clark 2002: 121.
68 Robinson Journal, 1847 in Clark 2002: 121.
69 Clark 2002: 118–120. It needs to be pointed out that although Clark cites Derrimut in Robinson's Journal of 30 December 1836 as his source for these names, Derrimut is not mentioned in the journal for this date and the citation is incorrect.

with his mother, was ten years old in 1837, working in Western Australia. This family structure fits the pattern of big men in early contact society, men such as Billibellary, Old Doctor and Old Mr Mann. Then there is the further detail from Dredge's account quoted above that Yankee Yankee escaped from Preservation Island: it makes sense if Munro's woman was his mother, and he had stuck with his mother until then. I would go even further and suggest that she encouraged him off the island to VDL, and thence hopefully to Port Phillip, and I suspect that there was contact between the abductees and the Bonurong, that Pinterginner's visit to VDL and his removing Barebun/Mary from the Smiths in June 1840 were related facts, exactly as Thomas wrote them in his journal.

And I suggest that we must look for further evidence regarding NAN-NAT-GOOR-RUK (see King Benbow's biographical details below, 7 January 1848) who had recently returned from VDL.

In the Barwick Papers is a photostat of a letter written in 1974 by an Aboriginal woman to a firm of solicitors requesting help about her grandfather's will. The photostat is accompanied by a covering letter from the solicitors requesting Barwick's help. There are two partial drafts of letters from Barwick back to the solicitors apologising for the delay and listing the immense amount of sources she had consulted in trying to work out the genealogy. There is even a partial draft of the article she wrote, its provisional title being 'Sealers, settlements, scandals: a biographical puzzle'. This is the article subsequently published as 'This most remarkable lady: a biographical puzzle'. Barwick's notes on the 1924 Hall and Taylor interviews with Mrs Louisa Briggs shed light on the Boon-wurrung foundation story. The original record of interview does *not* state that Louisa Briggs returned from VDL when Melbourne had but three houses, ie sometime between mid 1835 and mid 1836. It says the following:

> she returned from Tasmania to Melbourne when that city had more than three houses, but was smaller than Cumeroogunga and the Exhibition Ground was all forest. She was at that time a married woman.[70]

George Meredith (1806–c1835)

George Meredith's father, also named George Meredith, was a wealthy, well connected ex Marine officer who chartered a ship to emigrate to VDL, arriving in 1821 (Dr Francis Desailley, whose teenage grandsons looked after Hobson and Smith's sheep at the back of Rosebud, came with him). The family received the usual grants from the government and took up land in the Oyster Bay area on the mid-east coast of VDL. In addition to agriculture and pastoralism, the family subsequently established a whale fishery which prospered. The George

---

70   Barwick Papers, Ms 13521, Series BAR S 4007, Box 001, Folder BAR I 01634, SLV.

Meredith of our story was the errant son. Though his death was reported in VDL newspapers, his name was not mentioned in society out of respect for the feelings of the now distinguished family: his name is not even *now*, in 2010, mentioned in the *Australian Dictionary of Biography* online entry which lists all the other children of George Meredith senior.

According to Barwick, George Meredith junior stole the schooner *Defiance* after a quarrel with his father, and wrecked it near Twofold Bay early in September 1833. This has been checked from newspapers. The schooner *Defiance*, Captain Meredith, departed Sydney on 27 September 1833 on a sealing trip to the western coast of New Holland.[71] Nearly a month later, the schooner *Blackbird* left Sydney on a speculative trip in search of the wreck of the schooner *Defiance*.[72] According to Barwick, George Meredith then made his way by whaleboat to Kangaroo Island by February 1834 and was killed in the vicinity of Port Lincoln some time after September 1834,[73] but there is no indication how she knew that. Cawthorne, a recognised expert on Kangaroo Island society prior to official settlement (he lived locally, his father being the lighthouse keeper and he interviewed sealers), wrote a novel which he stated was a 'narrative of fact to a very large extent'. He mentions Europeans who are known in the historical records, such as Abyssinia Jack and Bumble footed Sal, and Big Bet, two Tasmanian women. In fact Cumpston states that Bumble footed Sal was Meredith's woman in 1833.[74] He gives the place of Meredith's death as Yankalilla, which is correct, but the year as 1827, which is clearly wrong.[75] Several secondary accounts, not rigorously researched but feeding off each other, and traceable to Inspector Alexander Tolmer's account in 1844,[76] locate George Meredith as a permanent resident on Kangaroo Island from 1827 till his death in 1832 or 1834. Tolmer's sources are undisclosed, and his account is written in terms of 'I heard' and 'it was said', but there were apparently sealers living on Kangaroo Island in 1844.

It is worth recalling that the Meredith family only migrated in 1821, and branched out into whaling after their pastoral activities were established, and that George Meredith senior built his first boat in 1828, the *Black Swan*.[77] It is George Meredith's residence on Kangaroo Island from 1827 till his death which appears not to be true. It places him as an outcast from society at the age of

---

71   *Sydney Herald*, Monday 30 September 1833: 2.
72   *Sydney Gazette and NSW Advertiser*, Saturday 26 October 1833: 2.
73   Barwick 1985: 231.
74   Cumpston 1970: 132, 191.
75   Cawthorne 1926[1823]: 87, viii. He has interesting detail about the women singing, coroborreeing, not sleeping with the sealers but in their own wurley village, children, grass tree hearts as food, all of which agree with known facts.
76   Tolmer 1882, vol 2: 6ff.
77   Mori Flapan, 'List of Tasmanian Boat Builders and Ship Builders from the Register of Australian and NZ Vessels', <http://home.iprimus.com.au/mflapan/TasmanianBuilders.htm>

21, just at the very time that the family was starting up the whale fishery. He is mentioned in the Hobart newspapers in 1826 as having recently taken two whales in the Straits.[78]

According to Plomley, George Meredith junior went to sea in small vessels trading and raiding in the straits. He built a house on Kangaroo Island, at Western River and lived there with a Tasmanian Aboriginal woman named Sal. He was involved in the abduction of New Holland women, both from Point Nepean and from the coast of South Australia adjacent to Kangaroo Island. These acts resulted in his death at the hands of the natives in South Australia in 1835 or 1836.[79] This is basically the received version inherited from Tolmer and I think it is true except for the date of death, if the first hand narratives of Matilda and the two English lads, plus the shipping intelligence all detailed below, are accepted as factual. The Bass Strait sealer, William Proctor, told Robinson as early as May 1836 that George Meredith had been killed by the natives off the coast of New Holland. Plomley and Henley state that he was killed at the hands of natives in South Australia in 1835–36.[80] Police Magistrate Stewart understood that Meredith was dead when he was at Port Phillip in June 1836.

The South Australian Police Historical Society has published an account by a local historian who has worked in South Australian Police Archives, Jean Schmaal:

> Another tragedy of those pre-settlement days concerns one George Meredith, the adventurous son of a prominent Hobart Town businessman who came to Kangaroo Island seeking his fortune among the sealers. He had with him, on landing on the island, a Tasmanian native woman named Sal. Later he 'acquired' two young native men from the Encounter Bay area, and these he trained to help him in his hunting expeditions. Meredith, much against the advice of his fellow sealers, decided to come across to the then unsettled mainland. Some time later, his companions came to find the reason for his non-return, and discovering Sal, were told that Meredith, on anchoring in Yankalilla Bay [Fleurieu Peninsula], had been despatched by a blow from a tomahawk by one of his native offsiders, who had then returned to his tribe. Meredith's father asked for enquiries to be made into the murder, but there being no European settlement in the country [pre-1836] nothing could be done. Years later,

---

78   *Hobart Town Gazette*, Saturday 10 June 1826: 2.
79   Plomley and Henley 1990: 90.
80   Plomley and Henley 1990: 90.

Police Commissioner Tolmer got onto the case and was able to locate Sal. However by that time the alleged murderer was himself dead.[81] [There are no dates in this article.]

George Meredith and the vessel he wrecked, the 24 ton schooner *Defiance*

There were two schooners named *Defiance* running up and down the east coast of Australia in the 1830s, but it is easy to distinguish between them. The *Defiance* which was *not* George Meredith's vessel was a schooner of 75 tons, Captain Kenneth McKenzie, built at Twofold Bay in 1832, registered Sydney; it must have been a comfortable vessel because it carried the carriage trade in its passenger lists for the few voyages which it made before being wrecked (for example Viscount Lascelles),[82] and it is always described with its tonnage 75 tons, and its Master and its passengers and its cargo. This 75 ton *Defiance* was wrecked on the night of 27 July 1833 on Cape Barren Island opposite Gull Island in the Furneaux group. She had been chartered by Captain Muggeridge of the *Courier* as a salvage vessel for his own wrecked vessel. Captain Muggeridge's *Courier* struck Gull Island on the night of 4 July 1833, and the *Defiance* had indeed salvaged most of the cargo of the *Courier* when *Defiance*'s own anchor parted and she herself was wrecked on Gull Island. The news of her wreck in 'Bass's Straits' reached Sydney on Tuesday 27 August 1833 via the *Hind*, Captain Scott, which left Launceston on 18 August.[83]

Every voyage up and down the coast can be tracked as this other vessel named *Defiance* plied between Hobart Town and Sydney: she is very visible in the records from being advertised as a new, fast sailing boat when her maiden voyage was advertised,[84] to being obliged to turn back due to stress of weather,[85] and having to be hauled up into the mud of the east cove at Sydney because she damaged her bottom on the run up from Hobart,[86] and finally being wrecked just 12 months after she was launched. She is clearly distinguishable from George Meredith's *Defiance*.

---

81   Jean Schmaal, The Place of the Woman's Tragedy being the story of Police Settlement at Normanville/Yankalilla, typescript, 1972, courtesy of Alan Peters, Historian, SA Police Historical Society.
82   *Sydney Gazette and NSW Advertiser*, 9 June 1833: 2; *Sydney Gazette and NSW Advertiser*, 9 July 1833: 3 quoting VDL news from the *Hobart Town Courier* of 21 June 1833, that the schooner *Defiance*, 71 tons, Captain McKenzie had arrived in Hobart from Sydney on 19 June 1833, with passengers including Rev Mr Manton; another passenger list included Viscount Lascelles.
83   *Sydney Gazette and NSW Advertiser*, 27 August 1833: 2.
84   *Sydney Gazette and NSW Advertiser*, Saturday 21 July 1832: 1.
85   *Sydney Gazette and NSW Advertiser*, Tuesday 14 August 1832: 2.
86   *Sydney Herald*, Monday 7 January 1833: 3.

George Meredith's *Defiance*, whose captain is sometimes listed as Meredith, sometimes as West, was only a small vessel of 24 tons.[87] If she was the vessel who abducted the women from under Point Nepean, and I, relying on the evidence of Matilda that both Meredith and West as Master, were aboard, have no doubt that she was the abducting vessel, then the date of the abduction becomes problematic: Meredith's *Defiance* was also wrecked in 1833, and Meredith's subsequent movements are accounted for, so the abduction could only have occurred prior to the wreck. Usually, in presenting evidence of a vessel's voyages, one would start at the beginning and work forward. But in this case, I have deemed it sensible to start with the fact of the wreck and work backwards, looking for any possible opportunity in time which the *Defiance* might have had for the abduction.

Her departure on the voyage during which she was wrecked is listed on 30 September 1833, for the western coast of New Holland (ie Western Australia), on a sealing trip, Captain Meredith.[88] The next mention of her is a month later when she is reported as wrecked:

> The schooner *Defiance*, Captain Meredith, which had left Sydney about a month ago on a sealing voyage was unfortunately wrecked on the coast, about 15 miles below Twofold Bay, all hands saved. The schooner *Blackbird* has gone in search of the wreck. The *Defiance* had about 600 worth of property in her when the accident occurred, and was not insured.[89]

The *Blackbird* arrived back in Sydney from Howe's Island on Saturday 2 November 1833 with part of the wreck of the schooner *Defiance*.[90]

From this time on, it does not seem that George Meredith had either a vessel or the opportunity to abduct anyone from Port Phillip before he died, because his movements are on record. His extraordinary tale is recounted in a West Australian newspaper two years later. Under the heading 'Two English lads' the newspaper published the following first person narrative account of two young crewmen who were wrecked with George Meredith:

> The following interesting narrative has reached us by the recent arrival from King George's Sound. The circumstances connected with the singular adventure of these two lads are not so fully detailed as we could have desired; the source, however, from whence our information is obtained, leaves no doubt of the accuracy of the statement as given

87 *Sydney Herald*, Monday 10 December 1833: 2.
88 *Sydney Herald*, Monday 30 September 1833: 2.
89 *Sydney Herald*, Thursday 24 October 1833: 3.
90 *Sydney Gazette and NSW Advertiser*, Tuesday 5 November 1833: 2.

by Manning one of the sufferers. On the 9 August last, two English lads, named James Newell and James Manning, reached King George's Sound from the mainland opposite to Middle Island, after experiencing the most bitter privations for nearly seven weeks on the main, and about two years on the islands in Spencer's Gulph. The account given of their perilous adventure runs thus:

They sailed from Sydney in the month of August 1833, in the schooner *Defiance* of about 25 tons burthen, laden with provisions for trading with the sealers on the islands on the southern coast of Australia,[91] and bound to King George's Sound and the Swan River, Captain Meredith. They were wrecked in September of the same year on Cape Howe Island. They went in a whaleboat with the commander, one man and a native woman to Kangaroo Island; the remainder of the crew of the schooner (six men) determined to make for Sydney, and accordingly started in another whaleboat; they never heard what became of them. They did not reach Kangaroo Island until February 1834, being five months, during which time, they state, they were doing their utmost to make a passage. [It is to be regretted that we have not here a more detailed statement of the manner in which those five months were occupied – it is idle to imagine that they were so long a time *'doing their utmost to make the passage'*!]

They established themselves on Kangaroo Island, built a house for the commander and *his native wife*, and made a garden. In September 1834 a black man named Anderson arrived at Kangaroo Island in a boat from Long Island, with another black man named John Bathurst. Manning and his companion took passage with them to Long Island. They were obliged to keep working in the boat, sealing, to obtain their provisions. In November 1834, George Meredith their commander, whom they left on Kangaroo Island, came to a bird island [mutton birds, Althorpe Isles, off the north coast of Kangaroo Island[92]] where Manning happened to be and accused Manning of robbing him of 4. 10. 0. There was another whaleboat on Long Island with four men in her, named George Roberts, John Howlett, Harry and William Forbes. In November [presumably still 1834], on Boston Island, the people in this latter boat caught five native women from the neighbourhood of Port Lincoln; they enticed two of their husbands into the boat, and carried them off to the island, where in spite of all the remonstrances of Manning, they took the native men in Anderson's boat round a point a short distance off, where they shot them, and knocked their brains out with clubs. Manning believes they

91   Maybe, but the authorities thought they were off to New Zealand.
92   Wells 1978: 77.

still have the native women in their possession, with the exception of Forbes, whose woman ran away from him shortly after they were taken to the island [Kangaroo].

Two of the women had infants at the breast at the time their husbands were murdered; an old woman was compelled to take them away, and carried them into the bush. Another native endeavoured to swim to the island to recover his wife but was drowned in the attempt. In January 1834 a small cutter the *Mountaineer* commanded by Evanson Janson arrived at the island [Kangaroo] in which vessel Manning paid 8 for his passage to King George's Sound; Janson being always drunk, by some misunderstanding Manning lost his passage. Both Manning and his comrade frequently begged of Anderson to land them on the main, that they might walk to King George's Sound but he refused. When Manning landed on Middle Island from the *Mountaineer* he had 50 L. in his possession, in Spanish dollars and English specie. This money Anderson stole; he was seen counting it with a man named Isaac, who also had another lot of money rolled up in canvas. Early in April, Janson the master of the *Mountaineer* arrived at the island in a boat with six men and two women, the vessel having been driven ashore in Thirtle Cove. About the end of May, five of these people left the island in a boat, without any provisions, intending to proceed to King George's Sound. On 23rd June, Anderson at the solicitation of Manning and his fellow traveller James Newell, landed them on the main but would not give them powder. They subsisted chiefly on limpits [sic], and on roots of grass, but were sometimes for several days without little or anything to eat. They found at all times sufficient water, although they never left the neighbourhood of the coast. Arrived at Henley, Oyster Harbour on the 9th August [1835] reduced almost to skeletons and having almost lost all power of articulation.

It is interesting to know that these lads owed their safety entirely to the humane treatment they met with from the natives of the White Cockatoo, Murray and Will-men tribes. From the moment they fell in with them, their exertions were unabated to restore them sufficiently to continue their journey; they nursed, fed, and almost carried them at times, when from weakness they were almost sinking under their sufferings. This is a return which could scarcely have been expected from savages, who have no doubt been exposed to repeated atrocities, such as we have related in a previous narrative. Indeed, to the acts of these white barbarians, we may now trace the loss of some valuable lives among the Europeans, and more especially that of Captain Barker, which took place within a short distance of the scene of these atrocities.[93] We are happy to hear that Sir Richard Spencer, Government Resident at King George's Sound, so soon as he was satisfied of the services the natives had rendered to these lads, issued a small portion of flour to each native, and gave presents to those who were most active and kind in the journey. The gentlemen in the settlement to their credit were very liberal in their subscriptions, to obtain the lads blankets, clothing and other necessities. To the natives they gave a bag of sugar and of rice.

The general vagueness of this report, more especially the five months delay unaccounted for, has left an impression unfavourable to the lads statement; but on reference to the *Sydney Herald* of the 24th October, 1833, two months subsequently to the departure of the *Defiance* from that port, we find the following paragraph: 'The schooner *Defiance*, Captain Meredith, which has left Sydney about a month on a sealing voyage (the variation in the lads' statement of a month, after so long a lapse of time, may be reasonably accounted for) was unfortunately wrecked on the coast about 15 miles below Twofold Bay, all hands saved. The schooner *Blackbird* has gone in search of the wreck. The *Defiance* had about 400 worth of property in her when the accident occurred, and not insured.'

It is to be regretted that our informants were not more minute in their enquiries; a little acuteness in the enquiry would have opened to us the conduct and characters of those employed on the southern coasts as sealers, by our neighbours in Van Diemen's Land. Passing, as they represent they did, along the coast in a whaleboat, with ample time for observation – five months – although we cannot doubt the fact, indeed we believe it to be fully confirmed, leaves an hiatus in the narrative, which may be gratifying to some of our readers, but is annoying to us, searching as we do for facts.

A further inspection of our files of the Sydney Journals may throw more light on this subject, which our leisure, in a future number, will enable us to disclose. The habits of the men left on the islands to the southward, by whaling, or sealing vessels, have long borne the character given them by Manning and Newell; it appears therefore, deserving of some consideration by what means their practices can be checked, as future sealers in the neighbourhood of Port Lincoln will be made to expiate the crimes and outrages of these lawless assassins.

---

93 Kangaroo Island, where 'atrocities' is a correct term for sealers' behaviors towards mainland Aborigines. Captain Barker's death is well known, believed to be a case of mistaken identity, a revenge killing as a response to the atrocities, but of an innocent man.

Quite apart from the present pleasure of reading an 1827 newspaper doing investigative journalism, this account leaves George Meredith last met with in November 1834 on Althorpe Island in the vicinity of Kangaroo Island, South Australia, without his vessel, without Master West and without his crew.

A chronology of sealers on Kangaroo Island makes the statement 'There are many stories regarding Meredith's death but most seem to agree that it was on the mainland near Yankalilla around 1834'.[94] As the Commissioner of Police Alexander Tolmer subsequently investigated the death (and arrested two native women but subsequently discharged them), and no-one has apparently attempted research in the South Australian archives to find these records, if they exist, this is one further step that could be taken to confirm the year of Meredith's death. But I accept 1834.

As Meredith was in no position to abduct anyone from anywhere between September 1833 and his death, it becomes necessary to follow the *Defiance* backwards in time so to speak, from September 1833, bearing in mind that Yankee Yankee has proved himself to be an impeccable witness, and he said that the abduction was in 1833. Even if Meredith died a year later than I believe, that is he died in 1835, I doubt that he could have abducted the women. Batman and Fawkner established themselves in the middle of 1835 at Port Phillip, and the abduction certainly did not happen after that. And if it occurred in the first six months of that year 1835, it would have been fresh news, a recent event for the Bonurong to inform the Europeans about, not something that happened more than a year ago.

George Meredith's *Defiance* recorded sailings are as follows:

- 6 December 1832 – Arrived Sydney, 28 November, from Hobart Town, schooner *Defiance*, 24 tons, Farley [Master], Learmonth and Sims agents, cargo sealing stores.[95]
- 10 December 1832 – Sydney. Departure, for New Zealand yesterday, schooner *Defiance*, 24 tons, Captain West with stores.[96]
- 21 March 1833 – Sydney. Departure for New Zealand yesterday, the schooner *Defiance*.[97]
- 28 May 1833 – Sydney. Arrivals, from a sealing trip on Sunday [ie 26 May] the schooner *Defiance*, West Master, with 536 seal skins, 2500 kangaroo skins.[98]

---

94   Copland 2002; Counterpoints, Flinders University Online Journal of Interdisciplinary Studies Conference Papers. Note that the published version did not include the 18 page chronology, available only online.
95   *Sydney Herald*, Thursday 6 December 1832: 4.
96   *Sydney Herald*, 10 December 1832: 2.
97   *Sydney Gazette and NSW Advertiser*, Thursday 21 March 1833: 2.
98   *Sydney Gazette and NSW Advertiser*, Tuesday 28 May 1833: 2.

There is no record of the *Defiance* between these two dates, and this voyage between March and May 1833 is almost certainly the one during which Meredith and West abducted the women from under Point Nepean. The defining evidence is the cargo on return – both sealskins and kangaroo skins. Matilda's evidence (above) specifically states that Meredith went sealing after abducting the women and names the islands in 'Bass's Straits'. This vessel had been in Bass Strait, the only place where it was possible to obtain together, both sealskins and kangaroo skins. It was the practice of the island sealers to shoot kangaroos to trade their skins[99] as well as sealskins, and so destructive to food resources for the VDL Aborigines was this practice of shooting kangaroos that Robinson banned it.[100]

In fact in his journal entry of 23 July 1836[101] which discusses this issue (the sealers were caught with 400 kangaroo skins from the Sisters Islands), he mentions the fact that Meredith is now dead, killed by the natives of the country adjacent to Kangaroo Island, and that Matilda was (yet again) an eyewitness. I am satisfied that the Meredith abduction took place between March and May 1833.

Part 2: the possibly separate issue of the Port Phillip women living at St Georges Sound in 1839

When Barwick wrote her original article on Louisa Briggs, published in 1985, she was interested in names, in genealogical links with ancestors. She did not even question that the women reported as living at King George's Sound in 1839 were part of the Meredith abduction. She saw the record of them in Thomas' journal, the evidence from Smythe, and she quoted it accurately, and footnoted the reference. Since then, everyone has followed her assumption, and no one has seen the original record, all writers citing Barwick as their reference, not the original record from Thomas.

But Barwick's interest was in the names, and she made no comment on the provenance of the information, or its detail. In fact, this record by its mere existence, challenges the assumption that the women living in Western Australia in 1839 were part of the Meredith abduction.

---

99   Plomley 1987: 38.
100   Plomley 1987: 624. I am grateful to Ruth Gooch for informing me that there were, strictly speaking, no kangaroos in the straits, that the animal to which the records refer is actually a wallaby.
101   Plomley 1987: 366–367.

It cannot remain unconsidered as one of the names, Eliza Nowen, appears on the list of apical ancestors from whom the Bonurong Land Council Aboriginal Corporation derives its authority to be the traditional owners of the Mornington Peninsula.

On 11 December 1839, in Melbourne, the surveyor George D Smythe, recently arrived from Western Australia,[102] informed Thomas that three Port Phillip females and their children were living in Western Australia. Thomas forwarded the information to Robinson thus:

> Mr Smythe, Surveyor at Swan River called … He also stated that there were 4 Port Phillip natives, 3 women and a boy at St Georges Sound who were stole away by the sealers in the year 1834. They were stole by the Captain of the George, the fourth Cutter,[103] which left Sydney touched at Western Port on its way to St Georges Sound. One lubra was cut over the face which she said was done by her father.
>
> One woman named Mary has two children, is 20 years of age, her husband is Captain Williams of Water —
>
> Eliza Nowen on Balls Island has 7 children.
>
> Julian Morgan aged 22 years has several children.
>
> These lubras are all anxious to come to Port Phillip to see their friends at Western Port.[104]

There is a brief mention in another journal 'In the evening a Mr Smyth, Brother to Captain Lonsdale [actually brother in law] gives me an account of Blacks at St George's Sound & in the islands in straits'.[105]

Some comments on Smythe's account

The report of this abduction is quite specific in relation to the year, 1834, a different year to the George Meredith abduction: it is also specific in relation to the abducting vessel, the *George*, the fourth cutter, a different vessel to Meredith's *Defiance* (as well, a cutter is a one masted vessel, rigged fore and aft, whereas Meredith's abducting vessel is specifically stated by the Aboriginal

---

102   According to Marten Syme's *Shipping arrivals and departures, Victorian Ports,* Vol 1 Index: 287, a 'Surveyor Smythe' arrived in Melbourne in the revenue cutter *Ranger* on 26 May 1839. This Surveyor Smythe however is almost certainly his brother Henry Hutchinson Smythe.
103   This seems to be saying that the women were abducted by a government vessel 'the fourth cutter'. There was a government vessel, a revenue cutter, the *Prince George*, engaged in government service operating out of Sydney in this period.
104   Thomas Journal, Monday 11 December 1839, CY 2604, item 4, frame 251, ML.
105   Thomas Journal, Monday 11 December 1839, CY 2604, frame 131, ML.

informant to be a two masted vessel); it is also specific in relation to the place of abduction, the body of water called Western Port, where the abducting vessel called in for water, and specific in relation to the destination, King George's Sound. And Thomas' brief mention in his second journal indicates that Smythe gave information about the women in 'Bass's Straits', which Thomas did not record, as well as information about the women at King George's Sound.

Where this brief account is incoherent is that it seems to attribute the abduction to two separate abductors – both to the sealers and to the captain of the *George*. And the number of children is a problem, for two reasons. It seems unlikely that sealers would snatch a woman with a number of children, yet if Eliza Nowen gave birth to one child per year for the five years from 1834 to 1839, it would be the first such record that I have ever come across.

Given the law of the sea, and the prevailing customs of the times, it would not be a matter of surprise to discover that a government cutter picked up people in distress and gave them a lift: there are quite a few records of government vessels picking up stranded seamen and carrying them to a port. Even international vessels did this, for example Commander Dumont D'Urville in *L'Astrolabe* picked up abandoned sealers at King George's Sound in 1826 and brought them to Western Port. Another example is Yankee Yankee himself who travelled in the revenue cutter *Prince William* from Launceston to King George's Sound (see below). But it *would* be astonishing to find a government cutter engaged in the abduction of native women.

It is such a small detail 'the *George* the fourth cutter', but considering the source, Surveyor Smythe, and the recorder, Thomas, my view is that both considered this fact to be noteworthy, possibly blameworthy. Then there is the detail that the cutter called at Western Port to take on water. This is a defining fact. No small vessels would call into Port Phillip to take on water, because there was no easy source inside the bay, whereas Western Port had a number of convenient and well known watering points. These women were taken from the shores of the bay called Western Port (not from the district called Western Port which included at the time Port Phillip), and they were taken *after* the initial settlement of Western Australia at King George's Sound in 1826, and *after* the revenue cutter *Prince George* arrived in New South Wales in 1833, so the firm date of 1834 may well be correct.

These women cannot be assumed with certainty to be part of the George Meredith abduction in 1834: they may be, but not until all the evidence is considered. It is worth drawing attention to the fact that Police Magistrate Stewart's report states that he embarked in the revenue cutter *Prince George* for the 'purpose of proceeding to Port Phillip', and mentions as well 'the settlement': it seems unlikely that he is using Westernport as a *district* name, but rather as a *place* name.

These women have been considered to be part of the George Meredith abduction only, I suspect, in ignorance of Thomas' primary record, because of the difficulty of accessing it, and then reading it on microfilm.[106]

In order to test the credibility of Smythe's account to Thomas, it is necessary to investigate the details.

George D Smythe

George D Smythe (1806–1857) surveyor … was brother to Henry Hutchinson Smythe. After the Smythe family arrived in Western Australia in 1829, Governor Stirling was able to use the Smythes' surveying skills … Smythe was surveyor with Captain Thomas Bannister's overland expedition to King George's Sound leaving in December 1830 and arriving at Albany in February 1831. Bannister was a difficult character and blamed Smythe for their getting lost; at one point he threatened to shoot Smythe. [The parents] moved to Launceston in March 1831. Henry departed in February 1833 to join his father in Launceston … In October 1834 Governor Stirling led a party of surveyors and mounted police to the upper reaches of the Murray River [the Western Australian Murray River] to deal with the Aborigines. En route they were joined by Smythe and some police. After spending the night at Thomas Peel's station Mandurah House, an assault was made on the Aborigines, the so called 'Battle of Pinjarra'. Eighty Aborigines were killed for the loss of one European life. Although Smythe is usually included in the party, he was not with the assault, for the archive reports indicate that Smythe had been bitten by a venomous insect and was forced to stay at Mandurah House with the Peels [sic] family at Mandurah House on the day of battle.

Smythe surveyed land around the Bunbury area and up into the Avon valley. By 1838 Smythe was in the Tooday area and still required soldiers

---

106   J D'Arcy believes they were part of the George Meredith abduction (D'Arcy, 2009, 'The Problem with Louisa Briggs', Draft Ms: 6); Barwick notes the existence of the women at King George's Sound but offers no opinion on whether or not they were part of the Meredith abduction – her text reads as though she did not think they were (Barwick 1985: 232, fn 18); Clark cites Barwick, adds further facts but offers no opinion as to whether or not the women at King George' Sound were part of the George Meredith abduction (Clark 2002: 113).

to protect him from the Aborigines. He is reported as accidentally shooting his Aboriginal servant, Narral in late 1838. In late 1838 or 1839 Smythe left Western Australia possibly due to this incident.[107]

The above biographical entry (not by an historian) leaves the reader with a vague feeling of unease about Smythe and the Aborigines. It is incomplete though: a newspaper search for Smythe reveals one entry only for Smythe, regarding his earlier experience with the Indigenous people of King George's Sound:

> The King George's Sound Natives. On Thursday last Mr Dale proceeded to Monger's Lake in company with Mr Smythe and two Natives of King George's Sound, Manyat and Gyallepert, in consequence of a wish to see the latter understood to have been expressed by Yagen and others of his tribe.[108]

This newspaper account continues on to relate that the two Aboriginal languages (of Perth and King George's Sound) were mutually unintelligible, and the Aborigines communicated mostly by gesture, but that both parties appeared pleased, and that the meeting ended with a corroboree. Unselected, (it is the only one turned up via an index name search of early Western Australian newspapers) it seems to fit better the fact from Port Phillip that we have seen earlier, that Smythe had good relationships, and in fact, was accompanied permanently by Aboriginal groups.

The friendliness of the relationships and the purpose of the meeting in Western Australia are confirmed in a recently published history (2009) of early contact in King George's Sound: a whole chapter is devoted to examining this meeting. It was a facilitative effort on the part of the authorities to please the Perth Aboriginal chief Yagan who asked to meet the 'chiefs' from King George's Sound. Smythe is confirmed as a surveyor with the Surveyor General's department, an escort of the two Indigenous King George's Sound men.[109] Smythe was experienced and trusted in Western Australia, knew the King George's Sound country and people, and unless and until there is evidence to the contrary, I take him to be a credible witness with his information about the women.

---

107   IM Stuart, in Forth 1998: 147.
108   *The Perth Gazette and Western Australian Journal,* Saturday 26 January 1833. The whole article can be read on National Library of Australia (NLA) Newspapers Online, <http://newspapers.nla.gov.au>.
109   Shellam 2009: 163.

Prince George

The problem lies in determining the meaning of the phrase 'the fourth cutter *George*'. The National Maritime Museum believes that it could have been the practice that names were re-used in the colonies as they were in the Royal Navy, ie there were four consecutive colonial revenue cutters named *Prince George* since 1788.[110] But the 'bible' for matters maritime for this colonial period[111] lists only one revenue cutter named *Prince George*, so that the most likely meaning of the phrase 'the fourth cutter' is that it was the fourth of four government cutters then in service around the Australian coast. Government cutters and Government revenue cutters in service around Australia in the period of the 1820s and 1830s include the *Charlotte*, the *Royal William*, the *Mermaid*, the *Sally*, the *Governor Arthur*, the *Opossum*, the *Swallow*, the *Duke of York*, and the *Prince Leopold*: some of these little vessels circumnavigated Australia in servicing the outlying settlements of Swan River, Port Essington and Moreton Bay.

The revenue cutter *Prince George* was a wooden vessel of 51 tons, built at Hastings, Great Britain in 1832 for the Port of Sydney. It arrived in Port Jackson on 30 August 1833 and remained in service till 1845 when it was sold out of government service. After being sold into private hands, she was wrecked in 1846.[112]

This *Prince George*, Master Roach, is recorded as lying off the dockyard, refitting, in September 1833, after arrival from its delivery voyage.[113] The other Sydney newspaper adds the further detail that it arrived in ballast, having left England on 17 April 1833, Master Roach.[114] It is next recorded in May 1834 as 'Revenue Cutter *Prince George* returned from a cruise'.[115] It was the *Prince George* which brought Mrs Eliza Fraser (of Fraser Island fame) the second mate, and five of the rescued crew back to Sydney after the wreck of the *Stirling Castle* on the Great Barrier Reef on 13 May 1836,[116] and it was the same revenue cutter *Prince George* which brought visiting magistrate Stewart to Port Phillip to report on the settlement in June 1836,[117] and the same vessel that 'went round to lay buoys in Western Port' during a ten day stay at Melbourne in 1837.[118]

---

110   Graham Thompson, National Maritime Museum, Greenwich, 1 December 2009.
111   Ian Nicholson, 'Ships of the "Colonial Marine" i.e. Government Vessels of NSW and VDL, 1788 to 1850s, together with Nominal Lists of Officers Afloat and Related Dockyard Officials etc', Typescript, undated, Launceston Library.
112   Jane Miller, SLV search, 23 October 2009.
113   *The Sydney Gazette and NSW Advertiser*, Tuesday 19 September 1833, NLA Newspapers Online.
114   *Sydney Herald*, Monday 2 September 1833: 2.
115   *The Sydney Gazette and NSW Advertiser*, Tuesday 1 May 1834, NLA Newspapers Online.
116   *The Sydney Gazette and NSW Advertiser*, Tuesday 18 October 1836, NLA Newspapers Online.
117   Bonwick 1856: 87.
118   *The Sydney Gazette and NSW Advertiser*, Tuesday 28 March 1837, NLA Newspapers Online.

It was the outward bound *Prince George* which transported the eight Port Phillip Aborigines to Sydney for trial in 1838,[119] and the same vessel for which tenders were called in Sydney for re-coppering its bottom,[120] and replacing its lower mast.[121] It was the vessel sent from Sydney to search for any evidence of the *Britannia* which left Melbourne on 9 November 1839 and was believed to have foundered off the Gippsland coast about a week later: Aborigines had seen a boat lying on the Ninety Mile Beach and footprints had been seen in the sand. The *Prince George* discovered a boat with a mast washed up on the beach near Cape Howe.[122] There is a plethora of reports from the *Prince George* in 1840 after it took government surveyor Hoddle to Portland Bay and to Western Port to report on soil type and minerals (it reported coal).[123] Two images exist, published in 1836: one is of the vessel enduring a great hurricane off the island of St Paul en route London to Sydney, and the other depicts the St George chasing the French ship *Victorine* on the same voyage – the *Prince George* merely wanted to hand over mail for England, but the French vessel fled in fear, and the *Prince George* chased her down.[124] This revenue cutter *Prince George* of 72 tons[125] accompanied HMS *Fly* on its charting of the Torres Strait islands 1842–1846, acting as its tender.[126]

The problem is that its service record lists voyages, 1834–1843, to and from the ports of Melbourne, Sydney, Western Port, Jervis' Bay, Moreton Bay, Howe's Island (modern name Gabo Island), Kangaroo Island, Geelong, Portland Bay, Port Phillip, Port of Melbourne, Williamstown, but *not* King George's Sound nor the Swan River settlement.[127]

Nor is the revenue cutter *Prince George* accounted for during the period from when it finished refitting sometime after September 1833 and when it returned from its cruise in May 1834: destinations and ports of call on its cruise were unrecorded in the Shipping Intelligence section of the newspapers of the period, where they would be expected – the ship is simply missing from ports, and presumably at sea. Unless evidence is found for the *Prince George* between

---

119   Commander *Prince George* to Lonsdale, 28 May 1838, 'have returned to Williamstown … bad weather … have landed natives under boat on deck … they have been under water since I left', VPRS 4, unit 4, 38/107, PROV.
120   VIC *Government Gazette,* 23 January 1839, no 384, p. 104, SLV.
121   VIC *Government Gazette,* 23 October 1839, no 460, p. 1182, SLV.
122   Shipwrecks of Victoria, <http://oceans1.customer.netspace.net.au/vic-wrecks.html>
123   Boys 1935: 103.
124   Both these images can be seen in the Rex Nan Kivell Collection, NLA; both can be seen online.
125   According to the National Maritime Museum, the discrepancy in tonnage is simply explained by the fact that the Royal Navy in 1835 changed its formula for measuring ships, and all vessels subsequently were accorded a different tonnage.
126   Nicholson 1988: 421; and google HMS *Fly.*
127   Jane Miller, SLV search, 23 October 2009.

these two dates, then I suggest that the evidence from Smythe, recorded by Thomas, must be kept in mind as possibly true, and that further research is required to confirm or refute it.

William Nairne Clark's account of native women with sealers at King George's Sound

This man was a lawyer and publisher whose entry in the *Australian Dictionary of Biography* asserts that his main claim to fame was that he fought a duel and was acquitted of manslaughter.[128] That may be so, but from our point of view, his several excursions between 1840 and 1842 to the south-west of the Colony of Western Australia and the series of articles which he wrote, provide another glimpse of the women abducted by the sealers. In the article published the week previous to this one about to be quoted, he stated that he would be revealing facts previously unknown to his readers.[129]

His account gives a different year and a different set of abductors, but it does agree with one of the names given by Smythe, and it offers an explanation of 'Captain Williams, Water— .' It is accepted by Plomley and Henley in their biographical notes on Gamble, Robert/Bob Gambell.[130] It is noteworthy that Bob Gamble worked as a pilot for Robinson in 1831 when he went round the Bass Strait islands, moving the sealers on and attempting to collect the VDL women whom they had with them. Bob Gambell was subsequently sent to Hobart by Robinson to be tried for killing two women.[131]

> The first sealers on the south-west coast of Australia came from the penal settlement of Van Diemen's Land ... one party landed in the district of Port Phillip, and forcibly brought away with them several native women, of a much more handsome and engaging appearance than those in this part of the island [Western Australia]. These poor creatures became reconciled to their lot, and attended on their white associates with a fidelity that might have put to the blush many of their sex. Several children were the fruits of this intercourse, some of whom are to be seen at King George's Sound, their complexions being much lighter than those of other native children. *Previous* to the foundation of the Colony [Western Australia founded 1 June 1829] the coast was likewise visited, according to the traditions of the natives, by parties in search of fur seal. They frequently made inroads into the

---

128 'Clark, William Nairne (1804 – 1854)', *Australian Dictionary of Biography*, vol 1: 227.
129 'Remarks respecting the Islands on the Coast of S.W. Australia', *The Perth Gazette and Western Australian Journal*, Saturday 8 October 1842: 3, 4. This whole article can be printed off NLA Newspapers Online.
130 Plomley and Henley 1990: 81.
131 Plomley 1966: 1013, 478, 468, 450, 392.

territory of the aborigines, and endeavoured to carry off the women, which infringement on their natural rights roused the natives to fury, and several collisions between the blacks and the whites took place. Even now, in talking of these marauders, the natives describe them with symptoms of loathing and innate hatred.

The first aggression on the rights of the natives by the sealers, since this Colony [Western Australia] was formed, occurred at Port Phillip in the year 1831. A marauding crew from Van Diemen's Land arrived on the coast and forcibly abducted several native women; afraid of the consequences, they left that part of the territory of Australia and steered in a westerly direction along the coast, where they had frequent encounters with the aboriginal inhabitants, which sometimes ended in the loss of human life on the part of the blacks. They have been described as a warlike race of men, chasing the sealers to the water's edge, and hurling their spears at the boats.

The great rendezvous of the sealers was the Archipelago of Islands to the eastward of Doubtful Island Bay, where they chiefly subsisted on wild geese and seal's flesh, and occasionally made a run to King George's Sound to purchase flour and other necessities and sell their sealskins. Another party of sealers was composed of the crew of the *Mountaineer*, a small craft from Van Diemen's Land, which was wrecked near the Archipelago many years ago ... One of the most daring of these people was a man of colour of the name of Anderson, and lawless as these men were, they looked up to him with a sort of dread ... [he] usually kept one or two black women to attend on him and minister to his wants, when not engaged in sealing ... The favourite resort of Anderson was Manduran Island ... [which] contains some natural salt pans from which immense quantities of that commodity might be annually obtained ... The late Mr Henty, when on that part of the coast, took away with him to Van Diemen's Land a considerable quantity of the salt as a specimen. Strange to say the salt on this island is of a reddish colour, formed probably by some vegetable substance. The last time that Anderson paid a visit to Manduran he had a full boat's crew with him, and a black woman, but neither he nor the woman were ever more seen. [Both murdered]. The person who has been the luckiest in sealing is one of the name of Williams who is still resident at King George's Sound. From first to last he has made from 1000 to1500 and his boat *Fanny* is well known as a remarkably fast-sailing, safe boat. She was built in Van Diemen's Land.

During the winter months, when not engaged in sealing, the sealers hunt kangaroo around the various bays, and supply the crews of

American and French ships with fresh meat ... it may be said with truth there is a considerable traffic carried on with foreign shipping in that part of the settlement. Others pilot foreign ships into the various bays where the whales are most abundant and receive a gratuity of about 50 for the season, according as the ships are more or less successful. Rather than be at the expense of living at the settlement, and going to work, some of these men prefer to lead an idling life on one of the islands with their black women and children, entirely excluded from human society, and sleeping away their existence ... Bald Island, about twenty miles to the eastward of the Sound has been inhabited frequently by them on account of the number of wallabees that abound on it. One of the sealers named 'Gemble' or familiarly 'Bob Gemble' originally from Van Diemen's Land, used to reside there with his black gin and his children for months together, and for aught that I know, he may be either there or somewhere else in the Archipelago to this day. He belonged to Anderson's party, and first let out the fatal secret respecting his murder, but it came in such a vague shape to the ears of the authorities that no notice was taken of it, and all the parties implicated have long ago left the Colony.[132]

Balls Island

It sounds as though Thomas just didn't hear the name properly. According to State Records of Western Australia:

Balls Island probably is Bald Island. The latter is located 50 kms east of Albany at the southern end of Cheyne Beach, then a popular haunt for American whaling vessels. The seamen on these ships operated beyond the writ of the Colonial government in Perth and Albany. Therefore one could surmise that George Smythe's contact with the women who lived with the whalers was on an informal basis.[133]

Summary

Clark believes that 'at least 20 women, girls and boys were abducted from the coasts around Port Phillip and Westernport in the 1820s and 1830s'.[134]

---

132   *The Perth Gazette and Western Australian Journal*, Saturday 8 October 1842: 3, 4.
133   Tom Reynolds, Archives Research Officer, State Records Office of Western Australia, 29 October 2009. Tom Reynolds searched the index to the correspondence between the Resident at Albany and the Western Australian Colonial Secretary in Perth, but these women were not mentioned. At the very least, nothing about the women was remarkable enough for the Resident to report on to the Colonial Secretary at the Swan River. As the Residents' correspondence is not itemised, it will be necessary for someone to go to Perth to follow this up, as well as Water Police and Customs records.
134   Clark 2002: 3.

D'Arcy, quoting Plomley, suggests 50.[135] The early settlers mention four, presumably because they were the wives of four men with whom the settlers were engaged at the time. The Police Magistrate Stewart mentions four. The first person participant witness Yankee Yankee mentions eight 'women' taken from Port Phillip; this number of persons apparently subsumes the young girls as women: and one of the women was pregnant. Surveyor Smythe gave an account of a further four females who were abducted from Western Port and were living in Western Australia in 1839. These may be a separate abduction.

Part 3: the return of Yaunki Yaunker

Yaunki Yaunker/Yankee Yankee/Yonker Yonker/Yanki Yanki/
Youki Youka/Yunk Yunker/Yonki-Yonka/Bob Cunningham/Robert
Cunningham/Robert You Yang Cunningham/Yang Yang Alias Robert
Cunningham

On 6 June 1841, Yaunki Younker strolled in to the encampment on the south side of Melbourne, though Thomas does not write it up on that day which was a Sunday.[136] He slept that night in his father's tent, as will be seen, and he was given a formal ceremonial welcome on the Tuesday. Following his arrival back in Port Phillip, Yankee Yankee abandoned the trappings of civilisation and immersed himself in local affairs: he was in everything. He married Bungurook, daughter of the Warworong 'chief' Billibellary. He was an excellent speaker of English and was offered good jobs but refused them. He was sought after for his information, and he divulged it to white people whom he considered trustworthy. He had influential friends who paid his fines when subsequently he was frequently before the courts on drunkenness charges. He was called the 'civilised black', and considered dangerous because he moved so easily between two worlds. He joined the 1842 Native Police Corps but stayed only a short time and was listed by Thomas as a deserter. He was highly critical of the fact that he was not taught to read and write during the years he worked for white people. He was equally critical of the broken promise to give the Bonurong their own reserve at Kullurk/Coolart.

---

135   Jacqueline D'Arcy, 8 September 2009, Draft Ms, p. 2, fn 7.
136   Thomas Journal, CY 2605, frames 283–284, ML.

Fig 44. 'Yonki Yonka'

Sketch, George Henry Haydon.

Assistant Protector William Thomas' two accounts of Yankee Yankee

Civilization does not alter the Australian Aborigine. Yaunki Yaunker after six years absence [Thomas has overwritten the word six with the letter 8] appeared in the Native Encampment S[th] of the Yarra, his appearance was intelligence & nought of the savage appeared in his countenance, he had fine eyes, Long black hair which appeared to have been taken much pains with, hung in curled ringlets on his shoulders, & waved each side on his face and on his brow. He was about 18 yrs of age and could not have been more than 10 yrs of age when kidnapped from Pt, just the age that would seem to be ripe for modelling [sic] the character. This youth was kidnapped with 8 lubras [Thomas annotates at the bottom of the page] one of these Toutkuningrook, afterwards escaped, jumped overboard when the craft was near the coast by Cape Howe, and got safe to her tribe and is still alive, on the coast between Arthurs Seat and Point Nepean, by the sealers.

Capt[n] West since dead of a government schooner[137] took Yanki Yanki to VDL. [Crossed out is the following: 1 lubra March run away.] Yanki was 1 year in VD Land. He was taken away from VD Land in the *Royal William*, cutter, Capt[n] Patterson, to Swan River where he was 4 years at wages of 15 shillings per week. He came from Swan River on the *Minnerva* Schooner, Capt[n] Reed, paid 9 for his passage to Adelaide. He left 3 lubras behind at Swan River with the sealers. He was at Adelaide 1 Year at 1 per week as Dairy Man & Stock Keeper. Yanki took his passage or worked his passage from Adelaide to Pt Phillip in the *Diana*, Capt[n] Skein.

His masters were, at Swan River, 1 & 2 Mr Barker, 3 Mr Phillips, 4 Mr Mundy. He gives Mr Barker the best character. His occupation at the Swan River was Shepherding and Stock-keeping. His master at Adelaide was Mr John Gombel. He stated that the sealers use the women very ill, making them get Mutton Birds etc by day & work by night.

However strange it may appear, this Yanki, the 2nd night was as the other blacks, naked and bedaubing himself over, and before a week, was in every respect as the other blacks. I was most anxious to secure him in order to aid me in some of the idioms of the language, & also to assist me in pressing upon the blacks the comfort of civilization, but no entreaties

---

137   It has to be asked if 'Captain West of the government schooner since dead' who took Yankee Yankee to Launceston is the same Captain West as the Master of the *Defiance*. Captain West does not appear on Nicholson's list of masters of Government vessels for either VDL or New South Wales.

could prevail. Other gentlemen, settlers, offered him good wages but Yanki would not be again entangled with again to live, and I verily believe that he has not from that period as a civilized man. He has now most awfully deteriorated in appearance, & is as filthy dirty & I think more so than his companions.

Now how can this be accounted for in any other way than their opinion that their life is the best. I was about to attribute this instance of Yanki to the Masters he was serving, find that during the 6 yrs he had never been taught his alphabet, or had any religious example, but in the evidence of Mrs Schelly it will be seen that such has been the case when every religious care has been taken of those who it was to be anticipated would have been good Members of Society. It perhaps may be urged now that the Sydney and many other Blks are about the country as Civilized, useful etc. I answer their case is like Yanki – they run away from home, & are afraid of being killed if they take to the bush, or have been taken in infancy and are not aware of their country and language.[138]

no date

Another version recorded by Thomas commences as a 'little history' of Bob whose native name is Yonker Yonker meaning far away. Yonki Yonker was kidnapped with eight women near Point Nepean when he was nine years of age, four years before the first settlers came to Port Phillip.

He appeared where I was encampt on the south of the Yarra in the afternoon. His appearance was intelligence, fine keen eyes, long black hair which hung in ringlets on his shoulders & which he appeared to have bestowed much care, He came to my tent and told me he was a native of this place which I did not believe at the moment but which a few hours convinced me was correct by the caressing and joyous formalities among the natives. He slept that night with his father [Big Benbow]. The next morning I got him to my tent where he related his history, which I communicated to His Honour the Superintendant and the following morning I introduced him to His Honour. Strange as it may appear but such is the fact on the 3rd day Yonker totally discarded all European dress and was bedaubed with grease and clay and his only cladding an opossum cloak – nor has any offer from that hour to this been successful in drawing him aside from the native habits of the Aborigs. Many in the district offered him most advant.[139]

138   Thomas Miscellaneous Papers, mf CY 3130, frame 35 ff, ML.
139   Thomas Journal, Ms set 214, item 2, CY 3126, frame 23 ff, ML.

James Dredge's Diary record of Yankee Yankee[140]

16 June 1841

During the week a young man of the Boonworongs arrived in the *Edwina* from Adelaide. It appears that about five years ago this Tribe was on the coast of the Bay near Arthur's Seat when a vessel came in, and having anchored, her crew went ashore. Early one morning they induced nine women and two boys to go into their boat and took them on board their vessel and sailed out of the harbour. One of the women contrived afterwards to make her escape and returned to her own people. The others were taken to Preservation Island in the Straits where they used very cruelly. The young man now returned, was, after a time taken to Launceston where he escaped in a vessel which he thought would take him home. Her destination however was Swan River settlement where he lived amongst Europeans and made himself useful as a Stock keeper and eventually obtained one pound per week wages. An opportunity offering he took his passage in a vessel bound to Adelaide for which he paid 9 and then hired himself on the *Edwina* to work his passage to Port Phillip where he joined his relatives and friends whose joy at his arrival was unbounded.

He is a fine youth and speaks English pretty well. He has however, assumed all the habits of his countrymen. It is to be feared that if his partial civilization is not turned to judicious account he will become an instrument of considerable mischief.

The blacks say that many years ago a vessel put into Western Port and attempted to carry off some of the women who saved themselves by running away; the whites however, fired upon them, killed two and wounded others. Some of them carry the shots in their flesh to this day.[141]

Verification of details in Yankee Yankee's story

Yankee Yankee states that one lubra ran away in March, and as she ran away from Wilson's Promontory on the voyage from Port Phillip to Preservation Island, the abduction took place earlier than March in whatever year. After one year in VDL, Yankee Yankee's story was that he went to the Swan River in the *Royal William*, Captain Patterson. The *Royal William*, 42 tons, cutter, modelled on Hastings lugger lines, was launched in 1832 from John Petchey's shipyard at Kangaroo Point, Hobart Town.

---

140   At the time of writing this account Dredge had already resigned from the service of the Protectorate.
141   Ms 11625, Box 16/4: 196, SLV.

She appears for the first time in shipping records as having left King George's Sound on 4 March 1834, returning to Hobart with a cargo of seals and salt, arriving 5 April 1834, her master being Captain Patterson.[142] Her departure for VDL for King George's Sound is not recorded, but given the roaring forties, the voyage towards King George's Sound would be longer than the voyage home with a following wind. She must therefore have left for King George's Sound early in 1834, perhaps January.

Given that this is the vessel on which Yankee Yankee sailed, then, considering that he spent a year in VDL before going to King George's Sound, the George Meredith abduction is pushed back in time to 1833. This agrees perfectly with Thomas' crossing out of 'six' years and substituting '8' in his first account of Yankee Yankee's narrative (see above).

Yankee Yankee's second intercolonial voyage is confirmed as well, as is the name of the Captain. The *Minerva*, an 89 ton schooner, Captain Reid, arrived in Adelaide from Leith, Scotland in January 1840:[143] she then made two return trips, Adelaide to King George's Sound and the Swan River in March and May 1840, her master being the same man Captain David Reid.[144] Importantly, her notice of sailing for one of these voyages specifically stated that she was to depart Perth on 13 April for King George's Sound and South Australia.[145] As ships were guided into King George's Sound by sealers, under the authority of Captain Williams (Nairne's account above) Yankee Yankee could not only have heard news of the Port Phillip women, he could have met them.

Yankee Yankee's last leg of his journey is also confirmed: Thomas must have heard the name of the ship incorrectly, but fortunately he recorded his version of the Captain's name and Dredge heard the name as *Edwina*. In the absence of passenger lists, the following account confirms that the ship made the voyage from Adelaide to Port Phillip in June 1841:

> The mainmast of the *Edina*, [Captain] Skinner, 557 tons from Greenock to Adelaide, shortly after her arrival in port was found to be deficient, so that a new mast was required … stringybark … mainmast for the *Edina* 75 feet in length, perfectly straight without a knot … [was obtained] … brought from the Tiers in a timber carriage drawn by 26 bullocks … shortened to 68 feet … prepared by the ships crew … in five days … stepped and rigged … cost 60 … the *Edina* sailed immediately for Port Phillip.[146]

---

142 Cumpston 1970: 131–132.
143 *The Perth Gazette and Western Australian Journal*, 4 April 1840.
144 David Leadbeater, *South Australian Passenger Lists (Shipping arrivals), 1803–1853*, Archives South Australia.
145 *The Perth Gazette and Western Australian Journal*, 11 April 1840.
146 *Sydney Herald*, 8 June 1841: 3.

The *Edina*, Master Thomas Skinner, 470 tons, with seven passengers and four steerage passengers, arrived in Port Phillip on 31 May 1841 from Greenock and Adelaide.[147] Yankee Yankee turned up at Thomas' encampment on the south side of the Yarra on 6 June 1841. His story checks out. Because Yankee Yankee's story is confirmed in every detail which can be checked, I take it to be truthful and accurate in those parts which cannot be checked. In particular, because Yankee Yankee was so specific about the four men for whom he worked at the Swan River, even giving them character references, I accept his time frame as well: he cannot be the boy reported by Smythe to be at King George's Sound in 1839 because he was working on a farm 200 miles away at the Swan River in 1839.

7 June 1841

Thomas breakfasted with His Honour and agreed to present Yankee Yankee to him at the wharf. In the evening, Yankee Yankee, Big Benbow and Thomas' men took Mr William Humphrey in charge but the case could not be substantiated because Wigal was not found on his premises.[148]

8 June 1841

Thomas sent 'Yaunki Yaunker', on horseback (?Bess, Thomas' beloved Arabian mare) to visit La Trobe:

> the bearer of this letter is the intelligent native of whom I spoke yesterday, who with his lubra was stolen from the beach between Arthur's Seat and Point Nepean about 6 years back. He states his story in good English and answers to the name of Yunki Yunker.[149]

On this day, Yankee Yankee was given a formal welcome back in a ceremony called Woolworkbullunberlin.[150]

Kobin Koolin or Embracement

> Kobin Koolin is a term given to the affecting embrace of one who has returned after long absence or confinement from his tribe. When the individual appears, his kindred fall on his breast and weep (tho evidently he has difficulty to restrain) but is, at it were, motionless during the scene which is truly affecting to behold. The one who receives the embrace is

---

147   *Port Phillip Gazette*, in Syme 1984: 62.
148   Thomas Journal, CY 2605, item 5, frames 283–284, ML. Wigal/Mary Anne was the wife of Burrenum/Mr Dredge. She was co-habiting with this man, a carpenter, in Elizabeth Street opposite the Bank of Australasia. When her relatives went to take her away, she was put in a box, and they found it impossible to prove that she was there (5 June). Wigal returned to the encampment in the evening of 7 June; Humphrey came looking for her. Wigal identified him.
149   Thomas to Superintendent, 8 June 1841, VPRS 10, unit 3/843, PROV.
150   Thomas Journal, CY 2605, frame 284, ML.

sometimes sitting; the one who embraces bends on his knees, presses his face to the breast of the preserved, weeps, mutters some expressions and remains weeping 3, 4, or 5 min. Occasionally the embraced cannot refrain droping [sic] a tear which falls upon the head of the embracer, but he never stirs or speaks to any till it is all over. When the embracer lifts up his head & takes his seat, when all due ceremony, the blacks come and sit round: the preserved will relate all that has happened to him, his whole adventures, which is eagerly listened to by his tribe with now and then ejaculations from his listeners – they in return relate what has happened, Deaths, fights etc during his absence. I have seen several such scenes, but the most affecting was one of Mr Parkers Blks from the NW who was liberated from Jail about 1840 – and Warree & his Father meeting at Nerre Nerre Warren in 1843, the latter different but equally affecting.[151]

Elsewhere, Thomas describes this ceremony as exactly like the situation described in the Bible between Joseph and his brothers. He witnessed a ceremony like this when Wigeculk/William was defended by Redmond Barry and acquitted by a jury in Melbourne on 15 July 1844. The ceremony affected Thomas so much that he wrote 'the greeting of the tribe cannot be described'.[152]

23 June 1841

Thomas' petition to Gipps states that eight lubras were abducted six years back, Yankee Yankee being the only one to get back to his native tribe.[153]

24 June 1841

The intelligent young man 'Yanki Yankie' said he would come soon but that first he was going with some blacks to the Barrabools.[154]

9 August 1841

Yankee Yankee taken ill; 'a black after being for years used to civilized habits is not able to bear exposure'. Thomas gave him a new blanket and a dose of rhubarb and magnesium.[155]

---

151 ML MSS 214/3, CY 2606, page 76, frame 49; I am grateful to Mark Hildebrand of the Mitchell Library for providing me with a large clear copy of this frame. I have added punctuation.

152 CY 2606, frame 206, ML.

153 VPRS 10, unit 3, 1841/909, PROV. Thomas is incorrect; his own narrative from Yankee Yankee states that Toutkuningrook jumped overboard, got back and was still alive at the time of writing.

154 Thomas to Superintendant, 24 June 1841, VPRS 10, unit 3/940, PROV.

155 Thomas Journal, CY 2605, item 5, ML.

29 September 1841

Yankee Yankee going to Arthurs Seat.[156]

19 December 1841

Yankee Yankee with Kollorlook, Yal Yal, and Beruke alias Gellibrand gave Thomas information including names of the blacks who had murdered an Adelaide Aborigine named Jemmy at Whitehead's station and removed his *marmulla* (kidney fat).[157] Jemmy had arrived on horseback to drove Whitehead's fat stock to market: he camped with a Monaro black working for Whitehead, apart from the locals. The two foreigners watched a Goulburn corroboree, then the Monaro black went back to their camp. The Goulburns and two Yarra blacks, Worrangulk and Terap, snatched the Adelaide man, crushed his head, removed his kidney fat, and flesh from the back of his thighs. Thomas arrived on the property, investigated, buried the Adelaide man and wrote two official reports on it.[158]

5 February 1842

'Mr Dana [Commandant of the 1842 Native Police Corps, in the process of establishing the Corps and feeding his enrolees even before official establishment] draws for five police only; Yankee leaves without leave'.[159]

24 February 1842

Yankee Yankee received blankets, clothes, equipment; enrolled in Native Police Corps and made his mark; drilled twice daily; remained at Nerre Nerre Warren until 28 March; the Corps then left because they ran out of water when Dandenong Creek stopped flowing in the big drought; marched in easy stages to Yarra Yarra opposite the surveyor's paddock.[160]

30 June 1842

'Yanker Yanker', male, aged 23, suffering 'from Pseudo Syphilis, treated internally with Liq Arsenic plus aperients and externally with Black Wash [Copper Sulphate]' is listed in the Medical Dispenser's reports for 1–30 June at Merri Creek.[161] Henry Jones' July report states in the remarks column that

---

156 Thomas Journal, CY 2605, item 5, ML.
157 Thomas Journal, CY 2605, item 5, ML.
158 VPRS 11, unit 8, items 417 and 418, PROV.
159 Thomas Journal, CY 2605, item 5, ML.
160 HEP Dana to La Trobe, 31 March 1842, VPRS 17, Box 28, 42/674, PROV.
161 Henry Jones Report, VPRS 4410, unit 2, item 48, PROV.

Yankee Yankee was for a long time on the sick list by the Yarra but he was perfectly recovered and was one of the ones who benefited from a three week excursion around the district with Mr Thomas.[162]

27 July 1843

'Yanki Junker' and a Native Policeman Murrummurrembean 'thwarted the ends of justice' by warning three Barrabools of a plan by the chief protector, the assistant protector and the chief constable to capture them.[163]

20 October 1843

Friday. Yankee Yankee, Ben Benger and a few Western Port blacks come in to encampment.[164]

9 December 1843

Saturday. Yankee Yankee accuses Thomas of writing a letter to the governor to put Billy Lonsdale and de Villiers in gaol.[165]

7 April 1844

Police Report, Melbourne.

> Woolorong was suspected of murder, and condemned to be speared by seven of the best men of the Western Port tribe; as he ran by them at a certain distance, he escaped the spears thrown at him; but a general fight took place and police had some difficulty in suppressing the affray, after many were seriously wounded.

Also: 14 April 1844

Police Report, Melbourne.

> Yang Yang (alias Robert Cunningham) brought up for obstructing the chief constable in his attempt to take Woolorong[166] (alias Lonsdale), a Goulburn black, for the murder of an Aboriginal boy in the service of Mr Manton at Westernport. Yang Yang pleaded to the bench that Woolorong was about to submit to the ordeal of spearing, viz. seven of the principal men of the Western Port tribe were each to throw a spear at him. If he warded them off he was no longer amenable. If he was killed satisfaction

---

162 Henry Jones Report, VPRS 4410, unit 2, item 49, PROV.
163 Thomas to Robinson, VPRS 11, Box 10/596, PROV.
164 Thomas Journal, CY 2606, item 2, ML.
165 Thomas Journal, CY 2606, item 2, ML.
166 The Police report is actually wrong in the name; it was *not* Woolorong and he was *not* a Goulburn black. It was the famous Poleorong aka Billy Lonsdale who undertook this ritual spearing with another Western Port man of great stature Warrador aka Jack Weatherly.

was complete. He further pleaded that had they not been interrupted, he would afterwards have induced Wooloorong alias Lonsdale to surrender himself to the chief constable, or aided to take him. Upon this occasion the Native Police refused to act. At the intercession of Mr Protector Thomas, Yang Yang got off with an admonition and forty-eight hours confinement.[167]

23 August 1844

Yankee Yankee, 'a disapproving' says 'Benbow[168] a baby go crying to the police office about his lubra'.[169] The circumstances of Benbow being a sook in going off to the Europeans for help are as follows: the account takes up three pages of Thomas' journal.

Marriage entitlement

Ningerranow, a Western Port black, aged 27, died at Pallemaramg (at the back of Mt Eliza) on 19 July 1844, with no cause of death recorded. His lubra Burdingrooc, aged 23 died six weeks later at the encampment south of the Yarra on 22 August 1844, 'of sheer grief', Thomas wrote.[170] The day after Burdingrook died of sheer grief there was serious trouble.

Ningerranow/Ingrianowl/Eggeranowl/Ningerranowl/ Ning-e-ra-non/Niggerenaul/Negronoule/Negre-Moule/ Negremoule

8 Dec 1835 – The Sydney blacks sent in Negrenoule to ask Mr Batman and Buckley to come and see them (Billot 1982: 20).

13 Jan 1836 – Derramut and Negrenoule reported seeing two vessels at Indented Heads on Tuesday (Billot 1982: 28); 16 Jan – Merape and Negre-moule Batman's stolen piece of iron (Billot 1982: 29); 6 Jun – Negremoule at the Head of the Blacks dug a good grave and interred Wir-ar-bill who died two days previously (Billot 1982: 87).

---

167   Smyth 1972[1878]: 81–82. There is a discrepancy here, probably Brough Smyth's error, in that Thomas' Journal gives the date of the spearing and Yamki Yamker's insolence to the Constable and subsequent arrest as February 1844, not April (VPRS 4410, unit 3/79, PROV).
168   This is not Yankee Yankee's father Benbow/Baddourup; it is his uncle King/Little Benbow/Bullutt.
169   Thomas Journal, CY 2606, item 3, frame 219, ML.
170   Sheer grief, Thomas Journal, CY 2606, item 3, frame 219, ML.

14 Jan 1839 – a fine young Aborigine his wife and 2 boys about 9 and 11 years old paid us a visit; the two boys threw the boomerang (here called a Wonguim) … the woman was dressed comfortable, had a fine opossum rug … wrapped around her; seemed very different to the naked wretches I had seen at Sydney; gave them tea, sugar and tobacco (Thomas Journal CY 2604, item 3, ML); 12 Feb 1839 – Ningerranow was the son of the old woman Dinoo and a brother to Derrimut, came into Thomas' camp with his wife suffering from influenza (CY 2604, item 3, ML); 12 Feb – 20 Mar 1839 – Ingrianowl alias Wooldelaruck, aged 28, Bonurong tribe; lubra is Plentybruthen, Susan, aged 18, Boonworong (Dredge census in Robinson Papers, vol 54, ML); Jul 1839 – Ning-e-ra-non/Jimmy, name taken in encampment (Thomas 'A' diary Jan-Jul 1839, set 214, item 1, ML); 17 Sep 1839 – Eggeranowl, aged 26, his lubra Susan aged 16, name taken in encampment Melbourne (CY 2946, ML); 22 Nov 1839 – his wife was recorded as Berbingrook, aged 20, wife of Ningeranook (VPRS 10, unit 1/ 242, PROV).

3 Jan 1840 – Four Waworong and Bonurong await Nigaranow's return from the Barrabools (Thomas to Robinson, enc to 40/2215 in 4/1135.1, AO of NSW); 7 Jun 1840 – Billy Lonsdale gave Robinson a list of blacks at Tubberubbabel including Niggerenaul, No 3 on the list after Derrimut and Pardynup (Robinson Journal in Clark 1998, vol 1: 344); 12 Jun 1840 – in a list of Aborigines at the head protectorate station Tubberubbabel, Thomas records Ning*, lubra and Dindow in a group of three (CY 2604, item 3, ML).

19 Jul 1844 – Ningerranowl, a Port Phillip black, aged 27, married, died at Pallemarangun [at the back of Mt Eliza], with no cause of death recorded, 'a black highly respected' (Thomas Return of Births and Deaths, CY 2604, frame 284, ML); 22 Aug 1844 – Burdingrook, age 23, married, Port Phillip tribe, at South Yarra, wife of the one who died on 19 July, this female had on my arrival in Colony a fine infant and has been twice pregnant since but has not left an infant behind Infanticide … (Thomas return of Births and Deaths, CY 2604, frame 284, ML).

At the encampment to the north of Melbourne, Benbow (Little/King, Chief Protector's messenger) complained that his wife (Kitty) had run away from him. Thomas found her and brought her back to Benbow's miam and only then discovered that she had not run away at all, but had been taken away from Benbow and given to another Western Port black (a son, at this stage unnamed, of Old Nern Nern) by her uncle Ningolobin. Ningerranow, whose death on 19 July triggered this sequence of events, was Benbow's wife's father, and as he, the dead Ningerranow had no father still alive, and no son,[171] it fell to Benbow's wife's uncle, Ningollobin, to dispose of her. Thomas argued vehemently with Ningollobin, on the grounds of the length of time – four years – that Benbow's wife had been with Benbow. Ningollobin countered with the fact that Benbow and his lubra had no piccaninnies. Thomas said that no black lubras have piccaninnies now so why was Ningollobin sulky with Benbow?

Thomas won in the end by heavy use of a threat: he had received a letter from La Trobe regarding Benbow's lubra: clearly Benbow had friends in high places. He told Ningollobin that he would take Benbow to the police office and take out a warrant to apprehend Kitty, and take into custody whoever had her, and that if Benbow could not have her, none other should have her. This produced the desired effect, causing Ningollobin to 'beg' Thomas not to do so, and he told Thomas where she was. Thomas found Kitty hiding in the back of her mother's miam but he could not get her out, so he started destroying the miam, only to find her packed between the boughs at the back. He returned Kitty to Benbow, then went and told Old Nerm Nerm how angry he was at him for allowing his son to have Benbow's lubra.[172] The son of Nerm Nerm (Old Billy) was Poligerry aged 18 years whose country was Konigo and the beach (Frankston).[173]

Thomas as a source for the anthropologists has been found wanting in the past compared to Robinson, partly because Thomas failed to recognise the principles that lay behind relationships. Here he did though. His account of the principles under which Ningolobin acted is constructed with perfect grammar, no spelling mistakes, beautiful clear writing and **underlined**: Thomas knew he was recording important information. But they never forgave him, he wrote later, for interfering in customary practice.

> It follows that a father has the disposal of his female offspring, for whom he will; in the event of not having the father, the eldest son; in the event of no father or son, that right devolves upon the uncles, in this case Benbow's wife's father dies and he has no brother, the uncle Ningolobin claimed his right and notwithstanding his niece has been four years married to Benbow, he not having had any children from her, the uncle claims his right and gives her to another.[174]

---

171 Ningerranow had his brother Derrimut still alive but Thomas does not mention any action of his, so, apparently, Derrimut had no rights or responsibilities in this matter. And the problem remains – where are Ningeranon's two fine sons? If their ages were estimated correctly by Thomas in 1839 as 9 and 11, they would be, in the normal course of events, initiated by now, putatively aged 14 and 16.
172 Thomas Journal, CY 2606, item 3, ML. Thomas recalled these events later, stating that La Trobe asked him to intervene, and though he got Kitty back to Benbow 'it was evidently far against the consent of the blacks and by them considered a great infringement on their rights', Thomas to Robinson, 8 November 1846, VPRS 11, Box 10/647, PROV.
173 Thomas Family Connections census, January 1846, CY 3083, ML.
174 Thomas Journal, CY 2606, item 3, frame 220, ML.

Fig 45. 'Boolutt/King Benbow'

Reproduced with the permission of the State Library of New South Wales.

Barlut/Bullut/Bollut/Boollutt/Little Benbow/King Benbow

Portrait in *HRV*, vol 2B: 546.

Harmless man, short time in Native Police Corps, not adapted by nature or disposition to police; seldom out of uniform; good and inoffensive, a chief (Thomas, no date, in Bride 1969[1898]: 406).

17 Apr 1836 – Benbow with Fawkner's party fishing (Fawkner's Journal in Billot 1970: 62); 24 Apr 1836 – With Derrimut and Fawkner's party fishing (Billot 1970: 65).

8 Mar 1837 – Governor Bourke distributed blankets and clothing to about 120 natives … gave 4 brass plates for good conduct to natives recommended by Captain Lonsdale (Bourke's Journal, MS 7759, Box 640/11, SLV).

Jul 1839 – Bul-lut/Benbow, name taken in encampment (Thomas 'A' diary, set 214, item 1, ML); Oct 1839 – Daniel Bunce who came from England originally as a collector of plants for Kew gardens, met Benbow on arrival in Port Phillip; he and his wife Kitty dwelt in a small hut of his own construction in a corner of Mr Batman's garden; everything within clean, in good order; Benbow often consulted by the settlers; always willing to impart information; the only teetotaller Bunce ever met (Bunce 1857: 64); Benbow – one of Daniel Bunce's guides, intelligent and really worthy (*Victoria, Legislative Council Votes & Proceedings*, 1858–59, Select Committee Report: 103);

6 Jan 1840 – With his brother Mangerrer and sister Lillernook, among the party who left Melbourne (Thomas CY 2605, item 1, frame 30, ML); 1840 – Little Benbow and his lubra are listed with Big Benbow as a party of three who are not going to Western Port (Thomas Journal, CY 2605, frame 8, ML).

19 May 1841 – Made drawings of native Benbo and placed them in Kerr's windows today; Benbo is chief of the Weraby tribe … agile … told me that last summer was the hottest for many years … is in want of a musquet … often goes out with me and I let him have it … turkey narrative; 23 May 1841 – Benbo and others prevented Derrimut Chief of the Melbourne tribe from murdering his wife (George Henry Haydon, mf, NL); no date – Benbo speaks English, wears a brass plate Chief of the Weirabee, wears the uniform of a Captain of Marines … expected homage to be paid … 'approached with a majestic step, as if treading on the neck of an emporer' … wears hair plastered with fat and ornamented with kangaroo's teeth tied to the hair in little bunches … wife a short woman about 18 years (Haydon 1846: 49–68).

27 July 1842 – Benbow, 2nd Div of Native Police Corps, on duty with CCL Powlett; rationed since 1 February (Dana return, VPRS 19, Box 30, 42/1143, PROV).

1 Feb 1843 – Sergeant, aged 35, married, 1 wife, no children, never punished, on duty at the Mt Macedon police and at the Loddon and Goulburn (*NSW Legislative Council Votes & Proceedings*, 1844); 23

Feb 1843 – Little Benbow's absence noted by Thomas from the full complement of the Native Police, daubed, in battle formation, with approx. 60 Yarra and Goulburns; they crossed river at the punt to fight with Western Port and Port Phillip (Thomas to Robinson, VPRS 11, Box 10/586, PROV); Benbo – Jul to Sep 1843 – at HQ; Oct to Nov 1843 – with CCL Tyers to Gippsland; 25 Dec 1843 – returned to HQ sick; Mar 1844 – sick; remarks – willing but worn out by his trip to Gippsland (Return, 4/1135.1, AO of NSW); 31 Mar 1842 – Enrolled not at same time as others but some time after (Dana to La Trobe, VPRS 19, Box 28, 42/674, PROV); 3 Nov 1843 – Benbo and Kulklo have I understand accompanied Mr Tyers party (CY 2606, item 2, ML);

29 Jul 1844 – Thomas questioned Benbow re murder of Taurang, aged 22, a Barrabool; Benbow confirmed it and Thomas went to the beach where he found Bobbinary who supplied further info (CY 2606, item 3, ML; Thomas to La Trobe, VPRS 19, Box 61, 44/1308, PROV); 23 Aug 1844 – Benbow's complaint to Thomas that Kitty has run away but actually she has been removed by her uncle (CY 2606, item 3, ML).

Jan 1845 – Chief Benbow who was once instrumental in saving his life farewelled George H Haydon at Williamstown – more regal than ever in the neat white uniform of the Native Police (J Whitlock, 'Gentleman Felix', unpublished Ms: 148); 29 Dec 1845 – Benbo, native place Yarra Yarra, enlisted May 1842, old and useless 1843 (Dana Return, VPRS 19, box 77, 42/2179, PROV).

Jan 1846 – Listed on Thomas' criticism of the Native Police as one of those from the Melbourne tribes who deserted (Quarterly report, enc to 46/3341 in 4/2745.1, AO of NSW); Jan 1846 – Thomas' family connection census lists Bollut, male, Little Benbow and his wife Mortkuningrook as a family of 2 (CY 3083, ML); 1846 – Thomas recalls a tragic case concerning King Benbow in which La Trobe asked him to interfere some years ago. Benbow's wife Kitty, her father died, her uncle claimed his right and insisted on it and Benbow's Kitty was given to another. Thomas got her back but 'evidently far against the consent of the blacks and by them considered a great infringement on their rights' (Thomas to Robinson, VPRS 11, Box 10/647, PROV).

Prior to 1846 when Yankee Yankee died – Old Bembo, Cunningham (Yankee Yankee) and Murray told magistrate William Hull of Port Phillip once being a hunting ground (*Victoria, Legislative Council Votes & Proceedings*, 1858–59: 12).

1845 to 1848 – Benbow sometimes named King Benbow is being rationed by the Aborigines Department; weekly chits signed by GA Robinson are recorded in the departments account book; 12 Mar 1847 – note says same scale as Native Police (VPRS 19, Box 78, unit 46/161 (a) and Box 77, 45/2183, PROV); rations for messenger Benbow, 1 Jan – 31 Dec 1847 (VPRS 26: 42, PROV).

20 Mar 1847 – King Benbow is introducing the Gippsland lubras to Europeans (Thomas Quarterly Report, 47/9842 in 4/2784, AO of NSW); Apr 1847 – Benbow told Robinson that Karn.jin.ditto, a young lubra belonging to Budgery Tom was taken by the sealers (Clark 2002: 121, referring to Robinson Office Papers, April 1847).

7 Jan 1848 – 'King Benbow obtaining a Passage by steamer *Aphrasia* to go to Geelong for the following purpose. Some time ago a white man near Mt Eliza took a black female NAN-NAT-GOOR-RUK down to Kings Island and thence to Geelong on board a ship, and King Benbow is proceeding to Geelong to see this woman and give information of the case to the Chief Protector' (GAR Office Journal of this date, A7079, vol 58, part 6, ML); 18 Mar 1848 – King Benbow accosted by a drunken man who wanted eels which he had caught; King Benbow said **'Me no sell em you, me catch them for gentleman Melbourne, the man took them2 and went off. Me go after him and take my eels out of his hand and he drunken man gave me knock on my mouth & kickd me. Me then put down eels and fight him'** [Thomas' quotation marks]; within five minutes the man came to Thomas and Benbow foaming at the mouth; Thomas sent Benbow on horseback for 2 constables (CY 2606, frames 497–498, ML); 31 Mar 1848 – King Benbow, 'dressed more than ordinarily fine' impressed Thomas with his acknowledgement of breaking a window **'Me been very bad; two Gentlemen make me drunk; me brake'm window; now going to pay for it or let the man take to the Police Office'** [Thomas' quotation marks]. Thomas offered to go with him but Benbow said in reply **'No. Man, a very good man, and me think he no sulky, me pay'** (CY 3084, no frame no, p. 44, ML); same story with the added detail that King Benbow dressed himself very stylish in the uniform of the Commissariat (CY 2606, frame 497, ML); 14 Aug 1848 – Thomas presses King Benbow to resume his duties at the Chief Protector's office as messenger (enc with 48/10697 in 4/2824, AO of NSW); 31 Aug 1848 – Signed memo from La Trobe to GA Robinson stating Benbow wants a blanket and some rations; if his requests are reasonable satisfy them (Papers of GA Robinson, vol 57: between 429–434, A 7078, ML).

28 Feb 1849 – Benbow and his party leave the Saltwater River and camp south of the Yarra. They press me very hard for a country to locate themselves upon (Thomas CY 2606, frame 470, ML); 20 Mar 1849 – King Benbow well equipped in his commissariat uniform waited at the entrance to the Royal Hotel in a queue to be introduced to Governor Fitzroy; he sent up his brass plate, **like white man's letter** [calling card] and bye and bye would see him – his object was to ask the Governor for a country for Western Port blackfellows – he was duped by the white men (Thomas half-yearly report to 30 June 1849, 4/2872, AO of NSW); 10 Apr 1849 – Benbow and his family connections are the only Aborigines permitted to frequent the town of Melbourne but Thomas has just permitted some others who came in for the races to stay until they were over, especially as the Native Police were also attending the races (VPRS 11, Box 11/716, PROV); 11 Dec 1849 – Thomas came to town to hear the case of King Benbow against a man called Thomas, a shoemaker at Brighton, for assault. It was proved that the King was a little the worse for liquor – a rare occurrence – and gave the first provocation. Case dismissed (Thomas Half yearly report 1 July to 31 December 1849, VPRS 10, unit 11, PROV).

25 May 1850 – Kitty and Benbow get blankets from Thomas; 3 Jun 1850 – Benbow asks Thomas for a pair of boots; Thomas says His Honour is out at the moment but when he returns Thomas will ask him; 6 Jun 1850 – Heard His Honour is back, requisitioned him for boots for King Benbow (CY 3127, frames 27–28, ML); 5 Aug 1850 – Thomas' census of the Boonurong or coast tribe lists King Benbow and Kitty at the top of a list of 26 (CY 3127, frame 36, ML); 31 Jul 1850 – Awful murder of a lubra at Geelong by a Geelong black – Benbow[sr] says it is his daughter Bourdgrook (CY 3127, frame 35, ML).

13 Dec 1851 – Thomas' census lists Boollutt alias King Benbow, wife Tallumungrook alias Kitty; Thomas has inserted later that he was dead by 1852 (Thomas Journal, set 214, item 12: 143, ML).

1 Jan 1852 – King Benbow, well known favourite of the old population was carried to Melbourne by the blacks in a helpless condition with rheumatics in every limb. After one months careful attention, he left well (CY 3078, frame 48, ML); 20 Apr 1852 – Thomas requisitions 24 blankets plus other food stores for King Benbow and the coast tribe who are now peaceably encamped within 15 miles of Melbourne (CY 3085, frame 22, ML); 5 Jul 1852 – King Benbow died at Little Brighton on his way to Mordialloc; his subjects were drunk for three days and neglected their king (Thomas in Bride 1983[1898]: 406).

No date – Benbow's wife Kitty died on his grave having refused to move away from it (Smyth 1878, vol 1: 139).

Death from sympathy

Thomas' original account from which Smyth took his story about Kitty dying of grief, not moving from Benbow's grave, lists a number of deaths from sympathy:

- The young lubra [one of three] of Bungerring, an old Mt Macedon black of great family who died 9 March 1848: she greatly burned her body and lacerated herself dreadfully … refused treatment from the Colonial Surgeon and Thomas … sat moping and smoking the whole of the day … said she would die to be with Bangorung … she died 16 days after her husband.
- Ningeranowl's lubra though hearty died a few days after him.
- The same with King Benbow … his lubra could hardly be kept from his grave … died within a few days.
- Pumpkin Murray's lubra died at the foot of Mt Disappointment and he died two days after.
- 'But the most remarkable case of sympathy in death was in two Portland Bay blacks who were brought to Melbourne gaol in 18..[blank]. One was taken ill no doubt through confinement. He was carefully attended to by the Govern^t D^r, but the sick black eventually died. Altho his companion in trouble was apparently in good health, he died the next morning'.[175]

27 August 1844

Tuesday. Thomas was reading the riot act to the blacks about murder … Yankee Yankee assured him that the blacks knew well our laws and that they would be afraid to kill blacks any more.[176]

30 August 1844

Friday. 'Talk to Yanki Yanker on the miserable way of living. What is his answer?'

> **If I like it what's that to white man? He said why not white man learn him to read when take him away. No, he stated, only make me work work and Blk Fellows no like work and never live like white men. He said he believed there was a God but did not believe there was a hell or else white men would not get drunk and swear, they would be afraid of going there.[177]**

175 Thomas Manners and Customs, CY 2606, frame 64, ML.
176 Thomas Journal, CY 2606, item 2, ML.
177 Thomas Journal, CY 2606, item 2, ML.

3 September 1844

Tuesday. Thomas told Yankee Yankee that great good might be done if he would prevail upon the Western Port blacks to settle down and cultivate the ground. His answer was:[178]

> **Where set down? Black Fellows want Kulluck[179] and white man would not let them have it. You know when you was at Tubbarubbabel[180] Black fellows stopped with you and worked and wanted to sow potatoes but you go away and go to the Yarra blacks.** These observations were so [illegible]. I am so often upbraided by the Western Port tribe for removing from them that it is useless arguing with them when I know I have not the power to accede were they so disposed. Go to my quarters for 2 hours and rest.[181]

28 January 1845

Tuesday. Two blacks, Yonker Yonker and Lanky got the body up of Mr Gaull drowned in the Yarra River; Thomas made an enquiry and found that they had behaved very well.[182]

31 June 1845

Yonker Yonker and Nerrimbineck arrive in Melbourne.[183]

3 October 1845

Friday. Yonker Yonker and others arrived this morning.[184]

5 October 1845

Sunday. 'Hear that Yonker Yonker was beastly drunk in the encampment but cannot find him in the encampment'.[185]

---

178   These are Thomas' own quotation marks, unusual for him; he must have regarded Yankee's comment as important.
179   The reserve at Western Port (now Coolart) which the Bonurong chose in June 1840.
180   Thomas' Protectorate Station on Tubberubbabel Creek, about one mile north-east of the crossover of Nepean Highway with the Freeway near Mt Martha.
181   Thomas Journal, CY 2606, item 3, ML.
182   Thomas Journal, CY 2606, item 3, ML.
183   Thomas Journal, 1 to 30 June 1845, Byrt 2004: 104.
184   Thomas Journal, CY 2606, item 3, ML.
185   Thomas Journal, CY 2606, item 3, ML.

7 October 1845

Tuesday. Three blacks – Yonker, Nerrimbineck and Bungarie – go as messengers for the Goulburn blacks.[186]

8 October 1845

Wednesday. Yonker Yonker and the other blacks return who left on Monday.

> A strange account in the *Patriot* this day touching Bob Cunningham. I read it to him; he denies the whole except the drunken part. I tell him that I will make enquiries and if his tale is correct I will contradict that part that is wrong, but not in the least extenuate his drunkenness.

In the margin Thomas noted that he reported this, presumably to the Chief Protector.[187]

8 October 1845

The *Port Phillip Patriot* news item reads as follows:

> The Aborigines. We feel assured that it is only necessary to point out to the Licensed Victuallers the injury which must necessarily arise from supplying the aboriginals with intoxicating liquors for them to abstain from the practice. All hope of bringing these benighted beings within the pale of civilised society must be at an end as they obtain a taste for and can procure supplies of, ardent spirits. So late as Saturday last an aboriginal, well known in Melbourne as Bob Cunninghame, and who is probably the most enlightened of his countrymen was reeling about Little Flinders St in a state of intoxication and beating his lubra with a waddie, who thereupon took refuge in the home of Mr Peacock, the teacher of the aboriginal school, and the door was closed upon her intoxicated husband. Cunninghame became furious, and putting a waddie under the door, forced it open, rushed into the house, overthrew a child six years of age, knocked down a nurse with an infant in her arms and frightened Mrs Peacock into fits, then [mf unclear and the original has a hole in it] his lubra by the hair, he dragged the unfortunate female into the streets towards his miam on the Yarra. Passing through Richmond he was so brutally using the poor woman that a sailor passing interfered and gave Bob Cunningham a sound thrashing. Thus, from the facility of obtaining ardent spirits by an aboriginal has also sanctity

---

186 Thomas Journal, CY 2606, item 3, ML. Messengers were men of status; they could travel anywhere on their job, were always treated courteously and never molested, no matter what the message. Thomas recorded that three messengers denoted an embassy of the greatest importance.
187 Thomas Journal, CY 2606, item 3, ML.

of the dwelling of a respectable citizen been violated – public decency outraged by a woman being beaten in the streets – and the demoralized habits of the black himself only the more strongly confirmed.

9 October 1845

Thursday. Early in the morning 'make an enquiry of Mrs Peacock [wife of the teacher at the Baptist Aboriginal school at Merri Creek], and find that Yonker's account was correct with the exception that he was very abusive and by his manner frightened Mrs Peacock's nurse, but he never maltreated his lubra or anyone'.[188] In the margin Thomas wrote that Mrs Peacock denies the assault attributed to Yonker Yonker.

10 October 1845

Friday. 'Yonker Yonker still in dudgeon on account of the paragraph. I tell him that he had better write to the journal and state it as he stated. I will forward any contribution'.[189]

11 October 1845

Saturday. 'Yonker tells me what to write and signs it with his mark'.[190]

12 October 1845

Monday. 'Yonker Yonker enquired if his letter had gone to the newspaper. I told him that it had'.[191]

Mid 1840s

Youki Youka, stolen from his tribe at Westernport (Haydon's spelling) and taken to an island in the straits; lived there seven or eight years; taken to Adelaide, overlanded to Port Phillip, received with joy by his tribe on his return. Haydon saw him in the 1840s and said he could be distinguished from others only by the good English he speaks; Haydon also said that he was 'a dangerous character ... half civilized and more mischievous'.[192]

January 1846

Yonker Yonker is listed as one of the Native Police who deserted in Thomas' criticism of the Corps.[193]

---

188 Thomas Journal, CY 2606, item 3, ML.
189 Thomas Journal, CY 2606, item 3, ML.
190 Thomas Journal, CY 2606, item 3, ML.
191 Thomas Journal, CY 2606, item 3, ML.. I read the 'Local Intelligence' section of the *Port Phillip Patriot* for the next ten days but could not find that the paper printed Yankee's letter.
192 Haydon 1854: 119.
193 Thomas Quarterly Report, enc to 46/3341 in 4/2745.1, AO of NSW.

6 January 1846

Tuesday. Yonker is one of six persons drunk last night in the encampment, sad this morning; Thomas scolded them.[194]

January 1846

On Thomas' Family Connections Census of the Boongurong of this date as Yonker Yonker, male age 23 years; father Buddurup aka Benbow; mother Mullingrook; sister, Bareboon, female 18 years, aka Mary.[195]

16 January 1846

Friday. Yonker Yonker and one lubra[196] at Thomas' encampment by Yarra.[197]

18 April 1846

Saturday. Yonker Yonker – his name is on a list requested of Thomas by La Trobe, of men suitable to send to King Island.[198]

20 April 1846

Thomas sent the list to La Trobe with Yonker Yonker's name heading it:

- Yonker Yonker – Bob Cunningham
- Kulpendure – Robin
- Gibberook – Net-krum
- Nunuptune – Mr Langhorne
- Poky Poky – Wor rung bare
- Davy – Kur-gun
- Warrengitalong – Ter-roo-urnin
- Yal Yal – Mr Merrick.[199]

18 May 1846

Monday. Yonker and Nerimbineck return from King Island.[200]

---

194   Thomas Journal, CY 2606, item 3, ML.
195   Thomas Correspondence and Returns set 214/10, CY 3083, ML.
196   On Thomas' Family Connections census of 1846, he lists a daughter of Billibellary named Bungurrook, aged 16, as married to Yankee Yankee, CY 3083, ML.
197   Thomas Journal, CY 2606, item 3, ML.
198   Thomas Journal, CY 2606, item 3, ML.
199   Thomas Journal, CY 2606, item 3, frame 347, ML.
200   Thomas Journal, CY 2606, item 3, ML.

23 May 1846

Yonker Yonker and Wigegulk have returned from a voyage to King Island with Mr Sutherland to recover portion of the wreck of the ship *Cataraqui*.[201] They told Thomas that 'there are 3 VDL black lubras there, plus 1 half-caste boy about 12 years of age, and an old Port Phillip lubra who *cried bitterly* and wanted to come away but the white men would not let her; that there were 5 white men living there and that in the scrub some distance from the white men were a number of casks of spirits – gin, rum and brandy'.[202]

The old Port Phillip lubra who cried bitterly

Clark has recovered a good deal of information about this old woman who cried bitterly (though not her name): the following is taken from his report:

> The identity of the 'three Tasmanian women, half-caste Aboriginal boy, and old Port Phillip lubra' seen by Yonki Yonka in May 1846, is revealed in correspondence of 20 June 1856 of William Wilson, from Collingwood Victoria to the Right Reverend the Lord Bishop of Tasmania respecting the welfare of Maria and Georgia.

> ...I would first mention that I did not apply to your Lordship's assistance for these people as a matter of right, but as a matter of charity, and being but an occasional visitor at Robbins Island, it certainly did not occur to me whether they were all natives of Tasmania or not, but knowing they had been on these islands for many years I took it for granted. When I visited Kings Island, three years ago there were two Aboriginal women there Maria and Gudague. The first a native of the East Coast of Tasmania, at Ringarooma River, the last belonging to the Oyster Bay tribe who died on Kings Island, and Maria was removed to Robins Island by Mr Howie.

> Upon making enquiry respecting the other aged woman under Mr Howie's protection I am obliged to admit, however it may militate against the poor creature's interest, that she is not a native of Tasmania, her history is this, she was brought over from Western Port, about thirty

---

201 The *Cataraqui*, an emigrant ship with 415 souls on board, was wrecked on reefs off King Island at 4.30 am on 4 August 1845, with only nine survivors. News reached Melbourne on 13 September and a special edition of the *Port Phillip Herald* was published (Loney n.d.: 12).

202 Thomas Journal, CY 2606, item 3, ML. Jack Loney says that Mr Sutherland was Alexander Sutherland, later the author of *Victoria and Its Metropolis*, who purchased the wreck and contents for £86. He also states that George Coppin held a benefit concert at the Queen's Theatre, which raised £160 for the survivors and the rescuers, Loney n.d.: 12–13.

years ago by a sealer named Munro,[203] with whom she afterwards co[h]abited, that she has one daughter an Aborigine born on the islands, and that daughter has also two girls by a white man who left them soon after their birth and whom they have never seen since, as they are all natives of Tasmania, except the old woman and she has lived there for thirty years I trust the Government will do something for them, the two old women have already reached the span allotted for human life and while I am writing may have one or both passed away. The information I have been able to get and which I believe to be correct is as follows

Maria, a native of Tasmania, Ringarooma River

Old woman, ditto Western Port, Victoria, but living on Kings and other islands 30 years

Pol, an Aborigine, daughter of the above, born on Kings Island

Robert Munro, son of the above, who has assisted in supplying his family for years, and needs nothing himself

Two girls daughters of Pol of 8 and 10 years natives of Tasmania.

Now my Lord, if they are not all positive Aborigines, they have been brought up and live the same, housed in a miam, hunt for a meal before they can eat it, and but for the kindness of Mr + Mrs Howie, would have gone positively naked, I will not presume to dictate to your Lordship, or the Government, but I do sincerely trust something may be done for these poor creatures, if your Lordship could see them, I feel my humble advocacy would be unnecessary.[204]

This letter to the Bishop gives the date of the abduction of Munro's woman as 'about thirty years ago', that is 1826, and the abductor as Munro himself, both facts which are quite contrary to the accepted version derived from Robinson.

2 July 1846

Thursday. 'Yonker Yonker returns from servitude'.[205]

---

203   That Munro brought her over from Port Phillip in the 1820s, or that Meredith brought her over and sold her to Munro is a key issue in the variant interpretations of the abductions.
204   Quotation taken in full from Clark 2002: 111–112. Clark cites the original as Wilson, 20/6/1856 in CSDI/92/2439, Tasmanian State Archives. It is this woman, Pol, about whom opinion differs.
205   Thomas Journal, CY 2606, item 3, ML.

18 August 1846

Yonker Yonker had up before Police this morning; spent the night in the watch house, 'does him good'.[206]

1 September 1846

Yonker Yonker, 'called by some the civilized black' was caught drunk, lodged in gaol, fined ten shillings which was paid by a gentleman.[207]

13 October 1846

Bob Cunningham put in watch house for drunkenness.[208]

14 October 1846

Wednesday. Yonker Yonker committed for assaulting a constable.[209]

14 October 1846

Yonker Yonker alias Bob Cunningham was caught drunk, far from the first time, obstreperous, committed to gaol for 14 days.[210]

15 October 1846

Thursday. Thomas visited Yonker Yonker in gaol and he expressed sorrow for his conduct.[211]

18 October 1846

Sunday. Thomas visited Yonker Yonker in gaol and had 'a serious talk' with him (Thomas says just that – he does not state what the serious talk was about).[212]

21 October 1846

Wednesday. Thomas visited Yonker Yonker in gaol. He was concerned that so many blacks were going to Gippsland and not him.[213]

23 October 1846

Friday. Thomas visited Yonker Yonker in gaol and found him very unwell – 'may this punishmt have its desir'd effect'.[214]

---

206   Thomas Journal, CY 2606, item 3, ML.
207   Thomas Quarterly Report, June to September 1846, enc 46/7609 in 4/2744, AO of NSW.
208   Thomas Journal, CY 2606, item 3, ML.
209   Thomas Journal, CY 2606, item 3, ML.
210   Thomas Quarterly Report, 1 September to 30 November 1845, enc to 46/9277, in 4/2745.1, AO of NSW.
211   Thomas Journal, CY 2606, item 3, ML.
212   Thomas Journal, CY 2606, item 3, ML.
213   Thomas Journal, CY 2606, item 3, ML.
214   Thomas Journal, CY 2606, item 3, ML.

1 November 1846

Sunday. Thomas visits blacks' encampment – 'Yonker a little indisposed like all others are after confinement in gaol – hope he'll be benefited by it'.[215]

4 November 1846

Yonker Yonker died south encampment: a Western Port black.[216]

4 November 1846

'Yonker, Western Port black, aged 23, male, married, died south of the Yarra. Remarks: The most civilized but a great drunkard, who after being reared by the whites to manhood, returned to his native habits'.[217]

5 November 1846

Yonker Yonker, a Bonurong member of the Native Police, while in jail told Thomas that he intended to construct his hut between the Assistant Protector's quarters and the Merri Creek Aboriginal school but did not get the chance, dying after leaving jail.[218]

5 November 1846

Thomas saw a fresh grave, and, aware no one was ill in the district got the district constable to dig it up; it was Yonker Yonker who but a few days previously was released from gaol for drunkenness and assaulting a constable; no marks of violence; he had been slightly poorly since release; reburied him; Thomas deplored the end of this young man 'who had been almost bred and matured to manhood under the whites … at one time he had one pound sterling per week plus rations'.[219]

6 November 1846

Friday. Thomas is concerned who died – no one was ill except Yonker who merely had a pain in his limbs 'on a/c of confinement in gaol'. Thomas got no answer to his question, who died? To his 'utmost surprise' it is Yonker. Thomas decides to have the body exhumed. The blacks are not in mourning.[220]

---

215 Thomas Journal, CY 2606, item 3, ML.
216 Thomas Journal, CY 2606, item 3, ML.
217 Thomas Return of Deaths, September to November 1846, enc to 46/9277 in 4/2745.1, AO of NSW.
218 Thomas Quarterly Report, 1 September to 30 November 1846, VPRS 4410, unit 3/93, PROV.
219 Thomas Quarterly Report, 1 September to 30 November 1846, enc to 46/9277 in 4/2745.1, AO of NSW.
220 Thomas Journal, CY 2606, item 3, ML.

9 November 1846

Monday. Thomas applied to the magistrate for permission to exhume the body, and the services of two constables to do the digging. Granted. They dug up the body but there were no marks of violence.[221]

17 November 1846

This day's entry in Robinson's Journal merely records 'Bob Cunningham dead'.[222] Robinson had just returned from a visit to the Goulbourn protectorate station from 10 to 16 November, but he was in his office all the previous weeks and failed to mention Yankee Yankee.

9 November 1858

William Hull JP gave the following testimony to the Select Committee in Melbourne:

> He was an authority on blacks beliefs ... Robert Yang Yang Cunningham, who was a very superior person indeed and a highly intellectual man, and spoke English fluently ... Yang Yang became very confident and I could get almost anything [information] out of him, but always with the strict injunction to secrecy ... Robert Cunningham told me [about the transmigration of souls] **'White fellow come from Pindye; black fellow when he die go to Pindye one way west then come back again east, jump up whitefellow'**... I may mention that one night I showed Robert Cunningham the pleides and he said they were children of the moon moon – moondick, and very good to blackfellows.

> Robert You Yang Cunningham is ... a very superior man indeed, and a highly intelligent man and spoke English fluently ... one of the blacks who told Hull that his progenitors recollected when Hobson's bay was a kangaroo ground ... the passage up the bay through which the ships sailed is the old river Yarra which once went out to the heads ... the sea broke in.[223]

---

221 Thomas Journal, CY 2606, item 3, ML.
222 Clark 2000, vol 5: 120.
223 Evidence of William Hull, Esq. J.P. to the Enquiry of the Leg. Co. Select Committee on the Aborigines, *Victoria, Legislative Council Votes & Proceedings*, 1859: 8–12.

12. Thomas' translations

Bunerong language, reproduced from Victoria Legislative Council Votes & Proceedings, 1858–59: 98–100

Aboriginal Language

Translations

The CXXI. Psalm

1. I will lift up mine eyes unto God; from Him cometh my help.

1. Murrumbeek woorunderoneit mynginiek kuding Pundgyl Marman; weda womonner nunlbeunnul.

2. My help cometh from the Lord, who made the heaven and the earth.

2. Murrumbiek nunlbeunnul womoner Pundgyl Marman, wellainer monkeit woorwoor bar beeker.

3. He will not suffer thy foot to be moved; He that keepeth thee will not slumber.

3. Kargee nier malbodoneit murrumbiek tinan; mungither wellainer koonark murrumbinner nier yemoner.

4. Behold! He that keepeth Israel shall neither slumber nor sleep.

4. Wa! Mungither wellainer Koonark murrumbinner nier yemee nier yemoner.

5. The Lord is thy keeper; the Lord is thy shade, upon thy right hand.

5. Pundgyl Marman kunark murrumbinner; Pundgyl Molariek ulbinner munung.

6. The sun shall not smite thee by day, nor the moon by night.

6. Nier ngervein tilbunner murrumbinner yellanwă nier mineam boorundut.

7. The Lord shall preserve thee from all evil; He shall preserve thy soul.

7. Pundgyl Marman nulworthun murrumbinner; nier nillam woman mungither moorupick nulworthununner.

8. The Lord shall preserve thy going out and thy coming in, from this time forth, and even for evermore.

8. Pundgyl Marman nerdoit murrumbinne yannon nulworthun, bar nerdoit womoneit nulworthun murrumbinner, netbo bar wootunno yearamboot tille mille nanbo.

The First Chapter of Genesis[1]

1. In the Beginning God created the heaven and the earth.

1. Ganbronin Pundgyl Marman monguit woorworrer bar beek.

---

1 Abridged in some of the verses, in order to simplify the chapter to suit aboriginal capacity, but the full perport is retained.

2. And the earth was without form and void, and darkness was upon the face of the deep. And the Spirit of God moved upon the face of the waters.

3. And God said, let there be light, and there was light.

4. And God saw the light that it was good, and God divided the light from the darkness.

5. And God called the light day, and the darkness he called night; and the evening and the morning were the first day.

6, 7. And God said, let there be a firmament. And God made the firmament; and divided the waters which were under the firmament, from the waters which were above the firmament, and it was so.

8. And God named the firmament, heaven; and the evening and the morning were the second day.

9. And God said let the waters under the heavens be gathered together unto one place, and let the dry land appear; and it was so.

10. And God called the dry land, earth; and the gathering together of the waters, called he seas: and God saw that is was good.

11, 12, 13. And God said let the earth bring forth grass, herb and trees, whose seed is in itself, and it was so; and God saw that it was good. And the evening and the morning were the third day.

14,15, 16, 17, 18, 19. And God said, let there be light above, to divide the day from the night, and let them be for lights to give light upon the earth, and it was so: and God made two great lights: the greater light to rule (or make) the day: and lesser light to rule (or make) the night. He made the stars also. And God saw that it was good. And the evening and the morning were the fourth day.

20, 21, 22, 23. And God said, let the waters bring forth abundantly of fish, great and small. And fowl that may fly above the earth. And God saw that it was good. And the evening and the morning were the fifth day.

2. Nier beek nowdin netbo, beek tandowring tarkate; nier boit, nier mill, nier taul, nier turrong, nier uungo; bar boorundara kormuk bumile. Bar Moorup Pundgyl warrebonuk narlumbanan parn.

3. Bar Pundgyl Marman tombuk, womear yangamut, bar yangamut woman.

4. Bar Pundgyl Marman nangeit yangamut, bar tombak boundup nge, bar Pundgyl Marman borungnergurk yangamut boorrundara.

5. Bar Pundgyl Marman nerreno yangamut yellenwo, bar borundara borundut; bar krunguine bar banbaneram nerreno ganbronin yellenwă.

6, 7. Bar Pundgyl Marman tombak, malwomear firmament. Bar Pundgyl Marman mongeit narng; bar borungnergurk parn kubberdon beek, bar nungonuk parn kuding karboit tandowring nowdin netbo.

8. Bar Pundgyl Marman nerreno firmament woorwoorrer; bar krungaine bar banban eram nerreno bengerrowlin yellenwă.

9. Bar Pundgyl Marman tombit, malwo mear parn kubberdon woorwoorrer kundee ganbony tombor, bar malwomear palletdebuk; bar nowdin netbo.

10. Bar Pundgyl Marman nerreno bidderup beek (earth), bar wotonno parn nerreno warreen-warreen: bar Pundgyl nangeit kooding nge marnameek.

11, 12, 13. Bar Pundgyl Marman tombit, warra wee boit, bar kunnulderbil kurrenum, bar, terrung willainer kooding nge; bar Pundgyl Marman ngerren bar tombak marnameek. Bar krunguine, bar banban eram yellingwă bengero ganmel.

14, 15, 16, 17, 18, 19. Bar Pundgyl Marman tombak, malwomear yangamut, karboit, bar nungonuk yellenwă bar borandut, tuduk yangamut beeker: tandowring netbo: bar Pundgyl Marman monkeit bengero bullito yangamut: koonge bullito narngate yellenwă, bar wyebo yangamut narngate borundut. Mungither monkeit wotunno topiram nowdin netbo. Bar Pundgyl Marman nangeit koodin marnameek. Bar krunguine bar banbaneram bengero bar bengerowlin yellenwă.

20, 21, 22, 23. Bar Pundgyl Marman tombak, malwomear tuat wootunno; wyebo bar bullito narlumbunner parn. Bar koyup woolwoin karboit beeker. Bar Pundgyl Marman ngerreen boundup nge. Bar krunguine bar banban eram, bengero bar bengero ganmelrowling yellenwă.

24, 25. And God said, let the earth bring forth all living creatures after its kind; and it was so. And God made beasts of the earth, and all cattle after its kind. And God saw that all was good.

24, 25. Bar Pundgyl Marman tombak, mallongener beek, wantagee umarko kunup togan nge; bar tandowring nge. Bar Pundgyl Marman monkeit tukin ungut tandowring nge. Bar Pundgyl Marman nangeit marnameek kuding.

26, 27. And God said let us make man in our image. And God made in his own image, man; in the image of God created he him, male and female created he them.

26, 27. Bar Pundgyl Marman tombak, mallun monkeit kooling tandowring murrumbuniek. Bar Pundgyl Marman monkeit tandowring kargeeiek koolinner, – nowdin kargeeiek monkeit munniger – kooling bar bagrook monkeit murrumnuller.

28, 29. And God blessed them, and said, increase and replenish the earth; and have power over the fish of the sea, and fowl of the air, and all living things. And God gave man every tree and herb bearing fruit and seed for man's food.

28, 29. Bar Pundgyl Marman tombit boundup murrumnuller; geanboon koolinge bagrook bar wootunno bopup kuding beeker; bar umanaro umarko tuat kuding warreen, koyup worworrow bar umarko yeareit togan. Bar Pundgyl Marman uminară koolin umarko turrung, bar umarko uungo tunganan koolinge bagrook.

30, 31. And God gave every living thing to man for food; and it was so. And God saw everything that he had made, and behold it was very good. And the evening and the morning were the sixth day.

30, 31. Bar Pundgyl Marman umanarer kunnulwarrable tuduk tanganan; kuding nge. Bar Pundgyl Marman ngarren umarko kargee mongon, bar wă tombak koongee boundup. Bar krunguine bar banban eram, nerreno bengero, bengero, bar bengerowling yellenwă.

The Creed

I believe in God the Father Almighty Maker of Heaven and Earth; and in Jesus Christ His only Son our Lord; who came down from heaven to save man, and die for his people, who was by wicked men killed and hanged on a tree; who was dead and buried; who rose again the third day from the dead, and ascended into heaven, and sat down at the right hand of God the Father; from whence He shall come again and make all mankind stand before Him; and separate the good from the wicked.
I believe in the Holy Ghost, the resurrection of the body, and the life everlasting – Amen

Murrumbeek nunurrunkella kuding Pundgyl Marman koongee palleek mongeit woorwoorrer bar beeker; bar kuding Jesus Christ Tindee mummum murrumbununner Lord; wellainer burrawee woorwoorrer mongonner koolinge bagrook marnameek; wellainer nillam koolinglilbuk wenkeit bar berbuk, narlumboon burrung; wellainer weagoulaneit bar numbuk; wellainer tinderbeek bengero ganmel yellenwă, kuding commargee nunnumo, bar kubboweer woorwooroit bar narlumby ulbinner munung Pundgyl Marmanieek; Uungo yellenwă Jesus Christ nerlingo mongoin umarko koolinge bagrook terridee kargeeiek; bar pindoner boundup bar meunga.
Murrumbeek nunarrunkellă Boundup Moorrup commargee murrum, bar moorrup, tillee millee nangbo – Amen

The Lord's Prayer

Our Father who art in heaven; hallowed be
Thy name; Thy kingdom come; Thy will
be done on earth like it in heaven. Give us
this day our daily food; and forgive us our
bad deeds, as we forgive them that do us
bad; and keep us from sin this day, and
from all evil.
Only Thou O Great Father can keep us
now and ever – Amen

Marmanellă Marman wellainer narlumboon
karboit; nerrīno murrumbinner koongee
boundup; woman trangbulk murrumbinner
mongon tandowring beeker. Umarleek nurnin
yellenwă tanganan; bar narlarnarny nurnin
nowdin murrumarter narlarnarny ungo; bar
kunark nurnin watticar koolin yellenwă nier
nillam womeit.
Tindu Murrumbinner, Boundup Marman,
nulworthen nurnin Netbo bar nanbo – Amen

From Church Service

My dear blackfellows – God's book tells
us in many places to acknowledge and
confess our many sins, and that we
should not hide them before the face of
Almighty God, but confess them with
sorrow, that we may have forgiveness
of them through His great goodness; and
though every day we ought to tell God
our sins, yet more so on Sunday, when
we all meet together; to thank Him for all
His goodness; to hear His good book; and
to ask all good for our bodies and souls.
So let us all, as many as are now here,
fall upon our knees, and pray to our Great
Father in heaven, saying – &c. &c.

Murrumbiek koolin, – kunne paper wă
Pundgyl Marman tombak wongonon, dado
pardogurrabun tomboon nillam nurnin koonge
meungo bar nier euletbee nillam nurnin tuduk
nier wongrunin pallat Pundgyl Marman,
tindee mardon mallun tombak mongderrewat
mardoneit kunnup Pundgyl Marman yangally
narrite umarko boundup rige; bar nelnwă
pardogurrabun banban eram bar krunguite
Pundgyl Marman, nerdoit bullito Sunday womon
wotunno pardogurrabun narlumby umarko;
thank Mungither tuduk umarko boundup
narngon kargeiek berkerk; tombarlarnon
yarrite boundup murrum bar moorup; netbo,
malpardogurrabun umarko, marlumbunun mihu
bullito Pundgyl boundup Marman narlumboon
karboti tom-der-run-en-er – &c. &c.

Hymn to Old Hundred

1. Pund-gyl Mar-man, bar mar-na-meek
   Nun-guk kub-ber-don mur-rum-beek
   Mong-der-re-wat koo-lin net-bo
   Tan-dow-ring koon-gee mur-rum-bo.

2. Mal-yeng-erk par-do-gur-ra-bun
   Tu-duk yar-rite ko-dun-un-un
   Ner-rem-bee bo-run, yel-len-wa
   Nul-wor-then bo-pup Koo-lin-er.

3. Ner-doit ye-men-ner mur-rum-beek
   Lack-boo-ding myng-ner kar-gee-iek
   Bar ner-doit yan-na-ner war-reet
   Kar-gee nger-ren-er mur-rum-beek.

&c. &c.

Catechism

Q. – Tell me, my child, who made you?

A. – The Great God who made the heaven and the earth.

Q. – Tombannerek murrumbiek bopup, wellainer mongeit murrumbinner?

A. – Pundgyl Marman weda mongut woor-woor-rer bar beeker.

&c. &c.

Afterword

This then, is what I have made of the evidence: there is no conclusion, no grand summing up. I have, it is true, done more than I set out to do, in the sense of ranging outside the stated period of research in search of meaning, but still... no generalisations.

The teacher whom I admired most in my far-off student days was the late Emeritus Professor Greg Dening. Over and over and over again, he taught that the historical effort was to *understand* and to *explain*: not to judge, not to label, not to take sides. In this task of *understanding*, one of the methods is called by the anthropologist Clifford Geertz 'thick description': it amounts to giving the reader as much detail and context as possible, so that the reader is offered the possibility of knowing nearly as much as the researcher. There is then no need to say 'they were this' and 'they were that' because the reader can make up his or her own mind. So... no conclusions.

Time will tell what the textbook writers make of it, amounting, as it does, to a contrarian view to the prevailing orthodoxy. The generalists will be obliged to fit the story of this amiable, intimate, non-violent coexistence on the Mornington Peninsula into their narratives of confrontation, massacres and victimhood throughout the rest of Victoria. There is no doubt that awful things happened in Victoria, but the fact that they didn't happen on the Mornington Peninsula is not explained by the facile 'our lot were a peaceful lot' of the past. If nothing else, this work demonstrates that matters were far more complex than that.

As with the Native Police Corps, *individuals matter, and their feelings shape events*. We are talking about 83 people who owned the land from Werribbee to Wilson's Prom, engaged in a relationship with a well intentioned European who kept a diary, of which a few months relate to our district. Yet what an impression Thomas has given us of their humanity.

There is no place to hide from their logic that the sheep eat the grass that belongs to the kangaroo, and the kangaroo are gone and therefore why can't we eat the sheep? The things that they wanted from Europeans were flour, meat, tea with sugar (from the vocabulary, it seems that even the children drank tea with sugar) and guns: I can imagine a different past for Victoria if only we'd paid the rent in sheep, according to *their* logic, instead of arresting them for sheep stealing.

Were I to dedicate this work, it would be to the old Bonurong woman on King Island who cried bitterly at not going home.

Were it not so politically incorrect and legally irresponsible, I would like to box Yankee Yankee's ears, and that response itself is a good lesson in bad history, because how do we know whether he *wouldn't* bring her back or really *couldn't* bring her back? (There is possibly more to be discovered about this episode in later records - in this case, in Superintendent's Incoming Correspondence, VPRS 19).

I stand silent before the logic of those women who would not raise children in a world which no longer held a future for them. What must they have felt? And I hope never to see in print again the falsity that 90 per cent of the Bonurong suffered from the venereal, or that they were the Tal Tals, or that they stole Willoughby's child. The chasing down of evidence in Chapter 11 is probably a bit obsessive, but asking questions, chasing down dead ends and ruling out possibilities is all part of research: in this case, we need to know who Margery Munro was because the foundation narratives of both contemporary claimant groups depend on her.

The biographical details are the platform for future work - every one of them probably leads to another story like this one. And I hope that the next story to be told will be that of the Protectorate at Narre Warren.

Bibliography

Manuscript sources

Aboriginal Affairs Records, microfilm VPRS 4467, Public Records Office of Victoria (PROV).

Barwick, Diane E, Papers, Ms 13521, State Library of Victoria (SLV).

Cheeseman, HA, 'A short Historical Sketch of the District', talk given to the Gardenvale Historical Society, 2 March 1925, in Cheeseman Family Papers, Brighton Historical Society, Victoria.

Cooper, John B, 'The History of Brighton 1842–1925', Ms, Brighton City Library, Victoria.

D'Arcy, Jacqueline, 8 October 2009, The Problem with Louisa Briggs, Draft Ms.

Dredge, James, Diaries, Ms 5244, SLV.

Franklin, Lady Jane, 'Diary of a Journey from Port Phillip to Sydney 3 April to 27 May 1839', xerox copy (original in NLA), Ms 7942, Box 640/10, SLV.

Haydon, George Henry, 'The Australian diaries and sketches of George Henry Haydon 1840–1845', microfilm July 1967, National Library of Australia (NLA).

Hobson Family Papers, Ms 8457, Box 865/3A, SLV.

Hollinshed, CN, undated, 'A History of the Mornington Peninsula to 1900', Typescript, Time Booksellers.

Kenyon, AS, Papers, Ms 7597, Ms 12173, SLV.

Lang, JD, Papers, A 2229, vol 9, CY 900, Mitchell Library, Sydney.

La Trobe, Charles Joseph, 'Memoranda of Journeys, excursions and absences, 1839–1854', Ms 130003, SLV.

Lilly, George, Papers, Ms 11879, Box 2400/2 (a–c), SLV.

McCrae, George Gordon, 'Reminiscences, vols 2, 3, 4', Ms 12018, Box 2523/4/ items b and c and Box 2523/5/d, SLV.

Meyrick, Henry Howard, Letters, Ms 7959, Box 654, SLV.

NSW and Port Phillip General Post Office Directory for 1839, 1987, Microfiche, NLA.

Nicholson, Ian, undated, 'Ships of the "Colonial Marine", i.e. Government Vessels of NSW and VDL, 1788 to 1850s, together with Nominal Lists of Officers Afloat & related Dockyard Officials, etc', Typescript, Launceston Library.

Port Phillip Association Papers, Ms 11230, SLV.

Port Phillip box 4/1135.1, Archives Office (AO) of NSW.

Rawson, Samuel, 'Journal of an expedition after some VDL blacks', and 'Journal from November 1839 kept while forming a new station at Western Port, on the southern coast of New Holland', Ms 204/1, NLA.

Rawson Papers, Ms 1029, folder 4, NLA.

Robinson Papers, vol 54, A 7075/1, ML.

Smyth, Robert Brough, Papers, Ms 8781, Box 1176/6, SLV.

Strode, Thomas, 'Annals and Reminiscences of Bygone Days: Historical, Statistical and Social, being some contributions to the early history of Port Phillip, together with incidents not generally known, By a Melburnian of 1838', Ms 19, (3 vols), NLA.

Strutt, William, 'Cooey or the Trackers of Glenferrie', Ms 5985, NLA.

— 'Autobiography Australia and New Zealand 1850–1862', Typescript, Ms 4294, NLA.

Todd, William, 'Journal June to November 1835 at Indented Head', Ms 7692, Box 28/11, SLV.

Thomas, William, Papers 1834–1868 (1902), uncat Ms, set 214, Mitchell Library.

Whitlock, Judith, 'Gentleman Felix: The Biography of George Henry Haydon' (1822–91), unpublished Ms, Broadstairs, Kent.

Maps

Fels Hughes Composite, Buckkermitterwarer, 25 June 2008.

Fels, MH, P Hughes and FDHS 2009, *The Boon-Wurrung Mornington Peninsula*.

Keble, RA 1951, *Geology of the Mornington Peninsula and part of Phillip Island*, Department of Mines.

Nutt, Thomas H 1841, 'Plan of a Special Survey selected by Hugh Jamieson Esq. in the Parish of Kangerong', SS 5, PROV.

Owens, W, *Map of Victoria with Pastoral Runs 1869–1870*, NLA.

Selwyn, Alfred 1854, *Mornington Peninsula*, SLV.

Smythe, George D 1841, 'Survey the Coast of Port Phillip from the Mouth of Tangenong Creek to Arthur's Seat', CS 81A, PROV.

— 1841, 'Survey the Coast from the west side of Port Phillip to Western Port', CS 17A, PROV.

— 1842, 'Survey of the Islands of Western Port', PROV.

Thomas, William, 'A Map of Western Port District', VPRS 4410, unit 3/67, PROV.

— 'Part of Western Port District', CY 2984, frame 300, ML.

— Sketch, Tuerong with surrounding stations CY 2984, p. 529, ML.

— Sketch of West Gippsland from islands of Western Port to Tarwin River, CY 2894, p. 523, ML.

— Sketch 'Blacks say burst from by earthquake', CY 2984, p. 543, ML.

— 'Boundary South of Yarra Blacks Country', CY 2984, p. 535, ML.

— 12 July 1840, Sketch from mudmap of journey round country, CY 2604, item 3, ML.

Published sources, Reports and Theses

Alexander, John 1994, *Nepean Limestone*, Nepean Historical Society, Sorrento, Victoria.

Amery, R 1996, 'Kaurna in Tasmania: a case of mistaken identity', *Aboriginal History* 20: 24–50.

Attwood, Bain 2003, *Rights for Aborigines*, Allen & Unwin, Melbourne.

— 2005, *Telling the Truth about Aboriginal History*, Allen & Unwin, Melbourne.

— 2009, *Possession: Batman's Treaty and the Matter of History*, Miegunyah Press, Carlton.

Barwick, Diane E 1962, 'Economic absorption without assimilation: the case of some part-Aboriginal families', *Oceania* 33(1): 18–23.

— 1971, 'Changes in the Aboriginal population of Victoria, 1863–1966', in DJ Mulvaney and J Golson (eds), *Aboriginal Man and Environment in Australia*, ANU Press, Canberra.

— 1972, 'Coranderrk and Cumeroogunga: pioneers and policy', in *Opportunity and Response: Case Studies in Economic Development*, T Scarlett Epstein and David H Penny, C Hurst, London.

— 1974, 'And the Lubras are ladies now', in *Woman's Role in Aboriginal Society*, Fay Gale (ed), Australian Institute of Aboriginal Studies, Canberra.

— 1984, 'Mapping the past: an atlas of Victorian clans, 1835–1904', *Aboriginal History* 8: 100–131.

— 1985, 'This most resolute lady: a biographical puzzle', in *Metaphors of Interpretation: Essays in Honour of W.E.H. Stanner*, Diane E Barwick, Jeremy Beckett and Marie Reay (eds), ANU Press, Canberra.

— 1998, *Rebellion at Coranderrk*, Aboriginal History Monograph 5, Canberra.

Bateson, Charles 1963, *Gold Fleet for California*, Ure Smith, Sydney.

— 1972, *Australian Shipwrecks*, vol 1, 1622–1850, AH & AW Reed, Sydney.

Bennett, Bruce and Arthur Woodley 2000, *Stony Point–The Heart of Western Port*, Crib Point, Victoria.

Billis, RV and AS Kenyon 1974[1930], *Pastures New; an Account of the Pastoral Occupation of Port Phillip*, Stockland Press, Melbourne.

— 1974[1932], *Pastoral Pioneers of Port Phillip*, Stockland Press, Melbourne.

Billot, CP 1970, *Melbourne: an Annotated Bibliography to 1850*, Rippleside Press, Geelong.

— 1982. See under Fawkner.

Bonwick, James 1856, *Discovery and Settlement of Port Phillip*, George Robertson, Melbourne.

Boys, RD 1935, *First Years at Port Phillip*, Robertson and Mullens, Melbourne.

Bride, Thomas Francis (ed) 1898, *Letters from Victorian Pioneers, being a series of papers on the early occupation of the Colony, the Aborigines, etc...*, Trustees of the Public Library, Government Printer, Melbourne.

— 1969[1898], *Letters from Victorian Pioneers...*, William Heinemann Ltd, Melbourne.

— 1983[1898], *Letters from Victorian Pioneers...*, 3rd edn, Lloyd O'Neil Ltd, Victoria.

Briggs, Carolyn 2000, *An Address to the Parliament of Victoria*, Hansard Transcript 31 May.

Brodribb, William Adams 1978[1883], *Recollections of an Australian Squatter*, Ferguson, Sydney.

— 1976, *Recollections of an Australian Squatter* (1883), together with Lavinia Hassell Bennett, *Account of a Journey into Gipps Land* (1844), Queensberry Hill Press, Melbourne.

Brookes, Mabel 1956, *Crowded Galleries*, Heinemann, Melbourne.

Brown, PL (ed) 1935, *Narrative of George Russell*, Oxford University Press, London.

— (ed) 1941–1971, *Clyde Company Papers*, 7 vols, Oxford University Press, London.

Bunce, Daniel 1857, *Australasiatic Reminiscences of Twenty-three Years Wanderings in Tasmania and the Australias*, Hendy, Melbourne.

Byrne, Gerald 1932, 'Early days of the Mornington Peninsula', *Victorian Historical Magazine* 14(4), December: 166–194.

Byrt, Pauline N 2004, *The Thomas Papers in the Mitchell Library: A Comprehensive Index*, (includes CD ROM), Centre for Australian Indigenous Studies, Monash University,

Campbell, Alistair H n.d., *John Batman and the Aborigines*, Kibble Books, Malmsbury, Victoria.

Cannon, Michael et al (eds) 1981–1998, *Historical Records of Victoria. Foundation Series (HRV), Volume 1, Beginnings of Permanent Government* (1981); *Volume 2A, The Aborigines of Port Phillip 1835–1839* (1982); *Volume 2B, Aborigines and Protectors 1838–1839* (1983); *Volume 4, Communications, Trade and Transport 1836–1839* (1985); *Volume 6, The Crown, the Land and the Squatter 1835–1840* (1991); *Public Record Office of Victoria, Melbourne; Volume 7, Public Finance of Port Phillip 1836–1840* (1998), Melbourne University Press, Melbourne.

Cawthorne, WA 1926[1823], *The Kangaroo Islanders: A Story of South Australia before Colonization*, Rigby, Adelaide.

Clark, Ian D 1998–2000, *The Journals of George Augustus Robinson, Chief Protector, Port Phillip Aboriginal Protectorate*, 6 vols, Heritage Matters, Melbourne and Clarendon.

— 1998b, *'That's my country belonging to me': Aboriginal Land Tenure and Dispossession in Nineteenth Century Western Victoria*, Heritage Matters, Melbourne.

— 2002, An Assessment of Boonwurrung Interest from Genealogical and Territorial Perspectives (Report 11 September 2002), Heritage Matters Pty Ltd, Victoria

— 2005a, 'Antecedent force: the Port Phillip Aboriginal Protectorate Domestic Europeans Constabulary, 1840–43', *Victorian Historical Journal* 76(1), April: 68–82.

— 2005b, 'Derrimut "traitor, saviour or a man of his people"', *Journal of the Royal Historical Society of Victoria* 91(2): 107–132.

Clark, Ian and Toby Heydon 2002, *Dictionary of Aboriginal Placenames of Victoria*, Victorian Aboriginal Corporation for Languages, Melbourne.

— 2004, *A Bend in the Yarra: A History of the Merri Creek Protectorate Station and Merri Creek Aboriginal School 1841–1851*, Australian Institute of Aboriginal and Torres Strait Islander Studies, Canberra.

Clarke, Keith M 1999, *Convicts of the Port Phillip District*, CPN, Fyshwick, Australian Capital Territory.

Cole, Valda 1984, *Western Port Chronology 1798–1839, Exploration to Settlement*, Shire of Hastings Historical Society, Hastings, Victoria.

Copland, Gordon 2002, *The Mysteries of Karta (alias Kangaroo Island), Creation, Colonisers and Crusoes*, Counterpoints, Flinders University Online Journal of Interdisciplinary Studies Conference Papers.

Cotter, R (ed) 2005, *A Cloud of Hapless Foreboding: Assistant Protector William Thomas and the Port Phillip Aborigines 1839-1840*, Nepean Historical Society, Sorrento, Victoria.

Court, BW 1980, *Prospector's Guide*, 10th edn, Department of Minerals and Energy, Victoria.

Coutts, PJF 1983, *Corinella: a Forgotten Episode in Victoria's History*, Records of the Victoria Archaeological Survey, no 15.

Crawford, Ian Maxwell 1966, 'William Thomas and the Port Phillip Protectorate 1838–1849', MA thesis, University of Melbourne, Melbourne.

Critchett, Jan 1990, *A Distant Field of Murder*, Melbourne University Press, Melbourne.

Cumpston, JS 1970, *Kangaroo Island 1800–1836*, Roebuck Society Publications no 1, Roebuck, Canberra.

Date, Val 1992, *Castles in the Sky: a Biography of the Family of Dr Edward Lutterell, Colonial Surgeon of Van Diemen's Land, 1816–1821*, Dromana, Victoria.

de Serville, Paul 1980, *Port Phillip Gentlemen and Good Society in Melbourne before the Gold Rushes*, Oxford University Press, Melbourne.

Evans, Heather 1983, *The Aboriginal People of Victoria: Select Bibliography of pre 1960 Printed Sources in the Collections of the State Library of Victoria*, SLV, Melbourne.

Fawkner, JP 1982, *Melbourne's Missing Chronicles*, CP Billot (ed), Quartet, Melbourne.

Fels, MH 1986, 'A quasi-policing expedition in 1838', *Aboriginal History* 10(2): 117–129.

— 1988, *Good Men and True: the Aboriginal Police of the Port Phillip District, 1837–1853*, Melbourne University Press, Melbourne.

— 1989, 'The La Trobe Library collection of the papers of Assistant Protector William Thomas', *The La Trobe Journal* 11(43), Autumn: 13–15.

Fleming, James 1979, 'The voyage of His Majesty's Colonial Schooner *Cumberland* from Sydney to King Island and Port Phillip in 1802–3', in *Historical Records of Port Phillip: The First Annals of the Colony of Victoria*, (Papers presented to Parliament 1878), John J Shillinglaw, Heinemann, Melbourne.

Forth, Gordon (ed) 1998, *The Biographical Dictionary of the Western District of Victoria*, Hyland House, South Melbourne.

Foxcroft, EJB 1940–1941, 'The NSW Aborigines' Protectorate, Port Phillip District, 1838–1850', *Historical Studies*, Pt 1 in vol 1 (April 1940-October 1941): 76–84 and Pt 2 in vol 1, no 3 (April 1941): 157–167.

Gooch, Ruth 2006, *Frontier French Island*, Warrangine Word, Hastings, Victoria.

— 2008, *Seal Rocks*, Warrangine Word, Hastings, Victoria.

Gordon, Malcolm 1997, *Victoria's Mornington Peninsula*, Loch Haven Books, Dromana, Victoria.

Gunson, Niel 1968, *The Good Country: Cranbourne Shire*, Cheshire, Melbourne.

Gurner, Henry Field 1978[1876], *Chronicle of Port Phillip now the Colony of Victoria from 1770 to 1840*, Hugh Anderson (ed), Red Rooster Press, Melbourne.

Hales, Jeremy and Marion Le Cheminant 1997. See under Meyrick, Henry Howard.

Hamilton, Anne 1937, *James Clow: A Memoir*, Ramsay, Melbourne.

Hardy, AD 1942, 'The early settlement of Port Phillip', *Victorian Historical Magazine* 19(3): 96–104.

Hart, Alfred 1929, 'Notes from an early diary of Sir Redmond Barry, 1839–1842', *Victorian Historical Magazine* 13: 133–145.

Hawdon, Joseph 1952, *The Journal of a Journey from New South Wales to Adelaide Performed in 1838*, Georgian House, Melbourne.

Haydon, George Henry 1846, *Five Years in Australia Felix*, Hamilton Adams & Co, London.

— 1854, *The Australian Emigrant: a Rambling Story Containing as much Fact as Fiction*, Arthur Hall, Virtue & Co, London.

Hibbins, Gillian 1984, *A History of the City of Springvale: Constellation of Communities*, City of Springvale, Lothian Publishing Co, Melbourne.

Historical Records of Australia (HRA), series 1, vol 26; series 3, vol 6 ('Instructions despatches and miscellaneous papers relative to Western Port 1826–7').

Historical Records of Victoria (HRV). See under Cannon.

Hollinshed, CN 1958, 'The Nepean Peninsula in the nineteenth century', *Victorian Historical Magazine* 28(4), December: 145–204.

Hopton, Arthur James 1960, 'A pioneer of two colonies: John Pascoe Fawkner Part 3', *Victorian Historical Magazine* 30(3), April: 103–169.

Hovell, William H 1827, 'Report 1827', *Historical Records of Australia*, series 3, vol 5.

Howitt, AW 1904, *The Native Tribes of South-East Australia*, Macmillan, London.

Howitt, Richard 1845, 'Account of my walk to Western Port and Cape Schanck in 1843', in *Australia: Historical, Descriptive and Statistic*, Longman, London.

Johnston, Anna and Mitchell Rolls (eds) 2008, *Reading Robinson: Companion Essays to Friendly Mission*, Quintus Publishing, Hobart.

Keble, RA 1928, 'Kitchen middens on the Mornington Peninsula', *Victorian Naturalist* 45(6), October: 151–159.

— 1968[1950], *The Mornington Peninsula*, Memoirs of the Geological Survey of Victoria No 17, Department of Mines, Melbourne.

Kerr, William 1841, *Melbourne Almanac and Port Phillip Directory 1841*, Kerr and Holmes, Collins Street, Melbourne.

Labilliere, Francis Peter 1878, *Early History of the Colony of Victoria*, 2 vols, Sampson Low, London.

Loney, Jack n.d., *Maritime Australia*, Quadricolor, Melbourne.

Lowe, Robert 2002, *The Mish*, University of Queensland Press, St Lucia, Brisbane.

McCrae, George Gordon 1911, 'The early settlement of the eastern shores of Port Phillip Bay: with a note on the Aborigines of the coast', *Victorian Historical Magazine* 1: 17–26.

— 1912, 'Some recollections of Melbourne in the forties', *Victorian Historical Magazine* 2(3), November: 114–136.

— 1917, 'A vocabulary of the "Western Port" Aborigines', *Victorian Historical Magazine* 5(4), June: 164–170.

— 1987, *Recollections of Melbourne and Port Phillip in the early Forties*, Sullivan's Cove, Adelaide.

McCrae, Hugh (ed) 1934, *Georgiana's Journal, Melbourne, a Hundred Years Ago*, Angus & Robertson, Sydney.

— (ed) 1966, *Georgiana's Journal, Melbourne, 1841–1865*, 2nd edn, Angus & Robertson, Sydney.

Macfarlane, Ian (ed) 1984, *1842: The Public Executions at Melbourne,* Government Printer, Melbourne.

McKay, A (ed) 1962, *Journals of the Land Commissioners for VDL 1826–28*, THRA, Hobart.

MacKellar, Maggie 2008, *Strangers in a Foreign Land: The Journal of Niel Black and Other Voices from the Western District*, State Library of Victoria and Miegunyah Press, Melbourne.

McLear, Colin 2006, *A Dreamtime of Dromana: a History of Dromana through the Eyes of a Pioneering Family*, Dromana and District Historical Society.

McLeod, I 2006, *Settlers California Bound and Returns, 1849–1850*, Genealogy Centre, State Library of Victoria, Melbourne.

Massola, Aldo 1968, *Bunjil's Cave: Myths, Legends and Superstitions of the Aborigines of South-east Australia*, Lansdowne Press, Melbourne.

Meyrick, F.J 1939, *Life in the Bush 1840–1847: A Memoir of Henry Howard Meyrick*, Thomas Nelson, London.

Meyrick, Henry Howard 1997, *The Letters of Henry Howard Meyrick, May 1840–November 1841, and January 1845–April 1847*, transcribed and introduced by Jeremy Hales and Marion Le Cheminant, JJB Publishing, Maffra, Victoria.

Mulvaney, Derek J 1970, 'The anthropologist as tribal elder', *Mankind* 7: 205–217.

Murray, John 2001, *The Summer Survey: Log of the Lady Nelson 1801–1802*, with introduction and notes by Valda Cole, Western Port Historical Society Inc, Hastings, Victoria.

Niall, Brenda 1994, *Georgiana*, Melbourne University Press, Melbourne.

Nicholson, Ian 1988, *Log of Logs*, (Volume 1), Roebuck Society Publications no 41, Roebuck, Canberra.

NSW Legislative Council Votes & Proceedings, 1843-44.

Parsons, Ronald 1982, *Australian Shipowners and their Fleets*, vol 7, *Sydney of 1840s*, Murray Bridge, South Australia.

Pascoe, Bruce 2007, *The Convincing Ground: Learning to Fall in Love with your Country*, Aboriginal Studies Press, Canberra.

Pascoe, Crawford 1897, *A Roving Commission: Naval Reminiscences*, George Robertson and Co, Melbourne.

Plomley, NJB 1966, *Friendly Mission: The Tasmanian Journals and Papers of George Augustus Robinson, 1829–1834*, Tasmanian Historical Research Association, Hobart.

— 1987, *Weep in Silence: a History of the Flinders Island Aboriginal Settlement*, Blubber Head Press, Hobart.

— n.d., *The Westlake Papers: Records of interviews in Tasmania by Ernest Westlake, 1908–1910*, Occasional paper No 4, Queen Victoria Museum and Art Gallery, Launceston.

Plomley, NJB and Kristen A Henley 1990, *The Sealers of Bass Strait and the Cape Barren Island Community*, Blubber Head Press, Hobart.

Port Phillip Expenditure Accounts for the year 1841 (1976), Public Records Office, Melbourne.

Rae Ellis, Vivienne 1981, *Trucanini: Queen or Traitor?*, Australian Institute of Aboriginal Studies, Canberra.

— 1988, *Black Robinson: Protector of Aborigines*, Melbourne University Press, Melbourne.

Reed, L 2004, 'Rethinking William Thomas, "friend" of the Aborigines', *Aboriginal History* 28: 87-99.

Rhodes, David and Stephen Compton 2005, 'Strategies for conservation and management of indigenous cultural sites in a rapidly developing urban environment: a case study from Melbourne', *ICOMOS Symposium*, <http://www.international.icomos.org/xian2005/papers/3-17.pdf>.

Russell, A 1840, *A Tour through the Australian Colonies in 1839*, Robertson Campbell, Glasgow.

Russell, Penny 2002, *This Errant Lady: Jane Franklin's Overland Journey to Port Phillip and Sydney 1839*, National Library of Australia, Canberra.

Ryan, Lyndall 1980, *The Aboriginal Tasmanians*, University of Queensland Press, St Lucia, Brisbane.

Selby, Isaac 1924, *The Old Pioneers' Memorial History of Melbourne from the Discovery of Port Phillip down to the World War*, Pioneers' Memorial Fund, Melbourne.

Selwyn, Alfred RC 1854, 'Report on the Geology, Palaeontology and Mineralogy of the country situated between Melbourne, Western Port Bay, Cape Schanck and Point Nepean', *Victoria Legislative Council Votes and Proceedings*.

Shaw, AGL 1989–90, 'Vandemonian influences on Port Phillip settlement', *Bulletin of the Centre for Tasmanian Historical Studies* 2(2): 15-33.

— 2003, *A History of the Port Phillip District: Victoria before Separation*, Melbourne University Press, Melbourne.

Shellam, Tiffany 2009, *Shaking Hands on the Fringe: Negotiating the Aboriginal World at King George's Sound*, University of Western Australia Press, Crowley.

Shillinglaw, John Joseph 1972[1879], *Historical Records of Port Phillip: The First Annals of the Colony of Victoria*, Heinemann, Melbourne.

Smyth, R Brough 1878, *The Aborigines of Victoria; with Notes relating to the habits of the Natives of other Parts of Australia and Tasmania. Compiled from various sources for the Government of Victoria*, 2 vols, Government Printer, Melbourne; Trubner and Co, London.

— 1972[1878], *The Aborigines of Victoria...*, John Currey, O'Neil, Melbourne

Strutt, William 1980, *Victoria the Golden,* with narrative by Marjorie Tipping, Library Committee, Parliament of Victoria, Melbourne.

Sullivan, H 1981, *An Archaeological Survey of the Mornington Peninsula*, Ministry of Conservation, Victoria.

Sullivan, Martin 1985, *Men and Women of Port Phillip*, Hale and Iremonger, Sydney.

Sutherland, Alexander 1888, *Victoria and its Metropolis Past and Present*, 2 vols, McCarron Bird and Co, Melbourne.

Syme, Marten A 1984, *Shipping Arrivals and Departures, Victorian Ports, vol.1. 1798–1845*, Roebuck Society Publications no 32, Roebuck, Canberra.

Symons, JC 1870, *Life of the Rev. Daniel James Draper*, Hodder & Stoughton, London.

Taylor, Rebe 2002, *Unearthed*, Wakefield Press, South Australia.

Thomas, WJ n.d., *Some Myths and Legends of the Australian Aborigines*, Whitcombe and Tombs, Melbourne.

Tolmer, Alexander 1882, *Reminiscences of an Adventurous and Chequered Career, at Home and in the Antipodes*, 2 vols, Sampson Low, London.

Tuckey, JS 2001, *An Account of a Voyage to Establish a Colony at Port Phillip*, Lavender Hill Multimedia, Red Hill South, Victoria.

Underwood, Robert 1972, 'Studies of Victorian seismicity', *Proceedings of the Royal Society of Victoria* 58(1): 27–48.

Victoria Legislative Council Votes & Proceedings, 1858–59.

Walker, Mary Howitt 1971, *Come Wind, Weather: a Biography of Alfred Howitt*, Melbourne University Press, Melbourne.

Webb, John 1996, *Coolart, a short history*, Friends of Coolart, Coolart.

Weber, Therese 2001, 'Port Phillip Papers: The Australian Journal of Georgiana McCrae', PhD thesis, Australian Defence Force Academy, School of Language, Literature and Communication, Canberra.

Wells, G Edith 1978, *Kangaroo Island: Cradle of a Colony*, Islander Newspapers, Kingscote, South Australia.

Wells, John (compiler) 2001, *Tooradin: 125 years of Coastal History*, Pakenham, Victoria.

Wesson, Sue 2000, *An Historical Atlas of the Aborigines of Eastern Victoria and far South-eastern NSW*, Monash Publications in Geography and Environmental Science, no 53.

— 2002, *Aboriginal Flora and Fauna Names of Victoria*, Victorian Aboriginal Corporation for Languages, Melbourne.

Select Index

Note that with a few exceptions of wide significance, the information contained within the boxed biographical details has not been indexed, and first mentions only are referenced for Chapter 11.

www.ingramcontent.com/pod-product-compliance
Lightning Source LLC
Chambersburg PA
CBHW061237270326
41928CB00033B/3347